10 0309865 3

KU-615-681

WITHDRAWN

Queering the Canon

Studies in German Literature, Linguistics, and Culture

Queering the Canon

Queering the Canon

Defying Sights in German Literature and Culture

Edited by

Christoph Lorey and John L. Plews

UNIVERSITY LIBRARY
NOTTINGHAM

CAMDEN HOUSE

Copyright © Contributors 1998

All Rights Reserved. Except as permitted under current legislation,
no part of this work may be photocopied, stored in a retrieval system,
published, performed in public, adapted, broadcast, transmitted,
recorded, or reproduced in any form or by any means,
without the prior permission of the copyright owner.

First published 1998
Camden House
Drawer 2025
Columbia, SC 29202–2025 USA

Camden House is an imprint of Boydell & Brewer Inc.
PO Box 41026, Rochester, NY 14604–4126 USA
and of Boydell & Brewer Limited
PO Box 9, Woodbridge, Suffolk IP12 3DF, UK

ISBN: 1–57113–178–7

Library of Congress Cataloging-in-Publication Data

Queering the canon : defying sights in German literature and culture /
edited by Christoph Lorey and John L. Plews.
    p.   cm. – (Studies in German literature, linguistics, and
culture)
    Includes bibliographical references and index.
    ISBN 1–7113–178–7 (alk. paper)
    1. German literature—History and criticism—Theory, etc.
2. Homosexuality and literature. 3. Arts, German. 4. Homosexuality
and art. 5. Homosexuality—Philosophy. 6. Gay and Lesbian studies.
I. Lorey, Christoph. II. Plews, John L. III. Series: Studies in
German literature, linguistics, and culture (Unnumbered)
PT71.Q44 1998
830.9'353—dc21   97-32471
                                                             CIP

This publication is printed on acid-free paper.
Printed in the United States of America

Acknowledgments

THE ASSEMBLING OF THIS EDITION has been an inspiring and empowering endeavor for both of us. We would like to express our appreciation to all the contributors for participating in this project by providing us with the excellent product of their research and reflection. For their help and active support, we wish to thank Dana Hope and Victoria MacLeod in the Department of Audiovisual Services at the University of New Brunswick, and, for administrative assistance, Jan Chalk and Scott L. Jensen in the Department of Modern Languages and Comparative Studies at the University of Alberta. We are also grateful to Diana Spokiene and Mirna Emersic-Barbeau for their work at the computer and to Angela and Heinz Spizig for their assistance overseas. For their help in applying for financial support, we extend our sincerest gratitude to Marianne Henn, George Lang, and Gary Libben at the University of Alberta. For her gift of energy, we would like to thank Jacqueline Doig, and, for their encouragement, kind wishes, and inspiring friendship, Henry Abelove, Rick H. Lee, and Andrew Brown. Finally, we are grateful to editors James Hardin and James Walker at Camden House for their warm reception of this edition.

We are, of course, most indebted to the University of New Brunswick Publication Grant and the Faculty of Arts at the University of Alberta. We also acknowledge the assistance of the Izaak Walton Killam Trust.

Contents

Queering German Culture

Defying Sights in German Literature and Culture: An Introduction to Queering the Canon

Christoph Lorey and John L. Plews

THE ROOT OF THE WORD *QUEER* means 'across', probably coming from the Indo-European *twerkw*, from which also derives the Latin *torquere* (to twist), the German *quer* (transverse), and the English word 'athwart'. Because the word *queer* can relate to whatever seems out of the ordinary, 'abnormal', 'unconventional', 'strange' or simply 'different' from our traditional or mainstream perception, *queer* resists any notion of being applied to or assimilated by one particular object, concept, person or group.

Among the many things to which *queer* can refer, writes Eve Kosofsky Sedgwick in *Tendencies*, is "the open mesh of possibilities, gaps, overlaps, dissonances and resonances, lapses and excesses of meaning when the constituent elements of anyone's gender, of anyone's sexuality aren't made (or can't be made) to signify monolithically" (1993, 8). *Queer* is often used to denote any form of representation of same-sex sexual object choice, lesbian or gay, as well as transgendered, wherever one may draw definitional lines.

"Almost everything that would be called queer theory is about ways in which texts — either literature or mass culture or language — shape sexuality," Michael Warner writes in "From Queer to Eternity" (1992, 19). "Usually, the notion is that fantasy and other kinds of representation are inherently uncontrollable, queer by nature. This focus on messy representation allows queer theory, like non-academic queer activism, to be both anti-assimilationist and antiseparatist: you can't eliminate queerness, says queer theory, or screen it out. It's everywhere" (19). However, current (academic and nonacademic) discourses suggest that *queerness* can or should no longer be associated only with a specific type of sexual orientation. As Dennis Denisoff states in *Queeries* (1993), although sexual preference might be considered a fundamental aspect of queerness, *queer* also refers to "political self-assertiveness and a dissension from heteronormativity and its support for rigid sexual (and therefore sociopolitical) classification" (2).

Indeed, much of the recent academic discourse around *queer* does not focus strictly on gender or sexuality, but rather on other identity-shaping elements and influences such as race, ethnicity, nationality, skin color, language, class, income bracket, legal status, etc., and on the way those elements relate to human sexuality. On a more political level, the term *queer* "rejects a minoritizing logic of toleration or simple political interest-representation in favor of a more thorough resistance to regimes of the normal" (Warner 1991, 16). Thus, *queer activism* has often been radical, 'in your face', and troubling in order to spark attention, reaction, and most importantly: debate.

Judging not only from the many questions that linger unanswered in the current, mostly North American, discourses on *queer*, but also from the great uncertainties and voids that surround traditional evaluations of German literatures and culture, both historically and contemporarily, it is high time to address and investigate the relations between questions of race, nationality, gender, and the expression of sexuality particularly as they intersect with the various artistic (music, film, fine art, as well as literary texts), political, and ideological projects of nation- and culture-building through the ages. The essays collected in this volume enter just such a debate.

As the recent public debate sparked by a series of newspaper articles published in *Die Zeit* in May 1997 shows, the literary canon is still largely considered and expected to be a representative documentation of standards or experiences common to a people or a group of people. It is held to be a constant body of knowledge, of everlasting truths which one is to "know" not just to place oneself among the educated, but also to know one's own culture, one's own history, and, above all, to know oneself. Literature is, after all, the "keeper of the dreams, fears, and hopes of people" of all ages (Greiner 14). At the same time, the canon is to represent not that which is commonplace, but that which is distinct, special, peculiar, novel, and inimitable. The ongoing deconstruction of what is considered to be *das Elitäre* (the elite) over the last three decades is much lamented by some and, as the responses to the *Zeit*-questionnaire clearly document, witnessed with disdain, disbelief, and even anger.

There can be little doubt that the 'canon', whether dead or alive, taught year in and year out in schools or meticulously revised in the curricula of liberal institutions, very much repeats and even reinforces existing public opinion, systems of thought, and the structured ways of imagining the experiences and desires of the community, known as 'standard truths', 'traditional values', 'common sense', or 'normal behavior'. And it goes without saying that the canon constructs itself with authority. In the very attempt to define its distinctive authority or value, the canon requires distinctiveness as its authority, that is to say, both the elevated social position of the most literate, the critics, ever-ready to pass judgment, as well as the peculiarity of each artistic production. Needless to say, the *Zeit*-debate constitutes such a discourse of authority, as can be seen by the fact that only distinguished members of the literary profession, established writers and eminent critics from within and outside of the academy were asked to respond to the intriguing question: "which literary works of German literature should a high-school student have read in a German class?" Following John Guillory's post-Marxist/postmodern analysis, the canon can be recognized as cultural capital and hence a material element in a system of power: "the distribution of cultural capital in such an institution as the school reproduces the structure of social relations, a structure of complex and ramifying inequality" (1993, 6).

Yet, the collected body of works forming the canon of any national literature or field of literary or cultural study at any one time is neither the comprehensive nor the qualitative representation of the cultural production of that community it often purports to be. Much rather, the canon is the effect of a dialectic process which defiantly acknowledges deviation and variation in culture in spite of, perhaps because of, its own guise as the emblem of the hegemony defined by a small intellectual elite. As a margin among parallel margins, a segment of a continuum of possibilities, chosen both as a result of and as a reaction to the ideologies of the day, the canon is an insecure centerfold. Its construction results from a fashion discourse in which any elect form transpires as but one stage in an ongoing civilizing process. Indeed, it functions in much the same way as the 'sociology of fashion' as discussed by René König in *The Restless Image*. For its own purpose of tradition in the development of civilization, the canon requires the 'recognition', 'integration', and 'acknowledgment' of another tradition and constituent part of orthodox views and values, namely precisely the assessment and influence of those forms commonly held to be 'deviant'. To point out that in the last two centuries the canon-system has followed not only the fashion of fashion, but first and foremost the fashion of sexuality, is to insist quite properly on the tautological relations between a hegemony and its means of assuming power.

The construction and reconstruction of the canon tells us how a given section of society requiring a system which naturalizes and authorizes its own set of values, assembles a literary inventory for itself and others in order to place itself in that position of authority, less as people who discern quality than as people of quality, who, in turn, authorize, that is, invent and assign value. Ironically, this canon-system of value-creation is not a normalization process which precludes difference. Difference emerges at the place where one asserts convention. As a set of albeit commonly recognized barriers and limits of a sociocultural and moral kind, the canon must necessarily transgress itself in order to become distinct and account for its authority. Indeed, the official limits of the canon which enable it to make claims of distinction, status, and value, and in turn assist it in becoming a vestige of power, must necessarily overcome themselves in order to integrate those very distinct and different elements which traditionally accumulate at the authoritatively deemed margins of society and beyond, or contrary to, the rule of the apparent norm. The canon is thus a system that incorporates into its own shifting body those endeavors initially *excluded* from the self-proclaimed sociocultural center. In fact, it seems to be the clandestine rule of the canon that *the barred* become *the standard*. A paradox, indeed, the once conspicuous *can* become an invaluable resource for the representation of everyday society: *the once excluded* can become *exclusive*.

Many canonical works, including those by Lessing, Goethe, Schiller, Hölderlin, Kleist, Heine, Kafka, Thomas Mann, Klaus Mann, Brecht (i.e., authors clearly posited as sacred cultural icons by virtually every contributor to the *Zeit*-debate), have at one time or another been tarred by at least one of an entire consortium of critical brushes. These have painted their conspicuousness, shown that they are apart from the community good, and have initiated their misreading as antisocial. They were, at some point in time, banned, burned, lost, suppressed or destroyed, considered blasphemous or heretical, politically irresponsible or dangerous, morally corrupt or lewd, intellectually pompous, irrelevant, difficult, inaccessible, elitist, nonsensical, unpublishable, unpopular, unread or unperformed, written and published only in exile. Their authors have been placed among the socially ostracized: the skeptical, the insecure, the melancholic, the suicidal, the mentally ill, the sexually depraved, the impotent. It was not necessary to brand them as national traitors and deserters in order to undermine the rank of their authorship or effectively ban their works. And yet, these are the very works now most on display. Whenever a new generation in society becomes conscious of its self-worth and feels the need to assert its identity, it realizes it cannot achieve self-assertion solely by duplicating established signs of power. Rather, the new (elite) class conceives its own revision of canonical reputability by at once recognizing and seemingly effacing deviations within its perusal of cultural production.

It appears that the successful entry of a text into the literary canon relies on an adherence to patterns of style set by heteronormative bourgeois culture which generally rule out the possibility of portraying same-sex, cross-class, crossfrontier, transgenerational love and desire and so prevent the demonstration of homosexual – or any other nonheteronormative – coupling or consciousness in a literary context. The functioning of queer authors in discourses validated by dominant culture – such as the ability to write in the fashion of the bourgeois understanding and use of Greek pedagogy as demonstrated by Thomas Mann in *Death in Venice* – appears to inevitably eliminate queer identity in favor of disease, decline, disappointment, disillusion, and death. In one instance, *Death in Venice* can be read as the imposition of a heterosexually validated discourse on beauty which dreads and denies homosexuality, relegating it to a hidden place, in other words, the *closet.* Ironically, as Sedgwick convincingly demonstrates, the very "foundational texts of modern gay culture" – and Mann's *Death in Venice* certainly counts among them – "have often been the identical texts that mobilized and promulgated the most potent images and categories for what is now visible as the canon of homophobic mastery" (1990, 49). In repeating the validated systems of bourgeois heteronormativity, literary writing obviously has the ability to write homosexuality out of the books as soon as it is mentioned.

This, however, is a repressive illusion which occurs both in literary documents and in their reception. Just as Sedgwick demonstrates, the petrified specter of homosexuality has to be raised, animated, and acknowledged, even – especially – if this is for the purpose of closeting. Thus the strategy of concealing often announces and proliferates the opposite intention and, in doing so, defeats its own. A queer dialectical approach to the canon-system itself reveals how the master relies on the acknowledgment of difference as a resource to construct itself not only by positing a difference but also by embracing that difference. Mann's *Death in Venice* may serve as a demonstration of how the act of cultural closeting inevitably brings homosexuality to the fore and how little the presence of queerness can dis-

appear from within the literary original no matter the strategy. The bourgeois style of the discourse of beauty, which routinely invokes Greek
pedagogy (as an intellectual barricade), always inevitably still signals Greek
love in learned circles, thanks not only to eighteenth-century celebrities
such as Johann Joachim Winckelmann, Johannes von Müller, Christoph
Martin Wieland and Wilhelm von Humboldt, but also to a long list of
nineteenth- and twentieth-century theorists, among them Karl Heinrich
Ulrichs, Friedrich Nietzsche, Magnus Hirschfeld, Hans Blüher, and
Thomas Mann himself. *Death in Venice*, which is only to serve as one example of many here, is in itself a confession, a defiant sighting, no matter
how much validated style has interfered with it. Indeed, same-sex desire
cannot be deleted unless it is written over in secondary literature, left out in
unfaithful editions or obscured by elusive translations.

Though the canon perpetuates the power system, a potential shift is
always present in the one-sided (mis)recognition of deviance, the awareness
of which by queer theory enables the recognition of the importance of
deviance more for its own sake. Homophobic spaces are always also sites
of resistance. As Sedgwick remarks: "Insofar as the problematics of the
homo/heterosexual definition, in an intensely homophobic culture, are
seen to be precisely internal to the central nexuses of that culture, the
canon must always be treated as a loaded one" (1990, 54). In other words,
the closet — defined by Sedgwick as "that curious space that is both internal and marginal to the culture: centrally representative of its motivating
passions and contradictions, even while marginalized by its orthodoxies"
(1990, 56) — when opened by queer analysis, exposes not only the repressive mechanisms of a dominant culture, but the reputable place of queerness in that dominant culture's own existence. The 'nonsense' dominant
culture makes of difference by making it justify itself in the terms of the
dominant culture is at the same time a recognition of the limits of dominant culture — limits, which by its own admittance it needs to overstep —
the resourcefulness of alterity, and the prerequisite of the margin for the
center.

To queer the canon is thus to continue a twofold exercise of civilization: a 'pincer movement' of pointing out queer distinctions and lining
up conspicuous queers. First, to remark upon the canon's position as a
hegemonic bastion of the reinforcement of dominant views and yet to
note that this is the very place where deviation and a multitude of subject
positions can and must necessarily occur. In doing this, one draws atten-

tion to the points of queerness, marginality, and alterity already incorporated and surreptitiously acknowledged within canonical structures. Second, to continue the practice of difference and differentiation, to promote it even by introducing further deviations as resources for the canon's distinctiveness and thereby cause an ongoing shift in opinion.

To queer the canon, then, means on one level to deconstruct these mechanisms to reveal how the canon — by dint of its own system and will to authority — is inherently, fundamentally queer, relying, as it does, on the very distinctions from its own posited norm, and, on another level, to exceed the material limits of the canon's own historical position. The queer rethinking of the literary canon operates according to a Hegelian dialectic in which it self-reflectively seeks to transcend the errors of its past. In other words, the task of queer theory is the very task Hegel assigns to philosophy and, as Charles Altieri has put it, "to position truth claims within specific modes of thinking, to dramatize the limitations each mode reveals over time, and to show how subsequent acts of spirit are capable of negating, preserving, and sublating those limited perspectives so that the reflexive mind can appreciate the more comprehensive positions that become available as spirit works beyond its own fullest self-expressions" (370). If it is true that, as John Guillory points out, "the canon participates centrally in the establishment of consensus as the embodiment of a collective valuation," then it is correct to follow that "it is in the interest of canonical reformations to erase the conflictual prehistory of canon-formation or to represent such history as the narrative of error" (1984, 358).

Fixing one's sights on queerness has been the project of both the adherents of heterosexuality and the canonical movers and shakers. After all, *queering* merely prescribes a manner of reading or viewing which attempts to ignore the belligerent blinkers of heteronormativity and which takes pleasure in the presence of precisely that which is hidden. Supposedly recognized — yet most often misrecognized or wrongly perceived — queerness coheres heterosexuality and the canon. But by being acknowledged — correctly or otherwise — by moving into sight and taking up diffuse positions, queerness occupies spaces in which it is possible to create polyvalence where both sexuality and textuality are concerned. Thus, returning the gesture, allowing its own acknowledgment and even contributing to it, queerness is not assimilated, rather it questions the validity of, corrects, partly erases, and partly rewrites the very norm it is called upon to assert: it is deviance that civilizes the norm.

Dominant discourse, however, which has already incorporated deviance in order to become distinct and authoritative in the first place, has interpreted works in ways which conceal, condemn, or excuse queerness. Not listing them in anthologies and bibliographies, in literary histories and library catalogues, often seemed an exercise sufficient enough to blot out queer authors such as August von Platen, Helene von Druskowitz, Christa Winsloe, Anna Elisabet Weirauch, John Henry Mackay, and countless others from public awareness and serious inquiry.

Many articles in this collection reveal how severe the processes of eradicating such 'inherent' queerness have been in the past. In cases where homosexual desire is being alluded to or clearly expressed, both anthologies and translations of texts — particularly by those who have ranked high on the list of 'canonized' authors, including Goethe, Schiller, and Thomas Mann — have actively obscured and falsified. A few examples will suffice to illustrate this point: Martin Blum retraces the legacy of misrepresentation of Dietrich von der Glezze's *Der Borte*, a late medieval comic tale 'cleansed' by an entire series of nineteenth and twentieth-century editors. Robert Tobin's translation of parts taken from Schiller's *Spiel des Schicksals* (*The Sport of Destiny*) inadvertently reveals that previous translations, such as the one by Marian Klopfer (1933), can be of little use for readers interested in Friedrich Schiller, let alone for serious scholarship. David John's analysis of performances of Goethe's drama *Egmont* points to the tradition of cutting out the character and cross-dressing of Margarete von Parma from early performances of the play. In her essay on Goethe's *Faust*, Silke Falkner charts a classic example of the homophobic accounting for male-male desire in academic reception which has only very gradually and painstakingly been turned around in recent years. Numerous excerpts taken from Thomas Mann's diaries in the article by Harry Oosterhuis had to be translated by the editors in spite of the existence of a select English-language translation. Mann's original diary entries concerning his homosexual desires had been edited out.

Queering the Canon does not make claims to provide guidelines for any form of separating that which *is not* from that which *is* canonical, a division that, particularly in light of feminism, has been reinstated at various levels of institutional practice in the last twenty years and which has, in fact, only perpetuated and exposed the same mechanisms of canon formation that were instrumental in the establishment of the 'closed' canon one tried to 'open up'. Nor does *Queering the Canon* attempt to become a mouthpiece for identity politics, or seek to raise heretofore unknown or forgotten queer authors from the dust of hidden library basements to their 'proper' place in the literary canon. Regardless, however, of whether or not the category of social identity qualifies as an acceptable key to canon entry (cf. Guillory 1993, 10), they, too, must be seen as representatives of social identities that have been denied free expression but deserve attention and critical investigation.

It is important to detail the integration of queerness in the established canon inverting it as acknowledgment of difference. We feel that it is vital to continue this process of shifting limited perspectives by placing about the central canon the cultural experience of further openly gay and lesbian works, as they dislocate the master canon's claims of universal validity and authority. Whether intentionally or only by their mere presence, the articles in this volume challenge the established canon of German literatures, music, film, and art history on a wider scale. Besides reexamining texts by well-known authors, including Goethe, Schiller, Thomas and Klaus Mann, Ingeborg Bachmann, Christa Reinig, and Elfriede Jelinek, many essays also (re)discover works and approaches that have thus far rarely been subjected to scholarly inquiry.

The first of three sections, "Queering German History and Thought," is of a theoretical nature. Keenly aware of historic differences and shifting ideologies, the authors engage in conceptual and epistemological questions, tracing not only the history and development of queer theory, but also its influence on German aesthetics, musicology, sexology, law, and gender studies. Holger A. Pausch researches the trends and limitations of queer theory as it has left and continues to leave its mark in philosophy, politics, sociology, psychology, and literary studies, and so offers an introductory historical purview which is complemented by Neville Hoad and Michael Scherzinger's exploration of 'inversion' in the interdisciplinary context of sexology and musicology. Angela Taeger's discussion of the demographic, sociomedical and family-ideological positions that sparked the turn-of-the-century debate on the legality of homosexual activities confirms our contemporary understanding that sexuality structures and destructures the social and political as much as the private sphere. Further contextualizing the influx of queer theory into the German academy, Evelyn Annuß reflects on the controversial reception of Judith Butler and examines the popularity of queer politics as an expression of academic struggles within the university hegemony, specifically within the field of gender studies.

As the title "Queering German Literature" suggests, the following section offers current readings focusing on lesbian, gay, and transgendered themes in canonical and marginalized texts dating from the Middle Ages to the present. While Helmut Brall, researching reflections of homosexuality in medieval poetry and chronicles, extrapolates the various clerical and secular conceptions of same-sex desire in their historical context, Martin Blum, investigating instances of transvestism and sodomy in Dietrich von der Glezze's *Der Borte* (*The Belt*), demonstrates how the genre of the comic tale contributed to the perpetuation of patriarchal feudal power structures by promoting heterosexuality and homophobia. Both essays give testimony to the long-held suspicion that the 'outing' of homosexual acts in the Middle Ages was more or less effectively used in the ruling classes' struggle for political power. The recognition of the fact that earlier expressions of queer identities and desires provide a constant source for future artists is central to the contributions focusing on late eighteenth- and early nineteenth-century drama. By tracing explicit signals of gender inversion in the text and stage/screen productions of Goethe's *Egmont*, David G. John exemplifies how inspiring, confusing, and disturbing the enigmatic, queer identity of Margarete von Parma has been to past and present producers and stage directors. In her queer reading of Goethe's *Faust*, Silke Falkner traces Mephisto's homoerotic desire, the primary threat to his identity as a devil, as a factor that makes possible not only the redemption of Faust but also, if only momentarily, the salvation of the devil himself. Robert Tobin shows in what way and how much the still underdeveloped boundaries between homosociality and homosexuality in late eighteenth-century Germany enabled Thomas Mann and other twentieth-century writers to appropriate Friedrich Schiller's writings for their own devices. Tobin's essay, then, conveniently sets the investigative scene for Harry Oosterhuis's detailed comparison of the significance of politics and homoeroticism in the lives and works of Thomas and Klaus Mann, particularly in relation to the role of homoeroticism in the rise of German nationalism.

In a close-reading of Anna Elisabet Weirauch's three-volume novel *Der Skorpion,* Nancy P. Nenno exposes the complex negotiations of lesbian identity in Berlin across the period of the Weimar Republic. Karin Bauer, exploring the role of fantasy in the constitution of the gendered subject in Ingeborg Bachmann's "A Step Towards Gomorrah," shows how the

Austrian writer visualized contemporary social, cultural, and institutional limitations imposed upon women's sexual fantasy. The application of lesbian feminist theory enables Cathrin Winkelmann to unveil the lesbian subtext in Christa Reinig's "Ein Sonntag im Krieg," a short story portraying a heterosexist, patriarchal world in which women's social, political, and sexual expression is inevitably inhibited. While Ralph J. Poole analyses the unusually emancipatory role of the lesbian vampire as mother and artist in a comprehensive selection of Elfriede Jelinek's writings, Amanda L. Mitchell discusses the ingenuity of representations of lesbian pornography in Regina Nössler's *Strafe muß sein*. Denis Sweet, who examines East German queer writings published between 1989 and 1996, contributes further to a vocabulary of queer pleasure by delineating lines of resistance developed in works which thematize the bankruptcy of administrative language in a totalitarian regime and the arbitrary use of power in the social enforcement of roles for gender, sex, and personality.

The final section with the open-ended title "Queering German Culture," locates the inherent queering of post-World War II German film, soundtracks, and the paintings of the once Berlin-based Canadian artist Attila Richard Lukacs. Les Wright's dialectical analysis of the genre-film cycle of gay coming-out narratives focuses on the role of both social identity politics and, specifically of the outsider in the development of New German Cinema. James W. Jones, confronting the history of gender roles portrayed in Frank Ripploh's *Taxi zum Klo*, shows how the film makes a radical break with the history of cinematic representations of homosexuality by integrating and subverting stereotypes and paradigms derived from history. Caryl Flinn demonstrates how the soundtrack of Rosa von Praunheim's film *Anita. Tänze des Lasters* contributes to a complex queer camp aesthetic and raises questions regarding the historical contexts of the film score's camp practices and queer identities. Sunka Simon demonstrates how Monika Treut's film *Die Jungfrauenmaschine* and Percy Adlon's *Bagdad Cafe* share a prevailing tone of uncanny comedy that transgresses sexual, gender, racial, and cultural identities as well as genre boundaries and conventional narratological rules. Ute Lischke-McNab discusses the wider significance of the role of queerness in New German Comedy by seeking answers to the question why homosexuality has become such a central focus, both as caricature and parody, in contemporary German cinema. Piet Defraeye unveils the symbolism behind the performances of masculinity in Attila Richard Lukacs's series entitled *E-Werk*, paintings which are intricately linked to German history and European art history.

All essays offer unique interpretations providing invaluable, often radical, insights as they, at times provocatively, engage in debates surrounding the multitude of issues of male-male and female-female erotics, male and female domination, misogyny, and homophobia, in an attempt to fuel further investigation and study. Together they join queer theory in transgressing the mysterious boundaries of the social and power mechanisms informing sexuality and thought, and in disrupting traditional perceptions of the canon and German literatures and culture as a whole. The essays share a fierce awareness of, but also a certain fascination with, the multitude of acts that can be, have been, and are being sexualized, genderized, politicized, and marketed in the German cultural sphere.

Queering

German

History

and

Thought

Queer Theory:
History, Status, Trends, and Problems

Holger A. Pausch

> *When man gave all things a sex he thought, not that he*
> *was playing, but that he had gained a profound insight:*
> *— it was only very late that he confessed to himself what*
> *an enormous error this was, and perhaps even now he*
> *has not confessed it completely. — In the same way man*
> *has ascribed to all that exists a connection with morality*
> *and laid an ethical significance on the world's back. One*
> *day this will have as much value, and no more, as the*
> *belief in the masculinity or femininity of the sun has*
> *today.*
> —Friedrich Nietzsche, *Morgenröte*, no. 3

I.

SIX YEARS AGO, THE TERM *QUEER THEORY* would scarcely "have rung a bell" in scholarly circles in Canada or the United States. But since that time, beginning shortly after its inauguration, queer theory has become "nothing if not hot," and "part of the attraction is that queer theory isn't a well-defined field" of investigation (Warner 1992, 18). The appropriation of the term *queer* in the lesbian and gay community is still controversial, even if it has been around for ages ((charles) 97). Originally the word functioned as a term of derision; a contemptuous signifier for "eccentric," "odd," "unconventional," "unusual," "doubtful," "irregular," "questionable," "suspicious," "perverse," "different," "outcast," "deviant," "lesbian," "gay," "homosexual," etc. However, the linguistic strategy of investing a negative concept, such as *queer*, with positive connotations in defining a common social identity, has many predecessors. The social history of language has quite often observed that the early or conventionally negative meaning of a word engages in a semantic transformation toward positive connotations which are caused by its extended application in new situations and contexts. Signifiers like "Gothic," "baroque," "expressionism," "black" Americans, "Deutsche," the modern science "nerd" or computer "geek," slang expressions like "bad," "decadent," "cool," and many more, are typical examples of the so called reverse discourse theory and practice. Similarly, the semantics of the word *queer*, even though under fire from considerable conservative resistance, is also in the process of undergoing such changes, including the reshaping of its use-value. Cherry Smyth, in *Lesbians Talk Queer Notions*, informs that whenever "the word 'queer' is used it defines a strategy, an attitude, a reference to other identities and a new self-understanding" (20). Bristow and Wilson read this as a demonstration of "how activists resignified the meaning of queer, wresting it from the homophobes, and using it as an enabling point of definition against the extremely narrow identities produced by the hetero-homo binary" (9).

Although the origin of the label *queer theory* is not entirely clear, one might point to two possible sources. The earliest one implicates the launch of the influential political action group Queer Nation in 1990, which, for the first time, employed *queer* as a positive signifier. It opened the door to corresponding compound expressions like *queer theory, queer criticism, queer romance, queer cinema, queer politics, queer representations, queer philology, queer state, queercore*, etc. To my knowledge, except for a number of essays, there is still no anthology or history documenting Queer Nation, which formally dissolved as a group in 1992 because of internal conflicts. "Queer Nationality" by Lauren Berlant and Elizabeth Freeman, together with its bibliographical information, is one of the important examples of these few publications. (See also Bristow and Wilson 8–12.) The second source of the term is most likely Teresa de Lauretis's introduction "Queer Theory: Lesbian and Gay Sexualities" to a special issue of *differences* in 1991. The essays that comprise this edition under the title "Queer Theory," de Lauretis explains, "were generated in the context of a working conference on theorizing lesbian and gay sexuality that was held at the University of California at Santa Cruz in February 1990" (iii). She goes on to inform that "the term 'queer,' juxtaposed to the 'lesbian and gay' of the subtitle, is intended to mark a certain critical distance from the latter ... formula" (iv). The possible use of the adjective *queer* had been suggested to her during a conference in which she had participated earlier. However, her *queer*, de Lauretis continues, "had no relation to," and thus was terminologically not motivated by, "the Queer Nation group, of whose existence [she] was ignorant at the time" (xvii, n. 2). In the context of her intentions, the term *queer theory* was arrived at by de Lauretis in an effort to avoid fine, and often politically necessary, distinctions in discursive practices regarding lesbian and gay "life-styles, sexualities, sexual practices, communities, issues, publications, and discourses" (v).

Queer theory is not based on a specific methodology of investigation and analysis. It deals with and scrutinizes a whole spectrum of human interaction in the sociocultural space from central topics such as sexuality and power relationships down to minute details in the realm of popular culture. Therefore, because of its thematic diversity and methodological pluralism, it is probably not possible to define clearly queer theory's epistemological object, or to construct a comprehensive theoretical system. However, it should also be noted that at this point in time such an undertaking might even be seen as undesirable because it is above all the methodological and thematic nonspecificity of queer theory, its protean ability to change and metamorphose according to the status and demands of the cultural text under investigation, which constitutes its analytical strength, educational effectiveness, and political presence. In a way, the analytical strategy of queer theory can be compared to guerilla warfare because in many cases it is impossible to predict in advance which cultural phenomenon will be targeted next. Such seemingly random targets include: the female opera singer, military infrastructure, fashion design, the language of politics and power, law, education, tourism, books, films, television, magazines and other new 'queer spaces', such as those about and within the construct of the literary canon. However, because queer theory does not have a defined object of investigation, it is engaged in a continuous process of dialectically questioning the sociocultural space. It might take quite some time before its long-range goal, which is implicated by the dynamics of the process, has been achieved.

It is the objective of queer theory to destabilize heterocentrism and its power position as norm-giver, to communicate the fact of its historical construction, to clarify its moral and ethical relativity and incidental structure in the social order, and, last but not least, to break down the barriers of racism, sexism, and homophobia. For these reasons, queer theory is essentially and fundamentally political (Sedgwick 1993; Alcorn, Sinfield, Smyth; Burston 1992). Furthermore, since attempts to define its specific *object* of investigation have been all but given up, even though the *objective* has been identified, queer theory resists deconstruction and dialectic inversion. In other words, it basically withstands its own most important analytical tools precisely because queer theory is not based on defined systemic principles. This approach is nothing less than a highly effective move in its political agenda. In a permanent reaction to the changing dynamics of a queer political economy, queer theory continuously proceeds to correct itself, to modify its approaches, and to adapt to new situations. When Steven Seidman attempted "Deconstructing Queer Theory" in 1995, his otherwise informative essay contained in essence little more than a critical reading of Eve Sedgwick (1990), Diana Fuss (1991), and Judith Butler (*Gender Trouble*), which hardly deserves being called "deconstructing."

Queer theory is generally interested in all phenomena of culture and its multifarious forms of reification of human desire and oppression. But it focuses especially on the question of why lesbian and gay culture is "so strangely integral to the selfsame heterosexual cultures which obsessively denounce it" (Dollimore 28). Seidman believes that queer theory originated in the United States, chiefly among English and Humanities professors in the 1980s (1995, 138), in other words, at a time, when the term *queer theory* had not yet been coined. For these reasons, it seems appropriate to use the term *queer theory* cautiously as an umbrella term for, or at least synonymously with, lesbian and gay theory and cultural studies. From my point of view, *queer theory* should be the preferred term, because it is not gender specific, because its applicability is general and inclusive, and, most of all, because *queer* cannot be assimilated or appropriated by means of sublimation. Its ability to integrate diffuse and antagonistic lesbian and gay political factions should outweigh the problematics of its definition and use. It is interesting to note that the prominent *Johns Hopkins Guide to Literary Theory & Criticism* (1994) omits the term preferring the label "Gay Theory and Criticism," which is then further subdivided into "Gay Male" and "Lesbian" (324-32). An ideological analysis of the implications of the Johns Hopkins's category "gay" in the light of the theories of Walter Benjamin or the School of Frankfurt — which is yet to be attempted in a separate study — would furnish a number of key arguments in favor of the use of the term *queer,* because it is, above all, as Bristow and Wilson point out, "the deployment of the term 'queer' that promised to incorporate as well as create a whole range of sexual identities — including dissident heterosexual ones — within its political [and, one might add, theoretical] project" (9).

II.

Michael Warner has written probably the most illuminating initiation to queer theory with his 1992 article "From Queer to Eternity. An Army of Theorists Cannot Fail" and his introduction to the trail-blazing edition *Fear of a Queer Planet. Queer Politics and Social Theory*. In order to circumscribe its central function, Warner argues that:

> almost everything that would be called queer theory is about ways in which texts — either literature or mass culture or language — shape sexuality. Usually, the notion is that fantasy and other kinds of representation are inherently uncontrollable, queer by nature. This focus on messy representation allows queer theory, like non-academic queer activism, to be both antiassimilationist and anti-separatist: you can't eliminate queerness, says queer theory, or screen it out. It's everywhere. (1992, 19)

Therefore, in Warner's view, it is the main ambition of queer theory to bring "sexuality, academic expertise, state politics, and public media into a more mutually critical relation" (1992, 19). The pathway to this aim, however, is deflected by a basic problem: the appropriation, colonization, and reifications of sexual culture and desire by the dominant discourse. Warner points out that:

> because the logic of the sexual order is so deeply embedded by now in an indescribably wide range of social institutions, and is embedded in the most standard accounts of the world, queer struggles aim not just at tolerance or equal status but at challenging those institutions and accounts. The dawning realization that themes of homophobia and heterosexism may be read in almost any document of our culture means that we are only beginning to have an idea of how widespread those institutions and accounts are. (1993, xiii)

In order to make his point, Warner scathingly examines the "cartoon image of human society devised by Carl Sagan (and drawn, appropriately enough, by his wife Linda) for use on NASA's *Pioneer 10* spacecraft" (xxi) which was the first 'man-made' object to leave from the solar system with this kind of message in a bottle. The two nude figures of a man and a woman testify in Warner's analysis "to the depth of the culture's assurance (read:

insistence) that humanity and heterosexuality are synonymous. This reminder speeds to the ends of the universe, announcing to passing stars that earth is not, regardless of what anyone says, a queer planet" (xxiii).

For the most part, that is, in the realm of questions that do not undermine the dominant heterosexual ideology (d'Arcy and Landa 1996), the abovementioned problems would have been posed by the left of social and political theory in the tradition of Marxism and dialectic materialism. However, materialist thinking about society has in many cases reinforced heterosexual ideology after having "posited and naturalized a heterosexual society" (Warner 1993, vii; cf. Parker). It has been unwilling to deal with, in its perspective, "subjective" and "individualistic" problems which could not be reduced to the class struggle itself. Indeed, sexuality, gender oppression, desire, etc., do not belong in the general category of social conflict in the light of such partiality (Wittig 1981, 107). Having understood social theory's disinclination to ask such questions, it did not take long before queer experience and politics were seeking their own paths to a theoretical narrative of the social environment, especially since the emerging discipline of 'queer left social/sexual theory', in regard to its essential problematics, is not a new postmodern construct but a topic in the history of social thought with quite an illustrious tradition (Abelove, Barale, Halperin 656-58; Burg 198-203; Warner 1993, viii).

However, the desire of queer theory to query, question, and dissect all phenomena of the sociocultural space has not necessarily led to a consensus about what queer actually is. In order to illuminate somewhat the complexities of this problem of searching for a more general understanding, it should first be pointed out that, to a great extent, queer theory is a product of the situation of lesbian and gay politics in the second half of the nineteen-eighties. After the first Gay Power meeting in New York in July 1969 — eleven days after the legendary Stonewall riots (Rutledge 3) — lesbian and gay politics was mainly one of identity. In the course of the second half of the nineteen-eighties, however — and because of unsolvable theoretical problems such as gender issues and opposing philosophical positions — identity politics was largely superseded by a politics of difference, diversity, and dissident sexualities. The theorization of such notions led finally to the concept of queer theory, even though the expression caused considerable terminological difficulties along the way. On the one hand, queer theory's dedication to diversity guarantees that it is not concerned with establishing new orthodoxies or conforming to established philosophical doctrines. On the other, its primary noncommitment to the practice of the academy, to a theory of learning, indeed, not even to the methodological requirements of the concept *theory*, has generated a pluralism of subjective applications of the term *queer* in critical studies. This can be observed throughout the literature, and it is astounding that this fact did not cause even more complication and confusion. A few examples will suffice.

Jonathan Goldberg, the editor of *Queering the Renaissance*, a collection of remarkable essays, agreed along with his collaborators on a more generic use of the term. In other words, for these historians "to queer the Renaissance" (3) means to challenge the period "within the perspective of gay and lesbian studies" (back cover). It is their goal to "call into question the accomplishments of the Renaissance as foundational for modernity" (1). An attempt to define the term is waived by Goldberg because Eve Kosofsky Sedgwick's "elaboration of an epistemology of the closet provides a supple analytic tool for investigating the regimes of unknowing and unacknowledgeability that structure the place of homosexuality in Renaissance culture" (5). Thus, it can be said that Goldberg's concept of *queering* in the context of queer theory only claims to indicate the general mode of inquiry and analytical procedure.

In a fashion similar to Goldberg, Paul Burston and Colin Richardson also stress the general intent of queer theory without giving much consideration to analytical methodologies or theoretical requirements. "Part of the project of Queer," they state, "is to attack, as Judith Butler does, the very 'naturalness' of gender and, by extension, the fictions of supporting compulsory heterosexuality" (1). Therefore:

> Queer Theory is both 'political' and 'cultural': political, because it seeks to expose and problematise the means by which 'sexuality' is reduced to the definitions and relations of gender; cultural, because just about everything we might call Queer Theory concerns itself with the ways in which cultural texts — books, films, television, magazines, etc. — condition understandings of sexuality. (1)

Thus, queer theory not only "seeks to locate Queerness in places that had previously been thought of as strictly for the straights," it challenges most of all "a theoretical model which privileges gender as the category of structuring perspective" (2) in the sociocultural space, the infamous heterosexual gaze (Evans and Gamman). For this reason, the queer project or queer reading of cultural texts "can take many shapes," as Burston writes, but "what they all share is the understanding that cultural texts do not have single meanings, that what is denied at the level of narrative (i.e., queerness) can often be deciphered through closer inspection of the textual codes" (1995, 120). A leaflet circulated in London in 1991 did explain the origin of such pluralism rather bluntly, as to queer: "means to fuck with gender. There are straight queers, bi queers, tranny queers, lez queers, fag queers, SM queers, fisting queers in every single street in this apathetic country of ours" (Quoted in Smyth 17). Mary McIntosh, taking a feminist point of view, opposes the all-encompassing status of queer theory. In her essay, "Queer Theory and the War of the Sexes," she explores "the separate development of lesbian and gay male history" (46) and arrives at the conclusion that, even though both "could have learned a great deal" (46) from one another:

> 'queer theory' has an odd relationship to pre-existing lesbian and gay male theory. For queer theory, being *de*constructionist, has much in common with the more radical forms of social construc-tionism represented in the male gay tradition. Indeed, queer theory may be said to be a development of that tradition, which has simply laid claim to a more all-encompassing status. (47)

It is this status in McIntosh's view that "is horribly reminiscent of what feminists have often found about 'male-stream thought'" (47). Toward the end of her essay she concludes that, "even though queer theory and queer politics ... are important for feminists, they do not replace feminism, which remains as a humanist and liberatory project with its own more structural theories" (49). Furthermore, McIntosh adds a very important observation to the abovementioned point, one which has been discussed and debated by lesbian and gay activists and academics for years: "queer theory should not forget that the heterosexuality, in terms of which we are defined as other is a highly gendered one, so that our otherness and the forms and meanings of our dissidence are also gendered" (47). With these few words she touches upon one of the most sensitive issues of queer theory, which has to be addressed sooner rather than later, as it undermines one of queer theory's claims to existence, namely the misguided assumption that it "is not gender specific" (Case 2).

Where McIntosh, together with de Lauretis, retains the categories "gay" and "lesbian" and some notion of gender division, Judith Butler and Sue-Ellen Case have argued that queerness is something that is ultimately beyond gender. Alexander Doty takes up the problems posed by this rhetorical dilemma in "What Makes Queerness Most," the introductory chapter to his remarkable study *Making Things Perfectly Queer. Interpreting Mass Culture.* Aware of the fact that, in the words of de Lauretis, queer discourse often seems "fuzzily defined, undecoded, or discursively dependent on more established forms" (1991, iii) and that at the moment "no particular definition or use of 'queer' and 'queerness' has gained wide currency" (Doty xiv), Doty discusses a number of influential definitional propositions (Warner, Queer Nation, de Lauretis, Butler, and Case). In the context of these terminological and conceptual problems he then states his goal:

> I want to construct 'queer' as something other than 'lesbian,' 'gay,' or 'bisexual'; but I can't say that 'lesbian,' 'gay,' or 'bisexual' *aren't* also 'queer.' I would like to maintain the integrity of 'lesbian,' 'gay,' and 'bisexual' as concepts that have specific historical, cultural, and personal meanings; but I would also like 'lesbian,' 'gay,' and 'bisexual' culture, history, theory, and politics to have some bearing on the articulation of queerness. On the other hand, it seems important not to have 'queer' and 'queerness' become the type of umbrella terms that implicitly position 'lesbian,' 'gay,' and 'bisexual' erotics, cultures, and politics as mere subsets of some larger, and seemingly more complex, progressive, or politically efficacious concept. This has already happened to lesbians in relation to notions of 'women,' 'feminism,' 'homosexuality,' and 'gayness.' (xvii)

Beyond the recognition of the abovementioned terminological and cultural considerations, queerness, in Doty's view, should ultimately "challenge and confuse our understanding and uses of sexual and gender categories" (xvii). Doty's attempt to be accordant with Richard Howard, and consiliatory toward a multitude of different views, and his ambition to conceptualize *queer* in a democratic manner is no doubt admirable. However, it should also be pointed out that, considering the present situation, the contours of a distinct theory and methodology have not surfaced.

Therefore, it is not necessary to artificially restrict the pluralism of the term *queer* in the variety of its applications, and this also goes for its use as an umbrella term. So far, the only common denominator of queer is the notion of being "nonstraight." Consequently, all other conceptualizations in reference to specific sociocultural phenomena could be open ended if no terminological precision is expected or demanded.

III.

The volume of available publications is nothing less than astounding if queer theory, in its present state, is understood as a comprehensive term for lesbian and gay theory and cultural studies. Even a cursory inspection of the Internet finds extensive databases of important research libraries; numerous homepages advise about the most recent publications, reviewed and nonreviewed, and developments in the ongoing debate. But most importantly for systematic scholarly research, a number of thorough bibliographies list according to various disciplines an amazing selection of available titles, materials, and sources.[1] Unfortunately, a comprehensive international bibliography on queer theory does not exist, and it remains a desirable and important project. A conservative estimate of publications since the sixties, including history, cultural studies, psychology, medicine, sociology, philosophy, law, and politics, would easily equal the sum of thirty to forty thousand books and articles.

Following the *Lesbian and Gay Studies Reader*, the accessible amount of literature can conveniently and comprehensively be divided into the subsequent categories: I. Journals and periodicals; II. The AIDS crisis; III. Contemporary testimony and memoirs; IV. Collections of source materials; V. Collections of academic articles by various authors; VI. History; VII. Anthropology; VIII. Sociology, Psychology; IX. Classics; X. Philosophy; XI. Politics; XII. Literary Studies, and XIII. Cultural Studies (Abelove, Barale, Halperin, 653–66). In light of such formidable sources of information and range of scholarly work, it is possible to touch only upon a few titles which, from my perspective, have been very instrumental in the development of queer theory, or might have deserved a greater degree of attention.

Historical cultural studies should probably be considered as one of the most important areas of engagement for queer theory because these inquiries challenge engrained traditional narratives of history, which still function in a broader context as universal fundaments of society. Above all, historical queer studies have been able to document their investigations and theses to such an astounding degree that one might be tempted to wonder if during the previous fifteen hundred years some kind of a conspiracy had not been in place which succeeded in silencing all relevant, positive lesbian and gay texts, not to mention suppressing their public reception beyond the knowledge of a few historians and specialists. In the last twenty years the results of gay historical studies have been fundamentally important for queer theory, and worth the effort, even though each and every one of the notable publications required an inordinate amount of work, even for relatively minor projects. In this respect, one might almost wish to defend the notion that the sociocultural space of history in all its complexities should actually represent the primary environment for queer studies, because all other investigations are connected with their conclusions. Until now, only the surface of the lesbian and gay genealogy and history, except for Greek antiquity, has been identified and described, whereas the major part of its narrative is still buried in the caves of the past, and under layer upon layer of hostile ideologies. This immense field contains sufficient problems to occupy legions of researchers for an indeterminate period.

In the period of 1925 to 1928, the renowned philologist Paul Brandt published under the pseudonym of Hans Licht the *Sittengeschichte Griechenlands* (*Sexual Life in Ancient Greece*), a groundbreaking and, later, internationally acclaimed classic which also caught the attention of Thomas Mann (1928, suppl. vol., vii). It contains an excellent discussion of homosexuality (188-244) and other aspects of Greek life as portrayed in Attic and Hellenistic literature and art, with extensive documentation, analyses of records, and considerable illustrations. Translated into English in 1932, the original third supplementary volume could not be obtained by the general public, but only by librarians and scholars who had first to sign a declaration of intent stating that the volume was to be used for research purposes only (iv).

Another example of the abovementioned category is John Boswell's brilliant study of the history of attitudes toward homosexuality in the Christian West over the first fourteen centuries A.D., *Christianity, Social Tolerance, and Homosexuality*, which challenges "received opinion and our own preconceptions about the Church's past relationship to its gay members" (back cover) over the first fourteen centuries. Much of his study

"is specifically intended to rebut the common idea that religious belief —
Christian or other — has been the *cause* of intolerance in regard to gay
people" (6) as it becomes more and more apparent that the history of
public reactions to homosexuality is "in some measure a history of social
tolerance generally" (17). However, using gay people to study social intolerance, Boswell points out that there are in addition to the advantages several
salient disadvantages. In my view, the recognition of these obstacles does
indeed represent one of the most important findings of the book, as
Boswell observes:

> The most fundamental of these [disadvantages] is the fact that the
> longevity of prejudice against gay people and their sexuality has re-
> sulted in the deliberate falsification of historical records concern-
> ing them well into the present century, rendering accurate recon-
> struction of their history particularly difficult. Distortion on this
> issue was little known in the ancient world but became more wide-
> spread with the dramatic shift in public morality following the fall
> of the Roman Empire in the West. Ignorance was the major force
> behind the loss of information on this subject in medieval
> Europe ... but the heavy hand of the censor was also evident. (17–
> 18)

Thus, Boswell reflects, it is little wonder that accurate analysis of gay people
in a historical context is so rare when such formidable barriers oppose
access to the sources (21; see also Ellis and Tixier). On the other hand,
from a contemporary point of view, the direction of future scholarship is
also identified through this situation, that is, it should be one of the principal tasks of lesbian and gay cultural studies to eliminate, if possible, the
heavy hand of the censor in historical documents in which homosexuality
has been written out of the script, and to reconstruct their original content,
an awesome but absolutely vital task.

When questioned, history seems to be full of surprises as seemingly
unshatterable truths and convictions quite often change considerably or
even dissipate into the realm of pure fiction. Such is the case with B. R.
Burg's remarkably detailed and well-documented study *Sodomy and the
Pirate Tradition* in which he dispels one such long-held and cherished
truth regarding buccaneer sexuality. Were pirates indeed such untamed,
wild and womanizing lovers as their modern image makes them out to be,

and as those most heavily romanticized and fabled characters in history seem to indicate? From Bluebeard and Blackbeard to Captain Hook and Captain Morgan, they have been the subject of countless cinematic love stories, books, and children's tales. The conception of pirates portrayed in such narratives, however, changes drastically when it is examined by a historian such as Burg as he investigates the social and sexual world of these sea rovers, a tightly bound brotherhood of men engaged in almost constant warfare with little heterosexual contact. What, he asks:

> did these men, often on the high seas for years at a time, do for sexual fulfilment? Buccaneer sexuality differed widely from that of other all-male institutions such as prisons, for it existed not within a regimented structure of rules, regulations, and oppressive supervision, but rather in a society in which widespread toleration of homosexuality was the norm and conditions encouraged its practice. (back cover)

In his conclusion, Burg reflects on what can be drawn from a study of those features of pirate society that make it truly distinctive. In his view, it:

> is not that homosexual and heterosexual can function comfortably together, but that homosexual communities can function virtually independent of heterosexual society. Aside from the production of children, homosexuals alone can fulfill satisfactorily all human needs, wants, and desires, all the while supporting and sustaining a human community remarkable by the very fact that is unremarkable. The almost universal homosexual involvement among pirates meant homosexual practices were neither disturbed, perverted, exotic, nor uniquely desirable among them, and the mechanism for defending and perpetuating such practices, those things that set the modern homosexual apart from heterosexual society, were never necessary. (172–73)

IV.

Whereas Burg studied sexual difference as a specific case in point, it is Jonathan Dollimore who engages in the imposing and complex task of developing a specific theory of dissidence. His cultural materialist critique *Sexual Dissidence. Augustine to Wilde, Freud to Foucault* (1991), an exercise in reading culture, is without a doubt one of the most important applications of queer theory to history, even though the term is not used. He explores the "complex, often violent, sometimes murderous dialectic between dominant and subordinate cultures, groups, and identities," and issues of sexual dissidence concerning "conceptions of self, desire, and transgression which figure in the language, ideologies, and cultures of domination, and in the diverse kinds of resistance to it" (21).

In trying to read the historical process within the social process, Dollimore starts with the notion that in terms of violent repression and cultural divisiveness discrimination can be said to be the very essence of culture. It is, in Dollimore's view, "only critical theory and history conjoined [which] can begin to reveal the tenacious yet mobile forms of discrimination, sexual and otherwise, which organize cultures" (24; see also D. G. Marshall). In this context, "history reads theory in a way enabled ... by theory" (25). Or more precisely, theory, and I would add, in combination with history:

> has helped us to see how ... the cultural can be freed from the tyranny of the natural; gender from biology; how social change has occurred, and how it can change again; how to reveal and defend ... cultural difference; how to make visible the 'political unconscious' of our culture. (24)

But, Dollimore continues, "if theory can show such things, it is because theoretical insights have already been struggled toward by thinkers, writers, activists, and others in specific historical and political struggles where the representative structures of oppression have been massively ... in place. More than ever before we need to recover those histories. In certain respects theory enables us to do just that" (24). In this area of the "complex dialectic between centres and margins, dominant and subordinate cultures, conformity and deviance" (26) — which gave "rise to the subversion/containment debate ... in contemporary cultural theory" (27) — it is Dollimore's goal to describe the concepts and mechanics of domination and dissidence, and to develop their significance as a specific theory of dissidence on this basis. One of his most thought-provoking conclusions is his suggestion of the inadequacy of "theoretical or pseudopolitical gestures" as well as "separatist or essentialist 'identity politics'" toward sexual difference, if seen from a historical perspective (355). Still, Dollimore insists that he has "no intention of prescribing a correct attitude toward difference, even less a correct theory of difference" as he admits that he does "not even know what the latter could possibly be." His consideration of difference "originated in a turn to history in order to repudiate one such theory — specifically, that which construed homosexuality as an embrace of the same because of a fear of the different" (355).

Dollimore's carefully phrased acknowledgement of the limit of theoretical speculation does not reduce the relevance of his study. On the contrary, it touches in fact upon one of the most important and central philosophical problems of queer theory: the dilemma that exists between the procedure of analytical methodology and the epistemological function of language. Put in another way, how do I talk about a phenomenon which came into being only through the process of talking about it? One which could have been established as an element of society in many different ways in other cultural contexts if it had been perceived and talked about differently? And last but not least, how do I grasp in this condition of profound instability and change the combination and correlation of the biological and mental process of human sexuality, if indeed it is at all possible to separate the two sensory systems? From the perspective of Ludwig Wittgenstein, these conflicts — which are discussed in the gender essentialist versus gender constructionist debate (see, e.g., Fuss 1989, 2-6 and ch. 6; Weeks 1977; Greenberg; Sedgwick 1990) — cannot be solved because the meaning of language is created only by its use and not through any other outside factors. Thus, again, an existential 'event horizon' emerges and outlines the limitations of discourse. Since this constraint can neither be changed, altered, nor avoided, it might consequently only be possible to modify or reconstruct the sociocultural area (see esp. Wittig 1975, 1992), and most likely by means of a political involvement alone, as the history of the Enlightenment seems to suggest. From a philosophical point of view, this is a frustratingly walled-in situation.

So far, because of overwhelming theoretical difficulties regarding the protean variability and discourse dependency of human sexuality, the philosophical-anthropological component of queer theory has hardly been developed at all. Among others,[2] Monique Wittig (1975, 1992) and Judith Butler (*Gender Trouble*) have published important contributions to the field, as has Diana Fuss, especially in her book *Essentially Speaking: Feminism, Nature, and Difference* (1989) in which she discusses the dispute between gender essentialists and gender constructionists. Of the three, it is probably Wittig's materialist thinking that leads to the most radical notion regarding the condition of human sexuality. She disputes the naturalness of 'woman' as a social category and the biological origins of both gender difference and inequality, with challenging consequences. For Wittig, "a lesbian society pragmatically reveals that the division from men of which women have been the object is a political one" and thereby shows that women have been "ideologically rebuilt into a 'natural group'" (1981, 103). The result was that women's minds and bodies, "as well as the category 'man', are political and economic categories, not eternal ones" (106). Thus, the political fight of lesbians and gays should aim to dismantle these classifications until they disappear and make room for "a new personal and subjective definition for all humankind" which can only be found "beyond the categories of sex (woman and man)" (108). However, this state of social affairs, she concludes, can be "accomplished only by the destruction of heterosexuality as a social system which is based on the oppression of women by men and which produces the doctrine of the difference between the sexes to justify this oppression" (108).

Butler follows the thrust of Wittig's argument in so far as she too calls for subverting the conditions of gender and heteronormative sexuality by destabilizing the categories that make them possible. In her view, "gender is a performance that *produces* the illusion of an inner sex or essence or psychic gender core" ("Imitation" 317). In the course of the splendidly played out development of her argument, Butler dialectically questions the regulatory imperatives of sexual identities in the general homophobic discourse of 'compulsory heterosexuality', which is continuously "in the process of imitating and approximating its own phantasmatic idealization of itself — *and failing*" in its "efforts to naturalize itself as the original" (313). Consequently, writes Butler, if it were not for the notion of the homosexual as copy, there would be no construct of heterosexuality as origin; heterosexuality here presupposes homosexuality. In other words, "the naturalistic effects of heterosexualized genders are produced through imitative strategies" (313). Once it is realized:

> that gender is a kind of imitation for which there is no original, that heterosexuality constantly tries and fails to reproduce its own ideal image of itself, and that sex and gender achieve their supposed 'naturalness' through social performance and psychic

scripting alone, then (according to Butler) you can come out as lesbian or gay without trading one straitjacket for another — and the lesbian/gay community can practice a politics that not only emphasizes a shared sexual identity by many kinds of sexual, social, racial, ethnic, economic, and gender difference. (Abelove et al., 307)

It should be noted that Butler's application of the dialectic method of investigation is admirable even within the frame of the best Hegelian tradition. She unfolds the process of change in which a fundamental concept of human sexuality passes over into, and is still preserved and fulfilled by, its opposite. It is possible to say that, considering its goal-oriented universal versatility, the Hegelian dialectic method, even more so than its derivative technique deconstructionism, is probably the most important analytical tool of queer theory.[3] From this point of view, it is again astonishing, to say the least, that a method as indispensable as the Hegelian dialectic, in spite of its widespread use and applicability, has received so little attention and is hardly ever discussed or, even more importantly, explained and communicated separately in a queer context.

Furthermore, the interest of queer theory in postmodern cultural theory[4] leaves much to be desired. Its indifference and lack of curiosity is, after all, not surprising if one considers that, in light of the postmodern condition, the seemingly consistent heteronormative and hostile society — the traditional target of queer theory — has already begun to deteriorate, or, more precisely, has already begun to grow and expand into a multifaceted social pluralism. Following Marx that, considering the human adaptability to new situations, what we produce is always miles ahead of what we think, then it is safe to say that many of the consequences of the postmodern condition have yet to reach the consciousness of the everyday mind, a fact which leaves, at least for the time being, the traditional target of queer theory still intact.

In the end, however, queer theory might have no choice but to realize and to adjust to the claims currently being made of our times, that is, claims to the effect that:

things have fundamentally changed in one way or another. The modern nuclear family has disintegrated, to be replaced by a diversity of individual arrangements. Class society has dissolved, leading to fragmented groupings and movements based on ethnicity, gender or locality. The nation state, the classic political embodiment of modernity, has gone, assailed by a combination of global and local forces. Parliamentary democracy has broken down; the age of mass electorates and mass political parties has passed. Democracy and citizenship have to be rethought; older concepts such as 'civil society' may have to be revived, and reapplied to current conditions. (Kumar 152)

Queer theory must adapt itself to the fact of this irreducible pluralism by abandoning the idea of consensual politics, or the view that the national sovereign state is the only arena of politics attractive to groups concerned with the politics of identity and difference. Correspondingly, the typical practices of the nation state are also weakened as mass political parties give way to the new social movements based on gender, race, locality, or sexuality. Queer theory will also have to come to terms with the likelihood that we are faced with a whole new way of thinking and feeling in the postmodern world as we now live in an endlessly 'contemporary' culture, a virtual world of 'hyperrealilty' or hyperspace dealing with such strange phenomena as the crisis of representation and historicity, the end of the original work of art and the arrival of the text, the simulacrum, the death of the author and the death of the subject, the structure of power and knowledge, the fiction of the self and the end of the bourgeois ego, problems of space, spatializing time, spatial logic, psychic fragmentation, that is, the fragmented or schizophrenic self, and last but not least, the media and the market. Queer theory may want to ask itself whether or not this space of postcontemporary cultural production with its multitude of postmodern artifacts and the abovementioned new social movements are, in the words of Jameson, "consequences and aftereffects of late capitalism" (326).

Are they new units generated by the system itself in its interminable inner self-differentiation and self-reproduction? Or are they very precisely new 'agents of history' which spring into being in resistance to the system as forms of opposition to it, forcing it against the direction of its own internal logic into new reforms and internal modifications?

Notes

[1]See, for example, Abelove, Barale, and Halperin 653-66; A. P. Bell; Bullough, Elcano, Legg, and Kepner; Damon, Watson, and Jordan; Dynes; E. Garber; Gough and Greenblatt; Maggiore; Roberts; Stern; Straayer 1993; Worth.

[2]See Abelove, Barale, and Halperin 661; Edelman 1994; Moon 1991; Sedgwick 1990; and Yingling 1990.

[3]Noteworthy are de Lauretis 1993; Frye; M. Garber 1993; Harper; Miller 1993; Joan W. Scott; and also F. Nietzsche, since his work is full of dialectic examples relevant to the queer gaze.

[4]Significant introductions are Harvey; Jameson 1991; Kumar; for an extensive bibliography see Madsen.

Homosexual Love Between "Degeneration of Human Material" and "Love of Mankind": Demographical Perspectives on Homosexuality in Nineteenth-Century Germany

Angela Taeger

I N THE NINETEENTH AND EARLY TWENTIETH century, neither advocates nor opponents of Paragraph 175 could deal with sexuality and morality without simultaneously bringing in one of the most exciting novelties of their times: the development of the nation state. It promoted the political discourse in the field of sexual criminal law. State interests, as will be shown in this article, were not limited to the historical moment, they had a universal effect — also with regard to setting sexual norms.

In the course of the nineteenth century, marriage — considered the basic principle of civil order — was methodically developed in Prussia and all of the empire. Since it was seen as a clearly arranged, small social unit which reflected the ruler-subject relationship, marriage became regarded as a guarantor for the development of a modern, powerful nation. It was protected by criminal law and by jurisdiction, which provided that sexuality was only acceptable in marriage, that is, extramarital, non-procreative sexual activities were considered an infringement of the law. This clearly represented a provocation to those contemporaries who doubted the moral, social, cultural, and demographic efficiency of the institution of marriage. This article first presents the position of those idealizing marriage, followed by, in a further step, an analysis of the arguments put forward by critics of marriage — arguments that were also, if not in the first place, aimed at decriminalizing homosexuality.

"Unnatural sexual acts between persons of the male sex or between humans and animals are punishable by imprisonment; moreover, the offender may be deprived of his civil rights." This is the wording of Paragraph 175 of the Criminal Code enacted in the year of the foundation of the German Empire in 1871. This wording is identical with that of Paragraph 173 in an outline of a criminal code for the North German Confederation of 1869. With regard to its content, it recalls Paragraph 143 of the Criminal Code of the Prussian State passed in 1851.

In 1868, in connection with preparations for a criminal code for the North German Confederation, the members of the "Royal Scientific Deputation for the Medical System" were asked to give their opinion on the punishability of "unnatural sexual acts." They declared themselves against punishment, saying that other kinds of sexual offenses were not punished either and, moreover, that no unhealthy consequences were to be feared as a result of sexual acts between men or fornication between humans and animals. Passing on this expert opinion in 1869, the Prussian Minister for Health and Education remarked that, in his opinion, it would be "inadmissible in the interest of public morality" not to make "sodomy and pederasty" a punishable offense. The minister considered "the explanations of the penal law (degeneration and degradation of the person; danger for morality), given in the rationale of Paragraph 143 of the Criminal Code of April 14, 1851, to be well-founded and that this is also true with regard to the opinion of the Scientific Deputation."[1] In 1870, the draft bill was submitted to the Reichstag for decision. In the rationale concerning Paragraph 173, which adhered to the respective regulations of the Prussian Criminal Code without reservation, it is said that it was necessary to take the "sense of justice of the people" into account.[2] The draft version of Paragraph 173 was passed without changes by the advisory commission of the Reichstag, although five petitions were submitted in 1870 demanding that the penal provision be discarded or changed, and the consultant responsible for section XIII of the draft bill asked to exclude the punishment of unnatural sexual acts. When the draft version of the law was passed by the legislative assembly, it was declared binding for the North German Confederation as of May 1870. The law was included into the *Reichsstrafgesetzbuch* (Criminal Code of the German Empire) as Paragraph 175 without any modification.[3] The penalization of homosexuality outlasted the nineteenth century in defiance of the numerous and committed critics, among them, jurists, medical experts, politicians, and the people most directly affected (Taeger/Lautmann).

Prussian militarism, a barely controllable nationalism, the politics made by *Übergangsmenschen* (transitional people), the machismo of the kaiser, Wilhelm II, and the arrogance of the heads of government whose moral impeccability was in the spotlight, this seemed to make it imperative to take an uncompromising stance against "unnatural sexual acts" between men (Doerry; Hull; Mosse; Taeger/Lautmann 586-89). For decades, historical research has concerned itself with the so-called mentalities suspected of lying behind the calls for the prosecution of homosexual acts. This research has led to detailed analyses of the lesser motives that made many contemporaries of the nineteenth century approve of Paragraph 175.

The bourgeoisie in the nineteenth century idealized the core family whose clear and strictly hierarchical structure made it easy to control all areas of the private sphere. The structuring of the private sphere depended on the requirements of those factors stabilizing the respective system of rule — factors such as demographical and economic growth, and social contentment. Homosexual relationships, among others, were seen as anarchic and thus considered subversive in two respects. First, they lacked a hierarchical structure and, thus, the traditional allocation of opposite gender roles, in other words, they were missing a functioning mediator between the public interest and private life. Secondly, same-sex sexuality — incompatible with reproduction — was not in accordance with the norms prevailing until the end of the nineteenth century, namely the belief that it was not pleasure but reproduction that mattered. Sexuality per se was seen as the means to achieving constant growth in the size of the population. Homosexual men were regarded by populationists, by family politicians, and race eugenicists as an issue of national policy and a demographical impediment, and were dealt with accordingly. Effectively, it was not until the last third of the nineteenth century that support was given to the Scientific-Humanitarian Committee, sexologists such as Magnus Hirschfeld and other medical experts, and jurists who were questioning the validity of political and demographical rationales for the prosecution of homosexuals. Although they were not able to shake the populationist and sociomedical positions by resorting to neo-Malthusian maxims and the first sexual-scientific theories, they could at least analyze them critically.

Friedrich Wachenfeld, professor in law in Rostock, described marriage as the outer form created by the state to regulate sexuality (1901, 140). Because of its valuable content — that is, marital heterosexual intercourse — the institution of marriage was to be protected above all, he argued. "Heterosexual intercourse is the expression of a level of development reached only gradually by living beings. Thus, homosexuality means to regress to a protozoan-like state of the past, and, as a regression, it contradicts the principle of a continuous progression toward perfection which a community ought to master" (1903, 62).

In general, however, the demands to prosecute "unnatural sexual acts" were not founded on mere descriptions of the phylogenetical status of the one or the other type of sexual orientation. Rather, they were based on calculations regarding the efficiency of homosexual and heterosexual marital relationships, respectively, for the general public. According to contemporary observers, only heterosexual relationships had a tendency to long-term stability; only this type of relationship tended to outlast "the period of sensual ecstasy" (Jentsch 90). It was only "normal intercourse" that led "to a lasting relationship ... that is of the greatest significance mentally, morally, economically, and politically" and that "forms the foundations of society and the state" (Jentsch 90). In comparison, it was inconceivable that a "relationship appropriate to our modern world ... could be the result of homosexual love" (Jentsch 90).

Sublimated sexuality or desexualized love of heterosexual partners were given preference over homosexual love which — unimaginable without sensuality — was said to lack stability. Instinctive promiscuity was contrasted with dispassionate monogamy. Only the latter was regarded as socially functional by the sexologist Karl Jentsch, and likewise by Friedrich Wachenfeld who, in line with Wilhelm Heinrich Riehl, Joseph Unger, and G. W. Friedrich Hegel, considered marriage — protected by the state as the long-term communion of heterosexuals — to be the basis of the family, an institution that, in Wachenfeld's opinion, was of even greater importance to the state. The family, he argued, was constitutive to the state, by which Wachenfeld meant, above all, the German state, the origin of which he saw in the extended family (1901, 141). A particular respect for the female sex was inferred by Friedrich Wachenfeld from the central importance of the family in the process of national development. This, supposedly, distinguished Germany in a positive way from the Orient and the countries of Ancient Rome: "Here, a genuinely Germanic characteristic emerges that can be traced back to the times of Tacitus and that contributed to making the German nation a first-rate civilized people" (Wachenfeld 1901, 141). Besides supporting the sanctioning and regulation of monogamous marriage by the state to produce stable and controllable social relations, Wachenfeld feared for the continued fundamental progress of culture if homosexuality were to spread. Since he equated the lack of sexual attraction for women with a lack of social appreciation for women, homosexual men seemed to him to express not only their lack of interest in family life but also disrespect for women (Wachenfeld 1901, 142). They refused to start a family and thus renounced the exposed position of the breadwinner that promised dominance. They dissociated themselves from masculinity which expressed itself only by way of power over a wife and children — mislabeled in contemporary terminology as appreciation for the woman. The commission working on the draft version of a new criminal code in 1909 seized such reasoning, including the claim that homosexuals adapt themselves insufficiently to the kind of role-behavior expected of men in the family unit and toward women: "Unnatural sexual acts, in particular between men, are a danger to the state, since they tend to damage the character and the bourgeois existence of men most seriously, and tend to destroy healthy family life."[4]

The state's control over the sexuality of its members served the purpose of consolidating power not only indirectly, that is, by means of family policy, but also directly. It was executed with the intention to suppress any behavior that might be detrimental to the national economy or civil obedience. It was in this connection that homosexuality first became a source of contention in the demographic balance seen as imperative to the prosperity of the state. It was said to contribute to a decline in the birth rate, thereby increasing the risk of a deficient demographic development. Then, it was argued that homosexuality threatened the *qualitative* demographic foundations necessary for economic growth, namely the health of the nation. Finally, homosexuality was regarded as a risk to national security by creating the dispositions and preconditions for revolutionary intrigues.

"The state reserves the right to prosecute this abnormal practice of the sexual instincts, because it has a great interest in the normal performance of this act. For, in one respect, the increase in population necessary for the existence of the state depends on it" (Gräf 97). Thus, by resorting to the good of the state that had to be protected from homosexuality, the interests of population policy became one of the arguments presented most often. It had been used since the beginning of the nineteenth century, and even after the turn of the century it seemed appropriate enough to convince the members of the Reichstag of the necessity to punish unnatural sexual acts (Feuerbach).[5] Obviously, the indispensability of a continuous increase in population and the advantages of high population figures were issues that did not seem to require empirical evidence or logical explanations. Justifications were neither consistent with the populationist discourse nor could they be sustained at all in view of the actual development of population figures (Charbit). The statements about the demographic relevance of homosexuality were consistent with the program of the "state-controlled production of men" that was maintained undisputedly and successfully without any objective cause, until the last third of the nineteenth century (Heinsohn et al.). It was only toward the end of the nineteenth century that neo-Malthusian countermovements became active, forcing populationists to use more differentiated arguments.

According to Friedrich Wachenfeld, the risk of depopulation increased with a growth in the number of homosexual men. Specifying the nature and the consequences of this threat, he mentioned that the dangers to national defense lay "particularly in a state dependent on a large army for its existence. Our continuous increase in population is the power which renders us superior to other countries with are rich in resources" (1901, 142). Only with a sufficiently large population – so we understand from statements made in 1903 – could a nation convincingly demonstrate its strength and, if necessary, vigorously put it to the test in conflicts with competing states. Wachenfeld limited the validity of populationist maxims to nations which, like Germany, did not possess other resources. France, for instance, could refrain from measures designed to stimulate population growth, such as the prosecution of unnatural sexual acts, without having to fear lasting consequences (1901, 142 and 1903, 57, 59).

Totally unaffected as yet by medical research on homosexuality, which did not become relevant until half a century later, Paul Johann Anselm Feuerbach characterized the unnatural satisfaction of sexual urges as an arbitrary act for which the individual is responsible and as a vice which results in the physical decline of the person affected. As early as 1801, Feuerbach warned that directing the political attention to the *quantity* of the population must not lead to completely neglecting the *quality* of the citizens' capacity for contributing to national achievements: "The nervous constitution of the citizens which makes them unable to contribute to the interests of the state: these is the rationale demanding that the police prohibit and prosecute these acts" (404). Feuerbach, however, did not clearly identify the immediate causes leading to such physical defectiveness. A causal connection was construed by way of association between unnatural behavior and health defects: the revenge of nature. Perhaps Feuerbach paraphrased the extensive contemporary literature on onanism, describing the nonprocreative waste of sperm and its devastating consequences. As long as advocates of political interests like Feuerbach regarded the nervous constitution of the citizens as a consequence of acquired homosexual acts, it was easy to justify the call for punishment: "Even the adversaries of Paragraph 175 admit that even a healthy, normal person will suffer physical and mental damage as a result of homosexuality ... Should homosexuality spread, the nation too, just like the individual, will lose strength and vigor" (Wachenfeld 1903, 58-59).

The health of the individual and of all citizens was regarded as an interest to be protected by the state and defended by the deterrent of the threat of punishment outlined in Paragraph 175. This is precisely the position to which Wachenfeld withdrew as late as 1903 — not, however, without having to admit that the results of the medical research carried out during the hundred years since Feuerbach conflicted with his arguments: "After the discovery of contrasexuality, when homosexuality, just like the former, was passed off as a regularly hereditary predisposition, it seemed no longer suitable for the law to counter the homosexuality of the perpetrator" (1903, 59). One strategy to avoid the dilemma of prosecuting a behavior for which the individual could not be held responsible and of imposing sentences that could have no remedial effect consisted in minimizing or simply denying the possibility of inborn homosexuality (cf. 1903, 60). Other contemporaries tried to redeem their position by means of a vicious circle: Anton Roemer, a physician, did not contradict the assumption that contrary sexuality was an inborn predisposition. But if it was possible for such a predisposition to develop, he concluded, this could only be so on the basis of moral depravity, of increasing nervousness, and of neuropathological and psychopathological states — in other words: on the basis of spreading homosexuality. According to Roemer, homosexuality not only led to illness, but was a sign of degeneration, was itself pathological, and, again, had to be fought in the interest of the self-preservation of the state: "It is exactly the same case as with compulsory vaccination, for instance, which must be continued and generally imposed even if it is not possible to avoid all damages completely" (Roemer 10). Wachenfeld followed: "We need a Criminal Code in the same way as we need an Epidemics Act. Whereas no Epidemics Act is required for illnesses occurring only sporadically, it is vital for those that may become epidemic. And this is the case with homosexuality" (1903, 62).

Paragraph 175 was thus also seen as a stronghold against an endemically spreading disease. It helped "to limit centers of infection to themselves as far as possible" and made it easier for the state to protect those who had not yet been infected — healthy heterosexuals (Wachenfeld 1903, 60). Around the turn of the century, eugenicists developed these thoughts in further detail. Visions of a race in decline, of a degeneration of human material, turned them into advocates of a strict imposition of Paragraph 175. Emphasizing the particular constitutional inferiority of homosexuals, eugenicists demanded that homosexuals — who, according to them, were "to be regarded both as the expression and the source of degeneration" (Loewenberg 733) — should be imprisoned for life. "From the point of view of racial hygiene it is impossible to regard them as a normal variant, and even less so as one in whose reproduction the race would be interested" (Loewenberg 733). They maintained that garnering the optimum quantity and quality in procreation was the guarantee for a "victorious fight against elements and fellow beings," such as "the extinction of mankind as such or the subjection of one nation to the other," both of which had to be "expected in the near or the distant future" (Rüdin 104, 107). Homosexuals compromised battle and victory.

Once it was established that homosexuals could not be utilized in the interests of the state, it was then only a small step to suspecting that they refused to contribute to building a powerful nation, and worse still, that they actively foiled the realization of the desire for national stability and international domination. Driven by sexual urges, hedonistic, unable to commit and reproduce themselves, not interested in marriage and starting a family, disrespectful of women and of male dominance, centers of epidemics, sites of dysfunction — with these characteristics, male homosexuals were stigmatized and turned into antisocial enemies of modern society. Yet, to maintain such a psychological background, it was necessary to regard homosexuality not as an innate predisposition, but rather as an acquired vice. In 1909, the commission preparing the draft of the criminal code declared that all claims to a congenital, biological origin of homosexuality were unproven and contradicted the experience of daily life. As far as behavior was concerned, the freedom of the will of homosexuals was not considered to be in the least restricted, and the damage done to their civic existence, the state, and the interests of society was believed to be self-imposed. Homosexuality, the commission stated, often went along "with shady activities and with seeking contact with the most suspicious individuals — neither of which will hardly be without effect on the overall moral personality of the person having gone astray."[6]

In the course of the eighteenth century, a "program for the production of men" became effective in the German-speaking countries that entailed endeavors which had been developed in France in connection with mercantilism (Heinsohn et al. 61). The program was based on the theory that the wealth of a nation varies according to the size of the population: the more subjects the larger the national wealth. Consequently, means and ways had to be found urging people to reproduce — in fact beyond the often narrow limits set by the economic situation of individual families; means and ways that make people forget the need for and the possibility of self-determined generative behavior. An important step in this was taken long before the eighteenth century: any knowledge about contraception had been wiped out around 1700 with the inquisition of witches (cf. Heinsohn et al. 46–48). In the eighteenth and nineteenth centuries then, the violent acts of the inquisition were replaced by the espionage of the Health Police (63). As a tool of the modern state, the Health Police attempted to fulfill the modern task of an unrestricted production of men by countering any form of extramarital and nonprocreative sexuality as well as subsequent birth control, while emphasizing ethical-religious principles. It was Protestantism in particular, but the Catholic Church as well, that prepared the ground for the ideology or the establishment of the Health Police. "While, until then, it is regarded in history as irresponsible to have children unless there is an inheritance securing their future, the Christian churches reverse this value in their sermons, designating as modern responsibility toward God that which used to be, traditionally, irresponsibility in the procreation of children" (Heinsohn et al. 16).

What the Christian churches regarded as sinful, namely sexual activity for the sake of pleasure, the state judiciary prosecuted as an offense against morality, as an offense against the basis of national prosperity. Indeed, having eliminated any knowledge of contraceptive practices and having popularized Christian sexual morals, there was no longer a need for modern governments to take draconian measures against saboteurs in the production of men. "From the eighteenth and nineteenth century on the highly differentiated criminal laws trying to force people into having and raising offspring are perfected. Now state control suffices to maintain the stability and effectiveness of the enforced family morality" (Heinsohn et al. 162).

Historical demographers have remarked upon a, or rather *the*, "population explosion" in the eighteenth and nineteenth centuries. The growth in population was the consequence of a high birth rate due to both an absolute increase in marriages and higher birth figures per marriage. This had a disastrous effect on the individual family since the number of children often exceeded the resources to support them. Governments were confronted with an army of neglected children, huge numbers of adolescents of no economic use, and impoverished parents. The countermeasures taken by governments, such as prohibiting child labor and introducing or extending compulsory school attendance, aggravated further the difficult situation of lower middle-class and working-class families. The prohibition of child labor meant that the children's contribution to the family income was lost, while, at the same time, sending the children to school often created new problems for the parents. "The expenses with which parents are encumbered finally compel them to find a way to avoid these expenses. Once again, sexual lust and reproduction are separated. The use of nonimpregnating techniques of satisfaction increases by the same rate as the use of contraceptives. The heyday of the police-controlled penal system enforcing reproduction has come to an end in the last third of the nineteenth century. From then on the birthrates in developed societies start to decrease" (Heinsohn et al. 95–96).

The discussion about the political significance of homosexuality intensified around the turn of the century. By this time, it had already become obvious that it was problematic, to say the least, to withdraw the generative behavior from individual decision-making and individual rationale in order to subject it to the nation's insatiable demand for people. The doubtfulness of these efforts intensified the debate surrounding the significance of homosexuality with regard to the state-directed production of men. Against better judgment, politicians and church leaders appealed to the viability of the traditional demographic principle; now more than ever, marriage and family were invested with the nimbus of a national shrine. Reproduction was praised as a natural inevitability and a phylogenetic achievement, the unlimited multiplying of citizens as an internal and external stabilizer. Against this background, engaging in same-sex sexuality could be turned into an act of high treason.

Another faction of authors dealing with homosexuality and state politics discussed, in a desperate attempt to eliminate it, the danger inherent in the program of the production of men. In the late nineteenth and the early twentieth century some race eugenicists believed that nervous diseases, physical and mental degeneration, and the deterioration of human material spread from homosexuals. According to race eugenicists, the internment of homosexuals was unavoidable from the viewpoint of race preservation. Since about 1870, anybody interested in demographic policy could hardly ignore the fact that the desired multiplication of human beings could only be effected with considerable losses in the quality of human material. Eugenicists argued that, under the pressure from the state, impoverished, unkempt, and feeble-minded parents would produce the same sort of off-spring – only in greater number. "This is where one may locate the histori-cal origin of bourgeois racism, made up of the fear of the decline of their own races and of being 'flooded' by 'inferior races'" (Heinsohn et al. 134). It was out of fear and concern that race hygienists took care to eliminate those elements assumed to impair the race and to maintain a stock worth reproducing. If in the course of this process their attention was drawn to homosexuals, it was not least because those who pleaded for the abolition of Paragraph 175 based their arguments on the pathological predisposition of the persons affected. Moreover, for rhetorical reasons, it made sense to blame homosexuals for the failure of the organized production of men since they had compromised the demographic program from the very be-ginning due to their nonreproductive sexual behavior.

The population explosion and the concern for society's well-being forced turn-of-the-century populationists onto the defensive, while strength-ening the voices of their opponents. In the last third of the nineteenth century, neo-Malthusians started to criticize the demographical strategies still dominant in a more and more emphatic way. Advocates of the aboli-tion of Paragraph 175 were often inspired by their arguments. They often left untouched the principle according to which a continuous growth of the population increases the national wealth. They confined themselves to questioning the extent to which homosexuality could be regarded as a factor worth discussing in this respect at all. As Karl Maria Benkert main-tained, with regard to their potential contribution to multiplying the popu-lation, homosexuals were the lesser evil when compared, for instance, with onanists whose fertility was believed to be irreversibly damaged (30). The example of other nations showed that not to prosecute homosexual inter-course by no means resulted in decreasing population figures (*Denkschrift* 13). Just as it could be assumed that, on the one hand, the threat of sanc-tions would reduce the number of citizens because it would make many homosexuals leave the country or commit suicide, so could it be taken for granted that, on the other hand, "by threatening and imposing prison sen-tences the desire of homosexuals for women will not be increased in the least" (Hiller 976-77). However, taking general recourse to demographical state interests which were supposedly violated by homosexuals was not convincing as long as other types of nonreproductive sexuality went unpunished (Benkert 26-27).

This objection showed the way for a comprehensive criticism of the populationist position; according to this criticism there could be no question of the danger of depopulation in the foreseeable future. Therefore, it was futile to attempt to counter this objection and unjustifiable to prosecute unnatural sexual acts for demographic reasons (Heimberger 707). In 1869, Karl Maria Benkert drew attention to the fact, that people in Germany in particular had been complaining for decades about a population that was too high, a fact which even led them to suggest to "the government as despicable a thing as 'infibulation'" (26). Considering such suggestions, it was absurd to punish homosexuals for abstaining from reproduction, for contributing to defuse the explosive demographic situation. It was "not even certain whether the wise Creator has not intentionally created people who love the same sex in order to preclude overpopulation" (*Denkschrift* 13). Even if it did turn out that homosexuals were not beings of divine providence, it was argued that one should nonetheless profit from their existence, for they made superfluous such "terrible means of regulation like wars, epidemics, famines that decimate humanity" (*Denkschrift* 13).

The populationists were, arguably, inconsistent in their debate over the punishability of homosexual acts. Yet not in the least did their credibility suffer from the obviously growing discrepancy between the demographic ideal and the actual demographic development. So were their arguments more than mere ideology? The close association of sexuality and reproduction was attributed to what they believed was an originally Jewish maxim that "not a single drop of sperm may be wasted wantonly from which a Jew might have grown, in order to increase the tribe and make it strong against its enemies." This original concept had been "carried to the extremes of original sin, of crime and impurity by *historical* Christianity only — not by the *teachings* of Christ." As a consequence, the prosecution of homosexuals was by no means justified by divine law but proved to be, in Benkert's own words, "dreadful, exaggerated nonsense" (77-78).

Heinsohn et al. characterize the early Malthusians as still swayed by the traditional demographic system. Unable to free themselves from the morality governing marriage and family imposed by the church, they could not find any new approaches in their endeavors to find ways of limiting the population growth: "In their search for possible means of birth control they usually suggest celibacy, lifelong sexual abstinence, instead of contraception-oriented hedonistic sexuality" (32).

A different line of thought can be found among contemporary advocates in favor of reforming the penal code punishing "unnatural sexual acts." Their play on thoughts, which presented homosexuality as a counterbalance — at least permissible, and perhaps even natural — to the potentially disastrous population growth, already expressed reservations against institutionalized (hetero-)sexuality, marriage, and having a large number of children. As yet, the majority of reform activists was reluctant to advocate hedonistic sexuality, and, if so, only to prevent dangerous overpopulation. Some authors, however, found better arguments against the conventional appreciation of institutions and the subsequent disdain for emotions and passion. Instead of the mere biological capability of reproduction, love was to become the basis of partnerships and the standard against which to judge the quality of the relationships. There can be no doubt, reform activists argued, that, compared to marriages, homosexual partnerships often came off better as far as mutual affection was concerned: "How many marriages approved by the state and sanctified by the church came about and are lived in such a way that they cannot be judged better than concubinage — and sometimes not even that!" (Katte 1900, 304). Although it was true that the church did not prohibit love, "it did not allow pleasure unless within the bounds of marriage" (*Eros* 9). Love and pleasure, however, are inseparable, an expression of the most elemental, vital needs of each individual. As such, the individual could not be controlled by the authorities and could not be limited to sanctioned lifestyles — a fact that was taken into consideration by the state insofar as "in general, extramarital intercourse between men and women went unpunished. Considering the fact that love and desire for men have been implanted into the homosexual just like the desire for women into the ordinary man, the former's behavior will have to be regarded and judged in the same way as are extramarital relations by the latter" (*Eros* 10).

The program of the production of men met with determined resistance. The "demand that those who are capable of reproducing must exert that capability" was not evaded by referring to abstinence (Katte 1908, 402). Those who entered the debate no longer tried to argue in defense of the prevailing demographic principles, but offensively adopted the opposite standpoint. The focus shifted to realizing individual desires, among them pleasure and love, while the supposed social obligation to reproduce receded into the background. Nature, Katte argued, "did not, first of all, instill beings with the drive to reproduce, but with the desire to come together sexually, in a more noble sense: to love one another; reproduction is a necessary but not — on the part of those having intercourse — an immediately intended consequence" (1908, 402). It was not difficult to render plausible this argument. For, if the sole purpose of the sexual act was to increase the population, it had to be performed "only once every ten months, to make a conservative estimate." And it was now recognized that "in any other case, intercourse between a man and a woman is determined by sensuality to no lesser degree than intercourse between homosexuals" (Katte 1900, 302–303; cf. Hirschfeld 1898, 53).

Dissolving the state-ordained conjoining of heterosexuality with marriage and reproduction, and confronting the limited biological reasoning toward sexuality with a hedonistic attitude meant creating a new foundation on which heterosexuality and homosexuality could coexist side by side. Both heterosexuals and homosexuals satisfied individual needs that, nonetheless, seemed legitimate. State interests were neither intentionally pursued by heterosexuals, nor systematically violated by homosexuals. The opponents of Paragraph 175 considered the public good and state interests to be categories that were either not at all applicable to sexuality or in need of a new definition considerate of the phenomena of homo- and heterosexuality. Obviously, Benedict Friedländer admits, no nation could survive in the long run if it consisted mainly of homosexuals abstaining from reproduction ("Bemerkungen" 219). However, before calling homosexuals inferior because of their unwillingness or inability to beget children, and before accusing them of being enemies of the state, it was necessary to examine whether they did not make up, perhaps even overcompensate for, this admitted deficit. In Friedländer's opinion "one of the most important characteristics of man is his social existence, without it there could be no culture" ("Physiologische Freundschaft" 186). On the basis of this observation, he continued, it could be ascertained that only the "most highly developed" (höchstsozialen) beings had achieved a "far-reaching differentiation of sexuality" and produced a "third sex," one that did not get involved in reproduction (186). As "exquisite social varieties," he concluded, they alone ensured a kind of division of labor between the "necessities of reproduction and the new necessities of socialness, the combination of which in one and the same individual would have been too much.

Physiological 'homosexual love'," Friedländer argued, was "necessary for every social species" (206). The existence of a 'third sex' was more than just necessary; it was *proof* of the specific quality of a culture. Male same-sex love was to be called "love of mankind" (193) in a comprehensive sense, the "basis of human socialness, and thus of culture and even morality" (187). He continued that compared to male same-sex[7] love, the love of one's spouse and maternal love were of inferior value. At best, marriage and family contributed nothing to the process of socialization, to culture and morality — at worst, they had a destructive effect on all three since they did nothing but administer egotistical interests. This cultivating aspect of homosexuality explained "why the percentage of determined homosexuals is particularly large among the great artists, poets, and statesmen," among people who are socially active, among creative artists and moral educators "in whom we have to assume a high, comprehensive, human affect" (188).

With his theory of "physiological friendship," Benedict Friedländer not only took the sting out of the reproaches accusing homosexuals of not contributing to the increase in population, he also provided arguments to parry attacks connecting homosexuality with the physical, mental, and moral degeneration of a nation. Their specific emotional orientation predisposed homosexuals to be particularly social-minded, sensitive, and ingenious (Wilhelm 423; cf. *Das Gemeinschädliche des §143* 15). "Socrates, Plato, Michelangelo, Shakespeare, Charles XII of Sweden, Frederick the Great, Count August von Platen — all of whom were men who were either extremely homosexual or whose character has, at least, a strong homosexual element — were surely no ignoble personalities?" (Kaiser 997). Friedländer added that it was not homosexuality that fostered the physical and nervous breakdown observed in some people. Neither could keeping suspect company or showing the tendency to hide away be called a direct predisposition of homosexuals. Constructs of this kind only showed "the same fine logic and the same nobility of attitude as in people reproaching animals in captivity for not jumping around merrily" (Hiller 978-79). Rather, it was the threat of punishment and manifest discrimination that gave homosexuals a tendency toward neurotic, deviant behavior. Friedländer concluded that the first step toward the social rehabilitation of homosexuals would be made by abolishing Paragraph 175. Then they would finally behave naturally according to their predispositions.

What was the aim of those voices who insisted on the prosecution of homosexuality as a violation of state interests? According to their own words it was the consolidation of national state power. Ironically, "civic and social freedom," the only roots from which "freedom of the state and the nation" could "grow organically," is exactly what an anonymous activist expected from the abolition of Paragraph 175 (*Das Gemeinschädliche des §143* 33).

Notes

[1] *Entwurf eines Strafgesetsbuches für den Norddeutschen Bund. Nebst Motiven und Anlagen.* Berlin 1870, 11.

[2] *Stenographische Berichte über die Verhandlungen des Norddeutschen Bundes. Anlagen.* Berlin 1870, 67.

[3] Strafrechtskommission. *Protokoll der Sitzung der Reichstagskommission.* 01.03.1870. Zentrales Staatsarchiv Potsdam, *Bestand Reichtstag*, Repositur 01.01., Akte 826 passim.

[4] Strafrechtskommission, *Begründung zum Entwurf eines neuen deutschen StGB* 1907. Zentrales Staatsarchiv Postdam, *Bestand Reichsjustizamt*, Repositur 30.01, Akte 5871, 168v. Freies wissenschaftliches Komitee, *Vorentwurf zu einem Deutschen StGB* 1909. Akte 5878, 2.

[5] See also *Stenographische Berichte über die Verhandlungen des Reichtags*, Plenum 31.3.1905 (Abgeordneter Thaler). Berlin 1905.

[6] Zentrales Staatsarchiv Potsdam, *Bestand Reichsjustizamt*, Repositur 30.01.1909, Akte 5871, 168v, 169v (Strafrechtskommission 1909).

[7] The words "homosexual" and "homosexuality" took on very different meanings in Friendländer's texts, particularly when compared to their use by Krafft-Ebing, Havelock Ellis, and other sexologists. See Harry Oosterhuis, *Homosexuality and Male Bonding*, and Jonathan N. Katz, *The Invention of Heterosexuality*, for details.

A/Symmetrical Reading of *Inversion* in Fin-de-Siècle Music, Musicology, and Sexology

Martin Scherzinger and Neville Hoad

> *Give me where to stand: And I will turn your system of*
> *persecution upside down.*
> —Numa Numantius[1]

Introduction

TOWARDS THE END OF THE NINETEENTH century, *inversion* and *inversional symmetry* evolved into fundamental concept-metaphors in various scientific disciplines, such as biology, physics, crystallography, music theory, sexology, and group theory. In mathematics, for example, the general idea of *symmetry* had evolved into perhaps one of the most significant contributions to the discipline at that time.[2] Although the very idea of mathematics is predicated on notions of symmetry, I. M. Yaglom argues, the post-Aristotelian period, under the influence of Euclid, witnessed an indifference and skepticism toward the concept. A lengthy hiatus in the use of symmetry in the mathematical sciences ensued. It was not until the new European mathematics of the late nineteenth century, particularly in the work of Felix Klein and Sophus Lie, that the mathematical apparatus began again to reflect symmetrical relationships.[3] At the same time, this era witnessed the emergence of new disciplines, such as scientific crystallography, that were deeply beholden to the idea of symmetrical inversions. Again, while the use of symmetric properties to classify crystals dated back to ancient times, Yaglom argues, "the mathematical theory of crystals ... was entirely a product of the 19th century" (206). An exhaustive list of crystallographic groups, two hundred and thirty in all, was achieved by the combined efforts of Efgraf Stepanovich Fedorov (1853-1919), Arthur Moritz Schönflies (1853-1928), and William Barlow (1845-1934) in 1894. Around this time, the literature on geometric symmetries, as they appeared in both science and art, abounded ranging from L. Sohncke's

Entwicklung einer Theorie der Kristallstruktur (1879) and G. V. Vulf's *Symmetry and Its Manifestation in Nature* (1908) to A. V. Shubnikov's *Symmetry: The Laws of Symmetry and Their Application in Science, Technology and Applied Art* (1939).[4] In fact, despite the divergent ways in which they were put to use, there was hardly a discipline that remained wholly untouched by the idea of *symmetry* and *inversion*.

This paper concerns itself with the deployment of these concepts in two of these disciplinary contexts in Europe between 1860 and 1910. Despite many affinities, *inversion* in musical discourse – both theoretical and compositional – was crucially involved in a significant stylistic shift, while in sexology, the *invert*, although a transitional term, inaugurates less a shift than a consolidation of the modern *homosexual*. What follows are speculations on both the convergence and the divergence of this concept in these fields and the implications this has for queer theory and musicology today. This will involve the telling of a less known history of the transition from chromaticism to atonality, on the one hand, and revisiting the transition from the *sodomite* to the *homosexual*, on the other.

Hence the paper narrates music's turn-of-the-century transition into modernism in terms of underlying generative modalities – inversional operations amongst them – instead of adopting the more widely-held view that this transition involved a saturation of chromaticism or an imperative to avoid the tonic. This it does by marking certain formal affinities between tonal syntax, as it came to be understood in the late nineteenth century, and early serial procedures. In an article entitled "Inversional Balance as an Organizing Force in Schönberg's Music and Thought," David Lewin also attempts to correlate notions of inversional balance with aspects of tonality. He shows, for example, how Schönberg employs inversionally balanced 'areas' in ways that relate to *key* areas in tonal music. Lewin also points out that, in important ways, the tonal system is based on inversional relations. Since the constituents of the *subdominant* cannot be generated by the overtones of a tonic note, it is posited by inversion: "Tonic-to-subdominant *inverts* the relation of tonic-to-dominant, and the force of the tonic involves its central character, as mediating between upper and lower dominants" (1968, 2–3). Although we identify a different trajectory from tonality to atonality via the work on inversional symmetries by nineteenth-century music theorists, Lewin's observations contribute to a similarly focused history of relations between these aesthetic periods.

Analogously, the paper narrates the shift in sexology, from the *sodomite* via the *invert* to the *homosexual* in less familiar terms, suggesting that more than taxonomy is at stake. That is, in this reading, the transition from *invert* to *homosexual* involves *more* of a transformation than the, now widespread, Foucauldian genealogy would have it. *Inversion*, as the conceptual tool used to understand the experience of same-sex sexual desire occupied a key moment in a European history of sexuality. Easily dismissed in current theory as biologically essentialist and empirically un-provable, this term is mostly understood as the simple forerunner of the *homosexual*. Rendered marginal in one domain, central in another, *inversion* has many confusing meanings and applications, which we will at-tempt to explore through a close reading of selected theoretical and com-positional works.

A word on our historical method: we advance the notion at various points in our examination that the explanatory force of *inversion* and *in-versional symmetry* — their ability to account for and generate new phe-nomena — was granted to such an extent that, even in situations in which the phenomena did not line up with the empirical situation, the empirical findings were nonetheless assumed to fit the pattern. On such occasions, it was felt that the data were merely still to be collected. The point to be ob-served about these moments of faith is that in an era of rampant positiv-ism, some truth claims were as deeply implicated in the symmetrical iden-tity as they were wholly empirical. In other words, the scientific discourse was thus charged with the energy of an aesthetic structure; its empirical content patterned by a form. We thus take Hayden White's configuration of "form-as-message" (204) as axiomatic in our account.

Our methodology also takes for granted the challenge to disembodied objectivity in the writing of history made by White, Stephen Greenblatt, H. Arom Veeser, and many others in recent years. We share with these writers an interest in exposing the manifold ways in which different aspects of so-cial, scientific, and cultural life affect each other, and particularly in reveal-ing the unsuspected regularities and borrowings that obtain in ostensibly distinct and unrelated activities, disciplines and institutions. However, un-like the New Historicists, we are not as much concerned with a differential analysis of local discourse, or of local conflicts in a specific setting, as might be expected. The concept-metaphors under investigation were, in fact, quite widespread and, in many cases, institutionally central. Thus, we have kept this general view in mind throughout our analysis, and paradoxically also strategically suspended an examination of the extent to which the form of the above scientific discourse, as well as our historical discourse, is the site of ideologically significant work. This is because not all manifestations of these forms, and thus their concomitant messages, yielded equivalent ideological meanings. While it is true that *inversion* in both sexology and musicology could be linked to certain modalities for the production of social norms and musical works respectively, we offer the idea that the concept also had a radical potential to undo gendered binaries that, in sexology, could not be managed in the end.

I.

By the late nineteenth century, leading German music theorists, such as Moritz Hauptmann (1792-1868), Oskar Fleischer (1856-1933), Arthur Joachim von Öttingen (1836-1920), Hugo Riemann (1849-1919), Bernhard Ziehn, and Hermann Schröder (1843-1909), sought to explain the duality of major and minor less in terms of the traditional masculine and feminine bifurcation and more in terms of a symmetrically inversional relation (*die symmetrische Umkehrung*). In Schröder's view, the major triad consisted of a perfect fifth and a major third above the fundamental, while the minor triad consisted of the same intervals below the fundamental (fig. 1). Minor was thus regarded as a mirror image of major and vice versa. While the empirical buttress for the major triad rested on the overtone series, scientific explanations of the minor were notoriously a good deal trickier. That is, the major triad was formed by the overtones closest to the fundamental, while the overtone series could not be relied upon to explain the minor triad, for the overtone yielding the characteristic minor

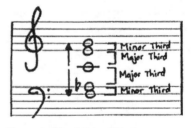

Figure 1. The Minor Triad as a Mirror Image of the Major Triad

third was not nearly among the first partials. Figure 2 reproduces Hermann von Helmholtz's representation of the overtone series in *On the Sensations of Tone* (1875). To complicate matters, partials occurring earlier in the series, than the lowest that could approximate a minor third, were already excluded from the (chromatic) system, presumably as too remote from the fundamental to be sensible.

Figure 2. The Overtone Series as Explicated by Hermann von Helmholtz (1877)

This lack of empirical support for the minor triad led the more tradi-
tionally-minded theorist Ernst Mach (1839-1916) to posit a single chord of
nature *(Naturklang)*, namely the major triad, in relation to which the minor
triad was explained as a modification or as an embellishment, weak and unstable in itself. This *harmonic monism* had a well-established eighteenth-
century precedent. For Jean-Jacques Rousseau, the minor triad lacked the
necessary resonance of Rameau's chord of nature *(corps sonore)*. It could
be "discovered only by analogy and inversion" (in Wheelock 202) and
thus, in the words of Johan Kirnberger, was suitable for the expression of
"sad, doubtful sentiments, for hesitation and indecision" (in Wheelock
202). The minor was thus judged either in the terms of a lack – Knecht's C
minor was "lamenting and longing," while his C major was "cheerful and
pure" – or the minor was judged in the terms of an excess; Galeazzi's G
minor was "frenzied," while his G major was "innocent and simple" (in
Wheelock 208). For the later nineteenth-century harmonic monists the subordinate place of the minor triad was maintained. Its failure to align neatly
with the overtone series rendered the minor triad a derivative of the harmonic monists' *Naturklang* and lacking in an empirical grounding in nature.

For the *harmonic dualists*, on the other hand, the minor triad was
equally as axiomatic, or fundamental, in their harmonic schemes as the major was. The minor, they claimed, was also based in nature. To impart an
acoustical foundation for the minor, Riemann invoked the *undertone*
series. As David Bernstein tells us: "A given complex musical tone, for Riemann, engendered both an overtone and a symmetrically related undertone
series" (380): the major sonority *(Klang)* was a mirror image of the minor
and vice versa. Thus we witness a moment in Riemann's empirical scheme
where the symmetry carries the bulk of the explanatory force and the
acoustics, not yet fully proven, were assumed.

Configuring the minor triad in terms of an inverted major has an extensive genealogy, beginning, perhaps, with Gioseffo Zarlino (1517–1590). For Zarlino, a fundamental C could, through the principle of *covibration*, generate the tones f, a-flat and c. While Zarlino's views preceded the common practice period and contributed to the then emergent principles of tonality, the work of Schröder, Riemann, and others marked the end of this period and contributed, in unforeseen ways, to the decline of these principles. Not surprisingly Riemann identified Zarlino's idea as the starting point of his own history of harmonic theory, praising him for "discovering" *harmonic dualism*, the "two possible forms of harmony" (506). Scott Burnham argues that Zarlino's understanding of major and minor had little to do with the nineteenth-century concept of dualism; that Riemann selectively reads dualism into Zarlino's work in order to justify the dualism which is the foundation of his own theory (8). In any event, Riemann chose to emphasize Zarlino's identification of major and minor as inversionally related and, in contrast, criticized Zarlino's adherence to the figured-bass school, claiming that the development of dualistic harmonic theory was thus hampered (425). According to Riemann, it was not until the late nineteenth century that dualism was rediscovered as axiomatic to harmonic theory. Thus, he maps a history of harmony that parallels that of mathematics and crystallography in terms of an early appearance, followed by the disappearance, and finally the reemergence of symmetrical inversions in the late nineteenth century.

Much of Riemann's dualistic theory seems to have been derived from a treatise written by Arthur von Öttingen in 1866 called *Dual Development of Harmony (Harmoniesystem in dualer Entwickelung)*. Öttingen's theory of harmony rested on the idea that elements of a *Klang* either have a common fundamental or a common overtone. The major triad represented *tonicity* because its constituents had a common fundamental, while the minor triad represented *phonicity* because its representatives all possessed a common overtone. For instance, in the phonic G chord (better known to us as the C-minor triad), c, e-flat, and g had a common overtone of which they were fundamentals, while the constituents c, e, and g of tonic C (known as the C major triad) were overtones of a common fundamental. These relations are depicted in figure 3. Öttingen's wording is interesting: "The tones of the major triad are common components of the tonic fundamental, those of the minor triad have a common phonic overtone" (39). In the spirit of the dialectician Moritz Hauptmann, Öttingen posited

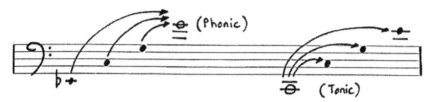

Figure 3. Arthur von Öttingen's Theory of Harmonic Dualism: Tonicity and Phonicity (1866)

an opposition between *Haben* and *Sein*. The phonic constituents *have* a common overtone, and the tonic constituents *are* overtones of a fundamental. On the one hand, Öttingen thus posited major and minor as inversionally symmetrical, and, on the other, he asserted ontological priority for the former. In other words, the phonic acted as a kind of back formation, or an opposite projection, of the tonic.

II.

In the contemporaneous realm of sexology, *inversion* enjoyed popular and scientific currency from the mid-nineteenth century to the early twentieth century. The origin of the term is unclear. Havelock Ellis and John Addington Symonds stated in 1898 that, a few years before, sexual inversion had not yet been named (35). They claimed that the term first appeared in the work of several Italian writers and then passed into general European currency in the last half of the nineteenth century. Karl Heinrich Ulrichs used the term *conträre Sexualempfindung* (contrary sexuality) in *Memnon: Die Geschlechtsnatur des mannliebenden Urnings. Eine naturwissenschaftliche Darstellung* (1868). Jean Charcot and Valentin Magnan introduced the term *inversion* in an 1882 article in the *Archives de Neurologie*. The term was also used by Karl Friedrich Otto Westphahl in his article "Die Sexualempfindung" (cf. Katz 55; and Chauncey 114–46), as well as by J. Chevalier in his 1893 study entitled *L'inversion sexuelle*. The meaning of the term broadly involved a description of a sexual desire that was projected in a direction opposite to the norm and additionally identified such a desire as a medical disposition. In its fully developed form, sexual *inversion* was a condition whereby sexual desire thus found expression toward not the opposite but the same sex, and suggested that a desire whose orientation had been inverted could be an essential component of a person's biological and social identity. This understanding of same-sex desire as innate and essential marked a radical break with earlier understandings of a related phenomenon, *sodomy*, which was understood as contingent, circumstantial aberrant behavior.

To rehearse Michel Foucault's almost axiomatic genealogy: the *sodomite*, an occasional sinner, became the *homosexual*, a species, through the medicalization of discourses around sexuality (43). Discourses regulating sexual behavior were increasingly no longer the exclusive concern of priests but came under the purview of doctors and lawyers. Participants in same-sex sexual acts were to be pathologized instead of being condemned as sinners. Yet the term *inversion*, as a liminal concept between *sodomy* and *homosexuality*, is not entirely interchangeable with *homosexuality*. Without contesting Foucault's genealogy in its broad outlines, one question nevertheless arises: is the *invert* simply the forerunner of the *homosexual*, the *homosexuel avant la lettre*, or does the term imply a different configuration, however slight, of same-sex sexual desire?

In *Sexual Inversion*, Havelock Ellis and John Addington Symonds reveal the social terrain in which the meaning of the term is contested. Ellis, claiming the mantle of science asked in 1898: "What is Sexual Inversion: Is it an abominable acquired vice, to be stamped out by the prison, a beneficial variety of human emotion, which should be tolerated or even fostered? Is it a diseased condition that qualifies its subject for the lunatic asylum or is it a natural monstrosity, a human 'sport', the manifestations of which must be regulated when they become anti-social?" (128). There was not just one kind of *invert* nor one kind of *inversion*. For Ellis and Symonds, while not all *inversion* was congenital, all *inverts* were born with a congenital disposition toward *inversion*. Although the term was disputed on legal, humanitarian, psychological, and evolutionary-scientific grounds, Ellis identified *inversion* as congenital at bottom. In his summary "Theory of Sexual Inversion," he concluded that "we must regard sexual inversion as largely a congenital phenomenon, or, to speak more accurately, as a phenomenon which is based on congenital conditions. This ... lies at the root of the right comprehension of the matter" (129). Keeping this empirical fact in mind, Ellis continued the chapter with an argument against regarding *inversion* as a disease.

What was new and significant was the claim for a natural basis for same-sex sexual desire. Like the minor triad for the harmonic dualists, the late nineteenth-century *invert* was also based in nature. Inversion was a congenital "anomaly" or "abnormality" given by "a peculiarity in the sperm or

oval elements or in their mingling" that could be likened to the "dissimi-
larities [such as] between brothers and sisters"(135). *Inversion*, in this
scheme, was thus grounded, even born, in a natural site. Addressing the
desire itself, Karl Heinrich Ulrichs explained that the *Urnings* and *Urningens* − Ulrichs's versions of the *invert* − were "naturally attracted" to men
and women respectively and were not "acting contrary to nature" (36). Re-
sisting the view that *inversion* was "eccentric," "melancholic," or "perverse," Ulrichs argued that *inversion* "is deeply rooted in human nature"
(77-78). The *Urning*, he claimed "act[s] according to his own nature ... following not only his nature but the nature of his own kind" (37).

Recalling the work of the harmonic dualists, *inversion* thus functions
as the concept-metaphor that challenged the unnatural basis of both the
minor harmony and scale, and same-sex sexual desire. In effect, minor
shifted from derivative, lamenting or frenzied to a phenomenon grounded
in the natural undertone series, while same-sex sexual desire shifted from
perverse, melancholic or eccentric to a natural inheritance − at least fleet-
ingly − in these accounts. Arguably, this congruence extends further than
the mere attempt to ground both phenomena in nature, and hence to grant
both equal status in compositional and social law respectively. But before
elaborating this deeper affinity, we must distinguish this project from, or
finesse its relation to, Foucault's broad genealogy, whose lineaments have
become widespread in the literature.

For example, Wayne Koestenbaum claims that the concept of inversion poses "homosexuality [as] the inferior and derivative mirror image of a
sound and uninverted normality" (1989, 43). One could possibly substitute *homosexuality* for sexual *inversion* in the quote from Ellis without
radically transforming its sense, in a way that would not be possible with
sodomy. However, the specificity of the meanings of *inversion* would be
lost in this substitution. Koestenbaum uses the term *homosexual* to explain *inversion*, and so anachronistically subsumes the one in the other. In
other words, by antedating *homosexuality* and, by implication, *heterosexuality*, he names the as yet unnamed.

In Jeffrey Weeks's *Sexuality and Its Discontents*, *inversion* appears in
its own right, but is identified principally with "sexological definitions,
embodied in medical interventions, 'creat[ing]' the homosexual," a "label,"
or a "social categor[y] whose fundamental aim and effect was regulation
and control" (93). Weeks is suspicious of the effort to account for abnormal sexual behavior in positivist terms because "the call upon science ...

becomes little more than a gesture to legitimise interventions governed largely by specific relations of power. The production in sexological discourse of a body of knowledge that is apparently scientifically neutral (about women, about sexual delinquents or offenders) can become a resource for utilisation in the production of normative definitions that limit and demarcate erotic behaviour" (79). Weeks argues that the scientific endeavor is thus dubious in itself, particularly when it is applied to the "imprecise domain of sex" (72). Sexuality, he argues, is social through and through and the scientific claims to facticity should be regarded as uniquely repressive and implicated in dogmatic social control. It is the scientific "seeking for truth" itself, Weeks suggests, "that is the problem" (62).

But the more seriously we take Weeks's claim that this form of scientific power was "spreading its tentacles of regulation and control ever-more thoroughly to the nooks and crannies of social life" (74), the more exactly are we presented with the terms of power with which any resistance at the time was forced to negotiate. Instead of ruling out positivism *tout court* as reactionary, an investigation into resistance requires a serious look at positivist modes of thought; in this case a rethinking of the common scientific impulse grounding both sexual *inversion* and the inversionally related minor triad. Given the predominance of positivist thinking and its attendant claims to authority in the late nineteenth century, we feel a danger in anachronistically projecting onto the period late twentieth-century terms of the debate — "sexuality is a social construction" as a phrase would have it — and thus overlooking the authoritative terms in which nineteenth-century theorists were then debating. Problematic as it was, the positivist ethos surrounded these writers. In other words, if there was resistance at the time, then it would have been specific and contingent upon the cultural field upon which it operated. And, in this case, if the resistance was to carry any persuasive power, the terms were set by positivism. To dismiss such science as necessarily in service of coercive control would be to overlook such a possibility. The point is not to regard scientific findings as fact — or to grant a dichotomy between positivism and politics — but to examine the conceptual forms that guided scientific narration, to heighten the tension between these forms and facts, and finally to gauge, even rediscover, their positive explanatory power and significance by comparing the uses of the same metaphor in diverse contexts.

What then was different about the narration of same-sex sexual desire and gender identity under the rubric of *inversion*? How did sexual *inver-*

sion work as an explanatory model, what were its internal arrangements and what, exactly, got inverted? One type of *inversion* theory depended on the idea of a biologically grounded sexual instinct, whose direction got inverted. In other theories gender identity was inverted. Ellis's *Sexual Inversion* embodied the oppositely-projected instinct while Ulrichs's *Urnings*, whereby a woman's soul coexisted in a man's body, inverted gender, resulting in a *third sex*. Similarly, Edward Carpenter explained *inversion* in terms of an *intermediate type* between opposite genders. For all the variations in these conceptions, the *inversion* theorists shared a resistance to the binary structuring of gender, Carpenter and Ulrichs using the poles of masculine and feminine identity and desire to call for a third category.

Arguably, there is something in the internal arrangements of the term that contributes to this undoing in ways that are closed down in the consolidation of the term *homosexuality*. The term brings the entire sex/gender system explicitly into play. As much as it may reify gender by insisting on masculine and feminine poles of identification and desire, *inversion* 'de-essentializes' gender by infusing one with the other. Ulrichs explains that the inverted Urning "is not a man, but rather a kind of feminine being when it concerns not only his entire organism, but also his sexual feelings of love, his entire natural temperaments and his talents" (36), and simultaneously that Urnings "are not fully ... women [and] that [they] are similar to men because [they] assume the masculine role in society and because [their] capacity for work is the same" (36). The *invert* emerges as either both woman and man or as neither woman nor man. Instead, the male body coexists with the female soul and vice versa.

Ellis echoes this kind of gender reversal, claiming, on the one hand, that in behavior "the male invert frequently resembles the normal woman" (108) and, on the other, that "the chief characteristic of the inverted woman is a certain degree of masculinity" (94). Furthermore, the question of gender origins is posed in explosive ways when Ellis disputes Ulrichs's claims. He says "to assert dogmatically that a female soul, or even a female brain, is expressing itself through a male body ... is simply unintelligible. I say nothing of the fact that in male inverts the feminine psychic tendencies may be little if at all marked" (132). The invert both does and does not resemble the opposite sex at different times in Ellis's text, while s/he emerges finally as the person who was incapable of "killing out those [germs] of the other sex" (132-33) as they appear at conception in all organisms. Ellis's organism at conception contained for all human beings "about 50 per cent of male germs and about 50 per cent of female germs" (132). The invert's germs, whose male or female components failed to "assume the upper hand" (133), remained, by implication, divided in later life. Empirically speaking, then, the point of origin, or conception, is paradoxically split in equal halves and the conceptual *inversion* relation was channeled into a symmetry that cut across the gender binary.

Many commentators have remarked on the constitutive force that the terms *homosexuality* and *heterosexuality* have for one another. For example, in *Between Men: English Literature and Male Homosocial Desire*, Eve Kosofsky Sedgwick writes: "The importance — an importance — of the category 'homosexual' comes not necessarily from its regulatory relation to a nascent or already constituted minority of homosexual people or desires, but from its potential for giving whoever wields it a structuring definitional leverage over the whole range of male bonds that shape the social constitution" (86). Judith Butler, in "Imitation and Gender Insubordination," argues for an understanding of gender and heterosexuality as imitations which lack originals: "The origin requires its derivations in order to affirm itself as an origin, for origins only make sense to the extent that they are differentiated from that which they produce as derivatives. Hence, if it were not for the notion of the homosexual as copy, there would be no construct of heterosexuality as origin" (313).

Without denying the potential for this kind of deconstructive movement, it is significant that, in Ellis's understanding of the organism's structure at conception, a symmetrical relation lay not only conceptually, but also empirically, at the origin. Thus the question of deconstructively marking the constituent derivative term in the opposition may not even arise: a gender symmetry is posited at the core. Also, in its as yet unformed state, Ellis did not specify which of the organism's gendered germs killed the other. To be normal required only that either were so killed. In effect, the female body in this empirical scheme was thus figured less in terms of the male person than in terms of a process of self-emergence. The same applied to the development of the male person. Neither gender necessarily assumed precedence.

We end this section with two speculations. First, perhaps this empirically given mirror relation was more readily accommodated in the theories of *inversion* and its promise of symmetry than in the later theories of *homosexuality*. Second, perhaps the shortness of the life span of *inversion* as the concept configuring same-sex sexual desire had something to do with this potential. Not surprisingly, later sexological and psychoanalytic theorizing discredited theories of *inversion* on putatively scientific grounds, claiming that *inverts* lacked empirical proof for their assertions which were made more in their political interests than in the service of science.[5] The emergence of the *homosexual* in this later body of theory should be considered against this background.

In this regard it should be noted that, at its inception, sexual *inversion* was concerned with giving public voice to increasingly pathologized and criminalized groups of people. Ulrichs and Carpenter's writings were as much manifestoes as theory. Ulrichs, for example, proclaimed in "The Rod of Freedom": "I am an insurgent. I decline to accept what exists if I believe it is unjust. I am fighting for a life free from persecution and scorn. I urge the general public and the state to recognize Uranian love as equal to congenital Dionian love" (109). The discourse of sexual *inversion* gave an insistent voice to the "love that dare not speak its name" decades before Lord Alfred Douglas coined the phrase. As a discourse of self-naming, *inversion* theory actively engaged a debate during a period in which sexuality was not publicly discussed as such. Weeks, for example, argues how the question of lesbianism remained "silent because unthinkable" (1989, 93) during the Victorian era. In England in 1889, the Director of Public Prosecutions expressed a concern for just such a public voice, noting "the expediency of not giving unnecessary publicity" to cases of sexual indecency. Paradoxically, the Director's concern for public silence on such matters extended to the point of advocating permitting "private persons — being full grown men — to indulge their unnatural tastes in private" (in Duberman et al. 201). Arguably, *inversion* theory partly broke such a public silence.[6]

III.

In subsequent music theory, a resistance to *harmonic dualism*, whereby minor was conceived as the symmetrical inversion of major, was raised in consonant ways. Öttingen's ideas were criticized for privileging what could not be heard in musical practice, for their lack of empirical grounding, and for their lack of applicability to specific musical examples and to actual compositions. Ernst Mach maintained that the ear did not perceive the inversional relationships expounded by Öttingen: "A reversal of musical sounds conditions no repetition of sensations. If we had an ear for height and an ear for depth, just as we have an eye for right and an eye for left, we should also find that symmetrical sound structures existed for our auditory organs" (in Bernstein 388). Some years later, Georg Capellen criticized Riemann in strikingly similar terms: "[The ear] rejects the inversion that is noticeable to the eye, since it hears all the tones in a simultaneity from the bottom up (in terms of a fundamental) according to a law of gravity which is also valid in music. *The external difference in direction entails a more profound difference in type*" (in Bernstein 388). According to Capellen, any chord's constituent tones were necessarily determined from the bottom up, in accordance with the natural model presented by the overtone series. Inversional equivalence between major — historically gendered as masculine — and minor was an impossibility, defying the 'musical law of gravity' upon which all tonal music was premised. Paradoxically, Capellen's observation that a musical structure that gave prominence to symmetrically inversional relations could lead to the demise of the tonal system, precisely culminated in the atonal musical language of Arnold Schönberg (1874–1951), Alban Berg (1885–1935), and Anton von Webern (1883–1945) a few years later. Hermann Schröder, albeit a harmonic dualist, also expressed an anxiety about the demise of diatonic music, but in an almost opposite way. Here inversion seemed to be a given, and other forces were leading to chromaticism even though chromaticism tended to wipe out the effect of inversion:

> An inverted painting of a battle results in a chaos of color blotches, it would not be much different for the inversion of wildly moving music, particularly with some of the new [compositional] directions, in which the clear, identifiable diatonic is crowded out by the, now fashionable, chromatic. The inversion of diatonic tone-rows yields an absolutely effective contrast in identity and character; major becomes minor and vice versa. On the other hand, with the inversion of a chromatic scale, little of the contrast in identity and character, that is, of major and minor, is recognizable — a proof that symmetrical inversion is notably more effective in the diatonic than it is in the chromatic. (6)

For Schröder, the new chromaticism disconcerted the opposition between major and minor because inverted chromatic lines could not be told apart in the same way that major and minor could. As a result, he claimed that inversions should be restricted to diatonic lines. Unlike Capellen, who recognized that symmetrical inversions potentially undid the opposition between major and minor, Schröder, paradoxically, used the logic of inversion in an attempt to safeguard this distinction.

Current theory takes little from Öttingen's inversional relations. Not only are his speculations scientifically unsound — the undertone series has never been proven definitively — but his symmetries, engendered by harmonic dualism, give rise to differences that are incommensurate with the tonal syntax of actual musical practice. In short, phonicity does not apply to any music of the time.[7] Kevin Mooney, in a recent presentation at Columbia University, claimed that Öttingen's project amounted to a rationalization of minor harmony that essentially fails to provide insight into music — where musical examples exist at all in Öttingen's writings, the doublings are strange and the progressions are unusual. Figure 4 is one such example.

What follows are partial analyses of two musical works precisely in Öttingen's terms. The analyses are mainly an attempt to challenge the view that Öttingen's inversional symmetries do not apply to actual musical examples, but also to question the idea that some things cannot be *heard* because their theoretical formulations lack empirical

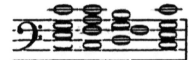

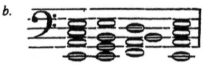

Figure 4. Öttingen's Characteristic Cadential Figure in (a) Tonicity and (b) Phonicity

proof. Before doing so, however, and in light of certain recent developments in musicology, the use of formal analysis in a project concerned with hierarchies of gender and sexuality calls for a methodological comment. In a recent collection of essays entitled *Queering the Pitch*, edited by Philip Brett et al., theories and methods attuned to questions of gender and sexuality are proposed for the study of music. Although it is a new methodological awareness that is principally emphasized throughout, the book's explorations cohere, perhaps unwittingly, around various 'gay' musical figures and composers. The approaches advanced in this book are set apart from the older, ostensibly narrower, formalist category of musical research. Jennifer Rycenga, for instance writes: "The first [methodology in present-day academia] is the time-honored analysis that is taught under the titles of musicology and music theory, in which music is considered exclusively in its own terms, but in such a way that it is reduced to meaning-lessness — its connectivity with social/historical, erotic, and personal dimensions is scorned and virtually ignored" (279).

This call for a musicology that casts a wider net — a call for the inclusion of what is traditionally regarded as extramusical data into the field of music scholarship — is part of a broader critical impulse in the discipline, commonly identified as the *new musicology*. We cannot take up this debate here, except to note that, in many cases, this new approach is predicated on an opposition between the work of music analysis — hermetically sealed from society — and that of a broader, culturally-situated study, and hence often does less to undo than to inaugurate this opposition. Such a gesture essentially accepts formalism's hermetic claims, instead of identifying the business of analysis as irreducibly social. Our project suggests a supplementary approach, by interrogating the, often unconscious, sex and gender determinants of the very language of music, analysis, and theory. Firstly, we are reluctant to consider only the work of (presumably) gay composers. Secondly, we are reluctant to cede the traditional territory of analysis, claiming instead that a strategically focused music analysis can also raise a host of questions relevant to queer theory.

The works selected are the first movement of Johannes Brahms's String Quintet in G, op. 111 (1890) and the last of Webern's Five Pieces for Piano and Violin, op. 7 (1907-1910). Both Brahms and Webern must have been familiar with the work of Öttingen.[8] These compositions, separated by less than two decades, are often held to be situated in sharply diverging aesthetic camps and periods. However, an application of Öttingen's notions of symmetrical inversion also reveals a generative affinity between them. This calls into question a *modernism* figured exclusively in the terms of a rupture with the past.

IV.

Brahms's Quintet begins a little like a cadential ending. The 'stable' root position tonic harmony in measure 1 is sounded on the weak last beat of the measure and moves, by a kind of inverted root movement — the leap of a fourth — to the dominant note D1. The stability of this harmony is thus at odds with its rhetorical function as an anacrusis. The first articulated downbeat of the piece (m. 2) is thus a six-four tonic harmony. The use of the 'unstable' six-four chord as a structural pillar is suggested by the placement of the repeat and can be traced throughout the movement. For example, the stability of the second subject (from m. 26), appearing characteristically in the traditional key of the dominant (D major), is offset in exactly the same way. D major is announced with a pizzicato A1. Again, the unstable six–four marks a structural point in the music. To further weaken its structural weight, it is not preceded by a definite dominant, but by a half-diminished seventh on ii, followed by a diminished seventh on vii. This seems to function, albeit not without ambiguity, as a predominant instead of as a dominant. A1 in the bass (m. 26) — the sound, perhaps, signaling the dominant function least ambiguously at this point — fails to move to its tonic root in measure 26. Instead, it is held as a pedal point for two measures. In effect, we get a cadential formula that cuts across the structural boundary ushering in the second subject group. By the time the not-quite cadence reaches closure (on the second beat of m. 27), the three-note viola motive is already implicated in a kind of descending line that propels the music forward, rather than bringing it to a close. Thus the voice-leading is 'out-of-phase' with the tonally normative cadential figure — an ending embedded in a beginning. While such overlapping effectively sutures the formal division at this point, how can the structural six–four chord be explained?

Let us have a look at Öttingen's representation of cadential formulae as demonstrated in figure 4. Despite his occasional efforts to allay its sounding incomplete, Öttingen's phonic cadence (fig. 4.b) ends with a six-four chord. This, if anything, is its point of repose. The chord is also preceded by what is called in traditional functional terms a *half-diminished* seventh chord on ii, only here it functions as a 'dominant' to the 'phonic'. In short, the progression from measures 24 to 26 is more closely aligned to the structural divisions of this sonata form if it is read upside-down or phonically. The prevalence of the half-diminished chord (a chord whose very name becomes ambiguous now) throughout the movement, and particularly in those positions where a dominant is called for in terms of tonal syntax, becomes differently coherent when read this way.

This casts a light on other passages in the movement, such as the strikingly colorful progression in measures 8 to 9 and 10 to 11. The sudden modulation to B major is effected on the third beat of measure 7 by a half-diminished seventh on C-sharp. This does not function as a dominant in tonicity but rather in phonicity. Even the characteristic leap of a fourth in the bass (sounded here by the second viola) from C-sharp to F-sharp invokes the cadential V to I, but articulates instead a half-diminished seventh on ii, followed by a six-four on I. As a rhetorical gesture, root movement is still given, but by different harmonic means. There are many ways of interpreting the progression that follows. For one, it could be conceded that tonal norms are momentarily disrupted here, and that it is the descending chromatic line in the second violin, beginning on a-sharp 1 in measure 8 that ultimately drives the passage. This line is continued after passing through an octave coupling in measure 9 and ends on e-flat 2 three measures later. The local contrapuntal scoring suggests such a linear projection in which the fleeting vertical harmonic formations are yielded secondarily. Alternatively, in traditional functional terms, the passage can be taken to pass in B major (V of vi) from I (six-four) to V to ii to iv (flat-3) to I. Perhaps the iv (flat-3) chord suggests a concealed invocation of B minor as the chromatic descent intermittently sounds the flattened seventh and sixth degrees of the descending melodic minor scale. The parallel progression in measures 10 to 11 casts an alternative reading: take the passage as a series of tonic/dominant relations in descending whole tones. The parallel progression beginning in measure 10 would thus read I to V in the keys G, F, and E-flat respectively: a consistent pattern, but a highly unstable sense of tonic.

What if this passage were understood as phonically in F-sharp instead of as tonically in B? The progression would now read: upside-down 'i', 'iv', 'VII', 'V', 'i'. The phonic F-sharp is strikingly unambiguous. In fact, the anomalous iv (flat 3) in tonicity becomes precisely the dominant function with a lowered leading note g-natural 1, or, more correctly, a leading note g-natural 1 raised in inverse pointing toward the root-tone f-sharp 1. Reading upside down thus results in the more economical account of the passage: phonically there are no anomalies. In other words, the passage, for all its non*diatonic* chords is arguably not non*diaphonic*. Also, the phonic progression is a stock i, iv, V, i (albeit chromatically inflected) while the tonic progression is more complicated, leaping back to I from iv with a lowered third. It is as if the inverted progression in F-sharp can make sense of the right-side-up progression in B.

Paradoxically, this phonic F-sharp is a minor triad *in* phonicity (or a major triad in tonicity). Such an interpretative gesture extends Öttingen's model beyond the purview of theorizing minor-as-phonic (or major-as-tonic). Instead, it recognizes that both modalities can be articulated as either minor or major. But even if we remain strictly within the terms set by Öttingen, the progression is more readily understood in his basic rules for chord transformations than in terms of traditional tonal syntax. In his theory of chord connections, Öttingen described a progression between two chords that were oppositely derived − that is, a move from phonic to tonic or vice versa − as *antinomic*. A special case of antinomy involved tonic and phonic chords that were built on the same pitch, such as the upwardly projected C major triad along with the downwardly projected F minor. Such a chord relation was termed "reciprocal" and amounts to what Riemann called a *Seitenwechsel* (changeover). Now, the progression under discussion precisely elaborates this special case of antinomy (fig. 5).

Figure 5. Mm. 8–9 of Brahms's Quintet as a Chain of *Seitenwechsel* steps

Ignoring for the moment the bracketed notes in the diagram, the progression − beginning now on the last beat of measure 7 − is a chain of *Seitenwechsel* relations. Such a pairing brings to the ear the implied 6/8 meter here. In the context of the progression as a whole, the bracketed notes, representing sevenths in their respective formations, can be read as a further symmetrical articulation marking the enclosure of the progression.

There are other places in the movement that can be read productively in a phonic terrain, as, for example, the uniquely quiet passage in measures 89 to 94 − the heart of the development − which can be construed as an extended cadence in phonic G. Phonality is suggested on the surface of the music as well. Firstly, Brahms generates motives through inversion. Instances include the start of the recapitulation in measure 106, where the opening ascending motive in the cello is presented in its descending form in the violins and the hypermetrically displaced descent on the second and third beats of measures 9 and 11, which ascends in measure 113. Second, Brahms frequently builds triads from the top down which suggests a phonic construction of the chord. In measure 79, for example, the cadence in G (the final tonic stated as an open octave) is immediately reinterpreted as the third of an E-flat major triad by means of a downwardly projected addition of chord tones.

As can be seen, a phonically conceived harmonic terrain, far from lacking applicability, can be mapped in various respects in this movement, alongside a tonic conception. In fact, in some places this inverted reading produces the simpler interpretation, and, in this way, could even substitute for tonicity. What would happen if two inversionally related strands coexisted with, instead of substituted for, one another, throughout a musical span? The last of Webern's Pieces for Piano and Violin, op. 7, offers one answer.

Here, the tonal system almost falls away completely and the unfolding of symmetrical inversions in themselves becomes the sole generating principle. The opening consists of two interwoven chromatic lines, one ascending, the other descending, that are sounded 'across-the-octave' (fig. 6). While d1 leads to d-sharp 2, which in turn leads to e3, g2 leads to f-sharp 1.

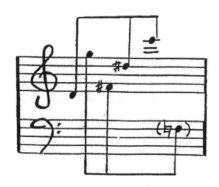

If the logic of the process implied here were to be continued, we would arrive at F, a pitch that cannot be played on the violin. The addition of this F would yield the symmetrically inversional hexachord 012345 around axis E/F and/or A-sharp/B. In the terms of David Lewin's notion of a 'generative lust', we can say that there is an urge to complete the inversional symmetry in this way.[9] But, instead of sounding F, the piano enters with a new sonority. In fact, the first F in the piece is in the middle of measure 3, in the middle of a piano chord. It is thus buried in another sonority and seemingly far removed from the opening violin figure.

Figure 6. (012345), m. 1

Figures 6–14. Symmetrical Inversions in Webern's op. 7, no. 4

There is one other way that the
opening 01245 could become inversionally symmetrical with the addition of
just one pitch class, namely G-sharp.
When added to this sonority, G-sharp
yields the symmetrically inversional
012456. The axis of inversion for this
hexachord would be F and/or B (fig. 7).

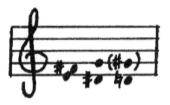

Figure 7 (012456)

Now, if we take the violin line alone, we hear just these tones, first g-sharp 3
in measure 3 which completes the 012456, and then the axis tones f3 and

Figure 8. Mm. 1–4, violin

b2. Not surprisingly, the registral
distribution, the chromatic line across
octaves, remains consistent. Figure 8
depicts the completed 012456 in its
actual register. Clearly, as axis tones, f3
and b2 cannot undo the inversion, but
simply extend — and, in so doing, confirm — an inversional sonority. The f-
sharp 2 in measure 4 also does not undo the inversion of the hexachord as
it simply repeats a pitch class.

In this way, all the tones of the violin part in measures 1 to 4 are an unfolding of this inversional symmetry. Near-symmetry 01245 is completed
in measure 3. Now, the g-sharp 3, f3, and b2 in measure 3 are duplicated in
the second right-hand chord in the piano with a change in spelling.
Instead of functioning as a continuation of a chromatic line, the a-flat of
this chord functions as an axis note around which b1 and f1 form an inversional symmetry. The surrounding voice-leading clarifies this symmetrical relation: c-sharp 2 and e-flat 1, also symmetrical around a-flat 1, move by
interval class 2 to b1 and f1,
and then back again. The axis
tone a-flat 1 is sounded
throughout (fig. 9). The relation
between the violin G-sharp 3, f2,
and b2 in measure 3 and the
enharmonically equivalent f1, a-

Figure 9. M. 3, piano

flat 1, and b1 in the piano becomes this: where g-sharp 3 is the result of a
chromatic line over the octaves of the inversionally symmetrical hexachord
012456, and b2 and f2 are the axis tones of the same hexachord in the

violin, a-flat 1 is the axis tone of the local voice-leading stated by the b1 and f1 of the piano chord. Their roles have been interchanged. In the upper line G-sharp/A-flat confirms B and F as axis tones, while in the lower chord the G-sharp/A-flat is the axis tone of B and F. The senses attributed to the three pitch classes has been inverted precisely.

This interplay between axis tones and the inversionally symmetrical collections surrounding them, between near-symmetries and their completion, between local voice-leading and voice-leading that spans more time, can be tracked throughout the piece. It would not be inaccurate to say that the unfolding of inversional symmetries spanning various durations *generates* the

Figure 10. (012456), mm. 10-12

piece, at least until the final section marked *ruhig,* "still" or "calm" Here, closure is achieved in the final measures with sonorities that are already inversions of themselves. The first four pitch classes in the piano in measure 11 recall the opening 0145 tetrachord. An analogous 01245 is formed with the addition of a1, which, together with c-sharp 3 in the violin, yields the inversionally symmetrical 012456. The two chromatic lines (broadly, still articulated across-the-octave) now interlock with one another (fig. 10). The piano pitch classes in measures 13 to 14 comprise the symmetrical 0167 collection, while the ponticello figure in the violin is comprised of two inversionally symmetrical tetrachords: 0145 and 0156 (figs. 11 and 12). There are no longer any "generative urges." The

Figure 11. (0145), m. 13

combination of all the pitch classes sounded in measure 13 in the piano and the ponticello figure results in the inversionally symmetrical 01234589 (fig. 13), while the collection on the last beat of the penultimate measure is a symmetrical 0158 (fig. 14). Finally, the piano is cut off in the last mea-

Figure 12. (0156), m. 13

sure leaving a fragment of the ponticello figure to complete the piece. Even this fragment is an inversionally symmetrical 0156. Webern states that the ponticello figure is to be played *wie ein Hauch*, "like a breath," and, finally, he places rests on the last two beats of the measure, as if to envelop this breath in silence; or is it as if to posit an index of inversion that remains unheard?

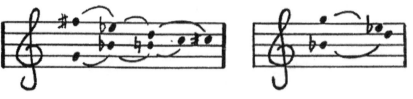

Figure 13. (01234589), m. 13   Figure 14. (0158), m. 14

What does the stylistic break between Brahms and Webern signify, particularly in the light of their historical proximity? As shown, both of the works analyzed embody substantial aspects of the theoretical conceptions of symmetrical inversions prevalent at the time, albeit in different ways. In Brahms's Quintet phonality operates alongside tonality, and occasionally substitutes for it, while in the last of Webern's Five Pieces for Piano and Violin, the temporal unfolding of inversional strands coexist. These works are not isolated examples of such procedures in the respective output of these composers. For example, downwardly projected harmonic formations can be usefully mapped in Brahms's Clarinet (or Viola) Trio in A Major, op. 114 (1891), or in his Intermezzo in B Minor. Webern's Symphony, op. 21 (1928), on the other hand, can be analogously analyzed as a symmetrical unfolding around shifting inversional centers. Webern's fascination with symmetrical inversions is persistently thematized in his *The Path to the New Music*. His very description of the Symphony, op. 21, centers around the question of unity made possible by "constant mirrorings" (56) in the form of inversion, retrograde, and retrograde inversion.

However, the crucial point is that major and minor seem to have collapsed in the music that mapped inversional trajectories in themselves. Ironically, this emphasis on inversional symmetries was the result of the very scientific imperative that was driving the new theorizing about the minor sonority. That is, *the desire by Öttingen, Ziehn and Schröder to ground the minor in empirical fact, to ground it in the immutable undertone series — the mirror inversion of the major — led precisely to the undoing of both major and minor*. Schröder, in fact, was resistant to the 'new chromatic' music, and harnessed acoustical claims about the scientific truth of inversional symmetries to safeguard *diatonic* music, unaware that inversional symmetries had the potential to undo the very system he aimed to protect – a danger that Capellen had recognized in his critique of harmonic dualism.[10] Brahms's harmonic language, where phonicity still operates as a crosscurrent in tonicity, gives way to atonality in Webern's more precisely symmetrically inversional syntax. In this respect, then, Webern is working with the same conceptual forms that are paradoxically stripped of the scientific content that was their raison d'être.[11]

Even Öttingen's attempt to grant privilege of presence to the major triad, is rendered nonpertinent by its own reflection. Just as, in Öttingen's terms, the constituents of the major triad *are* the overtones of a common fundamental, while the constituents of the minor triad *have* a common overtone, so too, when the model is that of inversion, does the fundamental of the major *have* the constituent overtones of its triad, while the constituents of the minor triad *are* fundamentals of a common overtone. As such, the major triad is rendered originally and essentially a symmetrical reflection, it is always already the inversion of its inversion. In this play of representation the point of origin is lost. As Jacques Derrida might say, "There are things like reflecting pools, and images, an infinite reference from one to the other, but no longer a source, a spring. There is no longer a simple origin. For what is reflected is split *in itself* and not *only* as an addition to itself of its image" (1976, 37). Which is prior? Overtone or fundamental? Which *is*?

V.

An analogous attempt to ground sexuality in physiology did not produce the same undoing of opposites, though it arguably had the theoretical investment in positivism to do so. To recapitulate, like Schröder insisting on grounding major, and its inversion minor, in nature, Ulrichs proclaimed in 1864: "The fundamental proposition upon which I base my entire system is the following: it is Nature which gives the feminine sexual love drive and a body built as a male to a large class of people" (51). Magnus Hirschfeld founded the Scientific-Humanitarian Committee in Berlin in 1898 to agitate against social and legal prejudices against same-sex sexual desire. He too believed that natural science rather than history or psychology was best equipped to address the injustices against sexual *inversion*: "I believe in Science and I am convinced that Science, and above all the natural Sciences, must bring to mankind not only truth, but with truth, Justice, Liberty and Peace" (in Weeks 1989, 71).

However, these ethical-scientific approaches to same-sex sexual desire never completely succeeded in grounding *inversion* in nature. They gave way to theories where questions of nature were mediated through evolutionary concepts; for the movement from vice to scientific discourse mobilized many evolutionary tropes, such as degeneration, arrested development and 'survival of the fittest'.[12] The insertion of evolutionary tropes was significant for it evacuated the implicit symmetry of poles in the *inversion* model of same-sex sexual desire. Poles of identification within evolutionary narratives in general were effectively hierarchized. The child and the adult, the savage and the civilized, while constitutively dependent on each other as categories, could not be symmetrical inversions of each other as they occupied different temporalities within a single telos: the adult subsumed the child; the civilized transcended the savage.[13]

For example, Max Dessoir, implying an evolutionist temporality, claimed that an "undifferentiated sexual feeling is normal, on the average during the first years of puberty — that is, from 13-15 in boys and 12-14 in girls — while in later years it must be regarded as pathological" (37). Consequently, Ellis, prefiguring Freud, asserted that "if the sexual instinct is comparatively undifferentiated in early life, then we must regard the inversion of later life, if it persists, as largely due to arrested development" (39). Similarly, he later defined morbid inversion as when "old men with failing sexual powers, or younger men exhausted by heterosexual debauchery are attracted to boys" (41). Within this evolutionist-inflected strand of *inversion* theory, the *invert* thus paradoxically occupied the position of both the underdeveloped and the overdeveloped, of both lack and excess. The evolutionary paradigm placed *inversion* in any position except that of the normative subject. Unlike its counterpart in musical practice, the inversion-relation in sexology was fractured by these displacements and never achieved an analogous symmetry. It resembled instead the earlier minor triad, unevenly figuring *inversion* as either too much or too little.

These asymmetries in theories of *inversion* were maintained in later theories of *homosexuality*. These theories maintained the general idea of directional drives in *inversion* but lost one significant figuration. They kept the understanding of same-sex sexual desire as a turning inwards (*narcissism*), a turning backwards (*degeneration*), a holding still (a *fixation* or *arrest*), but abandoned it as a gendered turning upside down (*inversion*). Psychoanalysis would treat homosexuality as *arrested development* and connect it to *narcissism*. The idea of the *homosexual* as a *degenerate* would have a long life in a wide range of scientific and popular discourses.[14]

We suggest that the political implications of radical gender disturbance in *inversion* theories may have encouraged their revision into *homosexuality*. For Freud, the aspects of *inversion* theory "which were formulated without regard for the psychogenesis of homosexuality" were precisely the "intermediate stage of sex or ... 'third sex'" (*Three Essays* 60), imagined as the man's soul in the woman's body or vice versa. Still today, even though *homosexuality* has been officially depathologized by its removal from the *American Psychiatric Association's Diagnostic and Statistical Manual (DSM III)*, *gender* nonconformity is still considered an illness and is a designated pathology — *Gender Identity Disorder*. Thus, *homosexuality* has been more easily 'normalized' than a proliferation of gender identities in a broader patriarchal gendered hierarchy. Seeing *inversion* theory only as the forerunner to *homosexuality*, as a medical discourse of control, as biologically essentialist or empirically untrue, loses sight of the utopian political horizon of embodied gender symmetry. This is where atonal music, considered also as imaginative thought, may point to such a horizon.

VI.

Like the theories of sexual *inversion*, the music and thought of Webern, Berg and Schönberg were, and still are, frequently regarded as inverting the natural order of things. This can be gauged in the surprising congruencies of the language of their respective detractors in the popular and professional domains. We cannot undertake a thorough examination of the proximity of these cultures of reproach except to note that, broadly speaking, like their contemporaneous *inverts*, the atonal composers were frequently charged with violations against nature. Schönberg was presenting "the constant succession of unnatural sounds from the extreme notes of every instrument" (*Manchester Guardian*, 1912) or Berg's music had "nothing to do with the natural enfoldment of melody" (*New York Times*, 1935). Additionally, the work of these composers was considered abnormal and perverse. In Berg's music "all is calculated ... to insult the esthetic sense of any normal and healthy human being" (V. Gorodinsky, *Music of Spiritual*

Poverty, Moscow, 1950) or "everything must be harmonically queer and perverse" (*Neue Freie Presse*, Vienna, 1925), while Schönberg offered a "most unaccountable jumbling together of abnormalities" (*Musical Courier*, New York, 1913). Webern is similarly characterized: "One is reluctant to utter the word 'abnormal', but on the other hand, one cannot assert that there is any connection [in Webern's music] with our accustomed ideas about music" (*Deutsche Allgemeine Zeitung*, Berlin, 1928).[15]

It was not uncommon for the abnormality of these works to be articulated in terms of a psychological disorder of an often explicitly sexual nature. Berg's work had "a prevailing flavor of a highly diseased eroticism" (*New York Times*, 1935), and Schönberg's was expressing "disordered fancies of delirium" (*London Globe*, 1912). While "it might deal successfully with neuroses of various kinds ... I cannot imagine it associated with any healthy and happy concept such as young love or the coming of Spring" (*Music and Letters*, London, 1951). As opposed to the happy coupling of the young heterosexual couple in the spring of their lives, Schönberg could offer only "quasi masochistic pleasure" (*Musical Opinion*, London, 1952). Relatedly, like same-sex sexual acts, these composers' abnormalities were figured as nonreproductive. Schönberg's theories were held to be "stillborn" (G. Schneerson, *Music in the Service of Reaction*, Moscow, 1950), Berg's music said to be "unfertile" (*New York Times*, 1935).

The emergent Darwinian evolutionary tropes, adapted to discussions of same-sex sexual desire in figures such as Max Nordau, Richard von Krafft-Ebing and Freud, were also applied to dismissals of this body of music in almost identical terms. It too was "childish," "infantile," "barbaric," "primitive," or "a bestial racket" (*Inter Ocean*, Chicago, 1913). In Schönberg, "the statue of Venus, The Goddess of Beauty, is knocked from its pedestal and replaced by the stone image of the Goddess of Ugliness, with the hideous features of a Hottentot hag" (*Musical Progress*, New York, 1923), while his theories were "calculated to destroy melody and harmony ... lead[ing] to retrogression ... in art" (Schneerson). Like the *invert*, this music was imbued with degeneracy and arrested development.

Occasionally, the invective invoked the trope of criminality: "I regard Alban Berg as a musical swindler and a musician dangerous to the musical community. We must seriously pose the question as to what extent the musical profession can be criminal. We deal here, in the realm of music, with a capital offense" (*Deutsche Zeitung*, Berlin, 1925). Recalling the criminalization of all same-sex sexual activity in 1886 by the Labouchere

Amendment in Britain, and the prohibitions of the same by the Prussian Civil Code over all of Germany in 1870, the body of the *invert* was already affixed with criminality. Posing a threat to the community on the grounds of practices that were unnatural, abnormal, perverse, degenerate, infantile, and unfertile, these musicians and *inverts* were faced with an alarmingly commensurate criminal oratory.

This is not to claim that hostility per se to both is sufficient to establish a substantive link between them, but rather to register the shared tropes of disapproval in the language of their respective detractors and thus to mark the nearly analogous awkward place these sub-cultures held in relation to the perceived musical/sexual norms. The founding of the Society for Private Musical Performances by Schönberg in 1918 cannot be understood apart from this public response. The secrecy surrounding the society's activities was linked to their wish to exclude any public reporting. In its statutes, Schönberg located "normal present-day concert life" as the practice which "the society intends to keep definitely at a distance" (in Reich 120). Thus Schönberg identified the norm as suspicious, and publicity, even the spoken word in general, as a "corrupting influence" (in Reich 120). Like that love, this music risked corruption by being spoken about; like that practice, this one thus sought a private performance space.

Most importantly, the conceptual form underlying both abnormalities was significantly enmeshed in the, then prevalent, idea of *symmetrical inversion*. It is just this concept that critics today identify as having led Schönberg and company astray. For example, echoing both turn-of-the-century newspaper reviews and the old arguments of the harmonic monists, William Thomson, in his aptly titled book *Schönberg's Error*, argues that the idea of *symmetrical inversion* contributed significantly to the mistakes Schönberg made. Imagining various triads, keys, and functions in tonal music to be in a relation of symmetry, Schönberg "yield[ed] to the temptation of the fictional *über-unter* mirror symmetry that became the nemesis of late nineteenth-century German music theory" (45). According to Thomson, Schönberg thus understood the tonal system within a specious *Über-klang-Unterklang* structure which he took on faith from his predecessors, and then erroneously applied to his own theories. Thomson writes:

> The roots of [his] concept-percept tension are manifestly traceable to Schönberg's controlling assumptions ... For instance, the insecure perceptual basis of his 'solution' can be detected in the way

he perpetuates the mythic symmetry of tonality by exploitation of inversional sets. In this he derives abstraction from pure myth: the very idea of dominant and subdominant as 'upper' and 'lower' balances for tonic was itself a hapless fiction motivated by conceptual ambition rather than perception. (193)

Once again, *inversions* can be seen but not heard as such. Ironically, it is not only Schönberg who perpetuates past beliefs in his theory but also Thomson. Like Mach a century before Thomson and decades before Schönberg, Thomson also believes that *symmetries* are perceptually suspect.[16] And, like Capellen, he also believes in a gravitational force given in the harmonic series which plays a "primal role in the conversion of auditory signal into musical meaning" (122).

Thomson concludes his argument for "the harmonic series as cognitive archetype" (122) with historically well expended imagery: "The series ... is decidedly bottom-heavy ... and constitutes a perceptual vector, a 'pointing force' ... The experience from birth of the tonal shape — the *hierarchical shape* — projected in the harmonic series leads to a powerful part of the structural inferences of harmonic roots, the tonic pitches of audition" (124; Thomson's emphasis). Thomson's suspicions about the perception of *symmetries* then echo disconcertingly familiar charges of abnormality about those who think they do hear them: "like the balancing power claimed for the subdominant degree of the major-minor tonal systems, these instances of 'what is there in the notes' lead dubious lives" (190). Resonantly, Thomson adds, "as evolution," the resulting music without pitch hierarchy "was an ill-conceived, though passionately propagandized, mutation" (176). Once more, we encounter the evolutionary anomaly in Schönberg, who, in his quest to "reject ... only the major-minor conventions of his immediate past," erroneously renounced "the primal tonal archetypes bequeathed him ..." (176).[17]

This figuration of atonal and serial music as working against "human nature" has not subsided in the current media either. In an article entitled "Does Nature Call the Tune?" Richard Taruskin writes: "bolstered by solid empirical work in cognitive psychology ... [Leonard] Meyer's counterparts today, increasingly aware and respectful of the mind's hard-wiring, are less circumspect in their critiques of those who ignore rather than explore human nature." Failing to "conform to the physics of sound," Taruskin concludes that the serialist position exhibits "the same optimism that drives all utopian thinking. It underlies the trendy academic claim that those things between our legs are not biological organs but social constructions." Biologically and cognitively hardwired, the normal subject's hearing and sex are irreducibly fixed by nature.[18]

Conclusion

When, how, and why is it that utopian thought is wished away; or music is charged with empirical error; or *symmetrical inversions* are figured as either not applicable to tonal music or not hearable in atonal music?[19] We have argued that these moments tended to be enmeshed in the question of gender hierarchy in various ways. Unlike the *symmetrical inversions* employed in late nineteenth-century crystallography and mathematics, gender was explicitly situated at the respective poles of the symmetry in contemporaneous music theory and sexology. Ulrichs's inverted Urningens and Urnings were constituted by the coexistence of both female and male components in a single individual. This resulted in his, equally natural, "sexual species ... a *third sex*" (36). Concurrently, major and minor, analogously gendered in traditional music theory, were increasingly regarded as nature-given *symmetrical inversions* of one another.

In fact, the two poles were consciously marked for dissolution into a third gender category by Webern himself. In plotting a history of scales in the *The Path to New Music*, Webern argued, first, that "accidentals spelt the end for the world of church modes, and the world of our major and minor genders (*Geschlechte*) emerged," and second, that the "new music ... has given up this 'double gender' in its progress toward a single scale – the chromatic scale" (28). Like Ulrichs, Webern thought the dissolution of gender produced a third category: "Double gender," he claimed "has given rise to a higher race" (37),[20] and elsewhere, "These two [keys, like genders] have produced something that's above gender, our new system of twelve notes" (43).

Embedded in the compositional method that would bring about the "dissolution of major and minor" (37) was the notion of *inversion*, a technique that permitted the equal status of basic sets, the "constant mirrorings" (56) that ultimately attributed apparent differences to "variations of the same idea" (53). "Considerations of symmetry," stated Webern, "are now to the fore" (54). Like his late nineteenth-century counterparts in music theory, Webern thus grounded this idea in natural law and regarded the new music, paradoxically, as born out of a deep theorizing of tonality: "Precisely because we took steps to preserve tonality — we broke its neck!" (48). Hence, tonality — or, more generally, "notes [as] natural law ... related to hearing" (15) — was/were transformed from hierarchy to symmetry. Webern ended his essay with a quotation of the Latin saying:

$$\begin{array}{ccccc} S & A & T & O & R \\ A & R & E & P & O \\ T & E & N & E & T \\ O & P & E & R & A \\ R & O & T & A & S \end{array}$$

which can be translated as "Arepo the sower keeps the work circling" (in Reich 136).

Such music, in which the dynamics of creation became necessarily internal, was clearly beholden to German Idealist romanticism. Throughout *The Path to the New Music,* Webern referred to the idea behind the surface chaos. Ironically, it is this kind of abstraction that is regarded by so many commentators today as reductively constraining social thought, as denying interpretative plurality, or as uncritically subscribing to the myth of ahistorical autonomy and high seriousness that was supposed to uphold a criterion of truth. Without abandoning this perspective altogether, we hope to have shown that such abstraction was less abstraction per se than it was a very peculiar engagement with social thought.[21] In fact, Webern encouraged us to engage such thought, calling for a listener "capable of imagining that music can have an idea, a thought, hidden in it" (14). Perhaps a close engagement with the embedded thought of the new symmetrical music, particularly in the context of the current figurations of modernism as abnormal, should give us pause.

Even though Webern, like many proponents of *inversion* theory in sexology, grounded his ideas in nature, we may not want to lose sight of the cultural context in which such thinking took place and the historical terms available for resistance. In other words, it may be worthwhile to listen closely to the view of reality that their 'laws of nature' purported to uphold. After all, could this not have been an affirmative form of resistance? Finally, the proximity of discursive cultures of musical and sexological thought — cultures in which participants and detractors had much in common — reveals some of the stakes involved in such resistance. What was lost in the transition from the *invert* to the *homosexual* in sexology was the idea of *upside-downness* and the promise of a certain reversibility. This is where a contemporaneous musical imagination usefully provided strategies for the undoing of oppositions.

Late nineteenth-century musicology and attendant musical composition was able to utilize the concept of *inversion* to undo the gendered hierarchy of major and minor and instantiate more symmetrical relations in a new musical language. *Inversion* in sexology was less successful, soon giving way to the lopsided homosexual/heterosexual binary in the figuring of sexuality, revealing a shift, rather than a displacement, of the masculine/feminine polarity, and unevenly doubling the telos of sexual subjectivity rather than interrogating teleological theories of sexuality. The use of *inversions*, one of the constituting trajectories of modern music, had no sexuality in terms of earlier gendered configurations. If it had one at all, it was probably a third category, musicologists and composers having achieved, knowingly and unknowingly, the task of turning conceptual categories and structuring principles upside down and back-to-front. For here, there is no longer any 'law of gravity' to keep things right-side-up. As Schönberg wrote in *Style and Idea*: "In [musical] space ... there is no absolute down, no right or left, forward or backward" (113).[22]

Notes

[1] This was the nom de guerre of Karl Heinrich Ulrichs. All translations are our own unless otherwise stated.

[2] I. M. Yaglom maintains that the history of mathematical symmetry does not extend further back than the late nineteenth century.

[3] For example, the new non-Euclidean *elliptic plane* attempted to eliminate the hitherto sharp distinction between spherical and plane geometry, by introducing two symmetrically inversional pairs of points to configure the sphere. By conjoining opposite points of these pairs (or hemispheres) the sphere is given in a symmetrical space known as *Riemann's elliptical space*.

[4] For a fuller bibliographic account of the literature, see Shubnikov, Belov et al. 249ff.

[5] In 1910, Sigmund Freud rebutted the claims of *inversion* and *third sex* theorists: "Homosexual men who have started in our times an energetic action against the legal restrictions of their sexual activity are fond of representing themselves through theoretical spokesmen as evincing a sexual variation, which may be distinguished from the very beginning, as an intermediate stage of sex or as a 'third sex'. In other words, they

maintain that they are men who are forced by organic determinants originating in the germ to find that pleasure in the man which they cannot feel in the woman. As much as one would wish to subscribe to their demands out of humane considerations, one must nevertheless exercise reserve regarding their theories which were formulated without regard for the psychogenesis of homosexuality. Psychoanalysis offers the means to fill this gap and to put to test the assertions of the homosexuals" (*Three Essays* 60). *Inversion* could be characterized as a discourse of self-naming — the *invert* declared himself as such — while psychoanalysis was the discourse of the expert. One effect of this was that the subject *invert* (in the manifestly political writings of Ulrichs and Carpenter) was rendered the object *homosexual* (in the scientific, and frequently pathologizing, writings of Freud, and also, more virulently, in later psychoanalysis). Even Ellis's objectifying stance in *Sexual Inversion* was mediated by the authorial presence of the *invert* Symonds. It should be noted that Ellis worked hard to erase Symonds as coauthor in subsequent editions of the work (Koestenbaum 1989, 43-67). This began to approach the subsuming of the experience of the analysand in the production of psychoanalytic knowledge.

[6]The informing context of these remarks is the Labouchere Amendment of 1886, which criminalized acts of gross indecency committed by men irrespective of whether they took place in public or in private. Not surprisingly, Ellis's *Sexual Inversion* was initially banned in Britain.

[7]The idea that inversions can be seen, but not heard, is also thematized in more recent theory. Modern pitch-class set theory, for example, offers a formal ground for viewing inversion as the nonhearable. When comparing, for instance, the representation of the formal operation of *inversion* with that of *transposition*, this difference is revealed. For transposition, the mathematical operation of subtraction represents, in musical terms, the difference between two pitches. The difference equals the interval of transposition. If $c_1 = 0$, say, then 5 minus 2 is equal to the interval from d1 to f1, that is 3 (or a minor third). Inversion, on the other hand, involves an opposite intervalic relation between two pitches. That is, a pitch M is as far below a pitch N as another pitch X is above Y. The addition of M to X and of N to Y yields the same (numerical) answer. In this way, the sum becomes a constant, and thus also a convenient determinant for inversion. Hence, the mathematical operation employed to formally represent inversion is addition. But what does the addition of two pitches signify in musical terms? Can it be heard? This sum, known as the *index number of inversion* in set theory parlance, is a theoretical construct which, useful as it may be, does not correspond to anything we hear. Visible to the eye, then, the index of inversion remains silent. We thank Joseph Dubiel for drawing our attention to this aspect of Milton Babbitt's set theoretical work.

[8]The relationship between artist and theorist can also be understood in terms of original and copy. Following Oscar Wilde, we posit here the *critic* (in some ways prior to the composer) as artist, suggesting an inversion of the traditional relationship between the two.

[9]Joseph Dubiel has pointed out to us that Lewin's concept need not be read in the sense of an *anticipation* for completion (in this case of an inversional operation), but rather in the (weaker) sense that, once completed, this operation defines the 'meaning', or the 'effect', of the sound *as* inversionally related. Instead of orienting the claim in the future, this articulation of the concept involves the future-perfect.

[10]Schröder wrote in 1902: "Every true art creates out of nature, she is and remains her best teacher. Unfortunately, the musicians are too little concerned with acoustics, with the nature of sound, as the original source of our art ... In sound we find the sonority with its aliquot parts, which served our tonal system as a basis, and in the symmetrical inversion of the the the sonic pillar [we find] its perfect opposite: There sounding together, here silent and concealed (latent), there major, here minor, there shadow, here light, there life, here death, etc." (4-6). In this schema, the difference between major, and its inversional symmetry minor, followed naturally from a proper sensitivity to the role of acoustics in music.

[11]This is not to say that Webern was hostile to science or that he considered his work to be unscientific. On the contrary, he felt that his works were beholden to the "unifying laws" (56) of nature, and that "when th[e] true conception of art is achieved, then there will no longer be any possible distinction between science and inspired creation. The further one presses forward, the greater becomes the identity of everything, and finally we have the impression of being faced by a work not of man but of Nature" (56). But Webern's appeal to scientific progress was concerned with nature's laws understood not as providing a scientific distinction between perceptions of oppositely projected constellations, but precisely as unifying these perceptions, recognizing them in terms of variations of the same idea. A musical idea and its inversion, say, may have appeared distinct on the surface but were, in fact, presentations of the same "primeval form," which, as given by natural law, "applies to every living thing [and] is at the bottom of everything" (53). Science, in Webern's world thus unifies both living things and musical ideas – whether retrogrades or inversions – even if they are different in outer appearance. Here it is also worth noting that Johann Wolfgang von Goethe, to whom Webern's views of science were significantly indebted in this regard, understood the physics of the relationship between major and minor keys as a "polarity in the theory of tone. The basic principle of both: the major key created by climbing, by an acceleration upward, by an upward extension of all intervals; the minor key by falling, by an acceleration downward. (The minor scale extended upwards would have to become a major scale)" (302).

[12]Evolutionary theorists of *homosexuality* usually subscribed to some form of Ernst Haeckel's biogenetic law that ontogenesis (the evolution of the individual) recapitulated phylogenesis (the evolution of the species).

[13]Very occasionally, evolutionary ideas were used to support the claims that same-sex sexual desire was normal. In *Intermediate Types Among Primitive Folks*, for instance, Carpenter claimed: "I think we may say that among primitive folk variations of sex-temperament from the normal have not been negligible freaks, but have played an

important part in the evolution and expansion of human society" (170). Interestingly, this claim relies on the hierarchy of races.

[14]Max Nordau's *Degeneration* (1893) was the classic late nineteenth-century example. More generally, the decadence of fin-de-siècle poetry (Mallarmé, Wilde, Verlaine) and music (Schreker, Pfitzner, Strauss) was often attributed to its invocation of a sexually degenerate milieu.

[15]For complete bibliographical information of these reproaches, consult Nicolas Slonimsky's *Lexicon of Musical Invective*. Listings are in alphabetical order by composers. The translations are his.

[16]Perhaps it should be noted here that Mach's empiricism also led him to believe that, because they could not be seen, atoms did not exist.

[17]For differently articulated theories advancing the same conclusions, see Helen Brown, Leonard Meyer, and Mary-Louise Serafine. Brown empirically 'verifies' the origin of the dominant/subdominant *symmetry* in myth.

[18]In his provocative article "Beyond Analysis," Edward T. Cone examines some of the limits of twelve-tone analysis by inverting three existing pieces — Schönberg's *Klavierstück*, op. 33a, and the first and last movements of Webern's *Variationen für Klavier*, op. 27 — thereby generating, in effect, new pieces that are the mirror of the originals. Because of the new "ambiguity between up and down" (42), Cone argues that structural values alone are not able to capture the "concrete musical values" (45) of the (right-side-up) pieces. These values can only be captured with reference to expressive, associative and representational elements that, strictly speaking, are beyond analysis. Cone's article is one of the early challenges to the discipline insofar as it opens a space for expressive and associative values in music research. This is a challenge that later culminated in the more sustained critical stance of the new musicology. But Cone is also doing something other than challenging the limits of the discipline here. For Cone, turning these pieces upside down, did not "improve on, or even ... equal, the original[s]" (39). To show this, he feels compelled to draw on "concrete values" that are beyond analysis. What are these values? He "call[s] upon implicit tonal functions to clarify [the] concrete values [of the original]" (47) in demonstrating its superiority, and shows how, for example, "in Op. 33a, the V-I effect created by the bass connection B-flat — E-flat from the development into the recapitulation [is] an effect signally, and perhaps disastrously lacking in [the upside-down] version" (47-48). Besides effecting a host of unstable binaries (absolute vs. analytic, etc.), here Cone reinstates, via his absolute values, a bottom-up auditory perception, in the very musical space that, for Schönberg, involved an "absolute perception" that knows "no absolute [up or] down" (113). The point here is neither to assert authorial support to challenge Cone's contention, nor to insist that tonal criteria are inapplicable in op. 33a — although it is far from self-evident what counts *as* a tonal criterion — but to draw attention to the possibility of a mirror to the original that is not automatically inferior to it. This possibility, implicitly held out by Schönberg, is paradoxically lost by Cone in the name of a project that aims to move *be-*

yond the purview of structural analysis. For Cone, it goes without saying that the original is superior to his inversions. Ultimately, this theoretical move clarifies the "ambiguity between up and down" (45) that he mentions at the outset of his article. There is, in the final analysis, a right-side-up, a correct "orientation" (47). Ironically, this, in many ways, recapitulates, in a later theoretical setting, the very debate surrounding Schönberg decades before, and, to our way of thinking, offers a vision that is not likely to give rise to a theoretical approach as imaginative as the music that it is analyzing. Perhaps this cluster of analytic concepts — mirror, inversion, right-side-up — was and is embedded in a discourse of sexuality, and perhaps we should consider that it is just such 'analysis' (whose limits Cone carefully exposes) that is provisionally, but more provocatively, queer, an analysis that is somewhere unable to tell apart an original from its inversion.

[19]Relating the commonly held notion that *inversions* do 'not apply' to tonal music back to sexology, it should be pointed out, that one of Ulrichs's motivations for writing his theory was to challenge the then current hypothesis that "in our species no class of born Urnings exists nor could exist ... no class of individuals exists nor could exist that is born with the sexual drive of women and has the body of a male, ie., whose sexual drive is toward men" (35). Perhaps the nonexistence of *inversion* was/is also a matter of not wanting to know. Thus Ulrichs felt compelled to let the public know.

[20]This comment, written in 1933, also has disturbing resonances with the, then emergent, nationalist socialist notion of an Aryan race. Against this, in the next section Webern identified an opposite attitude within the new political thinking to the dissolution of "double gender": "I don't want a polemic, but just now there's a lot of talk about this, in connection with political developments of course, and things are made to look as if it were all something foreign and repellent to the German soul" (37). In the end, the music of Schönberg, Berg, and Webern was rooted out under Nazism. There is not enough room to take up these important, and often paradoxical, questions here.

[21]For example, we do not want to overlook the fact that the protagonists we discuss were all male, nor the fact that the project of obliterating gender can be recuperated in a patriarchal project, since the universal, or the failure to distinguish between male and female, historically may have served the interests of men. Luce Irigaray's call for "sexuate culture" in *sexual difference* feminism is an example of a very different kind of utopic project in relation to gender. Our position tries to imagine a world without gender, or with radical gender parity, and thus takes a different route to reach the same place. Also, instead of underscoring the scope and authority of the patriarchal order, we have tried to read gender reversal as negatively constituent of, or a deconstructive *supplement* to, this order.

[22]Again, it should be stressed that this thinking preceded Schönberg in a paradoxical way. Schröder, the commited defender of diatonic music, wrote: "An inverted arabesque remains an arabesque ... An inverted painted flower-piece remains a flower-

piece and every single flower 'works' with equal charm. — The same applies to the inversion of simple melodies in music" (6). Schönberg, defending "*the emancipation of the dissonance*" (105) in "Composition with Twelve Tones" produced an uncannily similar figuration: "Just as our mind always recognizes, for instance, a knife, a bottle or a watch, regardless of its position, and can reproduce it in the imagination in every possible position, even so a musical creator's mind can operate subconsciously with a row of tones, regardless of their direction, regardless of the way in which a mirror might show the mutual relations, which remain a given quantity" (113). Webern similarly imagined the relation between tones: "An ash-tray, seen from all sides, is always the same, and yet different" (53). These similarities have impelled us to consider that Schönberg and Webern may have read Schröder, whose project was avidly in defense of diatonicism.

The Butler Boom:
Queer Theory's Impact on German Women's/Gender Studies

Evelyn Annuß, in collaboration with Robert Schmidt

Translated by Silke R. Falkner, Elizabeth Penland, and Cathrin Winkelmann

THE TRANSFORMATION OF GENDER CONCEPTS, which has accompanied the dissolution of traditional gender roles, and its subsequent questioning in academia is currently being interpreted as a radical shift (Maihofer 168). I would like to take this as my point of departure for an inventory of the contemporary German academic gender debate. After the shift from women's studies to gender studies in the eighties and its institutionalization in the nineties, the boom in queer theory is now precipitating a new crisis in this field. Although the deconstructivist approaches of queer theory thoroughly unsettle the previous essentialist models of explanation and homogenizing feminist political strategies, I would like to demonstrate the impact this critique of identity politics has on women's/gender studies: Overdetermined by the politics of theory and market strategy, the current battles over field-specific, academic capital are gradually obscuring much of the insight that was once part of what could be called critical common sense.

The shifts in discourse within German women's/gender studies have been determined primarily by the controversies surrounding Judith Butler's approach. Discussing these shifts on three levels, I will therefore: (I) examine Butler's theoretical framework; (II) position the concept of parody and multiple heterogeneous identities, characteristic of Butler's emphatic reception in Germany, within the context of contemporary processes of aestheticization. In the last section of this essay, I will (III) characterize the struggle between the traditional approaches of women's studies and the newer concepts of queer theory as an articulation of debates in academia about field-specific hegemonies.

I.

The recent Butler Boom highlights many of the controversies in the German women's/gender studies debate. The overwhelmingly positive reception of Butler's *Gender Trouble* on the one hand (Hark; Vinken), and its bitter rejection on the other (Duden 1993; Treusch-Dieter) may be seen as indicative of general processes of transformation affecting gender studies for some time now. Using Butler's texts[1] as an example, I would like to discuss some of the current questions and problems posed by queer theory.

Butler's approach is intended as a contribution to the politics of gender from the field of philosophical criticism. She uses examples of gender subversion from the aesthetic and cultural domain to deconstruct philosophical and psychoanalytical texts[2] focusing on symbolic articulations of gender relations. Her point of departure is the materiality of significatory practices, which are not qualitatively distinguished from social structures. There is no differentiation between the ideological, cultural forms of socialization and their material social conditions. As I see it, there appear to be some problems associated with this: Butler does not discuss the generation of the practices to which her approach refers; she fails to give her concepts of gender and the subject an historical and social context; she reifies civil society and its immanent contradictions into a hypercomplex structure of competing practices of signification; the political concept, which derives from this structure, is itself not grounded in the contradictory social reality, but remains on an exclusively symbolic level.

Butler does refer to cultural and historical relations throughout her texts and raises explicit questions about the preconditions and limits of agency. Nonetheless, these questions remain merely rhetorical, although Butler attempts to establish a materialist foundation for her theoretical approach in *Bodies That Matter*[3]: She does not see gendered practices as expressing 'facts of nature'; rather, she understands them as human activity. The abstract relation between sex and gender does not, however, explain the specific forms of gendered practices. Butler emphasizes iteration and materialization 'in time'. She does not reflect on the specific historical conditions under which 'true sexuality' is constituted (Foucault; Duden 1987). The social preconditions and the resulting cultural systematizations of the bourgeois body, namely bourgeois concepts of gender and their essentialization (Hausen; Honegger), are equally not enlisted for the critique of anatomical gender. Butler's work does not inquire into the category of the (bourgeois) subject, its engendering, and the social conditions of its potential decentering – all of which need to be historically qualified.

In her deconstruction of psychoanalytical conceptualizations of heterosexuality and gender differences, Butler treats gender primarily as a form of identity. The intrapsychic mechanisms for the production of gendered identities appear to be most relevant. Butler attempts to determine the (gendered) subject's self-relatedness (*Selbstverhältnis*), without incorporating its material social relatedness beyond its immediate interactions. The tension between the individual and society is therefore resolved in favor of the individual. I would like to elucidate this point by examining Butler's political objectives. Her aim is to broaden what is socially acceptable by integrating and pluralizing forms of identity, but not, however, to expose the underlying social mechanisms which produce identity and exclusion in civil society. Relatedly, Butler no longer identifies the problem of hierarchical gendered divisions of labor and the associated antagonisms of interests. 'Gender' as a structural category of civil society remains obscure.

The blurring of historically specific categories of social structure typifies not only Butler's approach. Beyond the philosophical trend of deconstruction in women's/gender studies, it is also indicative of some sociological approaches, which have recently been discussed on a broader scale. The proximity of Butler's theses to microsociological concepts has caused German scholars in the social sciences to demand empirical research on the claims being made within the current gender debate, which are often regarded as too generalized (Hagemann-White; Hirschauer). Ethnomethodology, in particular, is receiving somewhat belated credit within gender studies as a result of the Butler Boom (Gildemeister/Wetterer 207, n. 2). At the end of the sixties, Garfinkel emphasized the performative dimension of gender relations in his study *Passing and the Managed Achievement of Sex Status in an Intersexed Person*, and illustrated the relativity of physical characteristics for gender attribution in daily life. Garfinkel demonstrated the stability of our everyday construction of gender; Butler examines the destabilizing potential of 'gender trouble'. Ethnomethodologists are concerned with empirical research to determine the construction of meaning in everyday situations, whereas the discussions surrounding Butler's approach are primarily concerned with the philosophical deconstruction of traditional gender norms, the psychic basis of gendered practices, and the question of political agency. What both approaches have in common, however, is the shift in emphasis from biological 'nature' to cultural identity: Gender is no longer understood as an expression of anatomical destiny, of sex; rather, the gendered body is understood as a result of interactive practices. Instead of attempting to integrate these approaches, which are often seen as mutually confirming, I believe it is more productive to focus on the respective methodological and theoretical problems of empirical ethnomethodological gender studies and of Butler's deconstruction of the gender dichotomy and its regulation by the heterosexual matrix.

In both approaches, social reality is viewed as an amalgamation of contradictory constructions of meaning. According to the ethnomethodologists, social reality does not have 'its own objectivity beyond the intentional acts of perception and understanding of the interacting subjects' (Eickelpasch 135). Thus, in the ethnomethodological approach objective statements cannot be made; they appear as mere products of interactive constructions of meaning. This calls into question the claims for legitimacy of ethnomethodological research itself: If all aspects of reality ensue from subjective constructions of meaning, this is also true of the objects of ethnomethodological study itself; that is to say, these objects are constituted by the way in which ethnomethodology investigates them (Prodoehl 29).

This fundamental dilemma of ethnomethodology applies to Butler's approach as well, despite her emphasis on not only the situational but also the temporal dimension of significatory practices. Like ethnomethodology, Butler's deconstructive concept gets caught in circular logic. She understands every assertion of objectivity to be a subjective act of misjudgment. In contrast to the situational subjectivism of ethnomethodology, Butler refers to Lacan's psychoanalytical determination of *méconnaissance* and its radical democratic rereading (Butler 1993, 187-222).[4] Butler views *méconnaissance* as the precondition for shifts within the symbolic order. Correspondingly, contingency is understood as a constant instability in the ideological field, through which agency becomes possible, and the particular incoherent accounts of individual realities as the potential to act on the level of symbolic representation and resignification. With the rereading of what Lacan sees as the ontological failure of signification, the specific *content* of resignificatory practices can no longer be determined. Butler simply differentiates between 'good' anti-essentialist and 'bad' fundamentalist *forms* of identity. Consequently, the material content of these identities as social forms of existence is not considered; the critique of fundamentalism that attacks traditional identity politics remains formalistic. Due to its disregard of institutional, social, and historical conditions of interpretational perspectives, the transhistorical assumption of inevitable contingency becomes metaphysical. This idea of the fundamental contingency − a basic assumption in Butler's as well as in ethnomethodological work − can be derived from the ideological parameters of civil society. Prodoehl's criticism of the ethnomethodological concept of indexicality, which only addresses the situational-subjective constitution of reality, can also be used to critique Butler's assumption of contingency. In the ethnomethodological concept of indexicality,

> the historical fact is reflected that private individuals, who have been released from all immediate social constraints, must − as is the compulsory law of competition − interpret and functionalize all objective structures of reality for themselves in the context of their private calculations of interest as formally free participants in the market. Furthermore, these particular interests and the interpretations of reality of competing private individuals cannot be integrated harmoniously within a general and objective system of interest and interpretation. The ethnomethodological concept of indexicality and subjectivity proves to be necessarily disinterested in the question, whether and to what extent the formal freedom to constitute reality subjectively is itself a principal of the functioning of objective social relations and is for this reason subject to certain limitations regarding content. (Prodoehl 34–35, n. 17)[5]

The bourgeois "compulsory law of competition," as Prodoehl puts it, is disregarded in Butler's work; instead she reifies the social space to a conglomeration of competing significatory practices. Her understanding of the social is limited to the idea that contradictory or competing norms are actualized, reproduced, and transformed through the practices of the subjects in the form of bodily and speech acts, and that these norms participate in the production of the abject as the defining limit of the subject's domain. Thus, dynamics of oppression appear to be mere problems of signification and the search for agency is only explored on a symbolic level. The specificity of the content of speech acts and the particular social position of the acting subjects, as well as the prerequisites for legitimate speech acts remain underdetermined. After all, speech acts are not monological practices of resignification but rather the contested production of meaning within social context.[6]

Although Butler's deconstructive project offers valuable insights into the myths of identity politics, it appears to me to be the wrong alternative to essentialist arguments; the countering of ideas of sexual difference with only the irreducible multiplicity and incoherent identities of the gendered subject squanders the possibility to determine concrete relations of oppression and exploitation. Herein lies what I see as a fundamental problem, which the broader reception of queer theory poses: Instead of providing a sociotheoretical foundation for current developments – for example, the pluralization of gendered identities – the newer perspectives, often amount to nothing more than an affirmation of these developments, of which they are ultimately an expression. In order to examine the conditions and the boom in queer theory more closely, it is necessary to pursue the changes in social structure and culture, which contribute to the shift in perception of the (gendered) self.

II.

Butler understands the trend toward the pluralization of identities and the synthesis of incoherent subject positions to be an emancipatory process (Butler 1987, 128–42). According to her, the dissociation of the individual and even the decentering of its identity serve as constituents of anti-essentialist, radical democratic politics. The revolutionary gesture, however, with which the political program of the multiplication of meaning enters the debate appears inappropriate in light of the changes in forms of identity and gender roles. The political concept developed in queer theory should rather be situated within social and global processes of differentiation and restructuring, which virtually demand local political action. In the context of the current transition to a more flexible deployment of labor in post-Fordism and the simultaneous pluralization of consumer orientations and lifestyles, the political concept of queer theory conforms to the present social requirements of capitalist centers (Hirsch/Roth). In the course of economic and social structural changes, new posttraditional models of social relations have evolved, informed by lifestyles, cultural identities, and alternative cultures (Vester et al.). This has caused modified forms of consciousness and subjectivity to emerge, which the more differentiated new social movements have taken up. It is within this development in the Federal Republic of Germany that one can attribute a trend-setting role to queer politics.

Butler's approach can be read as an example of queer theory's attempt to render political the changed psychological foundation of the individual in postmodern culture (Jameson). In *Gender Trouble*, Butler uses Jameson's concept of pastiche for her parodic program of the destabilization of gender dichotomy — without, however, considering its embedment in the context of the postmodern as the cultural logic of late capitalism (Butler 1990, 138). Jameson situates postmodernism within multinational consumer capitalism and thus provides the key to a more precise determination of those forms of identity and thought which are the basis of both the parodic and the radical democratic project. He uses this reading to examine the replacement of previous experiences of alienation with fragmented subjectivities in capitalist centers. This replacement is accompanied by an aestheticization of both self-perception and social relations as evinced by its theoretical ratification within the Butler Boom.

Aestheticization is generally understood as a phenomenon of the increasing similarity between art and reality, an attempt to dissolve and simultaneously reshape social and cultural segregation aesthetically (Baudrillard, *Symbolic Exchange*; Bubner; Schulze). Butler sees this trend as a political concept. Aesthetic forms are transferred to the political sphere not only by the theater metaphors in her earlier texts and the concept of parody in *Gender Trouble*, but also by the form of the catachrestic speech act depicted in *Bodies That Matter*. In her approach, one can also find indications of differentiation in the new social movements and their subjects. Butler's references to newer gender politics reflect in turn the postmodern fragmentation and reconstruction of identities and viewpoints: Essentialist concepts are abandoned in favor of more pluralistic and heterogeneous forms of politics. Butler promotes local lobbyism with a dash of anti-essentialist coalition politics. The formal freedom to reinterpret the self and one's reality in civil society is used to justify a radical democratic concept in which individual identities and antifundamentalist modes of existence can compete virtually without conflict. The demand for wider acknowledgment of heterogeneous identities in no way criticizes, much less dissolves, the existing social antagonisms. Due to the 'radical' idealism of this political understanding, these antagonisms are not questioned and are therefore ontologized.

Although Butler advocates anti-essentialist politics, she limits herself theoretically to that which is politically feasible.[7] Antagonisms are considered unavoidable. While Butler interprets aestheticized forms of queer politics as potentially subversive practices, I would like to point out their affirmative aspects. As Creydt has demonstrated, borrowing from aesthetic practices helps to synthesize romantically the contradictory social demands (185). As a "softer medium" (184), the aesthetic competes with ideology to explain the world. The aesthetic veiling of social differences and the pluralization of culturalist self-positioning produces a variety of segregated symbolic communities. This development suggests a new differentiated form of sociocultural hegemony within society that maintains what Gerhard Schulze calls a "social peace of mutual non-understanding" (408). By means of this hegemony, structural social inequalities are reproduced even more imperceptibly, since the disavowal of the social increases and the veil of symbolic relationships becomes consistently denser and less penetrable (cf. Bourdieu 1984 and 1990). At the same time, the disposal of symbolic and cultural means for aesthetic self-performance is as unevenly distributed as ever. In the 'radical' democratic struggle for symbolic representation, not all marginalized groups are equally successful. Butler's demand for the aesthetic subversion of coherent meaning and identities in the context of queer politics becomes questionable insofar as it ignores the uneven chances in the competition for signification and representation based on social capital.

III.

The debates surrounding Butler's texts shed a new light on the symbolic battles for academic capital taking place within the field of German women's/gender studies. What many younger scholars downed as the newest theory-cocktail was considered by the majority of somewhat older scholars to be either yesterday's news with a new headline or an occasion to engage in embittered battles against heretical positions within their own field. In fact, the current attack on essentialism, of which Butler and her reception are representative, is the latest in a long series of such critiques. Even the demand to aestheticize gendered self-representations is not that new after all: For example, in her 1979 discussion of Wedekind's *Lulu* in

Die imaginierte Weiblichkeit (*Imagined Femininity*), Bovenschen already considered femininity a citation and, in this sense, promoted it as a strategy against essentialism (57–58). This makes it even more necessary to explain the harsh confrontation between the Butler Boom and Butler-bashing factions, which is commonly interpreted as a generational conflict.[8] My thesis is that the shift to gender studies and the current battle between queer theory and women's studies in the German academic context can also be attributed to changing market conditions within the university. Concealed behind extant geographic, disciplinary, and topical differences as well as the 'mere' generational conflicts, there are manifest battles for hegemony taking place within a scientific field in transition.

Up to now, women's/gender studies has been predominantly concerned with the critique of already established scientific fields. When reading Friederike Hassauer's *Homo. Academica,* one first gets the impression that not much has changed in academia in the last twenty years. According to her, the fields of knowledge produced in the alma mater continue to be gender-*blind* rather than gender-*neutral* (32) and there are fewer and fewer women to be found particularly in the upper levels of the system. Her argument addresses one aspect of this situation, an aspect on which participants in women's/gender studies most often readily agree. However, a reflexive look at the academic market, inspired by Bourdieu's *Homo academicus,* offers more: The "objectification of the objectifications" produced by scholarship, which Bourdieu calls for, can illuminate the social unconscious inscribed in the social logic of the academic universe and, thus, in women's/gender studies. In light of the discussions surrounding Butler, this self-critical view appears challenging and productive. It allows for a critique of the 'mere' generational conflicts within women's/gender studies as well as a critique of the mechanisms of exclusion, in which women are not only the victims of those mechanisms but also participate in their production.

According to Bourdieu, scholarly debates refer to symbolic representations of social reality, which they performatively produce. These debates constitute a battle over relations of representation with the concomitant disavowal of the actors' specific involvement in the larger social struggle. From this perspective, it is possible to examine subtle distinctions within the gender debate. Barbara Duden's reaction to *Gender Trouble* could be viewed as an answer of established women's studies to the crisis of the feminist subject within academia, as it has been theoretically ratified by

Butler: The bitter, confrontational attitude toward Butler in *Die Frau ohne Unterleib* (*The Woman Without a Womb*), in which Duden 'returns' to the sexual body and the reproduction of the species, would then appear in a different light. Her passionate polemic against Butler as a "woman, disembodied by the embodiment of theory" (Duden 1993, 27) is exaggerated and difficult to explain, considering the correspondences between Butler's theory and Duden's proposed sociogenesis of the body. Duden's polemic only makes sense when the discussions within women's/gender studies are seen as a sign of crisis in the context of changes in the university system.

In their study of social structure, Vester et al. describe the opening of the social space in West Germany since the sixties. The modernization of the income-structure, increased chances for consumption, the expansion of the welfare state, and the concomitant educational reform led to the widely discussed disassociation of social positions from ways of life, which in turn allowed for the feminization of education. It is not only the children of blue and white collar workers who have been able to take advantage of the newly available educational opportunities since the mid-seventies, but also and particularly younger women from primarily middle and upper class backgrounds. However, since the number of higher positions in society have not, on the whole, increased, the competition among those with upwardly mobile social ambitions has intensified. Since the end of the seventies, tendencies toward social closure have been growing, particularly in respect to those who initially benefited from the opening of the social space. Women, among others, have been the real losers in the more recent processes of change and crisis within the academic field.

Not only the demands for quotas, but also the fights for a separate scientific field were and are feminist political strategies to circumvent the mechanisms of closure. The fight for the representation of women in academia and the institutionalization of women's studies in the eighties was first characterized by its reference to the "authenticity" of the women's movement for legitimation.[9] However, this institutionalization and the simultaneous increase in the displacement of women from other scientific fields slowly led to stiffer internal competition. With the increasingly powerful mechanisms of closure in the face of financial crisis in all areas of the university, a differentiation in perspectives took place within individual disciplines and interdisciplinary areas of the already established field of women's/gender studies. As more women moved into this field, the need for the delimitation of academic territories increased. Women's/gender studies has developed into a scientific field in which there is indeed something to be either won or lost for the individual player. Especially for the 'younger generation', this directly effects imperatives of innovation and professionalism, and influences the respective theory design of the players' ante. To assume only an evolutionary movement from women's studies to 'more progressive' gender studies does not seem particularly convincing, especially in light of the market-driven forces within universities. Instead, the change in perspective accompanying the shift to gender studies illustrates the fact that the homologous positioning of women in the academy, which was discursively produced across all social differences, is no longer viable considering the new mechanisms of closure on the one hand, and the relative establishment of women's/gender studies that has already taken place on the other. Attempts are now being made from within women's/gender studies to open up new sites of competition and to conquer the hegemony in the established field.

The trend toward lending relative coherence to the different scholarly and social positions of women has now given way to widespread internal competition, which was made possible by the institutionalization of women's/gender studies in the first place. Evidently, the immanent crisis in women's/gender studies is erupting only now that it has gained academic status. Within this framework, Butler's approach — itself interdisciplinary — attacks the already fragile social peace in this comparatively new scientific field. The critical examination of the feminist subject in the German gender debate culminates with the Butler Boom in the insights and the oversights of queer theory which is now, in explicit competition with scholars of women's studies, attempting to take over field-specific capital. Thus, the current outrage of some women's studies scholars over the crumbling of homogeneous lines of confrontation in academic competition becomes visible. The effects of the current shifts in academic power can be likened to the confrontations between established academics and poststructuralist heretics in the events leading up to the events of 1968 in France, as described by Bourdieu (1988).

In this respect, it is particularly interesting that queer theorists are looking to new social movements and political arguments for legitimation in the confrontation with women's/gender studies. Thus, the political impetus has taken on a radical democratic form that corresponds to the societal trend toward aestheticization. In this form, it is particularly evident among younger scholars, who decisively contributed to the Butler Boom.

This is not only due to the progressive reconfiguration of horizons of experience, but also to the necessity for younger scholars of securing academic territory in the face of the market-specific logic of their scientific field. Like the pioneering women's studies scholars, queer theorists cannot situate themselves solely in academic discourse, due to their lack of academic capital. Instead, they necessarily fall back on the cultural and political capital of social movements outside the university. At the same time, academic competition demands that cultural and political capital be rendered scholarly with an enormous amount of intellectual exertion. From this perspective, the philosophical efforts, for example those in which Butler engages, to promote what is ultimately a political program suddenly seem much less surprising.

Although the current gender debate has exposed previous omissions and unsettled essentialist strategies for maintaining hegemony in women's/gender studies, the change in theoretical and political perspectives also conceals social inequality. Earlier attempts to position gender relations in the specific context of civil society have apparently been forgotten, at least for the time being, in the framework of contemporary aestheticizing theoretical and political concepts. As I have attempted to demonstrate in my discussion of Butler's approach, this act of omission is partially due to a specific, radical democratic variant of the linguistic turn, which reduces social practices to competing significatory ones. The critique of feminist identity politics has developed a dynamic of its own and detached itself from theoretical discussions in other domains. The current queer/gender debate has helped to weave the currently opaque veil of symbolic relationships in academia.

In view of the battles, which I have sketched here only in a cursory fashion, the question remains, to which extent and in what way a critical gender studies is at all possible. As the intense confrontation between some 'queer heretics' and established women's studies scholars demonstrates, a sociology of the shifting field of women's, gender, and now, queer studies should be established as epistemic reflexivity. This critical self-reflexivity could then address the market-specific logic of academia and the corresponding societal processes of transformation which influence the competing interests in this field. It could therefore examine and scrutinize the internal mechanisms of theoretical self-reproduction. The modernization of the field, which is constantly represented as a generational conflict, would no longer be understood in terms of theoretical and political confrontation based on changing horizons of experience, but rather as that which has always occurred in other areas of our alma mater: the battle over academic as well as cultural capital in the symbolic "dog-eat-dog" (cf. Bourdieu 1988). The 'exhibition battles of the sexes' and of the generations within the academy could thus be partially robbed of their ideological function. If nothing else, the crisis in the established field of women's/gender studies has demonstrated the prospects for a stricter separation of the subject and object of study, of feminist political strategy and academic work. This could also be taken further to a more thorough analysis of current anti-essentialist trends.

A critical gender studies cannot limit itself to a critique of the structurally 'gender-blind' production of knowledge, nor to the deconstruction of essentialist thought. It should at least attempt to reflect on and decode its own preconditions. This would entail deconstructive work on both antiquated and heretical strategies of self-legitimation and could perhaps even result in the insight that gender as an object of study is meaningful only as part of the larger picture of critical social theory.

Notes

[1] For a more comprehensive critique of Butler in the German context, see, for example, Eichhorn, Landweer, "Kritik," "Herausforderung," and "Jenseits"; as well as Nagl-Docekal.

[2] See Butler 1993, 121-66.

[3] Cf. the comments on Marx's first thesis on Feuerbach (Butler 1993, 250, fn.5).

[4] Cf. Laclau/Mouffe; for a critique, see Narr.

[5] In German: Im Indexikalitätskonzept "wird der historische Sachverhalt reflektiert, daß die aus allen *unmittelbaren* Vergesellschaftungszwängen entlassenen Privatindividuen als formell freie Marktteilnehmer jegliche objektive Wirklichkeitsstrukturen – als Zwangsgebot der Konkurrenz – im Horizont ihres privaten Interessenkalküls für sich selbst interpretieren und funktionalisieren müssen, und daß ferner diese partikularen Interessen und Wirklichkeitsinterpretationen der konkurrierenden Privatindividuen nicht konfliktfrei unter dem Dach eines objektiv-allgemeinen Interessen- und Deutungssystems integriert werden können. Das ethnomethodologische Indexikalitäts- und Subjektivitätskonzept zeigt sich notwendigerweise desinteressiert an der Fragestellung, ob und inwieweit die formelle Freiheit zu subjektiver Wirklichkeitskonstitution selbst ein Funktionsprinzip objektiver gesellschaftlicher Verhältnisse ist und aus diesem Grunde bestimmten inhaltlichen Beschränkungen unterliegt."

[6]In *Language and Symbolic Power*, Bourdieu refers to social and cultural capitals which first legitimize each speech act and are therefore its prerequisite. See also his critique of Austin's speech act theory (Bourdieu 1991), to which Butler alludes in her reference to Derrida (1993).

[7]Cf. Mouffe's understanding of democracy, as referred to by Butler (1992, 379).

[8]Cf. Landweer/Rumpf 1993 and Landweer "Generationen."

[9]Within German studies, for example, the eighties saw the establishment of so-called feminist literary studies (*feministische Literaturwissenschaft*) which set out to change the system from within by employing essentialist and poststructuralist components, fashionable at the time. Based on a tacit understanding, peaceful coexistence was possible between the old boys in traditional literary scholarship and the new girls of the school of sexual difference (*differenztheoretisch*), at least temporarily. The theory design of feminist literary studies was anything but coherent; however, the often surprising combinations of, for example, deconstructionism and essentialism obviously lent themselves to a more widespread establishment of the feminist approach within German studies. Cf. Weigel 1983, 1987; for criticism, see Hahn; Kolkenbrock-Netz; and Schuller.

Queering

German

Literature

Reflections of Homosexuality in Medieval Poetry and Chronicles

Helmut Brall

Translated by Amy Romig and Simon Marshall

T O ALL APPEARANCES, HOMOSEXUALITY was outlawed, scorned, and
ostracized throughout the Christian culture of the Middle Ages (cf.
Boswell; Hergemöller 1994; Kuster; Kuster/Cormier). Except for isolated literary evidences of homoerotic love in Latin lyrics (Düchting; Stehling),
most texts of this time which deal with this subject deny homosexual relationships between men any ideal or imaginary worth, and with it, any justification of its existence. Medieval writers, although interested in the manifold (including the bizarre) varieties of heterosexual love, dogmatically
judged homosexuality negatively and deemed homosexual relationships
threatening (cf. Bein; Beutin; Spreitzer). But, did that also mean that homosexual men were pushed to the edges of society? That they were burdened
with the fears of their sins and plagued by their consciences? That they were
discriminated against and persecuted? Did they necessarily have to lead a
wretched and endangered life because of their sexual longings?[1] As shown
by Philippe Ariès[2] and Michel Foucault ("Der Kampf"), such views transpose modern standards, modes of perception, and functions of sexuality
onto the conditions in traditional societies. For this reason, our concept
of the homosexual and homosexuality in the Middle Ages often seems
clumsy and wooden. The literary and historiographical sources on sexual
deviation are, however, subject to several rules; and it is therefore difficult to
throw all medieval authors together — be they clerical or secular — and
blame them for the outlawing and persecution of homosexuality in the
Middle Ages. Instead of making judgments in hindsight from the position
of an enlightened and liberal thinking modern world, and instead of the
forcible revision of a history of repression and prejudice — which has al-

ready been approached from different angles (cf. Bleibtreu-Ehrenberg 1978 and 1992; Hergemöller 1994, 362-64) – this paper intends to illuminate the conceptions and the meaning of homosexuality (as well as the function of accusing someone of sodomy) in several examples of medieval poetry and historical writings in their contemporary context. If one reads the texts as something other than stereotypical evidences of repression, the sources provide valuable information about the medieval preconditions of the modern attitudes toward homosexuality.[3] The development of the literary debate on homosexuality, on which I would like to shed light with a few representative examples, can be divided into three phases: First, the condemnation of homosexuality was of basic interest to spiritual counselors who wanted to make a clear distinction between the sex and gender oriented world of the laity, and the asexual society of the monks and clerics. Second, in the courtly and secular social structure, homosexuality was scorned, fought against, and placed on the same level as prostitution. This, however, was for other reasons: one could use the suspicion of homosexuality to spin webs of political intrigue, and sodomites were made responsible for the destruction of the ideal aristocratic social order. Finally, in cities of the late Middle Ages, homosexuals fell victim to the struggle for the enforcement of the power of the ruling class while the rulers themselves were able to escape the draconian punishments set aside for homosexuality.

I.

In his chronicle, bishop and historian Thietmar of Merseburg (975–1018) remembers in the obituary of his fellow friar Husward how this monk fought the temptations of the flesh:

> At night our cunning oppressor, the devil, often haunted my brother Husward when he slept beside me and asked him for some space to lie beside him. Finally he humbly begged him to become his paid servant. However, the pious man did not forget the vow he had given the Lord and demanded to see his reward before he gave an answer. The devil said: "If you agree, I will pay you in a similar way in which I recently rewarded my servant in the west." After the devil had made this offer, the venerable priest drove him away with the sign of the holy cross and harsh, scolding words as

he had done so many times before. When he heard that a clergy-man in the west had been hanged for serious offenses, he told us all about his experience. This venture of the devil is surprising considering that the true cross of Christ was carried into our dormitory every Sunday. (IV. 67, 183)

Thietmar is describing the violation of the chaste world of a monastic dormitory by a sexual element. His roommate Husward successfully defends himself against the temptations to which he felt especially exposed. Of which nature these temptations were apparently does not interest the historian. Due to his discreet description, it remains undecided if heterosexual wishes, wet dreams or masturbation, or homosexual desires are meant. The appearance of the evil seducer encloses the whole field of sexuality in such a way that a detailed investigation is superfluous. Even the devil's desire for personal proximity and warmth, for a place in the monk's bed, appears in a sexual light. The motives of sexual lust and desire are completely overshadowed, perhaps also because of Husward's age. Thus, Husward's part in the interaction with the cunning oppressor is hard to determine; even when the devil urgently asks him to become his paid servant, it remains obscure which duty the monk is to perform. From Thietmar's point of view, the practical side of the agreement is completely irrelevant because the devil's pay is always the death of the soul. According to this report, being a clergyman does not offer safe protection against sin and sexual misdemeanor. However, the monk in contrast to the cleric is saved from them and their consequences by a whole arsenal of spiritual weapons that Husward brings to bear in an exemplary and successful way: his oath, the sign of the holy cross, the exorcising words and the report of his experiences to his fellow friars.

A clear example of homosexual offenses in a monastery is documented in an example from the *Dialogus Miraculorum* by Caesarius of Heisterbach (approx. 1180-1240) (cf. Puff 47-49, for correlations between homosexuality, sin, and illness). In sharp contrast to his usual style, the Rhenish Cistercian monk does not reveal the scene of the action and the people involved. The success of the confession, that is, the deliverance of the young sinner, is not to be spoiled in the eye of posterity by an indiscreet description. Therefore, it cannot be said that homosexuality is being made taboo, nor that homosexuals are being oppressed. The single, yet extremely severe violation of monastic discipline by a dignitary of the convent is only the cause of the events. This feeble ordained monk had been tempted by the devil and had sinned with a young man who had often come to confess to him.[4] More disastrous than the actual deed, is the way the two sinners deal with the guilt that they both realize and regret. The father confessor has the unfortunate idea that they should confess to one another. This, however, contradicts the sacrament of penance because, instead of taking the thorny path of redeeming purification, the two try to do a cover-up even though they know better. Thus, the central matter of concern in this story is to demonstrate the possibilities and limits of the sacrament of penance and to warn against its devaluation.

This miraculous tale which gives an account of the two poles of human existence between ruin and salvation has been burdened with very important statements regarding homosexuality. "Firstly: Illness can be the actual consequence of homosexual acts. Secondly: homosexuality is like an illness, that is, homosexuality can be compared to an illness, is similar to it" (Puff 1-52).[5] With all due respect for an attempt to 'justify' homosexuality, several distortions of the reference text must be observed. From a contemporary point of view, the abuse of the position of father confessor comes close to what could be called child abuse. Caesarius, however, does not report this sin any less patiently or more fanatically than many other crimes deriving from greed, envy, or (heterosexual and incestuous) lust that must be expiated in purgatory if they cannot be forgiven through the power of confession (cf. LeGoff, esp. 258-60 and 365-67).

This priest, weak and susceptible to sinning, falls ill a short time later, and fearing that he would go to hell, makes a confession before his death. He does not, however, reveal the name of the other perpetrator involved. Although this will not save him from the horrors of purgatory, the confession helps the priest. This depends not on the gravity of the crime, but more on the lack of trust in the power of the forgiveness of sins. Since the youth was spared, death and illness were not in anyway seen as the punishment for homosexual activity by Caesarius, but rather as the ultimate summons to penance. The priest simply failed to realize while he was still alive that he would still be punished for this sin even after his death. Still, a healing contact between the living and the dead develops out of the relationship between the priest and the youth. The dead priest encounters the stubborn boy in a vision, explains the worthlessness of their mutual confession and the punishments in purgatory for the sexual sins. In this way, he helps the boy – who is still afraid to go to confession because he is too ashamed — to find the courage to acknowledge his sin and follow the path to salvation. The confession of the living is also of advantage to the deceased priest when it finally comes to be with the help of the wise abbot.

One might greatly object to this sort of disciplinary action for following sexual desires, but one must accept the fact that they developed out of the regulations of life in social groups and were enforced — as in this case — by long-suffering authority. The horrible threats of punishment and the tortures awaiting the sinner in purgatory served as instruments of education and character building. It is, however, inappropriate to condemn them from our modern point of view as mere instruments of oppression.

II.

In the vernacular poetry of the high Middle Ages, homosexuality was not made taboo, but was perceived from decidedly gender specific dispositions. In the following primary texts, homosexuality is presented first from a female, then from a male point of view, and finally in a dialogue on the correct conduct of men and women between a representative of each gender.

In the anonymous Old French novel *Le Roman d´Eneas* (v. 8565), and in Heinrich von Veldeke's *Eneasroman* (v. 10631), the hero is accused of homosexuality by an interested party (cf. Kuster 57–59 for similar accusations in Vergil). This accusation has the unconcealed purpose to cool Lavinia's love for the foreign Aeneas and to prevent marital bonds with him. During her intervention, Queen Amata, who charges the Trojan with sexual deviations (*des bôsen sides*, "bad habit," v. 10653), does not instrumentalize — even though she is wrong and mistaken — any of the collective and general resentments with which homosexuals are usually confronted. She is not concerned with morals, but with removing an unwanted suitor in a critical situation of marital politics. In her opinion, a man who does not desire women does not in any way fulfill the necessary preconditions for being a husband and king. Amata regards homosexuality mainly as an obstacle in marriage (*impedimentum*). Conveniently, she can denounce him in a way that should nip any subjective feelings of love in the bud: "with this you would dishonor yourself / and all of your kind."[6]

Even the lovesick Lavinia is tortured by doubts regarding the true erotic interest of her lover. When Aeneas lets her wait a long time shortly before the decisive battle, she remembers the rumors she had heard from her mother: "I am all the more convinced that he does not care about women. May God punish him for the fact that I have found out about him. What the devil does he love about men? That is a great disgrace."[7] Lavinia does not share her mother's aversion to Aeneas, but she nevertheless agrees with her conviction that a homosexual would be out of the question as husband and king. According to Lavinia, those men who do not love women should be banished from the country.

In the medieval romance of Aeneas, women evaluate homosexuality according to their own — more or less legitimate — interests with regard to status and life. They do not orient themselves mainly toward the norm propagated by religion or the church. In regard to a relationship with a homosexual man, they are much more afraid of a loss of power and social influence, and childlessness. Marital sexuality is not only regarded as an element of individual and private fulfillment of life and happiness, but, moreover, as an extensive and socially integrative contract comprising gender and generation. Therefore, from a female point of view, a homosexual appears to be the most unsuitable party to the contract and a serious threat to female concepts of life.

In Ulrich von Liechtenstein's *Frauendienst* (serving women), homosexuality appears in the context of political affairs. Playing the part of Venus, Ulrich refuses a duel with Hadmar III of Kuenring — for reasons of exhaustion — and puts him off until the next morning. However, the people around the rejected challenger, who similar to Ulrich von Liechtenstein belong to the group of politically influential landowners (*lantherren*) of his time, understand this refusal as an intentional signal for Kuenringer: since nothing of the kind has ever happened before, Venus's restraint is seen as a result of the circulating rumor that Herr Hadmar is homosexual.[8] Those who are publicly rejected by Venus, the universally recognized defender of female interests, must have done something wrong which makes them enemies of women. As in Veldeke's version of the Aeneas story — and Ulrich von Liechtenstein might have had the Trojan's image in mind at this point — homosexuality also had its value in the representation of status in *Frauendienst*. The slanderous report is supposed to publicly humiliate the man in question, as well as to make him 'impossible' as a man of rank. The slander also signals political opposition to the point of bitter animosity, that is, it serves an important purpose in the publicizing of the building of political fronts.

In Ulrich von Liechtenstein's allegorical, imaginary world, courtly love and the service to women associated with it are the gauges for the allocation of prestige in a representative public (cf. Habermas 16–17). In this text, the function of the service to love is to represent dominion, the ability to rule, and the virtues of a ruler. This is because the courtly love cult and the courtly-knightly code of behavior compose the only means of regulating life that *Frauendienst* allows. All sorts of mishaps, silliness, and inconveniences, both public and private, appear legitimate under the auspices of courtly love and knighthood. Homosexuality, on the other hand, is overburdened with negative connotations like no other abnormality of habit or behavior of a high-ranking member of nobility.

The reputation of being homosexual could apparently do especially long-lasting damage to the political and social position of a man in the ritualized system of this representative public. Thus, the attitudes of the sovereign landowners toward homosexuality seem to be impressed upon by justifiable fears of loss of influence in politics and prestige in their group of peers by rumors targeted at them. The *rede* (slanderous speech) was more effective than a conviction on moral grounds; while morals refer to a consensus in the confirmation of permissive behavior against which homosexuality goes, the *rede* cuts to the heart of social prestige. Therefore, rumors like those about Hadmar could trigger serious hostilities[9] caused by the resulting defamation and public humiliation of the person in question.

This obsessive overestimation of the situation can be found in all of the literary works by Ulrich von Liechtenstein, who returns to the subject of homosexuality in his *Frauenbuch* (book of women) written in 1257. These precepts for love, marriage, and status serve to ascertain social norms and intend to make both sexes keep to the common goal of a successful representation of status. The *êre* (honor) of the women and the *êre* of the men can develop fully only in mutual reference to one another. For this reason, the rules of love and marriage and the honor of rank are the standard and nucleus of all actions. Unfortunately, this goal is thwarted by gender specific passions (Ulrich von Liechtenstein means, for example, men's lust for hunting and drinking or women's requirements for tenderness and piety) which fuel the prejudices against the other sex, and lead to misunderstandings and hardening of positions. The accusation of homosexuality parries a targeted attack on the honor of the female sex in the context of the debate between the knight and the *frouwe* (lady). The knight argues that the women behave in an undisciplined way, that their love is venal, that they allow themselves to be showered with little valuables for their favors, or that they waste their love on men who are not in accordance to their social rank, but who are more than willing. In the counterattack, the *frouwe* expresses her suspicion that men practice their sexuality without paying any attention to social order or norms:

> Is that supposed to be acceptable, that men are now doing with one another what neither birds nor beasts feel like doing and seems so monstrous to all creatures? You know exactly what I mean: It is so atrocious that I cannot say it out loud. The lives of such men are cursed. Tell me if it is a heinous deed if a man does that with a man for which God also created women.[10]

Should the rule-governed interaction of the sexes be raised to a binding code of status-exclusive behavior (cf. Glier 16-18) — as demanded by the precepts of love at the time — then this model of behavior must be protected against two dangers. Firstly, against the independence of the woman from the prestige of the man, that is, against the separation of service and person. Secondly, against the independence of the man from the woman's rewards. Just as the purchasability of a woman's love impersonalizes and devalues the man's service to her, the man's desire directed at members of the same sex destroys the erotic and socially integrative action of the woman. Women who sell their favors and homosexual men have no place in the world of the aristocracy. Rather, they are perceived as the inveterate destroyers of an artificially regulated system of social intercourse. In terms of homosexuality, the knight then unreservedly ensures the *frouwe* of his solidarity (Ulrich, *Frauenbuch* 616, 14-617, 11).

The concept of the rendering of service in courtly love as outlined by Ulrich von Liechtenstein ignores the legal and hierarchical pillars of societal order and gives them a playful and ceremonial tinge. It is supposed to appear as if the nobility's obligation to the reciprocity principle is the only reliable basis of all actions. Service and reward must retain their delicate balance if the social life of the aristocracy is to function properly. This fragile concept is incompatible with any extra privileges; *minne umbe guot* (love in exchange for money) and homosexuality weaken the symbolic gestures of harmony, they thwart the means by which the social elite want to (and should) understand themselves. The aristocratic feudal society cannot afford to represent, nor imagine themselves representing, "something inferior or worthless, something lower" (Habermas 17; cf. Schmitt 208-210).

More important than the men's fears of suffering injury or disadvantage by rumors, as well as the possibility of profiting from them, is another result in the context of this study. Since the middle of the thirteenth century, homosexuality was not judged an exception or a marginal phenomenon of sexuality by the lay people, but rather was simply declared an enemy of the system and the social order. This particularly revealing fact is supported by additional evidence[11] which can be found when researching the subject of homosexuality in the Middle Ages. From the standpoint of literary history, the following factors can be taken into account for the excessive reaction to homosexuality both by the lay people as well as in courtly society. Talk of the abnormal evil of homosexuality gets its most important argumentatious (as well as metaphorical) support in the deterrent and disciplinary tracts written for clerics and monks. The historical dispositions for keeping them up to date can be seen in the self-perception of the courtly lay society. Hypersensitivity toward deviation necessarily follows when the status and the way of life of the elite is construed and expressed to such a great extent through the axioms of heterosexual love. It is only this disproportionate evaluation that gives reason to see dangerous and destructive elements of social life in both suspected as well as actual homosexuals, and to mobilize the whole force of law and order against them. Therefore, the rejection of homosexuality must be regarded as a considerable part of the concepts of courtly love.

To love men in a way which slights both the women's monopoly on love as well as the natural right of reproduction was understood as an opposition to the two forms of order established by rank and gender. In *Frauendienst*, Ulrich von Liechtenstein openly changes gender roles, both of which he embodied unambiguously, and yet did not come under any suspicion that he was indulging in some kind of forbidden or secret desires behind his masquerades and role-play. A homosexual, on the other hand, had to appear as a deeply ambiguous existence in the forming and formulating of a courtly/lay concept of society. He must have appeared a mixed being, perceived neither by women nor by men as an integral part of their society. From a male, as well as a female, point of view, a homosexual did not match the patterns of the courtly representation of status. Thus, without any status, he soon gained the reputation of being a sworn enemy of the 'natural' order. Homosexuality was therefore not a taboo, but rather an instrument of defamation. It is then no wonder that influential authors of the time, such as Der Stricker, as early as the mid-thirteenth century saw and branded homosexuality as a danger to the continuity of society in a way that we can not perceive today (cf. Brall, esp. 16–17). In this respect, the author who is commonly regarded to be very repressive actually takes the same point of view as the women in the *Eneasroman*. He does, however, also see the fear of the male side, when he laments the decay of order through spreading homosexuality in the style and with the rhetorical means of a penitential sermon.[12] It seems that the homosexuals are being made responsible for the courtly/lay discourse on homosexuality, which appears to be dominated by hostility, distrust and suspicion. From a modern standpoint, they were mistaking the cause for the effects; in the perception of dealing with homosexuality, we mainly see a construed, extremely volatile self-depiction of the social elites, and only secondarily, a prosecuting instance interested in controlling male sexual activity.

Even such a critical observer of social conditions as the Seifried Helbling satirist, who wrote in Austria toward the end of the thirteenth century, categorically mitigates the debate on homosexuality, the importance of which had been artificially built up by courtly literature and society. He argues with biblical patterns: Ninive, so he ponders, had eventually been able to cleanse himself. Sodom and Gomorrah, had they been given a chance to cleanse and improve themselves, would not have gone under either. With regard to Austria, there remains a lot to be ameliorated, "but I absolve this land from there being any sodomites in it."[13]

Let us then draw a short conclusion of what has been said thus far. There is much more in the literary debate on homosexuality than only the unrestricted validity of those powers inimical to lust which suppressed sexuality on principle and made homosexuality especially a taboo persecuting its perpetrators. Even in the realm of art, one finds more than simply the effectiveness of repressive norms. Regardless of the generally negative evaluation, the ways in which homosexuality is dealt with must be fanned out; the rejection of homosexuality by women in the antiquitizing novel appears to be linked to the protection of female interests. The way men deal with this topic in the courtly world has other hurdles, and creates different fears and desires than the way homosexuality is treated in churches and monasteries. Despite the reciprocity between these spheres, it seems advisable to carefully examine the differences between the various interests and motives in the social areas and in the different epochs. The 'meanings' of homosexuality depend on complex processes of attribution that were made in various social contexts and are determined by heterogeneous political and historical conditions.

The tendency toward correspondence between vernacular poetry and the clerical ban of homosexuality[14] from the middle of the thirteenth century was the result of complex social and literary-ideological formation processes. Ulrich von Liechtenstein's poetic and parodistic autobiography contributed to this by weaving the social life of the privileged class into patterns and types of literary tradition (cf. Birkhan, esp. 23–24; Knapp 112–14; J.-D. Müller). Despite all the poetic freedom and distance from everyday life, *Frauendienst* and *Frauenbuch* acknowledge the essential rules of status representation and their social reality without condition. The attitude toward sodomites documented here can claim a certain validity for the courtly/lay area: the secular society and its ruling elites considered this deviation to be an especially serious violation of their obligatory duty to demonstrate and represent the ideals of courtly lifestyle. The more precise the prescription of the rules to be obeyed, the greater became the pressure for order. Infringements carried more weight and were punished more drastically. Ulrich von Liechtenstein's work proves this historical tendency in the development of civilization. Education and amelioration in accordance with the loyalty to monastic rules could not be transferred to the conditions of the courtly/lay society without palpable sanctions; the punishments of purgatory were literally applied on earth already in the form of ostracism and animosity. However, at least the offenders and victims, judges and the judged belonged to the same rank and felt obliged to the same set of rules. From the point at which offender and victim were members of different political or social parties the view of homosexuality actually changed quite decisively.

III.

According to original sources, the criminalization of homosexuality and the persecution of homosexuals began in the middle of the thirteenth century (cf. Boswell; Hergemöller 1994; Wittkower/Wittkower 162–64). This intensification was obviously a side effect of a wide-ranging social boost of modernization that brought about an enormous pressure to conform, especially in the towns.[15] What turned homosexuality into such a severe crime in the eyes of the contemporaries? Must this development be ascribed to increasing intolerance by the secular and clerical authorities? Were the 'sodomites' really the male counterparts to witches, pitiable victims of suppressed lusts and unreasonable campaigns of annihilation (cf. Hergemöller 1994, 392)?

The severe sanctions against homosexuals served mainly, as I would finally like to point out, the demonstration of legal power. This bestowed additional legitimacy on the local authorities which arises out of the consequent emergence and establishment of public order. Sexuality thus became – following Michel Foucault – the place of events, where the balance of power was determined in a new way and power struggles between the authorities and the population were carried out (1978). This thesis can be proved with the help of some evidence from accounts of the persecution of sodomites originating from the realm of the late medieval German town historiography.

No less than four chronicles from the town of Augsburg, which are all partially dependent on one another, report of a case of heresy by sodomites that is unique in the history of the town. In the first supplement of the first continuation of the year 1409, the oldest *Chronik von 1368 bis 1406* (1447) links the assumption of office of Graf Eberhart of Kirchberg as bishop of Augsburg and of Ulrich Könczelman and Lorencz Egen as mayors with this spectacular demonstration of uncompromising legal authority.[16] Contrary to the outward chronology and the actual dates of the investiture – the appointment of the bishop already occurred in 1405 – the position of the entry at the beginning of the supplement attributes the events with great importance. On March 2, 1409, four priests were put in a cage called the 'bird house' on the outside of the Perlach tower and it was welded shut. The evil-doers were Jörg Wattenlech, a dominican, Uolrich der Frey, the chaplain of the Church of St. John, Jackob der Kiß, a member of the convent of the Church of the Holy Cross in Augsburg, and a Mr. Hans, the pastor of Gersthofen: "They practiced heresy among themselves. They lived without food until the friday and then they were all dead."[17] A layman, Hans Gossenloher – "he was also one of them"[18] – had already been burned at the stake on the previous Saturday when the priests were put in the cage.

According to this notice, the city authorities rigorously enforced their claim to punishment for five clerical and lay people and sentenced them all to death for the same crime. The reason that the punishment for the clerics was so much more tortuous is due to the fact that members of the clergy could not be executed by fire or sword. Because of their higher degree, they were left physically untouched, but died miserably of thirst in public for all to see. The crime itself remains unclear in the books and further details are not given. The names and ranks of the sentenced men were more important for the chronicler, the more so because there were ordained priests among them. Whether the layman Hans Gossenloher had homosexual contact with the priests, or if he was just regarded as a homosexual, is also not clear. The document's position, its connection to the bishop's ascension to power, and the naming of the mayor, implies that this is meant to serve as an example of the authority's executive power, and is meant to document the decisiveness of the city council to enforce their power. The excited echo of this event in later chronicles reinforces this impression.

In Burkard Zink's chronicle, the second book of which was written between 1450 and 1460,[19] the clerical rank of the convicted men and the conflict with the bishop of Augsburg about the right to judge the perpetrators takes the foreground. The crime itself – "they imprisoned them for the heresy which they had practiced together"[20] – is not more graphically described whatsoever. But, because the bishop, according to Burkard Zink, gave the citizens *gar schnell ... vollen gewalt* ("the full power immediately"), even the bishop's veto written later indicating his position could not protect the delinquents from the severity of the city's civic authority: "But the citizens of Augsburg did not want to comply and said that he had given them the full power, therefore they wanted to continue as had been planned. Thus, they welded them fast in the 'bird cage', and therein they had to die. And their companion, the tanner, was burned to death in the year 1409."[21]

Two further documents recall this action of urban administration of justice. The first is the *Chronik des Erhard Wahraus 1126-1445* (1462).[22] Erhard Wahraus was later a member of the city council and could have been a witness to the event described. He precisely documents the status and rank of the convicted, while at the same time he is rather indefinite about the names and dates. In his chronicle, the convicted men are more clearly a homogenous group of heretics. Lastly, one must mention the *Chronik von der Gründung der Stadt Augsburg bis zum Jahre 1469,*[23] which was most likely written shortly after the year 1469. This chronicle is mainly interested in the unusual form of the enforcement of punishment and the technical details of its carrying out. Names, dates, and the crime itself are pushed out of the spotlight by this outstanding example of such an inventive art of execution. For the chronicler, this event belongs to one of the deeds of glory in the history of the city of Augsburg.

This extreme example of late medieval persecution of homosexuals is countered by a case documented by the local scribe for the city of Co-logne, Edmunt Frunt, in which a process against notorious homosexual fornication was quashed (cf. Hergemöller, "Die 'unaussprechliche'"; Irsig-ler/Lassotta 198–99). While the mayor and the council of the city of Augs-burg achieved a memorable exemplary gesture of power over the members of the city's clergy (and we can hardly doubt its effectiveness as a deterrent), a pastor's attempted campaign against homosexuals among the citizens of Cologne failed miserably. In 1484, during a feast at the house of a prelate, the pastor of St. Apostles publicly accused a leading man of the city of Cologne of repeatedly committing unnatural fornication with a member of his parish. The pastor, who had gathered this knowledge about the accused man and a circle of homosexuals numbering more than two hundred people from the confession of one of his parishioners, repeated his accusa-tions before the city council. The city council, however, was unable to reach a decision to take punitive measures and instead, requested expert theological advice, which was to discourage them from any further inves-tigation into the matter. Even when the accused, former councilman and tower guard Johann Greefroide, was further incriminated by the testimony of other witnesses, including persons involved, of having to an extent forcibly committed sexual acts with young men, the testimony had no legal consequences. Although the city council used the opportunity that this legal case offered to investigate thoroughly the sexuality of the citizens of Cologne, the protocols of the testimony of the thirteen clerics who were called to testify before the investigation committee (which the city council had called together to research the spread of homosexuality in Cologne) were just as conflicting as the opinions expressed by Ulrich von Liechten-stein and the Seifried Helbling satirist on the spread of homosexuality in Austria. Since no one made any further use of the results of these investiga-tions, it can be assumed that the entire matter, even then, was regarded merely as a question of power and opportunity.

The persecution of the sodomitic *Unnatur* in late medieval cities, as the above examples make clear, served the setting of political goals as well as the struggle for the enforcement of legal jurisdiction. The aim of outlaw-ing homosexuality was to set a legal political trap for unpopular people or groups. If it were not for these preconditions, then there would not have been any official interest in initiating legal measures. The Cologne example is striking evidence for the fact that moral indignation and clerical demands alone could not trigger a wave of 'cleansing'. Sodomy was perceived from the perspective of an urban power machine already far away from the societal bonds of the high middle ages. This machine proceeded with brutality against outsiders and marginal groups in society when political power interests came into play, or when the efficient organization of the ruling class was to be enforced.

Notes

[1]Frantisek Graus expressly rejects the sociological attribution of homosexuals to a fringe group, rather they were fully part of 'normal' society so long as this fact was not discovered (399).

[2]"The attitude of ancient communities toward homosexuality—about which we know very little and which we should study with fresh eyes and a disregard for the anachronisms of psycho-analysis—seems more comlex than the very strict and detailed codes of religious morality would lead us to believe" ("Thoughts on the History of Homosexuality" 71).

[3]The modern conception of homosexuality seems to be mainly determined by a legal and moral, that is, public, condemnation on the one hand and by a scientific exploration of its causes, especially by social psychology and psychology of individualism, on the other hand. Political control over sexuality and with it the classification of views positive toward (homo)sexuality and those inimical against (homo)sexuality lead into a dead end because they always imply a concept of good and justified sexuality. This concept, however, cuts out the pathological 'lust for evil' and places it into a different, that is medical, discourse. Only on the basis of a clinker-free, scientifically investigated and theoretically clarified sexuality that is compatible with the ways of life in the societies of the twentieth century, the struggle for social and legal tolerance even of sexuality through the centuries appears to be a chronicle of tyranny, superstition, and hostility toward lust. Compare also the unsurpassed outline of this problem in Michel Foucault (1978, 11-13).

[4]The source text does not state that the priest had "sexual intercourse with the youth during confession" nor that "the short lust during the confession costs the consecrated priest and father confessor his life," as Helmut Puff writes (47-48). The editor of the *Dialogus miraculorum* is not called Stange (cf. 48, n. 5), but Strange.

[5]Incidentally, a certain liberalization in the evaluation of mortal sins emerges from precisely this imagery that draws the sin onto the level of an illness (cf. Schwaibold 111).

[6]"dâ du dich mite entêrest / und allez dîn geslehte!" (v. 10636-37). As it is known in the Old French novel, Amata phrases her accusations against Aeneas more explicitly: "Onkes femme n'ot bien de lui, / nen avras tu, si com ge cui, / d' un traitor, d' un sodomite" (v. 8581-83). [Never did a woman have any good from him, nor do I think you will have, from a traitor and a sodomite.] Moreover, she views sodomites to be sexually obsessed and to be pederasts: "il prise plus le plein mestier; / il ne vuelt pas bische chacier, / molt par aime char de maslon; / il prisereit mielz un garcon / que tei ne altre acoler. / A femme ne set il joer, / ne passereit pas al guichet; / molt aime froise de vallet. / En ce sont Troien norri" (v. 8569-77). [She prefers the opposite trade: he will not eat hens, but he loves very much the flesh of a cock. He would prefer to embrace a boy rather than you or any other woman. He does not know how to play with women, and would not parley at the wicket-gate; but he loves very much the breech of a man. The Trojans are raised on this. (Engl. Trans. Yunck 226)]

[7]"deste baz getrouwe ich des / daz im unmâre sîn diu wîb. / sô hazze got sînen lîb, / daz ich sîn kunde ie gewan. / waz tûfels minnet her an dem man? / ez ist ein michel bôsheit" (v. 11442-47).

[8]"man sprach: 'diu künegîn hât verseit / hern Hademâr ir tjoste hie. / daz tet si für wâr ritter nie. / ich waen siz dar umb hât getân, / daz man des giht, er minn die man'" (Ulrich von Liechtenstein 266, 4-8).

[9]For Ulrich it was because of herzenlîchen leit (heartfelt grief) that he came under suspicion of having nourished such a rumor. He was therefore herzenlîch gehaz (hated from the heart) by Hadmar (266, 4 and 12), and Hadmar announced his revenge.

[10]"stât daz wol daz nu die man / mit ein ander daz begânt / des vogel noch tier niht willen hânt / und alle crêature / dunket ungehiure? / ir wizzt wol waz ich meine: / ez ist sô gar unreine, / daz ich sîn niht genennen tar. / ir leben ist verfluochet gar. / sprechet ob daz sî missetât, / daz man mit manne daz begât, / dâ got ouch zuo geschuof diu wîp?" (614, 20-31).

[11]Above all, the laws against sodomites in the Italian city states have to be mentioned here (cf. also Boswell 293; Hergemöller 1994, 367).

[12]"Ich chlage uber die vercherten, / die verfluochten, die geunerten, / die verworhten und die verlornen, / die verteilten und die verchornen, / die in den waren schulden stent, / daz si daz mit mannen begent, / da got diu wip zuo geschuof" (Der Stricker, in Moelleken vol. 5, v. 417-23).

[13]"doch sag ich ditz lant wol frî, / daz dar inn iht Sodomiten sî." Seifried Helbling, in Seemüller II, 10, 21-22.

[14]The suppression of sexuality by the church, the way it is outlined by Schwaibold (127), following J.-L. Flandrin's Un temps pour embrasser, seems nevertheless to have been perceived as being too schematic. This view of making sexuality dependent on penance does not sufficiently take into consideration the functions of desymbolization and secularization.

[15]One has to consider, however, that at the beginning of the thirteenth century this rigid attitude was not only applied to homosexuality in particular, but to sexually devious activity in general. The laws against sexual offences have to be seen in the context of the influence communities had over the whole domestic life. Compare also Ariès/ Duby 289-91.

[16]*Die Chroniken der deutschen Städte vom 14. bis in's 16. Jahrhundert,* 4th vol., *Die Chroniken der schwäbischen Städte,* 1st book, Augsburg (Leipzig 1865) 111.

[17]"si hetten keczerey triben mit ainander. die lebeten ungeessen biß an den freitag, do waren sy all tod."

[18]"der was ir auch ainer gewesen."

[19]Compare the introduction of volume 5, 2 of the town chronicles (*Die Chroniken der deutschen Städte,* Leipzig 1866, page XVIII). For the chronicles of Erhard Wahraus and Burkard Zink, see also Hergemöller, "Homosexuelle" 86.

[20]"die fieng man umb ketzerei, die mit ainander getrieben hetten."

[21]"aber die von Augspurg wolten sich daran nit keren und sprachen, er hett in gewalt geben, also wolten si auch mit in tuen, als sie dann erkent hetten. also schmidet man sie in das vogelhaus, darin muesten sie sterben; und iren gesellen, den lederer, ließ man verprennen im 1409 jar" (*Die Chronik des Burkhard Zink,* in *Die Chroniken der deutschen Städte* 5, 2: 67).

[22]*Die Chroniken der deutschen Städte* 4, 1: 230.

[23]*Die Chroniken der deutschen Städte* 4, 1: 317-18.

Queer Desires and the Middle High German *Comic Tale:* Dietrich von der Glezze's *Der Borte*

Martin Blum

TRANSGRESSIVE SEXUAL DESIRES AND THEIR regulation are central to Dietrich von der Glezze's *Der Borte* (*The Belt*, 1270-90).[1] The paradox that these wishes and desires take a pivotal position within the text and the simultaneous attempt by the author to efface them offers an almost unique chance to explore the negotiations of late medieval conceptions of sexual behavior. It is certainly no coincidence that Dietrich chose to follow the tradition of the humorous comic tale *(Märe)*, since it is one of the most candid of medieval genres[2] in its treatment of sexuality.[3] One of its predominant characteristics is the direct translation of sexual desire into sexual activity (Muscatine 124-25; Nykrog 180). Although *The Belt* seemingly follows the pattern of the topsy-turvy world of the *fabliau*-like, humorous *Märe*, it is unusual in that it thematizes 'deviant' sexual activities; the text establishes a taxonomy of legitimate sexuality, that is, heterosexuality, which is placed into direct opposition to sodomy, its disavowed counterpart. In more than one sense, Dietrich's *Märe* deserves a special place among the number of extant medieval narratives: the text acknowledges the existence of queer desires as an alternative to heterosexuality, and one might argue that through this recognition the narrative has already been 'queered' by its own author. Drawing on feminist and queer theory, I intend to subvert the text's normative authority further, and to give voice to its sociohistorical context which provides the framework of my reading; then by arguing that social developments, which occurred on the Continent between the twelfth and thirteenth century, form the subtext to two emerging and closely related literary traditions, namely that of courtly love and the fabliau-like *Märe*. Since Dietrich's text is little known, I shall begin with a summary of the story.

Dietrich tells the story of a knight's wife, who is approached by another knight while her own husband is away, fighting a tournament. At the sight of the woman, the strange knight falls in love with her, confesses his *minne* — the Middle High German term for courtly love — meets with her refusal, and in order to gain the woman's sexual favors, he offers her his valuable falcon as a gift. When the woman refuses his offer, he also adds his two hounds, his horse, as well as a studded belt, the infamous *borte*, all objects endowed with magical powers (279-315). The woman finally agrees to have sex with the stranger and later ridicules him for parting so easily with his precious possessions (365-68). A squire, however, witnesses the woman's adultery and tells Kuonrât von Schwaben, her husband, what has happened. He in turn, deeply shamed by his wife's unfaithfulness, decides to leave, and travels to foreign countries to seek adventures (392-400). After two years the woman decides to find Kuonrât; she buys a horse and armor and cross-dresses as a knight (487-96). After having adopted the name Heinrich von Schwaben (541, 545), the previously unnamed woman now passes as a man. Soon after, s/he meets Kuonrât, who is taken in by the disguise, and they become close friends. At one point Kuonrât expresses his interest in Heinrich's hounds, his falcon, and his horse. Initially Heinrich refuses to give them to him, but then, conceding that he loves only men (739-40), is willing to give Kuonrât the falcon — if Kuonrât did what he wanted and if this were to happen in absolute secrecy (744). After a brief expression of dismay, Kuonrât seems quite willing to grant Heinrich his wish (760-61). Immediately before the sexual act takes place, however, Heinrich reveals his identity as his lover's own wife, exposes Kuonrât's queer desire to ridicule, and in addition accuses him of heresy (775-77). In the following speech the wife contrasts the venial nature of her own adulterous act with the serious nature of her husband's declaration of his queer wishes (791-803), and all that Kuonrât can do is ask for forgiveness for his offense. The narrative ends with a lament about the degeneration of the morals and an admonition to take the precepts of courtly love more seriously (835-88).

I.

One of the main characteristics of the humorous *Mären* is the variety of the characters and their ability to plot and scheme in order to satisfy sexual desire. Also characteristic is the development of more or less successful counterstrategies; together these contribute to the humorous nature of the genre.[4] The controlling and normative effect of medieval comic narratives is situated precisely at this critical juncture of humor and sexuality: by marking certain sexual activities as unorthodox and undesirable, and by making them the object of humor, these texts pursue a didactic aim "to preserve and enforce a status quo" (Lacy 37). In contrast to the notion of the liberating or subversive nature of laughter,[5] humor or laughter function as key strategies to pass judgment on a violation of norms or normative behavior.[6] In the *Märe*, humor and laughter, one might argue, become instruments of oppression.

The discursive practice of the telling of disparaging jokes is thus part of a tactic which affirms cultural norms and values at the cost of those who are not represented by or stand in opposition to these norms.[7] By virtue of the joke's dialectic structure, operating on a principle of inclusion and exclusion,[8] the joke deprives those whom it disparages of their own voice, reducing them to the status of passive objects of the discourse. This denial of one's own discursive space represents a form of violence which becomes manifest as a penalty for the insistence on sustaining a visible otherness. The medieval comic tale is part of this long tradition of narratives that resorts to the silencing of deviant sexual positions in order to reinscribe the myth of heterosexuality as the sole building block of cultures, past and present (cf. Wittig, "Straight Mind" 24-25). It can be historicized as a medieval example of precisely such a normative discourse on sexuality, and it can be read specifically from an ideological vantage point.[9] The following – in parts – structuralist reading emphasizes that a text functions as a trajectory of ideology.[10] Given the fact that, as Hans Robert Jauss claims, the social function of a medieval text is determined by its "*locus* in life" (102-103), one might argue that notions of amorality and subversion, often associated with the genre of the comic tale, do not hold true if one examines how the genre constructs its negotiations of sexuality.

In the *Märe*'s discourse on sexuality, violations of conventional morality are, in fact, limited to some very clearly defined scenarios. They are often determined by the antagonists' difference in age or social rank and, if anything, emphasize the normative impulse of the genre. These and similar violations of norms all take place in a highly controlled environment and reinscribe rather than question the genre's conservative values: social mobility[11] and control over sexuality are the two most predominant themes which illustrate the position of the comic tale as a literary commentary on social phenomena (Hines 33; Lacy 37; Muscatine 151). These kinds of narratives reflect some of the social underpinnings of medieval feudal society with is its strong reliance on homosocial bonds. The consequence of this reliance is the establishment of a system of allegiances between males who inhabit positions of power. One essential means to consolidate these relationships between various families and to guarantee a horizontal succession of power and property from one generation to the next, that is, from one man to another, is the passing on of women between the men of power (cf. Lévi-Strauss 52–68). Thus a central part in the creation of these homosocial bonds, which are so essential to the patriarchal system, is marriage. The significance of this exchange of women for medieval European societies, in particular from the twelfth century on, is underscored by the number of politically motivated marriages to consolidate allegiances between various houses and families of power. Gayle Rubin in her critique of Lévi-Strauss draws attention to the fact that these exchanges do not merely shape and maintain political structures, but that at the same time they become sites of oppression, with men as givers and receivers of women, and women as mere objects of exchange in this relationship.

Social historians, in particular Georges Duby, have argued that the twelfth century with its strong emphasis on primogeniture caused a number of social changes which affected the history of marriage and ultimately led to a novel code of behavior between men and women: since only the eldest son of a family could expect to play a role on the marriage market, a large number of younger sons were essentially turned loose as landless knights, roaming the country. The parallel rise of the phenomenon of courtly love spells out an acute awareness of an aggressive sexuality among the increasing number of young, unmarried male members of the nobility, who were denied the establishment of their own households through marriage and, thus, the succession of their elders. The resulting aggressions were then reigned by means of formalizing relationships between the genders to compensate for the frustrations of those unmarried young men whose lack of access to wives and status did not match their chivalric achievements (Duby, *Medieval Marriage* 11–20). Consequently, rituals, such as courtly love evolved.[12] They became "a test in the course of a continuing education" (Duby, *Love and Marriage* 57) for all youths who wanted to succeed their elders.

It is precisely at this critical juncture — the era when youths were challenging the privileges of their seigneurs, and the elders attempted to preserve them — that I want to situate the medieval comic tale: here the *Märe* becomes a literary expression of the attempt to defuse the potentially harmful confrontation between the generations in order to stabilize the feudal system. While courtly love propagates the impossibility to attain of the seigneur's wife, the sexual politics of the *Märe*, dealing in a way with the 'flip-side' of courtly love,[13] offers possibilities for the release of the frustrations caused by the pent-up sexual desires[14] of these young men, for the *Märe* advocates the relatively uninhibited use of girls or women of the lower classes.[15] Duby enumerates some inhabitants of the shadow world of courtly society, the peasant women, servant girls, maidens, widows, and the whores (*Medieval Marriage* 13). The inventory of this assembly shows an uncanny resemblance with many of the characters one encounters in medieval comic tales. If we read these narratives as a set of proscriptive rules for the sexual behavior of young noblemen,[16] the seemingly permitted transgressions of conventional morality make sense indeed: all violations of moral injunctions turn out to be sanctioned in order to preserve the bonds between youths and their elders, permitted to safeguard the continuation of their allegiances, the backbone of feudal society.

It may be seen as politically shrewd to permit, and even encourage, young men to have sexual relationships with lower-class females, who are of no real interest in the economy of the marriage market. The advantage of granting them some degree of sexual license lies elsewhere, namely in the fact that it ensures their elders' largely unchallenged positions as guardians of the feudal, patriarchal order. However, allowing liberties and making exceptions can be tricky: the upkeep of the status quo demands that these violations be as closely controlled as the rules of feudal relationships themselves if the danger of a general rebellion of the young is to be avoided. The main objective of this control is, after all, to ensure that the homosocial bonds, the glue to the patriarchal, feudal system remain intact.

A corollary of patriarchy's dependence on the exchange of women — apart from the prohibition of incest — is its reliance on a strictly enforced heterosexuality.[17] Within a heterosexual matrix,[18] homosocial bonds as sites of power and agents of exchange are dependent on clear demarcations between a lawful, that is, a heterosexual valence of desire, and its unlawful counterparts. These social constraints also find their expression in discourses, where, as Judith Butler argues: "the repressive law effectively produces heterosexuality, and acts not merely as a negative or exclusionary code, but as a sanction and, most pertinently, as a law of discourse, distinguishing the speakable from the unspeakable ... the legitimate from the illegitimate" (*Gender Trouble* 65).

This observation lends itself well for the analysis of the medieval feudal system and the texts it produced. In regards to the sexual politics of the

Märe, it explains why and how heterosexuality can be sanctioned even out-side the bounds of conjugal relationships, while at the same time transgres-sive sexualities[19] must be disavowed: for as long as the sexual behavior of young noblemen does not pose a threat to the system of feudal male bonds, which could potentially jeopardize this carefully guarded rupture between homo*social*ity and homo*sexual*ity. Thus, the medieval *Märe* func-tions as a societal regulative by passing judgments on specific sexual activi-ties. The sexual politics of the *Märe* reinscribes heterosexuality by represent-ing what I term *queer acts* in order to immediately foreclose them as possi-ble expressions of sexual desire. Judith Butler argues that it is precisely these foreclosed possibilities of alternate expressions of sexual desire which con-stitute one of the means to enforce normative sexual positions:

> For if we accept the notion that the prohibition on homosexuality
> operates throughout a largely heterosexual culture as one of its de-
> fining operations, then it appears that the loss of homosexual ob-
> jects and aims (not simply this person of the same gender, but *any*
> person of that same gender) will be foreclosed from the start. I use
> the word "foreclosed" to suggest that this is a preemptive loss, a
> mourning for unlived possibilities. (*Melancholy Gender* 27)

The specific discursive strategies used to erase queer acts and desires from the text come in the form of their depiction as the result of misunderstand-ings, deception, ignorance, or simply of misdirected sexual desire.[20] In the medieval comic tale, however, these strategies are not merely self-serving, they also utilize the suggested transgressive acts as a source of laughter which, in turn, justifies their (often violent) chastisement and, finally, ex-poses them as agents to humiliation and ridicule.

II.

Dietrich's *The Belt* has received scant critical attention since it was first edited in 1850 by Friedrich von der Hagen in his *Gesammtabenteuer,* a collection of Old German tales. A number of subsequent studies, if treat-ing the narrative's content at all, attempted to 'sanitize' the text in order to include it into the canon of Middle High German literature. Most at-tempted to avoid any reference to the queer act which forms one of the crucial scenes of the text. Ehrismann deliberately obscures and misrepresents the plot to erase all traces of homoeroticism. Van Stockum and van Dam reduce the *Märe* to a conventional story about marital unfaithfulness and merely mention a married couple, who prove each other's unfaithfulness (169). De Boor also skirts around the issue of male homosexuality, though he mentions the "unnatural desires" (277), which he, however, attributes to the woman. Only the more recent Hotchkiss (100–104), Hoven (69–71), and Rosenfeld (138) give brief and accurate accounts of the scene, although Hoven does add the somewhat puzzling conclusion that the knight's wife does not seem to be very familiar with the phenomenon of pederasty (72). Unable to falsify the actual content of the *Märe*, most critics thus seem to have depended on either misrepresentation of the original in their own critical work, or the tactic of exclusion operated by the academic phenomenon of canonicity to deny instances of homosexuality or its predecessors. In a way curiously similar to their medieval precursors, they resorted to more or less elaborate constructions in order to erase any possible allusion to queerness.[21]

Rather typically for the genre, Dietrich's *Märe* is concerned with sex. It is, however, special in that it establishes something of a taxonomy of sexual acts. While heterosexual adultery is considered excusable, sodomy of any kind is depicted as a grave offense. On the surface Dietrich is primarily concerned with the wife's adultery: her cross-dressing and her attempt as a transvestite to seduce Kuonrât are all discursive strategies used to restore the woman's honor. The representation of an alternate desire is subsumed under a heteronormative ideology, commonly found in the genre: in its function to justify the breach of the sixth commandment by comparing it with the more serious offense of an (attempted) act of sodomy, the text's strategy is to shift blame from one offender to the other. In light of its function as a commentary on social phenomena, the text's way of reproducing power rests on its narrator, on his passing judgment on – and disavowing of – a contestable desire by exposing the 'guilty party' to ridicule and shame.

The most obvious means of the text's propagation of normativity is to set up the woman as the natural and obvious object-choice of any red-blooded knight. Instead of presenting the typically nondescript female character, as is often the case in the humorous *Märe*, Dietrich provides an elaborate description of a courtly lady who might very well be equally at home in a *Minnelied*, or courtly romance. Right from the beginning, perhaps rather ironically, the woman, whose adultery in fact initiates the conflict, is depicted as a model of nobility and moral rectitude: "He had married a woman, who with all her virtues came from a noble family, and those who knew her well had never seen a more beautiful woman."[22] Following the tradition of the *descriptio pulchritudinis*, or description of beauty, Dietrich then goes on for some thirty-five lines (35-70) to supply a veritable catalogue of the *vrouwe*'s physical qualities, which traditionally are outer signifiers of her inner, moral perfection.[23] The purpose of the exercise is not so much a self-serving celebration of beauty and virtue, but rather, as Dietrich's comment shows, to present the female as the superior and natural object of any knight's desire: "whichever knight had such a wife, he would be a blessed man indeed,"[24] a sentiment confirmed by the following scene which shows the knight and his wife in an intimate embrace.

In addition to the signifying description of the woman's physical beauty, Dietrich also invokes symbolic descriptions of nature where he makes reference to heterosexuality: the month of May is named explicitly when Kuonrât and his wife are in bed (93-101). The implied message, of course, is to emphasize the potential fertility of the sexual union. Nature symbolizes Dietrich's approval of the heterosexual union in the description of the adulterous act. The blooming flowers and the singing of the birds lend the scene a celebratory tone, making the reader almost forget that a sin and a crime are being committed. Heterosexuality is associated with fertility and order, here epitomized by natural harmony: "The trees began to creak, and the roses to laugh, and the birds started to sing about it when the woman sank down and the knight bent down after her. Love's salute made the knight forget all his sorrows. Many roses sprouted out from the grass when body embraced body. When the play was over, both roses and grass were laughing."[25] Dietrich's use of the trope of nature confirms the sexual act as being in accord with the laws of nature.[26] This literary device, probably a response to the emergence of courtly love, was widely used from the eleventh century on and is commonly found in texts as a commentary on questions of morality. As John Boswell shows, the medieval assumption that order and morality are reflected by a harmonious 'nature' is not of Christian origin, but is derived from pagan sources. Boswell documents how a harmonious concept of nature filled a void caused by the ever increasing demand for instructions on moral issues. As the meaning of this nature trope is not fixed, it becomes a convenient means for each author to pursue his own particular agenda (311).

It is precisely this strategy that allows Dietrich to juxtapose the heterosexual acts with the attempt of sodomy, and his later condemnation of it.
Notably absent this time is any authorial comment on Kuonrât's humiliation and his loss of honor. Though Kuonrât is dismayed when he learns
about his wife's unfaithfulness, the act loses something of its immediacy
against the background of its universal approval. Subsequently, Kuonrât laments the loss of his wife's chastity only rather briefly: "her chastity has left
her, she has deceived me," concluding his complaint with the somewhat
laconic statement, "I have lost my honor."[27] To add insult to injury, as the
cuckold, the deceived husband has to bear the ridicule as the consequence
of his wife's trespass. The underlying notion is to shift blame on Kuonrât
in order to set him up to become the negative example he is to exemplify
later on: his resignation to the *fait accompli* mirrors the crippling potential
of shame and the insidious way in which it is directed against him. His
'guilt' consists of simply being a cuckolded husband: "since she has put
me to shame, I will now leave the country."[28] After Kuonrât has taken his
leave, the woman concedes that her husband has good reason to deny her
his affection, but she immediately retracts, at least partially, and claims that,
in due course of time, he would come to his senses again (405-10).

To help him on his way, the woman thinks up the strategy of cross-
dressing in order to prove to her husband that her own trespass is of a
rather venial nature compared to the graveness of his own offense, his willingness and desire to have sex with another man. After Kuonrât's admission of his queer desire, his wife, still speaking as the cross-dressed Heinrich, seizes the opportunity to pronounce her moral judgment on the offender: "by God, you have revealed yourself as a shameful figure since you
want to be a heretic ... you unchaste person!"[29] The fact that she equates
sodomy with shame and heresy is pivotal. It represents an historically accurate classification of the crime and places the offender on one of the lowest
rungs of the ladder among the late medieval society of outcasts: the various
heretical sects (Boswell 283; Moore 93).

The legal consequences for a detected and convicted sodomite are directly comparable to those facing the heretic. In both instances the inquisition under the auspices of the mendicant orders provided the legal
machinery to deal with the offender and thus rather predictably produced
similar judgments — often recommending that the offender be burned at
the stake (Hergemöller, "Sodomiter. Schuldzuweisungen" 329; Richards
145-48). In Dietrich's *Märe* this form of punishment is not only men-

tioned, but clearly exerts pressure on Kuonrât to bring him back in line and to ensure his future conformity. The woman gives the offender a lecture on the vastly different nature of the sins committed by both of them: "You have brought shame upon yourself; what I did was human, whereas you very much wanted to act against Christian morality: you have become an unclean man."[30] While she perceives adultery as a human failing, she sees the man's queer desires not only as deeply shameful and defiling,[31] but also as being in opposition to Christianity. The implied difference to the woman's adultery is that while she can be pardoned, her husband has forfeited all hope of redemption. The more immediate consequence is that the husband is excluded from the mainstream of medieval society. As indicated by the signifier "unclean," indiscriminately attached to a number of marginal social groups (Moore 100-101), the husband is associated with lepers, prostitutes, and heretics. The fact that the husband admits his offense at the conclusion of the *Märe* reflects his precarious position as a convicted heretic, who is completely at the mercy of his wife. His declaration of his moral bankruptcy has to be understood in light of the very real possibility that his wife can, in fact, denounce him and hand him over to the authorities of the church and the state.

In the end, the narrator exposes the offender to ridicule; his authority to ensure that the sodomite steps back in line is based on a thinly veiled threat of blackmail or on what Moore terms "the language of fear" (100). The husband's final words may be as much a token of his own terror as the author's admission of his anxiety about the power of transgressive sexualities, a power that cannot be conceded and that the text attempts to deny by relating the fiction of Kuonrât's contrition: "forgive me my lechery, my dear lady of clean birth!"[32] Ultimately, these words, admitting Kuonrât's shame, reflect the ideological tethering of the *Märe*: nonnormative sexual desires are preempted by the text's own forestalling of their mere possibility. A man's readiness to have sex with another man is not a discursive possibility, and has never been one, since the text's ideological stance cannot admit the possibility of same-sex relations. In the concluding statement of the *Märe*, Dietrich addresses his courtly audience directly and makes it clear that heterosexuality is the only possible expression of sexuality. To substantiate his claim, Dietrich moralizes and then resorts to the well-proven method of invoking fear: "You men, I want to teach you that you have to honor women, and to serve them; since their red mouths and white cheeks can save you from serious trouble."[33]

III.

Despite this seemingly homophobic ending the text provides two important clues which allow us to read Dietrich's *Märe* against its own agenda: the clear enunciation of the friends' desire for each other, and the woman's cross-dressing. The first betrays the text's dependence on its queer desires, while the second reveals the inherent instability of accepted male and female positions.[34]

The episode of the woman's cross-dressing is initiated as a search. On the foreground, echoing the tradition of the cross-dressed female minstrel, her search seems to be for her absent husband; in reality, however, the search only serves her own interests, as is revealed shortly afterwards when the woman sets off on her quest — together with her servants, the sum of five hundred marks, and all the presents she has received from the foreign knight. She takes shelter with a nobleman in another town, dismisses her entourage, and confronts her host with an unusual revelation: "I am a knight and not a woman, and although I appear to be weak, I am nevertheless of great strength whenever I want to make use of it. I had numerous strong enemies, who did me great harm, and who are the reason why I wore this dress while traveling through foreign countries."[35] In her own words, the woman is in reality a man, dressed up as a woman in order to escape his/her enemies. To (re)construct herself as a man, the woman demands that her host supply her with a number of props that signify the knight, that is, one of the most masculine identities the Middle Ages had to offer. She asks the host to supply her with squires, horses, and a knight's armor: "Get me a knight's outfit, an armor bright and shiny."[36] The transformation of the woman into a man, as the narrator assures, is an easy and remarkably successful one to boot: putting on the knight's armor and cutting off her hair is all that is needed to dress up a passing transvestite: "When the noble lady was ready, she cut off her hair, and together with her squires she took leave from her host in male clothing: how well it suited her!"[37]

The text's attempts to naturalize the woman's cross-dressing by invoking the story of the knight in distress and by the narrator's final comment on the suitability of the disguise must appear more than queer, particularly in light of the fact that by now the text has clearly established the normativity of heterosexuality. Transvestism here provides the key to the construction of transgressive sexual desires in the *Märe*: on the one hand the text's repeated mention of how well the woman looks in her male outfit affirms the cross-dresser's passing; on the other hand it signifies a sign of lack, the deliberate attempt to negate the act of passing. This ambiguity undercuts the text's own attempt to uphold normative categories. By passing as a man the woman successfully obliterates all traces of "a difference, which is not quite visible, not quite unknown, not-quite non-existent" (Tyler, *Passing* 212), and thus creates something of a troubled category: Heinrich is thus 'not-quite' a man, but also 'not-quite-not' a woman (cf. Tyler, *Passing* 212-13). This lack of a signifying ability points to the embattled position the cross-dresser inhabits, a fantastic space where the absence of an 'original' identity is located. In other words, the lack points to the fact that the idea of this original identification is nothing but a myth (Butler, *Gender Trouble* 138).[38]

The parody on the woman's original identity is underscored by the fact that the previously unnamed woman takes on a named identity only in the persona of a man, and, remarkably, at the very moment she meets the desired knight: "then the woman said: Sir, my name is Heinrich."[39] The naming of Heinrich is the clearest indication that the character's quest is primarily the search for a self, one that is more complete as a cross-dressed man than it is as a wife. That clothes do indeed 'make the man' becomes clear from the fact that Dietrich — albeit unwittingly — dresses up an extraordinarily handsome man who also equals and even excels the best of knights. Heinrich, then, is vastly superior to any other knight, including Kuonrât, as it turns out when both fight in a tournament against a fierce warrior from Britain: it is Heinrich who conquers him despite Kuonrât's previous warning not to challenge the Briton who, in comparison to Kuonrât, is much stronger: "he is strong and you are not; compared to him you are a mere dwarf."[40] The conquering of the Briton, a deed previously deemed impossible, makes Heinrich the best combatant at court; one should note the irony here that it takes a transvestite to demonstrate to the other knights what a 'real man' is. Heinrich's powers, though no doubt derived from the magically endowed objects, such as the belt, can indirectly be attributed to his drag, since only by wearing it he can enjoy its benefit. Heinrich's act of impersonating the supermasculine hero among the assembly of knights effectively deconstructs the very notion of masculinity as a stable signifier by revealing its reliance on fictions of supremacy, thus effectively subverting any claim to a stable masculine identity.[41] The subversive potential of parody and pastiche brings about the opposite of its desired effect, which is the exclusion of "marginal genders from the territory of the natural and the real." As Butler argues, "there is a subversive laughter in the pastiche-effect of parodic practices in which the original, the authentic, and the real are themselves constituted as effects" (*Gender Trouble* 146). Such a confusion of 'real' and impersonated men affects the whole personnel in the *Märe*. Dietrich tries to counteract this destabilization of signifiers[42] by referring to Heinrich as "vrowe" (lady) and looking "*through* rather than *at* the cross-dresser" (Garber, *Vested Interests* 9). However, the author soon abandons this strategy and does indeed start to look *at* the transvestite, as all the other characters in the *Märe* do.[43]

Apart from Heinrich's cross-dressing, the exchange of presents is another opportunity where the text betrays wishes that are decidedly queer. During a hunt Heinrich has the opportunity to show off the presents he has received from the foreign knight, and which promptly catch another knight's eye, who then asks him whether he intended to sell them for a substantial sum of money. Heinrich, however, declines the knight's offer and puts the matter to rest. This, however, is not the last time that Heinrich is asked about these possessions, as some time later his friend Kuonrât also asks for them, this time offering his love and his gratitude instead of any financial compensation: "thus love's stream would have flown to me, grant my wish, and I will show you my gratitude."[44] Heinrich refuses at first, but Kuonrât is not that easily deterred. He repeats his offer, only to emphasize his commitment to his friend: "... my dear companion, now give me your whole faith, I want to be your one and only, and (in) my heart's shrine I shall carry you with all my love."[45]

Perhaps, as in the first encounter with the cross-dresser, one should look *at* Kuonrât's response, rather than *through* it. His repeated plea shows a degree of affection that foreshadows the possibility of a future intimacy with the other man — yet another indication of the text's underlying queer wishes. Having heard this second offer, Heinrich decides to grant Kuonrât's wish, thereby declaring his *own* desire to have sex with the other man: "I love men; I have never had a woman in my entire life. If you do what I want, I shall give you the hounds and the falcon; all this has to happen in silence."[46] Heinrich's declaration is immediately followed by a word of caution that their sexual union has to take place in absolute secrecy — a warning which, in its stark realism, not only reflects the extreme risk both men take and the serious repercussions they would face if they were found out,[47] but which also pays tribute to the seriousness and the genuine nature of Heinrich's declaration. The call for secrecy, in turn, signals to Kuonrât in no uncertain terms that Heinrich has, in fact, those physical pleasures in mind that society deems indecent. Although Kuonrât expresses some dismay about Heinrich's wishes, his very words, nevertheless, simultaneously betray the pleasure he feels in sight of his friend's physical perfection: "I will always lament that your proud body loves men and not women."[48] Despite these seemingly strong words one has to wonder whether Kuonrât's objection is not of a merely perfunctory nature; his consent to have sex with his friend comes remarkably soon, and, together with his greed as his sole and only motivation, can be seen as part of the text's attempt to police transgressive desires. This passage offers a possibility to counter the text's own "heterosexual presumption" and its attempt to equate contestatory sexual practices with shame and punishment precisely by eroticizing these very practices, and thus making possible a "pleasurable insurrection" (Butler, *Bodies That Matter* 110). These pleasures are declared almost immediately afterwards when Heinrich tells his friend that he wishes to have sex with him: "You have to lie down with me, and I will love you in any possible way I can think of, and I want to do (with you) what every husband does with his wife when they are together in bed at night."[49]

The parallel placement of this love scene in relation to its heterosexual equivalent can be read as the text's own admission that queer wishes are a recognized, if dangerous, expression of affection; a mentionable and, equally important, viable alternative to the heterosexual paradigm. In short, queer desire and queer sex are possibilities which the narrator seemingly tries to deny. Furthermore, the narrator's reliance on a vocabulary appropriated from the domain of normative (hetero)sexual activity exposes, in a way not unlike the invocation of the cross-dresser, the arbitrariness of positions of orthodox and transgressive sexualities. Stripped of its ideological baggage, we have to acknowledge the text's discursive possibility of both sexual acts. In addition, the narrator's own peculiar linguistic practices reveal its supposedly firm footing on a self-declared normative position as yet another parody. While Dietrich postulates the primacy of his own heteronormative ideology as the 'original' by contrasting this with his representation of transgressive sexualities, he nevertheless achieves precisely the opposite by exposing the very assumption of 'the original' and 'the normal' as the sham it is.

To sustain the fiction of its normative sexual position, the text is ultimately dependent on its own queer wishes, a fact, which its narrator tries so hard to denounce. This reliance on a conceivable form of otherness seems

to preempt a process which Butler sees as instrumental in modern constructions of heterosexuality: "for heterosexuality to remain intact as a
distinct social form, it *requires* an intelligible conception of homosexuality and also requires the prohibition of that conception in rendering it
culturally unintelligible" (Butler, *Gender Trouble* 77). While the narrator
propagates the exclusive supremacy of heterosexual relations over other
forms of sexual desire by subjecting queerness to abjection and ridicule,
his reliance on a fictitious position of normality reveals the fallacy of the
whole enterprise of Dietrich's *The Belt*: the text's dependence on the selfsame desires its narrator attempts to police and prohibit can be read as
having precisely the opposite effect, namely that of generating the very
queerness he seeks to suppress.

Notes

[1] On Dietrich von der Glezze (Glesse) see Hans-Friedrich Rosenfeld (137-39). For
matters of convenience all citations of the text are based on Spreitzer's *Die stumme
Sünde*. Translations are my own.

[2] The authoritative study on the various types of the genre is still that of Hanns
Fischer. For a more recent discussion of the term see Joachim Heinzle. See also the
article by Mark Chinca who defines the *Märe* as "fabliau-like narratives in verse ...
which formed part of a European tradition, and were cultivated in Germany from
the early thirteenth century to the beginning of the sixteenth" (187).

[3] In this essay, I intend to make use of the term "sexuality" to denote the valence of
sexual desire, and not to define an essential sexual identity. Although David Halperin
argues that the use of modern terms, such as "heterosexuality," is anachronistic when
talking about premodern societies (15-40), I am following here the examples set by
other medievalists, such as Carolyn Dinshaw, who adopts a "middle ground" (206)
between essentialist and social constructivist notions of sexuality, and, to some extent,
Simon Gaunt, who sees in particular medieval attempts to regulate the correct
"'courtly' object choice" as indicative of the fact that "some men are represented as
having an irrevocable and immanent sexual orientation towards other men that tran-
scends their acts" (441). See also Jonathan Goldberg's "Introduction" to *Queering
the Renaissance* where he addresses the political aspect of "the failure to raise questions of sexuality in these texts [which] has often meant nothing less than the tacit
assumption that the only sexuality that ever obtains is a transhistorical heterosexuality" (6). For a useful and lucid introduction into the history of classifying sexual
categories see Jonathan Ned Katz's chapter "Before Heterosexuality" (33-55).

[4]See for instance Bédier's long-lived minimalist definition of fabliaux as "contes à rire en vers" (30), funny narratives in verse.

[5]On this, see for instance Mary Douglas's discussion of "Jokes" in her study *Implicit Meanings*.

[6]Bergson, for instance, sees one of the reasons of laughter in the countering of eccentricity, which he defines as "an activity with separatist tendencies, that inclines to swerve from the common centre round which society gravitates ..." (19); laughter then becomes a "social gesture," which draws its strength from "the fear which it inspires," and thus "restrains eccentricity" (20).

[7]Bloch (120) and Brewer (130) both argue for a double function of the comic tale which not only subverts the social hierarchy, but affirms it as well. Suchomski (162) emphasizes the "didactic" quality of the joke by drawing attention to nonconformity.

[8]In his structural analysis of the disparaging joke Martineau identifies the dichotomy between an "ingroup," telling the joke, and an "outgroup" against which the joke is directed; a basic structure entails a double function of discriminatory jokes: "when humor is judged as disparaging an outgroup, it may function as follows: 1. To increase morale and solidify the ingroup. 2. To introduce or foster a hostile disposition toward that outgroup" (118-19).

[9]For an apolitical reading of the genre, see for instance Beyer, who claims that fabliaux neither represent a certain world picture (*Weltbild*), nor an ideology (*Weltanschauung*), but rather an inner-worldy view of a fragmented universe, an infinite row of empirical encounters (118).

[10]Here, I am following Todorov, who perceives shared discursive strategies and their codification as the common denominators of generic categories, as well as in particular Jauss, who stresses the connection between the community which produced a particular text and the norms and values shared by this community (100).

[11]A similar situation is presented in Garin's old French fabliau *De Berangier au lon cul (The Long-assed Beranger)*. A wife, the daughter of a "chastelain," devises a means to punish her churlish husband, himself only the "filz d'un vilain," the son of a peasant, for his failure to live up to the social convention of knighthood, a status he acquired through marriage. The implicit competition between two societal regulatives shows that violations of social rank justify transgressions of gender boundaries. In contrast, it is highly questionable whether in a courtly environment where both partners are of equal rank the wife would have been able to transgress the limitations imposed on her gender, openly rebel against her husband, and be justified for doing so.

[12]Duby interprets the ritual of fighting for the favors of the courtly lady as expressing both hostility toward the institution of marriage and the great importance that was attached to it: "The favours of the lady thus became the stake in the competition among the bachelors of the court, a game that was similar in every point to the tournament, for it was aimed at attaining a mock capture that derived much of its

excitement from flouting the strict prohibition of adultery and was tantamount to a kind of revenge against the common seigneur" (1978, 13-14).

[13]On the close relationship between the fabliaux and courtly genres see for instance Busby (67-87), Cooke (142-46), and Nykrog (72-104).

[14]While Duby acknowledges the importance of the competition for wives and status as the main reason for feelings of jealousy and frustration among the wifeless young men (1994, 59), I disagree with his claim that sexual frustration does not play a significant role in this context. I would rather argue that "finding an outlet for that" is precisely what is regulated by the fabliaux.

[15]In his treatise on love, Andreas Capellanus suggests rape—among other things—if a nobleman wants to have sex with a peasant girl. See for instance Parry's relatively close translation of this passage in *De amore at amoris remedio*: "And if you should, by some chance, fall in love with anyone of the [peasants'] women, be careful to puff them up with lots of praise and then, when you find a convenient place do not hesitate to take what you seek and to embrace them by force" (150). The Latin *violentu potiri amplexu* denotes not merely a rough embrace, but is a direct reference to rape.

[16]On the nobility as the primary audience of fabliaux, see for instance Nykrog (72-104), and Chinca specifically on the audience of the German *Märe*: "Yet in spite of their contents and their popularity the *Mären* were never literature of the people. They remained a literary form whose public was originally to be found among the nobility and higher clergy, though from the later fourteenth century the audience became increasingly urban" (187).

[17]For historical examples, see Boswell's discussion of the condemnation of Edward II of England's relationships with Piers Gaveston and Hugh le Despenser (298-300), as well as Richards who identifies the young nobility as prime targets of "accusations of sexual misconduct" (137).

[18]I am following Judith Butler here, who devised the concept of the "heterosexual matrix ... to designate that grid of cultural intelligibility through which bodies, genders, and desires are naturalized" (*Gender Trouble*, 151n.).

[19]For a similar argument, see for instance Christopher Baswell's discussion of the utilization of the homophobic passages in the Old French *Roman d' Eneas* as means to ensure the proper genealogical succession of the Angevin court under Henry II (162-63).

[20]A particularly obvious example for the use of these narrative techniques can be found in Gautier Le Leu's Old French fabliau *Del sot chevalier* (*The Stupid Knight*), where a misunderstanding forms the basis for a number of allusions to sodomitical acts without ever actually mentioning them.

[21]To my knowledge this distortion of the content of the *Märe* in critical works has never been commented on. Apart from the ideological implications of canonicity, a further explanation may be that most of the critics wanted to prevent their academic

reputation from being 'sullied' by talking about an unacceptable topic for contemporary scholars and students. [Editors' note: But just perhaps their reputations might have been considered all the greater for their dismissal of homosexual themes.]

[22]"Er hete ein wîp zer ê genomen, / diu was mit ganzen tugenden komen / Von edelem geslechte; / der si bekande rehte, / Der gesach nie schœner wîp" (31-35).

[23]On the significance of the *descriptio pulchritudinis* for the courtly genres see for instance Tervooren (171-98).

[24]"Swelch ritter het ein solich wîp, / der wære ein sæliger lîp" (87-88).

[25]"Die boum' begunden krachen, / die rôsen sêre lachen, / Diu vogelîn von den sachen / begunden dœne machen, / Do diu vrouwe nider seik / und der ritter nâch neik, / Von der rehten minne gruoz / wart dem ritter sorgen buoz. / Vil rôsen ûz dem grase gienk, / dô liep mit armen liep enpfienk. / Dô daz spil ergangen was, / dô lachten bluomen unde gras" (345-56).

[26]The significance of this affirmation of the law of nature becomes apparent against the background of its opposite as for instance described in the opening lines of Alain of Lille's *Plaint of Nature* where the poet mourns the loss of order and the subsequent chaos: "I turn from laughter to tears ... when I see the essential decrees of Nature are denied a hearing, while large numbers are shipwrecked and lost because of a Venus turned monster, and when Venus wars with Venus and changes 'hes' into 'shes' and with her witchcraft unmans man" (67).

[27]"der ist ir kiusch' entwichen, / si hât mich beswichen" (395-96); "ich hân verlorn mîn êre" (400).

[28]"Daz si mich sô hât geschant, / dar umbe wil ich daz lant / Rûmen immer mêre" (397-99).

[29]"weiz Got, / ir sît worden mir ein spot: / Welt ir nû ein kezzer sîn ... Vil untugenthafter lîp!" (775-77, 799).

[30]"ir habt iuch selben geschant; / Daz ich tet, daz was menschlîch: / sô woltet it unkristenlîch / Vil gerne haben getân; / ir sît ein unreiner man" (794-98).

[31]See for instance Mary Douglas's discussion of contamination as an expression of, and a threat to, a perceived social system of order (1966, 29-40).

[32]"Vergebet mir die unzuht, / vrouwe liebe, reine vruht!" (805-06).

[33]"Ir man, ich wil iuch lêren, / vrouwen sult ir êren / Und sult in under tænik sîn; / wand iriu rôten mündelîn / und ir wîzen wengelîn / diu bringent iuch von grôzer pîn" (869-74).

[34]I want to take issue here with Valerie Hotchkiss's discussion of the nature of the male disguise in *The Belt*, which she sees in purely functional terms, enabling the wife to move freely in the foreign country as well as to shame her husband in order to excuse her own trespass (103). This reductive view of cross-dressing disregards its potential for disrupting established orders, be it intended or not.

[35]"Ich bin ein ritter, [und] niht ein wîp: / al eine schînt mir krank der lîp, / Ich hân doch sterke harte vil, / swen ot ich sie ueben wil. / Ich hete starke vientschaft / diu

tat mir grôze über kraft, / Durch daz vuort' ich diz gewant / verre her durch vremdiu lant" (471-78).

[36]"Ritters kleider gewinnet mir / harnasch glanz unde zier" (487-88).

[37]"dô die vrouwe wol getân / Bereit wart, und ir hâr ab geschriet, / mit den knehten si dô schiet / Von dem wirte in mannes wât: / wê, wie wol ir daz stât!" (492-96).

[38]It should be noted here that Butler later qualified her assumption of the subversiveness of all forms of cross-dressing and refers to films, such as Victor, Victoria and Tootsie which employ drag to effect the exact opposite, and function primarily as mainstream entertainment, as "boundaries against the invasion of queerness" (Bodies That Matter 126).

[39]"dâ sprach diu vrouwe sâ ze hant: / 'Herre, ich heize Heinrich'" (544-45).

[40]"Er ist stark, und ir niht, / ir sît gegen im en wiht" (633-34).

[41]For a more detailed discussion of masculinity as a troubled category and its dependence on specific fictions see my examination of masculinity in Chaucer's Miller's Tale.

[42]In this aspect I disagree with Carole-Ann Tyler's notion that authorial intention is indicative of the credibility of the parodic nature of a particular act of drag: "parody is legible in the drama of gender performance if someone meant to script it, intending it to be there" (Passing 54). Dietrich quite certainly did not intend to parody the cross-dressed knight's prowess, and yet, I would argue, the scene lends itself to a parodic reading.

[43]Marjorie Garber invokes the notion of the cross-dresser as producing a "third category" (Vested Interests 11-12), outside the male/female dichotomy, a notion which I find highly problematic since it sidesteps the issue of the transvestite's revealing of the parody of all normative positions of gender and sexuality by simply supplementing the dominant system with another 'hold-all' category, and thus effectively reaffirming its self-defined delimitations.

[44]"sô wære der liebe vlôz / Gevlozzen wol her ze mir / gewere mich, ich danke dir" (716-18).

[45]"... geselle mîn, / nû tuot mir ganze triuwe schîn, / Ich wil iuwer eigen sîn, / unde mînes herzen schrîn / Sol iuch in ganzer liebe tragen" (725-29).

[46]"Ich minne gerne die man, / nie dehein wîp ich gewan; / Tuot ir daz und swaz ich wil, / winde unde veder spil / Gib' ich iu mit willen; / diz muoz geschehen stille" (739-44).

[47]Butler's claim of a modern notion of "homosexualized abjection," based on the threat and subsequent fear of punishment finds something akin to its precursor in the medieval injunctions against sodomitical practices and their punishment as crimes, as stipulated by the "law," here in its original, legal sense (Bodies That Matter 95-111).

[48]"ez muoz mîn klage immer sîn, / Daz iuwer stolzer lîp / minnet die man, und niht diu wîp" (746-48).

[49]"Dû muost dich nider zuo mir legen, / sô wil ich mit dir pflegen / Aller der minne, / der ich von mînem sinne / Gedenken und ertrahten kan, / dar zuo swes ein ieglîch man / Mit sîner vrouwen pfligt, / swenne er nahtes bî ir ligt" (755–64).

Margarete von Parma in Goethe's *Egmont*: Text and Performance

David G. John

IN HER STIMULATING COLLECTION OF ESSAYS, *Outing Goethe and His Age*, Alice A. Kuzniar includes a contribution by W. Daniel Wilson, "Amazon, Agitator, Allegory: Political and Gender Cross(-Dress)ing in Goethe's *Egmont*." This provocative treatment of the play reinterprets all of its major figures and concludes generally that the two principal females, Margarete and Klärchen, have been undervalued and misunderstood by critics, and that some of the males have received undeservedly positive interpretations. Wilson's discovery of so many fascinating instances of cross-dressing and gender-bending among the main characters provides convincing evidence for his argument that "all the cross-dressers in the play hope to partake in the power represented by the opposite pole" (144), that is, the social and political power held by the other national group or sex, especially the political power traditionally held by males. For example, Wilson sees the famous scene in which Egmont dresses "in Spanish garb" for Klärchen as a masquerade, a signal of Egmont's divided loyalties between his own people and their oppressors (143).[1] Cross-dressing is thus not always a matter of gender crossing, but can be a political transfer even within one sex. Still, the pattern of gender crossing is mostly related by Wilson to sexuality, including Goethe's own inclination to homoeroticism and cross-dressing itself, both in his life and writings.[2] Wilson demonstrates Klärchen's femininity in her relationship to Egmont, but her masculinity in the final act as she attempts to take control of the political situation. Egmont's essential passivity, by contrast, is feminine in nature, despite his role as folk hero and political leader (141), and this passivity is combined with homoerotic suggestions in his relationship with Ferdinand (137f.). In terms of gender roles, Wilson concludes that Egmont's "performance [of gender] is unconvincing; he merely reveals the performativity of this masculinity" (145). This insightful comment leads me to explore the very notion of performance with a focus on Margarete von Parma.

One of Wilson's provocative contributions is his discussion of Margarete's apparently ambivalent sexuality, as evidenced by her "manly dress" (130), though she is "only partly cross-dressed" (131). He recalls Goethe's principal historical source, Famianus Strada's *De Bello Belgico* (1578) and the essentially negative characterization of her there (130 and 260, n. 9), which left her for Goethe and others as some sort of "*Mannweib* or virago, not androgynous but simply an abomination of nature" (128), taking this further to demonstrate that "Goethe reverses Strada's poles by presenting Margarete as a cross-dressed woman, not a cross-dressed man, and by marking her *Mannweib* characteristics as Egmont's invention" (130). Wilson argues that this results from Egmont's sexual ambivalence toward her, his dismissal of her as masculine, yet his suppressed subconscious erotic attraction to her at the same time, part of which is an attraction to her masculinity (132f.). Thereby, Wilson rescues Margarete from her freakish role in Strada, winning her a position of dignity, while at the same time lowering the title figure from his masculine pedestal.

To some extent, Wilson links his arguments about *Egmont* to the sociological fabric of Goethe's age (127), but his study is based primarily on Goethe's text, so much so that it is important to him as a conscientious philologist to determine "the authentic text" of the play (259, n. 5). This he sees as the manuscript version which has been reproduced among modern editions only in the Akademie- and Münchner-Ausgaben. The Weimar edition includes Herder's emendations which, Wilson points out, were not in fact authorized by Goethe (though it might be argued that a tacit authorization took place). Although Wilson's attention to the detail of critical textual history is admirable, it does raise a distinction of crucial importance for what follows now. It would amount to petty scholarly squabbling to dispute his choice of the Akademie- or Münchner-Ausgabe versions, for the manuscript and publication history of the text of Goethe's *Egmont* are so unusually clear and straightforward that there are very few differences among the printed texts of the major editions anyway. However, focusing our attention on Wilson's idea of *authentic text* raises two questions which must be answered. First, should modern scholars be interested foremost in interpreting a dramatic *text*, or rather a dramatic *work*? And what are the consequences if the text upon which we base our observations is a single "authentic" one, as Wilson defines it?

Wilson refers to Friedrich Schiller's version of *Egmont*, first performed on the Weimar stage with August Wilhelm Iffland in the lead role in 1796, noting that it "entirely deleted Margarete!" (260, n. 15), but commenting no further. We might question the importance of Margarete at all if in fact she was absent from the premiere on Goethe's own stage, after he himself had invited Schiller to rewrite the play?[3] We need not stop here, for it is well known that in his version Schiller allowed extensive further manipulation of Goethe's *authentic* text and even added a few new scenes.[4] Some would claim that Schiller's version should be considered only as an adaptation, but we could make a similar argument about *Egmont* productions that claimed loyalty to Goethe's text as well.

Since the object of discussion in this case is a sexually ambivalent character, we are involved in far more than an academic debate about the authority of texts. The adaptation and performance of *Egmont* and Parma occupy a classically Foucauldian queer space. In his *History of Sexuality* Foucault points out that sexuality is inevitably linked to power and politics (6), and that the relationship between sex and power is characterized by repression (8), especially in ages and societies with a strong bourgeosie. Foucault's "repressive hypothesis" well suits late eighteenth-century Germany when sex became a police matter and the policing and regulation of sex part of the public discourse (24f.). Foucault's discussion includes so-called perversions and their definition, and, within these, hermaphrodites who were categorized as criminals "since their very anatomical disposition, their very being, confounded the law that distinguished the sexes and prescribed their union" (38). Julia Epstein's study of sexual ambiguity shows the intensity of medical research on the anatomical nature of hermaphrodites throughout Europe from as early as the sixteenth century, and among the many treatises she cites are some from German presses, such as Casparus Bauhinus's *De Hermaphroditorum monstrosorumque* and Georg Arnaud's *Anatomisch-Chirurgische Abhandlung über die Hermaphroditen*, both with striking illustrations (110-11).

Foucault's theories have laid the groundwork for many scholarly investigations of sex and gender since, for example Judith Butler's discussion from a feminist point of view of the hermaphrodite Herculine Barbin, whose journals Foucault edited and published (*Gender Trouble* 95-106); and the contributions of Steven Seidman, Lauren Berlant, and Elizabeth Freeman to Michael Warner's *Fear of a Queer Planet*, both relevant for our contemporary debate about gay culture. Seidman considers it a fundamental problem that "Much of current lesbian and gay studies remains wedded to a standard Enlightenment scientistic self-understanding that … is inconsistent with its social constructionist premises. Gay identity politics moves back and forth between a narrow single-interest-group politic and a view of coalition politics as the sum of separate identity communities, each locked into its own sexual, gender, class, or racial politic" (105). In contrast, he advocates escape from this unproductive compartmentalization and the social empowerment of gender categories. He frames his argument still, in part, in Foucauldian terms, but goes further to recommend the viewing of "identity as a site of ongoing social regulation and contestation rather than a quasi-natural substance or an accomplished social fact," and argues that such identities "are not only self-limiting and productive of hierarchies but are enabling or productive of social collectivities, moral bonds, and political agency" (134). Berlant and Freeman discuss the concept of nationality in queer terms, taking as their starting point a scene at the end of Sandra Bernhard's *Without You I'm Nothing* in which the diva wraps herself in the U.S. flag (193). There follow many examples in which activists have used the American flag to cover or expose their bodies, creating images that explore gender and queerness within the framework of nationalism and patriotism. They make explicit "how thoroughly the local experience of the body is framed by laws, policies, and social customs regulating sexuality" (195).

Although it is a long way in time and place from modern America to the Netherlands of the sixteenth-century, or eighteenth-century Weimar, the issues of nationalism and patriotism are fundamental to the action of *Egmont*, except that the overt connection to gender was then repressed. Was Parma's sexual ambivalence intended by Goethe to contribute to the contemporary discussion of sexuality? Foucault cites as one of the many fora for public discourse of sex at the end of the eighteenth century a festival organized in 1776 (when Goethe was writing *Egmont*) by the philanthropist Johann Bernhard Basedow (1723-90). Foucault claims that Goethe was one of the many dignitaries invited, and one of the few to decline (29).[5] As we proceed now to discuss adaptations of *Egmont*, both the authority of the text and the consequences within the context of the history of sexuality should be kept in mind.

Before the Weimar production of 1796, Goethe's *Egmont* played briefly in the Nationaltheater in Mainz, in Frankfurt, and in Weimar (before Goethe's directorship). This review was among the first following the

Mainz premiere of January 9, 1789: "Recently there was a production of
Goethe's Egmont with some changes. Naturally, the vision scene with Klärchen had to be deleted. The play has been reprinted here at a good price
and consequently was in the hands of everyone in the audience. They read
along, but were dissatisfied that much had been changed, especially that
the scene just mentioned had been omitted."[6] Obviously, Goethe's *authentic* text (the critic must have been referring to the Göschen edition of 1788,
or a pirated copy, which is the same as the manuscript printed in the
Akademie- and Münchner-Ausgaben) was not respected closely even for the
play's premiere. Audience dismay, in fact, seems to have resulted, as if their
lexical umbilical cords had been severed. Clearly the actors and their director, Siegfried Gotthelf Eckhardt (1754-1831; pseud. Koch), were unwilling
to depend entirely on Goethe's text for artistic sustenance. A second reviewer commented:

> At today's performance so much was lost because of the mutila-
> tion of the original play. Many a play may be too long or have
> superfluous scenes or characters, which could be deleted without
> disturbing the whole. Other plays have perhaps moments of
> genius, isolated portions that may offend, which must be omitted
> for the sake of the general public ... But one cannot ascribe either
> of these to Goethe's Egmont ... so I don't comprehend why one
> could adapt Egmont so mercilessly here, so that most of the parts
> that speak of pangs of conscience and the new way of thinking,
> which are so closely connected to the depiction of Egmont's
> character, and which direct the action and motivate the catastrophe
> could be deleted, and the wonderful monologues mangled as well.
> (*Dramaturgische Blätter* 2.1, 8. St., 123-25)

The changes to Goethe's text were extensive, a general slashing, including what the critic considered key monologues for character depiction and
development. Such mutilation was in fact perfectly common at that time,
and things have not changed much since. From the beginning, producers,
directors, and actors never respected the sanctity of Goethe's *authentic* text,
and indeed were simply following the pattern of their age. The director and
actors in Mainz were using as a basis for their production what should
rightly be called a *performance text,* that is, an adaptation, and this is always
the case to some degree for performed dramatic works. Many such manu-

scripts of performance texts from Goethe's age and beyond are extant today and can provide us with insights into their production, reception and significance. An outstanding example of such a performance text in the present context is that of Schiller's 1796 adaptation of *Egmont* in the theater collection of the Reiss-Museum, Mannheim.

At times, Wilson provides the lead for critics to go in a direction other than his own text-based argument. We saw above his remarks on Egmont's unconvincing "performance" of his own gender. He also alludes to gestures and pantomime (129), an acknowledgement of the actor's role in character depiction. A comment like "the Margarete *whom we see on the stage*" (129-30) recognizes the split between stage character and actor persona. We may go further to enquire about her costume, make-up, and bearing, for in matters of performance, these visual elements are obviously important. Strada characterizes Margarete as "a man in women's clothing" (Wagener 47), but the only reference to her costume in Goethe's text itself is at the beginning of the first of two scenes in which she appears in conversation with Machiavell: "Margaret of Parma in hunting costume" (act 1; Passage 299). Her second appearance likely involved a change of costume, but there is no indication in the text (act 3). Wilson refers to a contemporary description of an "Amazon dress" when discussing Parma, claiming that such fashion was suppressed after about 1789: "A prerevolutionary encyclopedia defines women's 'Amazon dress' (Amazonenkleid) as 'women's clothing, which is half masculine, namely on the upper half of the body. A kind of men's vest with sleeves, worn over a customary women's skirt, usually buttoned up, but sometimes open and flowing'; it is green and is worn not with a bonnet, but with a man's hat, gallooned with feathers" (264, n. 35). The encyclopedia Wilson cites includes no picture of the dress, but includes this additional information: "The name has its origin in the Amazons, just described, who in fact wore an entirely different costume. They left the right side of their upper body naked to below the breast, covering the rest with a short garment reaching down to the knee." (*Deutsche Encyclopädie* I: 416).[7]

This additional information leads to an entirely different dimension: the mythological, classical figure, which cannot be separated from the eighteenth-century version. Their juxtaposition demonstrates first that the eighteenth-century notion of such clothing was far removed from its source; it was a contemporary fashion, a costume. Two of its distinctively 'manly' parts, the vest and hat, had nothing to do with the original Amazon dress of classical mythology, but the green color, which alluded to hunting, can be seen as connected, the original Amazons being associated with the hunt. Other encyclopedias of Goethe's age describe this fashion as a broad European phenomenon with only a slight connection to the original. Having largely traced the classical model, they conclude their entries with a note on "Amazonian *habit* ... a dress formed in imitation of the Amazons ... Some also apply *Amazonian* habit to the hunting dress worn by ladies among us."[8] In contrast, the Amazons of Greek mythology wore the type of tunic described above, with left breast exposed (most accounts claim that the right breast had been sliced or seared off to facilitate shooting arrows with a bow and increase strength). They were known for their bellicosity and depicted usually with weapons (bow and arrows, axe, sword), often in a hunting or battle stance and on horseback. Many detailed studies of their origin and nature exist, and most modern encyclopaedias contain a picture along with an overview of their heritage.[9]

Did Margarete von Parma actually wear a costume alluding to either the original Amazons or the eighteenth-century Amazon dress on stage? As far as individual productions are concerned, we must look for hints of costuming in reviews and contemporary accounts. The over one hundred and fifty reviews of *Egmont* I have consulted contain extremely few references to costume at all, scarcely any in detail.[10] Moreover, in the vast majority of these productions, Margarete von Parma had usually been deleted from the script, until about 1825 when she reemerged with some regularity. In these instances, however, there is no reference to her appearance, and the descriptions of her character are uniformly positive: "a clever duchess" (Frankfurt performance of November 20, 1825); "The duchess is portrayed masterfully, strictly religious, even ecclesiastically minded, with good intentions and politically experienced, but nevertheless a woman" (Frankfurt performance of April 7, 1827); "Miss Thum, a powerful figure, played Margarethe with considerable dignity" (Kassel performance of June 1, 1830).[11] If indeed she appeared in a costume alluding to Amazons in any of these productions, it did not attract the attention of reviewers, unless perhaps they felt such observations indiscrete and veiled them with double-edged compliments like "politically experienced, but nevertheless a woman"!

We might speculate whether Margarete's reemergence was in fact a queer strategy of contemporary producers and directors, or whether she is better contained by hegemonic perspectives on and off the stage. After all, she was not the only Amazon figure on stage at the time. Inge Stephan has analyzed Schiller's Maid of Orléans and Kleist's Penthesilea as Amazon figures within the context of German philosophy of sexuality in the eighteenth and early nineteenth centuries. She demonstrates that Gottsched's, Schiller's, Wilhelm von Humboldt's, Fichte's, and Hegel's positions on women were essentially all variants supporting the patriarchal structure (23-32), in contrast to the argument for equal rights championed by Olympe de Gouges in France and the legion of feminist activists she inspired (27-28), those women whom Parma resembled in attire. Stephan argues that Schiller's treatment flies in the face of his expressed support of the French Revolution and attraction to the Maid of Orléans as a revolutionary figure (34-36). However, she interprets Kleist's Penthesilea differently, emphasizing the contemporary impact of this character's sexual ambivalence and its meaning for the author:

> Fascination and terror are the dominant reactions to this text — in a letter Kleist reported the dismay and emotion released when the play was first read to his friends. Kleist himself was fascinated by the figure of Penthesilea. In her he worked through his ambivalent feelings toward his sister Ulrike and his vacillation between dominance and surrender, which typified his relationship to men and women. Penthesilea is an ideal, but also a figure of terror, a self-image, as is Achilles, who in his submissive behavior gives rein to feelings forbidden to men at the time. (40)

Goethe's Parma was perhaps another figure to elicit such feelings and provide an opportunity to explore queerness in a climate of repression.

Beyond the reviews, contemporary pictures are a further source for determining how characters looked on stage. Drawings, etchings, and paintings of stage characters were common, with the literary and dramatic fame of *Egmont* resulting in at least two substantial series of prints. The first series appeared in *Urania. Taschenbuch für Damen auf das Jahr 1815*, which included prints from three of Goethe's plays, *Faust*, *Egmont*, and *Tasso*. The three *Egmont* scenes are "Egmont and Klärchen" from act 3 (Egmont revealing his Spanish attire), "Egmont and Klärchen" again in act 3 (Klärchen at Egmont's knee), and from act 5 "Egmont in prison" (the vision scene with Klärchen hovering above the sleeping protagonist). The *Urania* pictures of 1815 contained none of Margarete, perhaps a reflection of the fact that her role was almost always omitted from *Egmont* productions until the mid 1820s or the fact that *Urania* was specifically designated as a *Taschenbuch für Damen* — enough reason to ban her presence there. The second series appeared in *Minerva. Taschenbuch für das Jahr 1825*, the seventeenth annual of this well-established journal of politics and social intercourse.[12] Included are eight prints: from 1,1 Bürgerszene; 1,2 Margarete von Parma; 2,2 Egmont/Oranien; 3,2 Egmont; 4,1 Vansen; 4,2 Alba; 5,1 Klärchen; and the last scene of act 5, the vision. Of primary interest to us is the picture of Margarete reproduced in figure 1; its caption reads: "O what are we great ones on the wave of humanity?" (WA I, 8: 184; Passage 300). It is clear that Margarete's attire approximates the "Amazon dress" cited by Wilson and described in the *Deutsche Encyclopädie*, including the flowing skirts, the tight bodice or vest, and the plumed hat. Margarete also holds a stick, perhaps a riding crop, and we note the hunting dog at her knee, being dragged reluctantly from her presence. Wilson's claim that the Amazon dress was supressed from about the time of the French Revolution would have to make room for this 1825 exception.

When looking at Margarete here with hunting dog at her knee, one cannot avoid thinking of its compositional similarity to the famous, frequently depicted scene of Egmont with Klärchen at his knee, which appeared as the frontispiece to the first edition in 1788 and is so distinctively associated with this play that ubiquitous modern Reclam reprints since 1993 carry a reproduction of it on their cover (Reclams Universal-Bibliothek 75). The contrast jars between the intimate scene of a lover and his lady, pressing herself to Egmont's heart in a suitably feminine dress with curves and ample bosom, and the stateswoman in "Amazonenkleid" whose hunting dog is dragged off by servants, with soldiers on guard. The 'normality' of one relationship stands in stark contrast to the bizarre partnership depicted in the other, so that Margarete is isolated further from the mainstream of society.

How have modern actors, directors, and producers of *Egmont* depicted Margarete von Parma? *Egmont* has been produced on German-speaking stages in the Federal and former Democratic Republic, in Austria, and in Switzerland at least twenty-four times since 1970.[13] It is impossible to discuss all of these within terms of the present essay, but three examples — two productions from the former GDR (Potsdam, 1971; Weimar, 1979) and one from the FRG before the fall of the wall (Karlsruhe, 1980) — are of particular interest. Among the twenty-one others, a number excluded the character of Parma altogether, one of these was the 1990 production on

Salzburg's Elisabethbühne, the only one of the twenty-four directed by a woman (Renate Rustler-Ourth). Others depicted Parma in visual terms simply as a regal female, with no Amazon or masculine suggestions, and none of them portrayed Parma along the lines of her mythological ancestors, that is, with one breast displayed — surely a unique opportunity lost by modern directors inclined to show seminudity.

The 1971 Potsdam production in the Hans-Otto Theater (director Peter Kupke) claimed in its program to be the "stage adaptation by Friedrich Schiller, arranged for the Potsdam theater by Karl Mickel ... dramaturge Irmgard Mickisch."[14] Yet contrary to Schiller's version, the Parma scenes were included, rewritten by Karl Mickel. Evidently, despite his affinity to Schiller's version, the director felt them necessary. As they were performed in Potsdam, the two scenes were similar to Goethe's originals, but in the first, Goethe's text begins: "*Margaret von Parma in hunting costume. Members of the court. Pages, Servants.* PARMA. You are not hunting today, nor shall I hunt ..." (WA I, 8: 183). Clearly, a hunting costume is called for at this point; the Potsdam version begins the same way: "*Margarete von Parma, in hunting costume.*" But soon after his entrance, Machiavell is joined by Egmont's servant Richard, a diversion from the source, and then comes this exchange:

> PARMA. Today we shall go hunting, it's always worthwhile.
> *(Richard gives Parma a letter)*
> RICHARD. *(to Machiavell)* An urgent message. It informs our most gracious regent that the Prince of Orange has departed to his German territories, without leave or farewell, by night, with a small entourage. How will she react?
> MACHIAVELL. She has given herself over to a man's passion, hunting, and Nature has avenged herself of this transgression through a male affliction, gout. People will delay, and avoid confronting her with difficult questions about matters of state, explaining that pleasure must be sacrificed in the state's interest. At the same time they will make it clear that she is sick, and feign that they are protecting state interests by having us believe that the sickness is genuine and of no concern *(Parma doubles up in pain)*.
> (Potsdam performance text 26)

The mixed scene including Richard is new, as are Machiavell's words, "She has given herself over to a man's passion, hunting, and Nature has avenged herself of this transgression through a male affliction, gout." In Goethe, a similar passage occurs in the final scene of act 2 between Klärchen and Egmont, when he says of Parma: "She also has whiskers on her upper lip, and sometimes she gets a twinge of the gout. A regular amazon!" (WA I, 8: 242; Passage 337). This, of course, is cited and commented on by Wilson (128), but the Potsdam version changes the emphasis of the original considerably. Parma's inclination to the 'manly' art of hunting, in both versions cited as the direct cause of her gout, is labeled in the Potsdam production as nature's revenge for her 'transgression', and its consequences are severe: "*Parma doubles up in pain.*" I understand this to indicate genuine physical pain, for exactly the same gesture of agony is repeated at the end of the scene, *after* Machiavell has left (29), when Parma is alone on stage. Parma is made to *pay* for her 'transgression' of nature, so much so that her second scene is played in a sickbed with the introductory stage direction "*Parma in bed. Lady in waiting. Medical attendants. Machiavell.*" This new scene consists mainly of an interview between Parma and Alba, another change to Goethe's original. Here, Parma surrenders all authority to him, and immediately thereafter, "*Doubles up in pain, rings for attendant*" and is assisted by the "*Lady in waiting. Medical attendants. Machiavell*" (58).

Photographs of the Potsdam production show Parma in the first scene in a unisexual suit suggestive of the late Dutch Renaissance with its black hat and large white collar, trousers, tunic, long black boots identical to the leading male's in the play, and short hair which further de-emphasizes her femininity. The second Parma scene in her sickbed shows her in a white nightdress, appropriate for either a woman or a man in that age. Parma is desexed in this production. She has moved from femininity to neutrality, and by crossing the line toward masculinity is punished by the loss of her health and power. The physical penalty imposed for her *Grenzüberschreitung* (crossing the boundary) of nature then has a direct impact on the dramatic development as she surrenders her authority to Alba.

Similar elements can be seen in the 1979 Weimar Nationaltheater production directed by Fritz Bennewitz.[15] Although based on Goethe's version, including every scene and the two Parma appearances, the dialogue was severely cut throughout, so what remained gains in importance. Egmont's description to Klärchen of Parma's masculine features, quoted above ("She also has whiskers on her upper lip") is *not* deleted here, and the inclusion reinforces the nature of Parma's appearance: "*de Reese* [actor playing Parma] *moves with two mastiffs left rear. (Pause) slow advance forward right*" (Weimar performance text 13). The photographs of this scene make the image even clearer. Parma holds two powerful mastiffs on short leather leashes at her side (similar to the servant in the *Minerva* picture). Props, sets, and costumes were minimal, so these creatures are far more than trivial accessories. They are usually associated with men and aggression, they are stage-front signifiers of masculine strength. Parma is dressed in a long green velvet coat with gloves, wears a cap with protruding feather, her hair covered, all feminine features concealed. These elements recall the Amazon's dress in *Minerva* and along with Egmont's description to Klärchen demonstrate this production's desire to typify Parma once again as a masculine being. The Weimar production also included a live horse on stage, ridden by Egmont, so the two animal scenes were particularly forceful.[16]

The Karlsruhe *Egmont* of 1980 in the Badisches Staatstheater was the creation of guest director Hanns Zischler and dramaturge Peter Krumme. The program for this production contained the full text of Goethe's play, complete with all director's markings, showing deletions, insertions, instructions to actors, and production notes; in other words, it was the performance text.[17] Despite the many deletions, the Karlsruhe production remained quite faithful to Goethe's original. Egmont's description of Parma's masculine features is even enhanced: "She also has whiskers on her upper lip, and sometimes she gets a twinge of the gout. *A regular amazon!*" (Karlsruhe performance text 31). By underscoring the exclamation, Zischler and Krumme signal particular significance for this dimension of Parma's character, and their treatment of it goes beyond what we have seen so far. As in Goethe, her first scene begins with "*Margarete von Parma in hunting costume,*" but the motif is developed to link more closely with details of Parma as an Amazon. Near the end of her interchange with Machiavell, and again in words from Goethe, Parma says with specific reference to Egmont: "No let me speak! What I have in my heart shall, with this opportunity, be disburdened. *And I do not want to use up my arrows for nothing.* I know where his weak spot is — and he does have a weak spot, too" (9; WA I, 8: 192; Passage 305). Of course, the emphasis on "*I do not want to use up my arrows for nothing*" is not in Goethe's original, but was added by Zischler and Krumme. Beside this underlining are found the marginalia

"*Diana (hunting costume)* ... *(and Actaeon?)*." How are we to understand these underscored references?

Diana, Roman goddess of the hunt (the Greek Artemis), is of course an allusion consistent with "Margarete von Parma in hunting costume." Actaeon is a male figure in Greek mythology who was changed by Artemis to a stag for surprising her in the act of bathing and was subsequently devoured by his own hounds. Zischler and Krumme are playing intriguingly here with sexuality, gender crossing, and vulnerability. The stage character Parma was already sexually ambivalent as an Amazon figure. The link with Actaeon underscores her masculinity and also suggests a cruel penalty for this transgression: transformation to the animal status of stag, representative of aggressive male sexuality and even lust; and in keeping with Actaeon's ultimate fate a life-threatening vulnerability to the very creatures she seemingly masters. The allusion to arrows on the one hand is also in keeping with the reference to Diana and the hunt, yet beyond this is a return to the original classical mythological concept of the Amazon. Ancient pictures and sculptures show these figures repeatedly with sword, bow, and arrow, and it is indeed the bow and arrow that is this hunter's chief weapon. The Amazon's arrows thus become metaphors for Parma's words "I do not want to use up my arrows for nothing."[18] In their production, Zischler and Krumme reinforce Parma's timeless connection to her classical heritage, and by combining it with the myths of Diana and Actaeon draw attention to the problematic nature of her sexuality and the danger for her that results.

Certainly, the figure of Parma, as Wilson emphasized, should be connected to the Amazon tradition, but the textual and reception history of Goethe's play demonstrate that the nature of her sexuality remains enigmatic. The many examples of textual manipulation perhaps result not merely from the efficacies of dramatic production, but also from a discomfort caused by the nature of this character. Productions in Goethe's time often avoided the problem by eliminating her entirely, and later, when she was reintroduced regularly, emphasized the noble aspects of her personality within terms of the conventional social and sexual mores. Still, we are aware of the lively public and medical discourse on the subject of sexuality at the time, even if it was conducted within a climate of sexual repression. It is reasonable to suspect that directors and audiences, if not Goethe himself, were making a contribution to that discourse when representing Parma on stage. In modern productions she can be the object of aversion or fascination as well, as demonstrated by the many productions that still eliminate her; others that ennoble her and disregard her queer sexuality; still others that explore her masculinity and femininity both. Is she to be understood essentially as a masculine entity who chooses, or who is trapped in a female costume and role? Or should she be seen as representing the type of femininity that transgresses its social markers and calls into question the exclusivity of male characteristics? Whatever the interpretation chosen by reader, director or audience, it is clear that by going beyond Goethe's original version to explore the full range of texts, visual representations, and productions we discover connections beyond his verbal legacy alone.

Figure 1. Egmont. 1. Aufzug, 2. Szene.
Marg. v. Parma. O was sind wir Grossen auf der Woge der Menschheit ?

Notes

[1]The scene is located in the Weimar edition of Goethe's *Werke* (I, 8: 239). Future references to *Egmont* are from the same edition and will be cited with part, volume, and page number in parenthesis. Quotations from Goethe's text cited in English are taken from the translation by Charles E. Passage; other translations from German are my own.

[2]Wilson summarizes this inclination in Goethe, which has also been discussed by critics before (130-31, 258-59). Kurt R. Eissler's classic work is still the touchstone, but current scholars such as Kaus, Kuzniar (3 and 14) and Tobin (1996, 97 and 107-108) continue to add fresh insights.

[3]In 1794 Goethe invited Schiller, "to correct [korrigieren] *Egmont* for the Weimar theater," as reported by Schiller to his wife Charlotte (*Goethe über seine Dichtungen* II, 1: 226).

[4]A precise comparison of Goethe's and Schiller's texts is available in Schiller's *Werke* (NA 13) or in his *Bühnenbearbeitungen*.

[5]Foucault does not document this claim. There are in fact many references to Basedow in Goethe's works and private papers, all of which could be called positive. A lengthy section of his *Dichtung und Wahrheit* (*Poetry and Truth*) is devoted in large part to this man who counted among his friends (*Werke* I, 28: 271-95). For the period in question, Goethe's diary indicates that he visited Basedow on December 15, 1776, and again on May 26, 1778 (III, 1: 28, 67). However, Foucault's failure to document the claim does not mean that it is entirely without validity.

[6]*Theater-Zeitung für Deutschland* 10, March 3, 1789, 77.

[7]Reference to the right breast here is in error. Many reliable sources indicate that the left breast of Amazons was exposed, the right covered, and for good reason — see below.

[8]Here quoted from Chambers (1787, I: unpag.), but almost identical in *Encyclopaedia Britannica* (1797, A: 523) and Rees (1819, II: unpag.).

[9]As for example the eighteenth-century encyclopaedias cited above and the modern *Encyclopaedia Britannica*, the *Brockhaus Enzyklopädie* and *Meyers Enzyklopädisches Lexikon*. The lore of Amazons is extensive and fascinating, but most of it beyond the scope of this article. Many monographs have been written on the subject, the most elaborate and influential early European version being Pierre Petit's dissertation of 1687 which included numerous illustrations. Guy Rothery's more recent study (1910) traces Amazons from antiquity to "modern times" and includes a chapter on the "Amazons of Europe" up to the later eighteenth century (95-108). When establishing his "modern" examples, Rothery uses the term Amazon very generally as a bellicose woman, and his celebrated eighteenth-century example is the female French revolutionary who also had a distinctive dress, something like that described in the German encyclopaedia above. It was originated by Théroigne de Méricourt, commander of the third corps of the army of the Faubourg: a red riding habit, huge

hat, plume of feathers, and sword. Another famous revolutionary, la Maillard, and her female followers wore male attire (106).

[10]In this regard I have made use of the rich repository of theater materials in the Fambach archive of the Germanistisches Seminar, University of Bonn. The private theater scholar Oscar Fambach collected thousands of photocopied reviews, but I also consulted the originals.

[11]Respectively in *Didiskalia* 327, Nov. 23, 1825; *Didiskalia* 104, Apr. 14, 1827; and *Abend-Zeitung* 177, July 26, 1830.

[12]See extensive bibliographical documentation in Estermann, vol. 1, item 1.22. The journal *Urania* is not listed in Estermann, although a different publication with the same title appeared in 1838.

[13]Sources for assembling this information include individual issues of *Theater der Zeit, Theater heute, Die Bühne,* and annual issues of *Was spielten die Theater?* (1981-1990) and *Wer spielte was?* (1990-1993). Performance venues include (in chronological order 1970-1995): Potsdam, Zürich, Vienna, Dessau, Cologne, Bern, Innsbruck, Weimar, Karlsruhe, Munich, Vienna, Düsseldorf, Brandenburg, Eisenach, Greifswald, Bregenz, Vienna, Leipzig, Berlin, Frankfurt/M., Salzburg, Aachen, Bonn, and Berlin. Through the generosity of theater archivists I have been been able to inspect original production materials of twenty of these, including programs, photos, collected reviews, performance texts (for almost half), and a few videotapes of entire performances.

[14]I wish to express my gratitude to Frau Mickisch, still dramaturge in Potsdam, for supplying me with the materials for my research, including an original program, photographs, a copy of the performance text, and reviews.

[15]I am grateful to Karin Scheider, librarian and archivist of the Weimar National-theater, for her advice and access to the original program, photos, collected reviews, and the performance text.

[16]One can hardly resist mentioning the irony of this parade of animals in the Weimar Nationaltheater in view of Goethe's paranoia of them, especially dogs, on stage and the production of *Der Hund von Aubry* (*The Dog of Aubry*) in 1817 which effec-tively ended his career as theater-manager (*Intendant*).

[17]I am grateful to Ulrich Ried, librarian and archivist of the Badisches Staatstheater Karlsruhe, for generously furnishing me with an original program and reviews. Unfor-tunately pictures were not available.

[18]We should remember as well that the final vision scene includes Klärchen as free-dom goddess who leans over the sleeping Egmont and "shows him the sheave of arrows" (WA I, 8: 303; Passage 375), a symbol of his people's struggle for liberation. The arrow metaphor could thus be understood to arch from the classical Amazons, to Parma, to Klärchen, and to the Dutch people.

"Love only succors / Those who can love": Mephisto's Desiring Gaze in Goethe's Faust·

Silke R. Falkner

IN CONVERSATION WITH JOHANNES FALK, Goethe hinted that there is a possibility for even Mephisto's salvation in *Faust II*, and he also expressed his pleasure at the idea that his readers would never forgive him if by chance they arrived at this place in the text.[1] Although Mephisto's redemption seems a laudable project, Goethe's notion that readers might find it unforgivable is a curious thing in itself. However, after careful analysis of certain key scenes, the reason Goethe's readership might be more than a little perturbed becomes evident: the possibility for Mephisto's redemption is inextricably linked to his homosexual love[2] for the angels in the Interment scene. For Mephisto to receive forgiveness from God, a change in his *identity* would have to occur, that is, the combination of attitudes and qualities that comprise his character and effectively distinguish him from nondevils would have to undergo some alteration. Examples of his devilish tendencies include a capacity for deceiving others, arrogance, and cruelty,[3] compounded by his own awareness of these traits.[4] No less of an authority than God identifies him as a spirit of "negation" (338). Another important facet of Mephisto's devilish self is his conduct in sexual situations.[5] Whether he contrives them at Faust's request or is a direct participant in them, his behavior indicates Goethe's intention to differentiate between Mephisto's homosexual and heterosexual desire. Throughout the play, desire is expressed by the 'gaze'; how who looks at whom informs aspects of sexual identity. Qualitative differences are evident in Mephisto's gaze vis-à-vis his objects of desire; the ways in which these changes are described, have major implications for both the general understanding of the text and the interpretation of the Interment scene in *Faust II*.

A climate of general misogyny permeates the heterosexual situations in which Mephisto appears. The constant detailing of his *intent* to satisfy only physical urges with women, captured in explicitly carnal language, serves to amplify his devilish identity. However, in the Interment scene

Mephisto craves that the angels return his gaze; this event actually undermines his identity hitherto characterized by a one-sided objectification of women.

The most transgressive and potentially liberating act for Mephisto, then, is homosexual desire. The creative power of Eros engenders a universe where even Mephisto can experience love, which goes to challenge everything else he reveals about himself in *Faust*. Although many critics acknowledge that Mephisto could be gay and that, as Goethe hinted, he can be redeemed, a glaring oversight requires a synthesis of these perspectives: his falling in love with the angels is a humanizing experience that transgresses his devilish identity, and therefore offers him a chance at redemption from the hell of which Mephisto is the central part.

Critical responses to the homoerotic passages in *Faust* can be classified into the following three groups, two of which certainly fulfill Goethe's prophecy that his readers would never forgive him for suggesting the devil could be redeemed. The main proponent of the first group, who rejects the existence of Mephisto's homosexual desires, is Hans Arens. His extensive and thorough *Kommentar zu Goethes "Faust II"* epitomizes this approach by stating that "Mephistopheles's infatuation has nothing to do with the angels, who happen to be male" and that it "is not 'perversity,' because this does not correspond to his inclinations as we know them" (984). He completely and conveniently ignores all references to homosexuality. Although recognizing that Mephisto has fallen in love, and conceding to a difference between Mephisto's homosexual and heterosexual attractions — like other scholars before him, Arens avoids discussing the range of meanings invested in what could be construed as Mephisto's reference to sodomitic pleasures. ("They're turning — see them from the rear! — / the rascals really whet my appetite!" 11799–800).

The second group distinguishes itself by commenting negatively about these crucial scenes. Ironically, Heinrich Rickert's and Ernst Traumann's homophobic devaluations of Mephisto's angelic infatuation as "degeneracy" and "perversity" acknowledge, at least, the existence of his same-sex attraction. Rickert bleakly depicts Mephisto's desire as "the lowest form of sexual sensuality" by which Mephisto remains "true to himself," and he dismisses Mephisto's "perverted concupiscence" as the antithesis of his salvation, as just another facet of his devilish identity (1932, 466 and 470). In the second volume of his work *Goethes Faust: Nach Entstehung und Inhalt erklärt*, Traumann acknowledges Mephisto's behavior in the confrontation with the heavenly host, even highlighting his confusion and loss of sardonicism. However, his analysis of Mephisto as "bankrupt" (1914, 356) is completely inaccurate. Mephisto's experience of the conflict in his essential nature is dismissed summarily as "perversity." According to Traumann, homosexual love intensifies Mephisto's devilish identity, making him "the most foolish of all fools, the most disgusting of all lovers," as the "heavenly element of love is turned into its opposite in the devil, it becomes *perverted*" (363; Traumann's emphasis).

The third group of scholars — including Paul Derks, Sander Gilman, Albrecht Schöne, and Robert Tobin (all contemporaries of Arens) — is characterized by an approach that is neither indifferent nor scathing. Schöne, for example, observes that "Faust's *Seelchen* escapes the claws of evil ... because [Mephisto] turns gay at the sight of the angels" (766), but, unfortunately, without commenting on exactly how it affects Mephisto. As comparatively daring as Schöne's reading seems, it fails to recognize the clearly redemptive quality of Mephisto's homosexual love toward the angels. My analysis examines Mephisto's apparently heterosexual desire, contrasts this with his change of desire in the pivotal Interment scene, and establishes definitively the place in the text where even the devil finds a possibility for salvation.

I.

Mephisto's heterosexual desire is staged in five crucial scenes throughout *Faust I* and *II*: "The Neighbor's House," "A Garden," "Nordic Walpurgis Night," "Classical Walpurgisnight," and "High Mountains." All of them are linked by Mephisto's contemptuous lust and misogyny. The fact that he never acts out his heterosexual desire underscores the suspicion that it functions merely to construct and maintain his identity as a *male* devil. A clear indication of this is given very early on in the play. As part of a strategy to win the fourteen-year-old Margarete, Faust asks Mephisto to "cultivate the woman who's her neighbor" (2858), Martha, an older woman, who is probably more responsive to courtship. Mephisto displays his savoir-faire in complimenting both women, ingenuously creating opportunities for Faust and Margarete to be together. He even offers Martha his hand in marriage. Mephisto's ironic mockery points to his basic dishonesty — and his actual fear of the possibility that Martha might accept his offer: "Upon my honor, given some such terms, / I would myself exchange engagement rings with you! / ... (*aside*) / It's now high time for me to leave — / she'd hold the very devil to his word!" (3001-05). A short while later, in "A Garden," the couples — Margarete/Faust and Martha/Mephisto — go for a walk. As Faust determinedly employs all his experience and skill in Margarete's seduction, Mephisto evades Martha's advances toward him.

In "The Neighbor's House" and "A Garden," Mephisto's contemptuous cynicism and cunning machinations are clear evidence of his misogyny. Mephisto only needs Martha for her matchmaking skills, feigning heterosexual attraction to advance Faust's scheme. The fact that Mephisto, despite his apparent obsession with sex, is disinterested in a woman of whom he could easily take advantage is, in the very least, extraordinary. During the "Nordic Walpurgis Night," then, Mephisto expresses pure heterosexual lust, emphasizing unadulterated carnal pleasure and indulging in a particularly lecherous objectification that is to reinforce his devilish identity. When the imbroglio on Brocken mountain overwhelms even the devil himself, Mephisto urges Faust to "escape this press of people" (4025-26) by joining a group of nubile witches Mephisto finds attractive: "I see some nice young witches over there, / Stark naked next to elders wisely veiled. / Be pleasant to them, simply for my sake; / A little effort gets you much amusement" (4046-49). What "amusement" refers to can be extrapolated from the following lines. As a "new dance" is called, Mephisto encourages Faust: "come on, we have our pick" (4127). The German "nun komm! Wir greifen zu" is more explicit, as *zugreifen* (literally "to have one's pick," but also "to grab," "to grasp") conveys the connotation of the physical touch. The dance thus denotes direct participation in "indecent activities" (Friedrich/Scheithauer 204).

During the dance, both Faust and Mephisto objectify the women at hand, although the language used for that purpose betrays the character of emotional investment in these attractions. While Faust is ready to get physical with a young and attractive witch, Mephisto shies away from sexual contact and resorts instead to mockery. When Faust imagines the breasts of the witch as "two apples" (4130) that tempt him "to climb the tree" (4131), Mephisto — in company with an old and ugly witch — caricatures Faust's fantasies. This lurid parody, which includes the crass reduction of a female to a "cloven tree," the penis to "the right-sized stopper," and the vagina to a "gaping hole," is couched in a literary tradition of vulgar language and overtly sexual allusions, and it conveys a preoccupation with the mechanics of penetrative sex (4136-43). Unlike Faust and Margarete, it is doubtful if they actually consummate their relationship. The Old Witch dares Mephisto to "Be ready with the right-sized stopper," concluding with a taunt, "unless big holes intimidate you," that crudely echoes his fear of Martha's designs on him earlier in the text.

Further evidence of the notion that the 'amusement' on the mountain refers exclusively to unbridled sexual activity can be reconstructed from the corresponding Paralipomena. In Paralipomenon 50, Satan extols the decidedly material nature of sexuality to a group of female witches, by associating the phallic "tail" with money: "For you there are two things / Of glistening allure / The shiny gold / And a gleaming tail / Therefore you women know / To love the gold / And even more than the gold / Enjoy the tails."[6] When a young girl, presumably a witch, bursts into tears because she fails to understand the exact meaning of the words, Mephisto 'comforts' her with advice laden with diabolical portent: "If you want to know what the devil is talking about, / you just have to reach into your neighbor's pants."[7]

In the Classical Walpurgisnight scene, this aspect of Mephisto's devilish identity is further sustained by his desperate pursuit of the ghostly Lamiae – and his itemizing them according to their physical charms: "I've chosen her who is the prettiest" (7769); "That one's petite – I'd like to make a deal with her" (7773); "Here's one who's stout – / perhaps she will afford more solace" (7779-80). The deceptive, elusive (albeit female) Lamiae, shape-shifters like Mephisto, are "lovely ladies" who "still flit roguishly along, / luring me toward them, then eluding me" (7692-93). Despite Mephisto's accusation that the Lamiae and (by implication) women are false (7713-18), their pulchritude still arouses him and inspires his attempt to "grab at them in any circumstances" (7695) – again testifying to the material nature of his desire. When he is unable to seize the ghosts, they caustically taunt: "Why harp so much upon your eagerness? / For all your swaggering and boasting / you are a pitiful gallant" (7763-65), and they punish the devil by making a fool of him by skillfully changing shape. Even the Lamiae hint at a growing suspicion that the subtotal of his machismo and misogyny amount to little more than an elaborate heterosexual hoax. As the "masquerade proves here, as everywhere, / to be but show that entertains the senses" (7795-96), Mephisto is free from having to act out his apparent heterosexual urges. Hence, he continues his hopeless pursuit of illusory women, as if chasing the unattainable would be sufficient to convince both himself and the reader of his pronounced heterosexuality.

Both the Nordic Walpurgisnight and the Classical Walpurgisnight scenes represent the respective philosophical principles of the Christian North, with its deeply ensconced moral precepts of good and evil, and the classical Antiquity of the South, where the aesthetic principles of the attractive and the repellent are more receptive of the sexual. Being a fully-fledged member of the Christian North (a 'Christian' devil), Mephisto is confounded by what he experiences as "a show that entertains the senses" (7795), as he enters the "Classical Walpurgisnight," the realm where the Christian construct 'devil' does not exist. The Sphinxes point out to him, "at home you feel yourself important, / but here, unless I'm wrong, you're ill at ease" (7143-45). Despite his confusion, Mephisto continues objectifying females only in the fraudulent hope of gratifying his carnal needs.

In "High Mountains," Mephisto engineers a fantasy in which the actual purpose is the complete opposite of its expressed intent. On behalf of Faust, he conjures a vision featuring special "residences / for rendezvous with lovely ladies," to "spend time without end / in pleasantly gregarious solitude" (10170-73). He uses this fantasy — ostensibly about enjoying further pleasures with women — to goad Faust into militaristic pursuits. Mephisto continues: "I speak of *ladies* for a simple reason: / I always think of beauties in the plural" (10174-75), thus potentiating the fantasy but also further objectifying women by dismissing them generically and not as distinct individuals. The deployment of this fantasy to encourage Faust to think about anything else *but* women is most revealing! Given that the staged heterosexuality exposes Mephisto's apparently heterosexual identity as inconclusive, it would come as quite a surprise if the conviviality of the fantasy harem actually were to interest him. As far as we know, Mephisto never satiates his lust, he is merely obsessed "with sex as a spectator" (S. Williams 95).

Mephisto's devilish identity has been constructed by immoral machinations and sardonicism ("The Neighbor's House"; "A Garden"), lecherous misogyny ("Nordic Walpurgis Night"; "Classical Walpurgisnight"), and finally with ironic ridicule ("High Mountains") calculated to challenge Faust into conquest and war. Although these attitudes and traits convincingly consolidate his devilishly heterosexual identity, the course of this tragedy will arouse another kind of amorous gaze, destabilizing and temporarily divesting him of his diabolical nature.

The conflicting values of North and South illuminate Mephisto's own metamorphosis. Enraptured by the ugliness of the fantastically hideous

Phorcides that share one eye and tooth amongst them, he transforms into one of them to contrive an affair between Faust and Helen. Despite his fears that he would "now be called hermaphroditic" (8029), Helen recognizes Phorkyas/Mephisto as female when s/he persuades her of the need to seek refuge at Faust's castle. Asked, "How does he look?" (9009) s/he replies: "Not bad! I rather like his looks" (9010-11). Mephisto's description of Faust's features has been interpreted as the first instance of homoeroticism in the play (Tobin 1994, 23) even though, or perhaps because, his desire may be the result of his transformation. Whatever the case, it becomes evident that, in the guise of Phorkyas, he can express his homoerotic interest in positive terms and direct his desire toward "Plenty of lively lads with golden curls / and youth's ambrosial breath" (9045-46).

Robert Tobin asserts that Mephisto's demasculinization in *Faust II* is linked to Goethe's creation theories developed in the poems "Prometheus" and "Ganymede," published in 1789. While Prometheus embodies the "masculine" principle of self-assertion, Ganymede incorporates the "feminine" principle of "dissolution of the self" (1994, 17), reflecting the eighteenth-century concept of "the feminine." A symbol for passive homosexual love,[8] Ganymede also serves to express an openness necessary to experience divine power. To this end, Mephisto progresses from a Promethean figure to one of a more Ganymedian nature; this begins with his description of Faust and his male entourage to Helen, and culminates in the Interment scene.

II.

After Faust's death, Mephisto presciently fears losing Faust's soul at the interment despite the contract in his hand and signed in blood (11614-22). As a precaution, the devil summons his own troops to capture Faust's soul upon its excarnation, "in the manner of a squad-leader" (11635-37) in a fantastic conjuration, like a flank man. The military term "flank man" ("flügelmännisch," 11635) is reminiscent of "weltmännisch," or worldliness, a character trait he consistently exhibits in the play. Mephisto displays his erudition by invoking his assistants with allegorical references to the Bible and Dante's *Inferno*. Goethe's contemporaries, including Madame de Staël, already saw in Mephisto the "civilized devil" (cf. Weinrich 61-67), who, as is the case in Friedrich Theodor Vischer's parodic sequel

Faust: Der Tragödie dritter Theil (1862), is sophisticated enough to enjoy expensive cigars (cf. act 2, scene 2).

The "Heavenly Host" (11676) proceeds to do just what Mephisto fears: to kidnap Faust's soul. Initially, the angels' "discordant, nasty tinklings" (11685) disgust him.[9] As Mephisto warns his minions to be watchful, the angels scatter roses, symbols of divine love, that confuse the devilish peons. Amidst the ensuing chaos, the angels confound even Mephisto; pushing him aside, the ethereal beings succeed in capturing and leading Faust's soul to heaven. Mephisto, for the first and only time in the play, completely loses what Thomas Mann has called "superiority of the Weltmensch" ("Über Goethes *Faust*" 310) and with it also his devilish self: his antipathy toward the angels has turned into love.

This stunning transformation has a humanizing effect on Mephisto, who has been rehabilitated by Erwin Ackerknecht as "certainly warmblooded" and "almost humanly tragic" (117). Mephisto likens himself to unrequited lovers (11757) whose "lovesickness" is located in those parts of the (human!) body where understanding and feeling are situated and where pain is felt: "My head's on fire, and I've heart-and-liver burn: / that superdiabolic element / is far more poignant than the flames of hell" (11753–55). Both the beauty of the angels and their overwhelming love arouse desire in him. The angels' song of divine love counsels Mephisto to open himself, invoking his Ganymedian potential: that which is contrary to divine love must be penetrated by precisely that love: "What you find alien, / be sure to avoid it; / what hurts your inward self, / you must reject it. / But if still it intrudes, / we must confront it. / Love only succors / those who can love" (11745–52).[10]

Mephisto's rhetorical question: "Is this the stuff that love is made of?" (11783) acknowledges a feeling both painful and pleasurable, hitherto unknown to him. As the angelic vision beguiles him and fills him with love, he now empathizes with humans suffering from unrequited love: "I see why you unhappy lovers moan so overmuch − / you who, although you're spurned, still twist / your necks to catch a glimpse of her you love. / My plight too! What's pulling my head in that direction, / when that's the side of my sworn foes −" (11756–60). Comparing Mephisto's infatuation with the Lamiae to that with the angels reveals critical differences. He states that he learnt nothing from his experience with the Lamiae (cf. 7713), whereas he admits to his infatuation with the angels (cf. 11765) immediately after he compares his feelings to "lovesickness." Although one can

argue that he objectifies both the Lamiae and the angels, his attraction is
reflected in the difference in language. His lust for the Lamiae is a linear
pursuit that needs no reciprocation. His infatuation with the angels, however, is ambivalent as Mephisto's hatred evolves into love — a process
which clearly destabilizes his identity — and then devolves into hatred
again.

Mephisto, whose "body is on fire everywhere" (11758), knows that this
new feeling is far more intense than anything he has experienced before. Although he claims to despise the heavenly beings, he remains riveted to the
sight of them. Previously described as hermaphroditic or sexless ("bü-
bisch-mädchenhafte," 11687), the angels are now defined by the masculine
noun "Wetterbuben" ("confounded rascals," 11767). Mephisto sees them
as "attractive" and "lovely" (11768-69); they are "pretty," he wants to "kiss"
them (11771), and this feeling is both comfortable and "natural" (11773)
for him. His pleading with them to "look at [him] at least once!" (11777)
ends with him being pushed aside in confusion. He describes his desire in
detail, and once more with a heartfelt appeal for reciprocity: "but just for
once I'd like to see your smile — / that would afford me everlasting ecstasy! / I have in mind the way that lovers look: / it only takes a little
movement of the mouth" (11790-93). Being entranced by the beauty of
one angel in particular engenders a love in Mephisto that can actually focus on an individual: "You, there, the lad that's tall, I like you best; / That
sanctimonious air is not becoming to you, / So please give me a slightly
wanton look!" (11794-96).

Mephisto's delight and erotic interest in the angelic vision initially
seems an insouciant — or, for the suspicious, a devilish — invitation to a
visual erotic exchange. However, what distinguishes the Interment scene
from heterosexual situations is Mephisto's desire for the reciprocated gaze;
this need actually undermines his identity, especially his unilateral concupiscence directed at the opposite sex. Furthermore, the language chosen
differs from that usually employed by Mephisto in heterosexual contexts.
These differences have an essential impact on the interpretation. While his
apparently heterosexual desire merely functions to construct and maintain
his devilish identity, he actually falls in love with the boyish angels in the
Interment scene. The homoerotic desire as expressed through his gaze transgresses the borders of his once conveniently heterosexual identity by sub-
stantially affecting his cunning 'man-of-the-world' posture, and therefore

offers him redemption, that is, deliverance from his own fraudulently heterosexual hell.

From a dramaturgical perspective, Mephisto's altered state offers a practical explanation for the actual transaction by which Faust's soul falls into the hands of the angels instead of his own. As Paul Derks assures us, the "dramaturgical necessity of the Interment scene is not questioned any longer today" (283).[11] Faust is granted divine mercy due to his lifelong activity and his constant striving.[12] It is the force of heavenly love in the form of an intercession by the female spirit (formerly Margarete) that delivers him. However, Mephisto's inaction regarding the rescue of Faust's soul is the direct result of the confusion caused by his falling in love with the angels. Gilman considers it a defeat (1989, 224), but Tobin reminds us that this scene "does not have to be seen as an unalloyed critique of homosexuality" (1996, 103–104), because Mephisto is, after all, always engaged in doing God's work (cf. *Faust*, v. 340–43).

III.

Unlike Mephisto's heterosexual infatuations, his desire for the angelic boys echoes the creative energy of Eros "the creator of all!" (8479). Like Goethe's unique creation myth, this homoerotic longing that Mephisto needs to have reciprocated is possible in a universe ruled by Eros with same-sex unions as part of its design. By adapting the creation myth of Plato's *Symposion*, Goethe invents a cosmos of constant renewal that culminates in the present complex and diverse world. In stark contrast to Paracelsus's rather sterile version of the formation of Homunculus, the creation scene at the end of the "Classical Walpurgisnight" is a lavish and sensual celebration of Eros, the embodiment of Desire and Love. Eros's combination of the elements synthesizes a completely novel universe, where even Mephisto's redemption through love is possible.

The creation scene is depicted as an all-embracing orgasm, in sexually suggestive language laden with phallic symbols.[13] Eros's creative powers are "pulsations of love" (8468); the constricting vial that contains Homunculus is a glass tube that easily resembles an erect penis; the fusion of the contents of the vial with the Aegean Sea is described as a cosmic orgasm: "Jetzt flammt es, nun blitzt es, ergießet sich schon" (8473). Atkins's translation "there's the flame, there the flash, and already it empties!" wipes out the sexual connotation of *sich ergießen* which — given the shape and size of the vial — also carries the meaning of "to ejaculate."

The common gender of the participants is also of consequence in Goethe's rendition of the creation myth. Creation occurs at the exact moment Homunculus merges with elements in the Aegean Sea. The process itself is energized by Eros and begins with the 'seduction' of Homunculus by Proteus. As Schöne points out, the meaning of *verführt*, although traditionally understood in a neutral sense to mean "led away," probably includes the erotic connotation "seduced" — an assumption which is further supported by the punctuation chosen by several editors and translators since the publication of the famous Weimar edition. With the exception of Ernst Beutler — who, in his Artemis edition, substituted the following ellipsis with an exclamation mark, thereby hermeneutically sealing any further interpretation of "verführt" — the editors of the Weimar, Hamburg, and Schöne editions, as well as Stuart Atkins in his English translation, have retained the ellipsis and thus left the interpretation of the verse "Homunkulus ist es, von Proteus verführt ..." (8469) open to the reader. Unlike the emphatic and limiting exclamation mark, the ellipsis leads the reader without interruption to the intriguing phrase, "Es sind die Symptome des herrischen Sehnens" ("Those are the symptoms of passion's imperative," 8470), which, in turn, allows us to keep with Goethe's all-embracing universe of Eros — a world in which even the devil's redemption becomes conceivable.

Goethe's reference to the possibility of Mephisto's redemption has not gone unnoticed (Ammer 153; Arens 988-89; Emrich 409; Oberkogler 682; Schöne 766-67). According to Wilhelm Emrich, the devil "has to save himself from redemption; because redemption for Goethe means fundamental enlightenment of the spiritual *vis activa et formativa*, darkened by alienation" (409). In Goethe's view, Emrich states, salvation and redemption revolve "around the problem of achieving pure nature. The nature of the devil, defined by negation of all nature and therefore in exact opposition to love, can only be overcome when the devil himself succumbs to the enemy, the 'alien' elements of love" (408).

When Mephisto, the "Spirit of Eternal Negation" (1338), introduces himself to Faust in the first Study scene, he describes himself as part of the force striving for evil, insisting that his "essence is ... sin, destruction, ... Evil" (1342-44). However, even Mephisto longs occasionally for release from this "awkward world" (1364) of Faustian adventures to dive into the preferred "Eternal Emptiness" (11603). Since Mephisto represents the antithesis of creation, the creative power of love contradicts his quintessential self. Yet, by inviting reciprocity, he becomes an object of desire himself, receptive to penetration by divine love. This destabilization of Mephisto's identity by homoerotic love for the angels is crucial to any informed interpretation of the Interment scene. The angels, clearly aware of their influence on Mephisto, wish that "truth cure all / who seek self-damnation" (11803–804). Shortly after, they celebrate in song the opposing tensions that characterize his suffering. This is depicted in the contrasts between both Mephisto's feelings and those of the angels. In astute observance they sing: "Spirits used to hellish torment / felt the pangs of love instead; / even the old Master-Devil / suffered agony all over. / Hallelujah! / We have won!" (11949–53). In the German original, the "piercing pain" that "penetrates" Mephisto alludes more specifically to the Ganymedian receptivity to divine power: "Selbst der alte Satansmeister / War von *spitzer* Pein *durchdrungen*" (11951–52; my emphasis).

The universe engendered by Eros constantly creates new life, as Goethe demonstrated with the creation of Homunculus; hence a new being could originate from the love between the rogue Mephisto and the praying heavenly host. Arens agrees that for Mephisto, "love is just as two-sided an experience as it is for humans ... it is implied that even the devil is not dammed without possibility for salvation because he, too, can change from experiencing divine love" (988–89). In the context of the classical South, beauty is the force of creation and inspiration. In Plato's view, Eros is roused by sensual recognition of beauty, inducing the search for the world of ideas. Thus the encounter with Helen anticipates the possibility of Mephisto's redemption, since Phorkyas/Mephisto claims to "know well what beauty is" (8912), displaying her/his abilities to distinguish between Beauty and Ugliness. The angels are beautiful, and so are the Nordic hero Faust and his male servants. His attraction contrasts vividly with his fascination with women on the basis of their ugliness: the Old Witch of the Nordic Walpurgisnight scene, the Lamiae, and the Phorcides. Mephisto barely notices Margarete's beauty which has Faust spellbound (2619–22).[14] Incontrovertibly, he directs what appears to be lust only at female objects of desire; however, love can only be released by male subjects of desire.

IV.

The Interment scene concludes with Mephisto awakening from his trance and noticing "a mass of boils / from head to toe" (11810). Significantly enough, this follows his invitation to the "lad that's tall" (11794) to dress a little more casually – and the infamous allusion to, perhaps, the pleasures of sodomy. Having temporarily lost his composure, he becomes aware of his confusion while he regains his devilish identity. As the 'man-of-the-world' again asserts himself, the question inevitably arises: what has happened to his opportunity for redemption? The answer can be found in the "healing rash" (11814).

The Biblical allusion to Satan covering Job with festering sores (Job 2,7) is perhaps a clue; however, the cultural historian Jeffrey Richards shows that, in the Middle Ages, diseases like leprosy and others with similarly visible symptoms were seen as a punishment from God. He refers to the "knowledge" that "leprosy was the outward and visible sign of a soul corroded by sin and in particular by sexual sin" (150), as the "excessive desire for sex had been associated with the disease" (159). Therefore, Mephisto's dermatological affliction could be seen as punishment for stepping out of a prescribed role, since the redemption of the devil means the redemption of evil itself – which would disrupt the given order of the world. In light of this, the boils are a clear signal warning Mephisto to resume the place that God has assigned to him.

Friedrich and Scheithauer liken the "healing rash" to what happens during "some feverish diseases, which are overcome as soon as they have caused a skin rash. Mephisto has overcome the influence of the divine spirit like a disease and now feels he is the devil again" (278). It is also conceivable that this plague emerges from within Mephisto himself; from a devil's point of view, the overpowering desire for the angels is a 'sin' of sorts, as this desire compromises his prescripted identity. In fact, Mephisto's 'man-of-the-world' self quite typically associates desire with disease. Since the angels nearly succeed in converting him, he was almost a quisling to the forces of hell. In either case the "punishment for moral failure" (Richards 160) serves to explain Mephisto's outbreak of boils.

Mephisto's relief at having resisted the angels' temptations and the resurrection of his devilish identity is celebrated as a kind of countersalvation too, where the "parts essential to a devil all are rescued" (11813). Most likely, Mephisto uses the line sardonically (cf. Tobin 1994, 24) to reaffirm his diabolical self. According to Arens, these "parts" represent the devil's inner self (987); however, they could also refer to the male sexual organs.[15] The revelry continues with Mephisto describing the "illness" that struck him as "love-illusion" ("Liebespuk," 11813). As "all those atrocious flames have now stopped burning" (11815), he can curse the choir of angels "as it is only proper" (11816), for a devil, one might add, and thereby reestablishes his devilish identity, for cursing is part of his role. Fully recovered from this love, Mephisto looks about in amazement and asks himself: "But what has happened, where can they have gone? — You stole a march on me, you puppies!" Then he concludes: "They are flying off toward heaven with my prey" (11827). Failing in his mission, Mephisto can only ignominiously lament "and so, o shame! a great investment's wasted" (11837) and exit in bitter self-reproach: "a seasoned devil overcome / by vulgar lust, erotic silliness! / If one possessing wisdom and experience / could get involved in childish madness, / it is indeed the very height of folly / that in the end defeated him" (11838–43).

A curious disconsonance exists between Mephisto's rapturous encounter with the heavenly host and his relief when his devilish identity reasserts itself. While his disappointment at losing Faust's soul is entirely reasonable, the extremely harsh manner in which he chastises himself for having been "overcome / by vulgar lust" might be a concerted effort to dismiss his profound experience of homosexual love and to trivialize his brush with redemption. Mephisto's 'defeat' comprises his failure to capture Faust's soul and the subversion of what he calls a "seasoned devil." However, by even allowing Mephisto an opportunity for salvation via homosexual love, Goethe has redeemed homosexuality not only for his contemporaries but for readers of all generations.

V.

Recent scholarship unveils that Goethe was no stranger to homosexuality (Derks, Gilman, Tobin). Goethe reveals in the *Roman Elegies* his "abandonment" of an "eighteenth-century hierarchy, the scale that exists between the permissible sexual act and the forbidden one, between heterosexuality and homosexuality" (Gilman 1989, 221–22). As a celebration of sexuality, the *Erotica Romana*[16] show Goethe's positive regard of sexuality, including the entire spectrum from purest pleasure to the act of procreation. As an expression of love, it is integral to the all-encompassing Eros.[17] The fact that

Goethe was open to, and even familiar with, homosexuality and homosexual practices[18] implies that all references to homosexuality and homosexual acts in *Faust* are deliberate. Moreover, in Goethe's opinion the male is "aesthetically far more beautiful, superior, more perfect than the woman,"[19] and therefore homosexual love between men, although an "aberration" is just as "natural" as heterosexual love.[20]

Robert Tobin has shown that Goethe's "positive understanding of homosexuality rests in large part on his belief that it points to heterosexuality" (1996, 109). While it is quite possible that Goethe sees homosexual desires leading to heterosexual desires (especially since the eighteenth century did not categorize the 'homosexual' as is done today), this does not apply to Mephisto, if 'pointing' is interpreted as an evolution from homosexual to heterosexual behavior. The only beneficial influence on Mephisto's devilish self is precisely homosexual desire; indeed, what could be more 'unnatural' for a devil — and therefore redeem him — than yearning for an angel's loving attention. A capacity for love is not part of the devil's identity because by loving he relinquishes his opposition to the 'Good'.

Goethe adapts the essentially Christian concept of the 'divine' by fusing it with classical thinking and rejecting Christianity's exclusion of nature's various forms. Based on this amalgamation and with a view of Eros as the ennobling and redeeming power, Goethe pursues his theory on creation, evolution, and death until its logical conclusion — openly embracing the role of homoeroticism in both creation and redemption. The homosexual gaze thus proves to be the more transgressive and potentially redeeming for the devil, since his love challenges his own identity *by negating the negation*. That this is possible was made clear in the very beginning: Mephisto is "a part of that force / which, always willing evil, always produces good" (1335-36). As Mephisto is both part of the divine plan and the antithesis of the Good, his opposition to the divine order is expressed in the heterosexual scenes, while in "Interment," Mephisto is closer to the divine than ever before. It is through homoeroticism that his redemption becomes possible — a logical conclusion within the classical context, where Eros between men is naturally a higher form of love than that between men and women.

Notes

*Some of these ideas were first presented at the "Body/Gender/Identity" Conference (McGill University, Montreal, April 1996). For her irreplaceable help editing this essay, I wish to express my gratitude to Janis Pereira and the editors of this volume. For the German Primary text and the Paralipomena, I have chosen Albrecht Schöne's superbly researched latest edition of *Faust*. Unless otherwise indicated, the translated *Faust* quotes are from Stuart Atkins, about whom McMillan notes: "Atkins's translation is lively and truly modern ..." (4). All other translations are my own unless otherwise stated.

[1] I am referring to a conversation with the writer and philanthropist Johannes Falk (1768-1826), as quoted in Falk's book: "Ja, wenn ich es nur je dahin noch bringen könnte, daß ich ein Werk verfaßte—aber ich bin zu alt dazu—daß die Deutschen mich so ein funfzig oder hundert Jahre lang hintereinander recht gründlich ver-wünschten und aller Orten und Enden mir nichts als Übels nachsagten; das sollte mich außer Maßen ergetzen" (91). "... wenn sie in der Fortsetzung von *Faust* etwa zufällig an die Stelle kämen, wo der Teufel selbst Gnad' und Erbarmen vor Gott fin-det; das, denke ich doch, vergeben sie mir sobald nicht!" (92). "Nahm doch selbst die geistreiche Frau v. Stael es übel, daß ich in dem Engelgesang, Gott Vater gegen-über, den Teufel so gutmüthig gehalten hätte; sie wollte ihn durchaus grimmiger. Was soll es nun werden, wenn sie ihm auf einer noch höheren Staffel und vielleicht gar einmal im Himmel wieder begegnet?" (92-93).

[2] I use the term "love" to define a caring or emotional attraction connected to sexual desire. "Desire" refers to sexual attraction. I understand "homoerotic" and "homo-sexual" placed on a continuum; one creating potential for the other, with "homo-erotic" referring to homosexual love or desire.

[3] One of the many examples is the murder of Baucis and Philemon in Act V of *Faust II*.

[4] This is expressed in many situations, for example: "I've had enough of this sober tone, / it's time to play the real devil again" (2009-10).

[5] Mephisto's character as a very sexual one is also indicated by ample references to *Faust* made by Leopold von Sacher-Masoch in *Venus im Pelz* (Venus in furs).

[6] Goethe, *Faust* Texte, Schöne Edition 553; my trans.

[7] Goethe, *Faust* Texte, Schöne Edition 554; my trans.

[8] Goethe uses the term in this meaning in *Götter, Helden und Wieland*, when Mer-kurius asks for Wieland with the words: "Und wenn er Ganymeds Hofmeister wäre, sollt er mir her" (HA 4: 205). Friedrich Maximilian Klinger invokes the same symbol-ism in *Fausts Leben, Taten und Höllenfahrt* (1791). Pope Alexander VI attempts to seduce Leviathan, who in this text is Faust's hellish aid. Leviathan, disgusted by the

offer from a contemptible human, greets him later in hell: "Ich hoffe, der Kitzel ist Euch nun vergangen, den Teufel zum Ganymed machen zu wollen" (223).

[9]He expressed his aversion to a musical offering in similarily derogatory terms during "Nordic Walpurgis Night": "There, listen, instruments start blaring! / A hellish screech! But soon one gets past caring" (4051).

[10]"Was euch nicht angehört / Müsset ihr meiden, / Was euch das Innre stört / Dürft ihr nicht leiden. / Dringt es gewaltig ein / Müssen wir tüchtig sein. / Liebe nur Lie-bende / Führet herein!"

[11]Adorno already pointed to the neccessity of this construction.

[12]Cf. Goethe's letter to Zelter of March, 19, 1827 (HA Briefe 4: 219) and his expla-nation to Eckermann on February 2, 1829 (Eckermann 279).

[13]Kurt R. Eissler interprets Goethe's poetic creation as a phantastic usurpation of the female power to give birth; he points out the many metaphors in which Goethe de-scribes this creative process as a birthing process (cf. 117ff.).

[14]It is true that, objectively, Margarete might not be much to look at, and that Faust only pays attention to her because he sees "in every woman a Helen of Troy" (2610). However, it is striking that Mephisto is never attracted to a woman's beauty at all, but pays so much attention to male beauty.

[15]Frustrated with the limitations of his mother tongue, Goethe invokes the pagan fertility god with an immense phallus in the thirty-eighth Venetian Epigram: "Give me not 'tail' but another word, o Priapus, / For, being a German I'm evilly plagued as a poet ..." (Roman Elegies 151).

[16]Regarding the history of these texts, see Ammer.

[17]Epigram 40 of the Venetian Epigrams suggests that even though Goethe preferred heterosexual relations, homosexual ones, and specifically anal intercourse, were not an alien concept to him. "Boys I loved, too, to be sure, yet I am fonder of girls; / if I have my fill of her as a girl, she still serves me as a boy." I am using Eissler's transla-tion here (1348). Eissler states for these Venetian Epigrams: "Remarkable, however, is Goethe's solution of the homosexual problem. As I have suggested, his relationship to Cornelia had the character of that to a mirror-image and afforded him the oppor-tunity to project the image of his own body onto that of a female body" (1347).

[18]See Derks and Tobin for a number of references about such documented knowl-edge.

[19]This translation is provided by Sander Gilman in Sexuality 1989, 226. He quotes from Goethes Gespräche, ed. Wolfgang Herwig, vol. 3: 1825–1832 (Zürich: Artemis, 1972) 603.

[20]Cf. Goethe's conversation with Hofrat von Müller, April 7, 1830 (GA 23: 686). From a similar perspective, Thomas Mann argues in "Die Ehe im Übergang," that precisely because "homoeroticism is erotic aestheticism" it is tied to death. It is the usefullness of love ("Nützlichkeit") that he evaluates—and a nonprocreative love (in the sense of begetting offspring) is therefore immoral (272).

Thomas Mann's Queer Schiller

Robert Tobin

TONIO KRÖGER, IN THOMAS MANN'S 1903 short story of the same name, offers his beloved Hans Hansen the gift of Friedrich Schiller's *Don Carlos*, a play so beautiful "that it gives one a jolt, that there is, so to speak, a bang ..." (210).[1] According to Kröger, it is a play about a lonely king, betrayed by a marquis out of love for a prince. Hansen, perhaps intrigued by violent images, does want to know how a play could have a "bang" ("knallen"), but otherwise does not pay much attention, preferring the more virile art of horse riding. Unlike Hansen, however, Mann's readers have paid attention to Tonio's analysis of *Don Carlos* — and usually found it wanting. While Anthony Heilbut, in his excellent new biography of Mann, describes Kröger's interpretation as "the homosexualizing of *Don Carlos* — to show the private uses of art" (161), most academics, more cautious by nature than freelance biographers perhaps, have simply viewed the boy's analysis as a misreading. Is this queer Schiller in Mann's text "homosexualizing" for a purpose or "misreading"? A closer reading of Schiller's texts themselves shows that *Don Carlos* lends itself willingly and elegantly to appropriation by Mann and indeed other queer and querying readers.

Thomas Mann's interest in Schiller's possibly deviant sexuality was openly discussed in his household. In a diary entry of August 16, 1931, Klaus Mann recounts the topic of conversation at one dinner party at his father's: "Was Schiller homosexual?" (*Tagebücher* 19). Nor is *Don Carlos* the only bit of Schilleriana that Mann uses homosexually in his writings. In *Schwere Stunde* (*Difficult Hour*), published in 1905, a couple of years after *Tonio Kröger*, Schiller appears as a bookish man, who must mentally tell his wife that he will never belong completely to her, because of the strong Hansen-like Goethe, hovering in the background (Heilbut). In one of the last texts Mann ever wrote, his *Essay on Schiller* (*Versuch über Schiller*), composed in 1955, he states more explicitly that the great love of Schiller's life was none other than Goethe:

The great adventure of his life, his experience of passion, of passionate attraction and repulsion, of deep friendship, deep desire
and admiration, of give and take, of jealousy, of melancholy, envy
and proud self-assertion, of lasting affective tension — was an event
between man and man, between him, the completely masculine,
and another man, to whom he wanted to attribute a feminine manner, while others, like Schlegel, emphasized precisely the masculine
in him — it was his relationship with *Goethe. (Leiden* 433)

For Mann, it is clear that Goethe and Schiller bring issues of gender and
same-sex relationships to the fore. Perhaps it is time to follow up on
Mann's hints.

Other readers of Mann's era agreed that there was something homosex-
ual in Schiller. The author was prominently cited in early homosexual
emancipation circles, which, incidentally, included a great-grandson of
Schiller, Alexander von Gleichen-Rußwurm. As early as 1891, a certain G.
Portig published a monograph entitled *Schiller in seinem Verhältnis zur
Freundschaft und Liebe, sowie in seinem inneren Verhältnis zu Goethe
(Schiller in his Relationship to Friendship and Love, as well as in his Rela-
tionship to Goethe)*. In his attempts to use the classics of German literature
to defend same-sex love, Elisar von Kupffer referred to Schiller in his work
*Lieblingminne und Freundesliebe in der Weltliteratur (Love of Favorites
and Ardor for Friends in World Literature)*. In an essay from 1930 entitled
"The Love of Friends as a Cultural Factor: A Word to Germany's Male
Youth," Adolf Brand, the editor of *Der Eigene: Ein Blatt für männliche Kultur (The Exceptional: A Magazine for Male Culture)*, a journal devoted to
promoting erotic male bonding, mentioned both Goethe and Schiller in a
list that also included Anacreon, Pindar, Virgil, Horace, Hafis, Michelangelo, and Shakespeare, all as proponents of male-male love (Oosterhuis
151). Another member of the circle, a physician named Otto Kiefer who
wrote for *The Exceptional* under the pseudonym "Reiffegg," specifically
discussed *Don Carlos* in an essay entitled "Über die Bedeutung der Jünglingsliebe für unsere Zeit" ("On the Importance of the Love of Youths for
our Time"), lamenting that "already now in our material, egotistical time,
boys and youths who let themselves be beaten bloody for their beloved
friend, as Schiller reports of Don Carlos, are becoming rare" (in Oosterhuis
171). *The Exceptional* reprinted Schiller's ode "Die Freundschaft" ("Friend-

ship"), an act that was deemed immoral in one of the many court cases against the journal. In 1914, the prominent homosexual sexologist Magnus Hirschfeld discussed Schiller's work, particularly the *Malteser*-fragment in his treatise, *Die Homosexualität des Mannes und des Weibes (Homosexuality in the Male and the Female)*, according to Paul Derks. In October 1927, a certain Herr Wegener published an article called "Die Homoeroten in Schillers Prosaschriften" ("The Homophiles in Schiller's Prose Writings") in the homosexual journal *Blätter für die Menschenrechte (Papers for Human Rights)*. As late as 1940, Gad Beck and his gay friends were reading and finding points of identification in Don Carlos and the Marquis de Posa:

> I consider both these figures gay, always this exalted Schiller –
> "O!", it doesn't get any gayer than that! When Carlos and Posa appear on the stage, they play a love pair, without any doubt, and whoever has not noticed just does not want to see it. (70)

So loud was the noise made in homosexual circles about Schiller that the satirical magazine *Jugend (Youth)* – not necessarily aimed at homosexual audiences – took note with a cartoon in which the statues of Schiller and Goethe in the Weimar Poets' Monument hastily withdraw their hands from each other, as Schiller whispers, "Wolfgang, let go of my hand! Dr. Magnus Hirschfeld is coming!"[2] An earlier image in the same journal, from October 16, 1897, showed two naked male youths resting together on an outcropping overlooking a bridge and a tower, accompanied by a quote from Schiller's ode, "Die Künstler" ("The Artists"). Thus, Thomas Mann's queering of Schiller is at home in a large body of early twentieth-century German thought.

The accusation that these early twentieth-century homosexuals were projecting their own historical biases into these texts by discovering "homosexuals" – products, after all, of mid to late nineteenth-century German medical discourses – in an eighteenth-century text loses some of its force in discussions of *Don Carlos*. Schiller, who had a chair in history at the University of Jena, knew his history well enough to write a lengthy book on the Spanish involvement in the Netherlands, in which he discusses historical figures such as King Philip II of Spain extensively. He knew perfectly well that he had changed historical dates to suit his fiction. (For instance, as Batley notes, Don Carlos, Elizabeth, and Egmont were all dead twenty years before the defeat of the Armada, an event which is none-theless mentioned in his play.) Schiller also knew that King Philip was actually forty-one at the time that the events with his son and his second wife were transpiring, not nearly sixty, as the play would have one believe (Kittler). He was also aware, as were many of his own contemporaries, of the anachronism of putting late eighteenth-century ideas about the rights of humanity into the mouth of the Marquis de Posa, a sixteenth-century Mal-tese knight (K.-D. Müller). Schiller himself concedes, in his *Briefe über Don Carlos* (*Letters on Don Carlos*), that Posa's belief in the freedom of the individual is the "favorite subject of our decade" (2: 251).[3] Historical accu-racy of this sort was in no way the prime motivator of his writing. This anachronism is not a problem for Schiller; in fact, to modern readers Schil-ler's own example suggests some possibilities for the uses of history in lit-erature.

Despite Schiller's own appropriation of history, and the queer tradition of appropriating Schiller, most responses to his plays have been decidedly straight. Since the nineteenth century, criticism has tended to see Schiller in terms of stirring defenses of liberty, humanity, and freedom or analyses of the concept of history and the characteristics of genre. The subtitle of Wolfgang Wittkowski's collection of essays on Schiller is typical: "Art, Hu-manity, and Politics of the Late Enlightenment." As far as the play *Don Carlos* goes, the most famous lines in criticism have been the Marquis de Posa's strident denunciations of monarchical abuse of power and ringing pleas for freedom of thought: "I cannot be a servant of lords" (3020) and "Give me / Freedom of thought" (3213-14). Reviews of productions of *Don Carlos* in *Theater heute* in the last five years suggest that the theatrical world has also seen nothing particularly revolutionary in Schiller's con-structions of gender and sexuality. K. D. Schmidt's production in Berlin's Maxim Gorki Theater in 1997 could deal with the male-male bonding in the play only in an embarrassed and embarrassing adolescent way. Simi-larly, a review of an English production of *Don Carlos* in *The Times Liter-ary Supplement* also suggests it was sexually quite conservative (Ashton).

As Jane Bennett points out, however, confining Schiller to the purely abstract, to concepts like liberty and humanity, vitiates some of his most heartfelt beliefs. Schiller was quite capable of writing abstract theses, and chose instead to write plays. In the abstract theses that he did write, he went to bat for aesthetics — for that realm of experience that attempted to bridge the gap between body and mind, that attempted to connect sensual pleasure with thought. Schiller's hope, in *Über die ästhetische Erziehung des Menschen* (*Letters on the Aesthetic Education of Humanity*), was that people could *will* to do what they *ought* to do. This 'willing' is ultimately a sensual, physical, bodily act. The drama attempts, as literally as possible, to flesh out the moral problems that Schiller confronts, by giving these problems to people with actual bodies. By ignoring the sensual, the physical, the bodily in Schiller's dramas, readers have tended to turn him into an intellectual, conceptual artist, who is at odds with his philosophy of art.

Schiller had begun his career with writings on the mind-body problem, inspired by medical models that denied the separation of mind and body. In *Don Carlos*, the connections between mind and body are made evident in the way the characters frequently turn scarlet or pale: the priest Domingo loses his color making a particularly nefarious suggestion (2102); Posa turns pale upon hearing of Carlos's love (2282); Posa refers to the blushes of embarrassed lady lovers (2379); Carlos turns red when he hears that the Queen will see him (2448); the King complains that the Queen made him turn red before his entire court (2623). This far from exhaustive list emphasizes the involvement of the body in Schiller's play. The moment in the play when the King cries succeeds in moving Tonio Kröger precisely because it is about the ability of bodily functions to break through strict intellectual and moral self-control. *Don Carlos* itself therefore avoids the reduction of themes to abstract concepts, such as freedom and humanity, and any exclusion of the body.

Certainly, Schiller's passionate devotion to friendship seems at times to move into the bodily realm. In addition to the ode "Friendship" (1782), which was originally going to appear in a novel with the mellifluous title *Aus den Briefen Julius' an Raphael* (*From the Letters of Julius to Raphael*), the 1789 short story *Spiel des Schicksals* (*Sport of Destiny*) demonstrates Schiller's powerful interest in friendship and its sexual implications. In *Sport of Destiny*, a prince is quite taken with a young man named G*, "the perfect image of blooming health and Herculean strength." Although the Prince admires G*'s mind, it is his exterior, his body, that really turns him on: "If the Prince was fascinated by the mind of his young companion, this seductive exterior carried away his sensuality irresistibly" (5: 36). This relationship clearly goes beyond friendship: "Equality of age, harmony of inclinations and character established quickly a relationship between both of them that possessed all the fire and violence of love" (5: 36-37). In the course of time, count Josef Martinengo (the only character with a name,

and an Italian sounding one at that, which makes him sexually suspicious
in eighteenth-century northern Europe), manages to insinuate himself into
the good graces of the Prince. In order to have the Prince all for himself,
the Italian count urges the Prince to indulge in unnamed "vices." Knowing that "nothing is more entitled to a bolder intimacy than the coknowl-
edge of secretly held weaknesses, the Count awakens passions in the Prince
that had until now still slumbered": "He carried him away to the kind of
excesses that tolerate the fewest witnesses and accessories" (5: 39). Derks argues convincingly that these unnamed, secret vices are very probably sexual; the fact that the Prince subsequently has a string of other male "favorites" allows one to presume that the vices are homosexual in nature.

The relationships related in *Sport of Destiny* are typical for many of
Schiller's works, which tend, as Kühnemann writes about *Don Carlos*, to
"wallow in men's greatness" (in Orton 250). In her outstanding piece on
Schiller, Stephanie Hammer argues that among the symptoms of the "diseased mythos" of masculinity in Schiller's plays are the "intermale relationships so passionate that they interrupt and violate the standard circuit of
male homosocial bonding" (155). In this world of "murky male desires"
(155), she maintains that Schiller implies "that men's relationships with
each other are, at least under patriarchy, both murderous and covertly
homosexual" (167). Because of the intensity of these male friendships,
many of Schiller's writings continue to be included in various compila-
tions of gay literature (see, for instance, Bullough et al.).

Hammer writes specifically about the trilogy *Wallenstein* (1798/99),
"the dramatic creation most overtly concerned with manhood, homosocial bonds" (161). Although they rarely mention the sinister sides of this
male bonding, it is certainly true that modern queer readers have frequently
looked to *Wallenstein* as a source for gay male history. To begin with, the
play is predominately masculine: its characters are mostly men primarily interested in the male world of war. Hammer is right to quote Eve Sedgwick,
who points out that, "for a man to be a man's man is separated only by an
invisible, carefully blurred, always-already crossed line from 'being interested in men'" (in Hammer 167). Indeed, Wallenstein does seem to wander
across that line. In *Wallensteins Tod* (*Wallenstein's Death*), Wallenstein approaches Max, reminding him of past help, and cries out: "I myself was
your nursing woman, I wasn't ashamed of small services, I tended you
with womanly caring activity" (2149-51).

In this passage, Wallenstein's femininity is emphasized repeatedly. Gender-bending is a frequent phenomenon in Schiller's other plays as well. Johanna, in *Die Jungfrau von Orleans* (*The Maid of Orleans*), possesses "a masculine heart" (196). Maria Stuart, in the play that bears her name, trumps Queen Elizabeth with the declaration: "*I* am your king" (2451). For an author who is always ready to attach gender to the binary oppositions he loves to create — see such notorious poems as "Kastraten und Männer" ("Castrati and Men," 1782) and "Würde der Frauen" ("Dignity of Women," 1796) — Schiller is surprisingly flexible.

Schiller's notes for his planned play *Die Malteser* (*The Maltese*) contain some of the most remarkably open discussions of male-male sensuality of any literary text from the eighteenth century, even if one hesitates to call them, as Hirschfeld did, proof of an intimate understanding of homosexuality. The *Maltese* was going to be about the Knights of Malta, an organization that Schiller perceived as an exemplary all-male secret society. In a letter to Wilhelm von Humboldt of October 5, 1795, Schiller wrote enthusiastically that the play consisted exclusively of male characters: "The plot is simple and heroic, as are the characters, who are at the same time exclusively masculine, and it is therefore the representation of a sublime idea, the kind that I love" (Seidel 1: 174). While, in his *Letters on Don Carlos*, Schiller denies that passionate friendship is at the center of *Don Carlos*, he states that that subject is reserved for a later project, which turned out to be the *Maltese*.

While many of Schiller's plays have large numbers of male characters, the *Maltese*-fragment goes beyond Schiller's usual generalized interest in the homosocial and masculine realm to address male-male love quite specifically. Two of the main characters, Crequi and St. Priest, were to be lover and beloved. In one projected table of contents, Schiller refers to a "Scene of the lover with the beloved" (3: 177). He clarifies the distinction between the two in a footnote to his plans for the project: "But only one is the lover, the active one; the younger and beloved behaves passively. But the lover acts with a blind passion, forgetting the whole world, and verges on the criminal" (3: 173). This understanding of male-male love as something inherently directional and not necessarily reciprocal or egalitarian is typical for the ancient Greeks, as both modern historians of sexuality and eighteenth-century classicists know. Therefore, Schiller alludes directly to the ancient Greeks in his notes on the two men: "Love of the Greek youths for each other" (3: 173).

Male-male love in ancient Greece was well known in the eighteenth century. In fact, it was one of the few arenas in which same-sex behavior could be discussed with any degree of openness. At times, the Greek love was regarded as asexual friendship. More often, though, it was understood as having a sexual component. Schiller did not steer away from this component. He refers to "the most dignified and accurate use of the motif of the love of the two young knights in its entire range" (3: 170). This range includes the sensual: "Their love is of the purest beauty, but it is however necessary not to remove from it the sensual character with which it is attached to nature. It may and must be felt that it is a transfer, a surrogate, of sexual love, and an effect of a natural drive ..." (3: 172). Although Schiller begins with the obligatory assurance that this love is "pure," his insistence on its sensual nature, its similarity to sexual love, and its naturalness is quite astonishing for this era. As remarkable as his beliefs are, though, his determination in arguing that this love has to be *felt*, rather than merely *thought*, fits in with his writings on aesthetics.

The *surrogate* nature of this male-male love appears elsewhere in Schiller's notes: "The love of men in the play is the completely valid surrogate for the love of women and replaces that love for poetic purposes in all parts, indeed, [the love of men] even exceeds the effects [of the love of women]" (3: 173). In another passage, Schiller equates Crequi's love with heterosexual love, or at least indicates that it is indistinguishable from such love: "His passion is true sexual love and manifests itself through a detailed tender care, through raging jealousy, through sensual glorification of the figure, through other sensual symptoms" (3: 173). This medical vocabulary also recurs frequently: "The love of the two knights to each other must have all the symptoms of sexual love" (3: 172). What these "other sensual symptoms" of love might be are not spelled out, but — especially since they are medical, and thus have to do with the body — it seems highly likely that they are the physical aspects of love. In any case, Schiller is willing and almost anxious to exhibit this love, even though it might arouse suspicions: "The lover may show his tenderness blatantly, even though that might appear suspicious" (3: 171–72).

Schiller's use of the words "surrogate" ("Surrogat"), "suspicious" ("verdächtig"), "appear" ("scheinen"), "symptom" ("Symptom") suggests that he ultimately differentiates between male-male love, a sickly surrogate with a suspicious appearance, and male-female love, which is presumably the real thing (it does not "appear" to be anything) and healthy to boot. At the same time, however, this male-male love, despite its sickliness, in other ways exceeds in merit the male-female love. Moreover, to compound the paradoxes that surround same-sex love in Schiller, the two categories of love are virtually indistinguishable — despite the difference between surrogate and original. The imitative, appearance-oriented, sickly-symptomatic side of this male-male love makes it difficult for modern readers (like Derks, for example) to accept Hirschfeld's view which understands Schiller's depiction of the love of the Maltese as a positive one. The quality of the homosexual counterfeit of heterosexual desire, though, is so good that same-sex desire becomes, in Schiller, as in Goethe (see Tobin), an apt symbol for the power of language to operate as a pharmakon, in the Derridean sense. In short: in Schiller's world, same-sex desire, like language, is a *surrogate* for the *real thing*, heterosexual desire, but it is not always possible to distinguish the original from the copy.

The classic *pharmakon* is the poison that cures, the curative that kills, the drug that can do both good and bad. The doubled nature of the German word *Gift* ("poison," but etymologically related to the positively charged English "gift") is thematized throughout *Don Carlos*.[4] Don Carlos refers to what he thinks is the Page's knowledge of his affair with the Queen as "poison" (1310); Domingo, who speaks eloquently of the two-sidedness of words (1974–78), believes that the "poison of the innovators" (2039) is already lurking in the hearts of the Queen and the Marquis. When Domingo suggests that the Queen and Carlos are having an affair, the King demands a "drop of poison" from him (2734). The Marquis hopes that Eboli's poison has not crossed her lips, equating "poison" specifically with words (4123). The King's knowledge that this "poison" can also be a curative makes it a pharmakon: "poison itself, / I find, can, in benevolent natures, / Nobly become something better" (3265–67). Conversely, the Marquis knows that some healing interventions are almost poisonous: "The remedy / Is almost as bad as the danger" (3458–59). As these characters learn about the positive sides of poison and the negative sides of cures, they are also learning the trickiness of language, the impossibility of determining its sincerity and authenticity, and the multiple, sometimes self-contradictory interpretations that it provokes, as well as the vagaries of sexuality.

The Grand Inquisitor, with his rhetorical questions, links the pharmakon specifically with issues of gender in a speech that begins when he grills the King: "Was ... poison no longer poison?" (5199–201). Connecting pharmaceutical poisons with fundamental truths, he demands to know: "Had between good and evil / And true and false the partition fallen?" (5201–02). Then linking these fundamental truths with gender, he compares masculine fidelity with feminine moodiness: "What is constancy, / What is male loyalty, when in a halfhearted / Moment a sixty-year-old rule / Melts like a woman's mood?" (5303–06). It is clear that the collapse of distinctions between man and woman has everything to do with sexuality because the point at issue is Posa's seduction of the King – a seduction that the King, almost maudlin in his dotage, could not resist because of the irresistibility of the younger man's eyes: "I looked in his eyes" (5207).

The Grand Inquisitor's questions are rhetorical, of course. While he argues for the one-sidedness of poison, denying its pharmaceutical power, the reader and the audience know that in this play the Inquisition has consistently stood for the manipulation of language and the constant reinterpretation of deeds based on context. It is, for instance, willing to countenance the sexual relationship between the Princess of Eboli and the King for the higher good that their relationship would bring, as the Princess points out: "although you have already proved to me / That cases were possible where the Church / Knew how to use even the *bodies* of her young daughters / For higher purposes" (2112–15). The Marquis specifically targets the false virtue of Eboli, as someone who does the right thing, but for all the wrong reasons – reasons having to do with the power of the Church. Thus, the Grand Inquisitor's insistence on absolute truths is only evidence for his willingness to manipulate language (and sexuality) to further his means.

To recapitulate, same-sex tensions exist in much of Schiller's work, and the difficulty of interpreting those tensions make them paradigmatic for the pharmakon, the fundamentally undecidable substance that characterizes literature and that is also thematized in his writings. How then do these same-sex tensions play out in *Don Carlos*? Why do Thomas Mann's character Tonio Kröger and some of the members of the homosexual emancipation movement in early twentieth-century Germany alight specifically on *Don Carlos* when queering Schiller? If one were to explode the play and pick up the pieces from the floor of the library or the theater, one would find a number of shards and fragments that ring queer bells and strike queer notes. When Carlos and the Marquis reminisce about their childhood days together, Carlos remembers Posa's sailor's outfit (208), which is the kind of detail that Thomas Mann certainly would remember – Tadzio, for instance, making his first appearance in *Death in Venice* in a sailor's outfit. A somber note rings out early in the play, when the Marquise of Mondecar expresses gruesome delight at the prospect of an auto-da-fé in Madrid. This may bring the etymology of "faggot" to the mind of some queer readers.[5] Furthermore, in act one, scene four, the Queen sees a blooming hyacinth, a flower that brings to mind the story of the mythological male athlete after whom it was named, who died as a result of the rivalry between Apollo and Zephyr, who both loved him (527). Finally, Don Carlos and the Marquis de Posa are repeatedly identified as queer fellows. The King, wondering whether to work with the Marquis, calls him a "queer fellow" ("Sonderling," 2848). The Marquis also uses the same word to refer to himself as the "queer fellow" (3387). The Princess of Eboli, trying to seduce Don Carlos, finds that her heterosexual charms have no effect and uses the same name for him: "all my efforts slide / Off this queer fellow, smooth as a snake" (1736-37). She asks him for the key to the "magically locked closet" ("zauberisch verschloßnen Schrank," 1742) that protects him. It is now our job to try to unlock that *closet* and see if it produces something more than a handful of queer fragments.

While the most obvious male-male erotics of the play *Don Carlos* might seem to be between the Prince and the Marquis, Tonio Kröger actually concentrates on the King, Philip II, whom he interprets as a lonely man desperately in need of a friend. Mann, of course, had done his homework. Schiller himself wrote that the dramatic tension of the play had to be in the King and his complicated feelings. Kröger in no way misreads the play when he sees that Philip II is in need of a friend. Indeed, the King pleads to God: "I pray to you for a friend" (2811). Carlos, who wants to be that friend and love his father, puts his desires somewhat more effusively than modern readers are used to, rejoicing in "the bliss of this kiss" (1040). The King, however, doesn't want his son, but rather his son's friend. In his superb essay on *Don Carlos*, Kittler writes about the ways in which the play — reversing normal psychoanalysis — recodes the bourgeois family to make comments about politics. Here, Schiller shows his virtuosity with familial constellations by neatly transposing the Oedipal complex: while the son desires his father's bride, the father desires his son's friend.

By the end of the play, the competition between father and son for the friend becomes quite explicit. The King cries: "He had a friend who died / For him — for him!" (5026-27). The King wants someone to die for him: "Had he died for me!" he continues, "I was fond of him, very fond"

(5047-48). This competition hinges on the issue of age. At first the King assumes that Carlos is too young to compete with him, but then he comes to realize that he has become too old to be attractive to the Knight from Malta: "Not / Philip does he sacrifice to Carlos, only / The old man to the young" (5065-67). (Interestingly, Philip is, in the play, about as old as the "sixty-year-old rule" that the Grand Inquisitor asserts has been abandoned in womanly moodiness.) Rejoicing in his youthful attractiveness, Carlos crows that Posa had compromised himself and died for him, not for the King: "...to save me, he / Wrote a letter to Orange — O God! / It was the first lie of his life! / To save me, he threw himself at the death / That he suffered" (4801-05).

Carlos admits that the Marquis might have dallied with the King: "Your scepter was the plaything of his hands" (4808). In these exchanges, the frequent repetition of the verb "buhlen" ("to compete, often sexually; to woo, to have an affair") lends them a physical and lusty nature that allows for a sexual understanding of the reference to the King's "scepter": "You dared to compete [buhlen] for his friendship" (4814). By the end of the play, the King too uses an unusually frank and physical vocabulary, saying that he is "lüstern" (sexually desirous, lewd) to speak with the spirit of the former king (5139). He justifies his attempted relationship with the Marquis with a similar expression indicating his physical desire for another person: "Desire arose in me for a human being" ("Mich lüstete nach einem Menschen," 5222). The excitement in this play then would be precisely what Tonio Kröger picks up on: the eruption of physical desire in an older man for another man, a desire that displays itself most dramatically in the issuance from the male of bodily fluids — fluids that happen to be tears.

If the relationship between the King, the Marquis, and the Prince is a kind of queer reversal of the Oedipal triangle, with the father competing for the son's friend, then is not the relationship between the Prince, the Queen, and the King a straight Oedipal complex, with the son competing for the father's bride? Not exactly, because the Prince is in love with a woman his own age, a woman whom he thought he was going to marry, and whom his father has only recently taken in marriage. He is actually in love with a step-mother. His story is strikingly similar to the motif of the lovesick prince which plays such a prominent role in Goethe's novel of 1796, *Wilhelm Meisters Lehrjahre* (*Wilhelm Meister's Apprenticeship*). In the novel, the prince is also in love with and pines for the young bride of his father. The similarities in the constellation of the homosexual and heterosexual triangles that confront both Wilhelm Meister and Don Carlos are striking: just as Wilhelm Meister identifies with the lovesick prince and at the same time clearly goes through homosexual phases, Don Carlos sees himself in the same position as the lovesick prince – in love with the young bride of his father – and will assign his love to a number of men, as we shall see. In addition, one of Wilhelm's lovesick phases, first mentioned in the sequel of 1832, *Wilhelm Meisters Wanderjahre* (*Wilhelm Meister's Journeyman Years*), is his love of the fisherman's boy, whose corpse also exerts a physical attraction on Wilhelm, in a way strongly reminiscent of the attractiveness to Carlos of Posa's "great beautiful death" (4796).[6]

The reader of Schiller's play can hardly fault the Prince for desiring his step-mother. The play however paints this love in the direst terms. Carlos himself tells Posa that his passion for the Queen stands in opposition to "the customs of the world, / The order of nature and Rome's laws" (276-77). By his own admission, it is a desperate and evil love: "I love without hope – viciously" (282). The Princess of Eboli refers to "this strange unnatural behavior"(1639). She puts it most exactly in her monologue in act two, scene nine: "So much / Is clear – he loves what he should not" (1890-01). Given the actual facts of the relationship, the play's insistence that such love is unnatural, forbidden, and a crime against nature and humanity seems overstated. This forbidden, hopeless, vicious, unnatural love – who could restrict it merely to the love of a step-mother who was rightfully one's own bride? Is it not more likely that this ostensible love for the Queen has, in fact, a slightly different constitution?

The Duke of Alba gives the reader a hint as to the true nature of the unnatural love. He relates that, when the Queen enters the room in which he and Don Carlos are fighting, the young man's alleged passion for the Queen curiously causes him to kiss the Duke: "The Queen, upon hearing the din, opens: / The room ... His arm freezes – he flies to my neck – / I feel a hot kiss" (1954-59). This suggests that the physical part of the Prince's relationship with the Queen tends to be carried out with men. The vocabulary about "crimes against nature" and "unnatural love" makes sense when one understands that the real object of Carlos's love of the Queen is the Marquis. Carlos's treatment of the Queen immediately after the death of the Marquis suggests strongly that the love of the Queen was merely a symbolic substitution for the love of the Marquis. Now that Posa is dead, he can no longer even befriend her: "I can give to you my friendship / So little as yesterday my love / To another woman" (5332-34). As soon as Posa is gone, there turns out to be no need for any love affair to explain Carlos's emotions.

When the Queen accuses the Marquis of pursuing admiration, using that sexually laden verb "buhlen," she strikes a blow at him that suggests an undercurrent of erotic jealousy between the two: "Oh, now — now I'm learning to understand you! You were / only competing for admiration" (4385-86). Upon plumbing the depths of the relationship between the men, she decides to give up on men altogether: "Go! / I'll never esteem a man highly again" (4392-93). The Marquis, interested only in his all-male world, is delighted: "O God! Life *is* beautiful!" (4394). The apparent Oedipal desires of the young Prince have turned out to be merely a cover for emotions that really describe the relationship between the two men.

The relation between the Prince and the Marquis is the most obvious homoerotic love affair in *Don Carlos*. It is the relationship to which Reiff-egg, for instance, alludes in his essay in *The Exceptional*. Although Tonio Kröger does not specifically refer to this relationship, he reenacts it in his love of Hans Hansen. But the understanding of the possible queerness of the relationship between the two men does not emerge first in the early twentieth century. Schiller seems to be reacting to anxieties about the nature of the relationship in his *Letters on Don Carlos*, first published in 1788. The "Third Letter" begins with the notion that passionate friendship is at the root of this tragedy: "You claimed recently to have found in Don Carlos proof that *passionate friendship* could be just as moving a subject for tragedy as *passionate love*" (2: 230). Although the construction of this statement suggests that there is a difference between "friendship" and "love," it is the very same difference that existed in the *Maltese* drama — a difference between simulacrum and original that is in fact indistinguishable. The fact that this friendship is as passionate as love, strengthens the suspicion that there might be something queer in this friendship. Schiller, admittedly, quickly rejects such a notion that "passionate friendship" is at the center of his tragedy — but perhaps readers should dwell on the question a bit longer.

It turns out that Schiller rejects the centrality of passionate friendship to the play because he claims that the Marquis de Posa is beyond friendship to a mere individual, even as a child: "already here Posa is the colder, the later friend, and his heart already embracing too widely to contract for a single being" (2: 231). Carlos, however, is a different matter altogether. Schiller concedes that the soft young Prince does want a passionate relationship of some kind with the Marquis. In relation to the Marquis, Carlos is "a delicate son of a prince, with lively feelings, receptive to [the Marquis's] outpourings and voluntarily hurrying toward him" (2: 231). Delicate and sensitive, the Prince seems to fit a lot of stereotypes about effeminate young men who are forever chasing after strong men, hoping to receive their (bodily?) outpourings. Compliantly and docilely, he clings to the Marquis: "the loving Karl snuggled up so submissively, so teachably!" (2: 232). So, by Schiller's own argument, even if friendship is not at the center of the drama, the desire for friendship could well be at the center of the character Don Carlos.

Carlos is full of love, pathologically so. His situation is a "state of *leisured enthusiasm, inactive observation*" (2: 232). Schiller's word for "enthusiasm" is "Schwärmerei," which was of major concern to the psychological physicians of his era. Carlos expends his energy, resulting in "a dark melancholy" (2: 232). He is "without energy, without occupation, brooding inwardly, exhausted by heavy fruitless battles, running scared between frightening extremes" and sinks into "a painfully blissful state of *suffering*" (2: 233). Kittler has already noted that Posa's awareness of the unnatural red on the Prince's pale face and his feverishly trembling lips (lines 148–51) reveal Schiller's medical studies of the effects of illicit sexuality on health. The *Letters* make explicit that Carlos is expending his (sexual) energy in a solipsistic, narcissistic way that would have seriously negative consequences for his health. From these descriptions of Carlos's physical and psychological state, it is clear that something is amiss with his sexuality.

Heterosexual libertinage is apparently not his vice. In a speech to the Marquis, the young Carlos admits that he has had no sex with women in his twenty-three years: "I am / Still pure, a twenty-three-year-old youth. / That which thousands before me unconscionably / Dribbled away in riotous embraces, / The best part of the spirit [Geist], male power, / I saved up for the future ruler. / What could drive you out of my heart, / If women could not do it?" (970–76). Schiller reinforces Carlos's age and innocence when the Prince exclaims: "Twenty-three years, / And still nothing done for immortality!" (1147–48). He has not done anything for immortality, because he has not expended his seed fruitfully (i.e., heterosexually). So, despite his pale looks, Carlos has not been wasting his seed — with women, at least. Carlos's lack of sexual interest in women becomes clear again when he has his disastrous encounter with the Princess of Eboli. He puts her off until he hears that she has resisted all the advances of her suitors. Then, upon learning of her asexuality, he becomes delighted with her. In contrast to all this borderline misogyny, Carlos seems to have a positive understanding of masculinity. Calling his seed "the best half of the spirit," he shows an appreciation for the value of the male body and its fluids.

But while Carlos is the weak, fawning prince, frightened of female sexuality, desperate for a father figure, and in love with the phallic masculinity of Posa, the Marquis is not quite as free of the taint of same-sex desire as Schiller maintains in the *Letters*, which, in their allusions to the play, are not — as the editor of the Hanser edition admits — "everywhere exact" (2: 1230). Posa is, after all, a Maltese Knight, a member of that organization that Schiller found so fascinating partly because in it male-male love was a surrogate for male-female love. In a letter written on June 13, 1787, to the Hamburg theater director Friedrich Ludwig Schröder, Schiller said that he wanted Posa played by a "lover" (NA 24: 100). Throughout the play, Posa is seen as a "sacrifice." There is something sexy about this image of the strong man, sacrificing himself for the sake of his friend, weak and pitiable. Carlos triumphs to the King: "The beautiful course of his life was love. Love / For me his great beautiful death" (4793-94). Similar to many of Aschenbach's characters in Thomas Mann's *Death in Venice*, Posa resembles the figure of Saint Sebastian, the beautiful male martyr, at the mercy of other men. In Schiller's play he is available, not only to the other characters, but also to the audience and the readers.

Posa, of course, cannot help it if others find him attractive, either in his strong or in his weakened state. But there are moments where he reveals that — with all due respect to Schiller in the *Letters* — he is the desiring subject as well as the object of desire. Posa calls Carlos the "favorite [Liebling] of my soul" (2370) in a discussion about Eboli. And later, he informs the Queen that his love for the royal son was a great joy: "To me was granted / A fortune the likes of which is only granted to a few: / I loved a lord's son" (4253-55). It is significant that these two admissions come in his discussions with these two women, for there are erotic tensions between each of them and him concerning Carlos. I have already mentioned the passages in which Posa and the Queen spar jealously. Jealousy is also the best explanation for Posa's reaction to Eboli. Posa's desire to kill the Princess in act 4, scene 17, is a serious overreaction, as even he admits: "Desperation / Made me into a Fury, an animal — I set / The dagger to a woman's breast" (4670-72). It is easy to interpret the implication of rape in this image of a dagger at a woman's breast, but one also wonders why Posa says that he was turned into a Fury, an archetypically feminine divinity, at the same time that he is turned into a beast, that is to say, a physical being without consciousness, without those ideals for which the Marquis is so famous. This gender-bending at the level of the body suggests that Posa's anger originates in the sexual confusion that is obvious in his physical response to Carlos. Posa's understanding of the relationship between Carlos and Eboli sounds like that of a lover suffering from self-inflicted wounds: "Abandoned by the only one, you throw / Yourself in the arms of the Princess Eboli — / Unhappy one: in the arms of a devil" (4658-60).

Here, too, there are odd gender reversals, for Eboli is a masculine "devil." Posa's anger at the women involved with the Prince, his blurring of their gender and his own, and his avowed love of the Prince all suggest that he too has more at stake at the corporeal level in his love for Carlos than Schiller admitted in the *Letters*.

Friedrich Kittler has the most convincing explanation for Posa's love of the Prince: it is the love of the teacher for his student, a teacher of the kind new to the eighteenth century, a teacher like the teachers in Schiller's own school, the Karlsschule, where teachers worked with youths who were "simultaneously pupils, friends, and beloveds" (265). Given the number of letters in the play, one could argue that Posa teaches Carlos to read and understand the manipulation of signs. But since the sign in its polyvalence is somehow akin to sexuality, one could also remain with the notion that Posa teaches Carlos to love, a theory that Posa himself supports: "my entire direction was / To explain his love to him" (4339-40). Posa discovers that his childhood friend thinks he loves his mother, and teaches him to return to the homosocial, if not the homosexual, world. This is the kind of pedagogical love that goes back to Socrates and Plato's *Symposium* and in which Thomas Mann would also delight: the pedagogical love that would always be sexually suspect.

In teaching love, Posa makes clear to Carlos that he, the Marquis, was the Prince's first love. The Prince's first love is an irritant in Schiller's writings. In the "Third Letter" of the *Letters on Don Carlos*, which is all about the relationship between the Prince and the Marquis, Schiller discusses the despondency that afflicts the Prince after the two are separated. After a long list of symptoms, Schiller writes: "thus the *first love* finds him" (2: 233). One might assume that the Queen is meant here — indeed, the Queen herself assumes as much when speaking to the Prince: "Elizabeth / Was your first love" (790-91). However, in Schiller's letter about the Prince's lovesickness, there is no reference to the Queen — only to the separation from the Marquis. Subsequently, in the "Eighth Letter," Schiller declares, with the same emphasis, that a "cheerful humane philosophy" is the Prince's "*first love*" (2: 252). Some have argued that Schiller is contradicting himself when he at first seems to suggest that Elizabeth is the Prince's first love and then asserts that it is philosophy (Crawford). But it is odd that Schiller would use so emphatically the same words in letters written a short time apart if he did not mean for there to be a connection. There is less of a contradiction if Elizabeth is *not* the Prince's first love. If that first love is the Marquis, then this philosophy, which is said to be "a child of friend-ship" (2: 252), would be a logical extension of that love. If the Marquis is the Prince's love — as he is the King's, who exclaims, "He / Was my first love" (5051–52) — then one can fully explain Posa's claim that he taught Carlos the meaning of his love. The Marquis first reminds the Prince that he is the first love; he then teaches the Prince to give up the object of that love and transfer his desire into useful societal channels.

In a letter from October 5, 1785, to the writer Ludwig Ferdinand Huber, Schiller exclaims, "let our hearts join manfully one with the other, enthuse little and feel much, project little and *handle* all the more fruit-fully" (NA 24: 25). Male-male bonding in Schiller's world must escape the realm of impotent "enthusing" (schwärmen) and become a fruitful act. In order to do so, it must be sublimated. Schiller's queer story does not end in the satisfaction of whatever confused erotic desires connect Don Carlos and the Marquis de Posa. Instead, it ends with the sublimation of those de-sires for the greater good. Most analyses of the play that argue that it ex-plodes the bourgeois tragedy by forcing its hero to move from the private realm to the public are correct (K.-D. Müller, for instance); they merely miss the homoerotic twist of private life in *Don Carlos*. But in emphasizing the importance of sublimating homosexual desire, *Don Carlos* plays into a long tradition that is still very evident in the first half of the twentieth cen-tury. The renowned psychoanalyst and Goethe expert, Kurt Robert Eissler, for instance, argues for the link between sublimated homosexuality and philanthropy in his monumental biography of Goethe. Essentially, Thomas Mann also believes that sublimated homosexuality lies at the root of artistic creativity (cf. Oosterhuis in this collection). Watching a young Argentine tennis player on the court in 1950, Mann contemplates in his diary "this mad and yet passionately maintained enthusiasm, which lies at the basis of everything, for the *incomparable* charm of male youth, *sur-*

passed by nothing in the world" (TB 4: 239). In assuming that his insane enthusiasm for male youth lies at the basis of everything, including his writings, he seems to be arguing for the presence of unsatisfied same-sex desire at the origin of all art. The implicit conclusion of Schiller's play, that male homosexuality must end in a "grand beautiful death" and a commitment to the greater good of humanity, would thus be attractive to Mann.

Mann also surely appreciated the specific way in which Schiller believes that male-male desire becomes sublimated. The "cheerful humane philosophy" that the friendship between the men engenders turns out to have another name: "The bold vision of a new state" is "the divine child of friendship" (4278–79). In the *Letters*, Schiller clarifies the nature of this new state: "All principles and favorite feelings of the Marquis circle around *republican* virtue" (2: 229). Schiller sees male-male bonding as the cornerstone of modern democracy. When Count Lerma, a Spanish grandee, expresses his condolences and support to the Prince, he links intense friendship with patriotism, which for Schiller would have been an antimonarchical, pro-republican category: "So loves / No friend anymore! All patriots cry / For you" (4932–34). Schiller hereby anticipates the concept of "adhesiveness," "'manly love' as a governing element of society," that Whitman would advocate (cf. Grier) and that Thomas Mann, Hans Blüher, and many writers for *The Exceptional* would find so appealing.

Homosexuality can be sublimated into writing, as well as politics, as Mann well knew. This is perhaps one reason why sexuality functions so well as a pharmakon. The sublimation of this sexuality appears in the exchanging, writing, and reading of all the letters in the play. When Eboli steals the Queen's letter, she practically violates her, forcibly breaking open her locked purse. When Posa asks Carlos for his letters, there is nothing more intimate he could request. When Posa wants a sign of the King's love, he asks for a signature on the secret arrest warrant.

This sublimation of same-sex desire into writing also functions at the real-life level of Schiller writing the play. The friendship between Carlos and Rodrigo and its relation to the greater good was an itch that provoked in Schiller an almost unending scratching of the pen on paper. The play, envisioned in 1782, took five years to complete. The first published version was thousands of lines longer than the edition Schiller authorized at the end of his life. Schiller shortened the drama several times, sometimes sending directors shortened versions with indications of possible further cuts, suggesting that much of the play was inessential, simply the froth produced by the churning of a writing machine fueled by same-sex desire. As in the case of the *Maltese* project, male-male friendship became a provocation to almost endless writing. On this issue, a secret sympathy would have existed between Schiller and Mann, who also found suppressed male-male desire to be the wellspring of creativity.

It is appropriate that Tonio Kröger specifically admires the style of *Don Carlos*. If Schiller's obsession with male-male friendship produces reams of poetry that can be cut practically at will, then the reader must assume that style, rather than content, must be Schiller's forte. There are several other elements that tie the short story *Tonio Kröger* closely with *Don Carlos* and show how well Mann appropriates the play for his own queer purposes. Like Carlos, Tonio loves his mother: "Tonio loved his dark and fiery mother" (208). But like Carlos, he really loves another boy, Hans Hansen. Like Carlos, the "queer fellow" ("Sonderling"), Tonio thinks of himself as "queer" ("sonderlich," 208) because of this love. In the play, Don Carlos is melancholy, soft, and alone, in love with the hard, active, sociable Posa; in the short story, Tonio Kröger suffers and desires painfully, while Hans Hansen is athletic, enjoys life, and has plenty of friends. While the Marquis sacrifices himself up for the Prince, however, Mann has written a more sobering story in tune with the oppressive nature of the dominant discourses of sexuality and desire in his day. Tonio Kröger must be sacrificed for his friend: "But when a third came, [Hans] was ashamed of [Tonio] and sacrificed him" (211). *Tonio Kröger* fantasizes less luridly about the self-sacrifice of strong men for the sensitive men who love them, but the story works within the same universe as *Don Carlos*.

There are other paths that connect Thomas Mann with Schiller via Tonio Kröger. His favorite teacher in school, Dr. Ludwig Bäthke, was a Schiller specialist. Thomas Mann fell in love with Schiller's *Don Carlos* — specifically its beautiful language — when he was a youth of fifteen, as he tells us in his final essay on Schiller. This love relationship between the reader Mann and the text of *Don Carlos* mirrors that between the author Schiller and the text. Schiller's understanding of his relationship to the text of *Don Carlos* is quite astounding. In a letter to the librarian, Wilhelm Friedrich Hermann Reinwald from April 14, 1783, Schiller embeds the play in male-male friendship: "In this splendid breath of morning, I think of *you* friend — and my *Carlos*" (NA 23: 78). Discussing the protagonist of his play, Schiller confesses that Carlos has replaced a heterosexual love interest for him: "I must admit to you that to a certain extent I have him instead of my girl" (NA 23: 81). Interestingly, although Schiller states here that Carlos is his "girl," he has just explained that the author needs to be the "girl" of his character: "The poet must be *less* the *painter* of his hero — he must be *more* his *girl*, his bosom buddy" (NA 23: 81). This kind of gender-blurring is not unexpected from the author of *The Maid of Orleans* and *Maria Stuart*.

Schiller provides further explanation for the love of the author for his characters. He argues: "Every poem is nothing other than an enthusiastic friendship or a platonic love to a creation of the head" (NA 23: 79). "Friendship" and "platonic" love may not sound particularly sexual to modern ears, but the pathological adjective "enthusiastic" ("enthousias-tisch" = "schwärmerisch") preceding friendship makes one wonder how this kind of friendship would differ from nonpathological, that is non-sexual, friendship. In eighteenth-century Germany — as Derks has shown — the adjective "platonic" in no way proved that a love was asexual: it could just as easily suggest that a love was homosexual. Schiller does not in fact seem to want to create strong boundary lines between friendship and love: "And are not all manifestations of friendship and love — from the soft handshake and kiss to the most heartfelt embrace — just so many expres-sions of a being struggling toward *mixture*" (NA 23: 80). For Schiller, the desire of the self to mix with the Other grounds both friendship and love. In any case, Schiller clarifies his notion of friendship and platonic love: "But what is friendship or platonic love other than a blissful exchange of being?" (NA 23: 79). In using the word "blissful" (wollüstig), Schiller em-phasizes that he is talking about a sensual, lusty, even lascivious exchange of being. Writing about a hero and loving a friend are for him similar activities: "If friendship or platonic love are merely the exchange of a for-eign being with our own, merely the passionate desire for his qualities, then both are to a certain extent only another effect of the power of poetry" (NA 23: 80). Thus the ardent romantic friendship that develops between the characters of *Don Carlos*, *Wallenstein's Death*, and the *Maltese*-fragment is a refraction of the intense desire that Schiller the author feels for his crea-tion.

The other answer Schiller gives to the question: "what is friendship or platonic love?" is "the contemplation of our self in another mirror" (NA 23: 79). One need not view this as mere narcissism. For Schiller, both love and writing involve a subjective investment in the Other, a blending and a merging of the self with the Other that is rooted in desire and borders on the sexual. Although he does not state it explicitly, reading too can perhaps be seen in this way — reading as a kind of rewriting that also involves the loving participation of the reader. Here then we have Schiller's blessing for Mann's reading or rewriting of *Don Carlos* in *Tonio Kröger* and all queer interpretations that are based on the highly subjective involvement of the reader. Schiller understands that any reader/author recreating a text will do so out of an erotic desire for that text, a desire that leads to a discovery of one's self in the text. Arguing that this creative activity, the lusty blending of the souls, this self-discovery in the other is also a characteristic of passionate friendship, Schiller seems not only to be endorsing queer readings, but also particularly supportive of queer readers.

Notes

[1] Thomas Mann's short stories are cited from *Die Erzählungen. Erster Band* (Frankfurt/M: Fischer, 1967). All translations are my own.

[2] The cartoon, entitled, *Panic in Weimar*, appeared in *Jugend* (Munich) vol. 11, no. 48 (November 19, 1907): 1089. Discussed by Steakley.

[3] Unless otherwise indicated, Schiller references are to Friedrich Schiller, *Sämtliche Werke*, Hanser edition. All parenthetic references from *Don Carlos* are to line numbers as they appear in volume 2. Translations are my own. Italics always indicate Schiller's emphasis.

[4] The positive charge of German *Gift* is still present in the word *Mitgift*, "dowry." In turn, the English word *gift* can have a negative meaning, depending on the context. See David Cheal and E. E. Evans Pritchard.

[5] It is an article of faith among many gays and lesbians that the use of the word "faggot" to describe gay men derives from the times of the Spanish Inquisition, when sexual deviants were burned like "faggots" (in the sense of pieces of wood). Some lexicographers, however, doubt the veracity of this folk etymology.

[6] See Tobin, "In and Against Nature," for more on homoerotics in Goethe's *Wilhelm Meister* novels.

The Dubious Magic of Male Beauty: Politics and Homoeroticism in the Lives and Works of Thomas and Klaus Mann

Harry Oosterhuis

Translated from the Dutch by Ton Brouwers[1]

HOMOSEXUALITY HAS A NOTABLE PRESENCE in the lives and works of both Thomas and Klaus Mann. Yet at first glance, when considering the ways in which each expressed his sense of homosexuality, it is hard to conceive of a larger difference between father and son. Thomas Mann (1875-1955), the prototypical German bourgeois paterfamilias, largely sublimated his homoerotic desire in his art and political writings. In many of his novels, novellas, and essays, he tended to broach homoeroticism in veiled language and to link it with one of his recurrent themes: the dichotomy between the ordinary man and the artist. But in his personal life he kept homosexuality at a scrupulous distance, despite — as his posthumously published diaries reveal — deeply felt homoerotic sentiments and several brief love affairs in his youth that continued to hold a fascination for him throughout his life. He confided his homosexual feelings only in his diary. One of the factors that prompted him, in 1945, to destroy most of his diaries written before 1933 may well have been that he felt that too many passages were too frank and would damage his reputation.

By contrast, the life of Klaus Mann (1906-1949) can easily be interpreted as an act of defiance against his father's conservative, detached stance. Whereas Thomas Mann chose to marry and to entrust his private feelings regarding his attraction to male beauty only to his diary, Klaus was more or less open about his own homosexual preference, seeking actively to make it an integral part of his private and public life. In response to his father's Wilhelminian, bourgeois milieu, he embraced an unconventional, bohemian lifestyle, feeling very much at home in the fashionable Berlin of the 1920s.

On closer inspection, however, and if their senses of homosexuality are seen against the backdrop of developments in their political thinking, the distinction between father and son seems less clear-cut. Following the rise of Nazism, both gave up their initially more or less apolitical stance, came to adopt similar political views, and publicly denounced Nazism. Both Thomas and Klaus Mann nevertheless did not connect homosexuality and democratic political activism. Focusing on the way both authors linked the personal and the political, I will argue in this article that it is not possible to understand their ultimately pessimistic perception of homosexuality without taking into account the development of their political views on National Socialism.

I. Thomas Mann: Erotic Irony

In one of Thomas Mann's early works in which homosexuality figures prominently, *Death in Venice* (1912), male same-sex desire is closely associated with decadence and a deadly Dionysian intoxication. The protagonist, Gustav Aschenbach, is a celebrated author who has produced an impressive oeuvre thanks to his ascetic way of life. But the price he has had to pay for success is his alienation from ordinary life: he lives in a purely intellectual world. While on holiday in Venice, however, he is completely thrown off balance by the physical beauty of young Tadzio. Aschenbach falls hopelessly in love with the boy and remains in Venice in spite of an outbreak of cholera. Just before he dies, he arrives at the conclusion that "we poets can be neither wise nor worthy citizens. We must needs be wanton, must needs rove at large in the realm of feeling" (72).

In *Death in Venice*, Thomas Mann offers a bleak image of how he might have ended up as an artist if he had not secured a bourgeois lifestyle through marriage. Before marrying Katja Pringsheim in 1905, he maintained a close friendship with Paul Ehrenberg, a painter one year his junior. Ehrenberg was instrumental in dissolving Mann's depression and the sense of solitude that troubled him during his early writing career. But from the beginning, their relationship — probably characterized by an erotic rather than sexual dimension — was also under much stress. Their personalities were quite different and Ehrenberg elicited contradictory feelings in Mann, feelings of affection but also of jealousy and contempt. More than once, his love for Ehrenberg caused him great despair, until his engagement with Katja put an end to their relationship.[2]

In contrast to the strong emotions that young men aroused in Thomas Mann, as countless entries in his diary demonstrate,[3] his love for his wife was mainly characterized by dispassionateness. Mann's homoerotic desires, however, seem never really to have threatened his relationship with Katja: their stable marriage provided him, as he claimed, with "sober happiness" (Mayer 1980, 477). He became the proud father of six children, and he eagerly posed as head of the family. In his 1925 essay *Über die Ehe* (*On Marriage*), he acknowledged that he had already opted for a marital relationship before meeting his future wife. Significantly, in this very essay he also set forth his views on homosexual relationships: they are bound to fail because of their precariousness. Whereas marriage embodies social morality and ordinary bourgeois life, based as it is on mutual faithfulness, responsibility, and fertility, homosexuality can thrive only on beauty. Mann reflected on homosexual relationships solely in terms of aesthetic fulfillment and barren *l'art pour l'art*, and as such, he believed, they can only result in loneliness, melancholy, and death. In *On Marriage*, he clearly indicated that as an artist he needed the stability and social security of marriage and family in order to protect himself from the tragic fate of Gustav Aschenbach.

Despite his critical view of homosexuality, Thomas Mann did not reject it unequivocally, even though he could write in a bantering tone about his "faible" (TB 4: 212; cf. Zijderveld). On the contrary, his diaries show how he cherished his homoerotic desires and felt they were important to him: "essentially, there is nothing 'more beautiful,'" so he wrote, "this absolutely fundamental, insane and yet ardently maintained enthusiasm for the incomparable, utterly unsurpassable charm of manly youth ... always my happiness and my misery."[4] In a letter to the poet Carl Maria Weber, he pointed out that male love may not be natural, but that that is precisely the reason for its spiritual and cultural significance (*Briefe* 178). Because homoeroticism lies at the root of both art and social ties, according to Mann, it is superior to ordinary, progenital, and essentially insipid heterosexuality (cf. Sommerhage 139). Clearly Mann's attitude toward homosexuality was ambiguous. On the one hand, he was infinitely fascinated by it, for it constituted, as I will explain, an important source of inspiration for his literary work as well as his political views. On the other hand, from a personal standpoint, he experienced his own desire as troubling, and as a bourgeois citizen he could only distrust it. He could never fully disavow his homosexual sentiments, though, if only because it would have meant a denial of his identity as an artist. He did, however, maintain a reserved stance: his stance toward homosexuality was that of the (ironic) observer. Producing literature and political commentary functioned as means of both expressing and controlling his desire (cf. Böhm 1991). The way he recreated his relationship with Ehrenberg in *Tonio Kröger* (1903) and, much later, in *Doctor Faustus* (1947) is indicative of this attitude.

Mann's representation of his friend is marked by a mixture of desire and contempt. Ehrenberg — whose appearance and charm captivated people's attention immediately — was to Mann a model of carefree life in which he, as an intellectual artist, a man of the mind (*Geist*), could never partake. Mann felt strongly, however, that Ehrenberg failed to understand what inspired him to be a writer; intellectually speaking, he had no respect for Ehrenberg. Because his love for him went hand in hand with contempt, he also felt somewhat humiliated (Feuerlicht 89-90). This split between art and life, which dominated his relationship to Ehrenberg, constitutes the main theme of *Tonio Kröger*. The novella's protagonist of this name, who, like Mann, considers himself an outsider because of his artistic aspirations, longs for friendship with the blond, uncomplicated, and sprightly Hans Hansen: "my deepest and secretest love belongs to the blond and blue-eyed, the fair and living, the happy, lovely and commonplace ... [Love] is good and fruitful. There is longing in it, and a gentle envy; a touch of contempt and no little innocent bliss" (*Tonio Kröger* 134). At the same time, however, Tonio understands that Hans remains beyond his reach: "I stand between two worlds. I am at home in neither, and I suffer in consequence" (133).

In *Doctor Faustus*, Ehrenberg reappears as the charming Rudi Schwerdtfeger, who tries to seduce the brilliant and unapproachable composer Adrian Leverkühn, the prototypical German artist. The boyish Schwerdtfeger, a blue-eyed "Blondkopf," who, according to Leverkühn's jealous bosom friend Serenus Zeitblom, lacks any sense of intellectual complexity or literary sensibility, endangers Leverkühn's artistic need for solitude. The lighthearted Schwerdtfeger evokes a "melancholy preference" in him that has all the characteristics of "ironic eroticism" (415). Eventually, Schwerdtfeger fails to break Leverkühn's self-chosen isolation.

A leitmotif in Mann's work is the opposition between artist and bour-geois citizen, or between a creative mind, *Geist*, and ordinary life. He tries to maintain a balance between the two by means of irony. This irony pri-marily betrays a relativist stance: the mind is seen as relative to life and vice versa. However, by using irony, Mann also evokes a certain amount of ten-sion that in his case is often charged with erotic energy. In *Betrachtungen eines Unpolitischen* (*Reflections of a Nonpolitical Man*, 1918), he de-scribes his use of irony as the voice of a creative mind that is life-preserving and inspired by Eros. He speaks of a longing which oscillates incessantly between life and mind. These two forces constitute, as he points out:

> Two worlds whose relationship is erotic without a clear sexual po-larity, without the one representing the masculine, and the other the feminine principle: this is life and intellect. Therefore there is no union between them, but only the short, intoxicating illusion of union and understanding, eternal tension without resolution ... It is the problem of beauty that intellect perceives life, and life per-ceives intellect, as 'beauty'. (420)

Later, in his essay *Schopenhauer*, Mann would characterize the artist not only as a mediator between mind and sensuality, but also between male and female: "The position of art, then, is exactly that which is between mind and life. [It is] androgynous like the moon, feminine in relation to the mind, but shows itself as masculine in life ... its essence is that of an enchantingly lunar meditation between the two regions. This meditation is the source of its irony" (GW 9: 535).[5] As a sign of his ambivalence with re-spect to homosexuality, irony plays a key role in Mann's work. Irony and aestheticism generally provided him the opportunity to keep a distance and express both fascination and mistrust. In terms of his sexual feelings, Mann was in fact quite sensitive and vulnerable. He could not dispense with these stylistic means for they provided the only way to simultane-ously conceal and express such sentiments.

II. Klaus Mann: Aestheticism and Politics

Whereas Thomas Mann sublimated his homosexual desire by hiding it be-hind a facade of respectable bourgeois life, Klaus Mann strongly resented his father's Wilhelminian milieu. "I prided myself on being disorderly and eccentric, as my father is punctual and disciplined. I reveled in mysticism, for I thought him a skeptic," he wrote in his autobiographical *The Turning Point* (1942, 196; cf. Härle 1988). During the 1920s he led a bohemian existence, emphasizing his role as outsider and openly parading his sexual preference. Like so many artists and intellectuals of the Weimar Republic, young Klaus Mann was skeptical about politics and bourgeois life with its typical sense of security: "... our sociopolitical responsibility – an irksome thing, but it just will not be settled for good. So long as we are dealing with this dreary nonsense (and sometimes there is no avoiding it) then let us be plain and simple! Once the tiresome social dues are dealt with, we will be allowed to amuse ourselves with our pleasures again" (*Der Wendepunkt*, 1949, 224).[6] The themes of his literary work involved personal and existentialist problems, such as love, eroticism, solitude, and death. He belonged to the post-World War I generation, which no longer had an optimistic belief in reason and social progress. Influenced by Nietzsche and such poets as Friedrich Hölderlin, Novalis, Oscar Wilde, Paul Verlaine, Walt Whitman, and Stefan George, he was attracted to a decadent sensuality, flirting with the irrational vitalism then popular among young Germans. In his first autobiography, *Kind dieser Zeit* (*Child of This Time*, 1932), he wrote that he preferred "The extravagant, the eccentric, the tainted over that which is kept moderate; the irrational and drunken over that which is tamed and governed by reason" (179-80).[7] In his early work, the collection of stories *Vor dem Leben* (*Before Life*, 1925), the play *Anja und Esther* (1925), and the novel *Der fromme Tanz* (*The Sacret Dance*, 1925), youthful rebelliousness goes hand in hand with an almost unconstrained experience of (homo)eroticism – an affront to most in the contemporary critical scene.

Thomas Mann was far from pleased with his son's unconventional way of life. The essay *On Marriage* may be read as a rejection of Klaus's lifestyle which, in fact, basically depended on his father's fame and financial support. However, his double-edged criticism of his son – as Thomas Mann was also fascinated by (male) beauty, sensuality, and decadence – soon lost its validity. After the rise of Nazism, Klaus gradually abandoned his apolitical aestheticism, irrationalism, and vitalistic glorification of youth and the body. Literary authors like Gottfried Benn and Ernst Jünger, for whom truth and justice were subordinate to style and intensity and with whose aestheticism and antibourgeois attitude Klaus had formerly felt a close affinity, were vigorously attacked by him in the early 1930s (cf. A. Kerker; Ipema). In a letter to Benn, Klaus Mann criticized his naive sympathy for the Nazi regime: "At present, there seems to be an almost inevitable law, [the fact] that too strong a leaning toward the irrational leads to political reaction ... First the great gesture against civilization ... all of a sudden one arrives at the cult of violence and then soon at Adolf Hitler" (in Spangenberg 1986, 45).[8] Earlier, in *Krieg und Sexualität* (*War and Sexuality*), he had attacked Ernst Jünger because of his vitalistic glorification of war as a source of renewal:

> Describe the atavism of the largest scale as 'progress'? ... Let's not make ourselves any better than we are. We have everything within us. In our dreams, every cruelty is ready and waiting. Nothing is animalistic, nothing perverse, but rather everything is natural: 'natural', of course, in the worst and deepest sense of the word. Man is not good, since nature is not. Cruelty and pleasure go together. When inhibitions fall, the orgy of sadism comes. Inhibitions are the foundation of the fabric of culture. One can will the catastrophe — and Ernst Jünger, for example, wants nothing but that — but it is decidedly hypocritical to consider this as progress. Back to the beast! would be the logical, anarchistic-warmongering catchphrase. It is only that the unleashed beast, in its bestialities, is more naïve and not half as imaginative as that human being, unleashed again, bereft of his inhibitions. (85-86)[9]

Clearly, following such an argument, it seems difficult to draw a line between unfettered sexual passion, glorified by Klaus Mann earlier, and the atavistic, destructive urges so characteristic of Nazism. Therefore, the aspects of homosexuality which he found so alluring — including its antibourgeois hedonism, flagrant promiscuity, excessive waste, and an unproductive and merely lust-oriented sexuality — were bound to become a source of anxiety to him.

Whereas during the twenties he lived largely a literary dandy's carefree, individualistic, hedonistic life, Klaus Mann changed into an antifascist political activist in the early 1930s, at a time when his father still hesitated to commit himself politically (cf. A. Kerker, E. Kerker). As a spokesman of the better Germany in exile, Klaus Mann edited two journals, *Die Sammlung* (The Collection, 1933-35) in Amsterdam and *Decision* (1941-42) in New York, both of which aimed at fighting fascism and increasing political consensus among émigrés. His 1936 novel *Mephisto* relates the story of actor Hendrik Höfgen, who after the Nazi takeover refuses to give up his career ambitions and thereby becomes an opportunistic supporter of the new regime. Despite his private dislike of Nazism, Höfgen is put in charge of the state theater company thanks to his friendship with one of the party leaders. Although Klaus Mann insisted from the beginning that his novel was not a roman à clef, suggesting that Hendrik Höfgen represented only a certain type of character — that of the artist-intellectual who, blinded by ambition, renounces his principles — it was clear to everyone that Höfgen was modeled after the actor Gustav Gründgens, who had become superintendent of the Prussian State Theater thanks to his good relationship with Hermann Goering. During the 1920s, Klaus Mann had worked quite closely with Gründgens: the two men admired each other and collaborated in the controversial performance of Mann's play *Anja und Esther.* Mann's sister Erika, who was also involved with the performance, was married to Gründgens for some time. Mann's thinly veiled condemnation of Gründgens in *Mephisto* was meant as a critique of the apolitical attitude of the many German artists who held on to the belief that art had an autonomous value that transcended everyday political realities.

III. Thomas Mann: Homoeroticism and German Nationalism

During the 1930s, Thomas Mann would arrive at a similar political point of view, yet the development of his political thinking was more intricate than that of his son Klaus. Thomas Mann's *Reflections of a Nonpolitical Man,* which breathes the spirit of Schopenhauer's and Nietzsche's philosophies, illustrates how much Mann was a product of the Wilhelminian *Bildungsbürgertum* (educated classes). This book appeared in the wake of the First World War and was a response to the democratic activism of his brother Heinrich — the prototype of the accursed *Zivilisationsliterat* (literatus of a civilized society). In *Reflections,* Thomas Mann reveals himself as a conservative nationalist who passionately defends German culture against Western liberal democracies — notably France — which he felt were displaying signs of moral decay. According to Mann, democratization entails the abolition of the distinction between internalized, spiritualized *Kultur* and the world of pragmatic politics directed solely toward superficial social and economic realities. The collapse of this distinction results inevitably in a lowering of artistic standards and a politicization of art. Basically, his defense of the authoritarian Wilhelminian German tradition is a plea for the autonomy of art. Mann supports his nationalist preference for (German) romanticism over (French) Enlightenment with an appeal to the spirit of irony. Irony excludes, as he puts it, all forms of political activism or efforts at improving society because such activism denies the rich and contradictory diversity of life. In addition, there is the danger of radicalism and fanaticism that inevitably results from univocal views or a simplistic moralism.

Mann's *Reflections of a Nonpolitical Man*, in which he defines conservatism as "the erotic irony of the intellect" (420), can also be read as his political pledge of affectionate allegiance to the blond, blue-eyed German male hero. The book's homoerotic nature derives from its misogynist stance and its celebration of heroic, militaristic masculinity and male bonding among soldiers. It is quite clear that Mann was fascinated by the German-nationalist ideal of the *Männerbund* (male alliance). Soon after the publication of his political essay, he saw his own views confirmed in Hans Blüher's two-part work on homoerotic male bonding, *Die Rolle der Erotik in der männlichen Gesellschaft* (*The Role of Eroticism in the Male Society*, 1917–1919). Blüher was one of the leading right-wing ideologues of the *Männerbund*: he favored a purification of German society under the guidance of elitist, all-male brotherhoods whose members would be bonded to one another by homoeroticism and charismatic leadership. According to him, sublimated homosexual feeling was an important factor in binding groups of men together, from the sanctity of religious orders to the masculine ethos of military organizations. Thomas Mann was deeply impressed by Blüher's work, which he praised as "certainly ... greatly and profoundly Germanic" (*Letters* 103). In his diary he noted: "... read Blüher. One-sided, but true. As for myself there is no doubt in my mind that even the *Betrachtungen* are an expression of my sexual inversion" (*Diaries* 66).

In many respects, the strong antifeminist and antidemocratic overtones of Blüher's ideal of male bonding are reflected in *Reflections of a Nonpolitical Man*. Mann saw a diametrical opposition between democratic progress and homoerotic masculinity. Whereas he assumed the German state to be homo*erotic* in nature, he pejoratively associated French cosmopolitan civilization with the feminine and a vulgar hetero*sexuality*: "One hardly understands democracy if one does not understand its feminine touch." The French political system he describes as "politics with ladies-in-waiting," adding: "'Freedom and the whore are the most cosmopolitan things under the sun.' What international *held on* even during the World

War? The horizontal one" (223).[10] Mann was in full agreement with Blüher who — contrary to common opinion — linked homosexuality with German culture's alleged innate masculinity. Moreover, he could identify with Blüher's views because the ideal of male bonding did not exclude the idea of the nuclear family. Blüher felt that the *Männerbund* and the family were complementary, that a man could participate in both spheres. In *On Marriage* it becomes clear that Mann applied this idea to his own situation by characterizing the artist as the (ironic) mediator between bourgeois life and the artistic mind, or between a heterosexual and homosexual sphere (cf. *Briefe* 178).

In the same essay, Mann suggested that the relationship between the (German) state and homosexuality was an ambiguous one. On the one hand, the state sought to oppose homosexuality for reasons that have to do with its population politics, but, on the other hand, the state's functioning was rooted in homoerotic bonds between men. This shows the extent to which Blüher's ideology of male brotherhood affected his political thinking, even after Mann went on in the 1920s to repudiate some of his conservative views as put forward in *Reflections of a Nonpolitical Man* (cf. Wisskirchen). His famous speech *Von deutscher Republik* (*On the German Republic*, 1922), in defense of a democratic Weimar Republic, also bears the stamp of the ideal of male bonding. Before an audience that included Friedrich Ebert, the former leader of the Social Democrats and first president of the Weimar Republic, Mann argued that homoeroticism was not only reserved for the reactionary *Freikorps* (volunteer corps) that fought against a democratic Germany in the aftermath of World War I, but that German democracy, too, had an erotic dimension. Mann explained how his republican sympathy was inspired by the poetry of Walt Whitman, who had glorified male love as the basis of American democracy. Whitman's homoerotic ideal, according to Mann, could serve as a guiding principle for the Weimar Republic because of the numerous similarities between the American poet's world view and the early nineteenth-century German tradition of romantic nationalism. The patriotic *Burschenschaften* (student fraternities) and German poets like Novalis and Goethe would have favored a "social eroticism" in order to do away with the gap between the personal and the political. In his speech, Mann called upon Germany's youth to link up with this tradition.

Thomas Mann was particularly interested in reaching the younger generation, because its members would be capable of displaying more openness in sexual matters than the older generations. In this context, he once again referred to Hans Blüher who, as a young man, had caused an uproar with his book about the German youth movement, *Die deutsche Wandervogelbewegung als erotisches Phänomen* (*The German 'Wandervogel' Movement as Erotic Phenomenon*, 1912). In this book Blüher claimed, on the basis of his own experience, that homoerotic friendships, fostered by sex-segregated education in Wilhelminian Germany, were essential for the cohesion and popularity of the *Wandervogel*, a youth organization which was founded in 1896 and quickly turned into a nationwide youth movement. Mann, however, also indicated that he no longer shared Blüher's rejection of the feminine. In *On the German Republic* and, again three years later, in *On Marriage*, he interpreted social tolerance toward same-sex relationships, which he felt was growing among young people, in light of the emancipation of women, the weakening of gender differences, and the modern ideal of androgynous beauty. Mann thought that in a democratic, egalitarian Weimar Republic, the so-called natural bisexuality of human beings discovered by Freud, could come to fruition and would fulfill an essential precondition for realizing "social eroticism." In contrast to his standpoint in *Reflections of a Nonpolitical Man* four years earlier, Mann demonstrated in *On the German Republic* a positive attitude toward the sensuous, that is physical, aspects of homoeroticism. Sensuality is no longer derogated as intrinsically foreign to spiritual German *Kultur*; instead, by bridging the gap between mind and life, it would guarantee its humanism. Thus, (homo-)sexuality is seen as a social phenomenon.

Despite his siding with democracy and his positive outlook on increased sexual freedom, and although there was a multifaceted sexual reform movement in Germany during the 1920s, Mann was far from advancing (homo)sexual emancipation. In his political essays, homoeroticism plays a prominent role. Yet, he was hardly concerned with the social position of homosexuals and their emancipation. He did sign a petition of the Scientific-Humanitarian Committee in which the German government was asked to abolish the illegality of "unnatural vice" (under Paragraph 175 of the Penal Code), but he spurned Magnus Hirschfeld's biological and emancipatory theory of the third sex, which understood homosexuality as a certain feminization of the man and a masculinization of the woman. Mann's only substantial contribution to the homosexual movement, a brief article objecting to Paragraph 175, appeared as "Protest der Prominenten gegen die Beibehaltung und der Verschärfung des Paragraphs 175" (Protest of V.I.P.s against the keeping and tightening up of the Paragraph 175) in *Eros*. This journal was published by Adolf Brand, whose *Gemeinschaft der Eigenen* (Community of the Exceptional) favored a cultural-aesthetic and masculine-nationalist approach toward homoeroticism, thus demonstrating an antagonism toward the views of Hirschfeld, a medical doctor and Social Democrat.

Homosexuality plays such a significant role in *Reflections of a Non-political Man* and *On the German Republic* because Thomas Mann regarded politics from the angle of aesthetics (Sommerhage 123, 222-23). It is in this light that we should read his comments on his altered political views but unchanged creed, which appeared in the preface to the book publication of *On the German Republic*: "Maybe I have changed my thoughts – not my mind" (116).[11] This unchanged conviction consisted of a call for a harmonic bridging of the contradiction between life and mind, a view largely derived from Goethe's humanist *Bildungsideal* (educational ideal).[12]

This essentially apolitical approach toward politics is also evident in *Der Zauberberg* (*The Magic Mountain*, 1924). In this novel, Mann presents the development of his views on homosexuality in quite a veiled manner.[13] The protagonist, twenty-three-year-old Hans Castorp, travels from Hamburg to a sanitarium high up in the Alps to pay a visit to his cousin who suffers from tuberculosis. His planned stay of three weeks will last seven years. Castorp breaks the habit of his Hanseatic bourgeois existence because he is fascinated by the alienating life of the sanitarium and by one of its patients in particular: Clawdia Chauchat, a young Russian woman with Asiatic eyes and wide cheekbones who enjoys slamming doors and despises all bourgeois conventions. Castorp falls in love with this woman, yet this love has clearly a homoerotic dimension, not only because of the boy-like features which Mann uses to describe her but also because of the phallic symbolism he employs. By meeting Clawdia Chauchat, Castorp retrieves a lost and forgotten youthful passion; half-dreaming, he discovers that she reminds him of Pribislav Hippe, a boy in school. to whom he was silently attracted ten years before. "How remarkably like her he looked – like this girl up here! Is that why I feel interested in her? Or was that why I felt so interested in him?" (*Magic Mountain* 123). Soon after he arrives at this awareness, his lungs appear to be affected, his temperature rises, and he falls completely under the spell of the thin air of the sanitarium, its atmosphere saturated with disease and death, as well as sensuality. Castorp's love for

Clawdia Chauchat, whom he adores from a distance and who serves as an object for projecting his memories of Pribislav Hippe, corresponds with features that Mann associates with homosexuality in *On Marriage*: it is insecure, infertile, unsocial, and without prospects. As the narrator comments: "For a man to take an interest in a woman inwardly diseased had no more sense than — well, than the interest Hans Castorp had once taken in Pribislav Hippe" (*Magic Mountain* 130).

After he has declared his love to Clawdia Chauchat, just prior to her — temporary — departure from the sanitarium, Castorp regains a certain emotional balance. With great interest he listens to the heated political debates between two fellow patients: the enlightened humanist Settembrini, who presents himself from the beginning as a sort of mentor to Castorp — suggesting a kind of pedagogical eros — and the sinister Jesuit Naphta, who seeks to undercut Settembrini's sense of rational certainty. Inspired by Naphta's religious background, Castorp becomes interested in male bonding. He perceives an analogy between Naphta's Jesuit order, the army in which his already deceased cousin was an officer, the Freemasons of which Settembrini is a member, and the fraternity which the bragging medical director of the sanitarium seems never to have left. Here, *The Magic Mountain* clearly betrays the influence of Blüher, since the second part of *Role of Eroticism in the Male Society* discusses these four male organizations as classical examples of *Männerbünde*.

When Clawdia Chauchat returns to the sanitarium accompanied by a lover, the Dutch coffee trader Peeperkorn, Castorp turns his back on male bonding and, consequently, on politics. The influence of male bonding can still be felt however, in one respect: he has — in a Freudian sense — sublimated his sexual desire. Clawdia Chauchat no longer confuses him as he reconciles himself with the idea that she — and hence Pribislav Hippe — is unattainable for him. At the same time, he downplays his masculinity by adopting a passive, detached stance regarding sexuality. This is expressed in particular through his aesthetic idealization of androgyny and his reflections on beauty and hermaphroditic phenomena in nature. Eventually, Hans Castorp is neither interested in embracing a male or female identity, nor a heterosexual or homosexual identity.

Autobiographical elements of Mann's life are echoed in the development of the protagonist of *The Magic Mountain*. The political discussions that fill a good part of the novel are a reflection of his own views during and after World War I. It is striking that Castorp, though closely following

and sometimes participating in the debates between Settembrini and Naphta, ultimately ignores politics. By and large, Castorp — characterized by
Mann as the "problem child of the times"[14] — remains aloof from all contemporary social issues during his stay in Davos. The isolated mountain
sanitarium, affected by disease and death, symbolizes a specifically German
view of culture of which Mann himself was an exponent. It was the tendency of German artists and intellectuals, and to some extent of the entire
German *Bildungsbürgertum*, to hide behind a sense of moral superiority
and inhabit a singularly intellectual and aesthetic universe. This resulted in
a rather naïve and impracticable understanding of actual political realities.

As pointed out above, Thomas Mann himself approached politics
largely from an aesthetic angle. In his comments on the democratic Weimar Republic in *On the German Republic* he did not invoke the ideals of
the French Revolution, liberalism, or socialism, but instead the world
views of poets like Novalis, Goethe, and Whitman, who couched their
humanism in various — partly erotic — aesthetic ideals.[15] Mann's siding
with democracy was based on the ideal of *Bildung* and homoerotic aesthetics, just like his conservative-nationalist appeal in *Reflections of a Nonpolitical Man*. Idealization of male beauty made him view homoeroticism as
an essential part of the identity of the German nation, irrespective of the
political status quo. Although he resolutely disapproved of National
Socialism from the beginning,[16] he claimed that this ideology's homoerotic dimension was abundantly clear in the prominent role that male
bonding played in the Nazi movement.

> As if homosexuality was not an essential part of it. It is not always
> about effeminacy. Rather, it is often also about excessive masculin-
> ity and is part of the style of military heroes and men of war ... It is
> a part of war, comes from war, and is at home among military peo-
> ples like the Germans, for instance, who — in contrast to the
> women-loving and galant French — are a homoerotic people.
> (*Leiden an Deutschland* 734)[17]

Evidently, this perspective was at odds with Klaus Mann's antifascist activism which came to the forefront in the early 1930s.

IV. Klaus Mann: Homosexuality and Antifascism

When Klaus Mann was about to emerge as one of the leading intellectuals of Germany's antifascist exile community in Europe, he published an essay entitled *Die Linke und das 'Laster'* (*The Left and 'Vice'*, 1934). In this essay he spoke out against the political use of homosexuality in the antifascist camp; he characterized homosexuals as the "Jews of the antifascists." During the early 1930s, German Social Democrats and Communists alike seized upon the homosexual orientation of some Nazi leaders, especially Ernst Röhm, with the aim of discrediting the entire National Socialist movement. They constructed a highly pejorative stereotype of Nazism by linking it with homosexuality. Antifascist leftists created the impression that homosexuality was widespread in Nazi organizations. The homophobia of German Social Democrats and Communists was bolstered by developments in the Soviet Union, where "pederasty" was criminalized in a new law, promulgated in 1934. Contrasting the purity and healthiness of socialist ethics with the moral corruption of Nazi Germany, the renowned writer Maxim Gorki placed homosexual activities on a par with bourgeois decadence and fascist perversion.

In his article, Klaus Mann put on record that in Western Europe as well as the Soviet Union, there was a general tendency among socialists in the 1930s to identify homosexuality with Nazism. He especially criticized the leftist ploy of automatically equating the fascist *Männerbund* with homosexuality. While acknowledging that male bonding played a significant role in the Nazi movement, Mann argued that it was not unique to fascism: the example of the American poet Walt Whitman provided evidence that the ideals of male bonding and friendship could also have a democratic character. He also referred to the German poet Stefan George, whose glorification of the *Männerbund* was aristocratic but definitely not fascist.

Klaus Mann's essay on homosexuality and Nazism bears testimony to his courage. The essay is important both as a document testifying to the homophobic atmosphere in leftist circles at that time and also because of Mann's attempt to critique it. In leftist circles, homosexual rights were scarcely acknowledged to be a valid political cause. On the contrary, prejudices against homosexuality were indeed part and parcel of socialist thinking which tended to regard homosexuality as something belonging to the antisocial domain of the unproductive, uncontrollable, and irrational.

Such beliefs became even more deep-rooted among leftists as a consequence of the ideological and moral confrontation with National Socialism. Against the presumed immorality and perversion of the Nazis, antifascists stressed their own rationality and purity. For Klaus Mann, the leftist,
antifascist strategy linking homosexuality with Nazism was all the more
embarrassing. For as a member of the socialist camp, he endorsed the Marxist analysis that capitalism was the underlying breeding ground for fascism
by arguing: "that Hitler could come to power not because 'German youth
is contaminated' [*verseucht*] but because Thyssen foot the bill" (678).[18]
Furthermore, Mann believed that a "humanist socialism" was the only alternative to fascism.[19]

   The leftist aversion to homosexuality — and in fact to all sexuality that
was not conventional, that is, monogamous and heterosexual — had dire
consequences for those antifascist activists who were homosexuals themselves. For most of them, criticizing the prejudices of their heterosexual
comrades in the struggle against Nazism was inconceivable — a fact which
makes Klaus Mann's essay exceptional. He himself knew how it felt to face
moral pressure from his fellow antifascists. One of his political friends, for
example, the writer Hermann Kesten, who gave him the idea for his novel
Mephisto, once proposed to him: "You should write the novel of a homosexual careerist in the Third Reich ... [a] satyre on certain homosexual figures" (in Spangenberg 85-86).[20] Although the protagonist in *Mephisto* was
modeled on the homosexual actor Gustav Gründgens, Mann transformed
him into a heterosexual masochist. "I tried to explain his terrible ambition
with an inferiority complex — caused in part by social, [and] in part by
erotic reasons," as Mann claimed, thereby suggesting that sexual aberration
was the psychological cause of political shortsightedness ("Selbstanzeige:
Mephisto" 53).[21]

   As far as his own lifestyle was concerned, Klaus Mann was forced to go
on the defensive and to pay lip service to leftist morals. In the twenties, he
had lightheartedly celebrated homoeroticism and decadence, but when he
turned to political activism after leaving Germany in 1933, his advocacy of
hedonism was supplanted by a far more reticent, cautious attitude, as can
be seen in the novels written in exile, such as *Symphonie Pathétique*,
(1935) and *Der Vulkan* (*The Volcano*, 1939), as well as his essay on the
Röhm affair, *The Left and 'Vice'*, and his second and third autobiographies,
The Turning Point (1942) and *Der Wendepunkt* (1949). In *Symphonie
Pathétique*, he suggests that homosexual intercourse can only be morally

affirmed if it is based on a stable relationship and a sense of inner connectedness. This view, however, does not square with his own life, in which casual sexual contacts were important, if only for their physical pleasure. In *The Volcano*, which is set in a milieu of German émigrés, the two male protagonists share in a rewarding homosexual relationship until one of them becomes a drug addict and dies. The surviving friend arrives at the insight that he has been leading a loose and parasitical life, and he decides to go to Spain to fight Franco. "He had become a man after all," Mann concludes. No more attention is paid to homosexuality, the message being that political activism requires the suppression of such desire.

It is striking that Klaus Mann chose not to publish his polemical essay *The Left and 'Vice'* in *Die Sammlung*, the journal he himself edited in Amsterdam, but instead in a less prominent Prague journal, so it could be ignored by the German exile community and sink into oblivion.[22] Mann felt that *Die Sammlung* was to be a broad-based forum for antifascists, which also meant that prejudice against sexual orientation would not constitute grounds for refusing any article. He appears, however, to have expressed to a German Communist his willingness not to stir up any dispute about this subject, thus seeking to avoid the impression that he placed a higher priority on his personal interests as a member of a sexual minority than on resistance to Nazism (Naumann 72).

Moreover, in this essay he described homosexuality only in abstract terms, not as an overtly practiced lifestyle. From a socialist perspective, the body was primarily a tool for labor and production; lust was suspect as an antisocial force, and sexual liberation as a cause in itself could only be viewed as a symptom of bourgeois decadence and selfish individualism. Therefore, Mann was under strong pressure to justify homosexuality socially and morally so as to neutralize socialist objections to its uselessness and unproductiveness. He defended homosexuality only as an innate phenomenon, emphasizing that it could be useful to the community because of its cultural fertility and should therefore be integrated into a future socialist society. He had little to say, however, on how this integration could be implemented (cf. Mattenklott). In fact, Klaus Mann, like his father, always paid scant attention to the social repression and discrimination of homosexuals. He evidenced no activist concern at all for emancipation. Although Klaus Mann, unlike his father, did not hide his homosexual preference, he did refuse, for example, to accept an invitation from Hirschfeld to give a lecture on homosexuality and modern literature at his

Institute for Sexual Science. Likewise, he regarded the praise he received in Adolf Brand's journal *Der Eigene* (*The Exceptional*) as "compromising" (Zynda 49). Yet he was far more positive about Hans Blüher, whom his father also admired. Because of Klaus Mann's independent and privileged position as a bohemian and artist, he never felt any need to justify or defend his sexual preference. Essentially, he embraced quite an elitist stance by adopting an eccentric lifestyle and writing about "important men," such as Alexander the Great in the novel *Alexander* (1930) or Tchaikovsky in *Symphonie Pathétique*.

Although Klaus Mann was courageous enough to expose the homophobia of his fellow antifascists, he could not escape tormenting doubts about his own sexual proclivities. The mixed feelings with which he looked back upon his youthful celebration of sensuality in *Der Wendepunkt* (1949) is typical of his ambivalence. The chapter in which he records his first love affair with an athletic, "strong and supple" fellow student begins with an elaborate description of his generation's world view in the years right after World War I, thereby casting an unfavorable light on sexual candor:

> Was my generation ... which grew up during the First World War
> – less disorganized and more frivolous than youth is in general?
> Did we carry on especially carelessly and licentiously? ... The moral
> and social crisis in the midst of which we stand ... was already in
> full swing back then ... The depths of organic life are disorderly –
> a labyrinth, a swamp of deadly lust and creative power. The roots
> of our being reach down into the turbid, muddy, into the morass
> of semen, blood, and tears, where the orgy of lust and decay repeats
> itself forever, never-ending pain, never-ending bliss ... From our
> poets we adopted the disregard for the intellect, the accentuation of
> biologically-irrational values at the expense of moral and rational
> ones, the overemphasis of the somatic, the cult of Eros ... Back
> then, of course, in the days of political innocence and erotic
> exaltation, we lacked any idea of the dangerous aspects and poten-
> tialities of our puerile sexual mysticism. Nonetheless, I could not
> help but noticing that our philosophy of 'body-sense' was at
> times preceded and exploited by fairly unpleasant elements. The
> glorification of physical virtues lost any attraction for me and any

power of persuasion, when it was joined with a militant-heroic pathos, which, unfortunately, was often the case. (125–27)[23]

In a similar vein he wrote rather guiltily about his sexual experiences in the Turkish baths during a 1937 visit to fascist Hungary:

> Something was going on ... in the baths decorated in a Turkish style, whose dim light — lecherously satiated by the steams of the hot and healing waters — was an invitation to the shamelessly collective orgy. Who wanted to play the spoilsport there? Not me, who was quite fond of these excesses of a vulgar, commercial sensuality, which, then again, was also marvelously primitive and hypertrophic in a classical Asian style. Satisfied lewdness, coarsely enjoyed to the full ... amused me as the only innocent, or at least relatively harmless, manifestation of our animalistic components ... Of course, I know — and even in frivolous Budapest I was not frivolous enough to forget it: the animalistic, which I like, is not very far from the bestial, which horrifies me. If it is true, then, that the satisfaction of urges diverts from destructive impulses or transforms them into positive libidinousness, then it is also undeniable that unleashed sexuality has in its own right the fatal tendency to degenerate into that which is sadistic and destructive. The mass orgy, in which I find my half ironic-bitter, half sweet-crass pleasure, contains in itself the germ of mass murder; every ecstasy is potentially the frenzy of the kill, a statement by which I do not want to revoke, but indeed modify properly my eulogy of debauchery. (390)[24]

Klaus Mann's antifascist activism gave rise to a reconsideration of his view on homosexuality. Although he criticized the homophobia of Social Democrats and Communists alike, he did endorse the leftist ploy to expose Nazism as a pathological and irrational political system, in which barbaric passions reigned and brutish lusts were satisfied by violence and destruction. For antifascists, it seemed easy to prove that fascism was a sign of perversion, sadism, and masochism, from which it was only a small step to homosexual vice. In light of this view, it was difficult for him to reconcile his earlier affection for what he called "the aesthetic-religious-erotic sphere" (453), for a life full of passion, with moral and political responsibility. Homosexual practices increasingly perturbed him. The way in which he voluntarily joined the American forces during World War II — it required quite some effort on his part to be let in — seems to suggest that this was a contrived attempt to avert inner conflicts as well. In *Der Wendepunkt* (1949), he associates homosexuality repeatedly with solitude and social isolation — a predicament which he tried to escape by his political activism. His army life was diametrically opposed to his earlier bohemian lifestyle, yet at the time, as his brother Golo Mann aptly put it, "the slavery of the army was a kind of liberation to him" (75). During this same period, Klaus Mann also seriously considered joining the Catholic Church. In 1949, he committed suicide.

V. Thomas Mann: Aestheticism and Nazism

Just as (homo)sexual lust became a problematic issue for Klaus Mann because he saw National Socialism as a movement that catered to the dark urges of people, so did homoeroticism become tainted for his father as a result of the fascist aestheticizing of politics. The rise of the Nazi movement forced Thomas Mann to seriously reconsider his views on the relationship between *Kultur* (or aesthetics) and politics. As a link between these two realms, homosexuality could not be left out of the equation. This is already clear in a 1930 lecture by Thomas Mann on the poet August von Platen (1796-1835) whom he much admired. In this lecture, delivered before the Platen-Society, he expressed his delight about the opportunity to speak freely of Platen's "exclusively homoerotic leanings" ("August von Platen" 271), the understanding of which he believed to be essential for a proper appreciation of both his poetry and his tragic, yet grotesque, life. Mann praised Platen's strictly classical poetry, but as he dug deeper into the poet's sexual preference it became clear that his lecture as a whole was far from an uncritical tribute. Implicitly Mann questioned the way Platen had viewed and experienced his homosexuality. Elevating it to a superior, singularly spiritual form of love, Mann argued that as Platen's spiritualized cult of beauty grew more masculine, the more he grew estranged from the ordinary life of his fellow men. Having become unapproachable, imprisoned in an ivory tower, Platen retained little of his humanism, disdain being his only response to ordinary life. Thomas Mann characterized Platen's radical aestheticism, which ultimately caused the severe solitude that brought his downfall, as amoral and adverse to life. As he put it in his lecture: "The knights of beauty are knights of death" ("August von Platen" 271).

In *On Marriage*, Thomas Mann had also established a close connection between death and a homosexual longing for beauty, but in this earlier essay he had associated homosexual aesthetics with artistic calling in a favorable manner through the use of irony. What stands out in his lecture on Platen, however, is the idea that from the angle of political morality an exclusively aesthetic attitude toward life, which had been his own all along, carries great dangers. It is significant that there is a striking silence about homosexuality in Mann's political writings that appeared after World War II. In these essays — some held as lectures — that mainly deal with Germany's recent past, Mann presented himself not only as a champion of humanist and democratic values but also as a critic of the infertile aestheticism that he considered so characteristic of German *Kultur*. This new attitude implied a tacit condemnation of his own political past, in which he had idealized the German state as a homoerotic phenomenon. This idealization had been grounded in the assumption that political and moral values could be based on aesthetic *Bildung*. In his opinion however, National Socialism proved that such an approach to politics was based on a horrible misunderstanding. In *Nietzsches Philosophie im Lichte unserer Erfahrung* (*Nietzsche's Philosophy in Light of Our Experience*), a lecture delivered in Zürich in 1947, Mann claimed that there is ample reason to reflect on the relationship between aestheticism and barbarism. He had touched upon this theme once before, in his novella *Mario und der Zauberer* (*Mario and the Magician*, 1930), which puts the magic of art on a par with the fatal attraction of fascism. Obviously, his comparison of Hitler and the artist in *Bruder Hitler* (*Brother Hitler*), as well as the devil's pact with Adrian Leverkühn, the highly gifted German artist in *Doctor Faustus*, should also be seen in this light.

After World War II, both in his political essays and his novel *Doctor Faustus*, Mann suggested that the German disaster had taken place partly because of the gap between political reality and the world of the artistic mind. According to Mann, most German artists and intellectuals lacked a sense of social responsibility and democratic pragmatism due to their "aristocratic solitude and their painful distance from life" ("Goethe und die Demokratie" 759).[25] Because they retreated so often into purely intellectual or aesthetic spheres, the humanism of German political life failed to be strong enough to counter the vitalist and aggressive tendencies of nationalism. In this respect, as he emphasized in his Nietzsche lecture, all those representing German *Kultur,* including the poets, philosophers, and composers, were equally responsible for Germany's atrocities. In this lecture, Mann described Nietzsche as a radical aesthete and compared him to the homosexual dandy Oscar Wilde. Wilde's view that there is no reality behind appearances, Mann argued, corresponds well with Nietzsche's view that spiritual and moral values contain as much truth — or as little — as works of art and myths. Both Wilde and Nietzsche saw life as a game that should be played with grace and, in the case of Nietzsche, with a sense of heroism. Mann further explored this theme in his final novel, *Bekenntnisse des Hochstaplers Felix Krull* (*Confessions of Felix Krull, Confidence Man,* 1954), which he called his "homosexual novel" (cf. TB 4: 295). The main character, Felix Krull, turns his life into art, considering it as if it were a work of art. Yet as an artist he is neither saint nor prophet, but a hustler who deludes the world, partly thanks to his (homoerotic) charms.

In his Nietzsche lecture, Mann pointed out the social dangers of such an attitude toward life. He criticized Nietzsche for his glorification of instinct over intellect and for his negative evaluation of morality as hostile to life. Mann argued that reason, morality, and a sense of proper living should be at the service of humanism and democracy, as a unified force against aesthetic intoxication, which in real life always entails barbarism and death.[26] "The real dichotomy lies between ethics and aesthetics. Not morality, but beauty is allied to death," he writes, adding that the Jewish people with their stern sense of morality have lasted longer than the "profligate little nation of aesthetes and artists, the Greeks" ("Nietzsche's Philosophy" 162). Although he never stated it directly, it seems clear that Thomas Mann no longer supported his former celebration of homoeroticism, as embodied in the German ideal of the *Männerbund* and modeled on ancient Greek examples. As a consequence of the terror of National Socialism and because of his own deep involvement with German history and culture, Mann felt it incumbent upon himself to take an ethical stance, one that was difficult to reconcile with ironic detachment and with an aesthetic approach to politics in which homoerotics played a key role.

Conclusion

It is striking that, in his political essays, Thomas Mann devoted so much attention to German culture and aesthetics and so little to the actual social, political, and economic realities. His analysis of National Socialism was largely conceptualized in the context of his changed perspective on aestheticism, decadence, and the two dichotomies of life versus art and beauty versus morality. Throughout his life, in fact, he continued to reflect on political issues from the (elitist) perspective of the artist. The same holds true for Klaus Mann, despite his lip service to the ideal of a socialist society in which social inequality — in his view one of the main causes of Nazism — would be abolished. Although during and after World War II both embraced some form of humanist socialism and flirted with communism, Thomas and Klaus Mann never showed signs of experiencing a deeper connection with active political life. They never involved themselves with leftist political parties or the labor movement, nor with other social emancipation movements. Social divisions played only a marginal role in their political analyses. Projecting public issues back to intimate needs and fantasies, the political thinking of both writers is indeed strongly marked by their own personal problematics. Their tendency to consider National Socialism primarily as the product of a deeply rooted cultural crisis, for which especially intellectuals were to blame, is closely tied to their preoccupation with the social role of the artist-intellectual. In choosing this perspective, I would argue that they tended to overestimate the influence of art and abstract ideas in modern mass society.

The similarity between homosexual sensibilities and the political concerns of Thomas and Klaus Mann is far greater than it may seem at first glance. For both of them, homosexuality belonged to an aesthetic sphere, one that was ultimately hard to reconcile with moral and political responsibility. Thomas Mann, who always privately struggled with his homoerotic desire, more or less discredited homosexuality as a phenomenon typical of German culture once he realized how easily the cult of physical beauty, in combination with a primitive vitalism, could turn its back on moral values. Starting from a similar line of reasoning, Klaus Mann soon found sexual liberation to be ethically and politically problematic. In his view, fascism proved how easily sexual instincts could be distorted, manipulated, and employed for atrocious political ends. This explains why as an antifascist activist he failed to link sexual liberation and democracy, and why he saw no way of integrating both into his ideal of humanist socialism. Whereas Thomas Mann believed that National Socialism thrived partly on the aestheticizing and homoerotic tradition of the *Männerbund*, Klaus Mann considered fascism a dangerous sexualizing of politics: National Socialism did not so much attract people on the basis of its ideology but, rather, because it played along with their emotions and subconscious urges. Based on their experiences of homosexuality – no matter how much or how differently valued by each in private – it was their individual stand against Nazism that caused them both to end up – and in Klaus's case tragically – with a pessimistic vision.

Notes

[1] The author would like to thank Ton Brouwers for translating this essay from Dutch into English. He is also indebted to James Steakley for editorial comments on an earlier draft and to the Koninklijke Nederlandse Akademie van Wetenschappen for financial support for the translation.

[2] See TB 1: 301, 652; TB 2: 411; *Lebensabriß* 107; *Briefe 1889–1936*, 27–28, 45–46, 53.

[3] For Mann's responses to young men, see TB 1: 111–12, 166, 181, 235, 282, 287, 290, 293, 379, 453–54, 470, 474, 530, 535, 540, 544; TB 2: 185, 296, 397–98, 411–12, 482; TB 3: 58, 306, 369, 409; TB 4: 207–16, 219, 220–21, 230, 238–40, 246–48.

[4] TB 2: 309; editors' trans. See also 412; TB 4: 239. Toward the end of his life, he wrote about his love for a young Swiss waiter: "I find world fame trivial enough, but it carries no weight at all against a smile from him, the look in his eyes, the softness of his voice!" (TB 4: 215; editors' trans.). Well on in years, Mann's homosexual sentiments often gave rise to melancholy self-reflection and sad pondering on his past life.

[5] Editors' trans.

[6] Editors' trans.

[7] Editors' trans.

[8] Editors' trans.

[9] Editors' trans.

[10] Earlier, in an essay on Frederick the Great, Thomas Mann had introduced the contradiction between German militaristic masculinity and what he thought of as French feminine civilization, thereby hinting at the Prussian king's homosexual preference: "Misogyny is now deep-seated in his nature ... It was not merely that the other sex left him cold. He hated it, he poured scorn on it, he could not endure it anywhere near him ... Frederick's masculinity was obviously not attracted in the orthodox way by the feminine counter-pole. Possibly the long years of soldiering contributed to this state of things and weaned his interests from the other sex. There are many cases of military who were or who became women-haters. This man, brought up in an atmosphere of French femininity, may have grown so accustomed to the maleness of camps that at last he 'could not stand the smell' of women. And this

was in the Frenchest of centuries, a woman's century *par excellence*, saturated with the perfume of the *Ewig-Weibliche* (eternal-feminine)" (*Frederick the Great and the Grand Coalition* 161–62). See also Th. Mann, *Gedanken im Kriege* 20–21, 23.

[11]Editors' trans.

[12]Cf. Th. Mann, *Die geistigen Tendenzen des heutigen Deutschlands* 229; and *Brief an Hermann Grafen Keyserling*, in GW 12: 603.

[13]For the next three paragraphs, I rely on Böhm (1985) and Härle (1986 and 1992).

[14]In *Die Wiedergeburt der Anständigkeit* (*The Rebirth of Propriety*), Mann calls the Germans "life's problem children" because of their tendency to turn to "the powers of the unconscious and the precosmic darkness so significant for life" which is a "tendency [that leads] to the abyss, the prototype, [and] chaos" (229; editors' trans.).

[15]Later, Thomas Mann acknowledged to his son Golo that his declaration of sympathy for the Weimar Republic was of a purely literary nature. "It was a combination of beautiful quotations from romantic poets, such as Novalis and others, with no relation whatsoever to reality," he remarked according to Golo Mann (see Hanssen 15).

[16]See TB 2: 470, 497, 592. Thomas Mann criticized the various "nationalistisch-völkisch" movements, Nazism in particular, for violating the values of German *Kultur*. Against the irrational vitalism they advocated (a one-sided and barbaric view of life in Mann's eyes), he emphasized from the mid-twenties onward that humanism and democracy were secured by the rational and enlighted spirit. He also came out in favor of closer ties between the German *Kultur* tradition and the Western European sense of Enlightenment, notably the French one. See: *Deutsche Ansprache. Ein Appell an die Vernunft*; *Deutschland und die Demokratie*; *Die geistigen Tendenzen des heutigen Deutschlands*; *Das Problem der deutsch-französischen Beziehungen*; *Die Wiedergeburt der Anständigkeit.*

[17]Editors' trans. While in exile in Bern, Mann wrote after seeing a German movie: "In which it struck me again that German films bring me something which those of another nationatity scarcely show: pleasure from youthful bodies, particulary male nudes. This is to do with the German 'homosexuality' and is missing among the charms of French and American productions" (TB 2: 308–09; editors' trans.). See also TB 3: 258.

[18]Editors' trans.

[19]In Klaus Mann's opinion, Marxist socialism was too one-sidedly aimed at economic relationships, thus failing to take into account the personal or existential problematics of people. The humanist socialism he advocated would put more emphasis on the individual's self-development. See his *Der Kampf um den jungen Menschen.*

[20]Editors' trans.

[21]Editors' trans.

[22]The manuscript was rediscovered and reprinted in 1969, and again in the 1981 as *Homosexualität und Faschismus.*

[23]Editors' trans.

[24]Editors' trans.

[25]Editors' trans.

[26]As early as 1926, in a lecture delivered in Paris, Mann had pointed to the danger-ous aspects of aesthetic intoxication: "The Germanic inclination toward ecstasy and intoxication can reveal itself as the holiest and as worst; it can mean the zenith of one's life or that fascination through death, which is of an aesthetic and orgiastic essence, which negates everything ethical and the thought of life's responsibilities as petit bourgeois, and which regards religion itself as in opposition to morality. Perhaps it is a sickness which one must have had, so, today, one can have something to say concerning life's affairs. Perhaps it is necessary to have served one's seven years of repentence in the magic mountain of romantic aestheticism to sustain true yearning according to a new conception and formation of the notion of humanity" (*Die gei-stigen Tendenzen des heutigen Deutschlands* 234; editors' trans.).

Bildung and Desire: Anna Elisabet Weirauch's *Der Skorpion*

Nancy P. Nenno

THE FIRST VOLUME OF ANNA ELISABET Weirauch's three-part novel of lesbian life, *Der Skorpion* (*The Scorpion*) appeared in 1919, nine years before Radclyffe Hall published *The Well of Loneliness*. The novel is unique in the history of lesbian literature in German because its publication spans almost the entirety of the Weimar Republic, the time between the repressive regimes of the *Kaiserreich* and National Socialism, when Germany was an El Dorado of gay and lesbian life. Indeed, it is precisely this visibility of homosexuality in a variety of spheres that has become emblematic of this period. Images of Marlene Dietrich as androgynous crossdresser and Anita Berber's bisexual exploits have come to occupy the central position of our field of vision. But what *The Scorpion* suggests is that this was not merely an era of joyous self-expression, but rather that the Weimar Republic was a time in which the contours of homosexual identity were being negotiated. Moreover, the discussion surrounding lesbian sexuality is complex precisely because of a diversity of venues for self-expression during the twenties and early thirties. As a result, the period has recently received scholarly and popular attention particularly in regard to lesbian life and feminist studies (cf. Kokula; Lengerke; Schoppmann; Vollmer-Heitmann).

The Scorpion appeared in three volumes: the first was published by the Askanischer Verlag in Berlin in 1919, the same year as Richard Oswald's ground-breaking *Aufklärungsfilm* (sex education film), *Anders als die Andern* (*Different from the Others*). The second volume was published in 1921, and was followed by the third in 1931,[1] which coincided with the conservative backlash against sexual difference that followed the stock market crash in 1929. The popularity and interest in the topic of lesbianism is further evidenced by the novel's translation into English.[2] During the late 1970s, Weirauch's novel was rediscovered by the German women's movement, which was looking for German texts that could serve, like *The*

Well of Loneliness had for decades, as a German 'lesbian bible'.[3] For many years, the second and third volumes were considered lost, only to reappear recently. Unearthed by the Lesbenarchiv Spinnboden during the nineteen-eighties, these volumes were only available as photocopies in women's bookstores until the Feministischer Buchverlag undertook the publication of a new edition of the novel.[4] In her introduction to the third volume, the editor, Anke Schäfer, addresses the importance of lesbian readership and thus the need to republish the novel, despite its somewhat "old-fashioned" aspects (4).

Anna Elisabet Weirauch had been an actress in Max Reinhardt's company in the beginning of the century and later became a prolific novelist. Weirauch was born on August 7, 1887, in Romania. During the Third Reich, she lived in Gastag, a town in Upper Bavaria, with her life partner. Although not a member of the National Socialist Party, she was, however, a member of the National Socialist organization for writers, the Reichsschrift-tumskammer (Schoppmann 1985, 15). After the war, she moved first to Munich, and then back to Berlin in 1961. She continued to write and publish popular novels into the mid nineteen-sixties, and died on December 21, 1970, in Berlin.

In the canon of lesbian literature in German, *The Scorpion* offers an unparalleled opportunity to explore the negotiation of definitions of lesbianism during the Weimar Republic. In many respects, the text registers the barometric pressure of social opinion on homosexuality – and specifically lesbian identity – during this period. Indeed *The Scorpion* is replete with (often oblique) references to sexologists' theories, as well as to the thriving lesbian culture of the nineteen-twenties in Berlin. The novel is also unique in its critique of the popular fetishization of sexual difference during this period. In a time that celebrated and feared the so-called New Woman, with the perceived willfulness of her self-expression of sexuality and independence, the lesbian became an icon of women's self-determination.[5] The novel sharply critiques this popular and fetishized image of lesbian identity and as such represents an intervention into the linkage between of lesbianism and identity performance.

In this essay, I will argue that the rediscovery of *The Scorpion* is significant insofar as it deviates from the usual fare of literature about gay culture during the Weimar Republic, which often looked voyeuristically from the outside in.[6] Instead of focusing on the image of the lesbian as a figure of resistance to heterosexual norms, in this novel the lesbian protagonist assumes a function as a model for lesbian self-discovery. The protagonist Melitta (Mette) Rudolf develops from a child who falls in love with an older woman, the exotic aunt of her friends, to a woman who chooses her own life by the end of the third volume.

Although it clearly belongs to the class of *Trivialliteratur* (popular fiction) — texts which are only beginning to enter the realm of German cultural and literary studies — *The Scorpion* might be described as an early lesbian Bildungsroman and as such represents an intervention in the canon of German literature. As is appropriate to a Bildungsroman, the novel focuses upon the self-discovery and coming of age of a young protagonist. But in contrast to the Bildungsroman of masculine identity, such as Goethe's *Wilhelm Meister*, the conflicts in *The Scorpion* stem less from the protagonist being pitted against the world than from the novel's internal, dialogic structure. Although the reader only rarely glimpses the tumultuous world of politics, the political repercussions of a marginalized sexual orientation reverberate throughout the novel. Indeed, Weirauch is less interested in the view that the world has of her protagonist, than in Mette's path to self-discovery.

In contrast to the homogeneous popular images of lesbian identity particularly as an 'inverted' or 'masculinized' woman, the multivalence of lesbian identity is a major theme of the novel. In a sense, the lesbianism of the protagonist accords much more strongly with the lesbian as a figure that rejects the fetishization and commodification of female sexuality and identity. Mette represents just such a site of resistance, albeit less toward the requirements of an explicitly heterosexual culture than toward quotidian inscriptions of what it means to be a lesbian. Indeed, the ambivalence of Mette's legibility as lesbian — her explicit femininity, her rejection of theories and practices of inversion, but also her flight from the Berlin scene later — refocuses the novel's search for a definition of lesbian identity from the performance of difference to the object of lesbian desire. The inscription of female homosexuality becomes less identified as a characteristic of a particular body than with a series of desires. To a significant degree, the lesbianism of the novel accords with Luce Irigaray's articulation of female sexuality as multivalent, part of what Blakey Vermeule has termed the "lesbian continuum": an overarching identity that encompasses all affective bonds between women (53-54).[7]

In the early part of the century, constructions of lesbian sexuality were just beginning to surface as the sexologists began to probe the depths of female sexuality. As one popular account put it: "Homosexuality in women remains, more than all other sexuality, concealed from the sight of the observer" (Brailowsky 202). The nascent discourse of sexology sought to pathologize female homosexuality much as it had already pathologized deviant male sexualities.[8] However, the major issues lay in the discussion not only of the origins of homosexuality, but also its social repercussions, so that at this time, the political ramifications of female homosexuality also came under scrutiny. Following the First World War and the rise of a diverse set of fears surrounding female sexuality and "masculinization," the invisibility of lesbians, in effect, the nonviability of their status as subjects in the eyes of the law, shifted. While female homosexuality never received the kind of politicized attention that male homosexuality did — attempts to place lesbianism under the umbrella of Paragraph 175 were ultimately unsuccessful — the awakened interest in "deviant" sexuality led to the establishment of an array of political groups both condemning and supporting gay and lesbian rights (cf. Schoppmann 1995).

In contrast to the dangers associated with male homosexuality, lesbianism was perceived to be insidious insofar as it was thematized within the domestic sphere. The threat seemed to stem primarily from nurturing, maternal figures who became the focus of schoolgirl crushes or who caused the kind of childhood traumas that "caused" lesbianism.[9] Indeed, much of the popular reception of these ideas during the early part of the century focused on childhood as the definitive moment of the homosexual's life. Even into the late 1920s and early 1930s, these models held as they were popularized in films like Mädchen in Uniform (1931, Leontine Sagan) and novels like Maximiliane Ackers's Freundinnen (1923).

In several of the most popular narratives of lesbianism during this period, the theme of the maternal body and the desire for this absent other acquires the status of the traumatic experience that in effect 'causes' lesbian behavior. And indeed, as Judith Roof has noted, the theme of the loss of the mother becomes a red thread in the literary representation of lesbian identity: "Lack of mother means lack of origins and vice versa. Beginning, instead, in media res, after mirror stage differentiation, lesbian novels avoid a mirror stage temporal paradox in favor of confounding post-mirror stage history itself, by denying the importance of origins, even as the protagonists seem to return to them" (108). Roof argues that it is no coincidence that this "desire to desire" constitutes the dominant maternal scenario in numerous lesbian novels. While it is not entirely true for The Scorpion —

Mette Rudloff's bourgeois, privileged origins are made very clear and indeed impinge with great force upon her development — the absence of the mother and Mette's desire for this absent ideal mother structures the narrative and thematic trajectory of Mette's *Bildungsreise* (educational journey).

Volume one of *The Scorpion* concentrates on Mette's search for someone to love in the face of the loss of her mother. The narrator suggests that this is indeed her own fantasy construction: "She had a fantastic conception of the essence of a mother, and always believed that the early death of her own was the cause of all the unhappiness in her life" (1: 9). Indeed, at those moments when Mette finds herself alone, her internal monologue turns to the mother and cries out for this figure of union and completion.[10] Her dramatic, excessive outcries seem to precede and echo Helene Deutsch's assertion that "the desire for the mother acquires the characteristics of a fantasy about the mother's body" (239), one that links the desire for the mother with the death drive. Following the death of her mother in childbirth, Mette lives with her father, Franz Rudloff, and his sister, Aunt Emilie, who oversees the household and the care of Mette. In many respects, both these adult figures function almost as caricatures, recognizable as stock characters in the family drama of female homosexuality during this period. Franz Rudloff closely resembles the father of Stephen Gordon in *The Well of Loneliness*: he is gentle and tolerant toward his daughter, and after his death, Mette, like Stephen, discovers his library of sexology texts (1: 373). Aunt Emilie is the martinet surrogate mother whose unloving demeanor and adherence to the codes and conventions of homosocial order represents the censure and punitive stance of society against sexual deviance. Aunt Emilie's fearful presence and her attempts to "cure" Mette of her "deviant" desire precipitates the implosion of the traditional family circle.

The loss of her mother thus functions retroactively as the decisive moment and organizing narrative in Mette's life, one that predetermines, acts as fate, for the rest of her life. That the novel, much like *The Well of Loneliness*, opens in an Edenic setting — the garden of Mette's grandparents' country house — is no accident, for the theme of the loss of innocence and the fracturing of wholeness dominates the entire book. This world of the proverbial pre-mirror stage remains the object of desire throughout the text. Mette's internal conflict surrounding her own identity is mapped onto the binary oppositions between city and countryside, artificial and urban spaces versus nature and rural idylls. Over the course of the novel, she moves from the idyllic space of a domesticated nature to the chaos of the city only to return, in the third volume, to nature.

The trope that governs Mette's search for a nurturing maternal figure is that of deferral, exchange. Her desire first falls on the maid who teaches her how to pawn objects, and who is eventually forced to leave the Rudloff household. Her desire is subsequently transferred to an aunt of some of her friends, a woman named Olga Radó. In the most superficial sense, Olga stands for the foreign element in Mette's insular world. An independent and educated woman, Olga represents both the danger and the attraction that the modern woman held for many.[11] A polyglot who becomes Mette's teacher, Olga's modernity is emblematized by her independence, her education, and her public smoking. However, Olga also conceals a dark past, and it is this past that precipitates the friends' forcible separation once Mette's family learns of Olga's disrepute. Mette responds by pawning some of the family silver in order to help Olga, after which she is sent to live with her uncle Jürgen and his family in the countryside. There too she finds escape to Olga through theft — an act which indirectly causes her father's death and leaves her an orphan. Olga disappears and it is only later that Mette learns from their mutual friend, Peterchen, that Olga committed suicide upon learning of Mette's (short-lived) engagement. At this point Mette closes the house, provides for Aunt Emilie, and leaves for the city of Berlin, taking little save Olga's pistol and her cigarette étui upon which is engraved a scorpion.

The novel's primary focus on the inner workings and opaqueness of desire is made explicit in the conflict between the discourse of sexology which opens the novel and the story that unfolds as a counterpoint. Mette's journey of self-discovery is framed by an introductory prologue, one that specifically engages with, and imitates, the objective, distanced perspective of the sexologist. From the first line this frame introduces Mette as something abnormal, curious, an object of fascination. "Were I to be honest — that I really wanted to make Melitta Rudloff's acquaintance came about because of her bad reputation. The straight, healthy and pure average person meant nothing to me. I sought out the sick, the lost, the outcasts" (1: 7). This fascination with Mette as a case study is clearly aligned with the objective gaze of the scientist, indeed of the sexologist who seeks to unearth the cause of deviance. Yet, this prologue which paints the plot of Mette's story in broad analytic strokes that elide the details of desire, the "clear and cold joy of the researcher" which seeks to "vivisect and analyze, to systematize" (1: 7) ultimately fails in the narrative. The rest of the novel attempts to delve into precisely those aspects of Mette's life which elude scientific categories. In this manner, the novel acts as a revelation of, and an attempt to fill, the lacunae that the scientific discourse had created in its narratives of female homosexuality.

On the surface, Mette appears to fit many of the sexologists' theories about the criminality and pathological behavior attributed to the homosexual: Mette repeatedly deceives those around her, and it is because of her "criminal" behavior — stealing and pawning some of the family silver in order to give the money to Olga — that a psychiatrist is brought in to consult on her case. However, what this scene reveals is less the inherent criminality of her behavior, the genetic or biological imperative of her theft, than the fact that society's marginalization and pathologization of her cause her to react in ways that are unacceptable in a homosocial environment. The extended discussion between Mette and the psychiatrist illustrates the fundamental inhumanity of such homogenizing scientific categorization.

In this interview, the psychiatrist mouths the widespread fear of the contagion of homosexuality and the threat that such deviant individuals pose to youth. Much of the discourse on homosexuality in the Weimar Republic was closely tied up with the *Jugendschutzgesetz*, the laws for the protection of the youth, which sought to protect children and minors from the potentially detrimental influence of sexual deviants. The casting of Olga Radó as Mette's object of desire and as the pedophilic temptress in the eyes of Mette's family and friends also accords with contemporary rhetoric about the danger of schoolgirl crushes on teachers. This becomes evident when the psychiatrist tries to convince Mette that Olga's influence over her is dangerous, and that she would be better off were she to forget Olga: "Do you really think that this is the first case that has come before us? You will be ruined for life, physically and emotionally ill, robbed of every chance of happiness — what will remain for you then? — Depending upon your inclination: murder or suicide! I have watched terrible tragedies of this sort occur ..." (1: 245–46). Indeed, the psychiatrist was not the only one to see "such terrible tragedies" on a regular basis. Such images of tragic and pathological behavior on the part of homosexuals and lesbians made regular appearances in the popular press during the Weimar Republic.[12]

As a counterpoint to this affectedly limited and effectively limiting conceptualization of lesbian identity as biological and deviant, the novel instead invokes an established and accepted tradition of friendships be-

tween women as its model.[13] In *The Scorpion*, the friendship between the
romantic writers Karoline von Günderode and Bettina von Arnim becomes
the positive counterpoint to the negative sexology arguments, serving as an
alternative model of identification. On the one hand, the epistolary nature
of this relationship becomes the model on which the relationship between
Olga and Mette is founded and which serves as a stylistic and thematic
model for the entire novel. Further, Olga's identification with Günderode
— whom she declares she loves and for whose sake she has endured unending suffering (1: 120) — is borne out by their parallel suicides.

   If on the one hand the novel appropriates German literary tradition to
legitimate the relationship between Mette and Olga, the device of the Gün-
derode/Bettina friendship also serves to divert attention from the construction of Olga as the pathological surrogate mother and contextualizes Mette
and Olga within a cultural and literary tradition of women's friendships.
The elaborate and often excessive language of the novel serves as a rhetorical
device that competes with the discourse of sexology for truth value. An
effective screen for the homosexuality of their relationship, the sentimentality of the rhetoric serves to add ambiguity to the interpretation of their
friendship at the same time as it eroticizes rather than sexualizes the interaction between the two.[14] Partially for this reason, *The Scorpion*, much like
Radclyffe Hall's *The Well of Loneliness*, has been considered by contemporary feminist critics to be outdated. However, within the scope of the
novel, such rhetorical excesses serve to encode the emotion and the desire
in an acceptable and recognizable form. Much like the letters exchanged by
the romantic women, the novel prefers the dialogic exchange between two
minds to the physical playing out of lesbian desire. In this way too, the
object of desire always remains out of reach, it is created only through language.

   The ultimate illustration of the serial deferral of desire in the novel is
represented by the figure of the scorpion and the cigarette étui. The importance of the étui is established early in the women's relationship, and it is
the object that precipitates their separation while continuing to link them.
After Mette has stolen the family silver to give the money to Olga, the latter
repays Mette with the étui. Mette subsequently returns the case to Olga
when she runs away from Uncle Jürgen and when they consummate their
love for each other. Furthermore, the étui is one of the two objects that
Peterchen then passes on to Mette as her legacy from Olga: both the pistol

with which Olga committed suicide and the étui symbolize, indeed stand in for, the constant deferral of desire.

Like the pistol, the scorpion is a figure of fate and destiny. As an harbinger of fate, it stands as an image of loss, for, as Olga tells Mette, the scorpion is the most tremendous of creatures because of its ability to kill itself. The significance of the scorpion is encoded in Olga's motto, engraved on the lid: *Qui vivens laedit, morte medetur.* This image appears to support the psychiatrist's claim that such deviance leads either to murder or to suicide, seeming to echo the discourse of a tragic fate which is the result of lesbian desire.

The linkage between tragic destiny and homosexuality was a popular theme in novels and movies of the interwar period. Certainly Richard Oswald's 1919 film *Anders als die Andern* (*Different from the Others*), which premiered in Berlin's Apollo Theater, tells the melodramatic story of a famous violinist whose homosexual proclivities lead to a seemingly inevitable tragic end.[15] The 1920s saw a veritable flood of novels and films explicitly addressing sexual otherness, and especially the fetishization and commodification of female sexuality. One thinks of Louise Brooks in G. W. Pabst's *Die Büchse der Pandora* (*Pandora's Box*, 1929), a film in which the first screen lesbian appeared. Christa Winsloe's successful play *Ritter Nérestan*, which was filmed by Leontine Sagan in 1931 as *Mädchen in Uniform*, and her subsequent novel *Das Mädchen Manuela* were popular not only in the lesbian community, but also with a broader audience. Following the early *Aufklärungswelle* of the Weimar Republic, Germany's first wave of sex education, homosexuality became a fetishized identity that was the object of spectatorship and identification. As one woman recalls, it was considered chic to act as if one were lesbian (Kokula 1983, 27). The fascination with the sight of difference, of the gender-bending with which we associate much of Weimar culture, became a trademark of Berlin's identity between the wars.

Indeed, this sexual deviance and decadence was capitalized upon by the tourist industry, as illustrated by a 1931 guide to "deviant Berlin." The "curiosity" and "desire for experience" (*Neugier und Erlebnishunger*) that drive the modern person also fueled the fascination with the risqué and titillating image that Berlin had during the interwar period. In Kurt Moreck's *Führer durch das lasterhafte Berlin* (*Guide Through Sinful Berlin*), lesbian clubs and bars become just another stop on the guided tour of the city's dark, sexualized side, which begins with afternoon teas, dance parties, and cabarets, and descends into the world of prostitution, gay and lesbian bars, and underworld hangouts: "The modern person's private life has been shifted more and more to the public sphere" (60). The perform-ance and flaunting of sexuality and difference provide spectacles of devi-ance, commodified for the paying guest into "dramatized comedies of vice" (133).

But in contrast to many of the gay clubs, Moreck notes that the lesbian bars of Berlin prefer an intimate atmosphere that eschews the flaunt-ing of homosexual identity. As opposed to the blatant fetishization and overt commercialization of sexual difference in popular narrative, the les-bian culture in Berlin during the Weimar Republic was a relatively closed community. Not homogeneous by any means, the lesbian circuit of events included everything from bars and elite, often separatist, clubs such as Klub Violetta and Monbijou in the fashionable Berlin West districts, to sports clubs, to lesbian publications such as *Die Freundin* (*The Girl-friend*).[16]

The second volume of *The Scorpion* takes issue with such popular images of the lesbian. In contrast to contemporary celebrations of this flourishing lesbian culture as a site of unambiguous self-discovery and lib-eration, the theme of the second volume ties this atmosphere to the themes of grief and mourning. Mette leaves her home and moves to a pension in Berlin, where she is introduced to the urban lesbian and gay cultures. In keeping with the tragic trope of the novel, the figures who populate this world are self-destructive and not particularly attractive as objects of iden-tification. The residents of the pension are divided between two social groups: one congregates around a painter named Luise Peters, while the other surrounds a cabaret artist named Fräulein Luigi. In the company of the former, Mette meets Gisela, a suicidal and narcissistic figure. Gisela is a spurned lover whose goal is that of forgetting, hence her addiction to mor-phine and cocaine. In many respects, she fulfills the negative stereotypes of the tragic lesbian who nowhere finds acceptance and love.

As Judith Butler has suggested, "identity categories tend to be instru-ments of regulatory regimes whether as the normalizing categories of op-pressive structures or as the rallying points for a liberatory contestation of that very oppression" ("Imitation" 13–14). Unlike the first volume in which the homosocial family constitutes the adversary to Mette's self-dis-covery, the only context to which Mette reacts in this second volume of *The Scorpion* is that of the lesbian and gay culture of Berlin. Mette's response to the decadent and performance-oriented world of the urban gay culture is a distinctly negative one. At a party she is surprised and shocked by the cross-dressing of men and women alike. She rejects the masculinization of lesbian women, and the overt, seemingly necessary, performance aspect of lesbian identity. In this volume of the novel, the text attempts to come to terms with the 'naturalness' or the 'artifice' of lesbian women. Mette's status as outcast is predicated upon her difference within the lesbian and gay community. Her education, or *Bildung*, takes place not in the adversarial world of heterosexual social norms, is not constructed as something different from or marginal vis-à-vis the dominant paradigm. Rather, her struggle for self-knowledge is fought out within a marginal culture that occupies center stage in this second volume of the novel. Weirauch thereby contests the myth of the homogeneity of lesbian identity, as she situates Mette's search for her own identity within the context of a fractured lesbian community.

Much as the dyad of Bettina von Arnim and Karoline von Günderode served as a model of domestic harmony in the first novel, Mette finds a counterpoint to the performative, excessive construction of lesbian identity in the couple Sophus (Sophie) and Nora. These two women, who have been lovers for many years, form a central point of confluence and stability for the younger gay and lesbian set. In effect, Sophus and Nora function as a modern, contemporary counterpoint to the Bettina/Günderode theme that runs through the first volume. The 'marriage' between Sophus and Nora appears ideal — again the image of the garden that they cultivate becomes an image of wholeness — or it is what Mette seeks: something that will last a lifetime. Yet, the specter of death and tragedy remains, for Sophie makes a living as an artist at sculpting tombstones, while Nora is critically ill.

Mette's ultimate rejection of the spectacular nature of this urban homosexual culture comes as she herself is positioned as spectacle. Toward the end of the second novel, Mette befriends a woman named Gwen and a man named Fred Wietinghoff. Finding herself maneuvered into a voyeuristic menage-à-trois, she departs Berlin for the countryside. In contrast to the chimerical urban gay identity, she asserts an inner core of selfhood as she discovers "the indestructible in herself" (2: 463).

In many respects, the withdrawal from the city that initiates the third and final volume of the novel mirrors the withdrawal into the home space that characterizes many of the narratives by women from the early 1930s

(Ankum 3). The third volume of the novel begins with Mette's desire for a space of her own. Upon arriving in the country, she sees a house with a wall and becomes enthralled with the idea of isolation: "'Such a wall!' thought Mette desirously, 'to have such a wall around oneself. To be protected from every glance, and to have only plants and animals and what is pleasant around oneself, hidden behind a wall. It must be wonderful'" (3: 15). As a counterpoint to the voyeurism and self-display of the urban sphere in the second volume, Mette's desire for protection and concealment is also a desire to avoid being looked at, to be protected from the gaze of others. Her house becomes a shell with which she shields herself from the world, withdrawing into an isolated, quasi-domestic sphere.

Mette subsequently buys a plot of land and builds a house, the house becoming a symbol of her own discovery of self-sufficiency. After years of chasing phantasms — whether the absent mother or Olga — Mette withdraws into herself to find comfort and to nurture her melancholic desire. She maintains sporadic contact with her friends Peterchen and Eccarius, whom she had met through Olga in Berlin. Her maternal instincts are fulfilled by the adoption of a puppy. The domestic sphere becomes a safe haven for her as she builds her house with a wall. In some respects, Mette seems to have taken Nora and Sophie's model as her own. On the other hand, like Stephen Gordon, she seems to acquiesce, even to embrace, loneliness as her punishment for her difference.

However, the ghost of Olga Radó continues to haunt her even here for Mette's search for the lost object of her desire, Olga, comes full circle as she meets Corona, who had given Olga the scorpion-etched étui many years ago. It is over the scorpion — the sign of death and the signifier of tragic life — that the scene of recognition takes place:

> Mette quickly took the cigarette étui out of her handbag, opened it and held it out. It was the broad, low, golden étui with the scorpion made of small rubies and Olga Radó's name on the interior. Corona von Gjellerström took a cigarette and, remarking "Oh, how lovely," bent a little closer to see it better.
>
> An incomprehensible trembling sound, joy, fury, complaint came from her lips.
> She laid her hand over the open box in Mette's fingers, the whole hand with a comprehensive movement: "My étui!" (3: 70)

It would seem that the étui and Olga were merely preludes to the meeting of Mette and Corona. The coincidence of this scene of recognition underscores the running theme of fate and fatality in the novel. The series of maternal figures/lovers in Mette's life become, in retrospect, "forerunners" to this fated pairing (3: 92).

Again the scorpion takes on a central metaphorical role, serving both as a symbol of the tragedy of life and as a sign of the intertwining of desire and death. When asked why she had had a scorpion engraved on the étui, Corona reveals that it is because of the meaning of the scorpion, Olga's birth sign: "Don't you know what this sign means? It is the sign of sexuality [Sexualismus] and the secrets of death" (3: 76). If Mette, who repeatedly contemplates repeating Olga's suicide through the novel, cannot die because she does not love death, then this becomes the scenario in which her death will be made possible. For Corona is modeled on popular images of the "Vampirweib," who sucks the life out of her lovers but gives nothing in return.[17] Her sexuality and energy are marked as narcissistic, and she declares herself incapable of fidelity or steadfastness.

Corona becomes a symbol of Berlin and of the urban life that Mette ultimately rejects. Her inconsistency makes her an object of desire that is constantly eluding containment. As a result, Mette ultimately returns to Olga as her absent object of desire, for it is this absence which conversely insures her presence. As she gives up her desire to control Corona, the links between the maternal body and birth become central metaphors once more, but this time as a form of self-assertion. Toward the end of the third volume, Corona discusses Olga's death as a "birth" (*Entbindung*, literally, a disengagement from the mother), in which she had set herself free (3: 319). The motif of birth and death again reappears and closes the novel, much as it had opened it. Mette, aligned with nature and nurturing the lost image of Olga, remains in the country as Corona returns to the city.

It is primarily the desire to see oneself reflected that has motivated the rediscovery of the Weimar period as a high point of gay and lesbian life. This was certainly a primary motivating factor in the reissue of *The Scorpion* during the nineteen-seventies under the auspices of the women's movement. As Anke Schäfer, the editor of the first volume of the reprint, phrased it: "We should also address those questions that affect us in the literary realm: what differentiates us from the lesbians, for example those who lived around the turn of the century — what did their existence look like, with what kinds of contradictions and problems were they confronted — to what extent can we recognize ourselves in them?" (5).

The value of a text such as *The Scorpion* lies less in its stylistic or artistic elegance than in its historical surplus value. While contemporary readers will undoubtedly find the relentless tragedy of the story to contradict the recent celebration of the Weimar period as a decade of liberation, the historical specificity of Weirauch's novels sheds light on the diversity of the definitions of lesbianism during the 1920s. Further, Weirauch's explicit appropriation of the friendship between the romantic women writers suggests ways in which lesbian writing has long sought not only to differentiate itself from the literary canon, but has also found points of connection to a predominantly heterosexually-oriented tradition, thus in effect *queering the canon* it had itself inherited.

Notes

[1]All references to the novel will be designated henceforth with volume and page number. All translations are my own unless otherwise noted. In the secondary literature around *The Scorpion*, there has been some discrepancy in these dates. I am adhering to the dates cited in the recent reprints by the Feministischer Buchverlag.

[2]The first two volumes appeared (unabridged) in 1932 and 1948 as *The Scorpion*, shortened in 1958 and 1964 to *Of Love Forbidden*. Volume three appeared as *The Outcast* in 1933 and 1948. Later, in 1964 and 1975, they appeared together as *The Scorpion*.

[3]Claudia Schoppmann's *Examarbeit* in German literature, which essentially marks the "rediscovery" of *Der Skorpion*, focuses not only on the novel, but also on lesbian themes in a range of literary texts in German.

[4]The reprint of volume one appeared in 1977 and again in 1992, followed by volumes two and three in 1993.

[5]Indeed, some sexologists perceived a direct connection between the women's movement around the turn of the century with lesbianism (cf. Pieper). On the creation of the image of the "New Woman," see Frevert.

[6]Perhaps one of the more notorious examples of this trend was *La Garçonne* (1922), a French novel written by Victor Margueritte and made into a film in 1925: *La Garçonne: Die Frau am Scheideweg*. See also Wendland.

[7]In this way, the novel also illustrates its ties to the German women's movement from the early part of the century. Anna Rüling explicitly addresses the connection between the women's movement and the homosexual question in her essay, "What Interest Does the Women's Movement Have in the Homosexual Question?"

[8]This fascination with female sexuality is detailed by Stephen Kern (132–34).

[9]For example, in *Das Problem der Homosexualität* (1917), Alfred Adler posited the homosexual as a "schwachmütiger Mensch" who had been turned from normal sexual development by a traumatic childhood experience (cf. W. U. Eissler 23).

[10]In one passage of the first volume, Mette cries out: "Dear, good mother, why have you left me alone, totally alone in the world?" (1: 234).

[11]An early German text that foregrounds the conceptual link between feminism, educated women, and lesbianism is Aimée Duc's *Sind es Frauen?*

[12]Alfred Döblin, for example, wrote a short novel entitled *Die beiden Freundinnen und ihr Giftmord* based upon trial of two women lovers. See also Siemsen. For a similar discussion of the murderous act of two women lovers, see Brailowsky.

[13]In her classic essay, Esther Newton suggests that this is the model against which Radclyffe Hall explicitly reacted in *The Well of Loneliness*, embracing instead "the image of the mannish lesbian and the discourse of the sexologists about inversion" (1985, 10). See also Strobel; Rauch; and on the paradigma of romantic friendship, see Faderman.

[14]The characterization of lesbian relationships during this period is often predicated upon the difference between eroticism and sexuality. Ruth Roellig wrote in the introduction to her book, *Berlins lesbische Frauen* (1928) that lesbian women were "more erotic and less sexual" (in A. Meyer 32). This eroticism has also posed problems for those critics who look for representations of "lesbian sexuality" as the defining marker of lesbian identity.

[15]In particular for a thorough exploration of these texts, see Dyer, "Less and More," Kreische, and Theis.

[16]*Die Freundin* was published between 1924 and 1933, except for a period in 1928 when its public exhibition was banned. For a more detailed history of this magazine, see Vogel.

[17]Peterchen laughingly comments to Mette that Corona is "Kannibalin in Reinkultur! Seelenraubtier − Vampir − Strige!": "Cannibal in pure culture! Predator of souls − vampire − witch!" (3: 63).

That Obscure Object of Desire: Fantasy and Disaster in Ingeborg Bachmann's *A Step Towards Gomorrah*

Karin Bauer

INGEBORG BACHMANN'S *A STEP TOWARDS GOMORRAH*, a story from the collection *The Thirtieth Year*, tells of the nightly encounter between two women: Mara, a young Slovenian student, and Charlotte, a successful concert pianist. Mara stays behind as the last guest at the end of a party at Charlotte's Vienna apartment, and apparently overstays her welcome. Charlotte is "dead tired" and searches for a "polite, appropriate sentence" to make Mara go (105; 106). Charlotte suspects that Mara wants something, that she has a request or "some story with which she wants to cheat me of my sleep" (106). Mara, however, seems to neither have a story nor a history, and her request is for Charlotte's love and attention. As the evening progresses, it turns out that it is Charlotte who has a story with which she cheats herself of her sleep. Mara's presence facilitates an existential crisis for Charlotte, a crisis that forces her to confront her mode of being and her seemingly comfortable place in society and in her marriage with Franz.

During the night and into the early hours of the morning, Charlotte begins to question her life and the choices she has made, she reflects upon the limitations of her present existence and briefly fantasizes about the possibility of leaving her marriage. Her crisis, provoked by Mara, does not follow a sudden discovery of dissatisfaction with marriage or a flash of insight into the possibility of a lesbian alternative, but rather is one of gender identification bringing to consciousness latent conflicts and resentments. In her thoughts and fantasies, Charlotte is unable to deal productively with these conflicts, for she cannot destabilize the construction of subjectivity and social hierarchy to a point at which she would be able to visualize herself as standing and acting outside present parameters of gendered, patriarchal consciousness. On the one hand, she fantasizes — in decidedly patriarchal terms — about conquering Mara and the world; on the other hand, she dreams about the invention of a new language and the utopian creation of counterimages to male history and the status quo. Charlotte perceives creation only within patriarchal structures and patterns of thought and behavior, that is, in terms of conquest and domination, and, paradoxically, as a complete 'leap' and withdrawal from precisely these structures. She fails to reinvent and revise her own position in both her marriage and society as a whole, because her fantasies of change are based upon two conflicting tendencies: the longing for an absolute break from reality and the drive to form a relationship with another women within the framework of existing patriarchal patterns of human interaction. Her inability to transform the norms of identity and gender construction in her fantasies reduces her reflections to a faint attempt at reassessing her life. Remaining caught in patriarchal structures, the imaginary relationship between Charlotte and Mara constitutes neither a utopian Other nor a true alternative to marriage. Furthermore, the fantasized relationship between the two women fails because of the absence of eroticism and sexual desire. It never develops into more than a brief fantasy of power.

Charlotte's reflections on her childhood and marriage, and her fantasies about a break from present cultural, social, and private-personal constraints dominate the story. The lack of action and the brief change of scenery — the women leave the apartment and go to a bar during the few late-night hours — accentuate the relatively narrow difference between narrative time and narrated time. Fleeing the scene of the party, Mara takes Charlotte to a seedy bar. Holding hands like two schoolgirls, the women run though Vienna which at that moment appears like an innocent, quiet village. The bar, however, is no place for innocent girls: it is airless, hot, hellish red, and reeks of smoke and alcohol. People are drinking and dancing without obvious pleasure and "Charlotte had the feeling that she found her way into a room of hell, to be burned and made to suffer by tortures as yet unknown to her" (108). The noises of the bar torment Charlotte, who is afraid of being seen in this place, having ventured from "her own world without permission" (108). Mara does not dance just for the sake of dancing; she is performing a dance for Charlotte. The atmosphere of the bar has a mesmerizing effect on Charlotte. She becomes immobile, speechless, and oblivious to the passage of time, and even the wine does not "come to an end" (110). She has to make an effort to utter the words: "Let's go" (111). Upon their return to Charlotte's apartment, Mara begins crying and asks Charlotte: "Why don't you want me" (112). She offers to leave if Charlotte tells her why she does not like her, but Charlotte keeps thinking that "it's mad-

ness" and reminds Mara to be "sensible" (113). Mara, however, has no intention of being sensible and reproaches Charlotte for calling her: "you
made me come to you, you took me with you again in the night, and now
I disgust you, now you don't want to admit that you called me to you"
(114). Mara then kisses Charlotte, and Charlotte compares Mara's lips to a
cat's muzzle and her kiss with that of a cat. To Charlotte, Mara's head
seems small and fragile, and "more insignificant than any head, any hair,
any kisses that had ever come over Charlotte" (114).

The comparison with a cat's affection and the insignificance of Mara's
kiss confirm to the reader Mara's suspicion of Charlotte's contempt for
her. While Mara's kiss is not significant enough to arouse strong feelings
of disgust, Charlotte's thoughts reflect a disregard and disrespect for the
other woman. Mara begs for a kiss from Charlotte, and recognizing that
Mara, because of her desire to be kissed and loved, is in the weaker position, Charlotte rather cruelly takes advantage of her own position of power.
Instead of kissing Mara, she looks at her wristwatch. Frustrated, Mara begins
to smash objects, and with this aggressive and destructive act she facilitates
Charlotte's momentary departure from the constraints of reality. Up until
then, Charlotte's "thoughts were still tramping to and fro like watchmen in
her head" (113); this changes with the scene of Mara's destruction: "Her
feelings, her thoughts jumped off the normal rails, raced without a track
into the open. She let them run wild. She was free. Nothing seemed to her
impossible any more" (116). However, closer examination of the fantasies
following this apparent derailment of Charlotte's feelings and thoughts
raises serious doubts about the narrator's postulation of a rupture. While
Charlotte's reflections might run wild, they certainly are not free, and while
Charlotte might think the impossible, the impossibilities remain squarely
controlled by the watchmen, that is, male society, in her head. In the end,
Charlotte is not able to fantasize the impossible in erotic or sexual terms.

In depicting Charlotte's thoughts, reflections, and fantasies, the text
discloses Charlotte's imaginary relationship with Mara as a failed homoerotic fantasy. Charlotte's fantasy is symptomatic of her failure to set the
stage for sexual desire as well as for constructive changes in her life. In the
fantasized relationship, Charlotte is not able to envision a break with fixed
subject-object relations and merely reproduces patriarchal patterns of
thought by imagining Mara as her "creature" (123). Charlotte's fantasies expose themselves as fantasies of power void of erotic content, and they
undermine Charlotte's aspiration to access an "untrodden zone" and find

a new "kingdom," where "she would no longer be at home in this city, in this country, with a man, in a language, but in herself" (123-24). According to Charlotte, all possibilities of self-empowerment hinge on her ability to love Mara: reality would disappear and she would enter a utopian 'no man's land', if only she *could* love Mara.[1] Yet Charlotte realizes that she neither loves nor physically desires Mara: "I don't want Mara because I want her mouth, her sex — my own. Nothing of the sort. I want my creature; and I shall create it for myself" (123).

Reading *A Step Towards Gomorrah* as a fantasy of power that fails both to act upon homoerotic desire and to engage in constructive change adds another conflicting dimension to the various interpretations of Bachmann's story. Karen Achberger insists that *Gomorrah* represents a utopian myth of femininity, "a new genesis, the creation of the female self, a counterimage out of the ashes of a male-centered world" (79). One of the leading Bachmann scholars in North America, Achberger's emphasis on the utopian dimension of Bachmann's work has contributed to the stylization of Bachmann into a cult figure of early feminist literature. Achberger traces the various biblical references in *Gomorrah* to argue that Charlotte progresses during the night: she has begun to destroy the old order, but "she cannot yet envision the present or future, a room with Mara, toward which, however, one difficult first 'step' has been taken" (85).[2] Upon a close reading of the text, it is difficult to see what Achberger means by "progress," for the story undermines its own brief utopian sentiments and ends with the same images with which it began. There is no indication that anything has changed or will change in the future. Late into the night, Charlotte sets the alarm, indicating that she will pick Franz up from the train station as planned. Achberger claims that *Gomorrah* is "a story of female creation and as such constitutes a deliberate countermyth to the patriarchal tradition of Judeo-Christianity," and she constructs her interpretation in opposition to readings that leave the reader with a "flattened, trivial account of literal lesbianism" (79). In a surprising move, she reads the references to the Old Testament not as critical, problematic, or ironic allusions protesting *against* the patriarchal tradition of Judeo-Christianity representative, but rather as a signal *for* "a breaking with the old covenant and advent of a new order and knowledge, a new race and gender" (79).

Dinah Dodds, for example, takes *Gomorrah* as a story of literal lesbianism and examines how a lesbian relationship is used "to call into question traditionally accepted sex roles in marriage" (431).[3] In a problematic confla-

tion of the narrator and Bachmann, Dodds identifies "Bachmann as a per-
petuator" of the "inability to view homosexual relationships as viable"
(431). She contends that "despite an apparently positive view of lesbianism,
Bachmann finally shows that love between two women is not a real alternative to the prevailing heterosexual norm" (431). Like Achberger, Dodds
equates the narrative voice with Bachmann's views, rather than recognizing
that the narrator has difficulty telling this story without resorting to clichés.
Both critics insist on decoding this overabundance of conspicuously trite
metaphors and symbolisms as Bachmann's hidden message to the reader.
While Achberger circumvents the issue of lesbianism, Dodds is clearly dis-
appointed by its treatment in the story. Dodds argues that "Bachmann
realistically sees the need for new myth, language, and roles," and that "she
retracts her solution" (438) to patriarchal modes of being. Their joint ap-
plause for the quest for a utopian potential blinds them to the subversive
and ironic quality of Bachmann's narrative and, especially, of the allusions
and biblical references. Achberger's approach reflects the aspirations of
feminist projects beginning in the seventies, namely, the search for a utopian countervision in women's literature. The proponents of a feminist
utopia in Bachmann's work have consistently overemphasized the utopian
moments at the expense of the author's relentless undermining of these
moments. Although Dodds finds the need for new, feminist myths to be
"realistic," she acknowledges – albeit with trepidation – the failure of
Gomorrah in this regard: "Creating myths, creatures, and language is, in our
Western Judeo-Christian tradition, seen as a masculine activity. God created
the heaven and the earth, and Adam named the animals. By performing
these activities, if only in her head, Charlotte is doing nothing more than
assuming for herself her husband's masculine role" (437). Charlotte,
Dodds concludes, is not able to create new roles and "thus the lesbian relationship is in the final analysis no improvement over Charlotte's previous
heterosexual one" (437).

Charlotte's imagined relationship with Mara leads merely to a reversal
of gender roles, because of the paradoxical fact that Charlotte can only envision her break from patriarchal society in patriarchal terms. In her fantasy,
Charlotte's will-to-creation constitutes itself as a masculine will-to-power.
While she thinks of the real Mara in diminutive terms, as a "little bother-
some animal" and a creature "playing the child" (118), the Mara of her fantasies has no identity of her own, but is a creature entirely of her own design: "[Charlotte] needed somebody around her, beside her, beneath her,

for whom she not only worked but for whom she was the approach to the world, for whom she set the tone, decided the value of a thing, chose a place" (118). In the imagined relationship, Charlotte wants complete power over Mara's thoughts and feelings. She does not consider an equal relationship, but one in which she completely controls Mara's access to the outside world. She "looks down at Mara" and imagines that "she would be able to subjugate Mara, to guide and push her" (127); Mara would be somebody "for whom the only important thing was to take part in [Charlotte's] life and for whom she was the measure of all things ... somebody, above all, for whom it was more important to think with [Charlotte's] thoughts than to have a thought of her own" (119). Outside of her domineering fantasies, Charlotte finds that she has no identity of her own, for she has always subordinated herself to the men in her life, a "subjugation that she herself, rather than [Franz], had carried out" (121). The impossibility of constructing a female identity is thus not caused directly by men, but rather by Charlotte's inability to envision a female identity at all: either one is active, creative, subjugating, and male, or one is weak, inferior, and female — in which case one gives up the claim to an identity. The negation of female identity in Charlotte's fantasies shows her incapable of projecting a constructive female identity for herself or for Mara. Charlotte's fantasized identity simply slides into the male role of the domineering creator; Mara's perpetuates the role of the weak and vulnerable female who must give up her identity altogether because the construction of male identity depends upon the continual obliteration of female identity. In her present reality, Charlotte concludes, "I don't even exist yet" (123), but in her fantasy, she sees herself as "no one's wife," with a partner who has no identity and thus does not exist either: "I want to decide who I am, and I also want to create my creature, to create my suffering, guilty, shadowy partner" (123). Charlotte's fantasized subjectivity is male-identified and can only construct itself at the expense of the disempowerment of women. The sacrifice of female identity — her own as well as Mara's — is the price that must be paid for adopting the male will-to-creation.

While fantasizing about dominating Mara's every thought and action, Charlotte begins to understand the mechanisms of her own subjugation to Franz. However, instead of rejecting these mechanisms of power, she reenacts them in her fantasies and never considers what it would be like for Mara to surrender her identity to Charlotte. Reacting to her own entrapment, Charlotte directs her resentment toward Mara, rather than pursuing a

course of action that would allow her to take at least one step toward
liberating herself from social and marital constraints. After the party, the
apartment — which is clearly Franz's because he has chosen all the furniture — is a scene of destruction: "disarranged chairs, crumpled table nap-
kins on the floor, the hazy air, the devastation, the emptiness after the onslaught. [Charlotte] felt sick. She was still holding a burning cigarette in her
hand and tried to stub it out in the pile of stumps and ashes" (105).
Building on the theme of Gomorrah, Mara smashes things and adds to the
destruction and disarray already present: Mara "destroyed one object after
another. The destruction seemed to go on for a long time like a fire, a
flood, a demolition" (116). The destruction in the wake of the party represents a self-destruction of and by the Viennese social order. Both this and
the further destruction of the patriarchal order by Mara — "the lucid order
that belonged to Franz" (119) — occur without Charlotte's active participation. Afterwards she attempts halfheartedly to straighten up, but in the end
leaves it to her domestic help, who is supposed to come in the morning.
It is Mara who externalizes and enacts the real destruction of the male order
that Charlotte keeps at the level of reflection.

Once she senses her superior masculine position, Charlotte claims not
to understand Mara's "words without muscles, these useless little words"
(117). She cannot make out what Mara is saying, for Mara is talking too
"vaguely," and Charlotte misses the "language of men" which "was such
that you could hold on to it" (117). Charlotte claims to recognize herself
in Mara's speech, the blackmailing tenderness and affection of the "sing-
song full of ignorance" (117). Projecting her own weaknesses onto Mara,
Charlotte forces her into the role of the submissive female. She does this
despite evidence to the contrary, for at the beginning Mara is quite aggressive and exhibits the traditionally masculine strength required for destruction. In order to affirm herself in the masculine role of the creator, as somebody controlling her own destiny, Charlotte projects the role of the female
onto Mara, who acts increasingly according to these feminine patterns of
behavior. Mara becomes Charlotte's "prey" and "victim," and she becomes
weaker, less aggressive, and takes on the role of the stereotypical jealous
female, who lays exclusive claim on her partner. Fixed by her female role,
Mara states that she wants nothing but love. Like Beatrix in *Simultan*'s
"Problems Problems," Mara claims to want nothing, to care about nothing, and to have no interests. Mara counters Charlotte's attempts to elicit
some response to her question about Mara's wants and goals: "I don't

want anything. I won't fall into the trap" (128). Her desire to love and be loved is exactly what puts Mara in a disadvantaged position, for Charlotte exploits Mara's desire. Her behavior toward Mara is cruel and calculated, and despite Mara's repeated requests, she refuses to send her away. Charlotte states that love does not seem so important, and toward the end of the story, Mara is gradually reduced to a creature without a will of her own. For a while still, Mara argues obstinately with Charlotte and repeatedly accuses her of lying; later she resorts to begging: "Don't be angry ... You are wonderful. I want to do everything, believe everything, that you want me to. Only love me!" (129). Once Mara surrenders her will, Charlotte's patriarchal utopia reaches its height and its breaking point: "It was time for the change of shift, and now she could take over the world, name her companions, establish rights and duties, invalidate the old pictures and design the first new ones ... First make the leap, leap over everything, carry out the withdrawal when the drum is beaten" (130). At the height of her envisioned power, Charlotte would be forced to take a leap out of present reality: "To hope for the kingdom. Not the kingdom of men and not that of women" (130). She, of course, does not take a leap, but resumes her former life. The shift change Charlotte envisions would require the impossible, namely, a complete break with reality. By basing her fantasies of liberation upon a withdrawal from patriarchal structures and languages, Charlotte creates an unimaginable scenario that renders futile any thought or action creating a viable alternative to and in the present, and, consequently, both women are now literally immobilized.

In the end, Mara cannot walk or stand anymore and pronounces: "I'm dead ... I can't go on any longer. Dead, I'm so dead" (131). The narrator states that "it was too late for everything," and Charlotte, too, is dead: "They were both dead and had killed something" (132). Charlotte sets the alarm indicating that she will pick Franz up from the station, and Mara looks at her indifferently. The fantasy has come to an end: Mara's "red skirt lay crumpled and insignificant by the bed" (132). The relationship with Mara is never consummated because, after hours of indulging in patriarchal fantasies of power, it is too late 'to hope for a new kingdom', too late even to contemplate a 'leap' into another reality.

From the beginning, the patriarchal structure of Charlotte's fantasy undermines its own utopian ambition and emancipatory potential. It is too late for a 'leap' into a sexual relationship with Mara because, throughout the night, Charlotte fails to establish an erotic space in her fantasies which could prefigure a sexual encounter with Mara. Charlotte does not desire Mara physically, although the narrator claims that she likes looking at women: "they frequently moved her or they pleased her visually, but so far as possible she avoided talking to them" (127). Charlotte's rather disinterested appreciation and her avoidance of any dialogue with women correspond to her disregard for them and the language she ascribes to them. Assigning language according to gender, Charlotte finds the language of women undignified and believes that "absolutely nothing, no insight, no observation corresponds to this language" (127). In her opinion, no intellectual or emotional exchange takes place with or between women, because women's speech articulates itself with an inherent discrepancy between the signified and the signifier.

The absence of the signified is seen as an undignified absence of identity, rendering women's speech vague and ignorant, and the lack of concepts, perceptions, and reflections relating to what is being said points to the potential meaninglessness of women's language. Although considered "bad enough already and doubtful," men's language is superior to women's because it conveys concepts and 'insights', and one can 'hold on to it'. Men's language is marked by the correspondence of the signifier and the signified, and the postulated presence of the signified legitimizes their language. Incapable of transmitting substantial claims to knowledge and power, women's language disqualifies women from participating in meaningful discourse and from utilizing language as a medium for establishing and expressing desire. Like the images of fantasy, language cannot provide an erotic, intellectual, or emotional space devoid of the mechanisms of exploitation and domination ascribed to masculinity and those of self-subjugation and emotional blackmail ascribed to femininity. While denigrating the linguistic expression of women, Charlotte falls into the trap of assuming a correspondence between signified and signifier in male language and identifies with it in her fantasies.

Following the argument of psychoanalysts Jean-Bertrand Pontalis and Jean Laplanche, who reject the separation between unconscious fantasies and daydreams, Teresa de Lauretis points out the significance of fantasy in the stage-setting of desire. De Lauretis states that, according to Pontalis and Laplanche, the origin of fantasy cannot be isolated from the origin of sexuality; fantasy "is not the object of desire, but its setting" (*Practice of Love* 26). She adds, "it is through their representations in fantasy that the drives become properly sexual" (83). Taking Freud as a point of departure,

de Lauretis maintains that sexuality "is not an innate disposition or configuration of the sexual instinct, but rather the result of particular negotiations that a subject manages to achieve between the internal pressures of
drives, the various component instincts and partial drives, and the external,
parental, and societal pressures" ("Habit Changes" 298). The object of desire, de Lauretis contends, is variable and chosen for its ability to satisfy.
With this move, de Lauretis disqualifies the interpretation of homosexuality as a deviation from nature and exposes it as a deviation from a socially
constructed norm. Within the context of *Gomorrah*, her argument becomes important in as far as de Lauretis emphasizes the involvement of
fantasy in the complex process of negotiations establishing sexuality and
sexual desire. Sexuality is "constructed or dynamically structured by psychic processes and forms of fantasy" which provide the scenarios for the
subject's desire ("Habit Changes" 301). The absence of erotic desire in
Charlotte's fantasies accentuates her male-identified drive to power that has
separated itself from and functions devoid of sexual desire. Thus, the scenario of Charlotte's desire exposes itself as an unerotic space of compulsory gender identification. In her negotiations, she identifies with masculinity and resists the restructuring of gendered subjectivity.

Judith Butler sees the constitution of sexuality as both an identification with sexual norms and a continuous process of citing the law. She insists that sex and gender — a differentiation she calls into question by
claiming that sex, like gender, is a constructed discursive category — are
repetitious rituals of citational performance. Butler argues that sex and
sexuality are assumed through complex identificatory processes, and the
performative dimension of the construction of sexuality is a "forced reiteration of norms" (*Bodies That Matter* 94). For Butler, like for de Lauretis,
fantasy is a constitutive moment in the construction of sexuality; however,
she denies that there is a conscious and controlling agent which actively
produces fantasies: "One does not have the fantasies, and neither is there a
one who lives them, but the fantasies condition and construct the specificity of the gendered subject with the enormously important qualification
that these fantasies are themselves disciplinary productions of grounding
cultural sanctions and taboos" ("Gender Trouble" 334). Butler's enormously important qualification merits further comment, for it reveals an
underexplored aspect that points directly to the failure of fantasy to
function as a stage-setting of desire. While fantasies condition and construct the subject's desire, they are constrained, restricted, and controlled by

private, political, social, and cultural norms which undermine their potentially productive and subversive dimension.

In *Gomorrah*, fantasies are censored images always already relegated to
the realm of the reproduction and reiteration of the norm. Charlotte's male-
identified performance continuously cites the law, and this citation undermines her attempt to fantasize a 'new kingdom'. Her gender performance
and identification make visible the limits of both the ability of fantasy to
set the stage for desire and the subversive dimension Butler accords to citational practice. The potential for a subversion of the private and public
realm is lost, for Charlotte's fantasies are caught up in the mechanisms of
domination, subjugation, and exploitation. The restrictive, gendered consciousness cites the law, conforms to and affirms it, while reenacting the
dissolution of female identity. Charlotte's fantasies of power give testimony to the impossibility of even thinking female identity: female identity
is sacrificed as a constitutive effect of a male-identified drive to power. As a
result, female desire is sacrificed, for it cannot be articulated either through
fantasy or in language. Charlotte's fantasy fails to function as a stage-stetting
of (homo)erotic desire, because it fails as a stage-stetting for a restructuring
of gendered subjectivity.

In Bachmann's text, gender identification exposes itself as a repressive,
rather than subversive, process of negotiation and makes visible the social,
cultural, and institutional limitations imposed upon fantasy. Charlotte's
male-identified performance perpetuates deep-seated misogynist perceptions
and ideologies, and exposes both fantasy's complicity with mimetic reproduction and the repressive function of gender identification. Far from erecting a feminine utopia, *A Step Torward Gomorrah* questions and undermines the very possibility of utopian thought and idealistic fantasy. In this
way, it indeed takes a step toward Gomorrah and immobilizes those who
glance at the site of destruction.

Notes

[1] By the use of the subjunctive, the German text emphasizes the hypothetical nature
of Charlotte's love: "Wenn sie Mara *liebte*, würde sich alles ändern," and "Wenn sie
Mara lieben *könnte*, wäre sie ..."

[2] Peter Beicken sees the first step toward change in an androgynous vision. He claims
that the text's utopian wish is the end of the struggle between men and women and

the erasure of sex and gender differences. He postulates androgyny as the utopian ideal in Bachmann's text.

[3]For other thematizations of the 'lesbian' relationship between Mara and Charlotte, see Madeleine Marti's *Hinterlegte Botschaften* and Rita J. Hoersley's article. Marti claims that Charlotte represses her lesbian desire, and Hoersley discusses the critique of heterosexuality.

Christa Reinig's Lesbian Warriors: *One Sunday During the War* of the Genders

Cathrin Winkelmann

> *Sometimes the gay shirt is closer to me than the*
> *feminist skirt*
> —Christa Reinig[1]

IN 1982 CHRISTA REINIG[2] PUBLISHED A collection of short stories entitled *Die ewige Schule: Erzählungen* (*The Neverending School: Stories*)[3] which reflects upon — among other problems surrounding lesbian themes — the difficulties encountered in establishing and representing lesbian identity. Set in Nazi Germany, *Ein Sonntag im Krieg* (*One Sunday during the War*) is one such story from this collection, which portrays a world clearly marked as heterosexual and patriarchal — a world in which women's social, political and sexual expression is inhibited. This situation is ironically depicted in the feminist narrative through Reinig's use of a lesbian subtext, as well as evasive language, symbolism, and the mimicry of the very control mechanisms which silence women, in general, and lesbians, in particular. Concentrating largely on the lesbian facet of the narrative, I will uncover the lesbian subtext of the story by examining Reinig's narrative strategies. *One Sunday During the War* clearly refers on the literal level to Germany during the Second World War; the reader, however, quickly discovers the ambiguity of the term *war*, which — on a figurative level — also refers to the war of the genders[4] and, specifically, to the difficulties two women in the story encounter when attempting to express themselves in a society clearly designated as male-dominated and heterosexual. It is precisely on this figurative level that my investigation will proceed. However, although my analysis is situated within contemporary lesbian-feminist thought, it is only by considering lesbianism in the historical context of the Third Reich that it is possible to demonstrate how this text both provides a general critique of the patriarchal structure of society, and portrays the problems confronted

by lesbians specifically in Nazi Germany. By applying feminist theory, I
will show not only how this story attempts to reclaim a history of lesbianism during the Third Reich and, thus, provide a critique of (male) oppression in Nazi Germany, but also how it simultaneously enlists all women
to engage in the war of the genders – a war, as suggested by the publication
date of 1982, that continues to be waged long after the capitulation of Nazi
Germany at the end of World War II.

This highly complex story describes the negative experiences of an
adolescent, Angelika, in Nazi Germany. The narration revolves around her
hiking trip along a river with Fräulein Ursula Beck,[5] a woman from Angelika's workplace, during which she shares her frustrations about the oppression she has experienced as a woman within patriarchy. Although the
young Angelika cannot express herself directly in such modern terms, her
accounts indeed demonstrate that she feels that she is a victim of male oppression. Angelika also relays to Fräulein Beck her recurring nightmare of
"Bloody Sunday," an historical, violent massacre in the Polish town of
Bydgoszcz (Bromberg) in 1939,[6] which she had learned about by overhear-
ing a conversation – significantly – between her father and uncle. The
story opens with this disturbingly violent dream in which soldiers cut
open the womb of a screaming pregnant woman, tear out her entrails and
the fetus, stuff a cat into her belly and sew her back up, while two crucified
women are suspended in the background. Fräulein Beck, who is at first
rather distrustful of Angelika and only eventually becomes more receptive
to her, serves as a spiritual guide to Angelika, particularly concerning this
nightmare. She recognizes a powerful energy in the younger woman and
ultimately encourages Angelika to use her rage toward perpetrators of patriarchy as a means to alter the fate of the women in her dream as well as her
own destiny. Reinig's language is too evasive, and her narrative techniques
are too subversive, for this ever to be stated directly in the text. However,
altering Angelika's dream necessarily means reconstructing a history of
women, finding an alternative to the dominant, phallocratic system, and
discovering the means to constitute a lesbian identity in this tyrannically
heterosexual society. Reinig suggests this, though not uncritically, as a strategy for women to emerge victorious in the gender war implied in her story.

The tyranny of heterosexuality is discussed by Adrienne Rich in her
1980 essay "Compulsory Heterosexuality and Lesbian Existence." Here,
Rich demonstrates in detail how "male power manifests itself" by "enforcing heterosexuality on women" (234). Drawing upon Kathleen Gough's

essay "The Origin of the Family," Rich amends a list of the characteristics of male power which oppress women by forcing them into heterosexuality and compliance with patriarchy. Included in this list are the restriction of women to marriage and motherhood, the restriction of women's access to knowledge and education, and the restriction of women's emotional and sexual self-expression through silence and rape (232-234).[7] In my analysis of Reinig's text, I intend to locate these male control mechanisms and demonstrate how they inhibit specifically the constitution of a lesbian identity. In *One Sunday During the War*, the difficulty in gaining personal agency originates with the inability of Angelika and Fräulein Beck to express themselves in this phallogocentric society.

Amidst the deep, painful silence in Angelika's violent dream comes a scream from a woman being assaulted by soldiers. When she awakens from the nightmare, Angelika, like the woman in her dream, has no words, no way to express herself other than by screaming. Though she can clearly envisage the scene and the actions of the men who cut the pregnant woman open with their bayonets, she cannot describe the woman when she recounts her dream to Fräulein Beck. She tries to describe the scenario, but needs the narrator's mediation: "She knows the words which had to be spoken here, namely, naked and pregnant and breasts and stomach and bowels and embryo, but she cannot voice them" (21). Fräulein Beck is also linguistically debilitated: "Ursula cannot say anything with precision either" (22). The paternal language — the only linguistic language available to Angelika and Fräulein Beck — is not designed to reflect the experiences of women as women experience them, because it is a male language developed from a phallogocentric value system (cf. Irigaray, Kristeva). Angelika and Fräulein Beck have no way of genuinely formulating their thoughts in the phallogocentric discourse within which they have been forced to think and communicate. As a result, they are confined within this system to a "silence ... so deep that it is painful to the ears" (7).

Angelika tries to break out of this silence by attempting to forge a voice. However, her efforts to speak ultimately cannot overcome the limitations and restrictions of paternal language on women and their experiences, because they are always still a product of patriarchal logic. Angelika recalls a conversation in which she reminded her mother that Angelika's childhood friend, Dagobert, had tried to rape her when she was younger. She explains that "he wanted to violate" her (11). Yet, Angelika cannot say the word "rape"; she must make use of a circumlocution. The reader must infer this violation against Angelika, since the taboo of rape cannot be revealed in the text explicitly, for that would amount to confessing to the heinous crimes committed in patriarchy. To this extent, Reinig's narrative technique intentionally mimics the limitations of the paternal language, in order to accentuate and paradoxically expose those very patriarchal control mechanisms in language that historically silence women's expression of their experiences.

In matters of sexual orientation, the negative effects of phallogocentric language on women become even more apparent. While Angelika and Fräulein Beck are on their journey, they chance upon a small restaurant where they notice a peculiar pair of older women who are attracting the attention of the other patrons of the restaurant. The couple is only indirectly identified by the narrator as lesbian by their clothes: one wears a straw hat and is dressed in a vest and man's shirt with a small necktie, "and the most conspicuous thing on her is her large cufflinks" (20). Fräulein Beck notices that Angelika cannot stop staring at these women, and, once again, it seems as though linguistic communication is impossible: "Ursula realizes that Angelika is looking precisely in the direction in which everyone else has discretely begun to stare. She wants to use the spiritual and intellectual guidance which she has won over the child to explain something to her ... However, Angelika is so taken, that it is impossible to have a conversation with her" (20). It seems that Fräulein Beck wants to make it clear to Angelika that these two women are lesbians, but, although she too may feel an innate bond with the couple, she can neither explain the situation nor describe her feelings about lesbian relationships. Angelika and Fräulein Beck easily converse about many subjects, but when it comes to sexuality, particularly female homosexuality, Fräulein Beck once again remains silent (cf. Marti 1990, 40), because she does not even know how to formulate the words outside of the male, heterosexual discourse which dominates not only sexual language but also male fantasies about women's (homo)sexuality: "She realized that in this instance she did not have any words at her disposal — except vulgarities which she had never uttered and which Angelika would not even understand. She wants to change the topic of conversation ..." (20). The narrator even informs the reader that Fräulein Beck is embarrassed.

It is not merely on the topic of sexual orientation that Fräulein Beck becomes silent. She is, indeed, generally hesitant when speaking to Angelika. This is expressed through her speech patterns and her thoughts which she does not communicate to Angelika and to which the reader is privy only through the narrator's mediation — particularly Fräulein Beck's belief that the trip with Angelika may have been a mistake. Historically speaking, patriarchal society often creates distrust between women through ignorance and prejudice; it attempts to weaken solidarity between women, so as to preserve its male hold on power. In Reinig's story, Fräulein Beck, who is also indirectly portrayed as a lesbian by means of her clothing, distrusts Angelika because she is uncertain about her ideological stance. The reader is surprised to discover that Angelika, dressed in regulation shoes worn by the *Bund Deutscher Mädel* (German Girls League), the corresponding female organization to the male Hitler Youth, observes Fräulein Beck's masculine attire and casts a disparaging glance her way. When Fräulein Beck feels the need to justify her 'peculiar' clothing, she uses the term *Frauenrechtlerin* (feminist) (14), which again causes an adverse reaction in Angelika, probably because her understanding of the term is the direct result of being raised in a misogynist society: "when she hears feminist, she becomes cold" (14). Fräulein Beck — like the reader — does not yet know what to make of Angelika. She is uncertain whether Angelika is a fascist and a homophobe. It is no wonder Fräulein Beck appears noncommittal when speaking with Angelika: she "laughs her usual little laugh which is supposed to signal agreement, but which can be taken back at any time through words" (14-15).

Reinig seems to acknowledge that, although women in this text are portrayed as victims, they are not necessarily or always innocent. Her portrayal of Angelika with her *BDM* shoes and disparaging glance signifying the inevitability of noncommunication between the women demonstrates that Reinig is aware of the complexities and subtleties that entrap and silence women. This also points to the complicity of women in their own oppression and thus reminds the reader that many women in Nazi Germany were just as guilty of crimes in fascist patriarchy as men. Reinig constructs characters that are multidimensional, exposing their strengths, as well as their weaknesses. Thus, because Angelika and Fräulein Beck are not homogeneously developed characters, the reader must contend with their occasionally seemingly contradictory, elusive and inconsistent positions.

Indeed, an air of elusiveness pervades the text. The narrator, like the two main characters, is not always completely forthcoming in her formulations. She provides the reader with only fragmented information about these women, their lives, and the National Socialist society in which they live.

The women's feelings and clear alternatives to the dominant system oppressing them are left out of the narrative altogether. The incomplete portrayal of either emotional or political lesbian representation, that is, the absence of an overt revelation of the sexual orientation of the characters and a differentiated account of their experiences in the narration, is a paradoxical attempt by Reinig to expose the structures which repress women, silence their experiences, and deny their history. She is targeting and subversively mimicking those very patriarchal control mechanisms which oppress women, and particularly lesbians, in an attempt to undermine them.

George Mosse states in his book *Nationalism and Sexuality* that during National Socialism the romantic male ideal of the heterosexual woman was linked to the potency of nationalism, whereby the "chaste and modest [heterosexual] woman ... fortified bourgeois ideals of respectability that penetrated all classes of society" (90). Lesbianism as an expression of female sexuality "was not merely a 'love that dared not speak its name' – it did not even have a name" (91). Claudia Schoppmann also remarks that "any self-determining female sexuality, including lesbian forms, was unthinkable within a centuries-old patriarchal tradition that identified passivity as a female sexual characteristic" (1995, 9). Though there were some concerns about lesbian sexuality such as tribadies and masculinization, lesbianism was not officially a punishable offense, because it was thought that most lesbians could be 'cured' and thus still serve the Reich by bearing children (1995, 9-17). Since Nazi population policies demanded procreation at any cost, heterosexual intercourse was turned into a compulsory national duty for both men and women, and lesbianism was seen as a crime against both nature and the state (1995, 8; 10-14). Female homosexuality was simply denied a visible existence by the strict enforcement of gender norms and the traditions of marriage and motherhood, a concept which manifested itself under Nazism in a national *Gebärpflicht* (reproductive duty) (1993:14 and 1995, 10, 14). Women who bore more than seven children were even bestowed the ultimate reward of the *Mutterkreuz*, the Iron Cross for motherhood, while those not abiding by the norms were labeled antisocial or mentally ill, and attempts were made to remove such "degenerates" from the public sphere (1995,14). For this reason many lesbians married (often gay) men in order to appear to be heterosexual (1993:15).

This historical fact of compulsory heterosexuality during the Nazi era and its suppression of gay and lesbian existence is reflected in Reinig's short story. Angelika is assigned a heterosexual role by her ideologically indoctrinated family because they do not even consider the possibility that she may be a lesbian, since for them such an option could not possibly exist. Her mother thus assumes she is heterosexual, as indicated by her heteronormative comments to Angelika about marriage and heterosexual relationships. Any chance of *openly* constituting and affirming a lesbian identity is denied from the start. This applies equally to the narrator's attempts to mediate. When describing the older lesbian couple at the restaurant, the narrator states that the secret of these women is clear and evident; however, it is never explicitly expressed in the text. In order to establish the couple as lesbian, the narrator must resort to describing their clothing, a coded and nonverbal form of communication outside of the paternal language, understandable only to those who can decipher the symbolism. She can imply their transgression of traditional gender norms as she claims with a tone of irony: "They are a completely ordinary old couple like any other" (20), but she cannot directly identify or declare their relationship as lesbian, because, as Angelika Bammer asserts, "there is ... no language for the experience of women, for the experiences between women. And that which cannot be named [in the paternal language] cannot ... be acknowledged as real" (123). In this case, a public lesbian existence is seemingly disavowed. The narrator may be attempting to blur and yet also simultaneously 'normalize' lesbian relationships with her comment by erasing the difference between homosexual and heterosexual relationships. Either way, however, lesbian experience is compromised because it cannot be openly and confidently acknowledged.

To ensure its control over discourses on lesbianism in the Third Reich, the Nazi regime denied women access to information regarding a history and culture of women that could provide them with either the resources to develop an alternative lifestyle to that sanctioned by the Nazis or with the possibility of expressing their homosexuality in an otherwise heterosexual society. This is demonstrated in the text through Angelika's reaction to the older lesbian couple at the restaurant. She seems to be perplexed and affected simultaneously by these women: "there is something about these two that deeply touches Angelika" (19). It appears that for the first time Angelika has perceived a viable alternative to heterosexual society. This scene illustrates Angelika's struggle to define her own sexual identity within a profoundly heteronormative society. Although this may be Angelika's first glimpse of a positive, engaging life beyond the paternal order in which she feels alienated, she and Fräulein Beck cannot even discuss the issue at hand. The possibility to engage in a fruitful discussion about female (homo)sexuality remains unrealized. They do not have access to the linguistic tools and information required for such a discussion, just as Angelika seems to lack the resources needed to understand feminism as defined by feminists. This scenario accurately mirrors the plight of emancipated women in the Third Reich, since the Nazi regime ensured the disbandment of all feminist organizations and extinguished feminist voices exercising criticism (cf. Hannelore Schröder 488).

Angelika's general lack of access to resources on female sexuality does indeed have profound effects. Although she vehemently rejects the institution of marriage and motherhood and thus appears to want an alternative to compulsory heterosexuality, her naïve views on sexuality render her seemingly powerless. She is unable to differentiate herself entirely from the power structure in place in that she fails to discover homosexuality as a viable option. With her limited knowledge, the only feasible alternative to heterosexuality is sexual abstinence. She swears her chastity to the ancient Greek goddess Pallas Athena, and thus in the process falls prey to the cultic role of the virgin. Forced into this position by the mere fact that lesbianism was not a socially accepted option, she is once again made a passive, nonactive member of society. Angelika seems to want an alternative as indicated by her dreams of freedom and her negative assessment of men, but she has been guarded from the knowledge of a different lifestyle and the tools by which she could attain it, and thus her potential aspirations cannot be realized. To protect itself, the heterosexist, patriarchal society of Nazi Germany has intentionally excluded lesbianism from the discourse on sexuality. By denying Angelika the resources and information needed to partake in such a discussion in a way that would best suit her desire, patriarchal society continues to strip her of her potential power to undermine the phallocratic system.

In regards to the relation of the sexes, Reinig ironically states in an essay: "The woman who is not saved through a man will be sent off to the dark side of the battlefield, where she must lose the war according to divine will" (*Blut* 206). With a sense of vengeance equal to Reinig's irony, Angelika and Fräulein Beck both adopt a rather separatist perspective in protest against the tyranny of patriarchy as their strategy in the war of the genders. This analysis of Angelika's and Fräulein Beck's assessment of and reaction to the phallocratic order is supported by the fusion of the theory of both radical-feminist and revolutionary-feminist lesbian separatism. The view of radical feminism postulates the complete withdrawal of women from men and male culture. Such an all-female society would be based on the very essentialist 'female' values men have traditionally ascribed to women such as nonviolence, community, nurturance, and ecological coexistence (cf. Andermahr 134–35). Radical-feminist lesbian separatism is based on the concept of a female nature, which positions "women as biologically and morally superior to men" (135). Revolutionary-feminist lesbian separatism, however, is an uncompromising repudiation of male-centered ways of thinking and being; it aims at undermining male power and the constructs created to sustain patriarchal structures by ceasing to cooperate with men on a daily basis. Although the text clearly associates males with violence and destruction, and females with nature, nurturance, and nonviolence, and thus resounds dangerously of essentialist notions, the story does not fall short of presenting a more contemporary social-constructionist critique of phallocratic society. By denouncing the violence that men perpetuate (rape, war) while also rejecting the paternal structures which edify patriarchy (marriage, motherhood), Angelika and Fräulein Beck seem to adopt a position which appears to fuse both essentialist and constructionist approaches to gender and sexuality.

It is through Angelika's voice that the separatist tone of the story first emerges. The reader discovers that both Angelika and her landlady have made a vow of chastity. The landlady comments every week on her own purity and vow of chastity in honor of the Virgin Mary. It becomes clear, however, that Angelika's vow is not motivated by Christian tradition, which advocates a heterosexual society, but, rather, is a protest against it. In opposition to the dictates of patriarchal norms, Angelika refuses to perpetuate the heterosexual social structures such as marriage and motherhood that Christian virginity is designed to secure. Her vow of chastity is a private homage to an ideal feminine form, Pallas Athena, the powerful virgin goddess of wisdom, fertility, the useful arts, and prudent warfare – a chaste figure indubitably more akin to the women of pagan myths than to the Christian ideal of the Virgin Mary. The manner in which the narrator portrays Angelika's renunciation of heteronormativity indicates that the young woman, although she has difficulty in defining and expressing herself, nonetheless does stand opposed to heterosexual society even despite her fears: "she would rather die than divulge this secret [the vow of chastity] to someone. Not even to mother, because mother belongs to the other side" (10), that is, the heterosexual world.

Through Angelika's separatist tendencies, the reader clearly recognizes the parallels between the war of the nations and the war of the genders. When responding to her mother's hope for and inquiry about a future son-in-law, Angelika adamantly rejects the institution of marriage through her allusion to male terror and violence. Her mother is appalled by her negative assessment of the "brave men" (11) who every day during wartime look death in the eye to protect the women. Enraged, Angelika replies that women, too, must look death in the eye every day. She recalls how Dagobert, a soldier himself now, attacked her "like a Russian" (11) when he tried to rape her. She asks rhetorically: "Why are we fighting against the Russians if our German men are just like them?" (11). Thus, on both the literal and the figurative level she links the war of the nations with the war of the genders by pointing toward men's deceitfulness, violence, and desire for control.

Reinig also transfers one level of war upon the other by incorporating a scene in which Fräulein Beck relays how she had once been sent to a Nazi concentration camp. Fräulein Beck tells Angelika how Herr Klein, their personnel manager, and Dr. Beese, the company physician, branded her as an addict because of her occasional use of morphine to alleviate her pain from a neurological illness. These people subsequently sent her to a concentration camp. Her addiction, however, can be considered merely as a pretense to deport her. Fräulein Beck was possibly incriminated because she is a lesbian and childless. Although there are a few sources documenting Nazi persecution of lesbians, women were only rarely imprisoned, at least not officially, on the basis of their sexual orientation, particularly if they had children (Schoppmann, 1995, 13-15). While the text does not state directly that Fräulein Beck was deported to a camp because of her lesbianism, the fact that her account of her detention remains strangely elusive points in that direction. For one, she does not provide details about the incident and never mentions how she was able to cope with the excruciating pain while in the concentration camp, nor does she mention any pain later. Moreover, it is questionable that she would be detained for the infrequent use of an addictive medication, especially since it did not interfere with her job, as it never caused her to miss even a day of work (24). Second, the very fact that Fräulein Beck is diagnosed as having a neurological illness can be read as an indication of lesbianism. Traditionally, the medical establishment pathologized homosexuality by associating it with nervous illness, and female homosexuality was admittedly a love "which dominant

prejudices and moral judgment consequently often equated with disease"
(Schoppmann, 1993: 26). Nervous illness and 'aberrant' sexuality, however,
were considered symptoms of degeneration and a threat to national health
– reason enough to be deported to a concentration camp. Thus, although
Fräulein Beck may indeed have suffered from "Trigeminusneuralgie," a
painful facial nerve disorder (23), Reinig could be masking the taboo of lesbianism in the story behind the trope of illness – a popular theme and device in German lesbian and gay literature.

Perhaps Fräulein Beck is afraid to divulge her lesbianism to Angelika
because she does not want to discourage this young, potential lesbian or
perhaps because she is not sure of her ideological disposition. Indeed,
when Angelika asks how the doctor could have sent her away like that,
Fräulein Beck replies: "She who drinks is a drinker, she who smokes is a
smoker, she who takes drugs is an addict" (24), a statement which may well
repeat a likely assumption by a misogynist Nazi physician. She continues
that the doctor "knew right away what this was about" (24). "People don't
see that any differently" (24), Fräulein Beck says, alluding again to Nazi
society's need to label and clearly distinguish its members as per its fascist
totalitarian agenda. In front of Angelika, she submits to the guilt instilled
in her by her oppressors: "I was the criminal. I violated the rules and had
to be punished" (25). Read in this way, Fräulein Beck's detention reflects
how the war of the genders became an ideological program within the war
of the nations. Thus, Reinig demonstrates how lesbians were not only silenced during the Third Reich, but furthermore how their persecution has
since been overlooked by predominantly male constructions of history
and overshadowed by the other victims of Nazism.

In support of a separatist perspective, Fräulein Beck utters a statement
that reinforces the idea of an alliance between nationalism and compulsory
heterosexuality but indicates that she and Angelika must refuse to cooperate with patriarchy in this alliance. When the two are about to part after
their day together, they pass by a flag factory. Angelika asks rhetorically:
"Who knows what kinds of flags are still being sewn here," to which Fräulein Beck replies: "What is being sewn here is of no concern to us" (26).
Fräulein Beck claims that she still believes in Germany as a nation (16) – it
is, after all, her home and the land in which she must live – but the flags
being sewn in the factory represent the oppressive, heterosexist, fascist society, to which it appears Fräulein Beck believes an alternative must be found.

The culmination of Angelika's day with Fräulein Beck is a testimony to the exigency with which women must confront their oppression. Without being able to name explicitly the injustice done to her in the concentration camp, Fräulein Beck nevertheless encourages Angelika to reevaluate her desire through the account of her detention and to think critically about the people who manipulate her. Angelika considers: "They aren't simply 'the people,' they are trustworthy superiors, I go to them with my fears and concerns, and what they tell me, I do ... but if Dr. Beese and Herr Klein do things like that, what do Papa and Heini, my brother and Uncle Willy do? ... And if a man that I do not know approaches me, is he then my friend or my foe. And if he is my foe, what then is in store for me?" (24-25). To further encourage Angelika, Fräulein Beck is emphatic when she explains to Angelika, that she must begin by altering her nightmare of "Bloody Sunday" for herself and for all women. She inspires Angelika by telling her: "Arm yourself with sacred sincerity and consider the suffering of the women as a martyrdom that must be acknowledged. Without fear and disgust, start to alter the fate of the women. Go into your own dream as a savior. Save the women ..." (26).

Considering the feminist theories prevalent at the time Reinig published this story and her admission to a political agenda in her writing (cf. Reinig, *Erkennen*), Fräulein Beck's urgent plea — formulated as a modern feminist concept — is a call for action against the oppressive, heterosexual, patriarchal society in general. Fräulein Beck acknowledges that women have not had a history that goes beyond the definitions and oppression put in place by men. Seen in this light, her subversive use of Christian terminology reflects the idea that Angelika, as her name suggests, is to deliver women from the grasp of men and men's domination over knowledge and the construction of history. Angelika is to liberate herself and give meaning to the martyrdom of other women by contextualizing women's experiences in a feminist history. More precisely, however, Angelika, as a savior, is to uncover alternatives to the heterosexual constructs of patriarchal society. She is to bring women to a space where they have access to resources, where they can constitute sovereign identities and live harmoniously beyond the sexual dualism of patriarchy — a space where women ultimately have the power to change their destiny. French poststructuralist Hélène Cixous suggests the constitution of the "subjective and affective guerrilla" in the form of the lesbian as the means to recast the fate of women.[8] Fräulein Beck sees that Angelika could potentially be that lesbian warrior, an Amazon, a disciple of Pallas Athena, a passionate figure who can lead women to a space where they have the freedom to find — even if not the ultimate panacea — an alternative to the dominant, phallocratic system, the freedom to find the possibility to constitute a lesbian identity. Empowered by her guidance, Angelika promises Fräulein Beck that she will alter her dream and shakes her hand. While criticizing the constructs of patriarchy, the story is meant as a critical and thought-provoking inspiration, but it does not claim to offer utopian solutions, as indicated by the fact that Angelika and Fräulein Beck still go their separate ways in the end (26).

Although Reinig's text mirrors the repression of lesbianism by veiling the lesbian theme, thus seeming paradoxically to perpetuate the silencing of the lesbian voice, I believe the text must be read as a reflection of her particularly critical, radical lesbian-feminist positioning. By centering her story around problems women confronted in trying to establish and affirm a lesbian identity during the period of the Nazi regime, Reinig, who experienced Nazi Germany first-hand, is reclaiming a part of women's history too often forgotten in both male and more recent broadly based feminist constructions of history. In the process, Reinig supplies a critique of the past which requires elucidation with the help of contemporary lesbian-feminist theory. Although I have focused on the lesbian subtext, this feminist narrative does not necessarily speak only to lesbian readers. Just as Fräulein Beck implores Angelika on the literal level, I believe *One Sunday During the War* appeals to all women to engage in the feminist cause. The story, indeed, calls for action today, because, although World War II ended half a century ago, the war of the genders is still being waged.

Notes

[1] *Müßigang ist aller Liebe Anfang.*

[2] For many years Christa Reinig struggled to establish an identity within the German feminist movement. With the publication of her novel *Entmannung* in 1977 came Reinig's self-proclaimed personal and professional entry into the feminist scene (*Mein Herz* 19). Reinig, however, had yet another challenging pursuit before her: establishing her identity as a lesbian within this movement. Coming out at the end of the 1970s while in her fifties, Reinig exemplifies the difficulties associated with defining oneself as a lesbian. In an interview with Marie-Luise Gansberg, Reinig admits she was, politically speaking, a "Dunkellesbe," or a silent lesbian, before and even after joining

the feminist movement (*Erkennen* 127): "I did not have a lesbian identity, I had a lesbian sexuality, I was happy that such a pigeon-hole existed for me. I was doing well, I enjoyed my life, but I shied away from presenting my lesbianism as my identity" (137; my trans.). Reinig did eventually confront these issues: she later became an avid lesbian activist and began exercising a lesbian voice of which *The Neverending School* is a product.

[3] All translations are my own.

[4] I argue that *Krieg* ("war") in the title *Ein Sonntag im Krieg* refers to both the war of the nations and the war of the genders. The German expression *Geschlechterkrieg* can be translated as "war of the genders," "gender war," or "battle of the sexes." However, I choose not to use the English collocation "battle of the sexes," preferring a phrase that avoids biology and cliché.

[5] Fräulein Beck's character is a monument to a woman with whom Reinig lived in solidarity in April 1945 near the encroaching front (Reinig, *Erkennen* 148).

[6] Bromberg was part of Reichsgau Danzig-Westpreußen, a district created by and incorporated into the Nazi Reich. All of the Jewish inhabitants were murdered upon the entry of the German Army, and the community was never rebuilt (*Encyclopedia Judaica*, vol. 4, 1547).

[7] The lists of both Kathleen Gough and Adrienne Rich include eight characteristics of male power. I refer only to three of these eight, because they are the characteristics relevant specifically to Reinig's story and prove instrumental in my textual analysis.

[8] Hélène Cixous, "Trennung," in Ricarda Schmidt 98.

"Ich gebäre nicht. Ich begehre dich": The Lesbian Vampire as Mother/Artist in Elfriede Jelinek

Ralph J. Poole

> *With this book, I have sucked me and my mother.*
> *Writers are vampires, you know.*
> —Elfriede Jelinek[1]

"**B**EWARE AND DUCK, THE TEXT IN FRONT of you is beginning. It slips from your hands, but that doesn't matter. Somebody else must carry me to fulfillment, a mountain guide, not you!" (*Kinder der Toten* 15). Indeed, Jelinek's latest novel, *Children of the Dead*, marks a new development: its high density assaults the reader. A Hebraic motto promises us that the ghosts of the dead, gone for so long, have come to greet their children. The ghosts reappear to satisfy their needs, be it as castrating cannibals or vengeful vampires acting out impetuous incest or phallic phantasmagoria. Jelinek summons the "dead, maggots in the fat of the living" (40), puts them on the stage of her Gothic enterprise, and spews them "out of our bloody jaws again" (652).

Vampires abound in Jelinek's textual work. In his excellent study on vampirism, *Fremde. Vampire* (*Strangers. Vampires*), Oliver Claes analyzes Jelinek's focus on female sexuality under the reign of man by looking at her use of the vampire motif. He sees her vampire figure as a metaphor for femininity that is defied and denied in a culture defined by male rules. It is the metaphor describing the destructive exploitation in both the political-economical and psychological-sexual fields. Moreover, he claims the vampire as metaphor for female art production or rather the sociocultural misgivings of such a production (65). In almost every text by Jelinek, Claes discovers vampiristic images that conflate the existence of woman as sexual person and artist with the nonexistence of the vampire.

In her novel *Die Ausgesperrten (The Excluded,* 1980), vampirism characterizes economic, psychological and sexual exploitative power in human relationships. Anna and Rainer, sister and brother, threaten to take revenge on their social and sexual oppression in childhood: "Unnoticed by the mass, the hands of brother and sister slink into each other, vampirically the milk-teeth are bared, wait only, Mom, until we're bigger, then we'll do the same to you and more" (48). Anna is the impotent vampire, she tries to resist the 'bloody kisses' of the proletarian Hans, but her vampiristic love-attack, "triggered by her surrendering to man's sexual authority" (Claes 71), is nothing but the fictive power of female dominance in the shape of the vampire. Anna tries to insert "her pointed vampire fangs" into Hans's flesh; he acknowledges this as tiresome foreplay (*The Excluded* 118).

Again, in *Die Klavierspielerin (The Piano Player,* 1983) vampirism as motif describes exploitation and submission. Family, art and sexuality, are the three power systems at play in the novel. All three lead to the figure of the mother and follow the economics of vampiristic 'sucking': either you suck or you are being sucked, instead. Overall, this is a death-ridden story: "Liveliness is not to be found anymore, the dead and mechanical determine the relations between the characters, and art participates at its own dying out" (Claes 73). The mother is the 'spider' sucking life out of her daughter, Erica, whom she keeps confined to her home and her piano practice. Erika 'escapes' through her 'blood-lusty' imagination. She is a suppressed vampire whose vampiric fantasies undermine her art:

> With one ear, SHE is always with the noises outside that her cousin produces with the girls. She listens for his healthy teeth to dig into time, greedily devouring it. For HER, every passing second entered her awareness painfully, like clockwork her fingers tick the seconds into the keys. The windows of the room in which she practices are wired in. The wires' shadows a cross, like withholding the gay bustle outside for a vampire who wants to suck blood. (41)

Vampirism is doubly constructed: it is life endangering to steal art's energy; but art itself is vampiristic in that it demands everything vital, leaving nothing for other activities. "From the perspective of life, art seems like a vampire stealing vitality and leaving back lifelessness, with a reversal of premises, art is vampiristically threatened by liveliness" (Claes 74). Both after the way she is treated by her mother and as an artist, Erika, the "formless cadaver" (*The Piano Player* 67), becomes a sort of vampire herself, taking control over her students (99). Furthermore, sexuality is to be damned for the sake of art, and the connection between art and sexuality is apparently wrong, even if artists' biographies reveal a different story: "Unfortunately, the biographies of artists, which are the most important parts of artists after all, all too often abound with the protagonists' sexual lusts and ticks. They evoke the misleading impression that it is only the compost heap of sexuality on which the cucumber bed of pure harmony grows" (198). In *The Piano Player*, the battle of the war of the sexes is fought out on the field of heterosexual vampirism. Both man and woman are vampires fighting — most often against each other — for the right to bite (190).

Oh Wildnis, oh Schutz vor ihr (*Oh Wilderness, oh Protection From Her*, 1985) metaphorically plays with the cannibalistic aspect of vampirism. The aspect of economy acts as an additional trigger. Two women — one an artist, the other a manager — try to conquer the same man, Erich, the "woodsman" and model of naturalness. Like a "praying mantis" who kills the male during sexual performance, the artist seeks to lure Erich into her cellar, into a love trap where she can devour him (104). But she fails and dies in her own trap. The manager, on the other hand, tries to 'buy' him like she has bought all the politicians on whose bribes she lives and calls "vampire juice" (266). But she fails, too, because he simply does not recognize her attempt at control: "Reversing the social and sexual roles did not succeed, it is inconceivable for man to be object only" (Claes 78). Again, the heterosexual union is represented as vampiristic: "Like the vampires, they are sucking blood and liquid" (*Oh Wilderness* 209).

The motto of *Lust* (1989) by a Christian mystic (Johannes vom Kreuz) draws an ambiguous picture of vampirism: "Deep down in the sunken room / I drank from the friend … When turning toward day, / there was until the farthest border / nothing that I yet knew - / the flock was removed with which I ran" (5). Depending on how we want to understand "flock," the vampiristic act can be seen as liberating or estranging. Could it be that this is a rare instance of utopia in Jelinek's work? The motto is part of the "Lied der Liebe" ("Song of Love") a mystic love song between a soul and her lover Christ. Here, it is the female bride longing for her lover. God reveals himself to the bride in the shape of a drink that completely fills her. This religious — and, indeed, sexual — image might mean even more than Claes suggests since he centers on the imagination of a male author fantasizing the union between a human woman and a godly man, putting himself in the position of the god-creator whom the loving soul has created (80). But could it not be that the author (vom Kreuz) imagines himself as the *bride* who longs for his/her god? This would be a homo-erotic fantasy not all that unusual in Renaissance, metaphysical, and puritan rhetorics.[2] Jelinek's citation does not show any sign of gender, the 'I' could be understood as either female or male. But would this make her text any more or less utopian? I must agree with Claes that the "beginning and end of this love relation is the assurance of man as god" (80), no matter how we want to look at it. There are two men, that is, two gods, in Jelinek's novel, both delightfully proving their potency by cohabiting with the same woman. All she can do — since she is no vampire, the motto bearing no utopian hope specifically for her — is play Medea: she kills her son, thus preventing him from becoming like his father, in fact, like any man. She breaks the chain of repetition, but gains nothing for herself.

Jelinek applies vampirism as historical-political metaphor in *Wolken.Heim* (*Cloud.Home,* 1990), a textual montage ranging from Hölderlin and Kleist, Hegel and Heidegger to letters of left-wing terrorists. History takes the shape of the undead that never can rest, that are doomed to return again and again: "Upon earth / we get no rest, even as / buried we remain present, and we / will return, we will return!" (24). Jelinek says that history is like vampirism: "It returns again and again, 'the memory of the soil' prevents the dead from remaining in the earth. They rise again and again." For her repression does not work: "The relicts crawl from out of the soil" ("Ich will kein Theater," "I Want No Theater" 155–56), for it is a *circulus vitiosus* of endless reappearances: "The dead want to be freed, but to regain their lives, they must kill the living" (*Children of the Dead* 456).

As these examples have shown, vampirism has been a constant focus in Jelinek's work, neatly fixed to assure the realm of heterosexuality. Her play *Krankheit oder Moderne Frauen* (*Illness or Modern Women,* 1992) combines all aspects of vampirism shown so far: "the art production excluding liveliness, the irreversibility of hierarchy between the sexes, woman as victim of male sexuality and power, and the prevention of a complete female existence as consequence of being unable to project oneself other than in dependency on ideas of femaleness marked by men" (Claes 82). I cannot disagree with Claes's view of Jelinek's pessimism, her failure to provide a positive or even utopian model of female existence — not even in the disguise of the vampire. Jelinek herself claims that she can only see the negative side of things: "The positive anti-model does not go together with

my literary techniques. In other words, all I can do is to highlight the negative side of things" (cf. "Access Routes" 111).

Nevertheless, one might ask whether it is necessary to follow Jelinek's
provision that her characters do not submit to psychological rules, that
changes only occur in the characters' speech, in their linguistic gesture,
never in their attitudes. What does it mean that her vampires have no secret
– the mysterious secret being the claim so inherently connected to vampirism – as Claes suggests of all characters in *Illness*: "Constantly, they talk
about themselves, define themselves or, accordingly, the other sex. This
volubility exempts nothing, all lies open and reveals the nonexistence of
individuals, they have no secrets" (84).

Enter the lesbian vampire. "Blood is a special liquid. At least it founds
kinship. It binds and separates, as it flows." These are the opening sen-
tences of Eva Meyer's essay "Den Vampir schreiben" ("Writing the Vampire") on the play *Illness or Modern Women*, Elfriede Jelinek's most challenging expedition into the realm of the undead on which I will concentrate.[3] Meyer points toward the fictional construction of the vampire: "The
literary invention of the chimeras, so as to recur in the script as something
that never has existed in reality" (98). Writing this powerful essay – in itself
one of the semifictional/part scholarly works for which she is famous –
Meyer turns the screw of Jelinek's own highly intertextual enterprise one
more twist. The vampire's entry is, according to Meyer, a formula "of a type
whose functioning is mainly based on the fact that you will not unveil its
mystery" (98). Jelinek's vampire is intriguing because he is not only a mystery, but 'he' is female and double. Meyer does not explicitly mention the
fact that 'she' is lesbian, too. However, even without addressing the lesbian
issue as such, I believe Meyer's essay to be a 'queerer' text than Jelinek's, for
it is Meyer who deconstructs Jelinek's narcissistic approach of the vam-
pire/lesbian.[4]

It is not easy to describe the vampire "because he is a sucking shadow,
one's own perhaps, always cast on what you desire to know better" (98). So
is the vampire a sucking and yearning shadow of one's own desire? A look
at Carmilla – the vampire in Sheridan Le Fanu's story after whom Jelinek's
vampire is modeled, and where the lesbian vampire's "particular 'queerness'
runs through it from beginning to end" (Gelder 58) – demonstrates the
mingling of self and other. From their first meeting on, Carmilla and her
future 'victim' Laura are fascinated by one another to the point of not
knowing who is who, who is to be feared more, whose desire for the 'other'

proves the strongest. However, Jelinek's play confronts us with a totally different Carmilla. The fascinating vampire-creature has become housewife and mother. She makes her own ketchup — much like the homely Doris Day of 1950s/1960s Hollywood — she is married to the hideous Dr. Benno Hundekoffer (Dogbag!), a tax consultant, has given birth to five children, and is preparing for the birth of a sixth at the beginning of the play. She is quite frankly the supermother. Meyer sees in the loss of the vampire's charisma a negative utopia if ever one wants to ask for it: "That the old myths have lost their bite and are now merely simmering in a housewifely way" (100). This is precisely a question we should consider: Why has Jelinek's vampire lost her bite?

Instead of relying on the vampire's mythical youthfulness defying all rules of earthly mortality, Jelinek refers to a different, philosophical myth, namely that of the enlightened Cartesian *cogito ergo sum*, which was meant to deconstruct myths, but it has become a myth in itself. Jelinek parodically plays with its lacking capacities when Carmilla announces: "I am ill, therefore I am." This is the reversal of the undead vampire: "I call at home, and nobody answers. Immediately, I have the notion: somebody else is ill, too! I am ill and therefore legitimate. Without illness, I would be nothing" (232). Such a statement may lead to a different notion of the vampire. In the restrictive age of Victorianism, vampirism and illness were closely related, as well as femininity and illness. Paradigmatically, this can be seen in Le Fanu's *Carmilla*. Here, the illness defining the vampire is her lesbianism. As Ken Gelder in *Reading the Vampire* points out, the "Victorian view of lesbianism conventionally saw it as 'unnatural', against Nature" (61). Carmilla refuses this position, however, claiming that "this disease that invades the country is natural. Nature. All things proceed from Nature — don't they?" (Le Fanu 95). Jelinek has parodically queered this notion's pitch. Jelinek's vampires are modern creatures, but does that make them post-Victorian? Eva Meyer reminds us: "If illness belongs to the self-fashioning of the modern woman, she lacks something. Normally, the man. In Jelinek's play it is the other woman. So much, that at the end they grow together" (102). The doubled creature at the end is not able to survive the bullets the men shoot. Can a woman not live on her own, does she need her double only to be extinguished, nevertheless, at the end? Here, doubled desire — lesbian desire — surrenders to male heterosexual desire. But, indeed, Meyer asks, is this all there is? Is there nothing left at the end but the extinction of this other desire? From a patriarchal point of view,

anything that cannot be proved has to be destroyed, among which is the
"Widernatur des Wiedergängers" (102), the perverse nature of the returning
vampire who turns everything upside down. She even eats her own off-
spring!

The ending of *Illness or Modern Women* has led to abundant speculations, of course. "(It) is pessimistic as is usual with me," says Jelinek ("Die
Lady – ein Vampir?" 35). Asked whether the male order is disturbed by the
resistance of the women, Jelinek answers: "Even if it were true that women
practice their own kind of anarchism by tricking men for some time as not
living, not dead in-between creatures, patriarchy finally triumphs, the brutal
male principle. The woman is hunted down with the holy silver bullet" ("I
Want No Theater" 145). According to Meyer, however, destroying the object of disturbance does not guarantee the extinction of its traces: the vampire was here, and she has left her mark. There remains the threat of repetition, of remembering.[5] Jean A. Luscher calls Emily and Carmilla's union at
the end "a merger of conflicting myth" (172). As the embodiment of countermyth, they can no longer be categorically and ideologically contained,
and therefore must be destroyed.

Jelinek creatively resists: her politics and aesthetics work against the
grain. Indeed, "You would have to work a lot to make me simple again,"
says Emily (*Illness* 210). The two leading female characters show ambivalent identities, especially Emily. On the one hand, she is autonomous. She
ironically repositions herself as writer in a way traditionally reserved only
for men: "I think, therefore I am. I drink, therefore I am well" (207). On the
other hand, she is a nurse, that is, a super-signifier of femaleness. As such
she is, at least at the beginning of the play, employed and exploited by
Heidkliff (Heathcliff), the dentist-gynecologist and her fiancé. Of course,
there is her vampirism and lesbianism, which are completely ignored by
Heidkliff as long as she collaborates in her sexually and economically subordinate role he prescribes for her (224). Luscher recognizes in the combination writer/vampire the invisibility of female authors within the male-de-
fined literary canon: "Just as her body casts no reflection, so too her voice
as a writer has no resonance" (170). She shares the common frustration of
many female authors and, thus, is undead in that her work exists but is not
read. Emily's ultimate threat as to compulsory heterosexuality is her motto
addressed to Carmilla: "I breed not. I crave for you" (*Illness* 208).

Carmilla has amply proved her reproductive qualities. When she dies
while giving birth to her sixth child, she becomes a vampire with the help

of Emily. Medea-like she devours her own children, taking revenge on her husband who has been possessed by her childbearing capacities (and by his abundant potency). Whereas Emily represents the sexual-political outlaw as artist/lesbian/vampire, Carmilla stands for the social-genderized minority of the category 'woman' as the ill mother/vampire, and her above-mentioned motto is thus most befitting the discourse about such a category. Illness and perversion are the overriding metaphors for woman, vampire, and lesbian. Thus, the union of the two women at the end is a multiplication of the blood mark. Benno's and Heidkliff's obsession with blood throughout the play culminates in this abundance of potentially flowing blood, be it the blood that flows in menstruation, in childbirth, or in the act of consummation. The self-controlled input and output of blood violently threaten male control over the female body because a blood (life) circle is being created that works without the help of men.

Yet each one of the four characters, not only the two females, is in an ambiguous state of existence. The men form an "essential mythic sameness" that is centered in their maleness. The two men share the bond of perceiving "woman as the blood-marked Other" (Luscher 167). Thus, in Benno's statement, "In a woman, everyone must involuntarily see the blood" (*Illness* 240), he means 'every man.' Theirs is a bond repressing obvious signs of homosocial desire. Their characters are structured around their fear of, and need for, women. Woman prevents male loneliness by providing social integration and, above all, by protecting them from the threat of impotence. Contrast Benno — "My sex strikes. She does not tempt me anymore! I believe: Due to the fact that my wife Carmilla now eats blood, she has taken on something male that I don't like" (239-40) — with Heidkliff — "Alone. It appalls me. Fuck. I want until absolute *finis*" (252). But their need to establish power over women to ensure male self-definition is counteracted in their envy of female productivity. They are asking for total control over reproduction. Again Benno: "I want one tiny thing more: Please, to be able to breed" (245). Paradoxically, total control of female capacities would erase 'woman as category' altogether and thus reveal an impasse. By showing the man wishing to possess women's essential biological characteristic, Jelinek leads the reduction of woman to her biological function as childbearer to its logical absurdity. "The illogic," as Luscher puts it, "comes full-circle as eliminating women eliminates men, because now the means for defining men — women — no longer exist" (169). Or to put it differently in Jelinek's words: "The sex convenes the dead, the male sex will survive alone, women will then have become men, too" (*Children of the Dead* 68). Men's victory at the end is a self-destructive one. In *Illness*, this can be seen in their gradual language regression toward illogical articulation: they shout and bark, produce animal sounds amidst an apocalyptic stage that is filled with waste and weapons. "At the height of power ecstasy, language as mode of communication has become superfluous. Heidkliff and Hundekoffer become puppets on the strings of their own unconsciousness" (R. Friedrich 88). The climax of this decomposing process is the infernal mixture of Goebbels and Goethe: "Me needs room! More room! Give! More light! More lights! More lighten! More hark! Bark! Bark! Bark!" (*Illness* 253).

Jelinek's experimental verbal artistry provokes and disturbs. In her essay on female vampires in nineteenth-century literature, Silvia Volckmann tells of an incident that occurred to her:

> Totally unexpected, I came across a new variant of my topic. The *Frankfurter Allgemeine Zeitung* [a German daily broadsheet newspaper] had invited Elfriede Jelinek to answer the questionnaire that Marcel Proust had developed as a parlor game. The writer, known for her biting tongue, accordingly presented herself eccentrically and maliciously: She prefers to live "in front of the TV," in men she especially appreciates "slavish submissiveness," and in her friends, "when they tell me everything." Of course, such answers are well-aimed gags, a pleasurable self-fashioning of the author who pleasantly sets herself apart from the usual dull sincerity (of authors). When Jelinek, however, includes as one of her "favorite heroines in literature" Carmilla, the "female vampire" of the Irish author Joseph Sheridan Le Fanu (1814-1873), this not only "fits" the picture, [but] it also means that female vampires need not be buried because male authors liked to kill them in the end after all. (175)

Obviously, Volckmann had no knowledge of Elfriede Jelinek's play *Illness or Modern Women* when writing her essay. It was published the same year that Jelinek's play had its premiere in Bonn (1987), featuring Carmilla as one of the two leading female roles. The change of the function of female vampires in literature during the nineteenth century is noteworthy concerning Jelinek's play. In pre-Christian millennia, vampires were female creatures, night demons, with both frightening and seductive characteristics. They lived on the blood of children, young mothers or beautiful young men. They had a strict mythological function as creatures caught between culture and nature, and as custodians of the mysteries of life and death, of sexuality and birth. They secured the fulfillment of the life circle. "'Femininity' and 'death' associate on the basis of female childbearing here, and female vampires are clearly discernible as the nurturing mother's negative" (155).

In the nineteenth century, there occurred a poetic revival of the female vampire that marks a redefinition of femininity. Until the end of the eighteenth century, the reign of androcentric Christianity executed a banishment of the 'female' from her archaic position of power. Before the age of Enlightenment, the power over life and death lay in the hands of an invisible male God. However, the superstition of vampires as wretched undead haunting the living never ceased, but it mostly remained outside gender boundaries. Vampires did not have the sexual connotation that we are used to ascribing to them nowadays.

Since individual bodily existence gained importance and, consequently, soon caused various problems, literary texts of the nineteenth century started investigating the question of death as one of gender. The consequent poetic evolving of the vampire motif is symbiotically coupled with the discourses of "woman" and "death" (157). Goethe's poem "Die Braut von Korinth" (1797), E. T. A. Hoffmann's vampire story in the collection *Die Serapionsbrüder* (1817/1819), Samuel Coleridge's *Christabel* (1816), Théophile Gautier's *La morte amoureuse* (1836), and Edgar Allan Poe's *Morella* (1836) or *Ligeia* (1838) are all literary examples that prove the exploration of the 'dark, feminine continent'.[6] The female body becomes tabooed as vampiric-ambiguous, as the place of the Other: it signifies death, disparity, nature, negativity, illness. Goethe's vampire was still sympathetic, pitiable. Yet, by the end of the nineteenth century, she will be the vicious vamp that has to be destroyed. This reinterpretation of gender codes calls for the total elimination of the vampire. The sexier she is fantasized, the more the urge to perform on her the old habits of impaling, decapitating, and burning. "Since Gautier, no vampire text lacks the detailed depiction of the execution fantasy; this is only one index for proving that the aspect of denial attributed to vampirism as the wish of dissolution and regression has become the focus of attention" (Volckmann 167).

Baudelaire — and before him already Poe — represents the vampire as the phallic woman. The battle of the sexes is now evident. The poem "Le Vampire" from his *Fleurs du Mal* begins: "Toi qui, comme un coup de couteau, / Dans mon coeur plaintif es entrée" (69). The radical differentiation of male victim and female vampire operates semantically with the metaphor of war. For, if the vampire becomes active, if, as woman, she even opposes the culturally enforced denial of the freedom of speech, that is, if, as absolute negativity, she dares to speak, then she steps into the position of absolute destruction. Baudelaire "thus names the psychological defense mechanism that has led her desire to be the tabooed textual center of the vampire topic" (Volckmann 170). This modern, medicalized focus on the female body reflects the change of attitude toward death during technological, psychiatric, and textual developments of the nineteenth century. Whereas in the seventeenth and eighteenth centuries, according to Philippe Ariès, the dead still had a sort of personality that suggested a "being," the medical discourse of the nineteenth century negates this belief. Now, death does not exist anymore, it is understood as deformation and 'not-life'. It has no meaning outside catalogued illness of whose last step it represents (cf. Ariès 1982, 460). The combining of femininity and death as illness, as prescription of the 'not-place' between life and death, provides the vampiric metaphor with another twist of meaning. The modern vampire — or the vampire of modernism — is synonymous with woman as illness. This is also Jelinek's position.

"'We are not dependent,' says Emily. 'We are undead, Carmilla! Will you remember that!'" (*Illness* 230). In her book on Jelinek's plays titled after a quotation by Emily from *Illness or Modern Women* (209), Corina Caduff points to the main difference in the treatment of the vampire in nineteenth-century literature and Jelinek. The female vampire as the creation of a male author is typically a character motivated by vengeance, mostly on her unfaithful lover. Her aim is to take him with her to her grave. Thus, the vampire demands something that has been taken from her, but that, according to ruling morals, she has the right to claim her own. The male vampire, on the other hand, does not follow any ethical rules, his existence is not emotionally defined. According to Caduff: "The difference between female and male vampire creatures thus shows in the *motivation* and *function* of vampirism: Whereas the appearance of the female vampire in general is grounded psychosocially and is meant to reestablish violated sexual morals, the male vampire functions as anarchic interference within these ruling

regulations" (123). Jelinek redefines this opposition: her vampires pursue
the traditional *motivation* of the female vampire, that is, they are deceived
avengers, whereas their *function* comes close to that of the typical male
vampire, that is, they disturb law and order.

There are many more differences between Jelinek's vampire play and the
traditional vampire narrative. Jelinek's text is consciously self-defeating in
that it plays excessively with tradition: intertextual references, fabricated into
a tightly woven web of collages, render the text almost inexplicable. Dagmar von Hoff says about Jelinek's theater texts that they "allow for no central interpretation to hit the heart of her texts; on the contrary, she develops
a textual structure that decenters. According to this structure, she dis-
embowels various textual bodies, carves them up and fuses them as new
textual particles" (112). Ute Margarete Saine speaks of "the poisonous collage flowers so brilliantly evident" in Jelinek's texts. In her "palimpsests of
patriarchy, the neat separation between reality and discourse is henceforth
impossible, the one bleeding into the other, and vice versa" (267). The
most obvious tendency toward negativity structures the play as a whole: it
is the reduplicated renunciation of any positive or utopian models. This
includes the paradox negation of theater as such. In her theater, Jelinek explains, blood is an essential: "In all of my plays, there is tearing and
bleeding ... Blood, for me, signals above all the ritualistic aspects of theater
which can thus evoke archaic conditions" ("Die Lady – ein Vampir?" 35).[7]
Vampirism and cannibalism seem to be leitmotifs signaling Jelinek's theatrical poetics.[8] In her programmatic text "Ich möchte seicht sein" ("I Want
to Be Shallow," 1990), she even characterizes the actors with vampiric vocabulary: they lead a 'double existence', they let themselves be multiplied:

> without taking a risk, because they don't get lost. Yes, they don't
> even fool around with their being! ... Become impossible, and
> need therefore not be prohibited, because they are not and nothing
> anymore ... There must be no theater any longer ... The actors sig-
> nify themselves and are defined by themselves. And I say: Away
> with them! They are not real. (160–61)

A theater without actors – alas, no theater?! Jelinek uses the metaphor
of the mirror inherent in vampirism. She creates a "stage as empty mirror"
(Haß 28). The actors are visible, but they do not embody anything. Like
Emily's mechanically constructed, unfoldable teeth – I will return to them

later — the stage is an empty mechanism to show off: "extendable, retract-able, clean" (Haß 28). Marlies Janz sees the vampire in *Illness* as a result of turning the feminine into the masculine, thus enabling the vampire to step into the mirror and to look at, "turn against," the spectator who has created the wrong image (94). Jelinek's texts reflect the interpreter back into the text "when he has to acknowledge that the possibilities for interpretation are al-ready founded within the dramatic figure" (von Hoff 112). Jelinek's work represents a late form of historical avant-garde. There, too — in dadaism and surrealism, in futurism and cubism — the cry to destroy the artifact was ut-tered in the shape of art (cf. Poole). Jelinek's contribution to representing a theater of the avant-garde à la Antonin Artaud can only be understood as parody. Ingeborg Hoesterey thinks that Artaud's "cruelty" — especially as read by Jacques Derrida ("Das Theater der Grausamkeit") as signifying the urgency of an utmost necessity — suits Jelinek's feminist agenda (Hoesterey 154).

Jelinek's avant-garde may be read as a parody of modernism. The am-biguous play with the idea of an original gains central importance. The paradox of such a parody lies in the fact that, on the one hand, the defects of the 'original' are deconstructed and that, on the other hand, the artist cannot dismiss the original, thus perhaps involuntarily presenting it wor-thy of recognition. Therefore, parody is not really only de(con)struction, since its inherent (self-)reflexivity points toward a relative reconstruction. This double function of avant-garde — destruction and renewal — should be kept in mind when looking at Jelinek's text. In Jelinek's work, it is gener-ally difficult to separate the destructive forces from the creation of counter-myth. "Thus in both the creative and destructive acts," as Luscher puts it, "myth accommodates a feminist aesthetic agenda not as a uniquely female-determined mode of expression, but rather as a means of articulating sub-versive critique" (174). To an extent, Jelinek performs gender parody by parodying the usage of the female vampire. As Judith Butler in her well-known study *Gender Trouble* has shown, the subversive laughter of the parodied performance exposes the original, the authentic, the real as effect, as deceptive or 'wrong' original. Such a 'wrong' original is the idea of a biologically given gender identity. Especially Jelinek's strategy of doubling — performed on all textual levels — may be read in this context.

Illness or Modern Women viciously parodies representations of femi-ninity. Emily, described as "*Nurse and Vampire*" (192) in the stage direc-tions, appears semantically ambiguous: "Out of her body, one, two stakes discretely protrude dripping with blood" (194). Is she a vampire already impaled as the traditional elimination procedure demands? In this case, she should not be appearing at all: for the impaled vampire marks the end of the story, when s/he is destroyed. Is this an anticipation of the female's final death (cf. Caduff 132)? Or do the pales demonstrate the martyrdom of Saint Sebastian, pestilence's patron (cf. Hoesterey 153)? Woman as vampire as martyr? Whether female Sebastian or vampire, Emily is marked as a woman who bears the stigma of illness. The course of the play proves the announced double existence of Emily: as mentioned before, on the one hand, she is nurse and fiancée of Dr. Heidkliff who, as a "*Specialist for Dental Care and Gynecology*" (*Illness* 192), is an 'expert' guardian of the female erogenous bodily orifices. On the other hand, Emily is a vampire and writer. Thus, Emily at once conforms to gender stereotypes as a helping, loving woman, and she breaks taboos as an artistically productive and parasitically bloodsucking woman. But soon we realize that she is, above all, a lesbian, which disgraces her as a liar in her function as fiancée and disqualifies her as a future wife — and, ultimately, as a nurse since as a lesbian she is considered 'ill'.

The object of Emily's lesbian desire is Carmilla, "*Housewife, Mother and Vampire, Austrian,*" according to stage directions (192), a not entirely accurate description at the beginning of the play, because she is not a "vampire" until after Emily's lovebite. But Carmilla does show the abundant signs of motherhood. When she first appears, she is pregnant and on the verge of delivery, the flock of children clinging to her manifests the fact that she has successfully given birth five times already. This time, Carmilla dies during delivery, fastened by her husband on Dr. Heidkliff's birthing chair, surrounded by the acoustic and optical convention of Gothic thunder and lightning. Emily enters and shows vampiric interest in Carmilla who willingly lets herself be bitten. Tenderly moaning and unnoticed by the men, Carmilla reawakens as undead.

The second act shows Emily and Carmilla living together as a couple. The surgery — the stage works with double effects, too — has changed into a "*lovely bedroom in the style of the fifties.*" "*Only: Instead of beds, there are elegantly manufactured coffins in the same fifties' style filled with earth.*" The scene is described as "*Idyll,*" later as "*Family,*" Emily and Carmilla lie "*cozily*" in their beds/coffins, "*the latter with curlers*" (229). Emily's prop is a portable typewriter. The women live on the blood of Carmilla's children until the men, now devoid of their function as bedfellows and breeders, discover their 'true' vocation and start hunting vampires. The last scene shows the two vampires combined into one "*huge, thick woman, the double creature,*" the "*Siamese twin Emily/Carmilla*" (261), surrendering to the men's bullets.

The doubles Jelinek presents are improper, that is, purposefully inaccurate and confusing. For example, she brings together Carmilla and Emily, an 'unclean' mixture of different intertextual levels. Carmilla, as we have seen, is the lesbian vampire of Le Fanu's tale. This story — written by a male author — is told by the female first-person narrator Laura, Carmilla's victim. "For the author must be woman to become a chronicler of arising horror," as Meyer cunningly notes (103). Then there is Emily Brontë, the female author after whom Jelinek's character Emily is named. Brontë wrote *Wuthering Heights* from the point of view of a male first-person narrator, Lockwood, "who above all distinguishes himself by representing the claim of probability" (104). Such gender inversions are not necessarily the norm in literary tradition. But Jelinek goes even further. She mixes her female herocouple out of a figure from inside and a figure from outside: one stems from a fiction writer (Brontë), the other from a fictional character (the vampire Carmilla). Literature is being performed "like a play." This is what the qualifier in the title of *Illness or Modern Women* tells us, like the actors who are not really there, the play acts as if it *were* a play, "for the use of the ghosts who have chosen it as a place of residence" (104).

Both, Carmilla and Emily rewrite 'originals' by vampiric misquotations: Carmilla's distortion of Descartes and Emily's own textual production. Like a vampire, Emily is able to disrespect borders. At the same time, she is an author and a quotation of another author, outside and inside her own text. Erdle calls this Jelinek's poetics of dirt and bad taste: "For the vampiristic misrecognition of known borders between various pre/texts, between real and fake texts, between genres, different sorts of texts, historical periods of time, semantic and syntactic units, indeed, creates an untidy, polluting mixture that is not so easy to cleanse" (339). The chaotic, 'dirty', destructive text implies a kind of female (queer?) authorship that corresponds to the negativity of the vampire. Emily says: "I am an authoress. I have no children, no time, no advice, no husband. Nothing and nothing else comes" (*Illness* 209). Her work is supposed to make visible what has remained hidden (*Illness* 211). The female vampire-artist is evil because she writes 'wrong', she is a "Schrift*ver*stellerin," a "woman *mis*writer" (Erdle 336; my emphasis), a writer queering writing. This marks the difference be-

tween her and her sisters, the other Brontës: "I used to have two sisters. Unlike me, they don't have to return. They are calm. Those unwicked. They
have long dissolved, simple riddles they were." Emily's mean riddles are a
combined textual inversion of the Christian revelation "I am Alpha and
Omega, the beginning and the end" and the Lord's Supper into the respective "I am the beginning and the end. Whoever I eat from, will live forever," and "I am the beginning and the end. I appear in-between a lot, too"
(*Illness* 210).

Vampires as literary figures are utter outcasts. They do not fulfill their
social obligations (Caduff 108), or put more positively: they create their
own living space on the boundaries of normality. In any case, it is a space
between threat and liberation, they are prosecuted and, at the same time,
they are provided with supernatural gifts. The vampire is a paradoxical creature: s/he can give life by making a new vampire, that is, there is a possibility of a sort of parthenogenesis. But s/he also spoils life by sucking it out
of others; the principle here is self-preservation by consuming and, thereby,
destroying others. From this perspective, the vampire lives, according to
Caduff "as a holoparasite with constantly changing hosts; he is utterly dependent on the system beside which he lives, because the product of this
system keeps him alive" (135). The vampire's characteristics are fluctuation
and absence. S/he is eternally wandering as undead, the lacking mirror
image proves freedom of time and space. All of these stereotypes can be
found in Jelinek — albeit distorted and deconstructed.

In the traditional vampire narrative, the vampire generally acts in the
dark, and whatever he or she does is forbidden and remains a mystery. The
masquerade makes the vampire the perfect image of normality enabling the
procurement of the victim's privacy. It is this horror that Victorian texts
like Bram Stoker's *Dracula* or Sheridan Le Fanu's *Carmilla* evoke. Jelinek,
however, turns the vampire's missing mirror image into her theatrical program. Before, the invisibility of the vampire in the mirror concurred with
the definitional lack of woman: both were nondescript. Now, the woman
emerges visibly stigmatized — note the stakes sticking out of Emily's body!
— and she seduces her victim not in the private chamber, but in the publicly accessible surgery, the site of woman's inscribed illness. Finally,
Emily makes no secret of her vampirism and lesbianism. Thus, "she decides *in favor of herself,* she will no longer be a projection" (Haß 27).

The dramatic action, however, lacks the main feature of suspense so inherent in classical vampire stories. Usually, the vampire appears unknown

in a given system, threatens it until he is recognized, hunted, destroyed, and the weakened order is restored again to strength. In this narrative structure, the vampire functions as a projection of fear, be it of sexual or social origin (cf. Craft 216). Jelinek's early story *Der fremde! störenfried der ruhe eines sommerabends der ruhe eines friedhofs* (*The stranger! troublemaker of the quiet on a summer evening of the quiet of a cemetery*, 1969) is a parody of this classical dynamic in the manner of Bram Stoker, etc. The vampire is considered the stranger in an unfriendly surrounding: "in a small town everybody knows everybody there all the people greet each other and chat about their small bigger and biggest problems there everybody is there for everybody. there inconsistencies cause mistrust, a stranger stands out immediately" (135). The gender of the vampire is ambiguous, he is male and female at once: "the stranger looks very athletic and very masculine," "the stranger himself is a very pretty girl" (136). After the intrusion into the village and the erotic entertainment the vampire provides, the text – like any vampire narrative, but particularly Stoker's – "expels or repudiates the monster and all the disruption that he/she/it brings" (Craft 216).

In *Illness*, however, Jelinek deals with the genre quite differently. When Emily 'outs' herself twice over as vampire *and* lesbian, thus casting the blind mirror back onto the spectator, the intertextually evoked Gothic romance is subverted. It has to be conceded that the tradition of vampire literature is a genre primarily shaped by male authors. Above all, there is no long-established lesbian vampire tradition created by lesbian authors, with the exception of Djuna Barnes, who in *Nightwood* alludes to the tradition of the Gothic novel. The fun play with ambiguities that gay readers have enjoyed for quite a while when reading vampire stories does not so much apply to lesbian readers, least of all to lesbians reading Jelinek. But gay male readers will probably also not enjoy the (rare) depiction of male homosexuality in Jelinek's texts. The vampire-threesome in *Children of the Dead*, for example, is a rather appalling sex scene between two brothers and a third male:

A pain like an instrument at the back, the loin, where some muscles are rotten already, gets weak. Look for yourself! the strained grin of this bared earthy ass appalls the elder still a little bit, but then his hunting device, that he knows well to operate, especially on himself, still beyond death when a target appears somewhere, disappears to the partially turned over shaft into his brother's well hole ... A heavy piece of meat, an empty stomach, innards all over, two hands from being put into their politely held little palms. Above bluish, carefree, wrapped in fine mist, the tunnel being watched by the thighs like idlers who don't have anything to do. Edgar's sex bone has tipped forward like a broken branch, a plug has been inserted into his notch and dangles directly into the widely open mouths of the forestry apprentices who from both sides snap at it. (299, 305)

However, as Richard Dyer so pointedly observes, gay readers may view the charismatic vampire figure as a metaphor for homosexuality. In his essay "Children of the Night: Vampirism as Homosexuality. Homosexuality as Vampirism," Dyer shows the genderized playfulness that structures both vampirism and homosexuality. The tickle of forbidden sexuality that the vampire triggers is experienced by the gay reader as pleasure instead of horror. He identifies with the vampire practicing a tabooed form of sexuality rather than with the victim who is torn from its bourgeois marriage and family life. An "enjoyable way of positioning oneself in this text-reader relation," as Dyer puts it:

is in thrilling to the extraordinary power credited to the vampire, transcendent powers of seduction, s/he can have anyone s/he wants, it seems. Most lesbians and gay men experience exactly the opposite, certainly outside of the gay scene, certainly up until very recently. Even though the vampire is invariably killed off at the end (except in recent examples), how splendid to know what a threat our secret is to them! (59)

However, gays could always enjoy the vampire tradition a lot more than lesbians. Until recently, this tradition provided lesbian readers with extremely negative examples. Indeed, (male) authors created female vampires and among them even lesbian ones with Le Fanu's *Carmilla* serving as an outstanding example. But contrary to the often aristocratic male dandy-vampire, the female vampire was a male-destroying vamp — at her best — or a mean manly teacher seducing her students — at her worst. This dichotomy may be observed in most films dealing with female vampires (cf. Burns; Hetze; Krzywinska; Perthold; Weiss; B. Zimmermann). Jelinek's Emily has a bit of both and, for me, it is Jelinek's strict denial to present a positive lesbian vampire-love story that overrules all her other refusals. Her text was written at a time, when lesbian writers started to redefine the figure of the vampire (cf. Morrill). Jelinek did not look in this direction. Probably because she has lost any notion of love at all: "One of the commonest tumors on account of which we fall ill, love, I take back this word and give you another one instead, only I don't know, where I have put it right now" (*Children of the Dead* 543). What would Case have made of Elfriede Jelinek's lesbian vampire? In her milestone essay for emerging queer theory, Case's search for the queer vampire brings her back to the roots of her own lesbian sexuality. She speaks of a "cross-gender identification" (1) that confronted her with her own ambivalent feelings toward her sexuality, oscillating between affirmation and shame. Her literary and related sexual development leads her on the track of the vampire. She finds herself, the lesbian woman, in the vampire's transgressive being between appearance and disappearance: "the identification with the insult, the taking on of the transgressive, and the consequent flight into invisibility are inscribed in the figure of the vampire" (2).

Case bases her argument on feminist film theory represented by critics like Linda Williams and Mary Ann Doane who analyze the relationship between the look of the female spectator and the representation of persons or actions that were originally meant for the male eye. What happens when a woman looks at a monster? For the female spectator, there occurs a breakdown of distance that normally guarantees the sublime pleasure of the male spectator. This breakdown grounds on identification: the similarity of woman and monster in the manner of their respective representation. Both are objectified. The sexual interest in the horror genre lies in the body of the monster, not in that of the often desexualized hero. Thus, there appears a sexual difference between monster and 'normal' male drawing the monster closer to the way femininity is represented: both are threatening to castrate the male hero/spectator. Case even goes further in her argument. She spots a lesbian desire in the process of identification. Case reproaches the film critics for clinging to oedipal, heterosexist structures leaving the same-sex taboo intact. The dominance of heterosexuality applies to the image of the vampire in the main discourse, too (11). Once more, the queer look only catches a glimpse of the center, otherwise remaining at the marginal fringes of prescribed heterosex.

It is astonishing that, although Jelinek shows again and again the impossibility of heterosexual relationships, none of her texts ever really emerges as a 'lesbian text'. She does not seem to believe in any such model of a woman-loving-woman relationship however close she may come to such a point.[9] Claes claims that, for Jelinek, lesbian love only exists as unreal vampire-love (89). However, even a lesbian relationship like that of Emily and Carmilla is far from ideal, even though we see moments of tenderness and affection. Already the description of their bedroom mentioned above can hardly be called a genuine lesbian space even though Jelinek sees this as the single positive scene of her whole play. The two women lying side by side in their coffins — which represent the "womb, earth, hole, death and life at once" — symbolize the illusion of solidarity ("I Want No Theater" 146). This copy of a typical fifties' bedroom points toward a nostalgic regression, instead, "thus reminding us of that decade where family ideology as reaction to war times was especially powerful within society" (Caduff 133). This bedroom scenario parodically manifests woman's topographical void. There are no new models, not even in a lesbian relationship. Woman biting woman may be transgressive, but there is no crossover of established power relations. Again and quite unoriginally, Emily is the phallic woman, she performs 'man'. It is a role that suits her perfectly. Of all persons, she chose her fiancé Dr. Heidkliff to install two extractable teeth that provide her with the long sought-after phallus: "I want these two main teeth to be made extendable! They should be able to peek and disappear. Like myself, too. I need a similar apparatus like you men have! I would like to impress. I would like to show pleasure! I have juices, but they don't count for very much in everyday life. I would like to function after a principle, too!" (*Illness* 222).

Neither Emily nor Carmilla occupies a new space. Carmilla's negation of the realm of motherhood is highly taboo-breaking, but does not lead to any new definition. Indeed, sucking one's own children is a brutal act of killing demonstrating a triple subversion: negation of life, destruction of (male) property, and radical denial of motherhood. Along with taking on the claim to determine the fate of her children, such a woman claims power over herself as well. This is a reversion of the mother-child relationship from the nurturing to the reincorporating function of the mother and is analogous to Emily's refusal to submit to the biological function of woman. Her choice of desiring instead of bearing is one of the truly radical moments of the play. "Ich gebäre nicht. Ich begehre dich," she tells her: "I breed not. I crave for you." Emily's positioning as vampiric woman, lesbian and artist is subversive: "There and everywhere: relentless opposition!" (210). Yet, it does not provide her with a new space.

Paradoxically, Carmilla's reductive and incomplete nonexistence as housewife and mother semantically corresponds to the vampiric forms of nonexistence. It is only together with the vampiric love bite that Emily recognizes Carmilla as individual (212). Perhaps one can agree with Claes that Carmilla's transformation from the nonexistent mother into the undead vampire is an incomplete liberation (94). It is certainly true that Carmilla's existence as mother was defined as disease, and now, as vampire, she is complete in her perfect sickness (94). This overdetermination of illness ironically creates a space of semantic freedom as seen in Carmilla's redefinition of the subject by Descartes (*Illness* 232). Like Emily, Carmilla destroys the idea of an original text by parodically misquoting it. "Because by falsely citing she drains the originals of their initial authority," and without creating a new, original meaning, "Emily and Carmilla undermine the Christian-patriarchal logic by producing a 'vampiristic' counterdiscourse" (Doll 67). They perform a vampiric contradiction, a conscious misreading (cf. Erdle 334). Carmilla's seemingly paradoxical 'and'-constructions resist the monocausal explanations exemplarily pursued by Benno and Heidkliff: "I am ill, and I'm feeling fine. I suffer, and I feel well. It takes very little to be ill. I know how to do it, and I feel very, very bad. Health is not all there is, and my body can't stand it any longer. In the face of all those good healths, I turn into a sieve through which everything seeps. I am pretty ill! Ill! Ill! Ill!" (*Illness* 233).

But is the vampire-existence a consequent continuation of the illness-metaphor (cf. Claes 95–96; Doll 68; Janz 90) and femininity a congenital venereal dis/ease (cf. Friedrich 84)? Jelinek reminds us of the seemingly productive aspect of illness for women who, for example, 'performed illness' to escape dull sexuality with husbands. Jelinek calls this a "conscious withdrawing-from-health," and "illness as a mode of female identity ... not in its negative connotation, but as productive refusal to the terror of healthiness." Seen from this angle, Carmilla recedes from her exploitation as birth-machine and moves to the realm of the undead: "Since women cannot live in this world, they have to try out another one" ("I Want No Theater" 147).

The artificiality of all vampires in Elfriede Jelinek's oeuvre is obvious. There is no way for them to be real, authentic, because they are deconstructed at any given moment. Their outspoken self-reflexivity acts as substitute for the blind mirror which fails to reflect a bodily image. They are at once the objects of desire and desire itself, they can never be possessed since desire always remains in the absent void. Jelinek's vampires are always threatened by their narcissism; like the monstrous double-creature at the end of *Illness*, the vampires in *Children of the Dead* are doubled. Dying they awake themselves:

> there the two young women unite, the still half-living (?) ghost of Gudrun with the freshly killed Gudrun ... While the student lies dazed ... on the floor of a country inn, a reawakened, a young murdered woman slips into this body shape offered to her, and we become one and a third, a noncreature of the third dimension, re-ceiving an annunciation ... Thus, Gudrun becomes the bride (bridegroom) of Gudrun, one climbs down the stairs and into the other like a puddle of dust and bones on which the spelt wishes swim and sparkle like oil streaks. At this moment, this intermediate creature is sent a power that reawakens its body. (245–46)

Vampires create themselves performing an incestuous and literal gender-fuck on themselves: "Accordingly, his body is but an appendage of his cock and not vice versa, and so he may applaud himself heartily. This lad has sought shelter with his entire sex that continuously sleeps with him and, therefore, with itself! This sex fucks itself ..." (385). The vampire is represented not as a creature of body, flesh, and soul, but as language, constructed and artificial. If at all, it is the men in *Illness* who occupy still some emotional space, otherwise they would not feel threatened by the vampiric double-creature. By shooting it, the men destroy their desirable objects, desire itself, and, ultimately, themselves. The women are long gone, and the men are left to search for their transcendental mirror image, for, as Jelinek most pointedly puts it: "At the moment of death, the woman with-draws her body from the man: he, however, doesn't know much about what to do with his own anymore" (*Children of the Dead* 277).

Yet, paradoxically, Jelinek denies the narcissistic doubleness of the vampire as woman/artist. She is her own 'I': "And this woman is she or am I: Gudrun B." (648). Jelinek connects 'woman' and 'vampire' according to an underlying female principle of in-betweeness:

> The woman like the vampire embodies the female principle of a never quite being-here and never quite being-away, within, or out of reality. This is elucidated by Chinese drawings where the old mas-ters entered their pictures and disappeared. The woman is no great

master and her disappearance will never be complete. She will always reappear, busy as she is with her disappearing. This is an image of the vampire, as it is one of the woman: an undead who never quite lives and is never quite dead. ("Die Lady — ein Vampir?" 34)

Jelinek does inspect the realm within which 'queerness' is represented after all. It is this realm where the connection between vampire and lesbian is maintained and where Case regards the vampire as 'queer' potential:

we can here re-imagine her various strengths: celebrating the fact that she cannot see herself in the mirror and remains outside that door into the symbolic, her proximate vanishing appears as a political strategy; her bite pierces platonic metaphysics and subject/object positions; and her fanged kiss brings her the chosen one, trembling with ontological, orgasmic shifts, into the state of the undead. What the dominant discourse represents as an emptying out, a draining away, in contrast to the impregnating kiss of the heterosexual, becomes an activism in representation. (15)

Even though Meyer insists "that there is attraction of which no one dares to speak," she is at the same time aware "that there is attraction of which one dares to write" (107). Not every displeasure must lead to a traumatized writing disability. Indeed, Jelinek has written three programmatic essays on female artistic production under the sign of pathology concerning Claire Goll, Sylvia Plath, and Ingeborg Bachmann (Jelinek, "Der ewige Kampf"; "Zu Sylvia Plath"; "Der Krieg mit anderen Mitteln"; cf. Doll 43-45; Erdle 323-25). Maybe 'writing the vampire' means the paradox of literarily repeating performances of a reality that we would want to get rid of: whenever the vampire shows up, she is destroyed before she can settle down, before she may find her mirror image, and yet, she always returns. As Emily once says: "I am the other that does not yet exist" (*Illness* 196). Perhaps, it is possible after all to discover traces proving the brief presence of the queer vampire.

Notes

[1] Elfriede Jelinek about her novel *Die Klaviespielerin* (*The Piano Player*). Quoted in Sigrid Löffler, "Der sensible Vampir." All translations are my own.

[2] See, for example, George Klawitter's study on John Donne's often 'genderless' lovers (both narrator and addressee). "It is my intent in this book to let the enigmatic narrator speak in his own voices and to suggest meanings for those voices that critics of Donne have in the past ignored or suppressed," meaning, above all, homoerotic possibilities (xii). See also Sue-Ellen Case who in "Tracking the Vampire" mentions the "works of John of the Cross, although not literally queer," as the beginning of a tradition "that will be taken up later as literal by Rimbaud, Wilde" (5).

[3] Most interestingly, it is Meyer to whom *Illness* is dedicated.

[4] Interestingly, Ingeborg Hoesterey compares *Illness* with Edward Albee's *Who's Afraid of Virginia Woolf?*, another highly charged text according to its inherent queerness (135). Most other studies on *Illness* astonishingly do not even imply the lesbian issue at all.

[5] One may be reminded of Gertrude Stein's authorial dictum: "When this you see remember me" that structures her opera *Four Saints in Three Acts*, signifying the author's coded queerness. See Poole, *Performing Bodies* 147–61.

[6] See also Elke Liebs, "Weiße und schwarze Magie," who mentions further examples of cannibalistic and vampiristic women.

[7] Hoesterey sees in Jelinek's "gaudiness" a reflection of the Austrian avant-garde tradition, the performances of the "Orgien-Mysterien-Theater" of Hermann Nitsch and Otto Mühl in the sixties and seventies. "Whereas Nitsch/Mühl performances, often lasting for days, were syncretic orgiastic rituals, animal sacrifice (a lot of real blood flowing), and various other archaisms in a naturalistic manner," Jelinek, according to Hoesterey, relies on devices of artificiality similar to Antonin Artaud's "cruelty" (Hoesterey 155).

[8] Noteworthy is Jelinek's cannibalistic radio drama *Präsident Abendwind* (1993) which is based on Johann Nestroy's play *Häuptling Abendwind* (*Chief Evening-Wind*, 1857).

[9] See her interview with Sigrid Löffler: "Ich mag Männer nicht, aber ich bin sexuell auf sie angewiesen" ("I don't like men, but I'm sexually dependent on them") in which she admits her inability to fulfill the feminist calling to be(come) a lesbian.

"Der Kitzel der bösen Gedanken": Representations of Lesbian Pornography in Regina Nössler's *Strafe Muss Sein*

Amanda L. Mitchell

IN 1994, REGINA NÖSSLER PUBLISHED A RADICAL new novel, *Strafe Muss Sein* (*There Must Be Punishment*),[1] in the midst of the ongoing pornography/erotica debate.[2] The first section of this essay is devoted to a narrative outline which orientates the reader to the topography of the text. Thereafter, specific literary themes are identified for further analysis: these include the depiction of control and violence within a lesbian partnership, the concept of the gaze, and the symbolic use of blood imagery. Finally, emphasis is placed upon a character review, with especial reference to the re-interpretation of the central relationship as primarily sadomasochistic. In conclusion, the extent to which the text may be read as pornographic is considered with respect to how far it is informed by the traditional conventions of pornography.

Nössler's narrative revolves entirely around the sexual (mis)adventures of Hildegard and Henriette who candidly and explicitly represent the multiversity of female sexual experience and desire. Through a chance rendezvous with an exciting and threatening stranger, Nössler addresses the concept of anonymous sexual adventure in a post-AIDS society. The author also brings to the fore issues surrounding the relational balance of power, as the narrative's dominant partnership seems to crumble in the face of individual jealousy and physical violence. The dynamics of group sexuality and the fetishization of the body are similarly played out in the text, specifically during an impromptu dinner party. Through the interaction of two characters, Nössler probes the concept of a malevolent female sexual deity during the penultimate section of the novel, in which secondary issues of fidelity and sexual freedom are also raised. The final chapter explores personal jealousy and the human need for revenge.

The publishers' note characterizes the primary protagonists as "ganz furchtbar liebenswert" ("absolutely terribly charming") which is, in itself, subjective. Seen from a conventional perspective, their behavior frequently borders on the conventionally unacceptable. Whether charming sirens or licentious vamps, a complex web of chance meetings, fatal attractions, and bizarre coincidences reveals layers of the women's lives in a process which poses challenges and dilemmas for the reader. Since ultimately the problematic issues raised remain largely unresolved, the purpose of the text is exposed: *Strafe Muss Sein* seeks to present a lighthearted but always graphic depiction of sexual adventure and conquest. Intended neither as a didactic nor critical work, Nössler's novel allows issues of contemporary relevance to arise without becoming ensnared in their wider political significance. Among the controversial themes raised are the use of 'rational violence' within the private sphere and lesbian sadomasochism. Depicting such realities devoid of critical commentary permits the work an enviable simplicity and innocence, belying the ferocity of debate otherwise surrounding some of the tenets upon which it is predicated.

In terms of its narrative structure, *Strafe Muss Sein* consists of five chapters, each relating specific events of an often confrontational nature. Situations are introduced by means of the sporadic incorporation of peripheral characters through which the lives of Hildegard, a television talk show host, and Henriette, a veterinary surgeon, are presented. The women, lovers for twelve years, maintain a complex yet essentially stagnant relationship, which apparently entails some measure of violence. Three secondary characters, performing catalytic functions, are depicted in a relatively one dimensional manner, defined solely in relation to the sexual game-playing of Hildegard and Henriette. Rubina, for example, is a protagonist of immediate significance to the primary couple since she ultimately becomes the sexual quarry of both women simultaneously. She is a pivotal character both in terms of her influence upon the central relationship and in the light of the vivid blood imagery Nössler develops in her text, a topic which will be discussed later. Marlene Gott, the second character, displays unusual, idiosyncratic traits and is less a cliché than her predecessor. Marlene, an enigmatic persona, is the earthly incarnation of an erotic goddess figure and presents herself as a woman with a mission. She is closely associated with the final secondary character, "die Außerirdische" ("the alien"), who is a malevolent female deity, physically resembling a huge vulva. She is woman-identified, but amuses herself by interfering and intervening in female sexuality. Sexual weaknesses, birth, and menstrual complications are also the prerogatives of this creature.

The textual order of presentation of characters corresponds to their relative depth of characterization. The representation of these secondary personae illustrates that they are mere satellites of the main protagonists. Rubina, for instance, illustrates this point since her significance to them depends upon her sexual availability. Even when she is depicted as separate from rather than in conjunction with the women, her ascribed actions are commonly of a prurient nature. This is also true of Marlene Gott who is depicted as a sexual being whose raison d'être consists of acquiring a full complement of erotic knowledge and experience. Endowed with allegedly metaphysical powers, Marlene bewitches all who enter her sphere, cloaking them in her sexual mystique. Similarly "die Außerirdische," ruler of all things sexual, influences the central couple absolutely, as their obsession with expressions of sexuality renders them her playthings. Her existence is entirely appropriate within the text, given that emphasis upon the assiduous pursuit of carnal pleasure constitutes the most blatant narrative motif. Sexual desire and expression permeate the text to the extent that its literary merit may be compromised, and the question arises as to whether Nössler's novel is an earnest attempt to portray female sexuality and sexual autonomy or simply undisguised and undistinguished pornography designed for intemperate excitation. In treading the fine line between a frank depiction of lesbian sexuality and overt pornography, does *Strafe Muss Sein* retain its erotic integrity or merely pander to pornographic gratuity? In considering these questions, a deeper understanding of Nössler's work is essential. Let us begin with a thematic analysis of the text per se.

One of the most significant but also the most ambiguous motifs within the work is the use of violence as a means of gaining power and maintaining domestic control. Within the second chapter, Nössler narrates an incident of violence perpetrated by Henriette upon her partner. Via a conflict born of verbal disagreement, domestic harmony apparently deteriorates rapidly into sexual assault and physical torture: Hildegard is overpowered, bound, forced into the position of a voyeur and of the sexual object. The ambiguity surrounding the issue of violence derives from two apparently equally convincing approaches to one textual event. While the first approach demands a complete acceptance upon face value of the events related, the second interpretation assumes the presence of a radical sexual subtext in Nössler's novel. There are two ways in which to read this scene. Firstly, as evidence of a partnership which embraces violence, facilitating for Nössler the opportunity to penetrate the social taboo surrounding a phenomenon which – in feminist terms – must not exist: lesbian partner abuse. The politics of denial associated with such violence are rooted in the idealization of lesbianism by feminists as the perfected practical implementation of theoretical goals. A second angle takes into account the portrayal of the women's abusive relationship as possibly symbolizing more than what the reader first would expect. I will return to the second reading later.

In the first reading, Hildegard is portrayed as a passive victim whose narrative reliability becomes questionable due to certain incongruities of perception and apparent reality. Incongruous, for example, is her assertion that "everything was possible in her relationship with Henriette" (58) despite the fact of her depiction in a relationship of seeming inequality. This lack of equilibrium is epitomized by Henriette's physical and sexual onslaught, during which patriarchal power roles are assumed and replayed. Ambiguity remains, however, as to whether this violent depiction parodies heterosexual roles, or represents the extent to which this paradigm of dominance infiltrates female existence. Hildegard's initial outrage concerning her treatment at the hands of Henriette – the same "skillful hands she liked to be touched by, to be taken by" (29) – is reiterated throughout the episode. Apparent physical and mental trauma is repeatedly highlighted as she finds herself degraded and humiliated by Henriette, who appears as a fiend, unrecognizable to Hildegard: "The monster ... a callous monster" (45). Initially almost palpable within the text, however, the anger and sense of betrayal are superseded by sexual arousal and desire. Controversially, Hildegard is shown as ultimately enjoying her rape: "Hildegard was by no means indignant. She was aroused. She wanted Henriette to do it to her. Right now" (49). Furthermore, at the climax of the scene, Hildegard's continued desire is described almost ruefully as she regrets the brevity of the experience: "She'd have liked to delay the blissful moment. To hold herself back" (50). The apparent incongruity of this development is problematic since Hildegard's reaction to the assault appears barely comprehensible. Indeed, it is only to be understood from within a framework of dependency and deference. In her domestic relationship with Henriette, Hildegard defers to her partner, delegating any personal responsibility and the overall maintenance of control. Clearly perceptible in the routine dynamics of their relationship, this voluntary disenfranchisement is rendered all the more acute and evident within the sexual arena. The women do not share a mutual living space, preferring rather to keep separate residences, spending leisure time together at Henriette's apartment. The choice of such a nonneutral and loaded location, privileging one partner above the other, permits Henriette a sense of ownership. She essentially comes to view Hildegard as intrinsic to the apartment, regarding her just as she would any other piece of furniture: "The armchair ... was Henriette's property. It was Henriette's apartment, in which the great and powerful Henriette was sovereign" (28).

The frequent repetition of Henriette's name in association with her material possessions serves to underline her ownership and the absolute significance this sovereignty holds for Hildegard. Since the text is focalized at this point through the latter, it is logical to assume that Hildegard is conscious of the imbalance. Her awareness and lack of attempt at transformation implies Hildegard's agreement to continuing the situation. In consenting to Henriette's ownership of the shared space, Hildegard additionally accepts her lover's right to determine that which occurs within that space. Since Henriette is permitted such a comprehensive usurpation of control, the "attack" which occurs following Hildegard's abortive attempt to regain a measure of authority is rendered more comprehensible.

From Henriette's perspective, despite her manifest strength of personality she reveals herself as latently insecure and afraid. This claim is evidenced by her need to control and her reaction to Hildegard's attempt to leave. Indeed, although the reader is explicitly told that "they were a nice couple" and that "they cultivated love" (28), the implicit message encoded in the text is one of a love conditional upon Henriette retaining charge. The escalation and intensity of the violence described above indicates the extent to which the relationship disintegrates when Henriette perceives a loss of supremacy. As the situation deteriorates, she is variously described as "furious," "perplexed" (31), "cruel and quiet" (32), and "brutal" (34). These differing stages of anger correspond with a growing realization of Hildegard's determination to leave: "cruel and quiet," for example, is the stage attained by Henriette when her lover firmly decides that although "Henriette has often kept her from leaving ... today, however, this would not happen" (32). As if reinforced by Hildegard's decision, Henriette's resolution also grows and she moves into another stage of aggression: "brutal." Preparing to prevent Hildegard from departing, her mood changes from an impassioned fury to a cold and calculating cruelty. It is significant that while Hildegard collects her personal effects from the apartment — that is, while she is active and present — Henriette merely follows her, remaining passive and silent throughout. When, however, Hildegard stands passively, debating her route of escape, her lover is spurred into action. With unruffled control, Henriette now resumes her active role: "'You deceive yourself, my love,' said Henriette even more calmly. 'You will not leave. In fact, you will never get out of here'"(33). Her words are underscored and rendered increasingly sinister by their context and the calm with which they are uttered. Henriette is now to be perceived as cold and heartless, devoid of sentiment or regard and Hildegard's situation is such that she now faces a jailer who was a lover, a prison which was a home.

Significantly, however, it was Henriette's strength which first attracted Hildegard. This same force of will, when turned against Hildegard, facilitates an attack in cold blood allegedly justified since Henriette knows "what is good" (36) for her. Throughout the novel as a whole, the issue of personal strength is repeatedly raised, always depicting one character as privileged above another. The authorial message is perceived as one of realistic acceptance of the practical improbability of the traditional feminist goal: the attainment of an equal partnership. In her portrayal of Hildegard and Henriette, Nössler indicates that theoretical and political equality is not realizable in practical terms, as one individual inevitably comes to dominate the other. The extent of the domination is, however, to be negotiated on an individual level. As is shown in the incident outlined above, when the fine line between benevolent control and sadism is breached a window for abuse is created.

The second major theme upon which we shall concentrate in this article is that of the gaze, and, in particular, the ways in which the gaze is used both offensively and defensively. Although Hildegard is reduced to *verbal* silence by the actions of her lover, there is one way in which she communicates particularly effectively: in the realm of her body language, specifically in terms of eye contact. In the beginning, Hildegard refuses to look her partner directly in the eye, thus erecting a shielding barrier between them. In so doing, Hildegard protects herself in part from objectification by the gaze of her aggressor. Such evasive action is important for Hildegard for two reasons. Firstly, it prevents Henriette from looking into her eyes allowing Hildegard to hide her feelings from her partner's cold analytic regard: "Hildegard avoided ... looking at Henriette. Hours ago, her own self-image had become that of a small, beaten creature" (29). The importance of this evasion also exists on a second, theoretical level, residing in the essence of the gaze. According to E. Ann Kaplan, the gaze differs depending upon the gender of the person who is looking. If the gaze is male, it "car-

ries with it the power of action and of possession"; if it is female, it lacks
these qualities (323). Women, contests Kaplan, can only receive and return
a gaze. Although originally using a cinematic framework as her backdrop,
her comments are justifiably transposed into the literary field and their
validity examined in terms of the female gaze within the narrative. To say
that Henriette's gaze lacks the power to act would be patently false: she regards her bound lover with the intention of allowing her to read what is to
happen. Her gaze is predatory and merciless: it objectifies and paralyzes
Hildegard, and it is for this reason that Hildegard shields herself from it –
protecting her feelings from Henriette and the judgment hidden in her eyes.

This issue is of particular significance when Henriette moves Hildegard's prone body closer to a window. In a situation of essential powerless-
ness, Hildegard's only form of control is that of her gaze and her speech.
At this juncture, attempts at verbal communication are met with aggression
and violence from Henriette: "'Let me go! Let me go! Go away!' Henriette's
grip became tighter. 'I'll smash your face in!' she panted and punched her
in the face" (36). Hildegard's sole recourse is, therefore, determining where
she rests her gaze. Henriette's motivation and behavior are schizophrenic
with respect to her lover's view: firstly, she actively arranges her with a view
of the outside world: "Panting, Henriette ... turned Hildegard's body
through 180 degrees. Hildegard could now see through the window" (36);
then shortly afterwards, she issues a direct command for Hildegard to look
instead at her: "Kindly look at this!" (37). In that she initially allows Hildegard a view of the outside world through the window, Henriette simultaneously licenses the intrusion of the external into their private reality. In other
words, she allows the public to merge to some degree with the private. In
sanctioning such a merger, Henriette also permits her partner a fleeting
sense of hope that this drama will yet end reasonably. It could almost be
said that by rendering permeable the boundary between the outside and inside domains, Henriette endorses the impression of a mediating influence
which may prove regulatory insofar as a view is rarely one-way and where
Hildegard can see *out*, others may be able to see *in*. Perhaps this implied
potential for intrusion and rescue is intended as a safety measure, an aspect
which will temper Henriette's conduct, in essence as part of the game. On
the other hand, it is perhaps an example of Henriette's perversity which demands the mental torment of Hildegard, by showing her a tantalizing view
of an unattainable outside freedom.

Whichever the case, the control of Hildegard's view, fundamental to Henriette's plan, functions upon three levels. The first, and most obvious, is that of psychological control: any individual relies upon general sensory input in order to conceive, understand, and analyze a given situation. Where Henriette determines her lover's visual sensory input, that is, what Hildegard can see around her, she also controls her lover's perception of the situation. It is easier to subject Hildegard to increased levels of stress, anxiety and fear, which in turn facilitates easier control — thus allowing a self-perpetuating circuit. The second level relates to Henriette's behavior once she has secured control over Hildegard's view: she proceeds to adopt the role of a stripper, undressing suggestively in front of her: "She sat down on a chair. So that Hildegard could see if she turned her head to one side" (36–37). Hildegard has to turn her head in order to see, an act which deliberately places her in a somewhat unclear position. It is this ambiguity which leads to the third major level concerning Henriette's need to control her partner's view: Hildegard's ultimate submission. What is Hildegard's motivation for turning away from the security of the external view? Why does she sever her link with external reality? In turning her gaze toward Henriette, Hildegard voluntarily breaks this link with the world outside of her private drama. Whatever this connection otherwise represented to her — the potential for rescue, the tempering of Henriette's actions, etc. — is lost. She deliberately submits and abandons herself to the will of her lover, although at this stage it remains uncertain whether this is desire or simply subservience. With regards to Henriette, we are told that she "sat there with her legs wide open ... lay one hand over her cunt and slowly rubbed her clitoris" (37), all the while being observed by her bound lover. Her attitude is neither one of embarrassment nor shame but rather of triumph and pride, a mood emphasized by her unwavering stare. Although Henriette has opted to become the object of her lover's gaze, she still maintains control of the spectacle. On different levels, she is simultaneously the active subject who determines events and the passive object who is watched. Within the conventions of cinematic and literary pornography, this is an unusual position: ordinarily, by virtue of the medium utilized, the object (that is, the performer) has no means of becoming an active subject, of returning and reclaiming the power of the gaze. Put simply, the conventional boundaries between the observer and the observed are firmly demarcated as to refuse fluidity of role.

In seeking to comprehend the significance of Henriette's refusal to allow her eyes to waver from those of her victim, it is useful to take account of the conventions of pornography. According to Thomas Waugh, it is a universal practice of heterosexual and gay pornography that in solo performances, such as the one instituted by Henriette, the object (i.e., the performer) maintains direct eye contact with the viewer. This point is of particular interest when examining this episode between the two women in the text, since the reader is constantly reminded of Henriette's unremitting stare. Every action undertaken by Henriette is done so "without letting Hildegard out of her sight"; as she begins to masturbate, she "kept her eyes on the tied-up woman"; and even at the point of orgasm, her eyes are fixed firmly upon her helpless lover: "Her eyes were half closed, until she suddenly opened them wide, fixed her unremitting stare upon Hildegard, and came" (37). Throughout the duration of the episode, Henriette achieves and maintains the unique status of the objectified-subject or the subjectified-object, refusing to fully relinquish either aspect of the identity. She refuses both the role of the (debased) female object of pornography and of its distanced (male) consumer, her position, at this stage, as being one of emancipation and liberation from the constraints of traditional pornographic convention. She has succeeded in defying accepted notions of the humiliated object and the aroused subject, arranging herself, instead, as an excited fusion of the two. The fact that she enjoys masturbating to an audience is highly indicative of her personal psychology, most evidently with respect to her exhibitionism. Tangentially, it is interesting that she has a preference for an apparently less than willing audience. Her confidence is similarly an important issue at this stage: despite Hildegard's protestations and appeals, Henriette persists in believing that she knows what is best for her lover. The reader is twice informed of Henriette's verbal acknowledgment of Hildegard's pleas: "Only I know what's good for you" (37). Perhaps most evident from this singular episode is Henriette's capacity for abuse. Although disturbing upon some levels, this aspect of her personality and of their relationship has important textual significance, in that it works toward allowing a perhaps more realistic portrayal of the partnership, an aspect to which we will return later.

The fact that Hildegard constantly watches her partner appears, at first glance, to be more immediately comprehensible. Initially she is curious, wondering what Henriette proposes to do next. Later her gaze is governed by a sense of fear: she needs to be alert to each new movement by Henriette in order to steel herself against the attack. Still later, she is mesmerized by Henriette's actions, to the point that her status evolves, almost imperceptibly at first, to resemble more closely that of the consumer of pornography. This is the stage at which watching her lover is no longer a choice, but a compulsion. She feels the act of looking to be inescapable: "She had to look constantly, unable either to turn her head away or to simply close her eyes, to forget it. Spectating − it was like a compulsion" (37). Hildegard's inability to avert her eyes and thus protect herself from her partner's actions is repeated just a short while later in the text. She realizes, however, her need to watch and her simultaneous repulsion at what she sees: "It disgusted Hildegard. She was ashamed ... It made Hildegard feel sick" (37), yet she cannot divert her gaze. Aroused by the spectacle, the excitement causes her still greater humiliation: "She too opened her mouth, involuntarily breathing more rapidly. Curiosity ... Hildegard sensed a tugging deep in her vagina and was ashamed. Curiosity: The whole time she had watched Henriette playing with herself on the chair. Now she turned her head away quickly" (37–38). Her embarrassment at witnessing the intimate scenario causes Hildegard to look away. She cannot, however, escape the scene, as Henriette chooses this moment to begin her physical assault upon her partner. Perhaps it could be said that Hildegard's gaze served to protect her in part from the excesses of Henriette's behavior: while she was an active viewer of the drama, she was physically outside of, and safe from, the skirmish. The act of looking away, of no longer paying attention to the spectacle, seems to be a catalyst, prompting Henriette to move from pure exhibitionism toward the sadistic enactment of rape.

The authorial choice of terminology throughout this episode is striking: it is seen that there is a predominance of sight- and vision-related terms, which serve to heighten narrative tension and to reinforce the inevitability of Hildegard's situation. Significant, also, is the position of the reader: just as Hildegard is obliged to look at and watch her lover's performance, constant reference to terms such as "to see," "saw," "look," and "compulsion" forces the reader into a similarly voyeuristic position. We are almost compelled, through the use of visual signifiers, to "watch" Henriette's activities and their effects upon Hildegard in our imagination. Again, in a similar way to Hildegard, we do so unwillingly, inextricably consumed by compulsive *Schaulust*, by the same sense of urgent fixation. The identification with Hildegard may be so complete at this point as to allow the reader to slip into her skin, as questions regarding Henriette's motives, her sanity, and the consequences of the situation inevitably surface and demand answers.

The reader's identification with the main protagonists is particularly interesting in light of the fact that Nössler, the author, appears to have a specific agenda which becomes increasingly visible through the depiction of Hildegard. Through a lack of detailed physical description, the image of a very singular couple is composed which does not rely upon external generalizations. That the women have been together for twelve years intimates maturity and stability. The quaint but stereotyped image of a loving and tender lesbian partnership based on equality, however, is exploded at the point where Hildegard and Henriette refuse to conform to such stereotypes. Monogamy, even in a post-AIDS era, is not integral to their plan; neither is politically-correct sex. Their relationship instead lurches from one sexual escapade to another, each in an apparent attempt to better the efforts of the last. Henriette's 'attack' upon her lover constitutes the pinnacle of these efforts.

Throughout the duration of this incident, Henriette persists in following her personal path, seeking to meet her own sexual agenda of domination. Her actions at this stage may be seen as a deliberate attempt to debunk the myth of the 'vanilla' couple: the lesbian partnership based upon mutual respect and gentle female affection. In presenting the women as she does, Nössler firmly underscores the idea that the vanilla couple is a stereotype based on discrimination and prejudice. A widespread misconception exists that lesbian couples are in some way inherently more evolved and exist on a higher emotional and political feminist plane than heterosexually-identifying women. This impression is culled predominantly from the Women's Movement of the late 1960s/early 1970s in America, where the slogan "feminism is the theory; lesbianism the practice" came to represent an idealized assumption. For some lesbian-feminists, including Sheila Jeffreys and Janice Raymond, lesbianism represents a political goal also for straight identifying women in order to escape from male dominance and sexual violence. This concept fails its adherents in perceiving the nature of lesbian relationships through rose-tinted spectacles as saccharine-sweet unions: perfect partnerships devoid of cruelty and oppression. Where such notions stubbornly persist, fault is rarely found in the idealization of the lesbian lifestyle.

Nössler's depiction of a lesbian who engages in such brutality is a deliberate move away from traditional representations of lesbianism, an attempt to portray a new generation of dykes. A new generation which is no longer constrained by or to old roles and which seeks to construct new sexual identities informed by 1950s butch/femme performance, by 1970s punk culture, and by lesbian-feminist politics. This new identity model has facilitated a reacceptance of the importance of roles, finding them to be "an erotic charge, a way of understanding sexual preferences, and of identifying and attracting potential lovers and friends" (Stein 478). In depicting the darker side of Henriette's personality, Nössler succeeds in contributing to the steadily increasing body of novelists "who convey a sense of lesbian life, warts and all, by constructing characters driven by anger, jealousy and revenge" (Stein 480). Additionally, she also contributes to a debunking of "the idea of a seamless, transhistorical lesbian identity that we all share" (Stein 480). Whether or not the reader identifies with Henriette's actions, the fact remains that Henriette refuses to conform to a prescriptive and proscriptive heterosexual stereotype of the pacific and solicitous lesbian. And it is precisely this realization that is intended in the ambiguous depiction of the character as a sometimes shocking but always honest individual. Henriette personifies a new breed of narrative personae who are "realistically developed characters" and who are not "just cardboard" (Rodgerson 277).

Moving away from thematic considerations, it is exciting to examine the use and function of the symbolic. Symbolism within Nössler's novel is largely understated, although one specific leitmotif does recur: the color red. Red assumes several forms, appearing either as blood or in personal names, but it can be found everywhere, as heavy textual emphasis is placed upon it. The early introduction of Rubina constitutes a good example. The significance of her name is inescapable: Rubina, derived from *Rubin* meaning "ruby." The associations accompanying such a name are manifold: the sense of the exotic, of preciousness and value, and also of sexual, especially clitoral, metaphors of the type used in Rita Mae Brown's *Rubyfruit Jungle*. Red is also the color of an amaryllis, designed as a centerpiece for the narrative dinner party — an event at which Rubina is the unexpected guest. This flower has a strong mesmeric effect upon her, enchanted by its pendulous leaves, she imagines red lips — a genital reference which also resonates earlier imagery. Throughout the meal, Rubina cannot avert her gaze from the sensual flower: "The red, fleshy leaves stretched themselves ... She would have enjoyed touching them. She'd have liked to have known what it was like to have them between her fingers, and to rub them. To penetrate their insides with her finger" (61).

The sexual imagery in this passage is not difficult to discern, but it is without doubt that the most striking use of the color red is in the closing pages of the second chapter. Here, tomato ketchup poured over Hildegard's food is adopted as a symbol of the treatment inflicted by Henriette. The sauce comes to represent that which is "disgusting" in Hildegard's view and that which is "good for you" (51) in Henriette's. In many respects, the ketchup is a cleverly symbolic allegory for the violent sex enjoyed by Henriette: within moderately prescribed limits, and with the consent of both parties, the ketchup is the perfect condiment with which to spice up the meal. When, however, Henriette smears it – unbidden and undesired – over Hildegard's food, forcing her either to eat or hunger, this is no longer acceptable. The amount of ketchup delivered unto the meal is also a point of contention: while a suggestion of the substance may be experienced as pleasurable, a surfeit revolts the stomach, rendering the meal entirely inedible – sticky, acrid, and nauseating. Of Henriette's actions in this regard it is said: "Maliciously she poured a stream of ketchup over Hildegard's potatoes. They were totally ruined" (51). She is aware of the symbolic meaning of the substance and carries through the analogy in order to express satisfaction at her actions. As reinforcement, she makes a most piquant and telling remark: "The potatoes turned out well again, didn't they? ... You see, I do know what's good for you" (51).

The synthesis of the images of blood and erotics which denote violent sex is first introduced with Rubina's fascination for dinosaurs as expressed by "a poster of a *Tyrannosaurus Rex*, with bloody jaws, that hung over her bed" (9). The location of this poster is of immense significance: hanging over her bed, it links power and sexuality. In terms of a character analysis of Rubina, this reveals to her the association of sex and power, although ambiguity remains as to her preferred role – the dominator or the dominated. The blood/poster motif recurs later when, upon a visit to a local museum, Rubina is seduced by Hildegard. The location of their rendezvous, the dinosaur exhibition, draws an implicit comparison of predator and prey. Against the backdrop of a carnivorous dinosaur with blood-slavered jaws, Hildegard initiates physical contact with Rubina, biting, pinching, and squeezing her. The only verbal communication is to express Hildegard's intention: "I want to have you now" (18). She neither seeks permission nor allows refusal, simply taking that which she desires. Her behavior with Rubina lacks any pretense of affection, but is instead predatory, as she stalks her victim and pounces. The setting for their union is appropriate as it evokes and mirrors the violence and savagery both of prehistory and of their experience. Brutal blood imagery continues during the climax of their meeting, with the detailed chronicle of Hildegard's manual penetration of Rubina. Vampiristic imagery is similarly in evidence here with Hildegard biting and sucking Rubina's neck and throat, although ultimately no blood is drawn and the only flesh consumed is that of a postcoital *Jäger-schnitzel* (hunters' schnitzel).

Vampiristic imagery persists throughout the work, emerging also during the dinner party, when Rubina declares the topic of her term paper or thesis (*Abschlußarbeit*): female vampirism as an expression of sexual ecstasy. The nature of her academic work reflects precisely her two primary interests: sex and power. The power she earlier associates with blood is presented again with this different focus, and the similarities between the two object choices are striking. By siting a locus of power in dinosaurs and vampires, Rubina chooses intangible creatures: while the former may have posed real danger in a distanced past, both are products of popular myth and folklore, alive only in the imagination. Both sites of power reside in the realm of the fantastic, distanced from common reality. It is this element of disjunction from actuality which renders the objects more significant for Rubina. Emanating from a magical sphere, they permit Rubina the full strength of indomitable prehistory and chimerical folklore in her attempt to resolve the conflict of sexual ecstasy. The connection between sexual vampirism and ecstasy is highlighted in two other scenes, both times occurring within a licentious context. The first of these is during the seduction of Hildegard by Marlene; the second is the seduction of Henriette. In Hildegard's seduction, Marlene embodies the vampire as she bites "so hard into Hildegard's neck that it crossed the pain barrier. Profane agony" (123). According to literary and cinematic convention in the horror genre, Hildegard's reaction is classically that of the vampire's victim: "She took a deep breath and turned: away from Marlene and her teeth, and simultaneously toward her. Spurred on, she pinched a nipple, which hardened immediately in response" (123). Henriette, on the other hand, does not experience the blood-sucking operandi of sex with Marlene, as the roles are reversed and it is Marlene who is considering the power of her partner's bite. During this encounter, the victim herself desires the bloodletting, while the projected "vampire" displays reluctance. Marlene ruminates: "She'd have no problem in biting through my carotid artery with those teeth ... Why doesn't she do what I want?" (150-51). Irritated and frustrated, Marlene remains unable to make Henriette comply with her wishes and takes sanctuary in fantasy.

From unrealized blood-lust, the narrative moves on to describe an incident of actual fluid transfer. The blood here appears no longer only in symbolic but in physical form: the menstrual blood of Henriette which she smears onto Hildegard's mouth and across her face. As it enters Hildegard's tightly closed mouth, the blood represents at once a sign of complete domination and the parody of a kiss. There is an intimation that Henriette has marked her lover as her own, the indelible print of her visceral blood, branding Hildegard publicly as the property of another. Conscious of this brand, her lover makes an ultimate gesture of submission: "Hildegard offered her throat so that she could sit on it if she liked. It made no difference ... Nothing made any difference now" (46). At the moment, however, when the blood runs down Hildegard's throat, a striking and apparently incongruous transition is effected. Suddenly she is intoxicated by the liquid and overwhelmed by her own lust: "All of a sudden she was swept away by her own passion, her lust ... The blood ran down her throat. Hildegard wanted it. More, more blood, more juice ... Since it had to have come to this, Henriette should enjoy it too" (46). In that it is accredited with an almost mystical power, the blood bridges the chasm between them, and Hildegard instantly takes an active role in her own assault, assuming the status of the mythical rape victim who comes to like it. Upon first reading, it is bewildering that Hildegard considers the pleasure of her persecutor: her concern evidences a potential sexual subtext, and it is to this second interpretation to which we must now turn.

The portrayal of the women's abusive relationship may well symbolize more than what the reader first expects as inconsistencies surround the explicit description of violent sexual scenes. Besides these inconsistencies there is much textual evidence that Nössler portrays a mature sadomasochistic relationship between two consenting adults. At this point I should like to emphasize that, while I am acutely aware of the divisive nature of this form of sexual expression, I choose to remain deliberately without opinion as to its moral and ethical justification.[3]

Observing that in sadomasochism, as in its literature, things are not always as they seem, it is wise to remember that Hildegard and Henriette have been a couple for a sufficient period of time to have probably sampled the full menu of sexual flavors and appetites. Hildegard cannot be unaware of Henriette's predilection for domineering sex — an appetite to which she later confesses: "My hobby is hard sex" (44). Similarly, if it is accepted that their relationship is sadomasochistic, Hildegard's acquiescence to the passive 'victim' role is clearly scripted, and she may no longer be regarded as the 'battered wife'. Conversely, she may thus be seen as the partner who holds the greater degree of control.[4] Equally, if we view the violence in this new light, we understand that the classical victim/conqueror roles adopted are, in fact, a deliberate and faithful play by the author who draws upon sadomasochistic practices. Hildegard's reactions to the unfolding events clearly expose that her masochistic role is penned: her humiliation, fear, and anger – all intrinsic to her role as the submissive partner – are superseded by sexual arousal. During the "attack" Hildegard's verbal communications are faithful to her role; her direct spoken appeals, for example, are without relative impact: "Let me go!" "Will you stop this!" (36), she exhorts weakly, but the format of these exhortations leaves their authenticity questionable. Pleading is fundamental to her masochistic play since without it the power of her opposite would go unrecognized. It is essential that Hildegard beg in order for Henriette to assume her full power. In the case of genuine attack, however, entreaties would be tailored to underscore authoritatively her demands. Equally, the majority of Hildegard's *internal* communications are either merely rhetorical, or they are affirmations of her lover's animal lust and less the products of a scandalized consciousness than the accentuation of a sense of helplessness which increases sexual arousal. The transition of Hildegard from prey to desiring victim is now easier to understand: the aim of the scenario is sexual gratification and the masochistic role is arousing to Hildegard. Indeed, her regret underscores her pleasure in the episode and reveals the scenario as action within mutual consent. The issue of consent, however, is problematic in Nössler's text, especially since no explicit verbal consent is given by Hildegard. May it still be argued that her agreement is implicit? In order to fully comprehend this point, the relational balance of power must be considered.

Hildegard's voluntarily disenfranchisement, her acceptance of Henriette's sovereignty and consent to her ethos of ownership clearly extend into the sexual arena. Since Hildegard is not portrayed as naive but rather as predatory and sexually aggressive, a point evidenced by her interactions with Rubina, it is fair to suggest that Hildegard remains passive, as the 'attack' is orchestrated with her consent. Close examination of Hildegard's character supports this interpretation. It reveals a personality prone to masochism. Publicly, Hildegard is forthright, with a professional life predicated upon personal confidence. Self-empowered, she is unafraid of her sexuality and narcissistic in its expression. Her love of self leads to a need for recognition, the legacy of which is exposure and isolation. As a personality with her own talk show, she is separated from her audience, appearing as a two-dimensional screen image that is never fully present to her viewers. Her inability to balance self-assertion and self-effacement is most apparent in the realm of her sexual behavior. While she adopts one strategy or the other, she fails consistently to produce harmony. Her pleasure in subservience stems from a desire to delegate responsibility which for her represents a personal (private) emancipation from the pressure of her professional (public) existence. It is, in other words, erotically transgressive for an otherwise responsible and strong woman to relinquish her power and to adopt its antithesis.

Henriette, aware of her lover's need for this release, becomes the embodiment of (controlled) violence and enacts this role upon her opposite. Henriette *does* display signs of regard for personal limitations. In this regard it is useful to examine once more Henriette's positioning of her bound lover in front of a window. The geography of the 'attack' assumes significance when issues of familiarity and feelings of security are addressed. Although sadomasochistic sex may seem to be predicated upon fear and anxiety, in reality safety and the security of a preestablished script are of paramount importance. Henriette ensures that her opposite is aware of her concordance with the script by the choice of locale. She deliberately places Hildegard's impotent body in front of the window, allowing her a view out of it. It may be argued that the importance is not so much what Hildegard sees from this vantage point, but rather the fact of her being in front of a "screen." The window may be regarded as a metaphor, the symbolic representation of a TV screen; and as Hildegard is familiar with being "on-screen," Henriette's actions place her again into this position. This action furnishes assurance as to her safety.[5] Similarly, there is verbal reassurance of Henriette's intentions in her frequently repeated phrase "I know what is good for you."

Clearly, ambiguity remains as to the nature of the scene enacted between Henriette and Hildegard. Since a variety of potential readings exists, interpretation becomes subjective. This is also the case when considering the extent to which *Strafe Muss Sein* is conventionally pornographic, and it is to this that we must now turn.

Thomas Waugh has outlined six elements which can exist simultaneously within pornographic narratives: seduction, profanation, incest, defloration, conversion, and nymphomania (320). In terms of the first narrative strand, seduction is a primal element which permeates the entire novel. The conquest of Rubina by Hildegard forms the main source of textual interest during the opening chapter, with another such scenario implied later when Henriette too attempts to seduce Rubina. The result of this encounter remains unclear as Rubina seeks to evade the clutches of her pursuer. Although depicted as a woman whose pleasure in life is obsessively sexual, she is unwilling to comply with Henriette's wishes. Throughout the text, the seduction of one of the protagonists by a stranger constitutes the narrative basis. Hildegard, for example, is shown as the willing conquest of Marlene Gott, with whom she initially has contact on a professional basis. Interviewing Marlene for a news report, Hildegard falls under the very erotic spell she is investigating, acquiescing to Marlene's alleged supernatural powers of seduction. Significant in light of a sadomasochistic reading is Hildegard's behavior at this time. As the two women rapidly adopt their respective roles, their dialogical tone is unmistakably that of dominatrix and seducible slave with noticeable reference made to such concepts as "right" and "permission." Significantly, these roles are reversed during Marlene's attempted seduction of Henriette. Unsatisfying for both women, the episode culminates nonetheless in their uneasy union and the first explicit incidence of infidelity upon the part of Henriette. Initially unwilling, she eventually succumbs to Marlene, balancing the scales of fidelity once more.

Profanation and incest play no significant role within the narrative. This is similarly true of the elements of 'conversion' and 'defloration': although the sexual orientation of Rubina is never stated explicitly, assumptions of heterosexuality or virginity are unlikely. From the very beginning, both her sexual appetite and experience are evident. Indeed, she personifies female sexual autonomy without apology: familiar with her own body, she understands how to satisfy it. Similarly, these concepts are invalid within a consideration of the main narrative relationship since Hildegard and Henriette are longtime companions, convinced of their sexuality. The sole way in which defloration may be perceived as relevant is upon a metaphorical level in the apparent unveiling of Henriette's latent sadism. In other words, Hildegard is deflowered of the perception of her lover as tenderly benevolent — a process which simultaneously occurs for the reader. Nymphomania, the final element discerned by Waugh, is usually restricted to heterosexual confines (i.e., women's insatiability vis-à-vis the phallus). Its transposition into a lesbian context however, is particularly appropriate to Nössler's novel since her characters are obsessed with sexual adventure and experimentation, and no realm is made taboo. From anonymous sex with strangers in public places to sadomasochism in private, little remains uninvestigated by the characters. The nymphomaniac tendencies of Hildegard, Henriette, and Rubina are so numerous as to be impossible to chronicle, since the entire narrative is consistently peppered with their episodic unions.

An elemental listing such as Waugh's is useful only insofar as it facilitates the recognition of narrative commonalities among works conventionally designated as pornographic. It does not, however, ascertain the extent to which these elements succeed in stimulating the reader. Sexual response must also contribute to any definition of the pornographic: if a text meets the above cited criteria and arouses the reader, it may be labeled pornographic. With regards to *Strafe Muss Sein*, the sexual episodes may certainly be interpreted subjectively as arousing, depending upon the predilections of the reader. The encounter between Hildegard and Rubina is essentially intended as exciting in order to establish an agenda, prepare the foundations of the novel and encourage the reader into the text. For readers of lesbian erotica, the appeal of this opening section resides in its presentation of refreshingly honest characters who refuse the prescriptions of vanilla coupledom. At last, in this work, Nössler depicts women whose lives resonate a potential reality rather than an idealization. Indeed, the actions of Henriette and Hildegard can be read as arousing to a particular readership: punctuated with acts of domination, submission, and sexual role playing, the actions of both women hold widespread appeal to a sadomasochistic audience.

Fundamentally, it is justifiable to understand *Strafe Muss Sein* as a pornographic text, in that it incorporates classical elements of pornography and is predicated upon consistent sexual underpinning. The ambiguity of interpretation (partner abuse vs. lesbian sadomasochism) permits the novel to function on more than one level. In addition, the text may be read as the realization of a new genus of lesbian sexual confidence and power reclamation, a modern revitalization of the celebration of polymorphous sexuality. Regarded thus, certain aspects of Nössler's text lose a measure of their prominence and the clever construction and passion of the work is revealed. In her novel, Nössler has succeeded in creating a text which forces a recognition of that which is commonly ignored: that the physical dynamics of lesbian sexuality are no more, and no less, correct than any other form of sexual expression. In their relationship, Henriette and Hildegard do not constitute a perfect symbiosis, but are as equally fallible and prone to excess as any other couple, regardless of their sexual orientation. Or, they are as interested in the full range of sexual practices and appetites as any other. Nössler has created characters whose potential for authenticity penetrates the two-dimensionality of conventional pornography.

The authorial emphasis upon genital behavior to the apparent detriment of other aspects of sex means that *Strafe Muss Sein* must be recognized primarily as pornography. The characters, however, are more fully 'fleshed out' than usual and this contributes to a heightening of narrative arousal. During the course of the novel, a marked absence of events not predicated upon sexual motive is in evidence and yet Nössler is able to cleverly weave a great deal of humor and an intelligence of style and suspense into the drama. It is precisely these elements which raise the work above the level of the merely pornographic, admitting it rather to the category of 'erotica'. Despite its lack of didactic intent, *Strafe Muss Sein* should be acknowledged as an important and serious work: in not devoting space to extraneous 'informative' material, it succeeds in attaining its primary objective — reader excitation. In the traditional sense, however, *Strafe Muss Sein* remains a problematic work. As a genre, erotica is based upon a nonsexual central narrative with a sexual subtext which allows the element of textual surprise: semi-unexpectedly, the reader chances upon an erotic episode and is 'taken by surprise' by its existence and form. Since the work is not peppered with such incidents, the reader devours the words, anticipating further excitement and arousal. Conventionally, this nonsexual narrative level dominates the work with the main site of reader interest as subtextual, located episodically and apparently at random. In Nössler's novel, however, we experience something of a reversal of the 'norm' in that a marked absence of surprise, of randomness to the sexual graphics instead permits a constant flow of genital interactions and interchanges. Unremittingly, the scenes collide with each other in what may be understood as a pioneering new female fusion of pornography and erotica. In *Strafe Muss Sein*, Nössler succeeds in balancing the exigencies of her genre — classic porn — with her own demands as a novelist of great promise. In deliberately blurring the boundaries between erotica and pornography, she challenges traditional paradigms and forces a reformulation of social, sexual, and literary perspectives. Her representation of the pornography of lesbian sadomasochism is certainly, as questioned above, undisguised. By no means, however, can it be perceived as undistinguished since the caliber of Nössler's work and her innovative deconstruction of genre lend authenticity and integrity to the novel and, if her work is duly recognized as a clear forerunner, herald a new age of erotic representation in queer German fiction.

Notes

[1] Regina Nössler, *Strafe Muss Sein* (Tübingen: Gehrke, 1994). All references are to this edition and will be given parenthetically in the text.

[2] Cf. Abrams; Allison; Dunn; Gibson/Gibson; Kappeler; Palmer; SAMOIS. I gratefully acknowledge the help and encouragement offered by P. Bagley, H. Jones, and E. Boa in the completion of this article.

[3] I am indebted to Robin Morgan ("The Politics of Sado-Masochistic Fantasies") for the idea of the inclusion of personal caveats preceding the discussion.

[4] Although this concept appears to be incongruous, it is a well-established convention of sadomasochism that the masochist ("bottom") controls the events. It is the bottom who decides the situational framework (where, when, how, etc. the meeting will take place), as well as the extent of the power available to the sadist ("top") and the means by which s/he may express this.

[5] The concept of the screen is particularly interesting in relation to sex and pornography. If the window in front of Hildegard is to be perceived as a screen, the actions a third party/viewer would witness could justly be described as pornographic, or perhaps obscene. Witnessing events through the screen/window, a voyeur would experience a number of scenes: the action, in other words, would be "on-scene." The traditional etymology of *obscene*, as described by Linda Williams (233–65), goes back to the ancient Greek word *scaena*, meaning "stage." Literally, obscene would mean "off-stage," that which could not be publicly shown. Given that the stage has largely been replaced in contemporary times by the screen, it is reasonable to transpose the two words, thus rendering *obscene* as "off-*screen*." Furthermore, given that the German word "obszön" is the exact cognate of the English term, it may be possible to understand Nössler's intentional repositioning of the "obscene" to firmly "on-scene" as a deliberate act. Perhaps by setting the pornographic depiction of the interaction between Henriette and Hildegard in front of a "screen" (window), Nössler is attempting to reposition the entire concept of the pornographic. That is, in her choice of an on-screen location for the *personal* actions of her characters, she forces on-screen the wider *political* context within which the women act.

Renegade Lit:
Gay Writing at the End of Socialist East Germany

Denis M. Sweet

> *The white Negro rehearses a state of affairs gone awry.*
> —Norbert Marohn[1]

The Second Wave

LET THE APPEARANCE OF AN EXPERIMENTAL, nonconformist, resistant, gay literature in the German Democratic Republic (GDR) serve as our point of entry. What follows is an interrogation, not of the first few gay-themed writings that were allowed to be published during the last years of the old regime, but of the second wave of East German gay writing, beginning with Norbert Marohn's *Plötzlich mein Leben* (*Suddenly My Life*), and ending with several texts that appeared between November 1989 and October 1990, in the brief period of euphoria that began with the fall of the Berlin Wall and the GDR's censorship apparatus and that lasted until Germany's political reunification: Detlef Opitz's *Idyll,* Thomas Böhme's *Die Einübung der Innenspur* (*Practicing the Inside Lane*), and Gino Hahnemann's *Ende der Utopien* (*The End of Utopias*). All of them are texts that originated under the old order of the GDR. But they are also works of transition caught between a socialist world that was already disappearing by the time of their publication and the new society of postreunification not yet come into being. Common to all are strategies of resistance against the hegemonic center. But first, by way of putting their significance into perspective, a brief and contrasting look back at the gay texts that had preceded them.

The taboo of silence surrounding homosexuality in the closely controlled mass media of East Germany had been lifted in 1987 with the onset of a carefully orchestrated campaign for tolerance and the integration of gay people into socialist society (Sweet 1997). Lesbians, for the most part, were not addressed in the media and continued to remain in the shadows of socialist society.[2] For the first time in the forty-year history of the GDR, writings with overtly gay themes by East German gay writers (as opposed to a few modern classics by foreigners such as James Baldwin's *Giovanni's Room*) could be published by the tightly controlled book publishing industry.

Every publication in the GDR was licensed by the state. Every author's opinions were screened by the Ministry of Culture's censorship mechanism before appearing on the printed page.[3] The first publications by gay men that began to appear in 1987, by the very fact of their existence, were sensational. There was Ulrich Berkes's *Eine schlimme Liebe* (*A Nasty Love*), a diary recording dreary everyday life in the GDR intertwined with a study of Lautréamont, the blasphemous, outrageous, nineteenth-century French *poète maudit* whose works were not then available. Then in the spring of 1989, Jürgen Lemke's collection of interviews with a representative cross-section of East German gay men appeared and became a bestseller. These works seemed to signal a new era.

But make no mistake; these are works that followed in the train of a new state policy: publicly propagated tolerance and integration of homosexuals meant to win over what was in actuality an increasingly disaffected gay male population that was applying to leave the country and joining gay liberation groups based in the Protestant church in record numbers (Sweet, "The Church"). These worrisome trends had prompted a two-pronged policy of co-optation and containment of homosexuals (Sweet 1997). Co-optation lay behind the new publications that took note of gay men's lives and projected a tolerant and integrated home for them in socialism. Parallel to it, a policy of stepped up containment was promoted by the state Security apparatus, whose apex was reached in a criminological study that constructed gay men as all-round security risks requiring ever greater surveillance and control efforts by the organs of State security (Sweet 1997; Fehr). It appears that the GDR wanted to have it both ways: covertly keep its gay sons under the wraps of the security apparatus and simultaneously project the public image of a nurturing and tolerant socialist homeland.

The first appearance of gay writings in East Germany, then, was made possible by a uniquely paradoxical and contradictory political constellation. Yet the fact of their publication does not present a complete picture.

There existed other gay writing, writing less visible because less likely to be co-opted for the purposes of integration into the status quo: unpublished literary works waiting for the day when they could appear in the open; or writings smuggled to West Germany and published there, and only there, and thus effectively unavailable in the East; or literature that appeared in the GDR itself but was strictly limited to clandestine, experimental art publications of very limited circulation. Such works could appear in the East German public sphere only after the state censorship apparatus had been dismantled in the wake of the mass street protests and government shake-up in the fall of 1989. Only then did the determining forces of the socialist state and its interests recede from the literary texts published in East Germany, and a very different kind of gay writing could make its appearance.

Yet a certain dynamic of its own had already built up in the policy of tolerance and integration of gays into the socialist mainstream. There is no other way to account for a publication in the fall of 1989 — a book planned and licensed earlier — that transgressed all of the rules hitherto in place. *Suddenly My Life*, a 146-page story by Norbert Marohn, a young, gay author from Leipzig, fails to provide the requisite pro-socialist message; indeed, practically all manifestations of a recognizably East German socialist society have been shunted aside by the massive presence of a cultural world of rock and blues imported from the West. Portrayed in this text is an East German world where socialism has already ceased to be a point of reference, where socialism has simply become irrelevant.

Fortified Language

Disjointed, aberrant, and elusive by design, linguistically playful, punning, and witty — all of the texts to be discussed in following are marked by an experimental language that resists conventional reading and the habits of expeditious understanding. Their language sets these texts in a space apart, from both the East German public sphere with its language instrumentalized in the name of a superior, socialist social order and from the ostensibly straightforward, 'authentic' language of everyday life (which, in turn, was also instrumentalized for public policy purposes, for example in the form of publications such as Jürgen Lemke's best-selling book of so-called representative interviews with 'ordinary' East German gay men).[4] Neither one nor the other, the language of these texts is literally and literarily marked off from both. In other words, their authors employ a distinctively

literary language to construct a textual redoubt written against the grain of
hegemonic discourse. Language here is resistance:

> His nice little songs. The verses that he's always composed instead
> of ... lips. Smiling Speaking Eyes Hands. Now they are open — the
> way the Stones have of playing. TATTOO YOU. Better to gulp it
> down alone than in the DRESDEN BAR. Beer, what else to the
> Stones? TATTOO YOU. Get a tattoo. Drum it into yourself. Bring
> me back up — worried about you. He's finally got it. At last. That
> at bottom it has to do with the same thing again and again. Only
> the way of doing it is the trick. Blues. Rock. Anonymous sex. Get-
> ting rid of inhibitions with the saxophone. The music hall a differ-
> ent kind of tearoom. Mick gets the masses high who get him high.
> Mick makes his voice, the masses, naked who scream him naked.
> The tongue to the the microphone, hard-on and clit. Mick's voice,
> singing his soul out. WAITING ON A FRIEND. The way Mick gets it
> across. Arnold never knew that voice can be so corporeal. At
> bottom it all heads toward the same thing. WAITING ON A FRIEND.
> To wait on. To wait. Until no text is left. Nothing left to sing. The
> saxophone is there, between a cry and a howl: I don't need no
> whore; I don't need no whiskey. WAITING ON A FRIEND. The
> saxophone is there. Between crying and a howl; no sense to it.
> Whoever hears it, hears too softly. The breast is in between. The
> saxophone inside it. (45)

The protagonist of Marohn's text, Arnold, whose cascading, associative
inner thoughts comprise this passage, is a twenty-six-year-old rock performer who, in his official capacity as doctoral student, is concurrently
writing a dissertation on the rock music of capitalism, specifically on
blues in the music of the Rolling Stones — hence the recurring references
to lead singer Mick Jagger and the titles and lyrics of specific songs by the
Rolling Stones. Despite the academic pretensions, the real fascination for
Arnold lies elsewhere. Blues ventriloquize in an acceptable cultural venue
his own — unacceptable, because homosexual — thwarted inner longings.
Blues in rock is the place where Arnold's performance as a musician on
stage, his as yet closeted gay passion, and the officially legitimizing, ideologically situated academic inquiry of his doctoral dissertation all collide.

The ensuing wreck is the dilemma of his life and the theme of *Suddenly My Life.*

Longing for sex, longing for love, Arnold finds the blues instead. Mick lights the way. Jagger has already, successfully, negotiated performance as (sublimated) sex, whose longings voiced in blues are also Arnold's longings and whose songs provide a means for situating (aberrant) desire in a recognized cultural tradition. Mick plays with what agonizes Arnold. He can strut his stuff in public – "Der Saal eine andere Art Klappe" ("the music hall a different kind of tearoom," 45) – where Arnold cruises furtively in real tearooms for the anonymous sex that is one of the leitmotifs of this text.

This language, this scene, and the entire story open up a parallel universe of rock, sex, and blues in the middle of East Germany, and it is not one framed and distanced by the ideological binoculars of a properly disposed academic study, at which the author of the tale jeers, but one by which the protagonist desperately seeks to give articulation to his own messy emotional life. The language employed to spin this tale resists the assimilationist strategies practiced by the first wave of East German gay literature of mainstreaming gays into the established order of socialist respectability. The values that inform the protagonist of this text – a floundering, horny, self-pitying, and sometimes cruel young gay man aching for fulfillment – are simply at odds with those expressed in earlier East German writings which viewed the erotically nonconforming as renegades to be pitied or punished but taken back into the fold. The language of this text, however, is the language of renegades.

Suddenly My Life is framed quite classically as a German Bildungsroman whose young hero learns the truth about himself. The question posed in the very first line of the text, "maybe I need a woman who is older" – because Arnold's amorous experiences with women up to now have been unsatisfying – sets an inquiry into motion on the theme of individual fulfillment. Through a great patch of turbulence, Arnold's trajectory takes him from musing on his unfulfilling amatory relations with women at the outset of the story to anonymous cruising in Leipzig bars and public toilets in the middle, to the affirmation of his relationship with a boyfriend in the very last sentence: "Benno, I'm going to stand by you." Strange, Marohn's story seems to be none other than a rather old-fashioned tale whose inner voyage takes the protagonist from a state of confusion to conviction, from playing a culturally and socially acceptable learned part to individual authenticity, from struggle to overcoming, from darkness to light. The paradigm is familiar. Yet the seeming fulfillment posited by the act of coming out that crowns Arnold's development of character toward the end of the story is belied by other, more ominous and more deeply flowing currents — ones not as neat as the affirmative last sentence.

Icons of Longing

Suddenly My Life is a text of intense unfulfilled longing, a longing only underscored, not cancelled out, by the tacked on nature of its happy end. Suffused with litanies that are repeated again and again, ineluctable idées fixes of Arnold's desire, this text reads like a mantra: lists of men's names, his sexual partners and former lovers, and those he wishes were his former lovers appear in his thoughts, on the page, disappear, and reappear in ever changing permutations. Lists of men's names, ever repeated litanies of longing for an imaginary fulfillment deriving from his memories as a sixteen-year-old schoolboy swimming, gazing at, and desiring the embrace of a naked chum. This seems to have been the *ur*-scene in his life: "Frank who for him was the summer, naked at the canal; he's sixteen, his images all proceed to Frank" (48). Like in a biblical genealogy, Marohn's text features a hero who is a progenitor of future longings: Frank begat Jürgen begat Sebastian begat Gunnar, etc. It is, however, an aberrant genealogy since it traces gay desire: "Stefan, Axel, René, Thilo, Christian, Arndt, Michael, Harro, Sven, Thomas, Rüdiger, Lutz, Steffen, Uwe, they are immediately present: his year with twenty-five, his twenty-five guys — his accelerated course" (31). As if in a fugue, these litanies of names — repeated again and again, invading Arnold's head and allowing no respite — are varied by a counterpoint of bitterness and disappointment: "His queer life story. Nothing for a long, long time — An old story, an old song — Blues Boy's song — Benno's song — a new song: his gig. Everyone there who was once important. Was. Sometimes. Most of the pressure you make yourself ... ILOVEYOU–NOT ... I wait on you. Like with Jürgen. With Sebastian. With Gunnar. His queer life's story. Like with Frank: Tomorrow! Tomorrow" (107-108). Here names no longer resonate as expectation and desire but as so many broken notes of disappointment. In this involution of the theme of longing, each name now represents a moment not of imagined fulfillment, but of bitterly experienced abandonment.

These mantras of names, recited first as longing, then as broken disappointment, embody a gay biography, but it is not a happy one. Each time the name of a gay bar (Café Presto, Dresden Bar, Ringbar) surfaces in Arnold's associations, sometimes in isolation as a single name, sometimes as chains of bar names strung across the pages of the text, there is a sting attached, a memory associated with each bar of nights of compulsive cruising, of competing with men he has already had and who disgust him for the ever sought but ever elusive sexual contact. During a conversation in Leipzig in April 1991, Norbert Marohn told me that the original cruising scenes, edited under pressure from the publisher, had been far more extensive. What remains are bitter enough dregs that make Arnold's predicament clear enough. This individual — at odds with his surroundings and longing for queer love, a renegade politically, culturally, linguistically, and sexually — persists in his quest for authenticity despite the odds. His story is an icon of longing.

Ineluctable longing makes its appearance again and again in the literature of the second wave. Perhaps its purest example is Detlef Opitz's short story LUST/IG. eine landschaft (Longing, a Landscape) in the volume Idyll. Born in 1956, Opitz had garnered a reputation as a dissident writer not easily cowed; he was under police order not to set foot in East Berlin. Arrested on several occasions in the eighties, he received a prison sentence in 1985 for gesellschaftliches Mißverhalten, for being a social misfit.[5] He was one of the first in the GDR who insisted on discussing homosexuality in public outside of church circles, a topic, as he put it, that "was not taboo [in the GDR], it simply did not exist" (Opitz 1988, 147). Hitherto confined to the clandestine publications of the East German underground art scene, Opitz was able to publish in the mainstream only after the Wall had come down. Idyll, a collection of shorter fiction, also documents Opitz's frequent run-ins with the GDR authorities. It is done with zany, slapstick verve by intertwining his letters to the police with deadpan commentaries.

"The possibilities that encounters and relationships possess in which role-behavior is not determined a priori, this is one of the most basic questions that is the stuff of exploratory literature," Opitz writes in an essay on homosexuality in 1985 (Opitz 1988, 157). In Longing. A Landscape, violence enters that equation — role-behavior determined by a priori boundaries enforced by a backdrop of threatened violence. The boundaries in Opitz's story are twofold and distinct, yet brought into an oddly and mutually informative juxtaposition: the injunction against homosexuality (the forbidden "longing" of the title) is one; the death strip along the German/ German border, its off-limits "landscape," is the other. Two fourteen-year-old kids who one summer's day amble off to a bar near the death strip and are served beers despite being underage are the protagonists of the tale, their heads already self-consciously crammed with the axiomata of de rigueur manly deportment as they sit, swagger, and drink beer.

> "Yeah, blindfolded," my companion commented, sticking his right thumb between index and middle finger in the direction of the babe.
> "Yeah, she shouldn't ..." I declaimed, making my voice heard above the juke box, knowing that my friend would get a charge out of it, "she really shouldn't spread her legs that way, it smells so ..." (97)

Yet the disdain for the woman the fourteen-year old voices is a calculated ploy, something said to impress the other with a knowing, perforce hetero-sexual manliness that reifies women as sexual parts. He is gambling on acceptance, calculating to impress with the swaggering vocabulary of ma-chismo, the tough guy stuff, while — as we learn from an interior mono-logue that runs parallel to the spoken dialogue — he really wants to run his fingers through his pal's hair and kiss him; what he aches for is amorous reciprocation from the other boy. All this, however, is precisely the weak, sissy stuff that must be left unsaid and undone. According to the rules of the man game that have been inculcated in him, the only way in which the boy can assert his sexuality is to resort to the tough-guy trope, that is, to denigrate women by alluding negatively to their sexual parts.

Both boundaries, the barbed wire of the state and the barbed words of the boy's tough talk, are overseen by constantly vigilant external and inter-nal administrators. Screwing up his courage to do what he really aches to do, "gotta be a man now, I decided ... I laid my hand on the hand of my friend and jeered, in order to relativize the gesture, something about the graffiti in the john. My friend removed his hand, lifted his beer, but placed it down again without having drunk any. He left his hand on the glass. Something hurt in me" (100). The boy's dilemma is clearly put here. It is summed up again in the story's conclusion when the boy, having come down with a fever after unaccustomedly drinking beer on a hot summer's day, has been put to bed by his mother. The blond hair refers to his friend whom he had left back in the bar: "I wanted to kiss blond, cool hair and knew that he was still sitting there perhaps. I knew that men sometimes got it on with each other, assfuckers, filthy, they called them" (101). This is the end of *Longing. A Landscape*, the tale of a boy's longing to kiss his friend's blond hair abruptly reigned in by the same macho language he had been employing in the bar that afternoon, the language of an injunction that threatens violence against transgressors (the assfuckers). What remains is the unhappy residue of ever present and ever unresolved longing. In this story, longing is thwarted under the injunction not to touch, not to cross over the stated boundaries; in Marohn's blues and rock novel, a longing for fulfillment remains forever unsatisfied despite working the pick-up scene of Leipzig's gay nightlife. In this world, gay longing is posed as unresolvable. If the longing boy is taken as the chrysalis for Marohn's later rock singer, then he has transgressed the injunction against becoming an assfucker to be sure, but he has not graduated into a world where queer longing can be satisfied. In *Longing. A Landscape*, it is society, as codified by macho language, that draws attendant behavioral expectations that are oppressive barriers to fulfillment. In *Suddenly My Life*, the impediments are all-pervasive. Becoming gay has not solved the problem.

Utopias Never Die ... People Do

Repressive violence versus gay identity is examined by Gino Hahnemann, the multimedia *enfant terrible* of the East German underground culture scene, in his short, spooky prose text *The End of Utopias*. Hahnemann releases the pent-up violence that had flexed its macho muscles in Opitz's *Longing. A Landscape*, juxtaposing two generations in a portrayal of a gay father in the Nazi period and his son in the then contemporary GDR of the late 1980s. At the outset of this text, set in the last few months of the Weimar republic before the Nazis come to power, two young men, Fritz and Ernst, meet in a gay bar and discuss the likelihood of same-sex sexual acts being decriminalized by the German parliament, a reform that had been recommended by a parliamentary committee in 1929. This discussion frames a chain of events that again and again culminates in violence. *The End of Utopias* unmasks gay delusions about the nature of power that excludes them: "The queens have got to disappear, Fritz says, they have publicly skewed the image of homosexuals. My father will introduce us to

the Führer in the fall. We will be the speakers of a new homosexual movement. Everything proceeding from the consciousness of race morality. Free
from prejudice and Jewishness. Against an effeminate, bolshevized eros, for
a male-male one!" (134). Couched in nazi-speak, Fritz's vision of a new
society is about conformity with power for the sake of gay life, a total error
of judgment in this case as history has shown. In 1934, alarmed by a direc-
tive that homosexuals in Nazi party organizations be reported to Berlin
forthwith, Fritz's father prevails upon his son, now a twenty-one-year-old
SA-Gruppenführer (Nazi Storm Troopers squad leader), to sever ties with
his nineteen-year-old friend Ernst and convince him, Ernst, to marry.

> A group of marching Storm Troopers. Four across. Six rows
> deep. In the front, next to the fourth man of the first row, Fritz
> Sellmann.
>   In front of 6 Hauptstraße, Fritz Sellmann draws his regulation
> sidearm and shoots the man marching next to him, [his friend]
> Ernst Glowatzki. The latter falls dead at once. Sellmann returns to
> formation. The group leaves Hauptstraße in the direction of Albert-
> platz. 12/1/1941.
>   "A member of the SS or police who practices indecency with an-
> other man, or who lets himself be misused by another man for the
> purposes of indecency, shall be punished by death. By order of
> the Führer for the purity of the SS and the Police — 11/15/1941."

Here a gay man acts as the self-manipulated accomplice to the Nazis
and murders his friend. From there, Hahnemann's exploration of violence
caused by homophobia moves on to the next generation in the contemporary GDR, culminating in a repulsive captor/captive victim scene set in a
public toilet highly evocative of the shower rooms in Nazi concentration
camps. After the war, Heribert, Ernst's now ten-year-old son from his marriage of convenience in 1935, befriends a twenty-five-year-old Soviet officer
and enthusiastically sets about learning Russian. The neighbor women are
incensed that Heribert's mother is "doing it with a Russian," "pulling the
poor child in after her." After his mother is driven to desperation by them
and commits suicide, Heribert is cared for by the officer until the women
accuse him of sexually abusing Heribert. The officer is transferred. For the
rest of his life, Heribert believes "that he is the cause of his friend's going
away because he had not divulged his father's Nazi past" (136). Cut to

Heribert, now a fifty-one-year-old invalid working part-time cleaning the men's toilet at the main train station. He wedges blocks of wood under the handles of the stalls so that the young men having sex with each other inside cannot escape. Then he climbs up onto the heavy wire mesh over the stalls and starts spraying his prey, locked and captive below, with a high-pressure hose. "You want tolerance, runs through Glowatzki's mind, while he played the jets of the hose with childish glee, but tolerance is only a waste product of the Enlightenment, never its outcome. Only one person has to be tolerant to gain power or to keep it ... Anybody can do with you as he likes. What kind of tolerance are you counting on" (136).

The events that this text relates and the thoughts and actions of its characters are compact, fragmentized, and constantly switching from one level of time and one person's consciousness to another; its language, style, and composition produce a far more unsettling and nightmarish effect than any recapitulation could provide. The original is written as a frightening puzzle which cannot always be immediately grasped by the reader as it unfolds. That is the horror of this text whose full meaning and implications often only dawn in retrospect. As for the question of homo-hating violence, any facile finger-pointing at a predetermined, all-encompassing Nazi guilt — they the perpetrators, we the victims — has been called into question. What remains is an enduring substratum of hatred of homos, perhaps self-hatred in this case. "An unresolved inability to deal with his own homosexuality, is what some say. Others say it was an act of desperate revenge" (136). This brief text explores gay complicity with power as a strategy for survival: in the 1920s through parliamentary decriminalization; in the 1930s as male-male love couched in *völkisch* and anti-Semitic terms supposedly acceptable to the National Socialists; in the 1980s as pleas for tolerance and acceptance by those perceived as different. But Hahnemann's text rejects them all in favor of a much more pugnacious and self-assertive stance.

In his writings, art works, and video installations, Gino Hahnemann eschews any form of complicity, either with the mandates of straight society or the accommodationist mind set of other gays. In a hilariously acerbic short prose piece entitled *Das Ghetto ist zu klein für uns beide* (*The Ghetto is too Small for Both of Us*), Hahnemann takes on fearful, accommodating, and conformist gays. Witness its opening sentence: "'Art changes nothing as far as existential anxiety is concerned, it merely reflects itself,' he said. I pull his dick out of my ass" (162). Hahnemann's provocative style courts outrage and confrontation. His stage decorations for the theater production in East Berlin of Jürgen Lemke's interviews consisted of blown-up graffiti from a notorious East Berlin tearoom. His in-your-face celebration of (homo-)sexuality marks a more strident variation on the theme of longing. For longing, however self-assertive, remains the constant.

Hide and Seek

Contrasting sharply to Hahnemann's provocative tactics, cast more in the mood of a highly aestheticized and enervating permanent soulache, stands the tightly hermetic world of Thomas Böhme, a poet and wordsmith of great wit. One might say that Böhme's long prose text *Practicing the Inside Lane* — subtitled "an imitation of a novel" — is studiously incomprehensible. But that is only a part of it; in fact, this text is an adroitly conceived linguistic game of hide and seek. What is concealed in it is a secret at once tightly guarded — Böhme's language is the most literarily fortified of all the texts under scrutiny here — and also revealed in fleeting glimpses, but one cannot gain entry without a key. Not the imitation of a novel, this text is a subversion, a deft deconstruction of any recognizable notion of a novel into mosaic pieces, each no more than a few pages each. It is a kaleidoscope with no progression, no order, and no plot; and yet it provides an entry into a hidden place: the imagining and longing mind of its only character, a scientist haunted by his forbidden passion.

Böhme's labyrinthine text is composed of passageways that lead nowhere, of false starts and elaborate chains of word games, of jokes in a gentle wry humor after the manner of the German romantic writer Jean Paul, of rambling and recurring reveries. The only apparent source of structure is provided by the calendar. *Practicing the Inside Lane* accompanies Felix Wurz, a scientist who produces precision-made crystalline structures, through the course of one year: from fall through winter, spring, and summer to another fall. Wurz is an ardent francophile who goes by the name Felician Laracine though he does not speak French beyond a few phrases. He is also a scientist losing interest in his exacting craft, perhaps because the crystalline silicon structures he produces are becoming obsolete in the trade. No, Laracine's passion definitely lies elsewhere, though it is never once unambiguously stated where. Böhme is playing a game, and it is up to the reader to parse the hints, in certain names that crop up among others, for example, as if at random: Enkidu, Patroklos, Antinous.

When the first politicized gay emancipation movement got underway in Germany in the early part of this century, that movement began a morally self-justifying tactic that the American gay liberation movement would pick up a half century later: fielding the names of famous historical figures as an argument that homosexuals cannot be all bad, for, 'see, these people contributed to human culture, too'. The first gay emancipation film ever made, *Anders als die andern* (*Different from the Others*, 1919), proceeds in this vein and ends its call for tolerance with a procession of the recognizably great – conspicuously featuring the most famous of the Prussian rulers, Frederick the Great (Russo 1981, 19). Subsequently, names came to serve as convenient signposts for those in the know, border markers signaling the zone of homosexuality beyond. So the alert reader of the ever cagey Thomas Böhme registers a veiled allusion to Hans Mayer's study *Outsiders*, or the mere mention of Pasolini and Hans Henny Jahnn with a growing sense of an insider's 'knowingness.' Yet the secret so artfully concealed in this text is not simply homosexuality, but an especially tabooed variety of homosexuality. An aside provides a hint: "[Laracine] heard a boy with a cross tattooed on his glans say, 'It's all a bunch of crap, this Jesus stuff' … When he asked him whether it had hurt, he answered chimerically, 'No pain, no gain'" (31). The giveaway lies not in the words of this exchange, but in the situation that underlies them – left vague, yet implied – the situation that revealed the cross to Laracine in the first place, namely the contiguity of the boy, his glans, and Laracine.

Yet in this text as well, homosex is encased in past memories, or in relentless longings for a sex/love that is forever out of reach. The resulting mood that predominates in Böhme's text is melancholy fatalism. "The disparity between wild fantasy and desire on the one hand, and self-imposed restraint on the other, had gradually deformed [Laracine's] being" (39–40). Böhme has recorded a protagonist paralyzed by fear of the consequences of acting on his desire, a desire, in consequence, forever restrained, quashed desire, from which has resulted a fundamental deformation of being. In the recurring hilarious confrontations between Laracine and his alter ego, the alter ego never lets up from peppering him with insults: "Knabenschänder!" ("boy molester") he hurls at him early on in the text, and before the reader can have any notion that this insult – unlike all the others in the broad stream of abuse in which it swims – functions quite specifically. Elsewhere, discussing the colors of the seasons, Laracine and his unnamed alter ego (it is never made clear whether the alter ego is another character in his own right or an internal voice of conscience) have this exchange: "But manifestations in the sky like that are quite unusual," says the alter ego, to which Laracine responds: "You know, I'm not constantly looking up as you seem to think. — Yes, I know. Your predilection for half-fledged bike riders" (68). This snide allusion is exceptional for its polite tone, for generally the matter is couched far more abruptly by Laracine's alter ego, as in this typical torrent of abuse: "you monkey-faced quack, you sodomitical alchemist, queer laboratory rat, voyeur of urinals, cannibalizer of children, polluter of the environment, possibly even a pacifist" (103). Curious, how the crescendo of insults builds up to "cannibalizer of children," but then collapses with the desperately dilute "possibly even a pacifist." Is this thrust, and the built-in parry that accompanies it, all just painful camp humor? Insults spun out of control and thus simply made ridiculous? This language ironizes the violence so bluntly signaled in Opitz's and Hahnemann's texts. The perfunctory strings of antiqueer insults in Böhme's imitation of a novel are served up half-decomposed, deflated, made idiotic.

It is a curiously dual text of slight and flight. The campy humor that poses, then deflates and ridicules threat, adumbrates the former; while flight into a grandiosely imagined imperial Roman past with the hermaphroditic teenaged emperor Heliogabalus serving as focus for a repeatedly occurring reverie on the possibility of acting out nonconformist sexual desire situates an imaginary place where queer desire can be lived out. Toward the end of *Practicing the Inside Lane,* Laracine resignedly admits to the imaginary nature of it: "I repeat myself ...Why do I love this butchered boy [Heliogabulus]? Because I can't love Jesus? Because Sören, because Mink [two boys with whom Laracine has had encounters and about whom he daydreams] do not enter my room? Because I am certain that I have missed my century? I am tired. Where should I go to rescue myself?" (158).

The desire hidden in the fortified castle keep of this text is posed as one constrained to unrealizable longings. It exists only in the mind, in a space marked by violent homophobia — formulated in this text ironically as half-decomposed insult — and reveries inspired by Stefan George's poems about a talismanic Roman boy emperor. Böhme's text identifies social and erotic deformation. Revelatory in its concealments, it acts as a savvy advocate for a love that 'dare not speak its name'.

White Negroes

In the last few years of its existence, the GDR instituted a new policy of simultaneous accommodation and containment of what was to them an increasingly worrisome gay population. For the first time, the government allowed gay writings to be published, ones that attempted to integrate gay East Germans into socialism. At the same time, however, another gay literature was being written, one that the state-controlled book industry did not publish and that appeared in East Germany only after the censorship apparatus was dismantled in the fall of 1989. This previously suppressed literature portrays a society fundamentally at odds with the subjectivities of its gay characters. What is valued and significant for this body of writing is the attainment of individual authenticity, and the denial or negation of collective orthodoxies of any kind. Its writers portray not a world of fulfillment, but one of longing and constraint. Although conceived and written under the old order, this literature has abandoned allegiance to the existing socialist society. Where institutions specific to East German socialism do appear, they are either treated as irrelevant (Marohn) or portrayed as a threat (Opitz). It is not a 'dissident' literature of political opposition, but a literature of self-reflective individualism written in a language of aesthetic resistance that claims the right to an individually defined sensuality in opposition to an oppressive and ever present hegemonic center. In a conversation in 1990 looking back on the GDR, the East German poet Bert Papenfuß-Gorek described the intent of the nonconformist writers of his generation: "They placed the emancipation of the senses and a sensual emancipation against the one-dimensionality of the hegemonic discourse. Against the vacuous rhetoric of speaking they placed a rebellion of material" (in Thulin 237). An emancipation of the senses and a sensual emancipation, though, for the literature discussed here, with the particular twist of homosexuality. For homosexuality remains written from the margins. Norbert Marohn's protagonist, grappling with his identity as an outsider, employs a telling formulation. He refers to himself as a "white Negro," a term that resonates with the historical concatenation in Germany of black musicians and jazz, but also points to the fundamental and a priori marginalization of the 'other', whether racially or sexually defined. Both are on the outside. "Der weiße Neger probt den Mißstand" (15), Arnold says of himself: "the white Negro rehearses a state of affairs gone awry." Writing from the margins of socialist society and against their marginalization, the "white Negro" writers of the second wave of East German gay literature portray a state of affairs gone awry in which their characters are trapped and against which they have written a literature not of integration but of intense longing and resistance, if not emancipation. It is not until after the end of the GDR that a third wave of writers comes forward to write a literature in which the hegemonic center has disintegrated in the new society of postreunification.

Notes

[1]"Der weiße Neger probt den Mißstand." This motto, taken from Norbert Marohn's *Plötzlich mein Leben* (15), is discussed at the end of this article. All translations from the German are my own.

[2]Ursula Sillge, an activist and important player in her own right, has written a detailed account of the lesbian emancipation movement in the GDR.

[3]*Zensur in der DDR* (Wichler/Wiesner), the accompanying catalog to an exhibition on the history and practice of the censorship of literature in East Germany, put together by the Literaturhaus Berlin in 1991, documents in compelling detail the all-pervasive hand of the state's censorship apparatus on East German literary publications.

[4]The best-selling collection of interviews with an ostensibly representative sampling of East German gay men that appeared in the spring of 1989, Jürgen Lemke's *Ganz normal anders*, is an apt case in point (see Sweet, "A Literature of *Truth*").

[5]Information provided on the dust jacket to Opitz's *Idyll*.

Queering

German

Culture

The Genre Cycle of German Gay Coming-Out Films, 1970–1994

Les Wright

> *Do you not hear the awful screaming all around us that*
> *people call silence?*
> —The Mystery of Kaspar Hauser[1]

IN A MERE TWENTY-FIVE YEARS (1970–1994) German filmmakers, pre-dominantly gay and predominantly independent, have generated a complete genre-film cycle of gay coming-out narratives. It is ironic that the distinctly U.S. American phenomenon of the identity politics of sexual orientation — coming out as gay — should have been treated more seriously by auteur filmmakers of New German Cinema than by their American counterparts.[2] The catalyst for the post-1969 *schwulenemanzipatorische Bewegung* (gay liberation movement) in the then West Germany was Rosa von Praunheim's polemical film of 1970, *Nicht der Homosexuelle ist pervers, sondern die Situation in der er lebt* (*It Is Not the Homosexual Who Is Perverse, But the Situation in Which He Lives*). In 1975, Rainer Werner Fassbinder released one of his most uncompromising films ever, a sort of gay Brechtian morality play *Faustrecht der Freiheit* (released in English-speaking countries as *Fox and His Friends*, but the original German title is suggestive of Kleist's novella *Michael Kohlhaas* and the strong-arm freedom of the robber barons). Only later would members of Germany's gay culture assimilate the jargon, the looks, the consumer-oriented cultural clutter of its American counterpart, as reflected in Frank Ripploh's autobiographical *Taxi zum Klo* (*Taxi to the Toilet*, 1980) and, to a greater extent, in Sönke Wortmann's *Der bewegte Mann* (*Maybe... Maybe Not*, 1994).

In the 1960s, the postwar New Left generation of the then West Germany adopted U.S. American pop culture as "a popular political form," representing "a remarkable break with the Frankfurt school's critique of popular culture — a form of mass deception by the culture industry" (Shattuc 86). New German Cinema began as a conscious break with the

immediate past of National Socialist filmmaking, making free and experimental use of Hollywood techniques. German gay films of the past
quarter century, at least initially, served as a staging site for the dialectical
working out of coming out as a political strategy of *schwulenemanzipa-
torisch*, or gay liberationist, theory and the auteur cinema as a mediator of
the *Erfahrungspraxis*, or experiential grounding, of New Left political theory. In essence, such films served both a traditional cathartic role, through
the gay male viewer's identification with, and emotional release through,
the film's narrative, as well as a didactic function exhorting the viewer
through the film's polemic to take action. Ideally, such action included
one's own *Selbsterfahrung* – the importance of learning to accept one's
own emotions as the primary authority of authenticity – while witnessing
the film as the auteur director's experiment in his own *Selbsterfahrung*.
Whether the viewer would then take social or political action at all, let
alone in accordance with the director's sensibilities, was at the heart of
these experiments in filmmaking.

The evolving relationship between sociopolitical realities and the practices of representation in these German coming-out films, that is, between
film as *Erfahrung* (privately knowable experiential knowledge) and as *Öffentlichkeit* (a consciously collective public experience), has grown increasingly problematic. The mainstreaming of gay identity in the United
States has subsumed the confrontational style and the oppositional position of gay liberationist politics. The German gay liberation movement of
the 1970s had never articulated specific, achievable goals, and over time its
energies dissipated in endless theoretical discussion. The movement has remained stagnant ever since, despite both the advent of AIDS and the end
of the Cold War. The bright promise of New German Cinema in the 1970s
proved short-lived. By the mid 1990s, both the gay movement and gay
films had been gradually co-opted, absorbed as another commercial niche
market, into the depoliticized consumer culture of the time. Questions of
identity, community, authenticity and the possibility of actual sociopolitical change seem to have collapsed into what Baudrillard has dubbed pure
simulacra. Such a view, however, will prove illusory.

The first part of this article poses the question: who is the 'I' in auteur
cinema? Following an overview of narrative structure and background
issues in the rise of New German Cinema, I will consider the fact of social
identity both as a private structure and as a public experience, the role of
social identity politics, and the role of the outsider – taking Kaspar Hauser

as its central metaphor — in New German Cinema. In the second part, I will trace the four-step evolution of the genre-film cycle of gay coming-out films of New German Cinema through four films, each one representative of one stage in that evolution. This study reflects narrative films with gay male content, and many of the historical specifics are about male homosexuals. To some extent, what is articulated applies as well for lesbians, bisexuals, the transgendered, and other queer individuals. This is but a preliminary study, and will hopefully encourage others to join me in pursuit of these dynamics in film history as they apply to the unique circumstances of each class of social outsiders.[3]

I.

Let us begin by exploring narrative structure and related background issues. *Auteur* theory presumes a fundamental understanding of the conventions of narrative film. Narrative plausibility in genre films, such as the western, science fiction, Gothic horror, or screwball comedy, depends to an even greater degree on conformity to conventions. As Will Wright argues in *Six Guns and Society*, narrative proceeds from an order to disorder, and then to resolution through the establishment of a new order. A commonly shared understanding of narrative structure in film explains how individuals in a society interpret the narrative actions in their myths. Narrative sequencing is essential, since that is how one can account for change in a given situation. Conventions of the genre film assume that given explanations cannot be questioned in their own terms and that everything in a narrative contributes to the explanation. To be considered a genre film, all — or almost all — the elements necessary to understand the film must be included within the narrative. Auteur films and, moreover, the coming-out films of New German Cinema require a grasp of the historical context in which the films were made and in which the viewer/participating moviegoer, in her or his role as active participant in creating narrative coherence, has presumably participated.

The mythic content of an auteur film will contain a conceptual analysis of society that provides a model of social action. All coming-out films serve to model social action or inspire the viewer to contemplate social action. Characters in a myth represent fundamental social types — archetypes, stereotypes — and gay characters in gay coming-out films serve to counter prevalent mainstream social clichés of homosexuals through either positive or ironic means. Narrative progression will lead the (soon-to-come-out) gay viewer to an authentic knowledge of what it means to be gay. The narrative will lead the viewer past the false stereotypes and thus negotiate the internalized (self-)hatred the viewer has to overcome as the first step in the process of coming out. So, step by step, the narrative accompanies its viewer/participant, as the latter achieves her or his desired goals of self-discovery, self-acceptance, social engagement, and a socially meaningful life as a self-identified lesbian woman or gay man. The role film plays as scripting for gay people's lives should not be underestimated. Consider, for example, the camp followers of *Mildred Pierce* (1945, Curtiz), *The Women* (1939, Cukor), and similar women's pictures or how gay male pornography scripts the sexual encounter for some gay men, who, in a real-life pick-up situation, come to realize that their sexual partner is obviously acting out scripts and dialogue from his favorite jack-off movies.

Geoffrey Nowell-Smith has made the anthropological observation that the point of narratives, whether as film, fiction, or oral storytelling, tends toward impelling consensus and social cohesion: narratives universally describe and promote heterosexual coupling, marriage, and procreation, while simultaneously warding off or containing homosexuality and incest (756). The transgressive nature of gay coming-out films arises, in part, in their channeling of explicitly homosexual desire into similar narrative patterns of social cohesion, holding up a mirror to the audience and challenging received notions of what is deemed normal.

The 1962 Oberhausen Manifesto[4] marks the start of the New German Cinema, and Fassbinder's premature death in 1982 the deathblow to the movement. This film movement, which was primarily in the style of *Autorenkino*, or auteur film, was driven by a need to invent a film language counter to the legacy of Nazi German propaganda, which had engendered widespread mistrust of received knowledge and official histories, particularly via the medium of film. Postwar German film had a disjointed 'feel'; in their search to break with the filmmaking of the Nazi era, directors drew upon the examples of Hollywood directors or German film from the Weimar era. Directors of New German Cinema grappled with problems of German critical history and ideologies, resituating German film history within the context of sociopolitical German history. But with an awareness of the international audience and reception of German film, they often also sought to create an artistically and economically viable alternative national cinema.

In terms of German history, two vitally important phenomena must be kept in mind. In an attempt to forget its recent past, a kind of cultural schizophrenia overwhelmed Germany after the Second World War. In a 1976 interview, Wim Wenders explained that "the need to forget twenty years created a hole, and people tried to cover this ... in both senses ... by assimilating American culture." Hollywood, from such a German film-maker's perspective, was both constructive as "an image of redemption and unparalleled technical proficiency," but also highly problematic as "the propagator of ideological and economic imperialism" (Corrigan 1). The original problem was also twofold, not just the conflict between primarily left-wing filmmakers and capitalistic financial backers, but also, as the French *nouvelle vague* auteur filmmakers had discovered a generation before, "all the best machinery and building materials are American-made" (Corrigan 2).

Thomas Elsaesser (1989) describes the dramatic shift in the expectations of the postwar generation of moviegoers caused by the politicization of the postwar generation following May 1968.[5] No longer seeking the entertainment of a Saturday matinee, as their American counterparts had sought, the generation of 1968 wanted legitimate information which the official media was — or was suspected of — ignoring or suppressing. As Elsaesser explains, revival screenings of Hollywood classics as self-conscious auteur films were no longer enough; "instead they sought cinemas that could function as a focal point for political opposition and protest — an anti-cinema, anti-television and anti-press medium" (1989, 155). Film, Elsaesser continues, was suddenly understood as "part of a collective act of self-expression and self-representation. The very media consciousness of the protest movement had helped the cinema, however briefly, to become 'naturalised' as a public arena for symbolic action" (1989, 155). The newly engaged moviegoer was more likely than not to be involved in the protest activities in Berlin and other major German cities and university towns. The story of gay moviegoers and how they were called to activism in or outside New German Cinema has remained virtually unexplored in the mainstream accounts by German film historians, such as Thomas Elsaesser (1989) and Anton Kaes (1996).

Along with Hollywood movies, U.S. American pop culture of the 1960s was absorbed by this increasingly politicized New Left culture, importing the consumerism of America's young generation: rock music, pop art, the fashions, style/atmosphere, and consumer habits of the American counterculture, and, in time, the urban American gay culture. More than one critic has characterized the German student movement in the 1960s as specifically antiauthoritarian. Richard McCormack identifies it as being based "on the ideal of personal refusal: each committed individual would refuse to cooperate with a system seen as authoritarian and immoral" (in Shattuc 85). German gays would join this antiauthoritarian movement in 1969 after the *Entschärfung*, or toning down, of Paragraph 175 of the German Criminal Code, which decriminalized male homosexual activities.

A second major shift arose out of the collective disillusionment with the utopian idealism of May '68, when hopes for an evolutionary revolution were dashed. West Germany in the 1970s may have looked very solid and prosperous to the outside world, but internally it was a time of widespread fear and paranoia, with severe limitations on civil rights, massive security checks, hysterical and absurd suspicion reminiscent of the McCarthy era in the United States, *Berufsverbote* (occupational blacklisting, a very real fear among German gays), and state-sponsored denunciation campaigns against radicals.[6] The *Schwulenbewegung* and the etiology of gay coming-out films emerged in this context. One of the weapons used against state-sanctioned repression − reflected, for example in *Fox and His Friends* sub rosa − was the (gay and straight) auteur cinema's reliance on subjective experience (film as autobiography) as authentic history in the face of official censorship and revisionist politics. Independent films were screened at communal cinemas in university towns and provincial capitals.[7]

The paranoia concerning terrorism − and particularly concerning the Red Army Faction (RAF), popularly called the Baader-Meinhof group − and the complicity of *yellow journalism* were captured in Volker Schlöndorff and Margarethe von Trotta's 1975 film *Die verlorene Ehre der Katharina Blum* (*The Lost Honor of Katharina Blum*), which was based on the eponymous Heinrich Böll novel, a kind of contemporary West German version of Arthur Miller's play *The Crucible* (1953). Anton Kaes correctly points out that the terrorist acts of autumn 1977 were an expression of the return of the repressed that "ultimately stems from the collective trauma of learning the truth about the horrifying German past, usually not from one's parents but from books or in school" (1989, 25).

For all these reasons, one may infer that melodrama would be the preferred genre for gay coming-out narratives, giving prominence to the emotional aspects of conflict between societal norms and discordant social identity. German gay filmmakers tend to rely on an explicit or implicit didactic approach as well, instructing the gay viewer not only how to come out, but making him aware of both the pitfalls and rewards of doing so. In the case of New German Film, explicit connections are made to the historical social problems of West German society. Gay coming-out films draw upon a psychology of filmic perception — which can be seen as the spectator's activity, such as integration of prior knowledge and experience into personal (if not social) transformation — and the material and structure of film itself (melodrama) (cf. Bordwell). In other words, a gay coming-out film does not merely record experience, but creates "its own kind of reality, and its own experience of time, memory, and duration of space, place, and occasion" (Elsaesser 1989, 208–209).

In 1982, German funding of film became very restrictive again, in part for economic reasons and in part for political reasons. Fassbinder's suicide in 1982 took the wind out of the movement; most German filmmakers left the country for Paris or for Hollywood. Thereafter, German cinema re-emerged as a "national minority cinema" (Kaes 1996, 626), often limited to late-night television and the art-cinema — or repertory cinema — circuit. It is within this context that Sönke Wortmann's 1994 film *Maybe... Maybe Not* entered mainstream theaters and ended up by 1996 as the highest-grossing German film of all time.

The politics of establishing a social identity on the basis of sexual orientation emerged during the 1960s in both the United States and Germany, as well as elsewhere. A key strategy of such politics is *coming out*. Coming out is understood as both an internal self-recognition and the public statement of one's social persona. The question of personal identity — who am I? — in gay coming-out films tends to speak in both mimetic and diegetic voices, that is, both dramatic and lyric exposition, telling someone else's story for its symbolic value to the (implied) narrator and the narrator's own story. Two distinct notions of otherness weave through the discourses of coming out. In his *History of Sexuality*, Michael Foucault has argued that society constructs an array of institutions and ideologies whose purpose is to define two classes of people — "the normal" and "the abnormal" — and to enable one minority group ("the normal") to maintain social control over those they have defined as social outsiders, or alien "others." Jacques Lacan, however, appropriates "the other" to describe a much different notion (*Ecrits*, 1977). For him, "other" marks a stage in the psychological development of an infant, namely when the infant realizes that its mother is not an extension of itself (self), but rather is not-itself (other). Bill Nichols argues that, for Lacan, the image of this mother as other "appears whole, complete, full, a plenum of realized potential;" it is "an ideal to which the child aspires" in order to develop its own identity (31).

Film narrative operates as myth, and filmic myth operates on a double perceptual dynamic. Each coming-out story tells one individual's tale ("I am me and not some other person"), but also invokes or traces the common path to self-fulfillment in a queer social identity ("I am like that person because we are of the same type"). Such narratives and social identities are paranoid or unstable because each is always in tension with itself and unresolvable. By coming out, a queer individual makes her- or himself and others conscious of the instability of social identities altogether. The queer person attains to a sexual maturity in which the bifurcated distinction of heterosexuality (men desire women and compete with other men; women desire men and compete with other women) is, for all practical purposes, irrelevant to queer realities, even though that queer person has been programmed to seek and make such heterosexualizing distinctions. In fact, the point of coming out is to turn the perceptual tables. The queer person realizes she or he is a Foucauldian other − "the abnormal" − in a normative heterosexual universe. However, by orienting her or his own perceptual point of view, the queer individual destabilizes the old order's center and creates a new center of her or his own. Following a quasi-Baudrillardian multiplication of sites of virtual reality, one might end up with an infinite number of centers. How often coming out as a strategy succeeds in recasting the natural given order of things is moot.

In Foucauldian terms, the queer individual − lesbian, bisexual, gay man, or transgendered person − is confronted with an internal split of being both social outsider and social insider. Self is both self and other. Or, in Jungian terms, coming out means claiming certain aspects of one's shadow which society has taught the queer person to repress. In the discourses of 1970s German gay activism, coming out meant literally to come out of the public water closets or 'tearooms' or 'cottages' (*Raus aus den Klappen!*), out of the bushes in the park, out of a compartmentalized private sphere, and step into the daylight of unobstructed public view. Coming-out films only underscore the reality apparent to gay men that, as socially marginalized and hence disempowered individuals, coming out would hardly cause the downfall of civilization. Instead, coming out fosters a new collective myth, both "abstract structure through which the human mind imposes a necessary order and a symbolic content through which the formal structure is applied to contingent, socially defined experience" (W. Wright 11).

In recent theorizing, the equation is between the resolution of sexual satisfaction (which is presumably the underlying impulse for a gay man to come out) and the psychological pleasure of narrative resolution. A coming-out narrative, for the gay man, offers resolution to the question, "Who am I?" The didactic intent of the coming-out film is achieved through a seduction by the narrative. If I can identify with the character in the movie, then I can identify with myself, I can become one with myself, I can transcend the acute sense of fragmentation within myself. This, at least, is the ideal. To paraphrase Marx, "the material conditions of existence determine men's consciousness and not the other way around" (Baxandall/Morawski). Critic Bill Nichols continues, "Althusser, in fact, defined this process of the setting into place of the self-as-subject as the ideology of ideology, the transhistorical first principles of socialization" (34–35). The desire and ideology of coming out are utopian projects, questions of how to imagine an ideal future and how to realize it in the present.

In contemporary capitalist consumer-society we are saturated by the visual media. Films offer images publicly for us to internalize. Films model the myths and fantasies we internalize. As Frederic Jameson has argued, "a work of art's vocation is to manage desire in social terms, negotiating between wish-fulfillment and repression, or arouse fantasy content within careful symbolic containment structures, which defuse the awakened (dangerous) desire" (1992, 25). In the brave new world of niche marketing, the cognoscenti viewers are defined as those who know how to decode the filmic messages. Over time, as gay film has been developed for a niche market, it has succeeded in manipulating and containing the emergent collective gay consciousness. As long as gay coming out draws upon a collective fantasy of a utopian sort, it will remain didactic. Once reduced to cliché, it is merely amusing and runs the risk of being dismissed.

The outsider figure stands at the core of New German Cinema, and the legendary (as opposed to the historical) figure of Kaspar Hauser in Werner Herzog's filmic treatment *Jeder für sich und Gott gegen alle* (*The Mystery of Kaspar Hauser* or *Every Man for Himself and God against All*, 1975) serves as arguably *the* central metaphor of the New German Cinema. The film expresses the problem of collective trauma denied through deliberate cultural amnesia — the search for identity, the sense of distancing which is an aftereffect of traumatic shock — and the embodiment of the other. The historical Kaspar Hauser appeared one morning on a public square in a southern German town. He could not write or speak, he could barely walk, and had never been among people before. The man-child grew up rapidly, making up for the childhood he had spent alone, chained to the floor, and deprived of virtually all external stimulation. Kaspar was never able to fit in, and rumors flew as to his mysterious origins. He was murdered within a few years by an unknown assassin. Kaspar's origins, the identity of his assassin, and the motivation for his murder remain an unsolved mystery to this day. Kaspar Hauser serves as a prototypical stand-in for the outcast of his age, not unlike the Jew, the guest worker, and, of course, the homosexual. The film offers one of the most vivid examples of how the subtext of homosexuality can function as the invisible but transparent marker of difference in postmodern Western society. Herzog's intent with *Kaspar Hauser* is to challenge the collective, normative mythmaking of corporate-controlled society.

Werner Herzog is at the core of New German Cinema, seeking to show a way toward true experience (authenticity), anti-intellectual, antitheoretical, and antirational approaches to express and arouse feelings. Fassbinder explicitly invokes Brecht's *Verfremdungseffekt* (alienation effect), to make the familiar seem strange, the strange familiar. This is what the homosexual is in postwar Western societies. "Herzog deplores our lack of images capable of assimilating the demands of the present and the brutal realities of the past. He has made it his goal to create in his films a wealth of imagery adequate to contemporary human experience" (Jansen/Schütte 110). In just such a way, gay coming-out films create new images. *Kaspar Hauser* frames this double problem of subjectivity and narrative — "subjectivity *as* narrative, and narrative *as* subjectivity," as Kaja Silverman suggests; the fact that Kaspar is never able to tell a "complete" story is "virtually synonymous" with Kaspar not being a "coherent" subject:

> [S]ubjectivity is in effect the dominant cultural narrative, a narrative which it is incumbent upon each individual to live through to the end of a linear and causal fashion. Kaspar's inability to find a conclusion to the story which he tells from his deathbed connects metaphorically with his inability to conform to the filial narrative with which he is equipped upon his entry into culture. (1981/82, 74)

Kaspar is unaware of the social expectations others have of him — in Silverman's model, he fails to pursue "Oedipal desire" and learn the lessons of "phallic signification and lack" (1981/82, 75) — in other words, he has failed to be socialized as a heterosexual man. In fact, Kaspar appears to be asexual. Kaspar learns by trial and error from direct experience, and several humorous moments in the film occur when his authentic perceptions are at odds with society's explanations. By degrees, Kaspar becomes aware of being under surveillance, both by members of society — at first he enjoys the attention, but gradually withdraws completely — and by being shadowed by an external, (probably) unknown agent who eventually murders him. Despite the relative safety and acceptance Kaspar finds in the community, the paranoia of his split consciousness proves well founded. Palpable but hidden forces (fearful individuals? paid agents? collective social disapproval? the very structures of a closed community?) conspire to destroy him, because he is different and because his undisclosed truth is a threat to others.

An important aspect of the Kaspar Hauser metaphor is the dynamics of "soul murder" and the analogy between the historical Kaspar Hauser, the homosexual outsider, and the social consciousness behind New German Cinema. "To deform a soul takes chronic and repetitive abuse," psychiatrist Leonard Shengold observes in *Soul Murder* (18). Shengold sets forth psychological parallels between the historical Kaspar Hauser as the survivor of chronic and severe child abuse, the soul-murdering effects of growing up a closeted (i.e., emotionally disconnected) homosexual in modern society, and the traumatized German nation which sought to 'forget' its Nazi past.[8] In all three cases, we are presented with an agent in desparate need and actively seeking to create a new language, forge new social bonds, and to 'forget' or shuck off the trauma and mutilation, the burden, of its own history and the stunted creature it has become.

II.

The genre film cycle is best divided into four stages: the primitive, the classical, the revisionist, and the parodic. Will Wright's analysis of the American western is often cited as exemplary of this paradigm. He traces an evolution (citing corresponding exemplars) from the primitive, *The Great Train Robbery* (1903, Porter), through the classical, *Stagecoach* (Gordon

Douglas, 1966), to the revisionist, *High Noon* (1952, Zinnemann), and finally the parodic, *Blazing Saddles* (Mel Brooks, 1973) (Gianetti, 345–54). The majority of westerns rarely rise above the level of being a vehicle for cliché plot lines, the narrative conventions of the genre obviating the need to be psychologically plausible. This is a defining characteristic of the genre film. In New German Film the gay coming-out cycle begins with corresponding genre exemplars, namely Rosa von Praunheim's primitive melodrama *It Is Not the Homosexual...*, Rainer Werner Fassbinder's classical polemical tragedy *Fox and His Friends*, Frank Ripploh's more subtle, that is, sublime and humorous, revisionist comedy *Taxi to the Toilet* which expresses the ambiguities and increasing awareness of the complexities of coming out, and, finally, Sönke Wortmann's parodic farce *Maybe... Maybe Not*, a film which reduces the conventions of the coming-out narrative to parody and cliché.

It Is Not the Homosexual... has become a seminal film, in part because it directly spawned the birth of the second German gay movement. Von Praunheim, self-identified avant-garde filmmaker and controversial gay activist, collaborated with Martin Dannecker, a self-identified gay sociologist, in producing the film as an ARD television coproduction. When the film first aired on German television, the Bayrische Rundfunk (Bavarian TV) blocked the broadcast in Bavaria. *It is Not the Homosexual...* tells the story of Daniel, a kind of gay Candide, who arrives in Berlin from the country and seeks his place in gay society. His journey is the archetypal 'new-gay-face-in-town' tale. "Daniel's various encounters present the film's audience with a catalogue of stereotypical gays: effeminate, garish, promiscuous, predatory men whose only concern with each other is as sex objects" (Kelly 116). He immediately settles down in a marriage with Clemens, only to traverse gay culture: from bourgeois sentimentality to luxury to the beach to the park to the bars, but – here is the new twist – winding up in a gay commune which will prove his salvation.

The film premiered at the Berlin Film Festival in 1971 and ran at the Arsenal Cinema in Berlin. Discussions followed the film, and gay men in the cinema audience were encouraged to join von Praunheim's organization, and in this manner the first groups were formed that would spawn the second gay movement in Germany. "When I shot my film *It Is Not the Homosexual...* with Martin Dannecker in 1970, we did not know anything about the American gay liberation movement (von Praunheim, *Armee der Liebenden* 7). "Raus aus den Toiletten, rein in die Straßen" (Out of the toilets, into the streets) and "Freiheit für die Schwulen" (Freedom for queers) were, clearly, indigenous slogans, independent from the rhetoric of the American Gay Liberation Front. Gay activist groups sprang up in university towns wherever the film was shown, drawing membership from students and junior faculty members.

Directly or indirectly, von Praunheim instigated several key shifts in both film and society. The German term *schwul* became widely adopted as the activist term of choice, employing the same tactic used by their American counterpart, who appropriated "gay," "faggot," and, a generation later, renewed the appropriation of "queer." His version of gender-fuck tactics is expressed through the choice of his camp drag name Rosa ("Rosie") and the jarring contrast in his hypermasculine black leather manner and dress. Von Praunheim's mandatory personal appearances at all screenings of his film, somewhat akin to author reading tours, expressed an essential value of auteur cinema, making filmmaking "a publicly accountable activity."[9] As Elsaesser points out: "It became a practical engagement with audiences on the one hand and social reality on the other, thus also conferring a different status on film viewing and cinema-going" (1989, 156).

Von Praunheim sought to subvert gay moviegoers as passive consumers and help create an *Öffentlichkeit,* or better *Gegenöffentlichkeit,* an alternative public space, where the audience is the filmmaker's equal and thus a group of social beings. However, this and other attempts by New German auteur directors fell short of their radicalizing and politicizing function. "My situation as a gay man," von Praunheim states in an interview:

> has not changed much even after the appearance of my film about gays ... I hoped for solidarity, for a group with whom I could work collectively to change my situation. I felt isolated in the hostile subculture (vain bars, dark parks, and toilets). The film forced me to take a position: I could no longer hide my problems or take refuge in bitchiness and complexes. It was not until a television interview that my parents found out that their son was a homosexual. I had not dared until then to talk with them about it. Although tolerant in a bourgeois way, one did not talk about sex at home. (1976, 18)

Indeed, von Praunheim describes in the same article how he found himself banned from various bars, threatened with knives, even beaten up as a result of his publicity by conservative gays, bar owners, and others. Right-wing gay groups formed in reaction to denounce von Praunheim as a communist.

Von Praunheim's film sets up a dialectical relationship with its audience, encouraging the viewer to actively put the pieces together. Its didactic purpose is manifested in von Praunheim's insistence that he (or another member of the production crew) be present at the screening. According to Keith Kelly, the film is "'descriptive' rather than 'analytical' ... The gay subculture is presented in a societal vacuum and the obnoxious behavior of the protagonists is never linked to its straight model" (117). In objecting to von Praunheim's emphasis of a gay versus straight dialectic over one of an oppressed versus a ruling class, Kelly hits upon the source of the ultimate failure of this utopian impulse. What is being modeled is a "special lesson for bourgeois gays" (117).

Von Praunheim's portrayals of homosexual stereotypes are deliberate caricatures, parodying mainstream heterosexual conservative behavior and values, and von Praunheim's own Berlin leather culture alike. Von Praunheim was committed "to mak[ing] homosexuality a highly visible reality without suppressing even its most hideous manifestations" (Bruce 28). He asserts that gay men hate each other, that gay culture is so foul, and that gay men lack solidarity because, in Richard Dyer's words, "they have such low self-esteem and that homosexual relations never last because to commit oneself to them means committing oneself to a loss of social status" (*Now You See It* 218). Gay men in Germany must join with such pressure groups as the Black Panthers and the women's movement, to change their social situation.

In the founding of the Federal Republic of Germany, the 1935 version of Paragraph 175 was adopted without modification. Historian Hans-Georg Stümke remarked that the Federal Republic's Supreme Court "even embraced the rulings in the legal judgments of Paragraph 175 made by the Nazi *Reichs*-court in its last days, whereby physical contact was no longer necessary to constitute an offense, merely 'looking with lascivious intent' sufficed" (133). It should be hardly surprising, then, that the *schwulen-emanzipatorische Bewegung* got off to a slow, even turgid start, that gays of the older generation refused to break their silence, and that much activism remained safely contained in theoretical discussions behind closed doors. Even von Praunheim's film was not possible until after the 1969 *Entschär-fung* of Paragraph 175. Most gay men did not identify with activism or leftist politics and instead perceived their new-found legal freedom useful for participating in the rapidly expanding commercialized culture of discos, clubs, bars, and bathhouses – much to von Praunheim's disappointment.

In the meantime, von Praunheim became very taken with the gay movement in the United States: "In America I was fascinated by the strength and the great organization of the gay groups, but no matter where I spoke about this, people soon lost confidence in me and I think it was right that my work was continued by many other people" (1976, 70-1). His later film *Army of Lovers, or Revolt of the Perverts* (1979) was an encyclopedia of queer America in the late 1970s. Von Praunheim was critical of his fellow auteur directors, in particular Fassbinder, whom he perceived as 'selling out to the System' as the latter became commercially viable. For all that, von Praunheim has continued to make numerous films, many of them with queer content, most notably *A Virus Knows No Morals* (1986), *Anita: Dances of Vice* (1987), and *I Am My Own Woman* (1992). At the core of the latter, there remains a paradox typical of his generation: an unintentional misogyny, rooted in a long tradition in Germany in which lesbians have been seen as and aligned with *women's* rather than *homosexual* liberation, that underlies the portrayal of the leathersex community's pansexual liberationist stance.

Rainer Werner Fassbinder's roots are in live theater, using *Verfremdungseffekt* in his epic "antitheatrical" approach, and mixing melodramatic overstatement with intimate psychological autobiography. Fassbinder continues the thesis put forth in von Praunheim's 1970 film regarding a dialectical material analysis of the social oppression of gays. He continues in the heretical tradition of critical analysis of gay male psychology and gay culture from an insider's point of view. Fassbinder appeals to the filmgoer's authentic experience and challenges his audience – not unlike von Praunheim – to actively put the pieces together, in order to get the message from his parable and to decide when and how to put theory into practice. In essence, *Fox and His Friends* is the story of a lottery winner and how he loses all his money. As the film opens, Franz, alias Fox, has been working as a barker for a *Kirmes* (traveling amusement park). When the operation is closed down by the police, Fox is left without work, which precipitates the break-up with his lover (a gay working-class relationship presumably based on chance circumstance). The film opens on a huge spinning wheel of fortune and the thronging blue-collar crowds at the midway; a progression of colors, from a kaleidoscope of bright colors and a dominant blue, culminate in the utterly solitary suicide of Fox, his body splayed across the floor of a sparkling new subway station, with empty and antiseptic white tiles and blue lights. The upper-middle-class lover who has bled Fox dry of his money, his self-esteem, his hope, and his ability to trust another human being, happens upon the body, but merely steps over it. Having outlived his usefulness to the lover, Fox is tossed away like another used-up convenience. The multivalent symbolic use of the color blue is in all likelihood also intended to underline Fassbinder's emotional appeal to his gay viewers. *Blau* (blue) is German slang for "drunk," an association the German viewer would automatically make between intoxication and going to a fairground.[10]

The wheel of fortune, along with Fox's lottery winnings, underscores the notion of chance. It is an ambivalent symbol of how chance events can radically change one's fate, of the role chance plays in someone turning out queer, even of the arbitrary nature of how society defines who or what is normal. Indeed, as the expression goes in gay German slang, "only 'normals' [heterosexuals] can be 'normal'." The ironic intent of the latter proposition is laid bare by the entire storytelling, which presents the relationship of two gay men of vastly different social classes within a realistic social context of 1970s West Germany. The irony is left to the moviegoer to work out for himself. Gays, as Paul Thomas points out, are subject to the same mechanics and dynamics as normal heterosexuals:

> Homosexual exploitation is still exploitation; an erotic exploitative relation between two people is no less exploitative for being erotic. And in this case, it is class, not sexual preference and "politics," that calls the shots. Fassbinder's way of presenting this reality is as original as it is harrowing. The melodrama is there, but it is not crucial; what *is* crucial is the portrayal of a homosexual relationship and swindle exactly as a heterosexual relationship and swindle would be portrayed (which cuts through jaded and naïve responses in much the same way). (8)

Fox and His Friends is suggestive of the corruptive nature of capitalism and how economics shape human relationships. Fassbinder attacks both the false myths of bourgeois sentimentality — romantic pairings are romantic fantasy, love is the most intimate form of betrayal, consumer comforts are dangerously seductive — as well as the empty rhetoric of solidarity and utopian vision – West German leftists are as much a product of a bour-geois-capitalist environment as their opponents on the right.

Most of Fassbinder's films are secular myths of small lives cast as archetypal or epic in scope. "Fassbinder does not shrink from centering his attention ... on those who *don't* cry out from under the wheels, who don't know how, who don't even see that the wheels are there" (P. Thomas 3). Fassbinder's films often acknowledge the filmmaker's debt to the German exile in Hollywood, Douglas Sirk. For that matter, Fassbinder reweaves autobiography into filmic fiction much as Thomas Mann did in his homoerotic stories *Tonio Kröger* and *Death in Venice*, and in his novel *Felix Krull*. Biographer Robert Katz suggests that Fassbinder modeled the film character of Fox on his real-life lover at the time, Armin, and that Fassbinder played the role of Fox as a kind of latter-day unspoiled noble savage. Fassbinder echoed Mann's ability to anticipate real life in his art in another way. Uncannily, Mann portrayed certain of his fictionalized characters committing suicide, foreshadowing the later suicides of the actual people from whom these characters were drawn. Similarly, Fassbinder portrays the suicide of the fictional Fox, foreshadowing that of his lover Armin.

Motivation for the fictional Fox becomes perhaps less strange to non-German viewers when the real-life Armin is taken into account. Armin had been the product of the Nazi *Lebensborn*, which Katz describes as a "sinister sexual fantasy hatched and put into practice by Hitler's SS chief, Heinrich Himmler" (85). The boy had encountered his mother only once, his father never. After the war, "Armin was brought up by nuns with conventional pretensions. He was still illiterate when at the age of fourteen he fell into the clutches of a country doctor, who took him as a domestic, went out of his way to arrest his mental development, and abused him sexually for the next twelve years. Shown the door when the doctor finally lost interest, Armin drifted into Munich and got a job in a slaughterhouse (Katz 85). Fassbinder had a sexual or romantic predilection for butchers, which he thematizes in several of his films, most memorably in the slaughterhouse scenes in *Berlin Alexanderplatz* (1979/80).

Gays, as Fassbinder portrays them, do not question their own behavior within the gay cultural context, nor the fact that they succumb to peer pressure and group conformity precisely because identification within the gay culture is their only salvation. Like von Praunheim and his fellow auteurs of New German Film, Fassbinder remains highly skeptical of dogmatic proselytizing and believes that only authentic experience can be trusted. For him, five years into the movement, gay liberationists who try to teach other gays or to lead them to liberation are members of an intellectual elite who presume insight into social dynamics, an insight which often turns out to be a self-aggrandizing view translated into so-called objective assessments of the situation. *Selbsterfahrung* is important – each must discover for himself and in his own way who he is, and communicate with his peers.

Fassbinder articulates Guy Hocquenghem's analysis of homosexual desire, a key text to gay self-understanding in western European societies of the 1970s. Much of this analysis was worked out by 1977 and published in book form as *Unfähig zur Emanzipation?* (*Incapable of Liberation?*). Here, sexual exploitation is equivalent to economic exploitation, which then in *Fox and His Friends* are expressed as interchangeable terms. Gays internalize and reproduce homophobic oppression, ghettoize themselves in a *sub-culture* of their own which consists mainly of gay bars and tearooms, where gay men recognize each other as fellow social outsiders and where they can pursue their sexual desires. The split between *homo faber* and *homo ludens* (man at work/man at play) – or the appearance of heterosexual conformity on the job and gay self-identity in the subculture – is a false dichotomy, since newcomers to gay culture remain unaccepted outsiders until they have learned and internalized the distinct social rules which demarcate this subculture. Fassbinder and von Praunheim both argue that this subculture merely reproduces mainstream oppression in a new guise. For Fassbinder the problem is how we can stop exploiting each other and survive. Survival, that is, being alive, comes "apparently only at the expense of integrity, honesty, intimacy, and love ... Insight into this harsh truth triggers either impotent rage or the awful, hopeless despair that characterizes Fassbinder's protagonists and, one cannot help but think, all of modern society" (Franklin 142).

Fassbinder's personal survival tactic was to strike back at this "unbearable reality." The result was defiant rage and his prodigious "furious productivity" (P. Thomas 16). Fassbinder confronted his society with its own logic, to make the viewer uncomfortable within his own skin. As Thomas remarks:

> In a society divided into classes and races, having an elaborate sexual division of labor into the bargain, all real communication, all

love, all compassion, is impossible; we can only engage in precautionary movements, gestures, rituals, habits. Fassbinder's films delineate these rituals. They compress, traverse the world they make up, and trace out their consequences. (16–17)

In the end, however, filmmaking was not enough to spare Fassbinder from the anguish of reality. Rentschler remarks that, "Like Walter Benjamin's 'urban individual', Fassbinder insulated himself by sealing his life off from reality" (1984, 193). He used himself, and used himself up ultimately, in his project. Even his body was conscripted into the cause, as was framed most explicitly in the Fassbinder segment of *Germany in Autumn* (1977, Brustellin et al.), where it functions as a commodity (a voyeuristic look at a public figure in the nude), as a weapon (an instrument of dominance and submission), as a narcissistic surface (the body as site of self-stylization), and as a potential corpse (presaging actual death and its meanings). To the end, Fassbinder literally and symbolically embodied the social outsider. In a revealing remark made upon Fassbinder's suicide, fellow director Werner Herzog stated that Fassbinder was *not* a German at all, he was a "wild Bavarian" (Calandra 9) — exactly the epithet used to describe Kaspar Hauser.

Fassbinder's legacy, rather than having an emancipatory effect, has been left trapped in the prison house of language. Franklin points out that "Modern society so perverts individuals and their language that verbal communication becomes nearly impossible and language becomes a social weapon, an aggressive instrument employed by the powerful against the weak" (135). Fassbinder's films contain long, silent, static takes in which we are confronted with the cold, silent stares of his characters. The conflict between the personal (good, unrealizable) and the social (bad, repressive, inhibiting, corrupting) cannot be resolved through art. Social change comes with understanding, not with mere feeling. Finally, the Fassbinder sequence in *Germany in Autumn*, in its singular merger of documentary confession and fictional self-stylization, "represents West German film's most provocative variation on the theme of the problematic *and* problematized subject, a preoccupation that in hindsight more and more looks like *the* central obsession of intellectuals living in the FRG during the seventies" (Rentschler 1984, 192).

Probably the most well-known and celebrated of the gay German coming-out films is Frank Ripploh's 1980 autobiographical *Taxi to the Toilet*.

This film represents the revisionist stage of the coming-out cycle, not only for its self-conscious reflections on gay filmmaking and the social progress of the gay movement in West Germany, but also for its more lighthearted, but nonetheless 'disarmingly honest' portrayal of one gay man's struggle for sexual emancipation. The film is solidly grounded in both psychological and social realities, and fulfills New German Cinema's desire for documentary authenticity in a fully realized fictional narrative form.

A realistic, 'slice-of-life' sensibility allows the auteur filmmaker to embrace the inherent contradictions between love and freedom. Gay liberation here is no longer abstracted and analyzed, but put into practice. Frank Ripploh (the character played by Ripploh) is a gay school teacher – placing him soundly within two suspect dissident groups of the 1970s – who tries to have it all, and who wants to live his vision of gay liberation. He is a sexual adventurer, an inveterate enthusiast of recreational sex. The film portrays him in an array of cruising spots – parks, public toilets, and streets – a commonplace of urban gay sociosexual habitats. His liberated lifestyle – by 1980, gay liberation had evolved into a civil rights movement, and the gay sub-culture increasingly into a public zone for commercialized pleasures – consists of attempting to harmonize recreational sex with domestic monogamy, and his private lifestyle with his professional persona. The basic plot line revolves around Frank meeting and falling in love with Bernd. As the two men have very different notions of romantic involvement, the relationship is full of conflict and leads to the inevitable argument. The crisis is reached at a drag ball. Frank is furious with Bernd's endless jealous feelings over Frank's flirtations, and after the argument on the subway ride home, Frank, still in full drag, ends up going straight to school the next morning to teach his class. Frank loses his job, he and Bernd lose touch, and Frank is left pondering 'where to go from here'?

Making this film became a mechanism of liberation for Ripploh. Since that time, the gay movement has clearly stagnated, and the sociopolitical analysis has been reduced to banter or replaced with the acrimonious insults gay men habitually throw at each other. Two countertendencies emerge: on the one hand, the film embodies the integrated consciousness of a mainstream gay man; on the other hand, the underlying conflicts raised by earlier filmmakers and activists have slipped away from surface consciousness. Not only in American society, where hippies became yuppies, and gay activists dinks and guppies,[11] but here, too, we find capitulation of the sort Fassbinder and von Praunheim had warned against, namely that a more mainstream acceptance of gays and tolerance for homosexual lifestyles would not resolve the underlying conflicts of class tensions nor fundamentally alter the outsider's marginal social status: Frank loses his job by coming to work as an identifiably militant homosexual. The social and individual conflicts remain unresolvable.

The didactic intent of earlier gay films is altered in Ripploh. He portrays *himself* seeking solutions through the process of making his film, he discovers the limitations of following one's emotional authenticity. In a sense, he 'can't have his cake and eat it too'. His desires to make a better world are much more humbly scaled down to making his own world a bit of a happier place. Gay American ideas, fashions, and jargon have begun to seep into German gay culture, and the question of gay community – as opposed to gay culture or subculture – makes its German film debut. Ripploh looks at gay life through the genre of comedy, thereby de-escalating the stakes in finding solutions. What is truly remarkable is a German filmmaker making a comedy in which he laughs at himself. In the broader context of German culture and society, serious comedy is a rare phenomenon. That a gay filmmaker should do so successfully suggests a major shift in the cultural crosswinds.

Two years later, Fassbinder committed suicide, taking the spirit of New German Cinema with him. AIDS, too, would make its first appearance, but would still be seen, for a very long time, as an 'American disease'. Social and political organizing around AIDS slowly altered and fundamentally changed the gay movement once and for all. Indeed, between a new generation of Germans attempting to blot out any consciousness of the new plague and the apparent victory of consumer capitalism made all the more unassailable with the collapse of the Soviet regimes, along with the reunification and privatization, the utopian vision was dispelled by the seduction of the material comforts of a globally commercialized gay culture. Being conversant in American English became even more indispensable, as Germans adopted en masse American gay jargon as their own.

Paul Thomas has suggested that the success gays have in modern capitalist society comes at a very high cost. In "Im Brei der Bewegung" (In the Sludge of the Movement), a widely discussed 1983 editorial in *TORSO* magazine, Matthias Frings argues that the depoliticization of German society has rendered "incomprehensible" the concept of *Schwulenunterdrückung*, the oppression of gays. Since the final striking of Paragraph 175 in 1994, the socially accepted liberal-tolerant view has held that, except for sex, gays are completely 'normal', and gay men, like heterosexual men, are being distracted by capitalist commercial culture, including the artistic scene. This trend parallels the broader transference of government control to the private sector. The gay liberationist vision disappeared in the face of AIDS trauma. The vision of more fully integrated queers in English-speaking societies became based upon the success of commercial exploitation. Gay desire was co-opted into advertising – such as the now famous IKEA ad in Germany which depicted a gay male couple choosing a dining table – and through newly emergent *queer theories* into mainstream academic discourses. In postwar Germany, only the Green Party treated gay issues as legitimate to mainstream political concerns.

Even while being superficially 'gay positive', Sönke Wortmann's *Maybe... Maybe Not* celebrates the commercial commodification of gay male sexuality as social identity and reasserts the superiority of heterosexuality in both oblique and not so subtle ways. On the one hand, one could argue that this film marks the interment of New German Cinema. The original German title captures and signals this shift: the term for "gay activist movement" has been abbreviated from *schwulenemanzipatorische Bewegung* to an adjectival *bewegt* – an activist gay man is *ein bewegter Mann*. On the other hand, the title is a play on the *Männerbewegung*, that is, groups of men who met to reassess their traditional masculinity in light of the *Frauenbewegung*, the feminist movement. This is depicted in the film when Axel goes to just such a group. Thus, *ein bewegter Mann* is one who has been 'moved' or 'shifted' by the women's movement as well as been 'touched' or 'swayed' by homosexuality.

Wortmann has the moviegoer believe that he can turn the social tables. *Maybe... Maybe Not* alleges to be the story of a straight man possibly coming out as a result of his encounter with gay culture. In fact, this assertion is specious, on the one hand nothing more than a gay fantasy, and on the other no more than a teaser to draw the consumer into the movie theater. The *bewegte Mann* of the original title is the intractably heterosexual Axel, whose sexual adventures eventually catch up with him: his girlfriend catches him having sex with another women in the bathroom of the restaurant where they work. As a consequence she throws him out of her apartment, and Axel ends up finding shelter at the apartment of a gay friend of a gay colleague from the men's discussion group, Norbert. Twin farce narratives are developed as Axel treads the naïf's path to gay cultural knowledge and Norbert unsuccessfully attempts to seduce his lodger with whom he has fallen head over heels in love. This ludicrous situation is strangely resolved, in typically *deus ex machina* fashion, when Doro, the girlfriend, shows up and, after first discovering the naked Norbert in the closet, tells Axel she is pregnant by him. Her ongoing fears and suspicions that Axel was turning gay eventually prove unfounded, and the heterosexuals live happily ever after. The fags, it turns out, were merely plot devices to propel the straight viewer through a tourist's eye view of gay life and safely back out the door of the funhouse ride.

The film is based on characters from two of Ralf König's gay comic books. König's lighthearted approach to using pop culture comics to explore serious issues in gay life is 'Hollywoodized' here, mined for those segments that lend themselves most easily to exploitation for a mass audience comedy. Postauteur cinema capitulates to Hollywood formula and, in my opinion, does so poorly. The film is, in many respects, a variation of the French/Italian coproduction *La Cage aux folles* (Molinaro, 1978) – originally released in Germany as *Der Narrenkäfig* in 1979. Indeed, its release in the United States preceded only by a short time that of *The Birdcage* (Nichols, 1996), in my opinion, a similarly weak but explicit American remake of *La Cage aux folles*.

The phenomenal commercial success of *Maybe...Maybe Not* in its domestic market would remain a mystery if it were not for Ute Lischke-McNab's article in this collection and the fact that the enormous popularity of Ralf König's comics among gay men and their friends in Germany probably acted as an instant springboard for the film into the mass market. Unfortunately, as a result, gay activism has been defanged and safely contained as cliché. Gays are embraced, once again as they traditionally have been, as fallguys. Axel is played by the very good-looking Til Schweiger. His immediate attractiveness serves as both an entrée into the gay world as well as a shield to protect him from unsolicited sexual advances. Even though Axel's rapacious sexual appetite is the cause of his temporary difficulties, this disappears before the stereotypical onslaught of gay male sexual predators all trying to 'bag' Axel. Norbert's hopeless infatuation with the more-often-than-not obviously unattainable Axel engages another cliché, namely, that of the hopeless homosexual desiring the socially superior and unobtainable heterosexual man.

The film nominally claims a gay insider's point of view, looking back at heterosexual society. Only to the extent that gays and straights alike embrace a common consumerist culture of objectified sexuality does this hold true. Again, such a point of view has merely been lifted for profitable intent by the film producers, who have been remarkably successful in that way (cf. Lischke-McNab). This seems to bear out my thesis that consumer-capitalism has co-opted the trappings, while containing and defanging the political or social import of gay film. Indeed, substance has been jettisoned and replaced with entertainment value. The German gay man has become a consumer product, the film itself a bit of reified homosexuality the consumer may purchase as a videocassette and thus have 'ownership' of the gay lifestyle — something befitting a parody by von Praunheim.

The film is just risqué enough for a straight audience to convince them of their tolerance — perhaps even condescending acceptance — of queers. This is the basis for any claims of being a sophisticated bedroom farce in the French tradition (cf. *La Cage aux folles*). The medium, clearly, is the message, for it has no content, and that message is: gay crossover films in the 1990s are marketable in Germany and can play to two separate niche markets, namely, to heterosexual middlebrow audiences while still appealing to the commercialized, sexual fetishized, assimilated gay male consumer.

Wortmann's film accurately reflects a postliberationist society in which the gay movement and political desire for social transformation have been utterly superseded by econosexual concerns. Nonetheless, the film does ring false, for the presence of any striving for authenticity is also absent. In such a manner this film reflects the broader cultural shift articulated in the writings of Jean Baudrillard. The film is no longer the product of an auteur director, but is a self-conscious media simulation of reality. Following Andreas Huyssen's line of thought, that "simulation has replaced production at the center of our social system" (175), we see that simulation has also replaced production in the realm of politics and history. It is as if the Frankfurt School's nightmare has come true, namely that the mass media manipulate the masses cynically for the ends of hidden, and presumably evil, forces. What has been abandoned is the reciprocity function so essential to New German Cinema. Such films — as seen through the first three examples — demand that the viewer wrestle with the content and seek dialectical resolution beyond the cinematic mise-en-scène. The fourth film under discussion here operates within a closed feedback loop, having already predigested all possible communication and mirrors back to the viewer what he has been made accustomed to expect. Film, having created expectations for the viewer, reconfirms those expectations over and over. Indeed, the videocassette the consumer-citizen has brought home can be viewed repeatedly, tracing the circuit of the always identical feedback loop, a fitting symbol for the spectacle as Adorno's frozen dialectic of modernism and mass culture. Writing in a similar vein about pop music, Frederic Jameson observes:

> The passionate attachment one can form to this or that pop single, the rich personal investment of all kinds of private associations and existential symbolism which is the feature of such attachment, are fully as much a function of our own familiarity as of the work itself: the pop single, by means of repetition, insensibly becomes part of the existential fabric of our own lives, so that what we listen to is ourselves, our own previous auditions. (20)

The collective viewing experience of *Maybe... Maybe Not* offers "instantaneous inclusiveness" (Huyssen 182). Exchange, response, participation, and the *Erfahrung* nurtured by the New German Cinema generation are rejected outright as fiction. The very notion of authenticity, not to mention the experience of it, is thought to be yet another fiction. The ahistorical, totalizing precepts of such principles, however, are highly misleading. Baudrillard has suggested that:

> only the bourgeoisie was a true class, and therefore the only one capable of negating itself as such. For it has negated itself, along with capital, and so generated a classless society, albeit one which has nothing to do with the classless society that was supposed to arise from a revolution and form a negation of the proletariat as such. As for the proletariat, it has simply disappeared – vanished along with the class struggle itself. (1993, 10)

But is this really true? And can the question of truth-value be condescendingly shrugged off as merely another mediated fiction? If so, it is doubtful that audience response too would not include such a widely experienced sense of falseness.

This false consciousness percolated into the gay movement during the 1980s. In 1985, for example, the *Bundesverband Homosexualität* (Federal Association for Homosexuality) was called into being as the first nationwide umbrella organization for gays, in part as an attempt to breathe new life into the stagnant *Schwulenbewegung* and in part in reaction to the extensive, nationwide setting up of AIDS help groups. Neither official government nor gay activist groups could be brought to take effective action as AIDS was growing into a national problem in Germany. The collapse of the German gay movement coincided roughly with the collapse of the Berlin Wall in 1989. Indicative of this is a 1988 editorial in *Du und Ich*, a longstanding glossy gay porn magazine which had long shunned any coverage of the gay movement. The editorial criticized the gay movement for only 'moving' around itself. On the one hand, such critiques had been leveled since the early 1970s. Yet, on the other hand, by running such an editorial, *Du und Ich* positioned itself as part of the gay movement, interpreting it as a civil rights movement which, with the repeal of Paragraph 175, was now superfluous and in no need of analysis and critique. To draw upon an analogy made by Donald Morton: "virtual reality situates both bomber pilots and cybersex users in an ahistorical space supposedly disconnected from actuality, and the subjects inhabiting that space are therefore beyond social responsibility" (*The Material Queer* 17).

In conclusion, I submit two propositions for consideration. The first regards the process of the material construction of gay male sexuality. Clearly, gay liberation has been co-opted into the machinery of consumer capitalism. Parallel to the transformation of the citizen into the consumer, commodities and their purchase now constitutes the entire machinery of citizenship. David Evans articulates this transformation in his 1993 analysis *Sexual Citizenship*, where he remarks that once one sees past the universalizing rhetoric of the free and independent citizen, "there stands a citizenship machinery which effectively invades and corrals those who by various relative status shortcomings are deemed to be less than fully qualified citizens. The state's management of these 'moral aliens' is exercised in social, political and economic arenas" (5). Liberationist culture – its vocabulary, its ideologies, its gestures and expressions of antiauthoritarianism, its paradoxical bind between freedom and fulfillment – was readily co-opted (as nearly everything is) into commodified consumer simulacra. The more battles it won, the more it went on losing the war. As Evans explains: "Sexual citizenship, to the extent that it guarantees differential market access, commodification of sexual immorality within 'private' environments, has served to largely maintain the purity of the moral community, conceal impurities and fragments and distract potential dissent, and to quite clear material and ideological ends" (8).

The second, and more important, of my propositions draws attention to the machinations of a forced historical amnesia underlying the pacifying and urgently desired message that 'everything is fine'. In the spirit of Baudrillard, one might argue that all we can do now is endlessly simulate liberation. At this point, one finds oneself at his fourth, "fractal stage" in which everything has been achieved (1993, 5), where one simply loops back upon oneself only to realize that values endlessly repeat themselves without going anywhere, and where there is a conviction that the revolution has occurred and humanity is at the end of Hegelian history (cf. Baudrillard 1993, 5). There will be no new antithesis to move beyond the synthetic stage one is now stuck in forever. But this is only the illusory world of advertising and mass media that is in a sense 'whistling in the dark', hoping — in the imagery of *The Wizard of Oz* — that no one will notice the man behind the curtain. Even as multinational corporate culture co-opts the historical left to manufacture its own fantasy reproduced as commercial come-on, not everyone is being fooled all the time, even if they go along with being fooled.

Indeed, the real question is, why is so much effort and so much complicity being willed into elaborately denying political realities, attempting to discredit authenticity as a value? Is it that the increasing segregation and isolation of the 'haves' from the 'have-nots' is so complete that — in the metaphor of *Metropolis* — the mind feels it can safely ignore the hands? Are we in a catastrophe so immense that we have collectively fallen back upon willful amnesia of a degree and kind last seen in the seventeenth century's flight from reality into the complexities of baroque aesthetics? The virtual world of simulacra is all form and no content, perhaps to an even greater degree than German baroque flights into abstraction, mysticism, and erudition in the face of that period's never-ending warfare and sociopolitical upheavals. In a more recent epoch, the 1920s and 1930s, similar flights from reality saw the working-class sensibility of Brecht's *Three-Penny Opera* replaced with the fascist mythologizing sensibility of Leni Riefenstahl's *Triumph of the Will*. Why so much effort to create the illusion of control over a situation that is completely out of control? And not least, why is it that the German intellectual community remains to this day blithely steadfast in its commitment to dismiss out of hand any gay scholarly inquiry as 'trivial'?

Notes

[1]Werner Herzog, quoting from Büchner's play *Lenz*. All translations are my own unless otherwise stated.

[2]Such coming-out narratives emerged as a distinct genre in America in realistic, 'coming-of-age' gay novels penned by gay-identified male authors during the 1980s.

[3]A companion piece including women filmmakers and lesbian-themed German films is forthcoming in the *European Journal of Cultural Studies* (1997).

[4]The Oberhausen Manifesto is a document signed at the Oberhausen Film Festival in 1962 by a group of twenty-six young writers and filmmakers who demanded freedom from industry conventions and commercial strictures in order to create a new German cinema. While ideologically and cinematographically diverse, these writers and filmmakers shared as a group a reaction of outrage to the quality of life in the young and highly affluent Federal Republic of Germany, as well as a humanistic, if often bleak, outlook on life.

[5]The first post-World War II generation reached maturity in the 1960s, and 1968 saw political uprisings across half the globe, including the student strikes in Paris which completely shut France down for a brief period, the Velvet Revolution which momentarily opened Czechoslovakia up to the West, and the radicalization of the civil rights movements in the United States which culminated in the Stonewall riots of 1969. For a discussion of the history, politics, and Zeitgeist of the New Left 'generation of 1968' on both sides of the Atlantic, see Paul Berman's *A Tale of Two Utopias*.

[6]I personally lived through this period of West German history — as an alien resident, university student, and gay liberationist radical activist. My phone was tapped, my mail was secretly opened and read by postal officials, and government security checks were run on me and my partner.

[7]I saw many first-run New German Cinema films, including *Fox and His Friends* and *Taxi to the Toilet* at the Arsenal Kino-Kneipe in Tübingen, and when traveling made the pilgrimage to similar movie houses in Würzburg, Bonn, Berlin, and elsewhere.

[8]Leonard Shengold has noted that the term "soul murder" was first used in connection with Kaspar Hauser, in Anselm von Feuerbach's 1832 popular account of the mysterious figure. "Soul murder is as old as human history, as old as the abuse of the helpless by the powerful in any group — which means as old as the family. But soul murder has particular resonance with the twentieth century" (3), in particular in the dynamics of the generational conflicts over collective suppression of Germany's Nazi past. The term was also used by D. P. Schreber, the celebrated Freudian case study, in whom Freud linked nervous illness, repressed homosexuality, and paranoia. See also Sampath, *Kaspar Hauser*.

[9]I first experienced the Praunheim film at a *Schwulen-Tagung* (gay conference) in Tübingen, October 1977.

[10]*Bleu*, as in *l'amour bleu*, is a familiar euphemism for homosexual love; and postwar Germans would be extremely familiar with the American musical idiom of the blues, a complex nexus of jazz music, nightclubs, isolation, social oppression (of Blacks, the poor, and working classes), and the deep pain, solitude, and hopelessness of such socioeconomic situations.

[11]See Stewart 70 and 108 for definitions.

History and Homosexuality in Frank Ripploh's *Taxi to the Toilet*

James W. Jones

RANK RIPPLOH'S *TAXI ZUM KLO* (*Taxi to the Toilet*,[1] 1980) was a
history-making film that was widely distributed in the United States
during 1981 and 1982, years which proved historic for gay and lesbian
American cinema as they provided such films as *Making Love, Personal
Best, Partners, Deathtrap, Tootsie,* and *Victor/Victoria* (another film with
German ties). The grosses for those with the most gay or lesbian content —
Making Love and *Personal Best* — were so disappointing and their attendant controversies so great that Hollywood dropped the theme. The sight
of two women or two men kissing in these films seemed to shock many in
the audience, for viewers of Hollywood products were accustomed only to
pity suicidal homosexual characters or to laugh at their stereotypical antics.[2] How then did they react to this West German, independently produced film which treated the topic with humor and went far beyond portraying two men merely kissing? A personal anecdote illustrates the general
response. When I ask friends about this film, they usually begin by saying:
"Isn't that the one with all the sex and where the guy urinates on the other
guy?" Their reaction might be summed up in the phrase 'grossed out'.[3]

Perhaps those scenes remain etched in viewers' memories because most
eyes are so unaccustomed to seeing gay life, much less gay sexuality, portrayed on the screen. There is certainly a pervasive sense that portrayals of
gay sexuality belong, if anywhere, on video screens in darkened bookstores.
But before addressing that question, one must first take a look at the rest of
the film and its origins. I quote a plot summary from *A Different Light Review*: "Frank Ripploh's firmly autobiographical, fiercely unapologetic film
describes the ups and downs of a relationship where one partner (played by
Ripploh) rejoices in cruising, leathersex and the freedom to pursue unrestricted sexual pleasure, while his partner (played by Ripploh's real life
lover) prefers monogamy, meatloaf and TV. Made in Berlin in 1980, this is a
wonderfully candid, witty and charming film" (44). The film follows Frank

over several months and shows him moving between his job, his relationship with Bernd, and his pursuit of sex with other men. Everything seems to fall apart at the *Tuntenball* (drag ball) where the lovers break up and Frank stays out all night which, in turn, leads to chaos in his classroom the next morning. A printed epilogue informs the viewer that Frank quit his job and became a filmmaker. (In the following, "Frank" shall refer to the film's main character and "Ripploh" to the film's author/director.)

Ripploh's film takes the next step forward from Rosa von Praunheim's *Nicht der Homosexuelle ist pervers, sondern die Situation, in der er lebt* (*It Is Not the Homosexual Who Is Perverse, But the Situation in Which He Lives,* 1970), a polemic, political piece about homophobia in West German society. At the same time, *Taxi to the Toilet* consciously rejects the melodrama of Wolfgang Petersen's *Die Konsequenz* (*The Consequence,* 1977), the story of society's destruction of a gay love relationship.

Vito Russo in *The Celluloid Closet* and Richard Dyer in *Now You See It* have analyzed the ways in which films have appropriated certain cultural myths about homosexuality. Cinematic representations of homosexuality have developed stereotypes congruent with those myths of the majority culture: male homosexuals are effeminate creatures who make us laugh or dark frightening men whose perversion threatens our boys; lesbians, however, have proven to be much more difficult creatures to appropriate for cinematic purposes. The "mythic mannish lesbian," as Esther Newton calls her, is not as much the stock character in film as is her male opposite — the sissy swish — but that is perhaps due to the lesser threat that women and female sexuality are perceived to pose to cultural mythology.

Cinematic representations of male and female homosexuality have generally been drawn from the realm of stereotype and those stereotypes arise from cultural definitions of acceptable male and female gender roles. Space does not permit a detailed examination of the critical discussion on stereotype, gender roles, and their cultural representations, but two points are crucial to understanding the role of history in, as well as of, *Taxi to the Toilet.* The British critic Simon Watney succinctly states them in his 1982 article, "Hollywood's Homosexual World." The first is that every representation of homosexuality is necessarily embedded within a cluster of signification at whose center lies a heterosexual paradigm. Therefore, "the overall construction of gender roles — that which is taken to be 'appropriate' to women and men — in film as a whole" must be placed into question in order for any representation of homosexuality to free itself of that superstructure

(Watney 108). That paradigm (or superstructure) of heterosexuality produces — indeed desires — stereotype, for stereotype supports the supremacy
of the paradigm. Watney provides a useful definition of stereotype as "a site
of ideological contestation ... of conflict between incompatible images of
what it means to be gay, black, [etc.]" (108). He goes on to state: "To identify stereotype is to signal one's rejection of a particular image, usually of
oneself" (108).

Ripploh's film makes a radical break with the history of cinematic representations of homosexuality by integrating its stereotypes and paradigms
— derived from history — in order to subvert them.[4] Whether or not they
persist is not the point; subversion is perhaps a first, necessary step.

The opening sequences begin this process. The viewer is confronted
with a black screen and the sound of a clock ticking, marking both the beginning of Frank's day and the start of a new view in German cinema from
an idiosyncratically gay point of view. In a voice-over, Frank introduces
himself and invites the viewer to accompany him on his adventure. During
this, the camera pans across the bulletin board near his bed, filling the
screen with images of photos, postcards and buttons from Frank's personal past and also from the West German gay liberation movement of the
1970s. Not only do the opening scenes establish Frank as a certain kind of
gay man — the *Szenentunte* of the late 1970s, what might be called the "gay
clone" of the same period — but they also integrate a specific gay past into
the present which the film is about to explore. The camera follows Frank as
he gets washed, dressed and drives to school. He dares his audience to be,
as Gertrude said in the cartoon (see note 3), "grossed out" by his actions:
climbing naked onto his balcony after locking himself out of his apartment, drying his posterior and then his face with the same part of the
towel, flirting with the gas station attendant, alternately grading essays and
having sex in a public toilet. All are scenes aimed at breaking down the
stereotypic representation of gay characters. They challenge that history on
film by refusing to eliminate sexuality from the lives of gay characters or to
accept the strict separation of private and public life.

Although Frank is an elementary school teacher, the film pursues no
obviously didactic purpose. But the central element in Ripploh's cinematic deconstruction of stereotype and reappropriation of homosexuality
is indeed a didactic film: *Christian und sein Briefmarkenfreund* (*Christian
and His Stamp-Collecting Friend*) is a short film made in the 1950s for distribution in West German schools. Based on the myth of older homosex-

ual men scheming seductions of innocent boys, the movie shows young Christian — what else *could* he be named? — lured into the upper-story apartment of his stamp-collecting friend, Herr Burkhard. After closing the curtains, Herr Burkhard tries to convince the naive youth that "even men can be tender with each other." He even goes so far as to grope the boy and to place the boy's hand in his own lap. At that, Christian flees and soon confesses all to his mother, who, it is clear, knows the right thing to do.

Two other scenes are intercut with this film. Frank's lover, Bernd, and Frank's friend, Wally, are in the living room viewing the movie. At the same time, Frank is in the kitchen tutoring Holger, a boy about the age of Christian, the 1950s victim. The tutoring session is supposed to consist of Frank helping Holger improve his spelling and punctuation by using *Lebensnahe Diktate* (*Authentic Dictations*). (The irony of the textbook's title soon becomes clear.) But the boy is in no mood to be tutored and tries everything he can to divert Frank's attention from the lesson. He offers Frank his toy horse to shorten the dictation; he climbs onto Frank's lap to play "horsey"; in short, he tries to seduce his teacher, and Frank resists his every move. The scene thus satirically shows the very opposite of what is taking place in the so-called educational film — where a scheming Herr Burkhard offers stamps and affection to his pupil — and of what the common myth is telling about homosexual men, namely that they cannot help preying on innocent boys.

Meanwhile, in the living room, Wally and Bernd are sharing an afternoon coffee and watching this movie. Wally is a transvestite and dressed in tea-time drag appropriate to his image of a proper, upper-middle-class lady: simple black dress, pearls, and heels. While Bernd presents the film as an example of miseducation according to stereotype, Wally reacts as the indignant bourgeois whom he affects to be. "Do *you* think that's proper?" he asks Bernd and then answers for him: "No." But he does not lose himself completely in his role. Reaction shots of Wally during the scene when Herr Burkhard tries to direct Christian's hand to his own lap reveal Wally's own lust. Wally even rubs his foot along Bernd's leg, imitating the attempted seduction on screen, but Bernd laughs and playfully pushes him away. Ultimately, however, Wally returns to the identification appropriate to his outfit: at the end he sympathizes with the mother. Thus, through the use of this "educational" film from the past and the technique of intercutting, Ripploh creates an ironic distance to the stereotype which undermines that myth.

Ripploh uses similar techniques to defuse the myth that defines any movie in which gay sex is portrayed as pornographic. Though Ripploh includes graphic scenes of gay sex, their context makes it clear that the filmmaker is deliberately playing with the convention that any graphic sex is pornographic. A look at four specific sequences in the order in which they appear reveals this intent. Early in the film, Frank goes after work to a public toilet where, in a stall, he alternates between correcting essays and having sex with someone on the other side of the wall. Ripploh intercuts footage from an old porn film (of the 1920s?) showing a woman masturbating. Later, at a birthday party for a female colleague, the teachers are getting drunk, and Ripploh intercuts scenes from another old heterosexual porn film of two couples drinking, dancing, and having sex. In the next scene, we watch Frank get a full body massage at his gay sauna, but instead of this becoming an erotic episode, we listen to his musings about what to get his mother for her birthday. Much later in the film, while Frank is driving, he thinks about women whom he finds attractive. Intercut with shots of him driving are scenes from another old porn film, this one with lesbian sex scenes.

Why does Ripploh insert these scenes into his movie? After all, they do not even depict gay male sex! It is likely that he uses these relics from the history of pornography to force the viewer to question modern definitions of the term "pornographic." Central to any definition of pornography is the aim of the work to arouse the libido (and not, for example, to engage the intellect). Through this intercutting of past representations of heterosexuality with his own depiction of a gay man's life that also includes but is not defined by sex, Ripploh throws definitions of pornographic film into question. In this respect, Ripploh's film should be understood as part of the redefinition of the image of the male body that was taking place in the late 1970s and the early 1980s.[5]

Even more interesting is how Ripploh uses conventions of pornography, straight and gay, to subvert his audiences' definitions as well as expectations. Soon after meeting Bernd, Frank takes him home and the two bathe together. This sequence shows their playful and loving eroticism, and the camera follows them into the bedroom, where viewers see the two men having sex. Expectations are aroused by what seem to be the conventions of gay porn: boy meets boy and the two quickly engage in sex for the satisfaction of the voyeur. But such expectations are not fulfilled — there is no orgasm — as they are interrupted by the screams for help of a woman ringing

Frank's doorbell. Desire is quickly replaced by sympathy as the film glides from one aspect to another in its depiction of this gay man's life. Here, too, Ripploh uses what might seem pornographic in order to attack the stereotype of gay men as driven solely by their aberrant sexual desires. In this, he is reacting against the usual way of depicting homosexuality on screen.[6]

It is only after Ripploh has confronted such stereotypes that he depicts sex between Frank and other men in what otherwise would normally be seen as a pornographic way. In the middle of the film, Frank picks up a stranger and has sex with him while Bernd, who by this time has moved in with Frank and become his lover, watches them through a crack in the bedroom window and masturbates. The camera moves between Bernd's perspective and a 'neutral', third-person point of view. Later in the film, Ripploh again intercuts two sequences. In the first, Frank talks with a female colleague about Bernd, her expensive furniture, and her recent trip to Morocco. This is contrasted with a sequence involving Frank being whipped by the gas station attendant. The sounds of the whipping then punctuate the woman's description of her furnishings. As she talks about Morocco, the film shows Frank urinating on his sex partner. His colleague's description of Morocco as "a totally different world" is an apt summation of the sequence between Frank and the gas station attendant, at least for most people in the film's audience whether straight or gay.

But that is exactly Ripploh's point. For most viewers, this cinematic representation of homosexuality is "a totally different world" because Ripploh refuses to cut it to fit the Hollywood myth of homosexuality. After all, people in the audience, one might argue, who know 'homosexuality' only from hearsay, that is, as a cultural myth inhabited by stereotype, believe 'homosexuals' to be creatures unlike themselves. It is *this* history that Ripploh confronts head on, and he refuses to capitulate to a politically correct rebuttal — that is, to perpetuate the argument 'we're the same as you, except for what we do in the bedroom'. Indeed, Ripploh drags his viewers into Frank's bedroom in order to confront them with gay sexuality and in an attempt to make them conscious of the ways in which they have been taught to look at the male body.[7] Thus, Ripploh breaks with the history of representations of homosexuality that believed one had to omit the element of sex from gay characters so as not to offend straight audiences whom the work needed to convince of the acceptability (i.e., normalcy) of homosexuality. Ripploh sees no need to plead for tolerance, even though his film is aimed, I believe, at changing attitudes. However, he wants to change through portraying reality, not a sanitized version of homosexuality that parrots the ways and means of heterosexuality.

Ripploh's questioning of the emulation of heterosexuality in homosexuality leads to the central conflict within the film, the argument between Bernd and Frank about monogamy. Essentially, their conflict is about male/female gender roles, roles that have historically determined how two people in a love relationship will act, regardless of their gender. Their historical definition must at the very least be questioned and, in Frank's view, cast aside as irrelevant to gay relationships. Of course, Frank's view is that of Ripploh, so the counterargument is never made with any conviction. Ripploh begins his rejection of a heteronormative history of sex roles and sexuality with a contrast between the old porn movies he intercuts and the scenes of sex between Frank and his various partners. The traditional conception and depictions are no longer relevant. Once again, Wally serves as the mouthpiece of (an admittedly somewhat skewed) bourgeois lifestyle. He poses Bernd the question that most gay men are too used to hearing from 'sympathetic' straight friends: "What do you *do* in bed? I mean, who is the man?" It is against such culturally defined (heterosexual) expectations that the film must be read. Simon Watney writes in support of Ripploh's critique that "the very concept of 'promiscuity' is clearly irrelevant to gay men, existing as it does solely and purposively in relation to the ideals of marital monogamy" (118). However, history is not so easily set aside, and not all gay characters in the film agree with Frank's ideology of unfettered sex.

Although Bernd refuses to answer Wally's question, he must take on the traditionally female role in the relationship with Frank. He offers the battered woman support, comforts her, and gets her to the women's shelter. While Frank is at work, Bernd stays home and cooks. After catching him having sex with someone else, Bernd argues with Frank about the definition of their relationship. Frank believes he is freeing himself of the shackles of heterosexually defined love relationships by continuing to enjoy anonymous sex, while Bernd struggles to get Frank to agree to monogamy. When Frank tells him he should have other sex partners, too, Bernd angrily responds: "You know what they used to do with unfaithful people? Stick 'em in swamps!" Frank answers: "We are not living in the Middle Ages, and I don't want to be like the heteros."

Frank does indeed have doubts about his choices. The following scene shows him driving and wondering why he is afraid of commitment. But this interlude is brief, and both men continue to seem to be trapped in someone else's roles — that is, the roles of heterosexual lovers. To be sure, Ripploh hit upon a major theme in gay male relationships of the late 1970s and early 1980s; indeed, one might refer to such difference in opinion on the relevance or political expedience of heterosexual-like monogamy as a crisis for homosexual relationships, and thus the film's resonance among gay viewers should come as no surprise. Ripploh conceptualizes this theme of monogamy versus promiscuity in part as a historical construct. Until that time, few had contemplated such an anomaly in gay culture, and certainly none had done so in German film. (The 1973 U.S. film *A Very Natural Thing*, directed by Christopher Larkin, set this dilemma at its center.) Yet, it must be admitted that Ripploh's film does not succeed in its attempt to remove the burdens of history placed on the backs of the two main characters, because, as Simon Watney writes, "the film is unable or unwilling to examine the basic conflicts" between the two men (119). The film treats Bernd snobbishly and with more than a hint of misplaced misogyny as it tries to frame him within a female-identified gender role.

The history of gender roles exerts a powerful, if ultimately unresolved, force in this film, but other aspects of history also become evident. Bernd's speech about drowning adulterers echoes the desire of Heinrich Himmler to return to the medieval practice of drowning sodomites in bogs. At the travel bureau, Bernd scolds the agent for not knowing where Caprivi is, namely in "the former German [colony of] Southwest Africa." "A fine patriot *you* are!" he tells her. But Bernd's politically conservative or perhaps simply unenlightened remarks become a parody, like his own role as hausfrau, due both to his acting — he can never quite carry these scenes off without a wink to the audience — as well as to the ridiculousness of the dialogue he at times is given to speak.

Whereas Bernd's ignorance of German history comes off as crass and not entirely believable, Ripploh makes a much more subtle statement about Frank's own ignorance of the German past. Before going out to the bars, Frank is seen idly watching TV and thumbing through a magazine. Flicking through the channels, he happens upon an interview with a German neo-Nazi. He is blond and wears a black leather jacket. Ripploh cuts to a shot of the magazine in front of Frank, open to a drawing of a blond man clad in black leather, intended to be sexually arousing. The neo-Nazi talks about wanting to set up "labor or reeducation camps" for "asocials and homosexuals." Frank calls Bernd to join him, and they express suitable indignation. This does not, however, deter Frank from putting on his black leather jacket and cap soon afterward when he is leaving for the bars. Although neither character makes the connection between past and present — between the National Socialist past and the reappropriation of the past in the present — the viewer is meant to do so.

Ripploh confronts one final aspect of history in the film's conclusion. The last scene has Frank wondering what to do about Bernd. He asks himself whether he should commit suicide. This would have been the solution prescribed by the history of gay and lesbian characters throughout literature and film in the twentieth century (cf. Jones; Popp; V. Russo). But Ripploh consciously rejects this historically determined fate and informs the viewer by means of titles at the end that Frank and Bernd did get back together.[8]

The film creates and negotiates paths between stereotype and myth, between political correctness and political conservativism, by refusing to posit one solution as the only possible answer for all gays. Critics agree that this is a highly individualistic work, and Vito Russo points out that "*Taxi zum Klo* disposed of the issue of homosexuality completely" (V. Russo 270). This is no 'problem movie' like *Die Konsequenz* or *Making Love*. Ripploh's characters are not intended to represent *the* truth about all gays. They thrive in their individuality, which makes it possible for Ripploh to undermine the constructs of history and the category of homosexuality.

Notes

[1] The usual translation of "Taxi zum Klo" is "Taxi to the Toilet," but one might also render "Klo" as "tearoom" or "cottage" to give the American or British term for 'restrooms' where men sometimes engage in sex with other men.

[2] As Russo details in his ground-breaking work, *The Celluloid Closet*.

[3] Russo includes a 1982 cartoon strip from T. Hachtman's series "Gertrude's Follies." Alice Toklas is reading bits of an article in *Gay Ciné Magazine* to Gertrude Stein: "'Gay Films Flourish While Hollywood Flounders,' 'Cage au Folle [*sic*] III a Smash,' 'Taxi zum Klo Out Grosses Ordinary People'." Gertrude cannot believe that the German picture was making more money than an Academy Award winning film, and

she grabs the magazine from Alice to read for herself. She finds that the article actually states: "Taxi zum Klo Grosses Out Ordinary People" (V. Russo 269).

[4]Also useful to theorizing this rupture are Chapters Three ("The Role of Stereotypes") and Four ("Seen to Be Believed: Some Problems in Representing Gay People as Typical") in Dyer's *The Matter of Images* and his article "Stereotyping" in *Gays and Film*.

[5]George Stambolian writes in his foreward to Allen Ellenzweig's *The Homoerotic Photograph* of "a burst of exhibitions in New York City [that] introduced the public to the richness of homoerotic and male nude photography" at that time (xv). The similarity between the critical reaction to these shows, as described by Stambolian, and the reaction to Ripploh's film, described at the beginning of this article, is striking: "What they saw were photographs of naked men that seemed to affirm both male sexuality and sexual desire for the male body, with all that this might imply about its subject and object — passivity, femininity, homosexuality" (xvi).

[6]Ellenzweig describes this point of view: "Equating the homoerotic with pornography is therefore a means to ensure that it is not taken for granted, that it remain, a priori, beyond the reach of mass media images in which heterosexuality is the constant, repetitive and accepted subtext" (207).

[7]In his article "Masculinity as Spectacle," Steve Neale provides a helpful analysis of the techniques that mainstream cinema uses to direct the viewer's gaze at the male body so as to de-eroticize that body.

[8]Russo enumerates this history for the cinema in his famous "Necrology" in *The Celluloid Closet* (347–49).

Camp, Music, and the Production of History: *Anita* and Rosa von Praunheim

Caryl Flinn

I. German Film, German Music, and German Queers

JUDGING FROM BOTH FILM PRODUCTION and recent scholarly activity, it is no stretch to say that the queering of German cinema already knows a certain tradition – in fact, if not yet in name. To broach the films of Rosa von Praunheim in general – and *Anita: Tänze des Lasters (Anita: Dances of Vice*, 1987) in particular – is to acknowledge even more rigorously that the German film canon has already been queered. *Anita* offers an unusual opportunity to explore how a queer, camp aesthetic operates in historically meaningful ways, and to note how a film's soundtrack, however disorderly or cacophonous, participates in this kind of historical camp.

As one of queer cinema's most outspoken participants, von Praunheim (born: Holger Mischwitzki) is about as out of the closet as you can be. Producing, as Vito Russo quipped, "home movies for the gay movement" (in Nash, "Not the Homosexual" 250) for some thirty years, von Praunheim is a key, and controversial, figure not only in German queer cinema – along with Werner Schroeter, Lothar Lambert, Monika Treut, and others – but in German culture more generally. On German television, he has outed public figures in government and show business communities; his films have been vigorously denounced and boycotted by gays; he and Rainer Werner Fassbinder never cloaked their intense mutual dislike.

Although the figure of von Praunheim makes evident how queer and contested German cinema is, it should be understood that German film history has never been *un*queer, historical limitations of queer terminology and methods notwithstanding. For as contemporary scholarship is demonstrating, queer authors, texts, and conditions of production and reception have shaped dominant film cultures throughout, even if most of that shaping was through censorship, omission, or displacement. Otherwise put, both as structuring absences as well as presences, same-sex 'deviancies' have been played out even in the most repressive film histories, and in the most tediously straight systems. But with German cinema in particular, even its most traditional histories and pedagogies have had to account for its tradition of conspicuously 'gay' films.[1] Even if they are not always apprehended as such, queer texts such as *Mädchen in Uniform* (Leontine Sagan, 1931) and Fassbinder's *Faustrecht der Freiheit* (*Fox and His Friends*, 1974) hold significant places within German film history. This is not to say that their reception has met with stable consensus or interpretative homogeneity, however — as 'gay', 'not gay', 'about' other things, etc. Indeed for years, *Mädchen* was read primarily as a treatise against authoritarianism or lambent fascism, until Ruby Rich's groundbreaking piece in 1981 helped critics pull it into queerness. Consider also the debate precipitated by *Fox and His Friends* among Bob Cant, Andrew Britton, and Richard Dyer, who objected to its use of homosexual lifestyle as a metaphor for economic exploitation, and Fassbinder's retort that the film should not have to be principally "about" gay themes.

If queer political readings are contested within lesbian and gay cultures, they are often fully denied in mainstream arenas. This very same denial is the justification for anthologies like the present one in German studies, a field historically slow to recognize exciting and rigorous new methodologies which address gender, class, and ethnicity. It is a reluctance which may partly explain why North American — particularly Canadian — German Departments are shrinking while, ironically, new scholarship is hitting great stride.[2] Part of the resistance comes from traditional scholars and programs that position German culture as immune to 'queering': for them its imputed purity must be protected at all costs, and recourse to preserve it will often be asserted by formal, biographical, or aesthetic approaches. Such assumptions of German cultural purity, made in the shadow of the Holocaust, run a rather sizable risk of courting other, more egregious notions of purity, such as national, ethnic, or racial.

The same kind of public intellectual drama has been enacted in musicology, which, like German Studies, has been notoriously reluctant to accept the assumptions and methodologies of poststructuralism and ideological and cultural criticism. To be sure, queering the musical canon, just like approaching it from any other ideologically derived lens, is not an easy task. Music is a recalcitrant object of study, a highly abstract sign system, one that does not denote or even connote with precision. This is not to say music falls outside the realm of meaning, of culture, or of ideology, but that its cultural and semantic functions are often very difficult to discern. In this way its formal systems seem more easily reduced to the realm of 'pure' aesthetics, with extraformal contexts and concerns dismissed as irrelevant or inappropriate (aside from classic examples such as biographical details of a composer).

Conventional musicology does much to preserve these notions, and thereby reproduces the hegemony and prestige of a specifically — if not actually designated as such — Germanic aesthetic culture. Consider, as Philip Brett has in his important account of Franz Schubert, the elevated status of Western art music in general: *it* is considered "serious," a worthy object of study, whilst the world's other musical forms and practices are devalued.[3] In this, Brett notes not only the value given to instrumental over vocal music (a debt to romanticism's interest in "vague yearning," in E. T. A. Hoffman's phrase, over the "confinements" of word and language), but the valorization of German music over all. Describing the conventional undergraduate plan of study that introduces students to music, he writes that they first follow courses in "musicianship and harmony," with material likely drawn from "the canon of German music (Bach to Brahms) towards which the [typical] syllabus generally leans. The acquisition of skill is dependent on the tacit understanding of the superiority of this repertory: it is here that the 'masterwork' ideology is first and most effectively instilled" (Brett 14). What Brett identifies as "Teutonic abstraction" is further emphasized, he argues, in the harmony course, "in which the chief ingredient is likely to be the four-part chorale settings of J. S. Bach" whose compositional techniques are taught as standard or normal, and not as the series of elaborations that they are, since most of the hymns Bach adapted had been previously adapted from folktunes. As Brett concludes: "The stage is set for the enormities of the Schenker system, in which masterworks are, as it were, Bach chorales writ large, or 'prolonged'" (14).

With the significant change of country establishing the norms of an entire discipline, the parallels between what Brett describes in musicology and film studies are striking. Like art music from Germany, classical film from Hollywood is standardly taught as a master language against which other cultural productions and practices are measured. Contained in such an approach is a glut of aesthetic, cultural, colonial, and national biases. Brett finds one particularly egregious example in ethnomusicology, which tends to treat even the most elaborate non-European systems, such as the sophisticated, intricate musics of Japan and India, as "primitive." Biases about sexuality are also involved: if German art music is the paradigmatic norm against which other musics are so measured, Teutonic culture is thus "straight" by traditional musicological standards, and only "others" can then be outed. As a "decadent, effeminate" Russian composer, for example, Tchaikovsky's homosexuality has hardly been perceived as threatening to many Western musicologists, whereas outings surrounding Schubert and Haydn have been treated as treasonous scandals. Consequently, German musical culture occupies the space not only of aesthetic rigor and excellence, but of regulatory heterosexuality at its most virile. "The central German canon," as Brett explains, "must at all costs be preserved in its purity. The closeting of Schubert is of a similar order as the papering over of Wagner's anti-Semitism" (15). In an interesting line that, as we will see, both affirms and refutes Brett's observations about Western art music and Germanness, Thomas Mann notes through a character in *Dr. Faustus*: "In Germany music enjoys that respect among the people which in France is given to literature; among us nobody is put off or embarrassed, uncomfortably impressed, or moved to disrespect or mockery by the fact that a man is a musician ..." (127).

Von Praunheim's *Anita: Dances with Vice* offers an exuberant repudiation of a pure national culture on musical and other levels. Though specifically German in its choice of subject, it is a fundamentally 'impure' text, boasting a compendium of formal and thematic references to international cultural productions: *Reefer Madness* (Louis Gasnier, 1936), the Ballet Russe, *Marat/Sade* (Peter Weiss, 1966), Christopher Isherwood, Divine, Rosa Luxemburg, and contemporary AIDS activism. Like other von Praunheim films, *Anita* takes a documentary topic for its starting point and quickly veers off into spectacular play and fancy. Its documentary component centres on the story of the historical figure Anita Berber (1899-1928), a nude dancer who was extremely popular in Weimar Berlin, who had small roles in *Anders als die Andern (Different From the Others,* Richard Oswald, 1919) and *Dr. Mabuse* (Fritz Lang, 1922), and who for von Praunheim was, "a symbol of the decadence, the perversity, and the bisexuality, and the drugs of her time. I like these exaggerated figures" (in Kalb 72). As with her character in von Praunheim's film, Berber, who died of tuberculosis at twenty-nine, dedicated her dances to "vice, horror, and ecstasy."

The scenes depicting Berber's story manifest anything but conventional documentary restraint. Portrayed in wild, heavily expressionistic, vi-

brantly colored and choreographed sequences, its events are conjured from
the mind of an elderly woman (Lotte Huber) picked up in contemporary
Berlin for exposing herself in public, claiming to be Berber. (She is identified as a Frau Kutowski near the film's end.) Institutionalized, she waltzes
into doctors' appointments she takes for adoring media interviews, and
chides fellow patient 'Rosa Luxemburg': "*My* revolution is to smash all re-
straints!" The psychiatric institution of present-day Germany – the less
documentary, more invented portion of the film – is shot in drab black
and white. It is a conspicuously less stylized space than the scenes of the
'past' – a past presented not as historically objective but as a series of delirious stagings that, as we shall see, highlight surface, performativity, and
impression over depth, authenticity, or veritability. The same actors portray
characters in both stories and periods: Anita of the 1920s is performed
both by Huber and, more frequently, by Ina Blum (who, along with cine-
matographer Elfi Mikesch, has worked with queer directors Treut and
Schroeter). Blum also portrays the hospital nurse, assistant to a rather lecherous doctor, portrayed by Mikael Honesseau, who performs as Berber's Weimar Berlin dance partner, Sebastian Droste, as well. An example of Brechtian
epic theater perhaps, the multiple roles not only suggest the subjective
nature of the alleged Anita's documentary story, but support the film's literal plays on identity and historical memory.[4] In fact, the blurred roles extend beyond the text, since, in her own youth, Lotte Huber was a dancer
whose career was interrupted by Nazism (cf. Rickels 47).

The fragmentation evoked by the film's performances and cultural references is matched by its equally diversified, collage-like use of music. *Village Voice* critic J. Hoberman aptly described the score as "honkeytonk
Schönberg," with popular American jazz, Igor Stravinsky, and Kurt Weill
helping to form its acoustic contours. Indeed, *Anita* is as brash musically
as it is visually, as brash as Anita herself is configured, and von Praunheim
is not unaware of this: "I love music's murmurs, its breaks, and its extreme
tones, like shrill bagpipes or violins, Chinese sopranos. I get a lot of satisfaction from the extraordinary because in it, I find interpretations of the
ordinary" ("Monologues" 16; my trans.). Theoretical support for von
Praunheim's preferences for the irregularities of music may be found in
Wayne Koestenbaum, writing on the vocal breakdowns of opera singers:

> vocal crisis is the diva's self-lacerating announcement that interrup-
> tion has been, all along, her subject and method. And in her in-

terruption, I hear the imagined nature of homosexuality as a rip in meaning, in coherence, in cultural systems, in vocal consistency. Homosexuality isn't intrinsically an interruption; but society has characterized it as a break and a schism, and gay people, who are molded in the image of crisis and emergency, who are associated with "crisis" (Gay Men's Health Crisis), may begin to identify with crisis and to hear the interrupted voice as our echo. (1993, 128–29)

The film's well-calculated 'lack' of musical control and borders succinctly and pointedly exposes another lack: the inability of formal institutional controls to regulate or fully suppress someone like Anita and the desires and sexualities with which she is associated – an idea that will be developed throughout this essay. Another, quite contemporary reference of the film's obstreperous soundtrack is that of AIDS activism's important slogan, "Silence = Death." For early in the film, Anita anguishes about "silence so loud that the eardrum explodes" in the hospital that, by the end, will be unable to "shut her up." At the risk of proceeding too literally here, one could read the film's refusal of silence and acoustic decorum as an assertion, a performance waged against the closet and against other institutions that would attempt to control, normalize, or medicalize.

This is not to say that the film score works beyond *any* sense of norm or constraint; indeed, much of its strength and originality derives precisely from its working within (and upon) styles, movements, and compositional techniques associated with Germany, such as serial music, cabaret and music hall jazz, and so on. Pulling the music (rarely soothing or harmonious) into the foreground, having it accompany otherwise silent scenes from Anita's "memory," stresses the function it serves as a part of stylised history. Coupled with the film's other emphasis on formal elements – most of which work to recall Berlin culture and the cinema of the Weimar Republic – the music participates in the larger camp strategies of the film which, through their attention to surface, sound, and matter, establish a peculiarly German text as quite queer and impure, formally and morally speaking. Within such a framework, the score need not be read against the grain, as is so often the case in queer hermeneutics, looking for "hidden" tracks or traces, checking under masks or vêtements: it is, in a real sense, already "out."[5] Moreover, the film's aesthetic strategies show a sensitivity to history not usually associated with camp, one with important repercussions for contemporary viewers and listeners eager to challenge the moral, physical, or mental 'defectiveness' still associated, seventy years after Weimar, with AIDS.

After Anita is taken away for exposing her rear to a small crowd on Berlin's Kurfürstendamm, we see her strapped to a hospital bed under a circular neon light which bestows a ludic, poignant halo over her (the camera even pans up to it). The image immediately conjures forth a number of references, some more celestial than others: the two male angels of Wim Wenders's largely black and white *Himmel Über Berlin* (*Wings of Desire*, 1987), although Anita distinctly lacks the privileged transcendence bell hooks and Tania Modleski have observed in Wenders' characters. Like the other hospital scenes — all without color — *Anita*'s early scenes also recall more the drab black and white "heaven" sequences of Powell and Pressburger's *A Matter of Life and Death* (1946), a film that, as we will see below, resembles *Anita* in other significant ways.

By coupling black and white sequences with static camerawork and barren mise-en-scène, both *Matter* and *Anita* suggest a coercive clinical, repressive space in which the fantasy life of a particular character becomes personal and political necessity, a means of survival. Importantly, in films as self-conscious as these, the purported symptoms of each patient are described like cinema itself: an "organized series of hallucinations which appear to take on a reality of their own," to paraphrase *Matter*; in *Anita*, "sometimes dreams are more vivid than life — [Fra Kutowski] seemed happy in her delusion." Both hallucinating the more stimulating alternate worlds of their respective films, protagonist David Niven masochistically believes he needs to win a court case against heaven to continue life on earth in *Matter*, and Anita creates a licentious past in von Praunheim's film. In a way, both characters escape the regulatory instincts of the black and white domain, by walking, literally, away from death sentences. But whereas Niven 'escapes' into properly socialized, Oedipalized and heterosexualized 'reality', Anita moves into a happier indeterminacy. *Matter*'s heaven finally offers less the release from, or reward of, a life of Christian moderation and repression than its institutional and symbolic reconsolidation: it is the punitive space of the law, where clocks, checks, and courts determine systematically which subjects 'arrive', when and how. (The sissy angel character, Conductor 71, for example, was symbolically emasculated during the French Revolution: "I lost my head," he says.) In *Anita*, the conservative institutional function of the hospital is no less punitive, if less orderly or

logically rendered: political and social undesirables such as Rosa Luxemburg have been made residents.

Matter treats these symbolic structures as forces to be reasoned with, if
Niven is to win more time on glorious, campy, Technicolor earth through
the culminating trial sequence. Yet although *Matter* makes its case in glorified appeals to humanism and romantic love (not unlike the end of Wenders's *Wings of Desire* in this regard), it seriously undercuts the symbolic
force of romantic love through its unglamorous portrayal of heterosexuality via Niven's newfound girlfriend, June (Kim Hunter). Indeed, the rote
heterosexualizing of Niven's character – who clearly shares more with his
mates and the paternal Dr. Reeves than with June – is unconvincing
enough to end up as rather camp and ludicrous. By contrast, von Praunheim's *Anita* is much less reactive to heterosexuality and other normalizing
scenarios, implying the existence of "other" alternatives through, among
other things, its critique of the (literally) black and white notions of sanity,
health, and sexual propriety represented by the hospital.

After we hear a couple of synthetically produced sounds (not quite
music) in *Anita*'s early hospital setting, we hear a few chords played rather
desultorily on a piano. There is a fuller breach with tonality, and the
chords become increasingly unstable (and loud) when Anita calls long-
ingly for "Music!" and "her" performance begins. Both she and Blum's
character are dressed in red in these first fantasy numbers, and there are
numerous graphic matches between the 'young' Anita's movements in the
color fantasy/history sequences and the 'older' Anita's in the film's contemporary, black and white portions – a scheme largely sustained throughout the course of the film. It seems that musically, the piano here is as
isolated as the older woman first appears, and the unstable chords would
seem the fitting acoustic accompaniment to the character's disjointed condition. In so far as the piano solo intimates her rupture with sanity, rationality, or standard issue behavior, it recalls the words of Adrian Leverkühn's
mentor in *Dr. Faustus*, Wendell Kretschmar, who maintained that the
piano was the only instrument "peculiarly suited to [music's] intellectual
nature" (61) which "can, indeed, like [other instruments] be used in a solo
performance and as a medium of virtuosity; but that is the exceptional case
and speaking very precisely a misuse" (62).

As "misuse" and through its suggestion of imbalance and impropri-
ety, *Anita*'s score[6] might seem to adhere to the classical (i.e., studio Hollywood) convention of providing parallelism by whatever means possible:

thematically (alienation of the ascetic hospital), formally (no clear organizing tonal center), graphically (sole figure/sole piano), and also as a means
of conveying interior character state (instability and "misuse"). At the same
time, though, when considered in conjunction with other formal elements,
the music functions more on the edges of that tradition. Its nonrepresenta-
tional evocation of unsteadiness or possible insanity, even in this brief
example, is very different from mainstream efforts of the same. Before the
1950s — when breakthrough work would emerge more frequently, like
Leonard Rosenmann's atonal score for Minnelli's melodrama situated in a
psychiatric hospital, *The Cobweb* (1955) — Hollywood scores tended to
depict unsteadiness in isolated moments of anguish, tied to individualized
characters, not as a fragmentation or disunity sustained throughout the entirety of the film. Moments of instability would be conveyed musically
through clichéd instrumentation, such as the theremin in *The Lost Weekend* (Wilder, 1945) and *Spellbound* (Hitchcock, 1945). *Anita* violates these
kinds of classical precepts further through its frequent, unexpected changes
in the kinds of music it employs. In one later sequence entitled "Nights at
the El Dorado," the music moves directly from a soft viola solo into a jarring series of notes played by wood instruments, to a syncopated, relatively
melodic song in the style of Kurt Weill, which is then interrupted by a
tango.

    Anita's fractured memories, such as they are, are constituted largely by
the dances she and her partner Droste, perform. With little linearity, they
follow the story of their careers, drug addiction, relationship, and deaths.
The soundtrack is composed largely in the style of popular music and art
music roughly contemporary to the time of Anita's history; particularly
evident is the influence of Kurt Weill and the atonal experiments of art
composers of the time. Importantly, the film does not use tone row per se
— although Schönberg was beginning to develop his dodecaphonic system in the 1920s — but is more reminiscent of the free atonality characterized by Berg and Webern (see also Scherzinger/Hoad in this collection). By
selecting free atonality over the more systematic dodecaphonic music of
Schönberg (a formal looseness echoed in the film's choreography), von
Praunheim shows his interest in stylized impression, and his disinterest in
so-called objective histories or notions of authenticity.

    With its countless cultural references, the film is a veritable grab bag of
Weimar Republic and First World War icons: a man with a horribly scarred
face and a heavily made-up, one-legged older prostitute seem to emerge

from the work of George Grosz or Alfred Döblin; Ina Blum's large-eyed Anita recalls Isherwood's description of Sally Bowles. As Anita and Droste's story unspools, we are also struck by the film's considerable visual impersonation of expressionist cinema.[7] Cragged handwritten intertitles appear during the "silent" scenes-within-the-film, and even the credit sequence, which periodically interrupts Anita's opening butt-bearing scene, is rendered in this fashion. The film also boasts unexpected camera angles, distorted lines, violation of Renaissance perspective, stark contrasts in color intensity, painted sets, and unconventional light sources above and below the figures. Its characters are heavily made up, particularly the kohl around the eyes – causing reviewers like Mark Nash to call Mikael Honosseau (Droste) "a Cesare lookalike" (*Anita*, 215), and another to refer to the "skull-headed" Honosseau as "a Conrad Veidt for the '80s" ("Weekend Movies"). The film's performance/flashback sequences are staged in a manner reminiscent of Max Reinhardt's anti-naturalist theatre in which "poetic space" (perhaps the space of Anita's fanciful reminiscences) spring to life not through realistic portrayals but through heavily stylized gesture, lighting, and set design. Like the dances they convey, these depictions create a strong sense of performativity and highlight the nonobjective nature of memory.

Combined, the tropes of German expressionist filmmaking accomplish a number of things. Most obviously, they set the stage for what is presented from out of the past, a past taken from post-World War I and Weimar Germany and located primarily upon the figure of Anita Berber. At the same time, its authenticity is gently mocked. Because these scenes are staged from the elder Anita's mind – whether as a consequence of the thorazine injections she is given, psychotic dementia, or actual memory is left significantly unclear – the film's expressionist packaging intensifies the subjectivity of the history it tells. This, of course, was exactly the aim of expressionist aesthetics, to represent an idea from 'inside' a character's head, a notion used to delirious effect in the infamous narrational frame of *Das Kabinett des Dr. Caligari* (*The Cabinet of Dr. Caligari*, Robert Weine, 1919). Expressionism's focus on subjectivity, though, should not be taken to mean an overesteemed, powerful individuality was at work; indeed, the works of Grosz, Döblin, or Murnau's *Der letzte Mann* (*The Last Laugh*, 1924) feature largely stunted, disabled characters. As commentators are quick to observe, expressionism gave form to a variety of anxious responses to modernity, rising urbanization, industrialism, changing gender roles, and the general political, economic, and social instabilities of Germany from 1919 to 1933. Its interest in restoring the internal life or soul of an object, to call up an inner or latent truth, seems more a utopian appeal to an imagined lost wholeness than to anything that subjectivities could actually absorb.

In this light, the visual and acoustic tropes representing 'Weimar' in the film might seem destabilizing. Yet for end-of-the-century viewers familiar with such expressionistic flourishes, the effect is clichéd rather than unsettling, a fact fully exploited by von Praunheim's camp aesthetic. It is also significant that a good portion of that camp effect is derived from Weimar Berlin icons of special importance to lesbian and gay subcultures: queer cabarets, bisexual figures, etc. As Dyer has noted, representations of "gays [were] part of the ambience of decadence in Weimar films such as *Mabuse*" ("Less and More" 6).

Although the score helps establish the historical and temporal setting of the film, only superficially does it unify image, sound, and diegesis, as in classical Hollywood practice. There is very much a sense here in which it refuses that function, less by contradictory, contrapuntal relationships between music and image than by sheer overload, with no dialogue in the past sequences, and indeed no overbearing narrative direction or aim guiding them. *Anita* takes great pains to present a disorderly compendium of aesthetic references: certainly no authority is conferred upon the musical bits that are scattered throughout the film, pieces which are at best approximations of earlier styles, and not direct quotes per se. In fact the film is best described as a repository of the acoustic and visual detritus of postwar Berlin, the irreverent use and abuse of its clichés and codes. Not unlike the soundtracks of Alexander Kluge, von Praunheim obliges the musical meanings of his film be 'filled in' through active listening.

Anita's evocation of war and *entre-guerre* cultures, while primarily national in focus, includes other European modernist phenomena such as the Ballet Russe. Though closely tied to the Parisian art scene, the troupe appeared in Berlin in 1910, and their new ballet (Schumann's "Carnaval") featured dazzling sets by Leon Bakst. *Anita*'s set design is heavily indebted to the saturated, bright blues, tent-like curtains, and the intense reds, blacks, and golds favored by Bakst. The loose choreography of Berber and Droste's dances, which often resemble a series of moving poses or friezes, moves chaotically with the music, not unlike the dance-music relationship of the Ballet's 1912 production of Claude Debussy's *L'Après-midi d'un faune*

(*The Afternoon of a Faun,* 1892/94). In fact, in the only black and white
sequence clearly set in the past,[8] "O, Wonderful Land of Dreams / What a
Horrible Opium Dream / The Incredible Power of Opium," Droste plays a
satyr-like faun to Berber's maiden in the woods.[9] Nijinsky, whose choreographic career had just started with *Faun,* whose lead he played, wanted to
make the ballet "like a moving frieze, to animate Greek and Egyptian reliefs
and Greek vase paintings" (Buckle 163). Similar to the "discontinuous
compositions as mosaics" (Kramer 175) that the Ballet Russe associate Igor
Stravinsky preferred in music, dancers would move from one static representation to the next in what Nijinsky called "stylized gesture," a term
which we might use also to characterize *Anita*'s choreographic style. One
scene in particular – Blum's first dance, performed largely on the ground
and intercut with matching shots of Huber in the hospital room – can
only be described as a series of frieze-like poses.

Despite its now secure place in the canon of modernist art, the ballet
production of Debussy's *Afternoon of a Faun* was immediately received as
morally and sexually degenerate. Again, this was less a consequence of
Stravinsky's music than Nijinsky's choreography and his performance of
the faun, which included a scandalizing hand-to-crotch movement as he
lay on an abandoned scarf at the conclusion of the ballet. Paris's *Le Figaro*
ran a scalding front page review, written by the editor himself:

> This is neither a pretty pastoral nor a work of profound meaning.
> We are shown a lecherous faun, whose movements are filthy and
> bestial in their eroticism, and whose gestures are as crude as they
> are indecent. That is all. [It] was greeted with the booing it de-
> served. (in Buckle 242)

Judging from film intertitles, spectators of Anita and Droste's dance
performances hurled similar invectives. In a progression recalling the structure of Isherwood's *Goodbye to Berlin* stories, *Anita*'s fellow Germans become less and less *offended* by what they witness and more and more
offensive and aggressive toward it. By the end, audience members are demanding Aryan purity in one form or another: one scene late in the film
portrays several beer swilling proto-Nazis – replete with German Shepherd
– pounding a table demanding, "Folk dance, not nude dance"; and dialogue titles are splashed, "Forbidden dances! Homosexual! Off with their
heads! Exterminate them!" The purported decadence of Berber and Droste

is then exoticized, made un-German. Not incidentally, for instance, Berber's final – and apparently fatal – dance is "in the Orient," as an intertitle tells us, in front of Arab men not accustomed to women dancing nude.[10] The notion of decadence as foreign, it should be recalled, was not unknown to the responses to *The Afternoon of a Faun* or *The Rite of Spring*; nor should we forget musicology's comments on foreign composers like Tchaikovsky, or the tedious speculations about Stravinsky's own sexuality.

In contrast, von Praunheim's film shows up the impossibility of these idealized fantasies of national, sexual, and aesthetic purity. The German body, for instance, is given no integrity (a one-legged prostitute is the hit of Berlin's streets), and sexuality is remarkably free-floating (the heterosexual businessmen are as rouged as Droste, whose makeup levels rival those of Tammy Faye Baker's). Although Droste and Berber perform "vice, horror, and ecstasy," the film insists upon the decadent and rather vile character of the bourgeois audience they are out to "shock." Audience members often resemble small boars about to be roasted, with white, round faces flushed red with drink. That performers and audiences alike are portrayed in androgynous, unstable, and decadent fashions shows that steady, uncomplicated, and unsullied norms and identities exist nowhere.

II. A Delirious Spread of Surfaces

However particular to early twentieth-century modernism *Anita*'s score may be, it constructs – in tandem with the film more generally – less a picture of historical authenticity than a delirious spread of surfaces, textures, and materials, something apparent in its treatment of body and movement. In this regard, it is not so much the exact quotes and cultural citations that have relevance (is this Schönberg or Webern? Sally Bowles or Lulu?) as the pieces, bodies, and fabrics out of which such references are built. The film lavishes in the sheer physicality of this matter: its 'rinky tink' pianos, crashing cymbals, drapes, kimonos, military uniforms, cigarette holders, and needles all demonstrate the indispensability of form and surface to the film's highly stylized erotics.

In the sense that it emphasizes appearance and the superficial trappings of different historical epochs, von Praunheim's project is quite postmodern. But other assumptions lie behind his exalted play of borrowed surfaces, mismatched texts, and collage: namely, his interest in camp, and the gay and lesbian cultures from which it has emerged. Indeed, the emphasis on camp's surfaces appeared well before the advent of postmodern queer criticism. As Susan Sontag wrote in her classic "Notes on Camp" in *Against Interpretation*: "Camp art is often decorative art, emphasizing texture, sensuous surface, and style at the expense of content" (278). Similarly, in an essay on cult films, Robin Wood notes how, like camp, these films draw the viewer/listener's attention to their own facades, to the surfaces especially of performers' role-playing.[11] This *Anita* does in abundance, with lavish attention bestowed on costume design, decor, and sundry beads, boas, velvet and leather. As we will see, it is not insignificant that so much of camp's intrigue with surface is found on the body of its human performers.

Because camp developed historically within gay and lesbian communities as a means of conducting aberrant readings off of textual surfaces — a practice now widely emulated by mainstream straight cultures — it is important to note the obsession with which homosexuality 'itself' has been associated with surface and appearance, as queer critics frequently note. As Diana Fuss observes:

> In its popular incarnations, the surfeit that marks off homosexuality from its normative other, heterosexuality, is "gleaned" from the surface of the body: homosexuals are said to distinguish themselves by their extravagant dress, their exaggerated mannerisms, their hysterical intonations, their insatiable oral sex drives, and their absurd imitations of "feminine" and "masculine" behavior. (1995, 70)[12]

Putting aside the obvious absurdity of taking such tendencies for ontological 'truths', Fuss's observation underscores the extent to which homosexual identity — so aligned (and maligned) with the play of appearance and facade — finds its theoretical parallel in camp, a cultural practice crucial to the histories of many lesbian and gay subcultures.

Camp's play with surface and its rich sense of display are just what von Praunheim is after. Not only does *Anita* acknowledge the campiness of its artifacts (indeed, Sontag lists "dresses of the 1920s" in her extended set of examples), but it appropriates, with great savvy, Weimar Republic icons that have proved important within certain lesbian and gay cultures. Rife as it is with androgynous and cross-dressed cabaret acts, the homoeroticism of the Ballet Russe, the hats of Djuna Barnes, signs of heterosex-

ual excess and hysteria, the film deploys such references in a more historically focused manner than the kitschy collection of "cast-offs and rejects"
Thomas Elsaesser justly identifies in Hans-Jürgen Syberberg's *Hitler. Ein
Film aus Deutschland* (*Our Hitler,* 1977), a film which appears to put the
whole of modern German culture up for grabs (1981/82, 136).[13]

As opposed to the melancholic reverence they receive in Syberberg's
Hitler, von Praunheim treats the historical signifiers of German cultural
identity with affectionate disrespect. As the older Anita says − in a line often repeated in reviews and promotion material for the film − "Berlin is the
capital of sin and I am her queen," out to "shock" her world. (One hears
in this utterance the echo of Divine from *Pink Flamingos* [John Waters,
1972] who also wants to reign as the "filthiest person alive.") It seems no
accident that the most stylized moments of von Praunheim's film occur
in Anita's past, and *Anita* bestows the visual and acoustic clichés of Wei-
marism generously upon her performance numbers. Stressing performativity over authenticity or immanence, Berber and Droste's numbers make
clear the ways in which the human bodies that pass through history are
always constructed, subject to revision and change. In fact, even the "off-
stage" scenes make this point, as can be seen when Berber's father abandons
the family when she is just a girl. The scenes are played as mock-Victorian
melodrama, filled with the requisite linguistic silences and the gestural,
musical excesses, with the elderly Huber portraying the young Anita.

Importantly, the film does not tie its materiality of signs and icons to
standard notions of production. Camp also operates in much the same
way, that is as a practice of consumption, a form of (re)reading made possible only in consumer cultures: even its enthusiasm for bad 'taste' raises the
question of exaggerated consumption. Critical discussions place considerable emphasis on the place of failed or outmoded production in producing camp effects: consider here the camp treatment of stars deemed 'past
their prime', for example, Elvis Presley or Elizabeth Taylor. Such a focus
tends to inflict the material facts of aging onto the once sexually 'productive' body whose years in certain camp forms are made hideously overpre-
sent, aggressively consuming.[14] Clearly bodies that consume and that produce are not so easily separated, although significant traditions (e.g., religious and economic) insist upon clear distinctions between production
and consumption, privileging the former (work) over the latter (waste). It is
precisely this opposition that grounds homophobic understandings of
homosexual and all nongenital sex as always-already perverse, since it fails

to lead to 'proper' reproductive output, a point echoed by Diana Fuss in identifying homosexuality's function in classical psychoanalysis as an "essential waste ingredient" (1995, 60). Von Praunheim is also aware of the perversity of this sort of bias; one need only recall the title of another of his films: *Nicht der Homosexuelle ist pervers, sondern die Situation, in der er lebt* (*It Is Not the Homosexual Who Is Perverse But the Society in Which He Lives*, 1971).

For its part, *Anita* boasts a dizzying array of nonproductive activity. Numerous items point to failed production or reproduction, such as newspaper ads for "suitable women wanted for experiments with male hormones" or images that show consumption in its various forms: eating, sucking, drinking, or drug-taking, which tend to appear in the conventionally productive public sphere (the couple's staged performances or in the commerce of prostitution). It seems that all that the young Anita can really and actively 'produce' is her nudity: audiences are distinctly hostile to her later efforts to assert her artistry, and to dance with clothes on. It is certainly not accidental that she dies of "consumption." The older, self-appointed Anita is deemed similarly counterproductive, with her useless, irrational, and unhinged fantasies that the institutions seem unable to suppress (actually, in a sense, it is through their medication that these fantasies are produced). Through the sheer size of the older Anita's body, with her self-proclaimed "big, beautiful ass," and her huge, generously made-up eyes, which can also be said to "take in" too much, the character is firmly tied to the assumption of excessive, out of control consumption. With her largeness, her unkempt hair, and considerable makeup, Huber's portrayal suggests a drag performance of Anita Berber as Divine.

Equally significant is the matter in which disease, contagion, and addiction are branded onto the film's campy, consuming figures. Droste, for instance, is represented in one scene as a skeleton and Anita performs a blood-soaked dance in another. In the equally performative offstage sequences of them at home, the two consume drugs and arrange for Anita to prostitute herself in order to acquire more. "I live in ecstasy," chants the elder, institutionalized Anita, "that gushes like a wave of blood," and indeed, blood emerges from the young tubercular Anita during her final dance in the "Orient." For the older Berber, disease is equally present, although her illness is not 'on' the body but 'in her head' (revealing an institutional obsession with impure interiors mocked by the character's own interest in asses and assholes). Furthermore, because AIDS has appeared to have given homophobic culture the go-ahead to pathologize homosexual bodies, *Anita*'s representations of disease and the body become especially important.

Like von Praunheim's 1989 *Schweigen = Tod* (*Silence = Death*), *Anita* opens with a performance that directly presents a pair of buttocks to the camera. *Silence = Death* presents the buttocks as the physical locus of homosexual pleasure and death, a symbolic double play dramatized by the eventual firing of a toy pistol into the character's rectum in mock suicide. *Anita*'s character happily performs in the street as the "great nude star Anita Berber," and reveals the "most beautiful ass in all of Berlin" to the jeering crowd. Just as she begins to sing, "Whoever says ass/has got to say hole," the police arrive and escort her away. Clearly, it is not just her diegetic stripping that poses a problem to the law, but the "hole" upon which she insists and in which she takes pride. For the anus demonstrates not only the difficulty of marking interior from exterior, waste from production, but it also marks the limit of reproductive sexualities. The discourse of anality operates throughout the film, primarily through Anita's dialogue: "Where do I find the shithouse?" she sings at one point; elsewhere she recounts the story of a man who "shits into the purse of the baroness" from which we learn that "No decent businessman will take shit for money." Later, she philosophizes, "The world is an ass, and we are its farts. Each of us stinks in his own way — that is the spice of life."

The anus has proved an especially crucial 'part' of contemporary gay male discourses of identity.[15] In this regard, Lee Edelman's rereading of the primal scene in Freud's Wolf Man case raises several interesting points. After noting the importance of retrospective, reconstructed memory in Freudian psychoanalysis, in what he provocatively calls the "view from behind,"[16] Edelman then examines Freud's ambivalence toward the primal scene regarding the possible sodomitical spectacle it avails. He notes that with the primal scene:

> as Freud [first] reconstructs the perspective of the infant at the moment he observes it, activates the pre-genital supposition 'that sexual intercourse takes place at the anus.' Thus in the first instance the primal scene is always perceived as sodomitical, and it specifically takes shape as a sodomitical scene between sexually undifferentiated partners, both of whom, phantasmatically at least, are believed to possess the phallus. (1991, 100-101)

Only later, in Freud's "revisionary rearticulation," is the subject's sexually indeterminate fantasy/history represented as heterosexual (1991, 102). Edelman stresses the extent to which this initial anal economy is "written over," censored in Freud's theoretical work as it is in other straight economies of representation. It is, of course, not only the purported inversion of male homosexuality which is censored, but the inability of the anus to confer fixed gender identity as well. Working from this same perspective, von Praunheim's film makes the latter point with special acuity, localizing the gay 'asshole' on a highly performative, campy *female* body. Significantly, the character's play with various dualisms of identity – sane/insane, young/aged, heterosexual/lesbian or bisexual, male/female, even dead/alive – is never 'straightened out' for certain in the film. Nor does Anita merely illustrate or *perform* the theoretical points made so astutely by Edelman and others. Not unlike the Wolf Man, whose view of the primal scene enabled a double identification with both mother and father, *Anita* offers a productive diffusion to its spectators and auditors. Nothing is fixed, be it at the level of character, time frame, history, locale, and sense of "truth."

Along with the film's economy of consumption and waste, its emphasis on indeterminate identities implies the dissolution of identity itself. Indeed, identification, as Fuss puts it, "invokes phantoms," and is a means of being "open to a death encounter" (1995, 1). Death and decay are everywhere in the film – as the institutionalized Anita states, "from every corner springs a hanged man ... corpses embrace." It is not incidental that *Anita*'s expressionist sets give no precise setting and frame their images in darkness, nor that the film's characters dedicate their dances to "death and sexlessness," conduct mock hangings, and so forth. To accentuate this morbidity is one early dance of Droste and Berber in which the two perform separately. Interspersed with black-and-white documentary World War I footage, Droste, dressed as a soldier, regards a bullet wound in his abdomen; an intertitle announces "It's over!" and we hear bass notes from a piano performed slowly and solemnly. The music abruptly erupts into loud attacks of brass instruments and a snare drum when we cut to war scenes. Interestingly, Berber is introduced as Droste's wound first appears in close-up. Standing against a plain geometric backdrop, she covers her white dress with blood, smearing it sensuously over herself. Coincident with this striking appearance of woman and wound, a gentle melody is introduced, one which will be used elsewhere in the film. Performed softly by clarinet, and

soon, piano, the melody continues as Droste goes on to 'remake' himself.
Sporting garters and makeup, and covering himself with powder — as if a
thick veneer will hide his mortal lack — he aspires, via intertitles, "to be the
most perverse of all!" a claim which hardly pleases the protofascist audiences von Praunheim situates alongside the film.

While some critics consider these masochistic, decadent displays as
important references to subjectivity in general, it is important to stress the
film's markedly Weimar Republic context, for it offers a historical precision not always acknowledged by film and cultural critics outside of Germany.[17] Moreover, the film's exploration of death and vice is as keenly attuned to audiences in the age of AIDS as it is to 1920s Weimar culture. A
panel at the 1988 Berlin Film Festival enabled critics, like von Praunheim,
to voice their criticism of bourgeois culture's inability to celebrate death.
As Jay Scott wrote at the time, ours is "a culture-wide abhorrence of sex on
the one hand and a denial of the inevitability of death on the other." Von
Praunheim's refusal to shirk from death and negativity is apparent in a remark he made to a French interviewer, "Stiffness, death, and immobility ex-
cite me" ("Monologue" 16; my trans.). Not only does *Anita* seem attuned
to lack and the negativity which ground any assertion of identity, it is
equally sensitive to the historical, institutional forms which regulate, encourage, and punish the bodies housing those identities. As is evident
from Droste's skeleton, young Anita's death bed, the 'corpse' of the older
Anita, the film's depictions of death are quite physical, material, somatic,
devoid of any transcendence. Von Praunheim makes no effort to uplift
through sounds and images, but offers a kind of tempered celebration of
the 'backside' of human and cultural identity.

Although Berber and Droste's performances offer the clearest elaboration of these kinds of alternatives, other characters are worth mentioning as
well. In an early parlor room scene in which Anita bares her chest, one
aristocrat cries out lewd with drink, "breasts as large as kaiser rolls!" By
melding obsessions with feminine, maternal bodies (her breasts) with the
most conventional of symbolic paternal authorities (the Kaiser), this figure
conjures an image not unlike that described by Klaus Theweleit regarding
the proto-Nazi *Freikorps* (volunteer corps) members. For these other exemplars of nationalist, seeming hypermasculinity were constituted in terms of
obsessive fantasies, projections, and anxieties: for the *Freikorps*, the establishment and violation of imaginary "ego-armor" was necessary to render
the ever-threatening morass of body fluids as "other" (feminine, Jewish,

etc.). Obviously these kind of projections were resolutely indissociable from the members themselves.

The topless Anita is approached by another soldier from the crowd. He grabs her and announces that "tomorrow I must go to the front," presumably in order to win her favors. Instead of patriotic pathos or compliance, however, her response is a mocking, "Well then, see you in the mass grave" — a gallows humor linking commerce, the heterosexual transaction, and the murderousness of war in no uncertain terms. One observes another sort of challenge to patriotic, male heterosexual desire in the fact of the soldier's imminent move to "the *front*," potentially leaving 'behind' an anal economy, and in so doing face near-certain death. That mortality is associated with the "front," where sexual difference is conventionally verified, rather than with the "view from behind," has strong repercussions for queer identities.

The film's emphasis on annihilation, negativism, and delirious consumption, along with its use of the historical past, is critical, and the selection of post-World War I Weimar Berlin in particular raises important conflicting cultural and sexual issues. For this is a period often constructed as a lesbian and gay utopia, given its relative (but by no means uncontested) social tolerance: its iconography — from the clubs to figures like Sally Bowles and Marlene Dietrich — has proved equally crucial to subsequent queer cultures. Yet *Anita* mediates this ephemeral queer utopia — whose significance as such is perhaps intensified by its very ephemerality — by the losses, lacks, and negativism on which it forcefully, if playfully, insists. For, Weimar Germany was marked by as many failures of leftist, alternative, and progressive activities as it was by their successes. Even the considerable support for homosexual rights lent by Magnus Hirschfeld, founder of the Institute for Sexual Science (1919), for example, was not without problems, particularly in his highly publicized theories on the detectability of homosexuality through measurable, physical signs. And, in another observation, Hirschfeld seems to have anticipated in 1927 some of von Praunheim's own frustrations with the nonpolitical stance of gay communities in the 1980s:

> It is untrue that homosexuals form a sort of 'secret society' among themselves with all sorts of code signals and mutual defence arrangements. Aside from a few minor cliques, homosexuals are in reality almost totally lacking in feelings of solidarity; in fact it

would be difficult to find another class of mankind which has
proved so incapable of organizing to secure its basic legal and human rights. (in S. Marshall 85)

Filmmaker Stuart Marshall has recently questioned the use of pink and
black triangles by gay and lesbian activists since the 1970s. He notes that
the black triangle, for instance, initially symbolized a wide variety of male
and female "asocials," including the "work-shy," and not just lesbians, during the Holocaust. He more forcefully questions the analogy to racial geno-
cide implied by the queer use of these symbols, especially in light of the
Holocaust of European Jews. Unlike Judaism, he reasons, homosexuality
was assumed nonprocreative, not a race that would multiply, and in this
way was treated as less of a threat to Aryan eugenics; for Marshall, this partially explains the less systematic punishment of gays by the Nazis, which,
he maintains through researched examples, was less categorical or absolute
than many believe (lesbianism was not officially proscribed, for instance).[18]
Marshall is, moreover, sharply critical of a group identity that is "affirmed"
by a symbol of annihilation. His emphasis on the historical complexity of
signs notwithstanding, it is important to stress that they are activated more
for their substantial imaginary weight rather than for any claim they might
make to historical authenticity.[19] With its own reactivation of an important,
but conflicted, queer epoch, *Anita: Dances of Vice* chooses less to oppose
the "false" identifications questioned by Marshall than to render them irrelevant.

III. Camp and the Inscription of History

Most commentators have constituted camp as a fleeting, ephemeral phenomenon, marked by fads and with no 'serious' relation to history. Some
do this to strengthen their claims for the difficulty of defining camp in the
first place, most others to set it off from notions of immanence or authenticity. Consequently, and in spite of the many existing histories *of* camp,
less attention has been paid to camp's contribution to historical representation or to the historiographic assumptions it upholds. One recent article
which begins to do this focuses — significantly — on New German Cinema, singling out the work of Fassbinder in particular and, more particularly still, the iconic status of Hanna Schygulla. For Johannes von Moltke,
Schygulla's image and acting style work within prevailing conceptions of

camp, that is, in which camp is a staging of gender as unstable, constructed performance rather than inherent, fixed property. Consider the instability of her image: is she hack actress from the hinterland? Dietrich reincarnate? decadent Hollywood glamour? ugly? beautiful? That Schygulla posed some of these questions herself also reveals camp's vouted self-consciousness.

Von Moltke goes on to observe how Schygulla's body has been linked to "Germanness" in two ways: as characters like Maria Braun or Lili Marleen, in films that graft the history of German war and postwar experience onto their eponymous characters, or as a result of Schygulla's public reception (people would say to her, "You were wonderful in your role as *Eva Braun*").[20] With films and reception thus nationalizing Schygulla's body with such conspicuous artifice, one can detect, as von Moltke does, a process to "represent the nation and its history as a drag performance put on by a particular body" (98). Nothing is rendered stable or natural, and although any number of New German films tie bodies to German history in stylized, self-conscious ways, rarely is the historical referent able to claim a stable, unassailably pure status. The strength of films like *Die Ehe Der Maria Braun* (*The Marriage of Maria Braun*, Fassbinder, 1979), *Karl May* (Syberberg, 1974), *Deutschland, bleiche Mutter* (*Germany, Pale Mother*, Sanders-Brahms, 1979), *Die Patriotin* (*The Patriot*, Alexander Kluge, 1979), and *Anita* resides in their peculiarly fractured treatment of memory and historical representation.

Von Moltke continues by recalling remarks made by critics on camp's obsession with detritus and with outdated artifacts and aesthetic standards. Developing Andrew Ross's claim that camp produces "surplus value from forgotten forms of labour" (Ross's example is Hollywood glamour), von Moltke adds that, for the New German Cinema, one such "forgotten form" was the "labour of remembering and forgetting" Germany's war and postwar past (102). In this regard, camp avails a textual strategy of remembrance that differs appreciably from the pervasive theoretical model of German remembrance asserted by the Mitscherlichs. Filmmakers and theoreticians alike have been massively influenced by Alexander and Margarete Mitscherlich's 1967 bestseller *Die Unfähigkeit zu Trauern* (*The Inability to Mourn*), and the authors' theory of postwar Germany's "inability to mourn" or to come to terms with the past. Mourning is not how camp commemorates the past, although like it, its representational work begins by turning to history. Instead, camp's "mnemonics put not only a 'cult of Hollywoodiana'

(Ross), but an abiding sense of spectacle and of performativity back into the representation of German history" (103), as von Moltke observes. For a cinema with as elaborate a sense of display and as sophisticated a sense of historical inquiry as the New German Cinema's, it is a fully convincing point.

Unfortunately, von Moltke minimizes camp's activity beyond American shores and comes close to saying that camp remains a purely American phenomenon.[21] This is partly a consequence of his choice of examples: Ross's work, with its focus on "Hollywoodiana"; Fassbinder's cinema, filtered as it was through Hollywood melodrama; or director John Waters's camp confession to secretly adoring Fassbinder. Once touched by American reception, it would seem, as in the instance of Fassbinder by Waters, German films can return home as camp. Von Moltke characterizes German audiences, by contrast, as having stuck more or less to the films' literal and more immediate references. Even one of his few remarks on von Praunheim, one of New German Cinema's campiest members, demonstrates this perspective: "Rosa von Praunheim's admiration for Tally Brown ... provides a good example of a kind of German camp which picks up on figures and iconographies that have already been made over into camp in the U.S." (101, n. 59). While there is no question about von Praunheim's savviness about U.S. camp figures,[22] von Moltke seriously underestimates the extent to which German (or other non-U.S.) artists can activate their own cultures for camp purposes. In fact, some of his own observations demonstrate the fundamentally German nature of Fassbinder's campiness, such as the over-the-top spectacle of Nazi machinery in *Lili Marleen* (1980); Schygulla's reincarnations of Dietrich, and so on. (We might add to his list the operatic, camp aesthetics of Schroeter, Ottinger, and Treut in their play with erotica and difference.)

By demonstrating that camp, however superficial or playful in appearance, can function as a form of historical representation, von Moltke puts the final nail into Sontag's long-attacked claim to camp's inherent "apoliticalness" (Sontag 277).[23] To psychoanalytic critics concerned with its relation to gendered identity, camp has political potential through its sheer emphasis on surface, image, and on the arbitrary, unstable 'nature' of human bodies and identity. Through its own recycling of clichéd icons of Germanness and of postwar and Weimar culture, *Anita*'s campiness insists on posing additional questions of national identity, challenging not only standard ideas of camp, but the notions of purity and uniformity which,

as we discussed earlier, tacitly ground a number of conceptions of Germanness and of 'proper' German culture. Von Praunheim's historical context
of his camp aesthetics include, in addition to that of postwar and Weimar
Germany, other histories, such as those of gay and lesbian cultures. Here it
is worth returning to music and the film.

For some queer musicologists, the concepts of 'homosexuality' and
'musicality' are linked both through definition and experience. Connections for gay men often take the form of popular riddles and codes: "does
he sing in the choir?"; "is he a musical lover?"; or, "is he musical?"[24] (In
this vein, the above quote from *Dr. Faustus* about the utter naturalness of
German men being "musical" resonates in delightfully queer ways.) For lesbians, the connection to musicality emerged with special force under the
influence of 1970s French feminism, which hypothesized a "feminine
language" characterized by corporeal, nonlinear, rhythmic, musical qualities which were contrasted to traditional, masculinist symbolic forms. In
this way, through recourse to musical qualities, Wittig, Cixous, Irigaray,
and, initially, Kristeva offered potential lesbian alternatives with their work.
To be sure, music's pleasures have long been construed in terms of femininity, even – and often especially – in nonfeminist writers, but, as lesbian
musicologist Suzanne Cusick writes, "For some of us, it might be that the
most intense and important way we express or enact identity through the
circulation of physical pleasure is in musical activity, and that our 'sexual
identity' might be 'musician' more than it is 'lesbian', 'gay', or 'straight'"
(22).

While the shared status of musicality and homosexuality serves historically sensitive and important polemical purposes, the equation remains
nonetheless vexed. Theoretical objections can be raised against the assumption that both homosexual identity and musicality deviate from standard
norms (of culture, of sexuality, or of subjectivity), a framework that, it
could be argued, flattens rather than confronts cultural notions of difference. Otherwise put, the linking of music and homosexuality easily roman-
ticizes as "other" *both* terms of the equation: as outsiders, as undervalued,
as abused or ridiculed victims, or, by contrast, as differences to celebrate. It
also invites the mutual essentialization of the arts as queer and of queerness
as artistic, notions as clichéd as they are simplistic.

Instead, I would maintain that the camp aesthetic *in* music works to
queer a text like *Anita*, not musicality per se. *Anita* extends camp's fascination with surface – usually described in terms of appearance and "cliché"

(a term taken from photographic reproduction) – beyond its prevailing visual conception into acoustic performance and reception. The tired, familiar signs of Berlin decadence – signaled visually through, for example, Berber's and Droste's dances – are also conveyed musically. Along with the acoustic clichés of Weimar cabaret culture, we also get familiar folk tunes, and clichéd *uses* of music: discordant pitches, loud, brief attacks, and/or unconventional instrumentation accompany diegetic moments of "shock" in scenes of incipient fascism and in moments of presumed degeneracy, such as when Anita first exposes her breasts (the 'kaiser roll' scene) or when Droste proclaims himself "the most perverse of all" at the mirror soon afterwords. Interestingly, these loud, brief attacks of music-shocks also occur independently of diegetic audiences that might motivate the outrage suggested by the music. In this way the shocks elicited by the display of unconventional sexualities exceed and outlive the film's diegetic setting, suggesting an important parallel to queer discourses and identities today.

Although musical examples have always been offered as camp, their contexts or manner of standard performance usually contributes more to their campiness than the music itself: Swan Lake, a Busby Berkeley musical, ABBA. Sontag acknowledged this by way of her own camp examples such as classical ballet, opera, and pop music. But she makes a curious exception: "concert music, though, because it is contentless, is rarely camp. It offers no opportunity, say, for a contrast between silly or extravagant content and rich form" (278). Some significant – in fact, obvious – counterexamples to this claim may be gleaned from the canon of symphonic concert music: the finale of Beethoven's Ninth Symphony, or the opening of his Fifth, both of which have been camped by Stanley Kubrick, Monty Python, and others. Sontag uncharacteristically bypasses the chance to explore the assumptions around such questionable notions as musical "contentlessness," its autonomous nature, and so on. *Anita*, by contrast, demonstrates that even the most abstract, absolute music is not immune to – and the metaphor is deliberate – cultural infection. For its cliché-ridden campiness helps dissipate some of the widely maintained myths of aesthetic purity and autonomy in Western, and especially German, art music.

At the same time, the German concert music with which *Anita* tinkers is quite different than the treatment of Beethoven's Ninth Symphony in, say, Alexander Kluge's *The Patriot*, or in Fassbinder's *Maria Braun* (with music by Peter Raben), or even Syberberg's *Hitler*. Unlike these films, the musical traditions with which von Praunheim works are not those of *official* German culture. Without diminishing the canonical status of Schönberg, Berg, Webern, and other modernists, it is important to note that, unlike titans such as Brahms, Beethoven, or Wagner, these composers never tapped the national imaginary with the intensity of their predecessors. Their music was deemed too abstract, too inaccessible, too difficult to achieve such overwhelming iconic status. Atonal music — be it the dodecaphonic system or not — has never specifically symbolized German nationhood in the way that Beethoven's or Wagner's has, even though it has been loosely aligned with a European modernism.

In this way, German modernist music suggests a productive counter-example to Philip Brett's observations on the German-centeredness of musicology. For here it is always-already excessive: at once too intellectual, too self-indulgent — in short, beyond the musicological norm. It is significant that von Praunheim's film uses German music composed in the style of 'high' art (e.g., Berg) with non-German art composers (e.g., Debussy, Stravinsky) along with popular forms attributed to more 'lowbrow' German tastes: the music of beer taverns and Berlin cabarets, American-influenced jazz, Kurt Weill, sing-along music and so forth. No type of music is rendered pure — or, to recall Sontag, "contentless" — all is over the top, campy, derivative. Their shared decadence also receives perverse historical confirmation, for both avant-garde abstraction and American influenced popular forms like jazz would soon be condemned as inferior, foreign, or decadent, whether through 'formal excesses', the non-Aryan status of the composer, or both, by the State. Although Nazi Germany was not alone in making these pronouncements (just as the critique of modernism was not restricted to the political right), *Anita* offers a metonymic compression of the near-global retreat from modernism in the 1930s as the proto-Nazis yell "folk-dance, not nude-dance" in their demand for traditional folk culture over aesthetic experimentation. In this way, as music about to be overturned, postwar and Weimar-era music, for all their purported excesses and indulgences, end up being, ironically lacking and ephemeral. Failing to uphold the virile, Western norm Brett locates in German music, *Anita*'s film score demonstrates the instability of such regularizing norms to begin with.

It is worth returning to the film's interest in disease and institutions, since here too discourses of normalcy are fervently played out. Purportedly sick at a number of levels, Anita leads a (literally) colorful alternate life compared to the austere, black and white setting of the hospital, whose repressive atmosphere is entirely devoid of energy – recall Anita's observation that "from every corner springs a hanged man." Its uncampy lifelessness is, quite conspicuously, unhealthy (patients complain of shit, shitty food, shitty drugs, etc.), although this is the institution that defines the "mentally ill" and, even more ironically, exists to improve or stabilize their condition. For the queer-identified Anita, this will not work, and she announces her boisterous reign as "Berlin's Queen." In his work on related queens – divas and opera queens – Koestenbaum notes:

> Divas, like gay people, fall under the sign of the sick, the maimed, the deranged. The diva is associated with disease and with injuries that prevent adequate voice production ... the produced voice is perceived to be a sort of sickness ... because it is an exception to natural law ... Diva iconography casts the successful, prominent woman (the [large] woman who makes a large fee and a large sound) as a diseased anomaly ... Diva voice production is a scene of sickness, an occasion for the body to appear nonconforming, internal, festering, underground, and interrupted. (1993, 102–103)[25]

The iconography of disease – which prevails in certain camp discourses as much as it does in opera insofar as women's bodies are concerned, and which dovetails with disturbing ease onto notions of the female grotesque[26] – is significantly overturned in the film. For it is not the aging, heavy Anita who falls victim to these deadly discourses, but the young, conventionally beautiful one: it is the young Anita who dies of 'consumption'. It seems to me quite crucial that the elder Anita is able to walk away from the hospital at the end of the film, not just as "a woman," the potential "female grotesque" (for she can be reduced to neither of these things), but as a representative for everyone affected by discourses of moral and somatic purity and disease – which is to say, all of us. As Koestenbaum maintains about divas, Anita succeeds in unsettling the terms of deviation and illness surrounding her.

> Singing, the diva interrupts our ideas of health, because what she produces is unnatural but also eerily beautiful. The diva ... exposes *interiority*, the inside of a body and the inside of a self; we may feel that the world of the interior that the diva exposes is a diseased place [as the hospital and police do], but we learn from the diva's

beautiful voice to treasure and solicit those operatic moments when suddenly interiority upstages exteriority, when an inner and oblique vision supplants external verity. (1993, 103; emphasis in the original)

Throughout von Praunheim's film, Anita offers precisely this kind of "operatic," "oblique vision." A crucial scene at the end reveals how what may be called an "inner vision" is branded onto, or "upstages," her present hospital reality. The scene, filmed in black and white, shows the body of the elderly Anita laid out on an oddly fantastic, chiffon-draped bed in a nonclinical, private hospital room. She then takes part in a seduction fantasy involving her nurse (Blum), who strips her uniform off to reveal a skin-tight evening dress. Vampire-like, the latter approaches and attacks Anita. There can be no doubt about Nurse Blum's sadism here, yet Anita's desires are far too indeterminate to reduce the sequence to a persecution fantasy — and indeed, as the 'corpse', it is far from certain that the fantasy is even her own. The character shows little of the "self-protective suspicions" that Leo Bersani describes in paranoia, even though she teases and rails against the nurse throughout the course of the film (1989, 108-09). Because this final fantasy sequence, unlike most of the others,[27] is situated in the hospital, there is a much stronger sense in which Anita's agency actively reinscribes the reality around her, offering less a refuge from its dreariness than an altered way of seeing, of hearing, of doing business with the self and with history. This remains the case in spite of our knowledge that Anita's fantastic vision of the past is unquestionably derived from her present institutionalized situation: for her 'autobiographical' presentation casts her current doctor and nurse in its two starring roles. Moreover, Anita's historical phantasms, possibly initiated by diegetic pharmaceutical treatments, are in actuality less the expression of *her* inner vision or subjectivity than those of larger, that is nondiegetic, critical and cultural forces and technologies, not the least of which are von Praunheim's efforts as filmmaker. From Anita's fantasies we can extrapolate, in a very basic way, how historical representations are molded by current prerogative and perception: the film offers a textbook illustration of the impossibility of objective history. In this way, Anita's 'oblique' perspective forces us to consider relationships between two historically and stylistically different contexts.

Anita's scrutiny falls upon the 1920s and the 1980s, both "period[s] of conservatism, following liberalism," as gay film critic Jay Scott has written. Von Praunheim describes it this way:

> After World War I it was a wonderful time of the Avant-Garde. But they went too far. [*sic*] It's very similar to now coming from the '60s and '70s. People have swung to the right and they think we have to go back to the status quo and security. I feel out of style. My whole existence feels out of place at the moment, because people aren't interested in politics and revolutionary ideas. (in Rubnitz)

Clearly, von Praunheim shares real affinities with the elderly, out-of-sync Anita (and his admiration of performer Lotte Huber is equally clear from interviews). In spite of his post 1970s disillusionment, however, he writes: "I need to remind people now that we can keep fighting even if the odds are hopeless" (in Nash, "Not the Homosexual" 250). With current and past obsessions over deviance, disease, and "improperly" sexed bodies, "it's very important to remember people [like Anita Berber] who had this kind of burning desire to try things out, to go to their very limits (Nash, "Not the Homosexual" 251).

Like his interest in the historical figure herself, von Praunheim is obviously very sensitive to the importance of his ficitional Anita's versions of the past, with their open exploration of desire and sexualities, to theorists and activists working today. For like contemporary AIDS activism, the film shows up the hypocrisy of those who try to bind physical disease with moral 'impurities', or who lay proprietorial claim to moral or sexual norms, projecting 'decadence' onto culturally devalued others. In this way the film shrewdly weaves together notions of sexual and moral norms with those of music: where is the norm? how stable, or how German is it? To be sure, the film does not, nor cannot, offer a full utopian escape from these regulatory ideas nor their institutional supports. The hospital, police, the tuberculosis of Anita Berber and the psychosis of the elderly Anita are all 'still there', but their ability, in the end, to impose punishing, incarcerative subjectivities on figures like Anita's is shown to be partial and, more emphatically, perverse.

Von Praunheim literalizes what T. Levin has called the "rhetoric of hyperbolized negativity" of the Weimar Republic's cultural expression,[28] forcing impurity and disease to their utmost conclusions through the interplay of medical, psychiatric, and camp discourses.[29] In its irreverent explorations of diseased negativity, *Anita* blurs the boundaries between a number of terms: present and past, documentary and fantasy, sane and ludic, objective and subjective, queer and nonqueer, and it shows the arbitrary nature of what connects as well as what divides these sorts of oppositions. Its diverse patchwork of aesthetic and cultural references, while wholly different than the elaborate compilation strategies of someone like Kluge, is no less historically sensitive.[30] It simply proceeds from a queerer perspective, using camp as a means of signaling relationships among its various elements.

In his notes for "Lost in the Stars," an album of rock covers of songs by Kurt Weill, Terry Southern acknowledges the collaboration of Weill and Brecht (whom he queerly calls "the original 'glimmer twins'") in the following way: "There is something in the German theatre music of the 20s and early 30s — something in the music of Weill, and in the words of Brecht, which speaks meaningfully to Americans in the 80s." The same is equally true for von Praunheim's film, whose score deploys music that to some was considered decadent and, to others even today, aesthetically inviolate, unassailably expert or standard. *Anita* blends these different musics together in ways that, while historically situated and contextualized, strips them of any accompanying myths of national or aesthetic purity. In its place the camp extends a campy messiness, a sense of indeterminate "contamination" present in the film's own desire to "shock the philistines," to use Anita's pet line. What von Praunheim offers in such colorful, boisterous play is the more serious suggestion of bringing music and camp into the fold of queer culture and into the realm of historical meaningfulness and responsibility.

Notes

[1] For one of the best overviews of early German films with gay and lesbian themes, see Dyer "Less and More." His essay includes extensive analyses of Richard Oswald's *Anders als die Andern* and Leontine Sagan's *Mädchen in Uniform* in particular.

[2] An unpleasant rumor has it that, to the regret of the authors, the section discussing the New German Cinema in Bordwell and Thomson's *Film History* will be cut from the next edition. In his recent *tour de force* on Friedrich Nietzsche, Geoff Waite trenchantly expresses the problem, objecting to German departments' reluctance to

confront contemporary issues or to form politically engaged positions, arguing that "departments of German and German studies are conceptually bankrupt, having outlived any more profound raison d'etre they might have had or have" (368).

[3]See also Gary Thomas's excellent analysis of Handel, about whose status he has this to say: "Though different in degree, Handel's image is constituted as a plenitude, one that as time went on got constructed increasingly in terms not only of Romantic hero ("heaven-sent genius"), but also of British national identity and religious purity. The myth could hold together, indeed be fortified, by such accretions, even in the presence of minor flaws in an otherwise seamless fabric ..." (170).

[4]The connection with Brecht has been raised by, among others, the anonymous reviewer for The New York Post, who, in "Weekend Movies," refers to the film's intertitles as a Brechtian device.

[5]Musicologist Gary Thomas, commenting on hidden information, and in particular, on the academy's weighted "silences" surrounding various musical figures and texts, writes: "On the most basic level closet knowledge depends on silence, an 'absence' out of which is generated a discursively elaborated 'presence,' the secret" (167).

[6]The film's music credits are to Konrad Elfers, Rainer Rubbert, Alan Marks, Ed Lieber, and Wilhelm Siebert.

[7]Von Praunheim used much of this same neo-expressionist style in his 1984 film Horror Vacui.

[8]Another black and white sequence in which the elder Anita dances with the dead Droste (she had just been talking to "his" skeleton) is situated in a highly ambivalent temporality. Droste appears to her from out of the past and in a displaced location, the hospital.

[9]The resemblance stops there, however, since the film characters' movements are more fluid and less disciplined than those of the ballet. This scene in particular emphasizes the tropes of silent film melodrama, from which it borrows heavily, down to its repetitive piano accompaniment.

[10]Berber performs in front of the men, who are playing Arab wind instruments and drums, after a belly dancer quits the floor. While certainly sensuous, traditional belly dancing is never vulgar; only Westernized variations on it oblige performers to move their hips in explicitly sexual patterns or to remove parts of their costume.

[11]In Wood's exact words, the cult audience "relies on film elements [that] directly relate to the human body" (157).

[12]Freud, Fuss continues, would abridge this perception by. shifting homosexual "excess" from exterior signs to internal unconscious "deviations," which would, of course, be less immediately perceptible.

[13]Here I cannot resist mentioning a key way in which kitsch has been distinguished from camp. As a recent reader of Esquire put it, "Straight people don't have camp, they have kitsch" (September 1993, 26). Even Sontag's 1966 piece referred to the basic "lovelessness" of kitsch (292). And Brecht continues the attack: "There are

effective films that have an impact on people who see them as kitsch, but there are no effective films made by people who see them as kitsch" (in A. Kluge 236).

[14]See Flinn for a fuller theoretical discussion of this point.

[15]In addition to Edelman's 1991 article discussed below, important essays include those by Miller (1990) and Bersani (1989).

[16]For related, film-specific uses of the term, see Kuhn and Silverman (1992).

[17]A notable exception is Thomas Elsaesser (1981/82), whose theoretical work on Fassbinder has consistently been informed by German historical experience.

[18]For Stuart Marshall, the figure of five to fifteen thousand homosexual deaths compared with the millions of murdered Jews is determinant. "Even if we focus on concentration camps," he writes, "it is inaccurate to describe Nazi regulation of homosexuality as a holocaust" (93).

[19]A similar point is made in a recent book by Jay Winter that explores the languages of mourning and remembrance after World War I. Winter recounts the story of the concrete shell made to commemorate Verdun's mortal "Trench of the Bayonets." The shell was not situated over the trench that had collapsed and killed the soldiers, but nearby, on an "imaginary site of heroism" (102).

[20]Quoted from Schygulla's *Bilder aus Filmen von Rainer Werner Fassbinder* (in von Moltke 97). Even now, a stubborn 'match' exists between Schygulla's current struggles with obesity and Germany's perceived 'fat cat' status within the emerging European Community — a reading often bestowed upon the body of Chancellor Helmut Kohl as well.

[21]Von Moltke writes "while I would not want to generalize to the point of saying that camp itself is inevitably American, there is a strong sense in which camp always involves the signs of America — its consumer culture and its fabrication, its star system, its glamour, as well as its own camp culture" (101).

[22]Interesting in this regard is the English version of the film, in which the very name of Doris Day appears to precipitate Anita's 'fatal' collapse after she is told to calm down and behave more like her. The original, however, cites the name of Ingrid Meyser, a camp reference more significant, given von Moltke's belief in camp's need of American definition, for its being German.

[23]Unlike some, however, I remain unconvinced of camp's automatic subversiveness, just mindful of its lambent potential.

[24]See Brett 23, n. 9. Indeed, elsewhere Brett, clearly addressing only men, claims that "All musicians, we must remember, are faggots in the parlance of the male locker room" (18).

[25]Koestenbaum's work offers a good example of exploring a variety of crucial connections between homosexuality and music, without reducing the two into essentialized, two-dimensional mirrors of one another.

[26]See, in this regard, works by M. Russo, Moon/Sedgwick, and Flinn.

[27]The other critical fantasy scene in which the elder Anita, after having scolded a skeleton on display (that she calls Droste), dances with Droste also occurs in the hospital and is filmed in black and white (see note 8). Beyond this, only the opium-influenced faun sequence is shot in black and white and does not occur in the hospital.

[28]As examples Levin cites Walter Benjamin's notion of "revolutionary nihilism" and "positive barbarism" and Siegfried Kracauer's appeal to the "revelation of the negative" (in Kracauer 20).

[29]Negativity and absence fuel many discussions of music as well. Perhaps most interestingly for the purposes of this essay is Wayne Koestenbaum's work on "opera queens": "Opera has the power to warn you that you have wasted your life ... This rushing intimation of vacuity and loss ('I mourn all I haven't seen, all I haven't said!') isn't a solely gay or lesbian experience, but unsaid thoughts and unseen vistas particularly shaped gay and lesbian identities in the closeted years of the nineteenth and twentieth centuries, the dark ages, when the shadow world of the opera queen flourished" (1993, 44).

[30]Queer director Stuart Marshall remarks on the use of collage form in his film *Bright Eyes*, which, he states, "allowed me to collide different historical episodes in such a way that the viewer would be presented with the problem of assembling their mutual relations" (67). While this assemblage work might be better said to pose a "challenge" than a "problem," the basic activity Marshall describes certainly characterizes *Anita*'s cross-historical stories.

Out of Hollywood:
Monika Treut's *Virgin Machine* and Percy Adlon's *Bagdad Cafe*

Sunka Simon

WHEN *DIE JUNGFRAUENMASCHINE* (*Virgin Machine*) and *Bagdad Cafe* appeared in the late eighties, hardly anyone would have placed them in the same category, much less considered them in a comparative study. Although both films feature their protagonists' frustration with compulsive heterosexuality, the differences simply seemed to outweigh the similarities. For starters, Monika Treut was the excitingly new and daringly experimental woman director of *Bondage* (1983) and *Seduction: The Cruel Woman* (1983–84). Both films located her at the fringes of the not-so-new New German Cinema and in the midst of the heated pornography debate launched by Alice Schwarzer in *Emma*.[1] Percy Adlon, the German-American equivalent of John Waters, had already established a cult following for himself with *Zuckerbaby* (*Sugarbaby*, 1985) which, like *Bagdad Cafe*, also starred Marianne Sägebrecht. As a result, *Bagdad Cafe*, filmed in the desert of California, could rely on the generous funding of the German Federal Film Institute in Munich. And the soundtrack of the film, mainly due to Jolietta Steele's hauntingly seductive "Calling You," brought in plenty of postproduction dollars. Money was scarce for Treut's project, and the director, who began in video, chose grainy black and white for her film, whereas Percy Adlon continued to work with his trademark candy-color prism. These differences, labeling *Virgin Machine* as experimental camp and *Bagdad Cafe* as popular cult, contributed to the diverging distribution of the two films in Germany and the United States, but *Bagdad Cafe*'s greater access to audiences in both countries hinges on its choice of the English language, its U.S. setting, and its lower level of sexual, especially homosexual, explicitness.

Precisely for their telltale structural variance, I propose to read *Bagdad Cafe* and *Virgin Machine* as semiotically and thematically connected films. At the time of their release in Germany, both were unique in visualizing not only lesbian, but an all-out queer sexuality through women's bodies, and in linking queer sexuality and race. Treut and Adlon intelligently fused some of the medium's most burning questions into one: how to out-smart, out-rage, and out-race Hollywood. Asking these questions from the vantage points of Hamburg and Rosenheim — the protagonists' origins — via San Francisco and the fictitious Bagdad, California — their respective destinations — also meant dealing with projections of U.S. and German culture, and inquiring about what authority these multiply mediated im-ages have on definitions of sex, gender, race, and class.

Both films share a prevailing tone of uncanny comedy that transgresses sexual, gender, racial and cultural identities, genre boundaries, and narra-tological rules. On both the narrative and symbolic levels, dissatisfaction with normative heterosexuality provides the necessary jolt for character and plot development. Both texts question the ability of dominant cinema to stir up rather than to reinforce heterosexual, racial, and class preconcep-tions. The disenchantment with methods of inquiry and available re-sources provokes an unorthodox quest for a quasi-utopian otherness and alternative lifestyles, a quest that self-reflexively investigates the limits and potentials of independent, queer, multicultural love- and filmmaking.

While they are involved in the same countercinematic project, each film employs a different generic approach to subvert the dominant order. *Virgin Machine* encodes the quest as a research expedition on romantic love that leads the protagonist, Dorothee Müller (Ina Blum), through a cinematographic universe constructed by elements taken from Greek trag-edy, William Shakespeare, the Brothers Grimm, Heiner Müller, Alfred Hitch-cock, and *The Wizard of Oz*. *Bagdad Cafe* encrypts its search in rebound-ing magic. These generic codes superimposed on homosexual desire allude to what one might call the bedrock argument of queer humanities: biol-ogy, chance, or choice. My individual readings of these two defiant films shall explore whether their utopias of otherness result in a *queering of the canon* and, if so, what kinds of histories, politics, philosophies, and ech-oes Treut's libidinal journey and Adlon's magical tour rely on and foster.

With her choice of title for The *Virgin Machine*, Monika Treut alludes to one of postwar German theater's most illustrious playwright-directors, Heiner Müller, whose *Die Hamletmaschine* (*Hamlet Machine*) saw its first stage production in Saint-Denis, France, in 1979. Both pieces demonstrate the economies of discursive power, the (re)production modes of images and cultural archives concerning sexuality, gender, politics, and history.[2]

Treut's leading character, Dorothee Müller, is not only Heiner Müller's namesake but also the Ophelia turned Elektra of his "Europe of Woman," acts three and five in *Hamlet Machine*. All figures in Treut's text are disconnected from their personal histories and instead rely on textual lineage, cinematic and dream images, and generic memories to inhabit their sense of identity until they can supplant these with desires and histories of their own. As a child, Dorothee Müller refuses to push her father over a cliff on her mother's drug induced orders. Instead of obeying her mother's command to kill her father, she turns the tables on her mother and asks her to do it herself. No solidarity, no pre- or postoedipal bliss here. The heterosexual past of Dorothee's life, supposedly fueled by family values, writes itself instead as a course in Western *decivilization*, a course which had been taught by Heiner Müller's tortured and suicidal young adults, Hamlet and Ophelia.

Out of disgust and boredom in her relationship to her lover Heinz, she sleeps with her half-brother Bruno, an affair which brings to the surface a supposedly well-mastered, that is, well-repressed, oedipal conflict. Since Heinz lets us know that Dorothee has never mentioned a brother, their more-than-platonic erotic games can also be read as Dorothee's engagement with her masculine side, a lesbian affair with herself that combines Freud's theories of female narcissism with bi- and homosexuality. Neither Hamlet nor Dorothee can ever quite manage to direct their passion toward the other sex. Treut and Müller present heterosexuality as a daunting public demand that propels their rebellious protagonists toward incest and homosexuality. Dorothee's disillusionment with her lover Heinz, coupled with the incestuous longing for her brother Bruno, literally unearths a desire to find her mother, who has disappeared to America. Hamlet, on the other hand, dances with Horatio and exclaims that he would rather be a woman or a machine than Hamlet. Both Dorothee and Hamlet are constantly struggling with an elusive yet materially abusive father and 'authoring' system. Dorothee, Hamlet, and Ophelia struggle to become authors of their own lives without authorizing themselves and others to (re)issue social and sexual taboos. The title of the film performs this double task. It takes out a postmodern loan on Heiner Müller's revolutionary Shakespearean *bricolage*, as both texts deconstruct their 'authors' and 'authorities'. Whereas Müller, the author, has his photo ripped to shreds in act four of *Hamlet Machine*, Dorothee, the character in the film, tears the images of her past apart, throwing them into the turbulent waters underneath the Golden Gate bridge.

But Treut's feature also criticizes Heiner Müller for subsuming Ophelia's gender-specific trauma under the rubric of "Hamlet." Although Ophelia takes to the streets in "Europe of Woman," she can only do so by wearing her bloodied skin as her revolutionary dress: "I walk into the street dressed in my blood" (41). Her outcry at the end of the drama is muted as her entire body is wrapped in bandages. She sits tied to a wheelchair like a mummy-bride, a woman undergoing plastic surgery to recycle herself according to male fantasies. Despite her physical refusal to be a virgin mother to these fantasies – "I choke the world that I have born between my thighs" – to give birth to the world objectifying her, she is forced to wait for another prince to kiss her awake, for yet another cycle of the "virgin machine." Monika Treut removes Heiner Müller's bandages, his conflation of gender with sex that 'biologizes' Ophelia's very attempt at revolution, and lets her, as Dorothee-Ophelia-Elektra, analyze the discursive sociopolitical processes that force-feed her and make her grow to become yet another virgin text to inscribe, conquer, and discard.[3]

What started with a cynical autobiographical frame at the beginning of Treut's film – "I had this fantastic illusion" – ends with: "I am Dorothee Müller, a German girl in America." The film as queer Bildungsroman becomes a Bilderstürmer (iconoclast) by necessity. Unlike the essentialist vein of German-style feminism of the seventies which was propelled by a positivistic interpretation of Enlightenment values, such as the search for a wholesome female subject, Monika Treut's film is generated by, and in turn facilitates, a poststructuralist reading of identity, desire, and sexuality. As Chris Straayer argues, "[s]ubverting romantic tendencies with a 'coming-of-age' ploy, [Virgin Machine] rejects true love and refuses to accept homosexual isolation" (1996, 24). Yet it does more than that. The film Virgin Machine claims that a virgin is a contradiction in terms. Starting with Mary, a virgin is defined as a woman and a mother without having had to undergo penile penetration. The issue here is one of images, of control over the production and representation of myth, story, history, and biology. As Müller's Ophelia states in "The Europe of Woman": "With my bleeding hands I rip apart the photographs of the men whom I loved and who used me on the bed on the table on the chair on the floor" (40). Similarly, the actor of Müller's Hamlet has to shred the photograph of the author before proclaiming the title line of the drama: "I don't want to kill any longer ... I want to be a machine" (45). Whereas Müller's Hamlet desires to become a machine without pain or thought, Ophelia desires to transform her womb into a tomb, to "take back the world."

Like Ophelia, Dorothee wants to "take back the world that [she] ha[s] born" (46), the world that is born with her and through her body, her image and her metaphoricalness. She wants to take the world back into her, to deny and undo its existence, yet she also wants to take back what she was made to give up, what she has never possessed in the first place. Ophelia acting as Elektra is the physical parallel figure to Hamlet's and Orestes' cerebral virginity, a virginity the boys lose once they step into their father's shoes and commit both patricide and symbolic incest. The metaphor of "eingebildete Schwangerschaft" (imagined pregnancy) with which Müller ends his play points to the construction and dissemination of images over which Woman has had little or no control. The images are literally *eingebildet*, engraved, built-in, internalized, and therefore naturalized. The hymen becomes the silver screen. One can read and view the family album of Western civilization with and through her body.[4] While Hamlet can change and don even Ophelia's clothes, step out of character and into his father's shoes, Ophelia has to walk the street "dressed in her blood." It is Müller's Hamlet who wants to make his mother a virgin again so that her king can have a bloody wedding night (39–40), who wishes that he could sow up all women for a world without mothers (39). Even when the virgin Ophelia/Elektra seeks to suffocate the world between her thighs, between those *Schamlippen* (labia of the vulva) that are made to speak of shame instead of desire, she is pregnant with hate, contempt, and death: "Down with the joy of submission. Hatred, contempt, resistance, and death shall live" (46). Even in her most severe negation of motherhood she is still a mother; her *Muttermund* (cervix) betrays her.

Instead of drowning themselves, 'wasting' themselves, these postmodern Ophelias seek to drain the wastewater forced into and out of their bodies in the course of Western civilization. In order to stop killing themselves, Dorothee and Müller's Ophelia are reinvestigating Woman's supposed origin as a by-product and dumping ground of phallocentric Adamic humanity. For Dorothee and Ophelia, it is not enough to stop committing suicide, but necessary to disrupt its aesthetic effect on the male voyeur. Alluding to and writing against the appropriation of Ophelia's death by modernist poets (Charles Baudelaire, Bertolt Brecht, Rainer Maria Rilke), the river in *Hamlet Machine* spits her out as refuse by not accepting her body as refuse (40). The "deep sea" is portrayed as just another sphere ruled by bourgeois imagination. Having nowhere to turn, not even to death, Müller's Ophelia recycles herself in an attempt to reprogram her "female ending": she begins destroying the sites of her sexual abuse in her domestic prison: "the chair, the table, the bed" (40). In her own Hamburg attic apartment, Dorothee, on the other hand, has to answer to a snooping Heinz's accusatory question: "Who has been sleeping in your bed?" Although the possessive pronoun indicates that it is, indeed, Dorothee's bed, his demeanor and the allusion to "Snow White," the fairy tale, de facto negate her ability to possess anything.[5]

Heinz, endowed with the master key, enters Dorothee's place at will and disturbs her work, most importantly the printout of her thesis on romantic love.[6] Criticizing her writing as "stuff," he proceeds to tell her that she should write on sex and prostitution, a topic that would sell better, inferring that the audience of the film and the manuscript is predominately male and heterosexual. Heinz's prescription, together with the obscene telephone caller later who flaunts a sexual fixation on academic women who, in turn, are to him so "fresh," so "cheeky," make it clear that even academic discourse, supposedly neutral and objective, serves to titillate and cater to the "straight mind," that the position of Dorothee as an academic has not enabled her to escape prostituting herself for the heterosexual machine at all.[7] Parallel to the obscene phone call – an act of impotency to which Dorothee responds by leaving both caller and receiver dangling ("hängenläßt") – the sink and tub in her apartment consistently spit up brown water. At first she taps the faucet with a hammer, then she tries to unblock the tub with a plunger, seeking to repair the system to ease the flow of water down the pipes.

The recurring image of waste refusing to go down the 'innards' of the house, the domestic Woman Machine, combined with the sound of dripping water and extradiegetic eerily spherical music also trigger an allusion to the most eminent film of psychological horror: Alfred Hitchcock's Psycho (1960). Both Ophelia and Dorothee are co-opted by the symbolic language responsible for their muted existence. Instead of being attacked with a knife while washing her hair, Dorothee turns the table on Heinz, who is turned on by his viewing of the Texas Chainsaw Massacre (Tobe Hooper, 1974) – a film which he describes to Dorothee in great detail, mimicking the character Leatherface, while playing with a plastic toy figure featuring a retractable erect penis. This neurotic activity indicates that the world of

Heinz's dreams and fantasy consists of photographic images which link heterosexual romance, sex, and violence: a flashback of a roller coaster ride with Dorothee brings together *Terminator* (a poster of Arnold Schwarzenegger hangs on Heinz's office door) and *Texas Chainsaw Massacre*. Heinz verbally projects his Hollywood-driven sexual fantasies onto Dorothee in the hope of finding a sounding board for his fetishistic desire in her. Treut, however, defies the straight look that would allow this projection machinery to continue unthwarted; she represents his verbal ejaculation as a masturbation with the symbolic and ruptures the easy interpellation of spectator into Heinz's position by swiveling him into full frontal shot, legs spread, while Dorothee attacks him with a pair of scissors, cutting his nose hairs as he drops the toy. Reborn as a postmodern Delilah, she cuts his and the spectator's filmstrip, engages in an act of defiance against her position as projection screen, sounding board or fetish, and catapults herself into the extradiegetic production process, reframing the mise-en-scène of masturbation as a castration in process. The fetish drops out of the frame and, thus, out of the symbolic. Along with the toy, the fetish falls to the ground and literally materializes as it disappears. In this scene, Treut has us watching filmmaking and viewing as a counterproduction, as a defiance against dominant cinema and its heterosexual register of visual pleasure.

This countercinematic defiance continues to develop and fine-tune itself in the montage sequence that begins with Dorothee, amidst her rebelling sewage system, staring off screen into the passageways of a microscopic close-up of a vagina. The female folds give way to a dark staircase in which she has to say goodbye to Bruno, her half-brother, who is next seen embracing another man in a public urinal. The night before, Dorothee had listened to a transvestite singing the Marilyn Monroe song "I wanna be loved by you." We hear an ominous "die Liebe" as the images shift. A decapitated fly-like mannequin suspended on a clothes line wildly flaps its wings but is not going anywhere. (Previously, Dorothee had ripped the wings off a fly counting them off as if they were the petals of a daisy: "he loves me, he loves me not.") This shot leads over to a clothesline carousel on which business suits rotate. In the next shot, Heinz rotates above Dorothee in a similar fashion. A microscopic close-up of what seems to be an ejaculating penis or a breast excreting milk gives way to Heinz blowing his nose.[8] This daydream of Dorothee's "undirected subconscious" stands at a crucial intersection for her development.[9] The off-screen/on-screen mental journey juxtaposes gender assignments and gender roles to stimulate her own and the spectator's analytical facilities. Treut parodies Klugean contrastive montage techniques by catapulting the viewer into the missionary position, a position traditionally held by women during sexual intercourse. We find ourselves underneath Heinz only to have him blowing his nose. He climaxes twice, and his blowing his nose on the second occasion parodies how intercourse with him must feel for Dorothee. Neither romance nor heterosexual activities get Dorothee aroused. The 'turn-on' is reduced to the 'turnstile' of heterosexual desire, circling around itself yet denying its built-in auto- and homoeroticism.

The only tender moments in the montage are reserved for the homosexual couple and the portrayal of homosexuality, which here appears as relegated to the public toilet of the individual (Dorothee's) and collective (the audience's) subconscious. While the particular image of Bruno and a stranger exchanging caresses symbolizes Dorothee's repression of homosexuality, it also opens the door for the pluralism of sexualities so evident in the second part of the film. Having to let go of Bruno as a lover, but daring to follow him mentally to his rendezvous, also points Dorothee in a new direction – her own – which from now on features homosexual overtones more prominently. After this montage dream sequence, she refuses to repress her anxieties and desires any longer just to make her life seem more harmonious. She refuses to treat herself and be treated as one form of vaginal discharge or other. Instead of becoming the entry and exit points of all sociopolitical, physical, and artistic ejaculate like Müller's Ophelia, Dorothee decides that she has had enough and packs her suitcase.

The last sequences in Germany take place on the roof of a high apartment building close to the Reeperbahn (Hamburg's red light district) and the Dom (an amusement park). Dorothee can see the capitalistic extraction of sexual and social pleasures from above, and surely connect them. Her new bewitching vantage point above the city lets her dream of an alternative, of the golden coast of Amazons, of California. Sitting on the edge of the roof, she begins to write her own fantasy: Dorothee goes to America. An abrupt, unceremonious cut, not unlike an accelerated tornado swishing Dorothy away to Oz, places her and the viewer at the end of a long urban street in San Francisco. What many have taken as a construction of a lesbian utopia, the maternal fairy tale about a golden island where the black amazons reign, is destroyed – first by a visual representation of the actual sociopolitical realities on this 'island' (in a graffiti mural, an African-American woman holds up her child while she herself appears to be drowning in

the flood waves of the American flag) and soon after by the actual encounter between Dorothee and one of these 'women warriors' in the poorer quar-
ters of San Francisco. When Dorothee assumes a female solidarity between
herself — the white European feminist — and the African-American woman,
her European-style curiosity, impertinence, and physical proximity quickly
force the cultural, racial, and social barriers into the foreground: "Back off
and cool it," responds the African-American woman. With the abrupt cut
whirling Dorothee from Hamburg to San Francisco, *Virgin Machine* rewrites an American classic. Treut's Dorothee is obviously not in Kansas,
and the easily colonized munchkins from the *Wizard of Oz* have transformed their exuberant welcome dance into a cautious and caustic distancing act, not at all interested in providing Dorothee with a guided tour or a
map home.

On her audiovisual travels through San Francisco — via TV and chance
meetings — Dorothee is repeatedly reminded of the fact that her identity
and desires are constructs of her gender, race, and nationality. At first, she
watches under the guise of her journalistic role. The most personal encounter with her study on romantic love is provided by the sex performer Ramona, who becomes her lesbian date for one night. Dorothee had seen
Ramona's ad about curing people of the illusion of romantic love and left
a message on her answering machine. Although the very portrayal of the
technologically mediated arrangement goes against the grain of the conventional ideal of spontaneous love-at-first-sight, Dorothee is glued to the
screen as she has never been before.[10] That Dorothee falls in love with
Ramona's image simultaneously mocks and subverts heterosexual first contact. The image, in this case, advertises the fact of its duality and irreclaim-
able Lacanian split, that it does not give what it promises, that it promises
to withhold what it appears to give. If visual pleasure lies in the very act of
deceiving oneself, of suspending disbelief, then Treut's usage of the TV ad
in her film demonstrates two things. First, it shows that Dorothee saw Ramona but did not understand her message, that the I/eye dominates the
text/object in an ontological framework that is prescribed by a heterosexual
dichotomy and simply takes the lesbian text as an/other object. This is exactly what Dorothee attempts to do with her case study of "Ramona" and
her lesbian love affair. Second, it reveals that the film needs to contextualize
Ramona's image and the visual code in which it is caught up in order to
arrive at an alienation successful enough to provide a lasting effect for both
Dorothee and the spectator. After the most idealized romantic set-up, com-

plete with limousine, picture-taking, sight-seeing, and dancing, they make love. When Ramona wakes her up and demands money for her escort service and disillusion cure, Dorothee's reaction proves that Ramona's treatment has begun to work. She reels with laughter as she finds out that she has lured herself into falling in love again and that, along with her, the spectators' voyeuristic gaze has been lured into a hegemonic position despite its shift in focus onto a marginalized sexual act. Dorothee's laughter chafes the glossy eroticism of their lovemaking and reinvigorates her and the viewer's skepticism about the authenticity factor of gender and sex, and of sexual identity.[11]

Appropriately, Dorothee's coming-out journey does not end with her lesbian encounter. Her further development and sexual experimentations do not achieve plot-oriented closure. She dances a striptease at "women only" night at the club (a contradiction in terms, since the transvestite gender-bending going on inside its walls marks the biological check at the door as rather counterproductive). She writes in the midst of a group of women dancing, singing, and cooking at a friend's house, and she bikes through San Francisco, for the first time dressed in butch pants and cap instead of her 'feminine' skirts, to throw her family-album pictures into the swirling waters under the Golden Gate bridge. The choice of locale indicates that her yellow brick road neither leads home to her old heterosexual German self nor necessarily to a place confined to American lesbian culture, but is made up of continuous transgressions, crossings, and gender-bend(ing)s. Her journey from the rooftops of houses to Golden Gate Park retraces and inverts the steps of Jimmy Stewart in Hitchcock's *Vertigo.* What *Vertigo*'s Scottie experiences as castration anxiety, the fear of losing himself in the 'speculum of the other woman', in the vaginal abyss of doubleness, becomes, in Dorothee's case, a chance to experience otherness without negating one or the other, without denying or harmonizing the differences.

This last sequence of shots also points back to Dorothee's dream montage before leaving Germany. In hindsight, the vaginal entry into her subconscious can also be interpreted as a replay of Hitchcock's *Vertigo* within *Psycho,* deconstructing *Psycho* with *Vertigo.* Dorothee challenges extroverted male aggression, including that of her household appliances and supposed amenities, by pursuing the spiraling blood down the Freudian plumbing system. She exposes her *Psycho*killers, including the voyeuristic gaze as such, to the vertigo of gender-bending. In the process, she gives birth to herself as "Other"; she produces herself as a queer virgin. Treut repeatedly shows her eye in close-up profile. Dorothee thus remakes herself in her own image; she literally beholds her own oppression and recreation, enabling her to be participant, spectator, critic, and filmmaker of her own story. The extradiegetic spectator, who, according to Laura Mulvey, shares dominant cinema's *male* gaze, does not even get a glimpse of her gendered body, and cannot set *his* eyes on a feminine surface other than the vaginal texture that defies conventional pornographic appeal because the image goes too deep. *His* production of Dorothee as "virgin-mother-whore-saint" is disrupted, the "virgin machine" reprogrammed and dispossessed under *his* very eyes.

While Treut exposes the spectator to an optimistic postmodern vertigo of queer gender-bending, she does not, however, deny the historically specific problematics of race and class, or national identity. She ties any empirical search, any mythical quest for gender identity to a necessary reappraisal of intertextual and intersexual movements, to a parodic cinematic practice that discloses the constitutive acts of gender and identity formation.

Percy Adlon's *Bagdad Cafe* or *Out of Rosenheim, a Modern Fairy Tale*, as it was subtitled and distributed in Germany, begins with a slanted shot of Johann Münchgstettner relieving himself behind the gigantic contours of his American rental car, from which one hears the oompah of stereotypical Bavarian *Volksmusik*. The camera then cuts to Mrs. Jasmin Münchgstettner squatting somewhat further away for the same purpose. The camera angle mimics the sharp, almost expressionistically slanted shape of the rusting metallic shed behind them. The color scheme is predominantly yellowish brown in this first mise-en-scène. From the very first sequence of shots, the camera's point of view and the lighting effects mirror the skewed relations between the sexes and link gender differences to toilet training. The segregation of the sexes manifests itself at the edge of the public sphere, between civilization and the 'call of nature'. The last fortress of biological determinism, toilet training, has men standing up and women squatting. The camera's point of view combines the two activities by tilting the frame; it achieves a half-way point between standing and squatting. In the car, the music drowns out Jasmin's statement that Las Vegas, where they are headed, is still one hundred and fifty miles away. Her husband downs beer after beer, opens one in her face, upon which she slaps him. She sits at a picnic table, her face in her hands to recover while he, reprimanding her to get under way, throws the empty beer cans at her. Meanwhile, at the Bagdad Cafe, Brenda, the proprietor, throws empty oil cans at her partner Sal, who sits sulking in the truck and threatens to leave her for being "too bossy." Back in the desert, Jasmin eventually gets in the car, her husband backs up into the metal pile, she demonstratively rips out her airplane ticket stub and some travelers' checks. The second time he backs up into the pile, the trunk magically opens just in time for her to take out what she believes is her suitcase. The double initials JM (Jasmin and/or Johann?) glitter like mirrors. The close-up shimmies as if both camera personnel and Jasmin were suffering from heat stroke, hallucinating or seeing double. He drives off with spinning wheels, leaving her to venture down the highway shoulder, pulling the suitcase after her, only to stop periodically to wipe sweat off her face.

Two tourists, clad in folkloric garb, stick out of the desert landscape like aliens who have just landed with their space ship.[12] The old and the new world are out of synch, even though Mr. Münchgstettner attempts to surround himself with a safety bubble of national identity like a turtle carrying its shell. His protective cover, a sign of his confusion and insecurity, assumes a rather belligerent mask. He drives like a tank brigade under Rommel's command, punching the steering wheel in rhythm with his favorite marching tune. His newcomer behavior is sharply contrasted to Jasmin's. Whereas he immediately invades the personal space of the 'natives' — sitting right in their faces, demanding beer and then coffee, enticing them to try his snuff, thanking them by slapping them on the back like a pal — Jasmin hardly speaks and takes a seat by the door.

The 'conqueror' disappears only to leave behind his legacy: his clothes, his magic kit, and his woman. At the beginning of Jasmin's life at the motel-cafe, this legacy leads to racist and nationalistic projections on both sides. The outsider/insider dialectic threatens to erase the similarities of Brenda's and Jasmin's conditions that first connect them as mirror images of another: both wiping their faces simultaneously, mixing tears and sweat, defiance and despair. Compared to the invasion performed by her husband, Jasmin's first contact with the other woman, the woman as Other, harks back to an anthropologist's description of 'natives' mimicking the habits of foreigners. Who is mimicking whom in this scene is deliberately left ambiguous. When Brenda (who has a pencil wrapped around locks of her hair on her forehead like a bone) asks Jasmin how she wants to pay for her two nights, Jasmin stares into Brenda's eyes and envisions herself as the main dish of the day. Later, upon seeing Jasmin kissing and hugging her grandchild, Brenda counters with a sardonically appropriate: "He'll be ready for dinner." As a married woman probably without any income of her own, Jasmin's racist stereotypes meet her deepest anxieties of being a woman alone in a man's world without any means to survive. Jasmin's angst of having to pay with her body is abated when she finds out that Brenda is her own boss. Brenda, on the other hand, sees even more reason to be suspicious because Jasmin comes out of Rosenheim with neither car nor man but has the room full of men's clothes and dangerous looking toiletry instruments.

These 'weird' objects, that scare the mother, delight Brenda's daughter who uses them as props for costuming herself. She has no fear, and instead seeks to incorporate Jasmin's doubly inherited clothes (they are her husband's and stem from a fatherland not particularly known for good race relations) into her own world via the fashion craze of the eighties. In another one of the many mirror scenes in the film, Jasmin picks up her costume play and combines pajama bottoms with shirt to create the leggings look of the time. The daughter's unencumbered experimentation with the ominous Bavarian wardrobe entices Jasmin to mimic her; it also allows Jasmin to distance herself from their nationalist, patriarchal, and sexist symbolism and to reassemble them instead defiantly in postmodern fashion.

The film's insistence on the uncanniness of common household objects is further elaborated by the significance of the coffee thermos. Left by the road side just like Jasmin and highlighted by Adlon's use of a slow-motion strobe light shot, the thermos is more strongly associated with Jasmin than with her husband. She prefers coffee to beer and is seen strapping it into the car to avoid its tossing about during her husband's drunken driving maneuvers. At the beginning of the film, Jasmin is constantly ordering, cleaning, vacuuming, and strapping things down; in other words, she is finding a means to control her new surroundings in the only way she knows how, namely by being a housewife. Just as she straps the thermos down, she continues to strap herself in, to reign in her fantasies and desires. This changes with her appropriation of the magic set, with which she literally teaches herself new tricks. The thermos has a cheerful yellow color with the label "Out of Rosenheim," denoting throughout the whole film Jasmin's point of departure and origin as well as her displacement.[13] After Jasmin leaves for Germany due to Sheriff Arne's belayed intervention on Brenda's orders, the thermos becomes her legacy to Bagdad, a legacy she never claims although she has several opportunities to do so. Although the carafe holds strong German coffee at the beginning, its adaptability to the different cultural palate makes it an immediate success. It never leaves its prominent place at the center of the counter of the Bagdad Cafe; it vibrates with the moods and rhythms of the cafe's inhabitants, yet never falls or breaks. The thermos' central symbolic value lies in its ability to satisfy calls of basic human need and desire not regardless but in spite of racial, national, class or sexual differences. It reduces the husband's bad temper and, once tampered with hot water, quenches the coffee thirst of its first cafe customer, the set painter Rudy Cox, who later turns into Mr. Münchgstettner's potential replacement.

It is easy to dismiss the playful and heavy-handed symbolism of the thermos by reducing it to stand for a general void in Bagdad. Likewise, it is too easy to close one's interpretation with the statement that the cafe is not a cafe until Jasmin's avid personality fills a need in Brenda's life, that Jasmin makes and keeps things 'hot' in more ways than one. I would argue that this obvious heavy-handedness, this clumsy attempt at making this national icon stick in the audience's mind is more of a structural device than a plot-related motif: the inability to look to the side, to take a household item such as a coffee thermos seriously, also stands for a misdirected male gaze. One could compare Adlon's practice to Sigrid Weigel's notion of der schielende Blick (cross-eyed glance) that has become so important for German feminist literary criticism and for a definition of écriture feminine (Weigel 83–137). Adlon adopts this notion for his countercinema for the mainstream audience. He goes to a great effort with the strobe and the pink lighting effects to force the general spectator, whose viewing habits have been structured by dominant cinema and its prescription of the male gaze to look askew and to register something as mundane as a thermos on the back of a pickup truck. Adlon's practice assists an audience trained to exclude marginal information, to zero in on the focal plane of the shot, and to develop a 'cross-eyed' glance. That Jasmin reacts as perturbed as she does to Sal's offer of a ride, besides revealing her racial prejudices, might well have to do with the fact that she has seen the thermos and connected its reemergence with her husband's possible reappearance. Her shocked reaction to Sal's offer also indicates her fear of either being 'stolen' like the thermos or of being taken for 'just another ride down patriarchy lane'. After all, Rudy Cox's old trigger-happy rifle accompanies the thermos on the bed of the pickup truck.[14]

As Sal, thermos in hand, walks into the cafe, Mr. Münchgstettner drives toward him like a madman, even forcing him to jump aside. Neither looking at Sal nor acknowledging his presence in any way, the German man stomps past him and in through the entrance. While Jasmin immediately recognizes the thermos upon entering the cafe earlier on, it is conspicuous that her husband does not, although he sits right next to it when Sal attempts to find the correct approach to open sesame, to produce the cup of coffee he demands. Although Sal is the manager, the German refuses to relate to him, unwilling and culturally unable to concede to his racist bias. Sal, on the other hand, is eager to serve him simply because Münchgstettner is a customer in his deserted cafe. Unable to deviate from their predetermined social scripts, the two men cross paths but never meet. The continuation of the story lies in the ignorance and xenophobia of the cinematic gaze. Had they actually talked, Jasmin would likely be back in Rosenheim with her husband. Therefore, the film's story is actually an investigation of the traditional relations of looking inherited "out of Hollywood," those made by, as well as ousted by, Hollywood. In order for the spectator not to reenact Mr. Münchgstettner's blind spot, Sal never disappears from the diegetic narrative. Like the sign in the Hollywood hills, which has come to represent Hollywood's domination over the world of international cinema, Sal remains on a nearby desert hill and mediates his binocular-aided view to the spectator at large. Sal's point of view treats the white Western European omniscient and voyeuristic heterosexual male gaze with irony, but also collapses the racial/sexual components of the relations of looking. The bifocal binoculars actually suture the individual images into one and the same. While in and through his look, the very medium of cinema is self-reflexively forced to consider its shortcomings, its constructions of racial and sexual stereotypes, Sal's narrative stance is empowered through its proximity to the spectators. The audience is coaxed into his shoes, moaning "Oh, Brenda" in shock or amazement, unable to draw their eyes away from Brenda, who, as the traditionally invisible or typecast black woman, retains the locus of the film despite Jasmin's impressive presence. At the same time, Adlon's framing device, which parallels yet also intersects Rudy Cox's painting sessions with Jasmin, allows a black man to look at a white woman (Gaines 208).[15] With the help of Sal's periodic commentary from the balcony, the spectator's position is ridiculed in its frustrated attempt to suture the cuts or to engage with the film as if it were real life. When Sal returns to the cafe during the last performance, he passes as one of the guys, just another spectator. Brenda does not even acknowledge his presence, and he soon fades into the background as the action on stage absorbs the camera's attention.

Instead of maintaining one focus like Sal's suturing look that locks the gaze into its heterosexual dichotomy, Jasmin and Brenda are and see double. Through them, the audience is forced to maintain two focal points. On the highway, turning away from the camera, Jasmin beholds two suns in the sky, one on either side of her, her feather-capped hat blowing in the breeze like a compass needle. Later, she will refer to this sight as "the lights in the sky" and "my vision." The "sign" reappears as Rudy Cox's signature on his paintings, one of which hangs in her motel room. It is no surprise, finally, that with her playful exposure of her second breast to his artistic gaze later in the film, the "Jasmin" series is finished. In order for the "vision" not to disappear into mainstream religious mysticism, Jasmin practices magic, employing the praying hands statue as a bookrest for her self-instructional sessions. Before, she had covered it up with her hat. One could argue with Luce Irigaray, that Jasmin "bastardize[s] the divine projects by making them obvious, making them apparent in their very conception" (*Speculum* 355). As Sal Junior performs Bach for her with a smile like Sammy Davis Jr., Jasmin's avisual spectatorship contrasts with Rudy Cox's audibly disturbing attempt to frame her visually. He wishes to preserve her magical saint-like illumination through a tinted window pane for his paintings. When he selects a painting of her for the bar that shows her in her 'native costume', her Bavarian uniform, his romanticization converts her into an icon and his visualization into a 'tinseltown' iconography of the male gaze: Woman appears as Madonna or exotic sexual object. Jasmin becomes the projection screen for the desires stirring in Cox and the inhabitants of the cafe. For them, her magic tricks — performed with such gaiety and indulgence of self-discovery — embody both the loss and regaining of paradisical magic in the ghost town Bagdad. While the Australian student's boomerang spins a magic circle around the giggling pair of Jasmin and Brenda's daughter during several sundowns, the boomerang stops returning after Jasmin leaves. It hits the water tower and falls to the ground. In Jasmin, Hollywood, Las Vegas, and Bavaria blend in a mischievous childlike way, with which Adlon, no doubt, infers that Hollywood needs to be reinvented, that experimental multinational coproductions have a creative momentum that puts the tired, canned Hollywood goods to shame.

Where specifically does Adlon locate this momentum? Even though Jasmin finally exposes her breasts in the last sitting with Rudy, she produces a rose to cover one of her nipples when he is painting her. She does not let him paint his fantasies of her vision; her two nipples do not bare the meaning of the two lights for her as they might for Rudy Cox. There is always a surplus of female sexuality, reproducing itself in the look, something more no matter how many times he paints her and how completely she strips. The playful music underscores that the experiment in undressing has been more of a discovery of herself, her body, and its sexuality than the discovery of their mutual attraction. The same vaudevillian music is later used for the magic wand dancing trick performed by Brenda and Jasmin in masculine garb. The music alienates the sensual scenes from any heterosexual romantic potential and turns them into slapstick performances. The most romantic scene in the film, initiated by the "Calling You" soundtrack, is reserved for Jasmin's return and her reunion with Brenda as friend and potential lover.

Together with the genre-specific reunion, the music nudges even the more resistant viewers toward reading Brenda and Jasmin's friendship as lesbian attraction. Why then does the film end with a marriage proposal? Was Adlon too concerned about mainstream middle American audiences to make the film's investment in queer sexualities more obvious? Did he play it safe? It is true that Jasmin's cross-dressing is less symptomatic of a gender-bending à la Monika Treut than it is symptomatic for a whole generation of German women daring to cross the dress and gender restrictions that their local communities, church, and public morals demand and foster. Jasmin's limitation to her husband's wardrobe allows her to discover that she can usurp its symbolic power without having to immediately convert to a "He-woman" or a "She-Butch" (Straayer 1996, 98) unless she chooses to do so. Her sexuality literally blossoms under the dual suns, under Brenda's and Rudy's gazes. While her outfits become more and more gregarious toward the end of her first stay at Bagdad, it is significant that she returns in a white loose fitting summer dress. Her return as a 'bride' signifies yet another gender reassignment, and this time one of choice.

The embrace between the two women is followed by the first shot of a relaxed and carefree Brenda outside of the cafe walls — she is talking and laughing with Jasmin in the desert grass — and soon gives way to the final performance at the Bagdad Gas and Oil Cafe turned Las Vegas vaudeville club. Brenda is dressed up for the first time, gleaming with joy and pride as she presents her magically blooming flowers. It is not by coincidence that Jasmin and Brenda, dressed in matching tuxedos, are wielding walking sticks, making them dance to their tune in one of their next acts. In compliance with the endeavor of the entire film, their sexual relationship has to be staged rather than voyeuristically screened. Just like the invisible threads allowing the two women to manipulate the phallus (the only signifier that always refers to but, by its own command, cannot collide with its own signified), their lesbianism does not reside in specific sexual activities or a politically validated lesbian identity, but in the power to transform the representational order of the "straight mind" (Straayer 1996, 79–80 and Wittig 1992). Rather than penetrating the film text with the lesbian equivalent of a primal scene, Adlon chooses to maintain a specular bisexual structure.

Although perhaps motivated by and contributing to a rendering of 'queerness' as metaphor, Bagdad Cafe proposes in 1988 that, in order to out Hollywood and to change viewing habits, queer desire needs to find a way to represent the discursive net that makes it otherwise apparently unrepresentable. As I have argued, successful queer filmmaking depends on the structural and narrative manipulation of the focal plane. Brenda and Jasmin's queer relationship falls outside of the double focus, the two eyes or two poles of hetero- and homo-sexuality. The dangers of "too much harmony," that cause Tattoo-Debbie to leave the newly formed community of Bagdad, are just as real as those of the straight look. All of Jasmin's cautious and inquisitive "yesses" to Rudy Cox's marriage proposal result in the requirement and demand for further dialogue and in an insistence on maintaining her multidirectional desire: "I'll talk it over with Brenda." Cox phrases his desire for Jasmin in the form of a heterosexual contract. With Jasmin's answer, the contract becomes publicly renegotiable. Adlon thus unmasks the legal constraints of heterosexuality and its sexual economics. With this precarious ending and the mixed audience, including the tattoo-crazed truckers and the returning Sal, participating and cheering for the female family performance on stage, Adlon creates new relations of looking. He configures a broad diegetic and extradiegetic audience for the defying sight and site of queer sexuality and identity. Bagdad Cafe, as the rest stop of heterosexual desires, initiates a public sphere for queering the cinematic canon.

Notes

[1]The sneak preview of *Virgin Machine* at the National Film Theater in London was sold out in 1988 (see Julia Knight 18, 170, and n. 54).

[2]Katrin Sieg's chapter on the playwright Elfriede Jelinek alerted me to another possible intertextual reference, a medical study of reproductive technologies called "MotherMachine," published in 1986 (162).

[3]In response to Michel Foucault's investigation of the discursive relationship between "sex" and "technology," Teresa de Lauretis (1987) coined the phrase "technologies of gender" insisting on the (re)production of the sex-gender system by dominant ideologies.

[4]Heiner Müller called the first act of *Hamlet Machine*: "Familienalbum" (family album).

[5]Treut demythologizes German-American fairy tales, and specifically their Hollywood equivalent, and takes them to task as the catalyst for childishly feminine heterosexual fantasies. Instead, she tailors them to conscious female desire in a multicultural and postmodern world: Heinz asks: "Wer hat in deinem Bettchen geschlafen?" (*Schneewittchen/Snow White*), Dorothee falls up the stairs to the doctor's office and loses a shoe (*Aschenputtel/Cinderella*), she always dresses like a girl and is side-tracked from her quest by Ramona and Susie Sexpert (*Rotkäppchen/Little Red Ridinghood*), her name is Dorothy and, in her search for the absent mother, she attempts to return home, that is, to herself, via the "golden island" (*Wizard of Oz*).

[6]The following close reading of the montage sequence draws from a paper I presented at the Kentucky Foreign Language Conference in April 1995, "De-Manning the Moon: Feminist Fantasy and Ideology from Else Lasker-Schüler to Monika Treut."

[7]Monique Wittig coins this phrase in her essay "The Straight Mind," in which she defines its "totalizing interpretation of history, social reality, culture, language" as "that which resists examination, a relationship excluded from the social in the analysis ... which is the heterosexual relationship. I will call it the obligatory social relationship between 'man' and 'woman'" (27).

[8]According to Chris Straayer's telephone conversation with Monika Treut, she actually used the microscopic detail of a coronary aneurysm for this shot (Straayer 38, and n. 33, 295).

[9]Elaborating on her choice of title in an interview with Renfreu Neff, quoted by Chris Straayer, Monika Treut pointed to Freud's thesis, that "the undirected subconscious works like a machine" (in Straayer 293, n. 12).

[10]In Hamburg, her TV and radio sets were on, yet not attended to as in this case.

[11]Here, Judith Butler's investigation of parody in *Gender Trouble* proves helpful: "What, then, enables the exposure of the rift between the phantasmatic and the real

whereby the real admits itself as phantasmatic? Does this offer the possibility for a repetition that is not fully constrained by the injunction to reconsolidate naturalized identities? Just as bodily surfaces are enacted *as* the natural, so these surfaces can become the site of a dissonant and denaturalized performance that reveals the performative status of the natural itself ... And yet this failure to become 'real' and to embody 'the natural' is, I would argue, a constitutive failure of all gender enactments for the very reason that these ontological locales are fundamentally uninhabitable. Hence, there is a subversive laughter in the pastiche-effect of parodic practices in which the original, the authentic, and the real are themselves constituted as effects" (146).

[12]I owe this observation to Dana Lemelin, in particular, but would like to take this opportunity to thank all the members of my 1996 Swarthmore German Cinema class for their enriching discussion of *Bagdad Cafe*.

[13]"Rosenheim" denotes that her relationship to her home is a prickly affair. Bavaria did not place her in a bed of roses like Sleeping Beauty (*Dornröschen*), although, from the American perspective, Rosenheim appears to have been forgotten by time. In an inversion of the fairy tale, Jasmin, as Sleeping Beauty, wakes up Brenda and herself by infusing the ghosttown Bagdad with her magic.

[14]Her reaction here is echoed by her cautious wait-and-hear stance in the last scene when Rudy Cox proposes to her. She woke up and 'smelled the flowers', and they are not necessarily 'all a girl wants or needs'.

[15]For an in-depth consideration of this important issue see Gaines 197–214.

Gender, Sex, and Sexuality: The Use of Music as a Collateral Marketing Device in *Maybe... Maybe Not*

Ute Lischke-McNab

IN 1987, WHEN RALF KÖNIG PUBLISHED the gay comic book *Der bewegte Mann*, followed by *Pretty Baby: Der bewegte Mann 2* in 1988, no-one would have expected the sensational success of Sönke Wortmann's film *Der bewegte Mann* (*Maybe... Maybe Not*) when it was released in Germany in 1994. Accompanying the release of the film was a new edition of the comic book in 1995 as *Das Buch zum Film* along with a large distribution of the video version of the film. By far the most popular item released with the film was the compact disc soundtrack, which brought almost instantaneous success to the Palast Orchester. Along with other paraphernalia such as T-shirts and posters, the release of this film was deliberately coordinated to be associated with these collateral tie-ins as a marketing device that would make money for all concerned, including the producers, director, and orchestra. This collateral marketing technique of movie tie-ins is a recent Hollywood technique that the current generation of German filmmakers has adopted exceedingly well.[1]

Maybe... Maybe Not is a unique film that incorporates three phenomena that are new to German cinema. The film is a comedy with immense domestic audience appeal that drew several millions of viewers to the cinema and made a very large profit. The film also uses, as part of the comedy technique and within its narrative structure, gay men who cross-dress, thereby opening up a level of public discussion on gay issues not seen since the post-1933 taboo against homosexuality in German films that lasted well into the 1980s. Lastly, popular songs and music of the 1920s and 1930s — enjoying a contemporary revival in Germany — are incorporated into the narrative structure of the film.

Beginning in 1992 with the runaway success of Sönke Wortmann's *Kleine Haie* (*Small Sharks*), followed by Katja von Garnier's unprecedented hit *Abgeschminkt!* (*Making Up!*, released in 1993) and by *Maybe... Maybe*

Not in 1994, the German film industry began to boom.[2] After the death of Rainer Werner Fassbinder in 1982, New German Cinema began to decline, and a few years later German film was pronounced dead by the critics. Producing only an endless staple of pornography and *Heimatfilme*, movies concerned with conveying a sense of national identity, Germans did not exactly rush to the movie theater; and when they did, they almost exclusively watched Hollywood imports. But the early 1990s produced a whole new generation of film school graduates who had developed a totally different concept toward film production. Like others of his generation, Wortmann wanted to prove that Hollywood was not the only place where entertaining and fast-paced films could be made. For example, in an interview with Stephen Kinzer in the *New York Times*, he confesses that: "When I was at film school in Munich, the great hero was Tarkovsky. Today it's Spielberg" (31). As did others, Wortmann mantled himself to a distinctive construct of filmmaking — cinema as a mass medium. This was criticized by some and despised by others.[3] Yet it improved itself through the embrace of the public.

The rise to prominence of the comedy in the 1990s represents a significant shift in German film production. To be sure, there have been comedies in German cinema from the Weimar Republic on, even in the Third Reich and down to the 1950s, which appealed to German audiences. However, New German Cinema generally lacked the capacity for comedy. Typically of long duration, and critically demanding of the audience, films by Rainer Werner Fassbinder, Ulrike Ottinger, and Doris Dörrie had no broad appeal for German audiences. Doris Dörrie's 1985 film *Männer* (*Men*) is one of the few exceptions. There is no question, then, that the New German Comedy (*Neue deutsche Komödie*) has drawn Germans back into the cinema to see productions by their compatriots.[4] The new comedies have also revitalized the domestic film industry. *Maybe... Maybe Not*, for example, grossed over forty million dollars in its first ten months, making it, along with von Garnier's *Making Up!* and Dörrie's *Keiner liebt mich* (*Nobody Loves Me*) one of the most successful German films since the early 1980s.[5] It is thus quite obvious that the appeal of *Maybe... Maybe Not* to German audiences is exceptional and needs to be studied within a broader cultural and historical context.

Sönke Wortmann was attune to this new concept of collateral marketing that was to win the domestic audience back from Hollywood imports. His films appeal to the young and hip generation of thirtysomethings through their concession to well-researched market demands and analysis. They seem to engage the young audience, moreover, in a critique of conventional attitudes about gender and sexuality, both homo and hetero, and their relationship to film. Consequently the new films are not merely pure comedy, but also – as von Garnier coined it in an interview with the newspaper *Berliner Morgenpost* in 1993 – *Samödie*, a combination of *Satire* and *Komödie* (comedy). Emulating traditional Hollywood-style narratives, these directors have also cultivated their own cadre of hip and sexy German stars on the make (Katja Riemann, Til Schweiger, Uwe Ochsenknecht, Nina Kronjäger). These actors have brought glamour to the German film industry for the first time since the 1920s and have added to the effect of commercialization.

The strategy of collateral marketing or movie tie-ins used with *Maybe... Maybe Not* is a Hollywood technique that has been developed over the last ten years to suit the German audience. The marketing strategy includes the packaging of popular and well-known stars with music that appeals to the teen romance/music generation with a blend of nostalgia which appeals to the older audience segments, and becomes a "Dionysian celebration of middle-class values" (Wyatt 1-3). Each element of the package must appeal to both young and old. The merchandising, tie-in comic book, video, and CD serve that purpose and relate strongly to the nostalgia for the 1920s and early 1930s. In addition, the video advertised the fact that the film had had over six million viewers at the cinema.

Maybe... Maybe Not was released unusually quickly on video on October 5, 1995, and was advertised as the film adaptation of the comic book. The release was timed to take advantage of Christmas sales and quickly became the most popular title both as a rental and as a sales item in video stores. The Ralf König comic book *Der bewegte Mann* which had originally been published by Rowohlt in 1987, reappeared in 1994 in combination with *Pretty Baby* as *Das Buch zum Film*. The CD appeared in 1994 as *Der Soundtrack zum Film*.[6] The film can also be located on the Internet on the Home Movie Line, as can Das Palast Orchester, the orchestra founded in 1987 with Max Raabe as its lead singer.[7] Wortmann, who has "shown German audiences that Hollywood is not the only place where snappy and entertaining films are made" (Kinzer 31), argues that his film has a message. He concedes that he wanted:

to say something about people, not necessarily about male-female relationships — although that's where people often show themselves most clearly ... Between the lines, I want to say something general. At the end of *Maybe... Maybe Not* the hetero and the gay guy go out drinking together. That's the message of the film. People close themselves off to what they don't know. I wanted to show the similarities between two worlds. (Kinzer 31)

In order to portray these *two* worlds, Wortmann takes us back to the swinging era of the Weimar Republic where the gay and lesbian worlds provided a backdrop for a way of life that was destroyed by the Third Reich.

The Berlin of the Weimar Republic was an exhilarating city of sex, prostitution, violence, and crime. In the 1920s, Berlin went beyond a mere metropolis to a modern myth, one reproduced, for example, by George Grosz in his numerous drawings, watercolors, and prints. This myth was also created by dramatist and poet Bertolt Brecht, by film directors Fritz Lang and Josef von Sternberg, by the English writer Christopher Isherwood, the actress and singer Marlene Dietrich, and the numerous artists of the era who vividly portrayed and epitomized this metropolitan jungle. Within the wild abandon of Berlin night life, sex — whether hetero, gay or lesbian — became part of the scene and attested to a collapse of bourgeois morality. When compared to the austerity of Nazism and the conservatism of the 1950s and 1960s, these lewd antics — so vividly reproduced in the comic book, film and music of *Maybe... Maybe Not* — are a direct throwback to the Weimar Republic. The film is an attempt to look behind the veneer of respectability and conformity in order to expose the lascivious passions that are part of the Berlin myth. Driven by the songs such as *Ja und nein* (*Yes and no*), *Schöner Gigolo* (*Pretty gigolo*), *Mein Gorilla* (*My gorilla*), *Was bin ich ohne Dich* (*What am I without you*), and *Fräulein, Pardon* (*Pardon, Miss*), the film exposes the "tierischen Triebe" ("animalistic drives," König 1988, 80) of contemporary German society, which are reflected, for example, by Elke's and Axel's consumption of "Bull Power," a sexual stimulant. This sexual promiscuity is linked to the more liberal era of the Weimar period which had been suppressed by the Nazis' assumption to power and the bestial acts committed by the administrators of the Third Reich not only upon Jews, but upon gays and lesbians. The Nazis had prohibited sexual promiscuity and perversion including the songs that celebrated it.[8]

Bestial violence and sex is the target of satire within the film in that it becomes an attempt to unmask the hypocrisy of society, tearing off masks to show the "animal" within. Whereas the most aggressive erotic fantasies often remain hidden, this was not the case in Weimar Berlin where they came very much to the surface and, in 1990s Germany, they are once again being discussed particularly via the medium of film. In the film, the audience is permitted to become a participant, not just an observer. The opening scene introduced by the Palast Orchester invites the audience to participate in a cabaret-like experience, it invites them to a *show*. While the guests at the Gloria Palast are dancing the fox-trot, the audience is taken into the washroom where they become the voyeurs – a sex act is taking place.

Since the end of the Third Reich, Germans have not participated in such large numbers to challenge these sexual taboos. Nazi society never permitted such liberties, finding them too threatening for their ordered society. Blatant consumerism, especially of sexual commodities, was discouraged. The only consumerism in the Third Reich was that of the melodramatic and propaganda films churned out by the UFA[9] dream machine, or "Ministry of Illusion" as Eric Rentschler has coined succinctly, aimed at keeping the masses mesmerized. For instance, Goebbels's seductive cinema already begins to exemplify the complex social role played by the mass media at the end of the twentieth century.[10] But, as Jean Baudrillard argues in *La Société de consummation*, the impact of mass media and informational systems ensured that the key dynamics of capitalism shifted from production to consumption and, as suggested by Antonio Gramsci, culture has now become a site of hegemony.[11] More and more, consumerism invokes society to participate in the complex systems of mass media.

The setting of the film in the commercial districts of a large city – in this instance Cologne, which has an open and sizable gay and lesbian population, with an active and commercially vibrant 'scene' (and where Ralf König makes his home) – reflects an environment where 'everything is for sale'. When Norbert takes a drive through the city streets, the headlights of his car highlight the advertising reflected by the neon signs of the shops. It is like grazing through a North American mall where the anonymous nature of life leads one to inquire about what is really happening *behind* the masks. Much like the setting from Woody Allen's *Scenes from a Mall* (1991), the profusion of advertising and images of goods for sale makes cities into huge twenty-four hour markets of pleasure where one seeks hidden desires and release of the beast within. Furthermore, Cologne

— as the carnival capital of Germany — adds to the flavor of the film of a large eroticized setting where 'anything goes' — a point also central to Doris Dörrie's *Nobody loves me*, which is also set in Cologne.[12] Mikhail Bakhtin, for example, coined the term *carnivalesque* to refer to a kind of activity that often takes place in the carnivals of popular culture where traditional hierarchies and values are overturned so as to allow for alternative voices to be heard (92). This is, in effect, a resistance to authority and could allow cultural and political change to occur. The use of camp and cross-dressing, particularly in the disco, reflects similar carnivalesque activities, especially during the performance of the song *My Gorilla*. Gender barriers are crossed and an outlet for ongoing social repression has been established. The erotic has also been politicized. Within the atmosphere of the disco, events are focused on the body, including physical realities such as eating, drinking, and sex. While these events become ritualized in themselves, their mimetic function remains open. What is clear, however, is that a transgression of the norm occurs and a drive toward liberation is in progress.

The music of *Maybe... Maybe Not*, the primary marketing tool used by Wortmann to achieve broad audience appeal, seeks to recapture the aura of the Weimar period, with its wide array of cabarets and variétés and *Tanzpaläste* (dance halls) where both performers and the audience achieved a similar sense of liberation from authority through the lyrics of the songs. The most important in this respect is the Palast Orchester, composed of thirteen musicians, which came into existence in June of 1987 precisely to invoke the nostalgia of the 1920s and early 1930s. The orchestra's success was based on two features. First, the original idea of playing the rhythmic fox-trot and tango. This had great appeal to an audience either enjoying a newly rediscovered music or reliving an unrestrained, emancipated past. Second, the talent of the musicians and the rhyming verses and *Trivial-Poesie* (light verse) of the lyrics, with their irony and double entendre, have an inescapable charm unto themselves. The music does capture the aura of the *Tanzdielen* (dance halls) of Berlin in the 1920s and 1930s, adding a hint of the varietés and the UFA studio hits, such as the song *Falling in Love again* from Josef von Sternberg's film *The Blue Angel* sung by Marlene Dietrich.

Maybe... Maybe Not, in which the music evokes that grand era, is also a sex farce with mix-ups reminiscent of Edouard Molinaro's *La Cage aux folles* (1978). It is striking that Wortmann chose a gay-themed tale against the musical backdrop of the 1920s for this is when Germany attained its peak in the production of aesthetically unequaled gay and lesbian films.[13] Wortmann's film also highlights the horror of the Third Reich, in which homosexuals were persecuted along with the Jews. This conjunction of smoothly and aesthetically restored and original music within the visual realm of a gay narrative is one of the highlights of the film. Wortmann thus, by means of satire and music, instantly evocative of another time, cleverly and subtly makes use of a modern high-jinx narrative to awaken the collective conscience of the contemporary German audience to one specific part of the German past, namely, the long silence concerning the atrocities committed upon gays and lesbians during the Third Reich. For example, the song *Pretty Gigolo* (1929), which is played nondiegetically while Norbert, Axel, and Walter are on their way to the disco, is ironic since it clearly establishes the redundancy of militarism.

Wortmann's film resurrects the *Swingmusik* of that era that contains songs with a *message*. Wolffram Knud has documented the revival of the music from this period:

> Old dance music is booming. When you turn on the radio in the evenings, when the talk shows have gone off air and only radio lovers are tuned in, you can hear the swinging vinyls [records] from the twenties, thirties and forties, and countless orchestras with names such as Dajos Béla, Oskar Joost or Kurt Widmann. At collector auctions, vinyls bring in dizzyingly high bids and at vinyl parties one is invited to dance to their sound. It is unimaginable that this music, unknown to most people, was once the music that was consumed, the music that was played in Berlin in hundreds of night clubs evening after evening for dancing and entertainment. That was fifty or sixty years ago ... In the early 1920s, dance halls had sprung up like mushrooms in Berlin, they surpassed each other with their ostentatiousness and diverse attractions and all brought in large crowds. The dance halls then survived in spite of, or perhaps because of political and economic catastrophes — people were crazy about dancing and diversity, entertainment and music. (7)

The film opens with a high establishing shot of the dance floor of the Gloria, reminiscent of the Gloriapalast in Weimar Berlin. As in any *Tanzpalast* of that epoch, couples are doing the fox-trot to the tune of *Ja und nein* (*Yes and no*), a 1939 Franz Grothe and Willy Dehmel song. Both the music and the dance hall recreated in Wortmann's film played an important social role in the Weimar Republic. These establishments were known to be frequented by the "underground of Berlin" (Knud 12) and were places with a "disreputable reputation" (Knud 15). The music that was played was, on the whole, instrumental. The reason for this was that in order to have a singer, a special license, or *Singspielkonzession*, was needed. The style of singing that was developed was consequently limited to the repetition of a refrain or two by the conductor approaching the microphone occasionally for special effect. In this way, the singing was secondary to the sound of the band (Knud 19). This effect is very noticeable in the film and on the CD of *Maybe... Maybe Not* in that most of the track is instrumental and when the songs do occur, they immediately attract the listeners' attention through the catchy refrains.

Many of the *Tanzlokale* in Berlin were places frequented by gays. In 1933, in some instances earlier, they were closed by the police, for example the famous *Eldorado*, "which was already closed in 1932 in connection with stepped up police sanctions against gay meeting places" (Knud 28).[14] There is no subtle irony in playing the "Comedia [Homo]sexualis" within the milieu of dance halls and discos.[15] By opening the film at the elaborate *Gloria* with the song *Yes and No* and continuing with the party in the relaxed atmosphere of the disco where the contemporary song *TAPP KNALL TAPP TAPP* is played, Wortmann has bridged the two eras from the 1930s to the 1990s, but reveals to the audience that the same cultural practices and rituals continue to exist. In his parody of accepted beliefs and practices, Wortmann makes it clear that his characters are striving toward a liberation from social constraints. This is an in-your-face coming-out film (namely Axel's) that relives the era of the more liberated days of the Weimar Republic and opens all topics of sexuality for discussion in contemporary Germany. The musical experience within the film is very much entertainment, yet can stand alone when listened to by itself, echoing the gay antics of the film perhaps, but wallowing in the silence between the two periods cleverly conjoined by Wortmann.

The film operates diegetically in such a way that the narrative includes the performance of several musical compositions which are played for audiences within the film. The opening suggests sexual ambiguity with the song *Yes and No*, and the song *My Gorilla* later played at the disco suggests the problems confronted by a man involved in both a gay and heterosexual affair, obviously alluding to Axel's dilemma. In this manner Wortmann has artistically achieved a fusion of both cinematic and real worlds. Linking the dance hall and cabaret to the contemporary party at the disco enables complicity too. As Edward Said has remarked:

> Clearly ... musical performance, with its narcissistic, self-referential, and ... self-consultive qualities, is the central and most socially stressed musical experience in modern Western society, but it is both a private musical experience for performer and listener, and a public experience too. The two experiences are interdependent and overlap with each other. But how can one understand the connection between the two, and, more interestingly, how does one interpret it? Are there particularly useful ways of doing so in order that the enabling conditions of performance and their connection with the sociocultural sphere can be seen as a coherent part of the whole experience? (1991, 12)

Performance thereby becomes, as Frith remarks, "an experience (or set of experiences) of sociability" (v), a social process. For example, Axel, the hetero, begins his *performance* in the public/private place of the toilet stall – ironically enough, usually more associated with illicit gay sex – which immediately brings into question the relationship between the "staged and the everyday" (Frith v). Performance always requires an audience and an interpretation. *Maybe... Maybe Not* has an orchestra that performs – the Palast Orchester – an audience within the film that also performs by dancing, and within that a man and a woman performing intercourse in front of an audience that is not immediately apparent to them. The movie viewers are instantly aware that Axel's performance is being watched by his girlfriend Doro. Axel's public act sets the stage for the *performance* or carnivalesque spectacle, in which the audience can participate in their imagination. From a sociohistorical perspective it would doubtless be relevant here to point to the increasing significance of performance in everyday life as an effect of urbanization and the decline of intimacy, industrial capitalism and commodity fetishism (Frith vi).

One of the recurring pleasures contemporary audiences seek in the consumption and production of popular culture lies in the thrill of the difficult or spectacular act, the drama of which lies precisely in its immediacy, in the resulting sense of risk, danger, triumph, virtuosity (vi). In this re-gard Wortmann, in seeking to capture the social questions of everyday life, has powerfully evoked, especially through the music, the intensity of urban life in Weimar Berlin. The audience identifies with this character who is doing something new, dangerous, and who is experimenting with some-thing. Axel is cheered on since he is liberating himself from middle-class and conventional social constraints, whether it is performing sex with an older woman in a public toilet, moving in with a gay man or trying to prove his heterosexuality with yet another woman. But none of the sex acts he commits is as appalling to Doro as being discovered in bed with an-other man.

The film explores a gay culture — or counterculture — which is in-tended, by the director, to affirm 'perversity' as an aesthetic impulse, espe-cially where society only sees a sexual impulse, and conversely, to explore sexuality thriving in representations other than those sanctioned by the aes-thetics of bourgeois culture. This becomes a mix of seamy, steamy, and sentimental elements situated within a situational comedy with a strong dose of self-irony. In the end, for example, while Axel's sexual transgres-sions with other women are forgotten, his apparent seduction by another man cannot be forgiven.

By using gay men who cross-dress, Wortmann brings out campy and ironic elements of *Sein/Schein* — existence and appearance, which play on the imagination and on the underlying and unexpressed sexuality through role performance. The mise-en-scène articulates visually that which is re-pressed on the narrative level. Judith Butler asks, for example, "what politi-cal possibilities are the consequence of a radical critique of the categories of identity?" (*Gender Trouble* ix). Wortmann acknowledges the complexi-ties and ambiguities of identity and, like Butler, argues that identity catego-ries are too regulatory and oppressive, that they need to become more fluid. Since identity, especially as seen during the carnivalesque sequences, is never fixed, one cannot have a single association with images. Politically, socially, and culturally, Wortmann's film challenges the fixed notion about gay, lesbian, and straight identities.

The cross-dressing that occurs in the film allows enough fluidity to en-able a change not only in appearance but also in identity. Judith William-son, in her remark to appear "in every possible outfit, just to say, how dare you think any one of these is *me*. But also, see I can be all of them" (91) has demonstrated just how fluid gender and sexuality identity can be. In the film, Wortmann explores these split identities by means of the meta-phor of gender-fuck where biological sex is separated from cultural gender. The performativity of sexuality, whether on impulse, whether or not cultur-ally acceptable, or whether or not within the 'norm' are revealed as apparent strategies that are organized according to certain power structures. Axel's deviation from Doro's perception of the 'norm' essentially leads to Axel's alienation from Doro. There is no subtle irony when Norbert, the *out* homosexual, is placed back *into* the closet to the refrain of Torsten Breuer's *Die verflixte Finsternis im Schrank* (*This blasted darkness in the closet*). While watching some slides, Norbert attempts to seduce Axel, but the two are surprised by Doro. Axel quickly hides Norbert in the closet, but Doro becomes suspicious. Axel has to explain to Doro what she wrongly per-ceives to be his *hetero*sexual betrayal while standing beside the closet. The necessity of a renewed 'coming out' of Norbert is painful to him and a great shock to Doro. Axel's attempt to clarify the situation fails. His remark "Look, Doro, everybody is really a little bit bisexual — we all know that" does not help the situation.

Consequently anxious and insecure, Axel attempts to prove his hetero-sexuality to himself. The inability to perform with Doro is explained away by her pregnancy. A chance encounter with an old classmate, Elke, gives him another opportunity. But her "bull-power" can of tricks, a sexual stimulant for bulls, has the opposite effect by immobilizing him. Axel — the hetero/homo? — later sits like a prize bull (or gorilla in the comic book), yet impotent, on the living room table, a sexed body, the object of the gaze (and desire) of Doro from the front and Norbert and Walter, a friend with a bloody nose, from behind. He remains immobile, but calls out the name of Elke, who has just seduced Norbert's lover, a gay butcher, in the bathtub. In the window to his right is suspended a bright-red heart-shaped balloon. Axel is unable to communicate any sexual desire. At this point, Doro goes into labor.

The film narrative begins with a classic tale of the woman, Doro, be-trayed by the man, Axel. But instead of finding a solution to this problem, the film poses another dilemma. Axel, who ends up moving into the gay world after being dislodged by Doro, experiences the tensions of sexual identity. Instead of a Hollywood happy end — a return to Doro and hetero-sexuality — Doro tells him to "get out" of the hospital room where she has just delivered their baby. Norbert, who had replaced Axel in the delivery room, assumed a surrogate husband/father role, until Axel was able to come out of his trance. Norbert and Axel are last seen leaving the hospital, swinging their hips together. The tension between the homosexual and heterosexual has disappeared because the gender barrier has been broken. Wortmann, through the satire of sexual conventions, has shown that men and women, whether gay, lesbian or straight, are trapped by social conventions, to perform according to heterosexual conformities. By mocking these conventions, he holds them up for analysis and criticism.

Maybe... Maybe Not is an exploration of sexual desire, both heterosexual and gay. As other artists — such as Bob Fosse whose film version of the stage success *Cabaret* (1972) was based on Christopher Isherwood's *Goodbye to Berlin* and Ute Lemper in her current revival of this powerful genre of satiric songs, written by Jews and performed by gays in Weimar Germany — Wortmann returns, albeit by way of allusion, to the cultural sphere of Weimar Berlin as a locale where contemporary social and political issues were examined in song. Yet the main attraction of the songs of this period is their role as medium through which social issues and taboos can be questioned. Songs are the vehicle through which political and social problems can be satirized and become a form of entertainment or light relief. Wortmann, therefore, is progressive in the use of this marketing technique in contemporary Germany. Not only does he evoke the aura of the Weimar past, but he highlights very similar critical issues concerning gender, sexuality, and identity for public debate. Such issues are relevant for many Germans in the 1990s and require rehearsal, in light of continued denial of queer rights and the denial to include, for example, the names of queer victims on a memorial of the holocaust.

Consider the irony when Norbert, Waltraud/Walter, and Norbert's partner, the butcher,[16] visit the Residenz cinema — an allusion to another famous Berlin *Tanzlokal*. The choice of films is Sylvester Stallone's *Rambo II* or Visconti's *Death in Venice*, the first being a commercial Hollywood triumph which deals with a victimized white male hero and the second, a coming-out film and an art film only modestly appreciated by audiences (Sorlin 156). The three end up alone, watching *Death in Venice* until three macho types, sent to the wrong theater, disrupt their enjoyment of the film. A fistfight ensues, during which Norbert receives a bloody nose. All this is accompanied by the 1940 Adolf Steimel song *Die Männer sind schon die Liebe wert* (*Men are certainly worth loving*). The Visconti film, of course, can be considered the 'outing' of Thomas Mann. There is no doubt of the entertainment value of this performance.

Fast-paced and relatively short, just under ninety minutes long, *Maybe ... Maybe Not* has borrowed from the North American marketing concept where directors have learned how to "pace films for success."[17] The pace, in turn, is controlled by the music. The songs move the film along from sequence to sequence and sustain the rhythm of the film. Nondiegetic instrumental music dominates the soundtrack. Vocal music usually occurs when the music is diegetic — such as the opening sequence in the Gloria or the disco sequence when there is a performance of the song *My Gorilla.* While one man plays the piano, another sings and a third puts on a gorilla mask. This parodies the Axel, Doro, and Norbert relationship. The music drives the film in various ways: it evokes the period of Weimar Germany and highlights the gay world in contemporary Germany. The two periods are fused through the artistic and smooth transition of melding contemporary compositions with original music.

The use of the music of the 1920s and 1930s in this film coincided, in Germany, with the rediscovery of the sound and the bands of that era. For the filmmakers this became an economic issue of profit-making: if these elements could attract moviegoers, then the domestic film industry was in for an important social change — as evidenced by the proliferation of other such films during this time. As Hollywood had only recently begun to demonstrate, production, distribution, marketing, and screening were important economic elements to consider when making a film.[18] Adding to the success of the revival of songs from the 1920s to the 1940s is the present vinyl record craze in Germany, which is also reflected in the film.[19] For example, Norbert fails to notice initially that his record player has been stolen when he tries to play a record, and a record is mounted over the bed in Doro's apartment which is seen during Norbert's attempted seduction of Axel.

The music frames the film's twin themes of sexuality and gender. As Norbert remarked to Axel in the film, "heteros should have a try at being gay and women should have a go at politics." In this film, the hierarchizing of male sexuality above gender concerns reflects Wortmann's attempt to liberate male sexuality from social constraints and open up a public debate on issues that negatively constrain sexual possibilities. Through viewing, the German audience is given an opportunity to begin to rethink such issues as sex and gender, as well as gender identity and identification, including male sexuality. All of these concerns much outweigh any consideration in the film over heterosexual gender issues. By bringing in the carnivalesque, Wortmann successfully challenges the rigid notions about gay and straight identity and the fact that they are determined only by biological sex. The carnivalesque, which has a universal leveling tendency, also eradicates distinctions, which highlights the fact that sexuality is a construct. Ironically, by having male sexuality dominate over the heterosexual genders, Wortmann is able to point out that queer politics has, much like its heterosexual counterpart, similarly complex sexual, social, and political hierarchies.[20] In the end, he has proven that people do close themselves off from what they do not know — and that the two worlds are, indeed, similar.

Maybe... Maybe Not, with its music as part of a collateral marketing device, has taken German film toward a new phase after the decline of New German Cinema. The New German Comedy heralds a positive revival of German cinema and cinematic attendance in Germany. German filmmakers have acquired an acumen second to none when it comes to producing this new art. As a result of commercialism, the German film industry too, like Hollywood, has realized that "a popular song [is] an effective device in marketing a motion picture" (M. Evans 17; cf. Gomery xvii).[21]

Wortmann has artistically revived an older art form and incorporated it into a new one to make it into a popular product. But, at the same time, *Maybe... Maybe Not* also brings to light social issues that need to be addressed. Germans, no longer preoccupied with *Vergangenheitsbewältigung* (coming to terms with the past), have been confronted with important issues in this film. The film concentrates on performance derived from history and recent memory to deliver a new form of public entertainment and popular culture that connects the present to ongoing silence around certain events in the past that need to be revisited. It remains to be seen whether this form of German cinema will be able to sustain its position as a vehicle for satirical criticism of universal themes of sex and gender. But there is little doubt that music will remain at its core.

Notes

[1]This paper was originally presented at the *10th Hollins Colloquium on German Film: Music and the German Cinema* on April 5, 1997. I would like to thank the participants for their invaluable comments. I would also like to thank my colleague in the Cinema Studies Program at the University of Toronto, Bart Testa, for reading the paper and giving me very valuable suggestions as well as the editors of this volume for their effective criticism.

[2]With the headline "The German Comedy, An Oxymoron No More," Stephen Kinzer declares in the *New York Times* that the "melancholy image" that had made German films difficult to sell overseas for a generation had disappeared with the appearance of *Maybe ... Maybe Not*. He also exclaims: "But now a younger generation of directors have emerged and, at least in terms of mass appeal, left their elders in the dust. They are making a kind of film new to Germany, the relationship comedy — light, funny, fast-paced, modestly erotic and enormously popular" (15).

[3]Bruno Ganz, the actor of such New German Cinema classics as Wim Wenders's *Wings of Desire* (1987) and *The American Friend* (1977) remarked "Let me put it this way, German film is now in a phase where it can get along very well without me. I'm not someone who could do *Superweib* (*Superwoman*), even if you tell me that this director is another Lubitsch [the famous actor/director from the Weimar era]. I saw the preview and I have to say that you'd need a squad of police officers to force me to see the whole thing" (Kinzer 31.)

[4]Andreas Kilb argues in *Die Zeit* that the new German comedy began with Sönke Wortmann's *Small Sharks*, continued with von Garnier's *Making Up!* and would end with Wortmann (n.p.).

[5]Both Dörrie's *Nobody loves me* and von Garnier's *Making Up!* achieved commercial and critical success and found U.S. distributors, unlike recent films by Volker Schlöndorff and Wim Wenders (cf. "New Pix tickle Teutons").

[6]Eight of the nineteen tracks are either original compositions from 1929-1940 or modelled on the same musical style. The other eleven tracks are original film music by Torsten Breuer.

[7]The marketing strategy for the film, CD, comic book and video is unabashed. The web sites for both the orchestra and the film refer to the various media that relate to *Maybe ... Maybe Not* and they promote each other. The web sites also have hot links to gay and lesbian organizations (Linkenbach).

[8]For a full discussion of gay and lesbian persecution under the Nazis see Grau, *Hidden Holocaust.*

[9]UFA, located in Babelsberg, was the largest film studio during the Weimar Republic and the Third Reich.

[10]Rentschler discusses the role of German feature films that premiered during the reign of National Socialism. He argues that the majority of these films were unpolitical melodramas with grand seductive potential. These elaborate productions with potent and destructive powers of fantasy show that entertainment is more than innocent pleasure.

[11]Like Antonio Gramsci, Baudrillard sees consumerism as a new form of alienation and another form of social control.

[12]One only has to look at the advertising in the comic book of the "Collection Manslip," men's underwear, which is accompanied by the ad slogan "You are responsible

for the content – we provide the wrapping" (König 1995, 86; subsequent quotations refer to this edition).

[13]Richard Dyer notes in *Now You See It* that "In Germany at more or less the beginning and end of the Weimar republic, the first gay and lesbian films appeared: *Anders als die Andern* (*Different from the others* 1919) and *Mädchen in Uniform* (*Maidens in Uniform* 1931). These are remarkably early dates. Not only are there no other lesbian/gay films before or during this period, there are also very few images of homosexuality in film – except in Germany. Even Vito Russo (1981) in by far the most comprehensive survey or images of gays in films has only a handful of examples, all of which only figure momentarily in the films, some of which could be seen as gays or lesbian at all – yet in Germany, 1919 and 1931, there are two films placing homosexuality centrally, unambiguously and positively" (7).

[14]These meeting places were ordered to close as early as 1933 but subsequently reopened intermittently. For example, by 1939 they were ordered not to open before 7 p.m. and permitted to open earlier for special occasions. They were, though, ordered to close permanently in January 1942 (Knud 28). See also Günter Grau, *Hidden Holocaust.*

[15]"Der neue deutsche Film liebt die Comedia Sexualis," "Das Lachen macht's," *Der Spiegel* 38 1996: 223–4.

[16]Norbert is a vegetarian and a very sensitive, peace-loving person. He has been abandoned by several lovers, who have taken advantage of him in some way or another. When Axel moves out of Norbert's apartment to return to Doro, he takes in a butcher for a lover. Dressed in black leather, fond of visually provocative violent movies, he is portrayed as macho and a "Rambo" figure. Norbert takes in partners that he can look after and care for, but in the end it is he who is always taken advantage of. The butcher is quite probably also an allusion to Frank Ripploh.

[17]Katja von Garnier remarks in *Der Spiegel* about *Making Up!*: "Außerdem: Tempo, Tempo, Tempo."

[18]One can only think back on the success of Frederick Hollander's 1930 composition "Fallin' in Love Again" sung by the new star at the time, Marlene Dietrich, in *The Blue Angel.* This film did not contain background music but featured several songs as well as the chorale theme based on Mozart's opera *The Magic Flute.* However, the use of other movie tie-ins is relatively recent, even in Hollywood. Here, the German film industry has indeed caught up very quickly with Hollywood marketing techniques.

[19]As Mark Evans notes, even though the quality of film music may have declined today, "the public's nostalgia for the film music of the Golden Age of the movies is at a high peak. This new interest is not limited only to old film scores (which people are buying in the form of new recordings), but extends to composers as well" (1975, 1).

[20]See, for example, discussions about the "other" in Edward W. Said's *Culture and Imperialism.* For a discussion on the importance of dance halls within different cul-

tures see John M. MacKenzie. What becomes apparent is not only that the dance halls evoke, for contemporary Germans, a nostalgia for the past, but also that the songs provide an opportunity to participate in a current debate about issues of sexuality.

[21] Evans talks about the inevitability of noted composers of serious concert music who became interested in sound films, composers such as Karol Rathaus, Paul Dessau, and Hanns Eisler. Many of those German composers arriving in the United States between the 1930s and 1950s were not trusted among the members of the classical music class and so were forced to look for other kinds of employment, initially considered below their talent, such as compositions for Hollywood films. Many German composers, among them Frederick Hollander especially known for his composition "Fallin' in Love Again," moved to Hollywood in the 1930s (M. Evans 17).

Performances of Masculinity in Attila Richard Lukacs's *E-Werk*[1]

Piet Defraeye

URING THE MID 1980S, BERLIN'S Bethanien Hospital, overlooking the then unrelenting Berlin Wall, was refurbished by the local government and made into an artist colony as a means of regaining control in the anarchic community of the Kreuzberg district. One of the early occupants of *Künstlerhaus Bethanien*, as it is since known, was the Canadian painter Attila Richard Lukacs, "the most significant and ambitious painter to have emerged in Canada [since 1987]" (Enright 14). Tucked away in his studio, subsidized by the Canadian government, Lukacs clearly enjoyed his displacement from the upper-middle-class suburbs of Calgary to the down and under of Kreuzberg's simmering cauldron of students, artists, squatters, outcasts, punks, nonconformists, and radicals. He obviously appreciated his new found locus as a source of inspiration: "You can smell the disaffection, envy, and rage that seethes and stews in this neighbourhood, you can notice it on the skin of people the moment you approach a *U-Bahn* station; you can see it on people's faces, and in the graffiti on store windows and facades — This is life, man!" (in Grubbe 244).[2] His collection of six paintings under the title *E-Werk* tries to recapture this performance of urban emotions, in a style that is both hyperbolic and reducing. I will analyze the performative aspects of these six paintings, and scrutinize the performances of masculinity which unfold themselves, and apply these observations to a more detailed discussion of one painting in particular.

Lukacs's huge canvasses are reminiscent of the German and Russian school of social realism; the muscle-bound giants that populate his tableaus are painted in stark colors of red, black, and orange. Although Lukacs has been praised as a keen portrait painter (cf. Gagnon 30), most of his faces are crude, and seem somehow unfinished. Some of his figures seem collated into the painting, rather than being an organic part of the tableau; others have been painted over, leaving an obvious *pentimento*. The greatest reduction, however, is in his selection of characters: the world in his paintings is almost exclusively male, with his masculine characters adopting various poses and postures that produce a strong rhetorical effect. His paintings are compelling: in Thomas Sokolowski's words, they engage "the viewer in a manner that both intoxicates and repells [sic]."

Because of its postmodern character, E-Werk stands out in Lukacs's oeuvre. The technique of eclectic juxtaposition of different elements, its assemblage of different historical references, its playful quoting and blending of high art and popular culture, its self-referentiality and its political ambiguity define this series of six paintings as commentaries on and illustrations of a postmodern consciousness. The postmodernity of E-Werk is most striking, however, in its preoccupation with the body and with the performances in which the body is engaged.

The notion of performance is a central element in these works, and it is present in numerous ways. With intriguing titles like In My Father's House (1989), Tomorrow and Tomorrow and Tomorrow (1991), and Everybody Wants the Same Thing (1993), the backgrounds of these paintings function as huge backdrops for the opera that unfolds in front of them. These operatic titles are a standard feature of Lukacs's presentation and highlight the performative quality of his work. Junge Spartaner fordern Knaben zum Kampf heraus (1988)[3] and Where the Finest Young Men (1987) are just two other examples of Lukacs's caption culture. Sometimes, the histrionic is made explicit, as is the case in Wild Kingdom (1992/93). The drawn curtain in the left part of this triptych and the suggestion of an orchestra pit in the central canvas create an obvious theatrical setting.

The figures in the canvases are seen on stages painted with trompe l'oeil perspectives. This is most obviously the case in This Town (1990), where the cobblestone layers/impersonators are working on their own set, the enormous square in front of Berlin's Altes Museum. The technique of the grid in perspective, as Lianne McTavish points out, "recalls the Albertian perspective squares of Renaissance painting" (5). Lukacs divides his canvas into two parts, a horizontal acting area and an enormous backdrop upon which an illusionistic perspective setting is painted, often, as in This Town, with a celestial glow illuminating the entire representation. Similar to the unforgettable designs of Renaissance set designers such as Girolamo Genga, Aristotile da San Gallo, Veridico di Somi, and Sebastiano Serlio,[4] this technique has an obviously manipulative effect. As in the early stage designs, the perspective's ground line resists both its abrupt beginning and end; it is "poised to extend forward" (McTavish 5) and, like a play set on a proscenium stage, the tableaus of *E-Werk* reach out to engulf the viewer.[5]

The histrionic aspects of Lukacs's world are most evident in the actual scenes that are depicted in the paintings, the tableaus dramatize performances of mostly male figures fulfilling certain roles, donning (or downing) specific costumes and select props. These figures assume particular poses and are distributed over the stage of the canvas in a strategic blocking. Their gaze is toward the audience of the spectacle, the viewer of the art, and whenever the gaze is toward their fellow actors/characters, there is always an awareness of the histrionic gesture. Their gesture or posture, including even the most intimate exchange of looks, is part of a performance, it is meant to be seen by a viewer who can be either part of the painting or standing in front of it. The smaller part of the diptych *In My Father's House*, for example, shows two men coyly and seductively looking at each other, while in *Tomorrow and Tomorrow and Tomorrow* two steelworkers on a raised platform are intimately staring each other in the face. Lukacs's *E-Werk* thus evokes an intriguing kind of intimacy, albeit it a very public one; one that is meant to be seen or watched.

Lukacs's figures play various culturally inscribed roles; they play their part in a predominantly male work environment, and we, the viewers, recognize these parts. We know these people on the canvas; we have seen them in the paper mill, in the gym, on the road in the summer, in fashion magazines, on TV. Through this recognition, we are, once again, drawn into a performance as it unfolds itself. While Lukacs's paintings are extremely static in their iconographic discourse — they are carefully constructed snapshots of his imagination — their effect on the spectator generates a more complex and dynamic dialogue. We are compelled to participate in the drama, and to play our roles. As we enter Lukacs's theater, we are startled, we hesitate, swallow, sweat, fear, avoid, and look around us at other spectators, who then become actors too. We watch. We recognize. We become part of the performance: we repress or confess!

Lukacs's iconography always consists of young, able-bodied males; his "paradigms of male beauty" (Headlam 84) find their incarnation in aggressive-looking skinheads, muscular construction workers or military recruits. While there is a strong sense of hierarchy within these male groups, the order is threatened by an intense rivalry or the ominous threat that whatever sort of structure may exist can be overthrown. These male worlds suggest "violence, confrontation and discipline, creating a dark and threatening

view of the post-modern psyche" (Cooper 329). The confrontational interaction that unfolds on the canvas is an exclusively physical one. Apart
from graffiti or the occasional tattooed phrase, and the one memorable
"Achte" in *Glamour Crew* (1993), these male environments are essentially
nonverbal. More importantly, the painter does not let his figures speak and,
instead, casts a disturbing silence over each and every scene. Perhaps with
the one exception of a youth in *This Town*, Lukacs's men only watch,
they gaze, at each other, at the spectator, and, we have the impression, also
at themselves. As in most of his other paintings, we are in "a zone in
which language has disappeared and been replaced by brutal histrionic gestures" (Mays). Like the hierarchical confrontation, the relationships between
these males are expressed in physical terms; while some paintings only suggest a sexual dimension to these relationships surreptitiously, others acknowledge the sexual rapport and bonding explicitly and unapologetically.
Sexual desire, with its intrusive dynamic between fulfillment and prohibition, does not only function as a threat to the assumed power structure
within the male environment, it also lies at the very basis of male social
interaction.

E-Werk conjures up a male world, in which women are either completely absent (as in *This Town, In My Father's House, Everybody Wants
the Same Thing*, and *Tomorrow and Tomorrow and Tomorrow*) or badly
battered and silenced (as in *Wild Kingdom*) or in which they play no active role in the drama (as in *Glamour Crew*, a painting which haunts us
with its slaughterhouse imagery and its gruesome depiction of raw flesh
dangling from meat-hooks, suspended from bloodstained metal rods). It is
not immediately clear whether this exclusion of the female constitutes a
kind of marginalization or disempowerment of women or whether, perhaps
more likely, it is merely a sign of Lukacs's lack of interest, as he suggests in
an interview with Robert Enright: "My world is very male so that a group-
ing of female figures held nothing that interested me" (21). What is more
significant, however, is the fact that females are let off the hook in his paintings, while males are anything but. This is quite literally the case in *Glamour Crew* which shows the decapitated head of a man, bleeding from a
meat–hook in the upper left corner of the painting (cf. infra).

Despite the horrific elements, we definitely sense the enjoyment, celebration, or *jouissance* that the painter experiences in depicting the male
anatomy, a certain delight which is absolutely missing in his depiction of
female bodies. But, whatever relish there is in the depiction of the male

body, it seems to be restricted to a distinctive quality of body: that of the youthful, muscular, powerful athlete, somehow untamed, untainted, uncompromized, and also, of course, uncompromising. Lukacs's males radiate a particular sense of threat, especially in the physical realm. They are Teutonic figures, whose apparent working-class social status is in sharp contrast with the painter's — and often the viewer's — middle-class, educated background. His characters, Christopher Hume points out, "are not the sort of young men you'd feel good about bumping into in a dark alley." His men, with or without clothes, look like scrappers, who would not be afraid of a fight. All of this is evident in their powerful physiques and in other attributes, which function as performances on the side or as subplots within the drama.

The costumes worn by these men are stereotypically male: a pair of Bavarian leather shorts (*This Town*), road construction vests (*In My Father's House*), orange coveralls (*This Town*), or bankers' suits (*Wild Kingdom*). The recurring jockstrap is the most distinctively male outfit. The men's activities, too, fit in the male paradigm: they act as cobblestone-layers or work in smelters, mineshacks, or in a slaughterhouse. The paintings present a particularly male discourse like the impressive and imposing backgrounds of museums and monuments in scaffolds, the presence of towering phallic columns, the elaborate timberwork of a shack, the red-hot glow of a foundry, the frigid coldness of the abattoir. Psychoanalytic readings of these elements might yield interesting results. It would be a mistake, however, to situate the manifestation of this male discourse only in what might be called hyperbolic statements of masculine physique, or the monumentality of a male *Lebenswelt*, a phenomenon which is reminiscent of social-realist art, and also, more disturbingly, of fascist art in Nazi Germany. Indeed, Lukacs flirts with Nazi and fascist propaganda imagery (cf. Enright 25), but his Teutonic imagery often borders on camp.

Male discourse is also present at a more intimate level. Performances of masculinity extend themselves to the omnipresent graffiti and, especially, the tattoos, sported by the most stereotypically masculine looking of Lukacs's males. A tattoo, like any scarification, is a kind of performance which works on an intimate level, despite the fact that, in some circumstances, it is acted out in public. In his study entitled *Bad Boys and Tough Tattoos*, Samuel Steward states that, "in a large sense, it may be presumed that any tattoo is an advertisement of some kind" (76). In Lukacs's case, the advertisement seems to be about masculinity and masculine affiliation, and the role males *play* to perform their masculinity. Some of his figures sport a drawing of a chained woman in a sadomasochistic scene, others have eagles across their chests, or swastikas, or Romanesque brassards on their biceps. Still others sport all kinds of text, alluding to their identity or ideology. *In My Father's House* shows a so-called redhead with the word "SHARP" on his back, an acronym for Skinheads Against Racial Prejudice,[6] while in *Tomorrow and Tomorrow and Tomorrow*, a strapping smelter shows off the word "Treue" (loyalty), again with an echo of the military and fascist exploitation of the concept. Another character, squatting on all fours, has "bum-boy," tattooed on the cheeks of his ass provocatively turned toward the viewer, thus eliminating any misunderstanding as to his function in the play. Just like the costumes, the jockstraps, the nudity, the props — from dog collar to heat-protection suit — the shaved heads, the piercings, the well-developed calves and biceps, and, of course, the opulent display of male genitalia, these tattoos function as mini performances, as plays within plays, and thus contribute to the multi-layered performances in which these males participate.

The result is an apposition of bodies that are made to serve a distinctly masculine semiotics. In spite of their organic appearance, Lukacs's bodies are consciously assembled and therefore, self-indulgently, form part of a typically postmodern discourse. In the words of theater critic Johannes Birringer, the body in postmodern performance is the product of an "artificial reconception." Birringer's description of this postmodern usage of the body is helpful for a better understanding of Lukacs's discourse: "The artifactual body, made-up, designed, perfected, and thus absorbed into innumerable, contradictory cultural codes of performance, style, and wholeness ('total design'), is an alien body, displaced from the subject that seeks to match a model not of her or his own production" (209).

The histrionics involved in this process are complex. Lukacs's gym bodies are part of a fashion-stimulated, code-driven culture of simulation and imitation — a discourse which is not exclusive to, but nevertheless quite prevalent in gay culture, and evidenced mostly in the phenomenon of the clone, a historically inscribed look that serves as a grooming and accouterment model. Lukacs's figures look like butch clones, gym queens or muscle Marys,[7] done up for their respective performances in a slaughterhouse, a smelter or a mineshaft. As with the gay clone — who is both the repetition *and* the paragon — there are additional layers of matching the model in these paintings: his representation of what is *already* largely a representation is, in turn, also the product of simulation and quotation. The artist's use of references to art history is well known (Enright 14, 16, 20-22; Gagnon 30-31; Headlam 84; McTavish). In the case of *E-Werk*, the quotations include Rembrandt, Pierre Subleyras, Caravaggio, John S. Sargent, as well as numerous faces and postures from popular magazines and advertisements. His technique of quotation even extends to quoting his own work. Some of the figures in one painting — his favorites, no doubt — reappear in another, barely disguised by a different garment or prop. Finally, there is the distinctly Lukacsian subject of the skinhead or youthful clone, continuously reoccurring in all of these works. These *répétitions* are intensely theatrical, both in their self-reflexivity and in their *re*-presentational force.[8]

Repetition, in any sort of discourse on gender, is a powerful instrument, for it can be used as a subversive technique of transgressive reinscription of traditional identities. In gay popular culture, camp and machismo are undoubtedly the two most popular reinscriptive styles. Lukacs's style is a variation on this macho style, which, in Judith Butler's view, through its theatricalization of the original, allows a so-called deviant sexuality to reinscribe itself. "The task is ... to repeat, and, through a radical proliferation of gender, to *displace* the very gender norms that enable the repetition itself" (*Gender Trouble* 148, cf. Dollimore 322).

Lukacs's subversiveness emanates to a great extent from the settings he chooses: they are conventional and recognizable male loci, logically filled with their male occupants. He recreates, in other words, prototypically male worlds. Gym showers, work-out rooms, factory floors, construction sites, abattoirs, as well as conference rooms, faculty clubs, private clubs, and the business section of national newspapers, all are familiar masculine environments. Lukacs's evocations of male worlds — though he sticks to the former rather than the latter type — allude to an existing phenomenon, namely, homosociality.

The homosocial realm refers to those spaces that allow men to socialize, more or less intimately, but at any rate exclusively, with other men. Loci like the hockey rink, the sportsbar, the hunting cabin, or the boardroom perform a crucial role within the male homosocial structure, because they offer chances for men to group together, notwithstanding the intense rivalries that operate in these places. As Eve Kosofsky Sedgwick has pointed out, within the male homosocial structure, men's heterosexual desires serve as a more or less perfunctory detour on the way to a closer bonding with other men. Women, in their conspicuous absence, serve as stepping stones to bring men together in an alliance from which women are then in turn excluded (cf. *Between Men* 1-27). This dynamic is typical of a patriarchal structure. Interesting in relation to Lukacs's paintings is the fact that homosocial desire is characterized by a fundamental homophobic prohibition: there is no touching, only looking! Any physical contact has to take place within the context of work, sports, or camaraderie. In other words, the unavoidable horseplay that goes on reinforces the homosocial structure, while it releases the tension of pent-up male energy and unaddressed neuroses. As Gore Vidal says, rather tongue in cheek: "The only time where heteros may openly enjoy what they secretly dream of is when watching handsome young men playing contact games" (34; cf. Pronger 182). And yet, like the hockey rink, so are the gym, the bar, the board room places of intense and, sometimes, celebrated homophobia. Vidal's observation is somewhat reductive of homosocial desire, which may well have sexual components, but seems to be primarily about power. However, it is the homophobia that characterizes male homosocial structures so fundamentally and that keeps patriarchy in place. Lukacs's choice of the skinhead as his central icon reinforces the corroborative dynamic between homophobia and the homosocial. They can, in many ways, be seen as extreme or freakish expressions of — straight — masculinity, and have a troublesome history when it comes to expressions of bigotry and hatred.[9]

In *E-Werk*, Lukacs subverts the homosocial structure, by overturning the sexual and, more specifically, the homophobic taboo. By exposing the attractiveness of symbols and institutions because of their overladen play on masculinity and male aggression, in both a heterosexual and a homosexual context, Lukacs not only subverts the homosocial, but also raises important questions as to the construction of homosexual desire. Homophobia itself is exposed as part of homosexual desire — a brilliant, if frightening, dialectic. As usual, Lukacs operates on several levels. We can start with the title, *E-Werk*, or Power Plant, which alludes to the potent vitality of the male homosocial world and introduces masculinity as a geyser of power, energy, and strength. At the same time, the title implies a certain destructiveness connected to the hegemonic structure of power plants and, by extension, of patriarchal structures. Finally, *E-Werk* is also the name of a gay bar in Berlin, a city which functions as the main background of the paintings. A gay bar is, of course, an altogether different exclusive meeting place for men: it serves as a subversive location of the homosocial.

Lukacs's subversiveness extends to the postures, gestures, costumes, and props he lends his male actors. The recurring jockstrap is an obvious example. Brian Pronger calls the jockstrap an essential prop in any commentary on gay identity:

> The jockstrap is perhaps the quintessential homoerotic ritual robe because, just as it enshrines the symbol of the myth of masculinity, so too the straps that originate in the top elastic circumscribe the buttocks and disappear in the anus, bringing us to that place where masculinity meets its mythic undoing ... there are two sides to the jock strap that symbolize the homoerotic paradox: the pouch in the front as the shrine of masculinity joined to the straps in the back framing its mythic violation. (160)

Lukacs makes ample use of the jockstrap, and he reinforces its dissident quality by having the characters who wear them pose almost exclusively from the back.

The tattoos on Lukacs's men perform a similar function. They situate the sexual in the discourse of the painting, primarily by drawing attention to the disrobed body and its potential attractiveness. However, tattoos in themselves can be seen as an intensely sexual phenomenon that is intimately related to the performance of masculinity of which they are a part. Samuel Steward's sex surveys, conducted on his tattoo-clients in collaboration with Alfred Kinsey, reveal a striking correlation between acquiring a new tattoo and the immediate rush of sexual desire or yearning for a physical expression of masculine power.[10] He describes the mystique of the tattoo as "a kind of temporary love affair between artist and customer" (41). It is an interesting observation, yet, I am inclined to go further and describe the tattoo as a love affair between self and body, which, in Lukacs's case, poses interesting questions concerning the performances of desire in which his male characters are involved.

One of the crucial questions, and perhaps the most difficult to answer in relation to *E-Werk*, is whether Lukacs's paintings are transgressive or, on the contrary, conformative in their commentary on masculinity and male identity. Does Lukacs try to break open a space within the repressive masculine performance, in which self-indulgent male-male desire is possible, or do these paintings celebrate a mere displacement and, therefore, continuation of oppressive forces? The machismo on display in the canvas is disturbingly recognizable, and seems to be painted with *Begeisterung* and avidity. Lukacs readily admits that his interest in these characters stems from "an erotic or sexual fascination" and that rather than having them as models in his studio, he would have preferred them in his bed.[11]

Do these paintings imply parody? *Wild Kingdom*, with its asinine exhibitionists, most obviously does, but what about the others? Arthur Kroker calls Lukacs "apolitical and non-theoretical ... an artist whose imagination is uncensored." Perhaps, we are very close to Leo Bersani's critique of gay machismo. Rather than parodying the prescriptive model, Bersani suggests that gay machismo entails a profound respect for *straight* machismo: "from within their nearly mad identification with it, *they never cease to feel the appeal of its being violated*" (1985, 208-209; Bersani's emphasis; cf. Dollimore 321). Lukacs's paintings provide a fascinating ambivalence in this respect, which is not necessarily a failure. *E-Werk* struggles with its own discourse, which is also the paradox of the gay skinhead, a phenomenon that has become more widespread in the 1990s, particularly in large metropoles. Murray Healy's recent study of gay skinheads elucidates the dynamic of these paintings. "Gay and skinhead," in his words, "demarcate the unacceptable opposite extremes of masculinity" (4).[12] Similarly, Lukacs's homosexualization of his working class icons brings out and conjoins polar opposites of masculinities. The repetition or simulation involved in the process is problematic and, in Jonathan Dollimore's words, impure, but it is a contamination that is almost necessarily there: "this impurity, for the fantasies of transgressive reinscription, is not the ground of its failure but the material upon which it works" (325). The greatest significance of Lukacs's *E-Werk* is the commentary it provides, not so much on the construction of *gender* – male gender in this case – but, rather more intriguingly, on the social and historical construction of *desire*. "All desire bears its histories, the desires of the exploited and the repressed no less than the desires of those who exploit and repress" (Dollimore 325). *E-Werk* does not avoid the intricate convolutions and complexities of the paradigm of desire, but brings them out throughout its bold performance on the canvas.

Looking closer at one of the six canvases, Lukacs's impurities, contradictions, and complexities become fascinating aspects of his work. *Glamour Crew* presents a dark horror scene, situated in a basement abattoir, with flanks of meat and a quartered carcass hanging from black metal hooks. A group of nude figures anxiously looks on, while in the background two butchers, diabolic looking with their glowing red dust sleeves, carve up the meat. The scene, dimly lit by a few sparse bulbs, presents itself as a nightmare with all the inconsistencies that a dreamworld brings with it. While we count only eight bodies, there are nine heads in the picture, one decapitated and bleeding head is gaffed onto one of the meat-hooks. Unlike some of the other more unpolished portraits, this face is painted with exact detail; and yet, with the stream of bloody veins hanging from it, its performance becomes a parody. The horror of the scene is further undercut when we realize that the dismembered head is a rare self-portrait of Lukacs: the painter's face looks out toward his audience. This is surely a reference to Caravaggio's self-portrait as the beheaded Goliath in his painting *David with the Head of Goliath* (c. 1609-10),[13] and is reminiscent of the Italian painter's only signature of his entire career: a name written in the blood streaming out of the head of Saint John in the *Beheading of St. John the Baptist* (1608).[14] The atmosphere of Lukacs's painting in general echoes Caravaggio's fascination with decapitation, violence, and exhibition of nude flesh.[15] The remaining characters in *Glamour Crew*, however, are undisturbed; their gazes are directed away from the head, toward the hanging meat and an empty meat trolley: are they waiting for their turn to be carved up?

As we allow the scene to unfold, our reading is momentarily halted by the ramifications of the foreboding "Achte," spelled out in Gothic script over the entrance to the carving cavern. Associations with the holocaust are unavoidable. Does *Achte*, as an ordinal number, refer to the eighth figure, which, after the ninth, is about to be beheaded? In numerology, on the other hand, eight is usually associated with "home, regeneration, redemption, felicity, harmony, transformation, [and] new beginning" (Peck 62). The biblical eighth Age is the eighth day of judgment and brings about the New Jerusalem, after the deluge (Peck 62). The painting portrays an apocalyptic atmosphere, but there is no suggestion of redemption here. A more acute echo of "Achte" is as an imperative warning signal or *Warnruf* of the verb *achten* (to pay attention), more familiar through its military version *Achtung!* It adds a sinister dimension to an already cold and bleak scene. What makes it even more sinister is that "Achte" may well be an erroneous variant of *Acht*, meaning *Friedlosigkeit* (the status of being outlawed, cf. F. Kluge 8), and still in usage in the expression *in Acht und Bann tun* (to outlaw). The sentence of *Acht* or outlaw-status "was given by a lay court. The condemned could thus be killed by anybody, without restraint" (F. Kluge 8).[16] Are these figures, then, outlaws waiting for their

execution, without any form of trial? The holocaust resonance rings louder
and louder, and yet, these figures look like Olympic champions, products
of a desiring imagination, rather than emaciated camp victims. Unavoida-
bly, we also associate the theme of death and decay, as it surrounds these
perfect bodies, to the toll of AIDS. The association between the holocaust
and AIDS is, of course, fatuous, which is thematized in the outrageous
depiction of some of the characters. One of the men, for instance, in a pre-
posterous imperial posture has a length of velvet fabric draped over his
shoulder; another one, a black figure – and one of the few non-Caucasians
to appear in Lukacs's work – wears white sneakers; another male wears Doc
Martens' boots. The allegorical implications are frighteningly contemporary for the 1990s, an epoch in which arrogant and ignorant sybaritism and
self-indulgence can thrive against a dystopian background of biological,
economical, and social destitution.

A group of figures in the left corner of the painting seem disconnected
from the rest. Like so many of the figures in the painting, the woman to the
extreme left looks familiar. She turns out to be a literal quotation from
John Singer Sargent's painting of a Spanish dancer, *El Jaleo* (1882).[17] While
in Sargent's painting the dancer is the central object on display, cheered by
a row of male musicians, as is customary in the animated Andalusian El
Jaleo dance, Lukacs's woman is shoved to the side and disappears on the
fringe as a frenzied spectator. While the motif of dismemberment is manifest throughout the painting, it is also formally present in the way the out-
stretched arms of the woman, through the technique of clair/obscure, seem
almost severed from her body.

What ultimately lingers on after having reflected upon the different elements of the painting is the forceful presence of body: Lukacs has succeeded in portraying the manic dance of the hysterical male, self obsessed,
objectifying and objectified, repulsive and seductive: the trappings of desire are all present. The ultimate irony of the painting lies undoubtedly in
the painting's original function as a backdrop for the dancefloor of a
popular gay bar in Berlin. Sweating designer bodies, performing the ritual
liturgy of seduction, dancing to the tune of death. The reeking smell of despair and desire of Berlin's Kreuzberg district is never too far off in these
paintings. Who said that Lukacs's oeuvre was not political?

Attila Richard Lukacs (b. 1962) *Glamour Crew* (1993). Oil on canvas.
153 x 239 in. (*Diane Farris Gallery*, private collection) © A. R. Lukacs

Notes

[1] I would like to thank Fenton Burke, Christoph Lorey, Ian Lumsden, Lianne McTavish, John L. Plews, and Tony Steele for their generous help.

[2] My translation.

[3] *The Young Spartans Challenge the Boys to Fight.* The painting is usually referred to with its German title, undoubtedly for dramatic and political effect.

[4] For further description of the work of these designers, see A. M. Nagler (71-110). The similarities between these designs and Lukacs's technique are striking. Even his use of costume, props, and posture is remarkably reminiscent of, for instance, Veridico di Somi (Nagler 102-107).

[5] *Everybody Wants the Same Thing* (1993) is significantly different from the other five paintings in its use of perspective, which may help to explain the often very distinct reactions to this canvas. The backdrop of the tableau is flat, and the acting area is virtually nonexistent. The virtual absence of perspective in this painting precludes the viewer's engulfment into the painting's fable, and allows for greater distance.

[6]Skinheads Against Racial Prejudice, formed in England in 1988, is just one of a series of skinhead groups that tried to mobilize resistance to "the far right's troublingly successful recruitment of the skinhead as a public image" (Healy 127).

[7]See William Stewart for definition of butch clone (37), muscle Mary (173), and clone (52). Stewart's definition of the latter concept seems to ignore the multiplicity and rapidly changing paradigms of gay clonal appearance.

[8]In a 1993 interview, while working on E-Werk, Lukacs suggests he feels self-conscious about the repetitive use of the skinhead image: "Maybe I've been tanking it. I don't want to become an imitation of myself. That gets pathetic." This potential change of course may have to do with a shift in his personal style of dressing and grooming due to his age: "It looks great on a young guy" (in Headlam 87).

[9]The skinhead movement in Germany in particular is customarily associated with violence against foreigners, gays, and ethnic minorities (Healy 206).

[10]For a tabulation of these surveys, see Samuel Steward 41.

[11]Quoted in Celina Bell.

[12]The skinhead style has also grown into a fashion, especially in large gay communities. The appropriation of masculine signifiers is thus depoliticized and, as the brand-name props become available in expensive stores, pushed from the periphery into the center. As Healy points out, the "skinhead-derived look [has] become the dominant urban gay uniform" (197). Lukacs's paintings situate themselves before this co-optation.

[13]Galleria Borghese, Rome. See also Hibbard, Illus. 173 and 175.

[14]Cathedral of St. John. Malta. See also Hibbard, Illus. 153 and 156.

[15]For further discussion of Caravaggio's fascination with decapitation and violence, see Hibbard (261-64).

[16]My translation.

[17]Isabella Stewart Gardner Museum, Boston. See also Ormond, Illus. 22 and 23.

Works Cited

A Different Light Review 3.1 (summer 1992): 44, s.v. Taxi zum Klo.

Abelove, Henry, Michèle Aina Barale, and David M. Halperin, eds. *The Lesbian and Gay Studies Reader.* New York: Routledge, 1993.

Abend-Zeitung nebst Intelligenzblatt für Literatur und Kunst. Ed. Friedrich von Laun. Dresden 1805ff.

Abrams, Rebecca. "The Pain for Pleasure Principle." *The Guardian,* 19 July 1994, 10-11.

Achberger, Karen. "Bachmann und die Bibel: *Ein Schritt nach Gomorrah* als weibliche Schöpfungsgeschichte." *Der dunkle Schatten, dem ich schon seit Anfang folge: Ingeborg Bachmann — Vorschläge zu einer neuen Lektüre des Werks.* Ed. Hans Höller. Vienna: Löcker, 1982.

——. *Understanding Ingeborg Bachmann.* Columbia: University of South Carolina Press, 1995.

Ackerknecht, Erwin. "Die Gegengestalten im Faust." *Goethe. Neue Folge des Jahrbuchs der Goethe Gesellschaft* 11 (1949): 117-33.

Ackers, Maximiliane. *Freundinnen. Ein Roman unter Frauen.* Hannover: Seemann, 1923.

Adlon, Percy, dir. *Bagdad Cafe* [*Out of Rosenheim, a Modern Fairy Tale*]. 1988.

——. *Zuckerbaby* [*Sugarbaby*]. 1985.

Adorno, Theodor W. "Zur Schlußszene des *Faust.*" *Gesammelte Schriften.* Vol. 2. *Noten zur Literatur.* Frankfurt/M: Suhrkamp, 1974. 129-38.

Alain of Lille. *The Plaint of Nature.* Trans. James J. Sheridan. Toronto: Pontifical Institute, 1980.

Alcorn, Keith, Alan Sinfield, and Richard Smith. "The Politics of Queer." *Gay Times,* May 1992, 20-29.

Allen, Woody, dir. *Scenes from a Mall.* 1991.

Allison, Dorothy. *Skin. Talking about Sex, Class and Literature.* New York: Firebrand Books, 1994.

Altieri, Charles. "Hegel, G. W. F." *The Johns Hopkins Guide to Literary Theory and Criticism.* Ed. Michael Groden and Martin Kreiswirth. Baltimore: Johns Hopkins University Press, 1994. 369-73.

Ammer, Andreas, ed. Johann Wolfgang *Goethe: Erotische Gedichte: Gedichte, Skizzen und Fragmente.* Frankfurt/M: Insel, 1991.

Andermahr, Sonya. "The Politics of Separatism and Lesbian Utopian Fiction." *New Lesbian Criticism.* Ed. Sally Munt. New York: Columbia University Press, 1992. 133–52.

Andreas Capellanus. *The Art of Courtly Love.* Trans. John Jay Parry. New York: Ungar, 1964.

Ankum, Katharia von. Introduction to *Women in the Metropolis: Gender and Modernity in Weimar Culture.* Ed. Katharina von Ankum. Weimar and Now 11. Berkeley: University of California Press, 1997. 1–11.

Arens, Hans. *Kommentar zu Goethes "Faust II."* Heidelberg: Winter, 1989.

Ariès, Philippe. *Geschichte des Todes.* Munich: dtv, 1982.

———. "Thoughts on the History of Homosexuality." Ariès and Béjin, *Western Sexuality* 72–75.

———. "Überlegungen zur Geschichte der Homosexualität." Ariès and Béjin, *Masken des Begehrens* 80–96.

Ariès, Philippe and André Béjin, eds. *Die Masken des Begehrens und die Metamorphosen der Sinnlichkeit. Zur Geschichte der Sexualität im Abendland.* Frankfurt/M: Fischer, 1986.

———. *Western Sexuality: Practice and Precept in Past and Present Times.* Trans. Anthony Forster. Oxford: Blackwell, 1985.

Ariès, Philippe and Georges Duby, eds. *Geschichte des privaten Lebens.* Vol. 2. *Vom Feudalzeitalter zur Renaissance.* Frankfurt/M: Fischer, 1990.

Arnaud, Georg [Georges Arnaud de Ronsil]. *Anatomisch-chirurgische Abhandlung über die Hermaphroditen.* Trans. from French. Strassburg: König, 1777.

Arnold, Heinz Ludwig, ed. *Die andere Sprache. Neue DDR-Literatur der 80er Jahre.* Munich: text & kritik, 1990.

Artaud, Antonin. *Selected Writings.* Ed. Susan Sontag. Berkeley: University of California Press, 1988.

Ashton, Rosemary. "Plots and Plotters." *Times Literary Supplement,* 11 September 1992, 18.

Austin, John L. *How to Do Things With Words.* Ed. J. O. Urmson and Marina Sbisà. Cambridge, Mass.: Harvard University Press, 1955.

Bachmann, Ingeborg. *The Thirtieth Year.* New York: Holmes & Meier, 1987.

Bakhtin, Mikhail. *Rabelais and His World.* Trans. Hélène Iswolsky. Cambridge, Mass.: MIT Press, 1968.

Bammer, Angelika. "Testing the Limits: Christa Reinig's Radical Vision." *Women in German Yearbook* 2 (1986): 107–27.

Baswell, Christopher. "Men in the *Roman d'Enéas*: The Construction of Empire." *Medieval Masculinities: Regarding Men in the Middle Ages.* Ed. Claire A. Lees. Minneapolis: Minnesota University Press, 1994. 149–68.

Batley, Edward M. "Zur Problematik der Glaubwürdigkeit der Geschichte. Mit besonderer Berücksichtung der Marquis-Posa-Figur in Schillers *Don Karlos* und dem *Malteser*-Fragment." Brandt 250–75.

Baudelaire, Charles. *Die Blumen des Bösen / Les Fleurs du Mal.* Munich: dtv, 1986.

Baudrillard, Jean. *La Société de consummation.* Paris: Gallimard, 1970.

Baudrillard, Jean. *Simulacra and Simulation.* Trans. Sheila Glaser. Ann Arbor: University of Michigan Press, 1994.

———. *Symbolic Exchange and Death.* London: Sage, 1993.

———. *The Transparency of Evil: Essays on Extreme Phenomena.* Trans. James Benedict. New York: Verso, 1993.

Bauhinus, Casparus [Kaspar Bauhin]. *De hermaphroditorum monstrosorumque, partuum natura.* Frankfurt: Oppenheim, 1614.

Baxandall, Lee and Stefan Morawski, eds. *Marx and Engels on Literature and Art.* New York: International Geners, 1974.

Beck, Gad. *Und Gad ging zu David: Die Erinnerungen des Gad Beck, 1923 bis 1945.* Ed. Frank Heibert. Berlin: Edition dia, 1995.

Bédier, Joseph. *Les Fabliaux.* Paris: Champion, 1964.

Beicken, Peter. *Ingeborg Bachmann.* Munich: Beck, 1988.

Bein, Thomas. "Orpheus als Sodomit. Beobachtungen zu einer mhd. Sangspruchstrophe mit (literar)historischen Exkursen zur Homosexualität im hohen Mittelalter." *Zeitschrift für deutsche Philologie* 109 (1990): 33–55.

Bell, Alan P. *Homosexuality: An Annotated Bibliography.* New York: Harper, 1972.

Bell, Celina. "Skinhead Esthetics: A Painter Puts His Favorite Subjects to Work." *Maclean's,* 28 February 1994, 61.

Benkert, Karl Maria. *Paragraph 143 des Preußischen Strafgesetzbuches vom 14. April 1851 und seine Aufrechterhaltung als § 152 im Entwurf eines Strafgesetzbuches für den Norddeutschen Bund.* Leipzig 1869.

Bennett, Jane. "'How is it, then, that we still remain barbarians?' Foucault, Schiller, and the Aestheticization of Politics." *Political Theory* 24.4 (1996): 653–73.

Bergson, Henri Louis. *Laughter: An Essay on the Meaning of the Comic.* Trans. Cloudesley Brereton and Frank Rotherwell. London: Macmillan, 1913.

Berkes, Ulrich. *Eine schlimme Liebe. Tagebuch.* Berlin: Aufbau, 1987.

Berlant, Lauren and Elizabeth Freeman. "Queer Nationality." Warner, *Fear* 193–229.

Berman, Paul. *A Tale of Two Utopias.* New York: Norton, 1996.

Bernstein, David W. "Symmetry and Symmetrical Inversion in Turn-of-the-Century Theory and Practice." *Music Theory and the Exploration of the Past.* Eds. Christopher Hatch and David W. Bernstein. Chicago: University of Chicago Press, 1993. 377–407.

Bersani, Leo. "Is the Rectum a Grave?" *October* 43 (1985): 197–222.

———. "Pynchon, Paranoia, and Literature." *Representations* 25 (1989): 99–118.

Beutin, Wolfgang. *Sexualität und Obszönität. Eine literaturpsychologische Studie über die epischen Dichtungen des Mittelalters und der Renaissance.* Würzburg: Königshausen, 1990.

Beyer, Jürgen. *Schwank und Moral: Untersuchungen zum Altfranzösischen Fabliau und verwandten Formen.* Heidelberg: Winter, 1969.

Birkhan, Helmut. "Ministerialenliteratur in Österreich." *Die Kuenringer. Das Werden des Landes Niederösterreich.* Wien: Niederösterreichisches Landesmuseum, 1981.

Birringer, Johannes. *Theatre, Theory, Postmodernism.* Bloomington: Indiana University Press, 1991.

Bleibtreu-Ehrenberg, Gisela. "Das Vorurteil gegenüber der Homosexualität im Abendland." Stemmler 9-42.

——. *Tabu Homosexualität. Die Geschichte eines Vorurteils.* Frankfurt/M: Fischer, 1978.

Bloch, Howard R. *The Scandal of the Fabliaux.* Chicago: University of Chicago Press, 1986.

Blüher, Hans. *Die deutsche Wandervogelbewegung als erotisches Phänomen. Ein Beitrag zur Erkenntnis der sexuellen Inversion.* Berlin: Bernhard Weise, 1912.

——. *Die Rolle der Erotik in der männlichen Gesellschaft. Eine Theorie der menschlichen Staatsbildung nach Wesen und Wert.* 2 Vols. Jena: Diederichs, 1917-1919.

Blum, Martin. "Negotiating Masculinity: Erotic Triangles in the *Miller's Tale.*" *Masculinities in Chaucer: Approaches to Maleness in the "Canterbury Tales" and "Troylus and Criseyde."* Ed. Peter G. Beidler. Cambridge, MA: Brewer, 1998.

Böhm, Karl Werner. "Die homosexuellen Elemente in Thomas Manns *Zauberberg.*" *Stationen der Thomas-Mann-Forschung. Beiträge seit 1970.* Ed. Hermann Kurzke. Würzburg: Königshausen, 1985. 145-65.

——. *Zwischen Selbstzucht und Verlangen. Thomas Mann und das Stigma Homosexualität. Untersuchungen zu Frühwerk und Jugend.* Würzburg: Königshausen, 1991.

Böhme, Thomas. *Die Einübung der Innenspur. Roman Imitation.* Berlin: Aufbau, 1990.

Bordwell, David. *Narration in the Fiction Film.* Madison: University of Wisconsin Press, 1985.

Boswell, John. *Christianity, Social Tolerance, and Homosexuality: Gay People in Western Europe from the Beginning of the Christian Era to the Fourteenth Century.* Chicago: University of Chicago Press, 1980.

Bourdieu, Pierre. *Distinction: A Social Critique of the Judgement of Taste.* Trans. Richard Nice. Cambridge, Mass: Harvard University Press, 1984.

——. *Homo academicus.* Trans. Peter Collier. Stanford: Stanford University Press, 1988.

——. *Language and Symbolic Power.* Ed. and introduced by John B. Thompson. Trans. Gino Raymond and Mattew Adamson. Cambridge: Cambridge University Press, 1991.

——. *The Logic of Practice.* Trans. Richard Nice. Stanford: Stanford University Press, 1990.

Bovenschen, Silvia. *Die imaginierte Weiblichkeit. Exemplarische Untersuchungen zu kulturgeschichtlichen und literarischen Präsentationsformen des Weiblichen.* Frankfurt/M: Suhrkamp, 1979.

Brailowsky, V. Review of *Krasnuschkin und Cholsakowa: Zwei homosexuelle Mörderinnen.* In *Monatsschrift für Kriminalpsychologie und Strafrechtsreform* 18 (1927): 202-03.

Brall, Helmut. "Geschlechtlichkeit, Homosexualität, Freundesliebe. Über mannmännliche Liebe in mittelalterlicher Literatur." *Forum Homosexualität und Literatur* 13 (1991): 5-27.

Brand, Adolf. "Freundesliebe als Kulturfaktor: Ein Wort an Deutschlands männliche Jugend." *Der Eigene*, no. 1 (1930): 1-8. Rpt. as "Friend-Love as a Cultural Factor: A Word to Germany's Male Youth." Oosterhuis 145-54.

Brandt, Helmut, ed. *Friedrich Schiller. Angebot und Diskurs. Zugänge, Dichtung, Zeitgenossenschaft.* Berlin: Aufbau, 1987.

Brett, Philip. "Musicality, Essentialism, and the Closet." Brett et al. 9-26.

Brett, Philip, E. Wood, and G. Thomas, eds. *Queering The Pitch: The New Gay and Lesbian Musicology.* New York: Routledge, 1994.

Brewer, Derek. "The Couple in Chaucer's Fabliaux." *The Making of the Couple: The Social Function of Short-Form Narrative.* Ed. Michel Olsen. Odense: Odense University Press, 1991. 129-43.

Bristow, Joseph and Angelia R. Wilson, eds. *Activating Theory: Lesbian, Gay, Bisexual Politics.* London: Lawrence & Wishardt, 1993.

Britton, Andrew. "Foxed." *Jump Cut* 16 (November 1977): 22-23.

Brockhaus Enzyklopädie in zwölf Bänden. 19th ed. Mannheim: Brockhaus, 1986.

Brooks, Mel, dir. *Blazing Saddles.* 1974.

Brown, Helen, "The Interplay of Set Content and Temporal Context in a Functional Theory of Tonality Perception." *Music Perception* 5 (1981): 219-50.

Brown, Jane K., Meredith Lee, and Thomas P. Saine, eds. *Interpreting Goethe's "Faust" Today.* Columbia: Camden House, 1994.

Brown, Rita Mae. *Rubyfruit Jungle.* Harmondsworth: Penguin, 1994.

Bruce, Bryan. "Rosa von Praunheim in Theory and Practice." *CineAction!* 9 (1987): 25-31.

Brustellin, Alf, Rainer Werner Fassbinder, Alexander Kluge, et al, dirs. *Deutschland im Herbst.* 1977-78.

Bubner, Rüdiger. "Ästhetisierung der Lebenswelt." *Ästhetische Erfahrung.* Frankfurt/M: Suhrkamp, 1989. 143-56.

Büchner, Georg. *Werke und Briefe.* Munich: dtv, 1965.

Buckle, Richard. *Nijinksy.* London: Weidenfeld and Nicolson, 1971.

Bullough, Vern L., Barrett W. Elcano, W. Dorr Legg, and James Kepner. *Annotated Bibliography of Homosexuality.* 2 vols. New York: Garland, 1976.

Burg, B. R. *Sodomy and the Perception of Evil. English Sea Rovers in the Seventeenth-Century Caribbean.* (1st ed. under the title *Sodomy and the Pirate Tradition.* 1983.) With a new introduction by the author. New York: New York University Press, 1995.

Burnham, Scott. "Method and Motivation in Hugo Riemann's History of Harmonic Theory." *Music Theory Spectrum* 14.1 (1992): 1-14.

Burns, Bonnie. "*Dracula's Daughter:* Cinema, Hypnosis, and the Erotics of Lesbianism." *Lesbian Erotics.* Ed. Karla Jay. New York: New York University Press, 1995. 196-211.

Burston, Paul. "The Death of Queer Politics." *Gay Times,* August 1992, 22-23.

——. "Just a Gigolo? Narcissism, Nellyism and the 'New Man' Theme." Burston and Richardson 111-22.

Burston, Paul and Colin Richardson, eds. *A Queer Romance. Lesbians, Gay Men and Popular Culture*. London, New York: Routledge, 1995.

Busby, Keith. "Courtly Literature and the Fabliaux: Some Instances of Parody." *Zeitschrift für Romanische Philologie* 102 (1986): 67-87.

Butler, Judith. *Bodies That Matter: On the Discursive Limits of 'Sex'*. New York: Routledge, 1993.

——. *Gender Trouble. Feminism and the Subversion of Identity*. New York: Routledge, 1990.

——. "Gender Trouble, Feminist Theory, and Psychoanalytic Discourse." *Feminism/Postfeminism*. Ed. Linda J. Nicholson. New York: Routledge, 1990. 324-40.

——. "Imitation and Gender Insubordination." *Inside/Out. Lesbian Theories, Gay Theories*. Ed. Diana Fuss. New York: Routledge, 1991. 13-31. Rpt. in Abelove et al. 307-20.

——. "Melancholy Gender / Refused Identification." *Constructing Masculinity*. Ed. Maurice Berger, Brian Wallis, and Simon Watson. New York: Routledge, 1995. 21-36.

——. "Variations on Sex and Gender. Beauvoir, Wittig and Foucault." *Feminism as Critique. Essays on the Politics of Gender in Late-Capitalist Societies*. Ed. S. Benhabib and D. Cornell. Cambridge: Polity Press, 1987. 128-42.

Caduff, Corina. *Ich gedeihe inmitten von Seuchen. Elfriede Jelinek – Theatertexte*. Bern: Lang, 1991.

Caesarii Heisterbacensis Monachi ordinis Cisterciensis [Caesarius of Heisterbach]. *Dialogus Miraculorum*. Vol. primum. Textum recognovit Josephus Strange. Coloniae, Bonnae et Bruxellis 1851. Distinctio tertia, Capitulum XXIV.

Calandra, Denis, ed. and trans. *Rainer Werner Fassbinder: Plays*. New York: Johns Hopkins, 1992.

Cant, Bob. "Fassbinder's FOX." *Jump Cut* 16 (November 1977): 22.

Carpenter, Edward. *Intermediate Types Among Primitive Folks*. New York: Kennerly, 1921.

Case, Sue-Ellen. "Tracking the Vampire." *differences: A Journal of Feminist Cultural Studies* 3.2 (1991): 1-20.

Chambers, Ephraim. *Cyclopaedia*. Dublin: W. Sleater et al., 1787.

Charbit, Yves. *Du Malthusianisme au Populationnisme*. Paris: Presses Universitaires de France, 1981.

(charles), Helen. "'Queer Nigger': Theorizing 'White' Activism." Bristow and Wilson 97-106.

Cheal, David. *The Gift Economy*. New York: Routledge, 1988.

Chevalier, Julien. *Une Maladie de la personnalité: l'inversion sexuelle*. Lyon: Storck, 1893.

Chinca, Mark. "The Body in Some Middle High German *Mären*: Maiming and Taming." *Framing Medieval Bodies*. Ed. Sarah Kay and Miri Rubin. Manchester: Manchester University Press, 1994. 187-210.

Cixous, Hélène. "'Trennung'. Gespräch mit Maren Sell." *Die Schwarze Botin* 2 (1977): 21.

Claes, Oliver. *Fremde. Vampire. Sexualität, Tod und Kunst bei Elfriede Jelinek und Adolf Muschg.* Bielefeld: Aisthesis, 1994.

Cone, Edward T. "Beyond Analysis." *Perspectives of New Music* (fall-winter 1967): 33-51.

Cooke, Thomas D. *The Old French and Chaucerian Fabliaux: A Study of Their Comic Climax.* Columbia: Missouri University Press, 1978.

Cooper, Emmanuel. *The Sexual Perspective.* London: Routledge, 1994.

Cornut-Gentille d'Arcy, Chantal and José Angel García Landa, eds. *Gender, I-deology. Essays on Theory, Fiction and Film.* Amsterdam: Rodopi, 1996.

Corrigan, Timothy. *New German Film: The Displaced Image.* Rev. ed. Bloomington: Indiana University Press, 1994.

Craft, Christopher. "'Kiss Me with Those Red Lips': Gender and Inversion in Bram Stoker's *Dracula*." *Speaking of Gender.* Ed. Elaine Showalter. New York: Routledge, 1989. 216-42.

Crawford, Ronald L. "Don Carlos and Marquis Posa: The Eternal Friendship." *The Germanic Review* 43.3 (1983): 97-105.

Creekmuir, Cory K. and Alexander Doty, eds. *Out in Culture. Gay, Lesbian and Queer Essays on Popular Culture.* Durham: Duke University Press, 1995.

Creydt, Meinhard. "Ästhetisierung und Ideologie." *Produktion Klassentheorie. Festschrift für Sebastian Herkommer.* Ed. Heiner Ganßmann and Stephan Krüger. Hamburg: VSA, 1993. 181-92.

Cukor, George, dir. *The Women.* 1939.

Curtiz, Michael, dir. *Mildred Pierce.* 1945.

Cusick, Suzanne. "On a Lesbian Relationship with Music." Brett et al. 67-83.

Damon, Gene [Barbara Grier], Jan Watson, and Robin Jordan. *The Lesbian in Literature: A Bibliography.* 1st ed. 1962. Reno, NV: The Ladder, 1975.

"Das Lachen macht's." *Der Spiegel* 38 (1996): 223-4.

Das Gemeinschädliche des § 143 des preußischen Strafgesetzbuches vom 14. April 1851 und daher seine notwendige Tilgung als § 152 im Entwurf eines Strafgesetzbuches für den Norddeutschen Bund. Leipzig 1869.

De Boor, Helmut. *Die Deutsche Literatur im späten Mittelalter: Zerfall und Neubeginn. 1250-1350.* Vol. 1. Munich: Beck, 1962.

de Lauretis, Teresa. "Habit Changes." *differences: A Journal of Feminist Cultural Studies* 6 (1994): 296-312.

——. *The Practice of Love: Lesbian Sexuality and Perverse Desire.* Bloomington: Indiana University Press, 1994.

——. "Queer Theory: Lesbian and Gay Sexualities. An Introduction." *differences: A Journal of Feminist Cultural Studies* 3.2 (1991): iii-xviii.

——. "Sexual Indifference and Lesbian Representation." Abelove et al. 141-58.

——. *Technologies of Gender: Essays on Theory, Film, and Fiction.* Bloomington: Indiana University Press, 1987.

Denkschrift betreff Aufhebung des Paragraph 175 RstGB. Berlin 1898.

Denisoff, Dennis. *Queeries. An Anthology of Gay Male Prose.* Vancouver: Arsenal Pulp Press, 1993.

Derks, Paul. *Die Schande der heiligen Päderastie. Homosexualität und Öffentlichkeit in der deutschen Literatur, 1750-1850.* Berlin: rosa Winkel, 1990.

Derrida, Jacques. "Das Theater der Grausamkeit und die Geschlossenheit der Repräsentation." *Die Schrift und die Differenz.* Frankfurt/M: Suhrkamp, 1976. 351-79.

———. "Signature, Event, Context." *Limited Inc.* Ed. Gerald Graff. Evanston: Northwestern University Press, 1988.

———. *Of Grammatology.* Baltimore, MD: Johns Hopkins, 1976.

Deutsch, Helene. "Über die weibliche Homosexualität." *Internationale Zeitschrift für Psychoanalyse* 18.2 (1932): 219-41.

Deutsche Encyclopädie oder Allgemeines Real-Wörterbuch aller Künste und Wissenschaften von einer Gesellschaft Gelehrten. Erster Band A-Ar. Frankfurt/M: Varrentrapp Sohn und Wenner, 1778.

Didiskalia oder Blätter für Geist, Gemüth und Publizität. Ed. J. L. von Heller et al. Frankfurt/M: Heller & Rohm, 1823-1903.

Die Bühne: Das österreichische Theatermagazin. Wien: Geyer. Jahresbände.

Die Chronik des Burkhard Zink. In *Die Chroniken der Deutschen Städte* 5.2.

Die Chronik des Erhard Wahraus. In *Die Chroniken der Deutschen Städte* 5.2.

Die Chronik von der Gründung der Stadt Augsburg bis zum Jahre 1469. In *Die Chroniken der Deutschen Städte* 4.1.

Die Chroniken der deutschen Städte vom 14. bis in's 16. Jahrhundert. Vols. 1, 4, and 5. Leipzig 1865-66.

Dieckmann, Christoph. "Die heilige Schrift. Eine Rede wider das Verschwinden der Sprache in der Gegenwart." *DIE ZEIT,* 35, 30 August 1996, 16.

Dietrich von der Glezze. *Der Borte.* Ed. Brigitte Spreitzer. *Die stumme Sünde: Homosexualität im Mittelalter.* Göppingen: Kümmerle, 1988. 248-73.

Dinshaw, Carolyn. "A Kiss Is Just a Kiss: Heterosexuality and Its Consolations in *Sir Gawain and the Green Knight.*" *diacritics* 24 (1994): 205-26.

Döblin, Alfred. *Die beiden Freundinnen und ihr Giftmord. Außenseiter der Gesellschaft. Die Verbrechen der Gegenwart.* 1924. Rpt. Frankfurt/M: Suhrkamp, 1971.

Dodds, Dinah. "The Lesbian Relationship in Bachmann's *Ein Schritt nach Gomorrha.*" *Monatshefte* 72.4 (1980): 431-38.

Doerry, Martin. *Übergangsmenschen: Die Mentalität der Wilhelminer und die Krise des Kaiserreichs.* Weinheim: Juventa, 1986.

Doll, Annette. "Weibliche Kunstproduktion: Die Frau als Zitat-Künstlerin." *Mythos, Natur und Geschichte bei Elfriede Jelinek. Eine Untersuchung ihrer literarischen Intentionen.* Stuttgart: Wissenschaft und Forschung, 1994. 43-68.

Dollimore, Jonathan. *Sexual Dissidence. Augustine to Wilde, Freud to Foucault.* Oxford: Clarendon, 1991.

Dörrie, Doris, dir. *Keiner liebt mich [Nobody Loves Me].* 1995.

———. *Männer[Men].* 1985.

Doty, Alexander. *Making Things Perfectly Queer. Interpreting Mass Culture.* London, Minneapolis: University of Minnesota Press, 1993.

Douglas, Mary. *Implicit Meanings.* London: Routledge, 1975.

Douglas, Mary. *Purity and Danger: An Analysis of Concepts of Pollution and Taboo.* London: Routledge, 1966.

Dramaturgische Blätter. Continuation of *Tagebuch Mainzer Schaubühne.* [Ed. Aloys Wilhelm Schreiber.] St. 1-13 [Frankfurt/M: Eichenberg, 1788 (1788-89 Eßlinger)].

Duberman, Martin, Martha Vicinus, and George Chauncey, Jr., eds. *Hidden from History: Reclaiming the Gay and Lesbian Past.* New York: Penguin, 1989.

Duby, Georges. *Love and Marriage in the Middle Ages.* Trans. Jeanne Dunnett. Chicago: Polity, 1994.

———. *Medieval Marriage: Two Models from Twelfth-Century France.* Trans. Elborg Forster. Baltimore: Johns Hopkins University Press, 1978.

Duc, Aimée. *Sind es Frauen? Roman über das dritte Geschlecht.* 1901. Rpt. Berlin: Amazonen Frauenverlag, 1976.

Düchting, Reinhard. *"Sonderlicher denn Frauenliebe:* Homoerotische Lyrik des lateinischen Mittelalters." Stemmler 89-101.

Duden, Barbara. "Die Frau ohne Unterleib: Zu Judith Butlers Entkörperung. Ein Zeitdokument." *Feministische Studien* 2 (1993): 24-33.

Duden, Barbara. *Der Frauenleib als öffentlicher Ort. Vom Mißbrauch des Begriffs Leben.* Hamburg/Zürich: Luchterhand, 1991.

Duden, Barbara. *Geschichte unter der Haut. Ein Eisenacher Arzt und seine Patientinnen um 1730.* Stuttgart: Klett-Cotta, 1987.

Dunn, Sara. "Voyages of the Valkyries: Recent Lesbian Pornographic Writing." *Feminist Review* 34 (1990): 161-70.

Dyer, Richard. "Children of the Night: Vampirism as Homosexuality, Homosexuality as Vampirism." *Sweet Dreams. Sexuality, Gender and Popular Fiction.* Ed. Susannah Radstone. London: Lawrence, 1988. 47-72.

———. "Less and More than Women and Men: Lesbian and Gay Cinema in Weimar Germany." *New German Critique* 51 (1990): 5-60.

———. *The Matter of Images: Essays on Representations.* London: Routledge, 1993.

———. *Now You See It: Studies on Lesbian and Gay Film.* New York: Routledge, 1990.

Dyer, Richard, ed. *Gays and Film.* London: British Film Institute, 1980.

Dynes, Wayne R. *Homosexuality: A Research Guide.* New York: Garland, 1987.

Eckermann, Johann Peter. *Gespräche mit Goethe in den letzten Jahren seines Lebens.* Weisbaden: Insel, 1955.

Edelman, Lee. "Seeing Things: Representation, the Scene of Surveillance, and the Spectacle of Gay Male Sex." Fuss (1991) 93-116.

———. *Homographesis.* New York: Routledge, 1994.

Ehrismann, Gustav. *Geschichte der deutschen Literatur bis zum Ausgang des Mittelalters.* Vol. 2. Munich: Beck, 1934.

Eichhorn, Cornelia. "Judith Butler. Zwischen Dekonstruktion und feministischer Identitätspolitik." *Die Beute* 1 (1994): 40-43.

Eickelpasch, Rolf. "Handlungssinn und Fremdverstehen. Grundkonzepte einer interpretativen Soziologie." *Soziologie. Zugänge zur Gesellschaft. Geschichte, Theorien und Methoden.* Ed. Georg Kneer, Klaus Kraemer, and Armin Nassehi. Hamburg/ Münster: Lit. Münster, 1994. 119-43.

Eissler, Kurt Robert. *Goethe: A Psychoanalytic Study. 1775-1786.* 2 vols. consecutively numbered. Detroit: Wayne State University Press, 1963.

Eissler, W. U. *Arbeiterparteien und Homosexuellenfrage. Zur Sexualpolitik von SPD und KPD in der Weimarer Republik. Sozialwissenschaftliche Studien zur Homosexualität.* Hamburg: rosa Winkel, 1980.

Eldorado. *Homosexuelle Frauen und Männer in Berlin 1850-1950. Geschichte, Alltag und Kultur.* Catalog, Berlin Museum May 26 - July 8, 1984. Berlin: Fröhlich, 1984.

Ellenzweig, Allen. *The Homoerotic Photograph: Male Images from Durieu/Delacroiz to Mapplethorpe.* New York: Columbia University Press, 1992.

Ellis, Havelock and John Addington Symonds. *Sexual Inversion.* 1897. Rpt. New York: Arno, 1975.

Ellis, R. and R. Tixier, eds. *The Medieval Translator: Traduire au Moyen Age.* Proceedings of the International Conference of Conques, 26-29 July 1993. Turnhout: Brepols, 1995.

Elsaesser, Thomas. "Syberberg, Cinema, and Representation." *New German Critique* 24/25 (1981/82): 108-54.

———. *New German Cinema: A History.* New Brunswick, NJ: Rutgers University Press, 1989.

Emrich, Wilhelm. *Die Symbolik von "Faust II": Sinn und Vorformen.* Bonn: Athenäum, 1957.

Encyclopaedia Britannica, The New. 15th ed. Vol. 1. Chicago: Encyclopaedia Britannica, 1988.

Encyclopaedia Britannica. 3rd ed. Edinburgh: Bell and MacFarquhar, 1797.

Encyclopaedia Judaica. Vol. 4. Jerusalem: Keter, 1971.

English, Deirdre. "Talking Sex: A Conversation on Sexuality and Feminism." *Socialist Review* 58 (1981): 51.

Enright, Robert. "Regendering the Garden. The Very Rich Painting of Attila Richard Lukacs." Interview with A. R. Lukacs. *Border Crossings,* summer 1992, 14-25.

Entwurf eines Strafgesetzbuches für den Norddeutschen Bund. Nebst Motiven und Anlagen. Berlin 1870.

Epstein, Julia. "Either/Or — Neither/Both: Sexual Ambiguity and the Ideology of Gender." *Genders* 7 (1990): 99-142.

Erdle, Birgit R. "'Die Kunst ist ein schwarzes glitschiges Sekret.' Zur feministischen Kunst-Kritik in neueren Texten Elfriede Jelineks." *Frauen-Fragen in der deutschsprachigen Literatur seit 1945.* Ed. Mona Knapp and Gerd Labroisse. Amsterdam: Rodopi, 1989. 323-41.

Eros vor dem Reichsgericht. Ein Wort an Juristen, Mediziner und gebildete Laien zur Aufklärung über die "griechische Liebe." Leipzig 1899.

Estermann, Alfred. *Die deutschen Literatur-Zeitschriften 1815 bis 1850. Bibliographien, Programme, Autoren.* 10 vols. Nendeln: Kraus, 1977-81.

Evans, Caroline and Lorraine Gamman. "The Gaze Revisited, or Reviewing Queer Viewing." Burston and Richardson 13-56.

Evans, David T. *Sexual Citizenship: The Material Construction of Sexualities.* London: Routledge, 1993.

Evans, Mark. *Soundtrack: The Music of the Movies.* New York: Hopkinson, 1975.

Evans-Pritchard, E. E. *The Gift. Forms and Functions of Exchange in Archaic Societies.* New York: Norton, 1967.

Faderman, Lillian. *Odd Girls and Twilight Lovers: A History of Lesbian Life in Twentieth-Century America.* 1991. New York: Penguin, 1992.

Faderman, Lillian and Brigitte Erikson, eds. and trans. *Lesbian-Feminism in Turn-of-the-Century Germany.* Weatherby, Missouri: Naiad, 1980.

Falk, Johannes. *Goethe aus näherm persönlichen Umgange dargestellt.* Leipzig: Brockhaus, 1832.

Fassbinder, Rainer Werner, dir. *Berlin Alexanderplatz.* 1979-80.

———. *Die Ehe der Maria Braun.* 1979.

———. *Fox and His Friends [Faustrecht der Freiheit].* 1975. Videocassette. New Yorker Video, 1989.

———. *Lili Marleen.* 1980.

Fehr, Gerhard. "Zu einigen Aspekten der Entwicklung der Risikogruppe der männlichen Homosexuellen und der Risikogruppe der kriminell-gefährdeten, nicht lesbischen, weiblichen Jugendlichen und Jungerwachsenen in der Hauptstadt Berlin." Dissertation, Humboldt-Universität zu Berlin, 1983.

Feuerbach, Paul Johann Anselm. *Lehrbuch des gemeinen in Deutschland gültigen peinlichen Rechts.* Gießen 1801.

Feuerlicht, Ignace. "Thomas Mann and Homoeroticism." *Germanic Review* 57.3 (1982): 89-97.

Field, Nicola. *Over the Rainbow. Money, Class, and Homophobia.* London: Pluto, 1995.

Fischer, Hanns. *Studien zur deutschen Märendichtung.* 2d. ed. Tübingen: Niemeyer, 1983.

Flandrin, J.-L. *Un temps pour embrasser. Aux origines de la morale sexuelle occidentale (VIe-XIe siècle).* Paris 1983.

Fleming, Victor, dir. *The Wizard of Oz.* 1939.

Flinn, Caryl. "The Deaths of Camp." *Camera Obscura* 35 (1996): 53-84.

Ford, John, dir. *Stagecoach.* 1939.

Fosse, Bob, dir. *Cabaret.* 1972.

Foucault, Michel. "Der Kampf um die Keuschheit." Ariès and Béjin, *Die Masken des Begehrens* 25-39.

———. *The History of Sexuality.* Volume 1: *An Introduction.* 1976. Trans. Robert Hurley. New York: Random House, 1978.

Franklin, James. *New German Cinema: From Oberhausen to Hamburg.* Boston: Twayne, 1983.

Freies Wissenschaftliches Komitee. *Vorentwurf zu einem deutschen Strafgesetzbuch nebst Begründung.* 1909. Zentrales Staatsarchiv Potsdam. *Bestand Reichsjustizamt,* Repositur 30.01. Akte 5878, Bl. 2ff.

Freud, Sigmund. *Leonardo da Vinci: A Study in Psychosexuality.* Trans. A. Brill. New York: Random House, 1947.

——. *Three Essays on the Theory of Sexuality.* Trans. J. Strachey. New York: Basic Books, 1982.

Frevert, Ute. *Frauen-Geschichte: Zwischen bürgerlicher Verbesserung und neuer Weiblichkeit.* Frankfurt/M: Suhrkamp, 1986.

Friedländer, Benedict. "Bemerkungen zu dem Artikel des Herrn Dr. Rüdin über die Rolle der Homosexuellen im Lebensprozeß der Rasse." *Archiv für Rassen und Gesellschaftsbiologie* 1 (1904): 219-21.

——. "Die physiologische Freundschaft als normaler Grundtrieb des Menschen und als Grundlage der Soziabilität." *Jahrbuch für sexuelle Zwischenstufen* 6 (1904): 179-211.

Friedrich, Regine. "Nachwort." Elfriede Jelinek. *Krankheit oder Moderne Frauen.* Cologne: Prometh, 1987. 84-93.

Friedrich, Theodor and Lothar J. Scheithauer. *Kommentar zu Goethes "Faust."* Stuttgart: Reclam, 1980.

Frith, Simon. Introduction to *Performance Matters* (London) 27 (1995/96).

Frye, Marilyn. "Some Reflections on Separatism and Power." In Abelove et al. 91-98.

Fuss, Diana. *Essentially Speaking: Feminism, Nature and Difference.* London: Routledge, 1989.

——. *Identification Papers.* New York: Routledge, 1995.

——, ed. *Inside/Out: Lesbian Theories, Gay Theories.* New York: Routledge, 1991.

Gagnon, Paulette. *Attila Richard Lukacs.* Montreal: Musée d'art contemporain, 1994.

Gaines, Jane. "White Privilege and Looking Relations. Race and Gender in Feminist Film Theory." *Issues in Feminist Film Criticism.* Ed. Patricia Erens. Bloomington: Indiana University Press, 1990. 197-214.

Garber, Erich. *Uranian Worlds: A Reader's Guide to Alternative Sexuality in Science Fiction and Fantasy.* Boston, MA: G. K. Hall, 1983.

Garber, Marjorie. "Spare Parts: The Surgical Construction of Gender." Abelove et al. 321-38.

——. *Vested Interests: Cross-Dressing and Cultural Anxiety.* New York: Routledge, 1992.

Garfinkel, Harold. "Passing and the Managed Achievement of Sex Status in an Intersexed Person." *Studies in Ethnomethodology.* Englewood Cliffs: Prentice-Hall, 1967. 116-85.

Garin. *De Berangier au long cul.* Ed. Jean Rychner: Contribution à l'étude des fabliaux. Vol. 2. Neuchâtel: Droz, 1960.

Garnier, Katja von. Interview. "Ich bin keine Komödientante!" *Berliner Morgenpost,* 1 July 1993, n.p.

Garnier, Katja von. "Tempo, Tempo, Tempo. Die Regisseurin über ihren Überraschungserfolg *Abgeschminkt!*" *Der Spiegel*, 6 September 1993, 214.

——, dir. *Abgeschminkt!* [*Making Up!*]. 1993.

Gasnier, Louis, dir. *Reefer Madness*. 1936.

Gaunt, Simon. "Straight Minds / 'Queer' Wishes in Old French Hagiography: *La Vie de Sainte Euphrosine.*" *GLQ: A Journal of Gay and Lesbian Studies* 1 (1995): 439-57. Rpt. *Premodern Sexualities*. Ed. Louise Fradenburg and Carla Freccero. New York: Routledge, 1996. 155-73.

Gautier Le Leu. *Del Sot Chevalier*. Ed. Charles H. Livingston. *Le jongleur Gautier Le Leu. Étude sur les fabliaux*. Cambridge, MA: Harvard University Press, 1951. 186-97.

Gelder, Ken. *Reading the Vampire*. London: Routledge, 1994.

Gianetti, Louis. *Understanding Movies*. Englewood Cliffs, NJ: Prentice Hall, 1996.

Gibson, Pamela Church and Roma Gibson, eds. *Dirty Looks. Women. Pornography. Power.* London: British Film Institute, 1993.

Gildemeister, Regine and Angelika Wetterer. "Wie Geschlechter gemacht werden. Die soziale Konstruktion der Zweigeschlechtlichkeit und ihre Reifizierung in der Frauenforschung." *TraditionenBrüche. Entwicklungen feministischer Theorie*. Ed. Gudrun-Axeli Knapp and Angelika Wetterer. Freiburg i. Br.: Kore, 1992. 201-54.

Gilman, Sander. *Inscribing the Other*. Lincoln, NE: University of Nebraska Press, 1991.

——. *Sexuality: An Illustrated History*. New York: John Wiley, 1989.

Glier, Ingeborg. *Artes amandi. Untersuchung zu Geschichte, Überlieferung und Typologie der deutschen Minnereden*. Munich: Artemis, 1971.

Goethe, Johann Wolfgang. *Egmont. Ein Trauerspiel in fünf Aufzügen*. Erstausgabe. Leipzig: Göschen, 1788.

——. *Egmont. Ein Trauerspiel in fünf Aufzügen*. Stuttgart: Reclam, 1993.

——. *Egmont*. Goethe, *Werke. Weimarer-Ausgabe*. I, 8.

——. *Erotische Gedichte: Gedichte, Skizzen und Fragmente*. Ed. Andreas Ammer. Frankfurt/M: Insel, 1991.

——. "Faust." Goethe, *Werke. Weimarer-Ausgabe*. I, 14-15.

——. *Faust*. Ed. Albrecht Schöne. *Sämtliche Werke. Briefe, Tagebücher und Gespräche*. Ed. Friedmar Apel et al. Frankfurt/M: Deutscher Klassiker Verlag, 1994.

——. *Faust I & II*. Ed. and trans. Stuart Atkins. Vol. 2. of *Goethe's Collected Works*. Ed. Victor Lange, Eric Blackall, Cyrus Hamlin. Cambridge: Suhrkamp/Insel, 1984.

——. *Gedenkausgabe der Werke, Briefe und Gespräche*. (GA) Ed. Ernst Beutler. Zürich: Artemis, 1949.

——. *Goethe über seine Dichtungen*. Vol. 2. *Die dramatischen Dichtungen*. Ed. Hans Gerhard Gräf. 3 parts in 9 vols. Frankfurt/M: Rütten & Loening, 1901-14; rpt. 1968.

——. *Goethe's Plays*. Trans. Charles E. Passage. New York: Ungar, 1980.

——. *Goethes Briefe und Briefe an Goethe. Hamburger Ausgabe in 6 Bänden*. 3d ed. Ed. Karl Robert Mandelkow. Vol. 4. *Briefe 1821-1832*. Munich: Beck, 1988.

Goethe, Johann Wolfgang. *Goethes Werke. Hamburger Ausgabe.* (HA) Ed. Erich Trunz. Munich: Beck, 1972.

——. *Roman Elegies and Venetian Epigrams.* Ed. L. R. Lind. Lawrence: University Press of Kansas, 1974.

——. *Sämtliche Werke nach Epochen seines Schaffens. Münchner-Ausgabe.* Ed. Karl Richter et al. Munich: Hanser, 1985ff.

——. *Scientific Studies.* Trans. D. Miller. New York: Suhrkamp, 1988.

——. *Werke. Akademie-Ausgabe.* Ed. deutsche Akademie der Wissenschaften Berlin. Berlin: Akademie-Verlag, 1952–66.

——. *Werke. Weimarer-Ausgabe.* (WA) Herausgegeben im Auftrag der Großherzogin Sophie von Sachsen. Weimar: Böhlau, 1889.

Goldberg, Jonathan, ed. *Queering the Renaissance.* Durham: Duke University Press, 1994.

Gomery, Douglas. *Shared Pleasures. A History of Movie Presentation in the United States.* Madison: University of Wisconsin Press, 1992.

Gough, Cal and Ellen Greenblatt, eds. *Gay and Lesbian Library Service.* Jefferson, NC: McFarland, 1990.

Gough, Kathleen. "The Origin of the Family." Toward an Anthropology of Women. Ed. Rayna [Rapp] Reiter. New York: Monthly Review, 1975. 51–56.

Gräf, Heinrich. "Über die gerichtsärztliche Beurteilung perverser Geschlechtstriebe." *Archiv für Kriminalanthropologie und Kriminalstatistik* 34 (1909): 45–122.

Gramsci, Antonio. *The Modern Prince and Other Writings.* Trans. L. Marks. New York: International Publishers, 1957.

Grau, Günter, ed. *Hidden Holocaust? Gay and Lesbian Persecution in Germany 1933–45.* Trans. Patrick Camiller. London: Cassell, 1995.

Graus, Frantisek. "Randgruppen der städtischen Gesellschaft im Spätmittelalter." *Zeitschrift für Historische Forschung* 8 (1981): 385–437.

Greenberg, David F. *The Construction of Homosexuality.* Chicago: Chicago University Press, 1988.

Greenblatt, Stephen Jay. *Learning to Curse: Essays in Early Modern Culture.* New York: Routledge, 1990.

——. *Renaissance Self-fashioning: from More to Shakespeare.* Chicago: University of Chicago Press, 1980.

——. "Towards a Poetics of Culture." Veeser 1–14.

Greenblatt, Stephen Jay and Giles B. Gunn, eds. *Redrawing the Boundaries: the Transformation of English and American Literary Studies.* New York: MLA, 1992.

Greiner, Ulrich. "Bücher für das ganze Leben. Eine ZEIT-Umfrage: Brauchen wir einen neuen Literatur-Kanon?" *Die Zeit* 21, 23 May 1997, 14–17.

Grier, Edward. "Walt Whitman." *The Encyclopedia of Homosexuality.* Ed. Wayne R. Dyers. 2 vols. New York: Garland, 1990. 2: 1389.

Grubbe, Peter. "Ein Haus für Künstler und Bürger." *Schöner Wohnen,* November 1987, 239f.

Grumbach, Detlef, ed. *Die Linke und das Laster. Schwule Emanzipation und linke Vorurteile.* Hamburg: MännerschwarmSkript, 1995.

Gubar, Susan and Jonathan Kamholtz, eds. *English Inside and Out: The Places of Literary Criticism.* New York: Routledge, 1993.

Guillory, John. "The Ideology of Canon-Formation: T. S. Eliot and Cleanth Brooks." *Canons.* Ed. Robert von Hallberg. Chicago: University of Chicago Press, 1984. 337-62.

———. *Cultural Capital. The Problem of Literary Canon-Formation.* Chicago: University of Chicago Press, 1993.

Gürtler, Christa, ed. *Gegen den schönen Schein. Texte zu Elfriede Jelinek.* Frankfurt/M: Neue Kritik, 1990.

Habermas, Jürgen. *Strukturwandel der Öffentlichkeit. Untersuchungen zu einer Kategorie der bürgerlichen Gesellschaft.* Neuwied am Rhein: Luchterhand, 1965.

Hagemann-White, Carol. "Die Konstrukteure des Geschlechts auf frischer Tat ertappen? Methodische Konsequenzen einer theoretischen Einsicht." *Feministische Studien* 2 (1993): 68-78.

Hagen, Friedrich von der. *Gesammtabenteuer: 100 altdeutsche Erzählungen.* Vol. 1. Stuttgart: Cotta, 1850.

Hahn, Barbara. "Feministische Literaturwissenschaft. Vom Mittelweg der Frauen in der Theorie." *Neue Literaturtheorien. Eine Einführung.* Ed. Klaus Michael Bogdal. Opladen: Westdeutscher Verlag, 1990. 218-34.

Hahnemann, Gino. "Das Ghetto ist zu klein für uns beide." *Vogel oder Käfig sein. Kunst und Literatur aus unabhängigen Zeitschriften in der DDR 1979-1989.* Ed. Klaus Michael and Thomas Wohlfahrt. Berlin: Galrev, 1992. 162-65.

———. "Ende der Utopien." Arnold 134-36.

Halperin, David. *One Hundred Years of Homosexuality and Other Essays on Greek Love.* New York: Routledge, 1990.

Hammer, Stephanie Barbé. "Schiller, Time and Again." *German Quarterly* 62.2 (1994): 153-72.

Hanssen, Léon. "Een gesprek met Golo Mann." *Maatstaf* 8-9 (1985): 13-22.

Hark, Sabine. "Queer Interventionen." *Feministische Studien* 2 (1993): 103-09.

Härle, Gerhard. *Die Gestalt des Schönen. Untersuchung zur Homosexualitätsthematik in Thomas Manns Roman "Der Zauberberg."* Königstein/Ts: Hain, 1986.

———. *Männerweiblichkeit. Zur Homosexualität bei Klaus und Thomas Mann.* Frankfurt/M: Athenäum, 1988.

———. "Simulationen der Wahrheit. Körpersprache und sexuelle Identität im *Zauberberg* und *Felix Krull.*" Härle, *Heimsuchung* 63-86.

———, ed. *'Heimsuchung und süßes Gift.' Erotik und Poetik bei Thomas Mann.* Frankfurt/M: Fischer, 1992.

Harper, Phillip B. "Eloquence and Epitaph: Black Nationalism and the Homophobic Impulse in Responses to the Death of Max Robinson." Abelove et al. 159-75.

Hart und Zart. Frauenleben 1920-1970. Berlin: Elephanten, 1990.

Harvey, David. *The Condition of Postmodernity. An Enquiry into the Origins of Cultural Change.* Oxford: Blackwell, 1990.

Haß, Ulrike. "Grausige Bilder. Große Musik. Zu den Theaterstücken Elfriede Jelineks." *Text und Kritik* 117 (1993): 21-30.

Hassauer, Friederike. *Homo. Academica. Geschlechterkontrakte, Institution und die Verteilung des Wissens*. Wien: Passagen, 1994.

Hausen, Karin. "Die Polarisierung der *Geschlechtscharaktere* — Eine Spiegelung der Dissoziation von Erwerbs- und Familienleben." *Sozialgeschichte der Familie in der Neuzeit Europas*. Ed. Werner Conze. Stuttgart: Ernst Klett, 1976. 363-93.

Headlam, Bruce. "Attila up against the Wall." *Saturday Night*, December 1993, 54-59f.

Healy, Murray. *Gay Skins*. London: Cassell, 1996.

Heilbut, Anthony. *Thomas Mann. Eros and Literature*. New York: Knopf, 1996.

Heimberger, Joseph. "Die strafrechtliche Behandlung der Homosexuellen." *Allgemeine Zeitschrift für Psychiatrie und psychisch-gerichtliche Medizin* 64 (1907): 704-10.

Heinrich von Veldeke. *Eneasroman*. Mittelhochdeutsch/Neuhochdeutsch. Nach dem Text von Ludwig Ettmüller. Ed. Dieter Kartschoke. Stuttgart: Reclam, 1986.

Heinsohn, Gunnar, Rolf Knieper, and Otto Steiger. *Menschenproduktion. Allgemeine Bevölkerungstheorien der Neuzeit*. Frankfurt/M: Suhrkamp, 1979.

Heinzle, Joachim. "Kleine Anleitung zum Gebrauch des Märenbegriffs." *Kleinere Erzählformen des Mittelalters: Paderborner Colloquium 1987*. Ed. Klaus Grubmüller, L. Peter Johnson and Hans-Hugo Steinhoff. Paderborn: Schöningh, 1988. 45-48.

Heller, J. L. von et al., eds. *Didiskalia oder Blätter für Geist, Gemüth und Publizität*. Frankfurt: Heller & Rohm, 1823-1903.

Helmholtz, Hermann von. *On the Sensations of Tone as a Physiological Basis for the Theory of Music*. London: Longmans, 1875.

Hergemöller, Bernd-Ulrich. "Die *unaussprechliche stumme Sünde* in Cologneer Akten des ausgehenden Mittelalters." *Geschichte in Cologne* 22 (1987): 5-51.

———. "Homosexuelle als spätmittelalterliche Randgruppe." *Forum Homosexualität und Literatur* 2 (1987): 53-91.

———. "Sodomiter. Erscheinungsformen und Kausalfaktoren des spätmittelalterlichen Kampfes gegen Homosexuelle." Hergemöller, *Randgruppen* 361-403.

———. "Sodomiter: Schuldzuweisungen und Repressionsformen im späten Mittelalter." Hergemöller, *Randgruppen* 316-56.

———, ed. *Randgruppen der spätmittelalterlichen Gesellschaft*. Warendorf: Fahlbusch, 1990.

Herr Wegener. "Die Homoeroten in Schillers Prosaschriften." *Blätter für Menschenrechte*, October 1927.

Herzog, Werner, dir. *Jeder für sich und Gott gegen alle* [*The Mystery of Kaspar Hauser*, alternatively: *Every Man for Himself and God against All*]. 1975. Videocassette. New Yorker Video, 1993.

Hetze, Stefanie. *Happy-End für wen? Kino und lesbische Frauen*. Frankfurt/M: tende, 1986.

Hibbard, Howard. *Caravaggio*. New York: Harper, 1983.

Hiller, Kurt. "Homosexualismus und Deutscher Vorentwurf." *Pan* 35 (1912): 973-83.

Hines, John. *The Fabliaux in English.* London, New York: Longman, 1993.

Hirsch, Joachim and Roland Roth. *Das neue Gesicht des Kapitalismus. Vom Fordismus zum Post-Fordismus.* Hamburg: VSA, 1986.

Hirschauer, Stefan. "Dekonstruktion und Rekonstruktion. Plädoyer für eine Erforschung des Bekannten." *Feministische Studien* 2 (1993): 55-67.

Hirschfeld, Magnus. *Die Homosexualität des Mannes und des Weibes.* Berlin: Marcus, 1914.

———. *Paragraph 175 des Reichs-Straf-Gesetz-Buches. Die homosexuelle Frage im Urteil der Zeitgenossen.* Leipzig 1898.

Hitchcock, Alfred, dir. *Psycho.* 1960.

———. *Spellbound.* 1945.

———. *Vertigo.* 1958.

Hoberman, J. "The Belly of an Audience." *Village Voice,* 19 January 1988, n.p.

Hocquenghem, Guy. *Homosexual Desire.* 1972. Trans. Daniella Dangoor. 1978. Durham: Duke University Press, 1993.

Hoersley, Ritta J. "Ingeborg Bachmann's *Ein Schritt nach Gomorrah*: A Feminist Appreciation and Critique." *Amsterdamer Beiträge zur Germanistik* 10 (1980): 277-93.

Hoesterey, Ingeborg. "A Feminist 'Theater of Cruelty': Surrealist and Mannerist Strategies in *Krankheit oder Moderne Frauen.*" Johns and Arens 151-65.

Hoff, Dagmar von. "Stücke für das Theater. Überlegungen zu Elfriede Jelineks Methode der Destruktion." Gürtler 112-18.

Honegger, Claudia. *Die Ordnung der Geschlechter: die Wissenschaft vom Menschen und das Weib. 1750-1850.* Frankfurt/M: Campus, 1991.

Hooks, Bell. *Yearning: Race, Gender, and Cultural Politics.* Toronto: Between the Lines, 1990.

Hooper, Tobe, dir. *Texas Chainsaw Massacre.* 1974.

Hotchkiss, Valerie L. *Clothes Make the Man: Female Cross Dressing in Medieval Europe.* New York: Garland, 1996.

Hoven, Heribert. *Studien zur Erotik in der deutschen Märendichtung.* Göppingen: Kümmerle, 1978.

Hull, Isabel V. *The Entourage of Kaiser Wilhelm II, 1888-1918.* Cambridge: University Press, 1982.

Hume, Christopher. "Ugly Paintings of Skinheads Beautifully Tell Tale of Our Time." *Toronto Star,* 30 June 1989, 23(E).

Huyssen, Andreas. *Twilight Memories: Marking Time in a Culture of Amnesia.* New York: Routledge, 1995.

Ipema, Jan. "Antipoden of geestverwanten? Klaus Mann en Ernst Jünger." *Maatstaf* 8-9 (1985): 87-90.

Irigaray, Luce. *Speculum of the Other Woman.* Trans. Gillian C. Gill. Ithaca: Cornell University Press, 1985.

Irigaray, Luce. *This Sex Which is Not One*. Trans. by Cathereine Porter. Ithaca: Cornell University Press, 1985.

Irsigler, Franz and Arnold Lassotta. *Bettler und Gaukler, Dirnen und Henker. Außenseiter in der mittelalterlichen Stadt* Cologne *1300-1600*. Munich: dtv, 1989.

Isherwood, Christopher. *The Berlin Stories: "The Last of Mr. Norris" and "Goodbye to Berlin."* 1963. Cambridge, MA: Bentley, 1979.

Jameson, Frederic. *Signatures of the Visible*. New York: Routledge, 1992.

———. *Postmodernism, or, The Cultural Logic of Late Capitalism*. Durham: Duke University Press, 1991.

Jansen, Peter W. and Wolfram Schütte, eds. *Werner Herzog*. Munich: Hanser, 1979.

Janz, Marlies. "Falsche Spiegel. Über die Umkehrung der Verfahren bei Elfriede Jelinek." Gürtler 81-97.

Jauss, Hans Robert. "The Theory of Genres and Medieval Literature." *Toward an Aesthetics of Reception*. Ed. Hans Robert Jauss. Brighton: Harvester, 1982. 76-109.

Jelinek, Elfriede. "Access Routes into Postmodernism." Interview with Donna Hoffmeister. *Modern Austrian Literature* 2 (1987): 97-130.

———. "Der ewige Krampf. Elfriede Jelinek über zwei Arsenleichen (weiblich) in der Literatur." *Wespennest* 44 (1981): 32-36.

———. "Der fremde! störenfried der ruhe eines sommerabends der ruhe eines friedhofs" [1969]. *Der gewöhnliche Schrecken. Horrorgeschichten*. Ed. Peter Handke. Munich: dtv, 1971. 135-47.

———. "Der Krieg mit anderen Mitteln. Über Ingeborg Bachmann." *Die schwarze Botin* 21 (1983): 149-53.

———. *Die Ausgesperrten*. Reinbek: Rowohlt, 1980.

———. *Die Kinder der Toten*. Reinbek: Rowohlt, 1995.

———. *Die Klavierspielerin*. Reinbek: Rowohlt, 1983.

———. "Die Lady N ein Vampir?" Interview with Roland Gross. *Theater Heute* 28.4 (1987): 34-35.

———. "Ich mag Männer nicht, aber ich bin sexuell auf sie angewiesen." Interview with Sigrid Löffler. *Profil* 13 (1989): 83-85.

———. "Ich möchte seicht sein." Gürtler 157-61.

———. "Ich will kein Theater – Ich will ein anderes Theater." Interview with Anke Roeder. *Autorinnen: Herausforderungen an das Theater*. Ed. Anke Roeder. Frankfurt/M: Suhrkamp, 1989. 141-60.

———. *Krankheit oder Moderne Frauen*. In *Theaterstücke*. Reinbek: Rowohlt, 1992. 191-265.

———. *Lust*. Reinbek: Rowohlt, 1989.

———. *Oh Wildnis, oh Schutz vor ihr*. Reinbek: Rowohlt, 1985.

———. *Wolken.Heim*. Göttingen: Steidl, 1990.

———. "Zu Sylvia Plath *Briefe nach Hause*." *Aufschreiben. Texte österreichischer Frauen*. Wien 1981. 43-46.

Jentsch, Karl. *Sexualethik, Sexualjustiz, Sexualpolizei*. Wien 1900.

Johns Hopkins Guide to Literary Theory & Criticism, The. Eds. Michael Groden and Martin Kreiswirth. Baltimore: Johns Hopkins University Press, 1994.

Johns, Jorun B. and Katherine Arens, eds. *Elfriede Jelinek: Framed by Language.* Riverside: Ariadne, 1994.

Jones, James. "German and Austrian Literature: Nineteenth and Twentieth Centuries." *The Gay and Lesbian Literary Heritage.* Ed. Claude Summers. New York: Henry Holt, 1995. 317-23.

Kaes, Anton. *From "Hitler" to "Heimat": The Return of History as Film.* Cambridge, MA: Harvard University Press, 1989.

——. "The New German Cinema." In Nowell-Smith, *The Oxford History of World Cinema* (1996): 614-27.

Kaiser, A. H. "Homosexualität und Strafrechtsreform." *Fortschritte der Medizin* 30 (1912): 993-1006.

Kalb, Jonathan. "Lotti Da." *Village Voice,* 18 January 1988, 72.

Kaplan, E. Ann. "Is the Gaze Male?" *Desire. The Politics of Sexuality.* Ed. Ann Snitow, Christine Stansell, and Sharon Thompson. London: Virago, 1983. 321-38.

Kappeler, Susanne. *The Pornography of Representation.* Cambridge: Polity, 1986.

Karlsruhe, Badisches Staatstheater. Program for *Egmont.* Performance text, 1980. 56.

Katte, Max. "Aus dem Leben eines Homosexuellen." *Jahrbuch für sexuelle Zwischenstufen* 2 (1900): 295-316.

——. "Über den Begriff der Abnormität mit besonderer Berücksichtigung des sexuellen Gebietes." *Zeitschrift für Sexualwissenschaft* 1 (1908): 385-404.

Katz, Jonathan Ned. *The Invention of Heterosexuality.* New York: Penguin/Dutton, 1995.

Katz, Robert. *Love Is Colder than Death: The Life and Times of Rainer Werner Fassbinder.* New York: Random, 1987.

Kaus, Rainer J. *Der Fall Goethe – ein deutscher Fall. Eine psychoanalytische Studie.* Heidelberg: Winter, 1994.

Kelly, Keith. "The Sexual Politics of Rosa von Praunheim." *Millennium Film Journal* 3 (1979): 115-18.

Kerker, Armin. *Ernst Jünger – Klaus Mann. Gemeinsamkeit und Gegensatz in Literatur und Politik. Zur Typologie des literarischen Intellektuellen im 20. Jahrhundert.* Bonn: Bouvier, 1974.

Kerker, Elke. *Weltbürgertum – Exil – Heimatlosigkeit. Die Entwicklung der politischen Dimension im Werk Klaus Manns von 1924 bis 1936.* Meisenheim: Anton Hain, 1977.

Kern, Stephen. Anatomy and Destiny: *A Cultural History of the Human Body.* Indianapolis: Bobbs-Merrill, 1975.

Kiefer, Otto [pseud. Reiffegg]. "Über die Bedeutung der Jünglingsliebe für unsere Zeit." Leipzig: Spohr, 1902. Rpt. as "The Significance of Youth-Love for Our Time." Oosterhuis 167-77.

Kilb, Andreas. "Ein letzter Versuch, die neue deutsche Filmkomödie zu verstehen." *Die Zeit,* Online 26 April 1996, n.p.

Kinzer, Stephen. "The German Comedy, An Oxymoron No More." *New York Times,* 23 June 1996, 31.

Kittler, Friedrich A. "Carlos als Carlsschüler. Ein Familiengemälde in einem fürstlichen Haus." *Unser Commercium. Goethe und Schillers Literaturpolitik.* Ed. Wilfried Barner, Eberhard Lämmert, Norbert Oellers. Stuttgart: Cotta, 1984. 241–74.

Klawitter, George. *The Enigmatic Narrator. The Voicing of Same-Sex Love in the Poetry of John Donne.* New York: Lang, 1994.

Kleist, Heinrich von. *The Marquise of O. and Other Stories.* Trans. David Luke and Nigel Reeves. New York: Penguin, 1978.

Klinger, Friedrich Maximilian. *Faust's Leben, Taten und Höllenfahrt.* Ed. Sander L. Gilman. Tübingen: Niemeyer, 1987. Vol. 9 of *Werke: Historisch-kritische Gesamtausgabe.*

Klopfer, Marian, trans. "*The Sport of Destiny. A Fragment of a True Story.* Johann von Schiller (1759-1805)." 1933. *Great German Short Novels and Stories.* Ed. Victor Lange. New York: Modern Library, 1952. 100-109.

Klug, Thomas. *Verboten, vergessen, verdrängt – Homosexualität in DDR-Medien. Zum Prozess der Herausbildung des öffentlichen Diskurses zum Thema Homosexualität in den DDR-Medien.* Diplomarbeit. Institut für Kommunikations- und Medienwissenschaft, Universität Leipzig, 1995 (unpublished).

Kluge, Alexander. "Pact with a Dead Man." *West German Filmmakers on Film: Visions and Voices.* Ed. E. Rentschler. New York: Holmes and Meier, 1988. 234-41.

——, dir. *Die Patriotin.* 1979.

Kluge, Friedrich. *Etymologisches Wörterbuch der Deutschen Sprache.* 22nd ed. Berlin: de Gruyter, 1989.

Knapp, Fritz Peter. "Literarische Interessenbildung im Kreise österreichischer und steirischer Landherrn zur Zeit des Interregnums." *Literarische Interessenbildung im Mittelalter.* DFG-Symposion 1991. Ed. Joachim Heinzle. Stuttgart: Metzler, 1993.

Knight, Julia. *Women and the New German Cinema.* London: Verso, 1992.

Knud, Wolffram. *Tanzdielen und Vergnügungspaläste. Berliner Nachtleben in den dreißiger und vierziger Jahren. Von der Friedrichstraße bis Berlin W, vom Moka Efti bis zum Delphi.* Berlin: Hentrich, 1992.

Koestenbaum, Wayne. *Double Talk: The Erotics of Male Literary Collaboration.* New York: Routledge, 1989.

——. *The Queen's Throat: Opera, Homosexuality, and the Mystery of Desire.* New York: Poseidon Press, 1993.

Kokula, Ilse. "Die 'goldenen Zwanziger' in Berlin – von unten gesehen." *LesbenStich* 4.2 (1983): 24-28.

——. "Freundinnen–Lesbische Frauen in der Weimarer Zeit." *Hart und Zart* 128-32.

——. "Lesbische leben von Weimar bis zur Nachkriegszeit." *Eldorado* 149-61.

Kolkenbrock-Netz, Jutta. "Interpretation, Diskursanalyse und/oder feministische Lektüre literarischer Texte von Frank Wedekind." *Weiblichkeit in geschichtlicher Perspektive.* Ed. Ursula A. Becher and Jörn Rüsen. Frankfurt/M.: Suhrkamp, 1988. 397-422.

König, Ralf. *Der bewegte Mann.* Reinbek bei Hamburg: Rowohlt, 1987.

——. *Der bewegte Mann. Pretty Baby, Der Bewegte Mann 2,* Comic. *Das Buch zum Film.* Reinbek bei Hamburg: Rowohlt, 1995.

——. *Pretty Baby. Der bewegte Mann 2.* Reinbek bei Hamburg: Rowohlt, 1988.

König, René. *The Restless Image. A Sociology of Fashion.* 1971. Trans. F. Bradley. 1973. London: Allen, 1973.

Kracauer, Siegfried. *The Mass Ornament.* Trans. T. Levin. Cambridge: Harvard University Press, 1995.

Krafft-Ebing, Richard. *Psychopathia Sexualis.* New York: Putnam, 1965.

Kramer, Jonathan. "Discontinuity and Proportion in the Music of Stravinsky." *Confronting Stravinsky: Man, Musician, and Modernist.* Ed. Jan Pasler. Berkeley: University of California Press, 1986: 174-94.

Kreische, Rosi. "Lesbische Liebe im Film bis 1950." *Eldorado* 187-97.

Kristeva, Julia. *Revolution in Poetic Language.* Trans. by Margaret Waller. New York: Columbia University Press, 1984.

Kroker, Arthur. "Attila Richard Lukacs: Painting the Hysterical Male." Exhibition Catalogue. Vancouver: Diane Farris Gallery, 1990.

Krzywinska, Tanya. "La Belle Dame Sans Merci?" Burston and Richardson 99-110.

Kuhn, Annette. *The Power of the Image.* New York: Routledge, 1988.

Kumar, Krishan. *From Post-Industrial to Post-Modern Society. New Theories of the Contemporary World.* Oxford: Blackwell, 1995.

Kupffer, Elisar von [pseud. Elisarion]. *Lieblingminne und Freundesliebe in der Weltliteratur.* Berlin: Brand, 1909.

Kuster, Harry J. and Raymond J. Cormier. "Old Views and New Trends: Observations on the Problem of Homosexuality in the Middle Ages." *Studi medievali* 25.2 (1984): 587-610.

Kuster, Hendrikus J. *Over Homoseksualiteit in middeleeuws West-Europa. Some Observations on Homosexuality in medieval Western Europe.* Utrecht: Privatdruck, 1977.

Kuzniar, Alice A., ed. *Outing Goethe and His Age.* Stanford: Stanford University Press, 1996.

Lacan, Jacques. *Écrits: A Selection.* Trans. Alan Sheridan. New York: Norton, 1977.

Laclau, Ernesto and Chantal Mouffe. *Hegemony and Socialist Strategy. Towards a Radical Democratic Politics.* London: Verso, 1985.

Lacy, Norris J. *Reading Fabliaux.* New York: Garland, 1993.

Landweer, Hilge. "Generationen in der deutschen Frauenforschung." *Konkurrenz und Kooperation. Frauen im Zwiespalt?* Ed. Ilse Modelmog and Ulrike Gräßel. Münster/Hamburg: Lit. Münster, 1994. 117-35.

——. "Herausforderung Foucault." *Die Philosophin* 7 (1993): 8-18.

——. "Jenseits des Geschlechts? Zum Phänomen der theoretischen wie politischen Fehleinschätzung von Travestie und Transsexualität." *Geschlechterverhältnisse und Politik.* Ed. Institut für Sozialforschung Frankfurt. Frankfurt/M.: Suhrkamp, 1994. 139-67.

Landweer, Hilge. "Kritik und Verteidigung der Kategorie Geschlecht. Wahrnehmungs- und symboltheoretische Überlegungen zur sex/gender Unterscheidung." *Feministische Studien* 2 (1993): 34-43.

Landweer, Hilge and Mechthild Rumpf. "Kritik der Kategorie *Geschlecht.* Streit um Begriffe, Streit um Orientierungen, Streit der Generationen?" *Feministische Studien* 2 (1993): 3-9.

Lang, Fritz, dir. *Dr. Mabuse.* 1922.

——. *Metropolis.* 1926.

Larkin, Christopher, dir. *A Very Natural Thing.* 1973.

Laun, Friedrich von, ed. *Abend-Zeitung nebst Intelligenzblatt für Literatur und Kunst.* Dresden 1805ff.

Lautmann, Rüdiger. *Seminar Homosexualität und Gesellschaft.* Frankfurt/M: Suhrkamp, 1977.

Le Fanu, Joseph Sheridan. "Carmilla." *The Penguin Book of Vampire Stories.* Ed. Alan Ryan. Harmondsworth: Penguin, 1988.

Le Goff, Jacques. *Die Geburt des Fegefeuers. Vom Wandel des Weltbildes im Mittelalter.* Munich: Klett-Cotta, 1990.

Le Roman d'Éneas. Trans. into German and introduced by Monica Schöler-Beinhauer. Munich: Fink, 1972. Klassische Texte des romanischen Mittelalters, Bd. 9.

Lemke, Jürgen. *Ganz normal anders. Auskünfte schwuler Männer aus der DDR.* Mit einer Vorbemerkung von Irene Runge. Frankfurt/M: Luchterhand, 1989.

——. *Gay Voices from East Germany.* Ed. John Borneman. Trans. Steven Stoltenberg et al. Bloomington: Indiana University Press, 1991.

Lengerke, Christiane von. "Homosexuelle Frauen: Tribaden, Freundinnen, Urninden." *Eldorado* 125-48.

Levi-Strauss, Claude. *The Elementary Structures of Kinship.* Trans. James H. Bell and Richard von Sturmer. Boston: Beacon, 1969.

Lewin, David. "Behind the Beyond: A Response to Edward T. Cone." *Perspectives of New Music* (spring-summer 1969): 59-69.

——. "Inversional Balance as an Organizing Force in Schönberg's Music and Thought." *Perspectives of New Music* (spring-summer 1968): 1-21.

Licht, Hans (Paul Brandt) *Sittengeschichte Griechenlands.* 2 vols. plus 1 supplem. vol. Zürich: Aretz, 1925-1928. Trans. J. H. Fresse. *Sexual Life in Ancient Greece.* New York: Dorset, 1993.

Liebs, Elke. "Weiße und schwarze Magie. Oder: vom romantischen zum dialektischen Kannibalismus/Vampirismus der Frau." *Argument-Sonderband Frauen Literatur Politik.* Berlin: Argument. 242-54.

Linkenbach, Alexander. "Die Aufnahmen des Palast Orchesters." Internet, Online 26. August 1997.

Loewenberg, B. W. "Über die Homosexualität." *Deutsche Medizinal-Zeitungen* (1903): 733-35.

Löffler, Sigrid. "Der sensible Vampir." *Emma* 10 (1985): 32-37.

Lorey, Isabell. "Der Körper als Text und das textuelle Selbst: Butler und Foucault." *Feministische Studien* 2 (1993): 10-23.

Luscher, Jean A. "Myth, Language and Power in Elfriede Jelinek's *Krankheit oder Moderne Frauen.*" Johns and Arens 166-75.

MacKenzie, John M. *Propaganda and Empire. The Manipulation of British Public Opinion 1880-1960.* Manchester: Manchester University Press, 1984.

Madsen, Deborah L. *Postmodernism: A Bibliography, 1926-1994.* Amsterdam: Rodopi, 1995.

Maggiore, Dolores. *Lesbianism: An Annotated Bibliography and Guide to Literature, 1976-1991.* Metuchen, NJ: Scarecrow, 1992.

Maihofer, Andrea. "Geschlecht als Existenzweise. Einige kritische Anmerkungen zu aktuellen Versuchen zu einem neuen Verständnis von Geschlecht." *Geschlechterverhältnisse und Politik.* Ed. Institut für Sozialforschung Frankfurt. Frankfurt/M: Suhrkamp, 1994. 168-87.

Mann, Golo. "Herinneringen aan mijn broer Klaus." *Maatstaf* 8-9 (1985): 61-82.

Mann, Klaus. *Alexander. Roman der Utopie.* Berlin: Fischer, 1930.

———. *Anja und Esther. Ein romantisches Stück in sieben Bildern.* Berlin: Oesterheld, 1925.

———. *Der fromme Tanz. Das Abenteuerbuch einer Jugend.* Hamburg: Gebrüder Enoch, 1925.

———. "Der Kampf um den jungen Menschen." *Woher wir kommen und wohin wir müssen. Frühe und nachgelassene Schriften.* Ed. Martin Gregor-Dellin. Munich: Heinrich Ellermann. 113-22.

———. *Der Vulkan. Roman unter Emigranten.* Amsterdam: Querido, 1939.

———. *Der Wendepunkt. Ein Lebensbericht* (1949). Berlin: Fischer, 1952.

———. "Die Linke und das 'Laster'." (1934) *Europäische Hefte* 36-37, 675-78.

———. *Heute und morgen: Schriften zur Zeit.* Ed. Martin Gregor-Dellin. Munich: Nymphenburg, 1969.

———. "Homosexualität und Faschismus" (1934). K. Mann, *Heute und morgen* 130-37.

———. *Kind dieser Zeit* (1932). Reinbek bei Hamburg: Rowohlt, 1982.

———. "Krieg und Sexualität" (1930). K. Mann, *Heute und morgen* 85-87.

———. *Mephisto. Roman einer Karriere.* Amsterdam: Querido, 1936.

———. "Selbstanzeige: Mephisto" (1936). K. Mann, *Heute und morgen* 50-54.

———. *Symphonie Pathétique. Ein Tschaikowsky-Roman.* Amsterdam: Querido, 1935.

———. *Tagebücher 1931 bis 1933.* Ed. Joachim Heimannsberg, Peter Laemmle, and Wilfried F. Schoeller. Munich: Spangenberg, 1989.

———. *The Turning Point. Thirty-Five Years in This Century* (1942). London: Oswald Wolff, 1984.

———. *Vor dem Leben. Erzählungen.* Hamburg: Gebrüder Enoch Verlag, 1925.

Mann, Klaus and Kurt Tucholsky. *Homosexualität und Faschismus.* Hamburg: Frühlings Erwachen, 1981.

Mann, Thomas. "August von Platen" (1930). *Gesammelte Werke* 11: 268-81.

———. *Bekenntnisse des Hochstaplers Felix Krull* (1954). *Gesammelte Werke* 7.

———. *Betrachtungen eines Unpolitischen* (1918). *Gesammelte Werke* 12: 7-589.

Mann, Thomas. "Brief an Hermann Grafen Keyserling" (1920). *Gesammelte Werke* 12: 593–603.

——. *Briefe 1889–1936*. Ed. Erika Mann. Frankfurt/M: Fischer, 1963.

——. "Bruder Hitler" (1939). *Gesammelte Werke* 12: 845–52.

——. "Das Problem der deutsch-französischen Beziehungen" (1922). Th. Mann, *Von deutscher Republik* 170–91.

——. "Death in Venice." Th. Mann, *Death in Venice* 3–75.

——. *Death in Venice and Seven Other Stories*. Trans. H. T. Lowe-Porter (1930). New York: Vintage, 1936.

——. *Der Tod in Venedig* (1912). *Gesammelte Werke* 8: 444–525.

——. *Der Zauberberg* (1924). *Gesammelte Werke* 3.

——. "Deutsche Ansprache. Ein Appell an die Vernunft" (1930). Th. Mann, *Von deutscher Republik* 294–314.

——. "Deutschland und die Demokratie" (1922). Th. Mann, *Von deutscher Republik* 213–22.

——. *Diaries 1918–1939. 1918–1921. 1933–1939*. Trans. Richard and Clara Winston. New York: Harry N. Abrams, 1982; London: Robin Clark, 1984.

——. "Die Ehe im Übergang." *Essays*. Vol. 2: *Für das neue Deutschland 1919–1925*. Ed. Hermann Kurzlee and Stephen Stachorski. Frankfurt/M: Fischer, 1993. 267–82.

——. *Die Erzählungen. Erster Band*. Frankfurt/M: Fischer, 1967.

——. "Die geistigen Tendenzen des heutigen Deutschlands" (1927). Th. Mann, *Von deutscher Republik* 222–35.

——. "Die Wiedergeburt der Anständigkeit" (1931). In Th. Mann. *Von deutscher Republik* 314–43.

——. *Doktor Faustus. Das Leben des deutschen Tonsetzers Adrian Leverkühn, erzählt von einem Freunde* (1947). *Gesammelte Werke* Vol. 6.

——. *Doctor Faustus. The Life of the German Composer Adrian Leverkühn as Told by a Friend*. Trans. H. T. Lowe-Porter (1948). New York: Modern Library, 1948.

——. "Frederick the Great and the Grand Coalition." *Thomas Mann. Three Essays*. Trans. H. T. Lowe-Porter. New York: Alfred A. Knopf, 1929. 143–215.

——. "Friedrich und die große Koalition" (1915). Th. Mann. *Von deutscher Republik* 28–88.

——. "Gedanken im Kriege" (1914). *Von deutscher Republik* 7–25.

——. *Gesammelte Werke in zwölf Bänden*. (GW) Frankfurt/M: Fischer, 1960.

——. "Goethe und die Demokratie" (1949). *Gesammelte Werke* 9: 755–82.

——. *Last Essays*. Trans. Richard and Clara Winston and Tania and James Stern. New York: A. Knopf, 1959.

——. "Lebensabriss" (1930). *Gesammelte Werke* 11: 98–144.

——. "Leiden an Deutschland" (1933–34). *Gesammelte Werke* 12: 684–766.

——. *Leiden und Größe der Meister*. Frankfurt/M: Fischer, 1982.

——. *Letters of Thomas Mann, 1889–1955*. Trans. Richard and Clara Winston. Vol. 1: 1889–1942. London: Secker & Warburg, 1970.

Mann, Thomas. *The Magic Mountain.* Trans. H. T. Lowe-Porter. New York: Alfred A. Knopf, 1927; New York: Vintage, 1969.

———. *Mario und der Zauberer. Ein tragisches Reiseerlebnis* (1930). *Gesammelte Werke* 8: 658-711.

———. "Nietzsche's Philosophy in the Light of Recent History." Trans. Richard and Clara Winston. Th. Mann, *Last Essays* 141-177.

———. "Nietzsches Philosophie im Lichte unserer Erfahrung" (1947). *Gesammelte Werke* 9: 675-712.

———. "Protest der Prominenten gegen die Beibehaltung und Verschärfung des Paragraphen 175." *Eros. Werbeheft der Kampf- und Kunstzeitschrift "Der Eigene"* 7 (1930): 97-98.

———. *Reflections of a Nonpolitical Man.* Trans. Walter D. Morris (1983). New York: Frederick Ungar, 1983.

———. "Schopenhauer" (1938). *Gesammelte Werke* 9: 528-80.

———. *Tagebücher 1918-1921.* (TB 1) Ed. Peter de Mendelssohn. Frankfurt/M: Fischer, 1979.

———. *Tagebücher 1933-1934.* (TB 2) Ed. Peter de Mendelssohn. Frankfurt/M: Fischer, 1977.

———. *Tagebücher 1935-1936.* (TB 3) Ed. Peter de Mendelssohn. Frankfurt/M: Fischer, 1978.

———. *Tagebücher 1949-1950.* (TB 4) Ed. Inge Jens. Frankfurt/M: Fischer, 1991.

———. "Tonio Kröger." Th. Mann, *Death in Venice* 76-134.

———. *Tonio Kröger* (1903). *Gesammelte Werke* 8: 271-338.

———. "Über die Ehe" (1925). *Gesammelte Werke* 10: 191-207.

———. "Über Goethes *Faust.*" *Schriften und Reden zur Literatur, Kunst und Philosophie.* 3 vols. Frankfurt/M: Fischer, 1968. 2: 290-322.

———. "Von deutscher Republik" (1922). Th. Mann, *Von deutscher Republik* 118-59.

———. *Von deutscher Republik. Politische Schriften und Reden in Deutschland.* Frankfurt/M: Fischer, 1984.

Margueritte, Victor. *Die Aussteigerin.* [Orig. *La Garçonne* (1922)] Munich: Matthes and Seitz, 1982.

Marohn, Norbert. *Plötzlich mein Leben. Erzählung.* Halle: Mitteldeutscher Verlag, 1989.

Marshall, Donald G. *Contemporary Critical Theory. A Selective Bibliography.* New York: MA, 1993.

Marshall, Stuart. "The Contemporary Political Use of Gay History: The Third Reich." *How Do I Look? Queer Film and Video.* Ed. Bad Object-Choices. Seattle: Bay, 1991. 65-101.

———, dir. *Bright Eyes.* 1986.

Marti, Madeleine. *Hinterlegte Botschaften: Die Darstellung lesbischer Frauen in der deutschsprachigen Literatur seit 1945.* Stuttgart: Metzler, 1992.

———. "Von 'Robinson' zur 'Angehörigen der Lesbischen Nation': Christa Reinig als lesbische Schriftstellerin." *Die Welt neu erfinden: Über das Schreiben und Lesen von Lesbenliteratur.* 2nd ed. Bremen: XENIA Lesbenliteraturverlag, 1990. 25-43.

Martineau, William H. "A Model of the Social Functions of Humor." *The Psychology of Humor: Theoretical Perspectives and Empirical Issues.* Ed. Jeffrey H. Goldstein and Paul McGhee. New York: Academic, 1972. 114-23.

Mattenklott, Gert. "Homosexualität und Politik bei Klaus Mann." *Sammlung: Jahrbuch für antifaschistische Literatur und Kunst* 2 (1979): 29-38.

Mayer, Hans. Outsiders. *A Study in Life and Letters.* Trans. Denis M. Sweet. Cambridge, MA: MIT Press, 1982.

———. *Thomas Mann.* Frankfurt/M: Suhrkamp, 1980.

Mays, John Bentley. "Skinhead Paintings Transcend the Erotic." *Globe and Mail,* 8 July 1989, 4(C).

McIntosh, Mary. "Queer Theory and the War of the Sexes." Bristow and Wilson 30-52.

McMillan, Douglas J. *Approaches to Teaching Goethe's Faust.* New York: MLA, 1987.

McTavish, Lianne. "Confronting the Work of Atilla Richard Lukacs." Unpublished Essay, 1997.

Meyer, Adele, ed. *Lila Nächte: Die Damenklubs von Berlin der Zwanziger Jahre.* Berlin: Edition Lit. Europe, 1994.

Meyer, Eva. "Den Vampir schreiben. Zu *Krankheit oder Moderne Frauen.*" Gürtler 98-111.

Meyer, Leonard. *Music, the Arts and Ideas. Patterns and Predictions in Twentieth-Century Culture.* Chicago: University of Chicago Press, 1967.

Meyers Enzyklopädisches Lexikon. Mannheim: Bibliographisches Institut, 1971.

Miller, D. A. "Anal Rope." *Representations* 32 (1990): 114-33.

———. "Sontag's Urbanity." Abelove et al. 212- 20.

Minerva. Taschenbuch für das Jahr 1825. Siebzehnter Jahrgang. Mit 9 Kupfern. Leipzig: Fleischer, 1825.

Minnelli, Vincente, dir. *The Cobweb.* 1955.

Mitscherlich, Alexander and Margarete. *Die Unfähigkeit zu trauern. Grundlagen kollektiven Verhaltens.* Munich: Pieper, 1967.

Modleski, Tania. *Feminism without Women.* New York: Routledge, 1991.

Moelleken, Wolfgang W., ed. *Die Kleindichtung des Strickers. Gesamtausgabe in fünf Bänden.* Göppinger Arbeiten zur Germanistik 107. Göppingen: Kümmerle, 1973-78. Vol. 5.

Molinaro, Edouard, dir. *La Cage aux folles.* 1978.

Moltke, Johannes von. "Camping in the Art Closet: The Politics of Camp and Nation in German Film." *New German Critique* 63 (fall 1994): 77-106.

Moon, Michael. *Disseminating Whitman.* Cambridge: Harvard University Press, 1991.

Moon, Michael and Eve Sedgwick. "Divinity: A Dossier/A Performance Piece/A Little Understood Emotion." *Discourse* (1990/91): 12-39.

Moore, R. I. *The Formation of a Persecuting Society: Power and Deviance in Western Europe, 950-1250.* Oxford: Blackwell, 1987.

Moreck, Kurt [Konrad Haemmerling]. *Führer durch das lasterhafte Berlin.* Leipzig: Verlag moderner Stadtführer, 1931.

Morgan, Robin. "The Politics of Sado-Masochistic Fantasies." *Against Sadomasochism. A Radical Feminist Analysis.* Ed. Robin R. Linden et al. California: Frog in the Well, 1982. 109-23.

Morrill, Cynthia. "Revamping the Gay Sensibility. Queer Camp and *dyke noir.*" *The Politics and Poetics of 'Camp'.* Ed. Moe Meyer. London: Routledge, 1994. 110-29.

Morton, Donald, ed. *The Material Queer: A Lesbigay Cultural Studies Reader.* Boulder: Westview, 1996.

Mosse, George. *Nationalism and Sexuality: Respectability and Abnormal Sexuality in Modern Europe.* New York: Fertig, 1985.

Mouffe, Chantal. "Feminism, Citizenship, and Radical Democratic Politics." *Feminists Theorize the Political.* Ed. Judith Butler and Joan W. Scott. London: Routledge, 1992. 369-84.

Müller, Heiner. "Die Hamletmaschine." *Revolutionsstücke.* Stuttgart: Reclam, 1988. 38-46.

Müller, Jan-Dirk. "Ulrich von Liechtenstein." *Die deutsche Literatur des Mittelalters. Verfasserlexikon.* Vol. 9. Berlin: de Gruyter, 1995.

Müller, Klaus-Detlev. "Die Aufhebung des bürgerlichen Trauerspiels in Schillers *Don Karlos.*" Brandt 218-34.

Mulvey, Laura. *Visual Pleasure and Narrative Cinema. Issues in Feminist Film Criticism.* Ed. Patricia Erens. Bloomington: Indiana University Press, 1990. 28-40.

Murnau, Friedrich Wilhelm, dir. *Der letzte Mann* [*The Last Laugh*]. 1924.

Muscatine, Charles. *The Old French Fabliaux.* New Haven: Yale University Press, 1986.

Nagl-Docekal, Herta. "Rezension zu Judith Butlers *Gender Trouble.*" *L'Homme. Zeitschrift für Feministische Geschichtswissenschaft* 4 (1993): 141-48.

Nagler, A. M. *A Source Book in Theatrical History.* 1952. New York: Dover, 1959.

Narr, Wolf-Dieter. "Vom Liberalismus der Erschöpften." *Blätter für deutsche und internationale Politik* 2 (1991): 216-27.

Nash, Mark. "Anita: Tänze des Lasters." *Monthly Film Bulletin* 57.679 (August 1990): 215.

——. "Not the Homosexual." *Monthly Film Bulletin* 57.680 (September 1990): 250-51.

Naumann, Uwe. *Klaus Mann.* Reinbek bei Hamburg: Rowohlt, 1984.

Neale, Steve. "Masculinity as Spectacle." *The Sexual Subject: A 'Screen' Reader in Sexuality.* Ed. Screen. London: Routledge, 1992. 277-87.

"New Pix tickle Teutons." *Variety*, 17 July 1995, 34-35.

Newton, Esther. "The Mythic Mannish Lesbian: Radclyffe Hall and the New Woman" (1984). *The Lesbian Issue: Essays from Signs.* Ed. Estelle B. Freedman et al. Chicago: University of Chicago Press, 1985. 7-25. Rpt. in Duberman et al. 281-93.

Nichols, Bill. *Ideology and the Image: Social Representation in the Cinema and Other Media.* Bloomington: Indiana University Press, 1981.

Nichols, Mike, dir. *The Birdcage.* 1996.

Nicholson, Linda and Steven Seidmann, eds. *Social Postmodernism. Beyond Identity Politics.* New York: Cambridge University Press, 1995.

Nietzsche, Friedrich. *Werke in sechs Bänden.* Ed. Karl Schlechta. Munich: Hanser, 1980.

Nordau, Max Simon. *Entartung* (1895). Engl. *Degeration.* With an introduction by George L. Mosse. New York: Fertig, 1968.

Nössler, Regina. *Strafe Muss Sein.* Tübingen: Gehrke, 1994.

Nowell-Smith, Geoffrey. "New Concepts of Cinema." Nowell-Smith, *Oxford History* 750-59.

———, ed. *The Oxford History of World Cinema.* New York: Oxford University Press, 1996.

Nykrog, Per. *Les Fabliaux.* 3d ed. Geneva: Droz, 1973.

Oberkogler, Friedrich. *Faust II. Teil von Johann Wolfgang von Goethe: Werkbesprechung und geisteswissenschaftliche Erläuterungen.* Schaffhausen: Novalis, 1982.

Oberstes Gericht. *Entscheidungen des Obersten Gerichts der DDR in Strafsachen.* Vols. 1 and 3. Berlin: Deutscher Zentralverlag, 1951 and 1955.

Oosterhuis, Harry, ed. *Homosexuality and Male Bonding in Pre-Nazi Germany: The Youth Movement, the Gay Movement, and Male Bonding before Hitler's Rise. Original Transcripts from "Der Eigene," the First Gay Journal in the World.* Trans. Hubert Kennedy. New York: Harrington Park, 1991.

Opitz, Detlef. *Idyll. Erzählungen und andere Texte.* Halle: Mitteldeutscher Verlag, 1990.

———. "Wie anders denn?" *Mikado oder Der Kaiser ist nackt. Selbstverlegte Literatur in der DDR.* Ed. Uwe Kolbe, Lothar Trolle, and Bernd Wagner. Darmstadt: Luchterhand, 1988. 147-64.

Ormond, Richard. *John Singer Sargent and the Edwardian Age.* New York: Harper, 1970.

Orton, Graham. *Schiller: Don Carlos.* London: Arnold, 1967.

Oswald, Richard, dir. *Anders als die Andern.* 1919.

Öttingen, Arthur von. *Harmoniesystem in dualer Entwickelung.* Dorpat und Leipzig: W. Glaeser, 1866.

Pabst, G. W., dir. *Die Büchse der Pandora [Pandora's Box].* 1929.

———. *Die Dreigroschenoper. [The Three-Penny Opera].* 1931.

Palast Orchester. *Der Soundtrack zum Film "Der bewegte Mann."* With Max Raabe and original film music by Torsten Breuer. CD. Constantin Records BMG, 1994.

Palmer, Pauline. *Contemporary Lesbian Writing. Dreams, Desire, Difference.* Buckingham: Open University Press, 1993.

Parker, Andrew. "Unthinking Sex: Marx, Engels and the Scene of Writing." *Social Text* 29 (1992): 28-45.

Parry, John Jay, trans. *Andreas Capellanus. The Art of Courtly Love*. New York: Ungar, 1964.

Peck, Russell A. "Number as Cosmic Language." *Essays in the Numerical Criticism of Medieval Literature*. Ed. Caroline D. Eckhardt. Lewisburg: Bucknell University Press, 1980. 15–64.

Perthold, Sabine. "Zeigt her Eure Zähne. Die monströse Darstellung weiblicher Vampire in der 'Verzahnung' von Religion, Mythologie, Medien und Film." *Rote Küsse. Film Schau Buch*. Ed. Sabine Perthold. Tübingen: Gehrke, 1990. 12–24.

Petersen, Wolfgang, dir. *Die Konsequenz*. 1977.

Petit, Pierre [Petri Petiti]. *De Amazonibus dissertatio*. 2d ed. Amsterdam: Wolters & Haring, 1687.

Pieper, Mecki. "Die Frauenbewegung und ihre Bedeutung für lesbische Frauen (1850–1920)." *Eldorado* 116–24.

Poole, Ralph J. *Performing Bodies. Überschreitungen der Geschlechtergrenzen im Theater der Avantgarde*. Frankfurt/M: Lang, 1996.

Popp, Wolfgang. *Männerliebe. Homosexualität und Literatur*. Stuttgart: Metzler, 1992.

Porter, Edwin S, dir. *The Great Train Robbery*. 1903.

Portig, G. *Schiller in seinem Verhältnis zur Freundschaft und Liebe, sowie in seinem inneren Verhältnis zu Goethe*. Hamburg: Voss, 1894.

Potsdam, Hans-Otto-Theater. Unpublished performance text of *Egmont*. Typescript, 1971. Pp. 77.

Powell, Michael and Emeric Pressburger, dirs. *Stairway to Heaven (A Matter of Life and Death)*. 1946.

Praunheim, Rosa von. *Armee der Liebenden oder Aufstand der Perversen*. Munich: Trikont, 1979.

——. "Monologue Interieur." *Cinéma* 252 (December 1979): 16–18.

——. *Sex und Karriere*. Munich: Rogner, 1976.

——, dir. *A Virus knows No Morals*. 1986.

——. *Anita: Tänze des Lasters [Anita: Dances of Vice]*. 1987.

——. *Army of Lovers or Revolt of the Perverts*. 1979.

——. *Horror Vacui*. 1984.

——. *I Am My Own Woman*. 1992.

——. *Nicht der Homosexuelle ist pervers, sondern die Situation in der er lebt [It Is Not the Homosexual Who Is Perverse, But the Situation in Which He Lives]*. 1970.

——. *Schweigen = Tod*. 1989.

Prodoehl, Hans Gerd. *Theorie des Alltags*. Berlin: Duncker & Humblot, 1983.

Pronger, Brian. *The Arena of Masculinity. Sports, Homosexuality, and the Meaning of Sex*. Toronto: Summerhill, 1990.

Puff, Helmut. "Die Sünde und ihre Metaphern. Zum Liber Gomorrhianus des Petrus Damiani." *Forum Homosexualität und Literatur* 21 (1994): 45–77.

Rameau, Jean-Philippe. *Treatise on Harmony*. New York: Dover, 1971.

Rauch, Christina. "Vom Umgang mit Krankheit und Natur in Radclyffe Halls *The Well of Loneliness*: Zur Rezeptionsgeschichte." *Forum Homosexualität und Literatur* 23 (1995): 71–81.

Rees, Abraham. *The Cyclopaedia; or, Universal Dictionary of Arts, Sciences, and Literature.* London: Longman, 1819.

Reich, Willi. *Schönberg: A Critical Biography.* Trans. L. Black. London: Longman, 1968.

Reinig, Christa. "Blut und Boden und das Tausendjährige Reich." *Die Überwindung der Sprachlosigkeit: Texte aus der neuen Frauenbewegung.* Ed. Gabriele Dietze. Darmstadt: Luchterhand, 1979. 203–9.

——. "Ein Sonntag im Krieg." *Die Ewige Schule: Erzählungen.* Munich: Frauenoffensive, 1982. 7–26.

——. *Entmannung: Die Geschichte Ottos und seiner vier Frauen erzählt von Christa Reinig.* Roman. Darmstadt: Luchterhand, 1976.

——. *Erkennen, was die Rettung ist: Christa Reinig im Gespräch mit Marie-Luise Gansberg und Mechthild Beerlage.* Munich: Frauenoffensive, 1986.

——. "Freitag, 24. Februar." *Müßiggang ist aller Liebe Anfang: Gedichte.* Düsseldorf: Eremiten-Presse, 1977.

——. *Mein Herz ist eine gelbe Blume: Christa Reinig im Gespräch mit Ekkehart Rudolph.* Düsseldorf: Eremiten-Presse, 1978.

Rentschler, Eric. *The Ministry of Illusion. Nazi Cinema and Its Afterlife.* Cambridge, Mass.: Harvard University Press, 1996.

——. *West German Film: In the Course of Time.* Bedford Hills, NY: Redgrave, 1984.

Rich, Adrienne. "Compulsory Heterosexuality and Lesbian Existence." Abelove et al. 227–54.

Rich, Ruby. "Mädchen in Uniform: From Repressive Tolerance to Erotic Liberation." *Jump Cut* 24/25 (March 1981): 44–50.

Richards, Jeffrey. *Sex, Dissidence and Damnation: Minority Groups in the Middle Ages.* New York: Routledge, 1991.

Rickels, Laurence. "It's a Wound-erful Life." *Artforum* (December 1993): 45–47; 97.

Rickert, Heinrich, "Fausts Tod und Verklärung." *Deutsche Vierteljahrsschrift* 3 (1925): 1–74.

——. *Goethes Faust: Die dramatische Einheit der Dichtung.* Tübingen: Mohr, 1932.

Riefenstahl, Leni, dir. *Triumph des Willens* [*Triumph of the Will*]. 1935.

Riemann, Hugo. *Geschichte der Musiktheorie im IX.–XIX. Jahrhundert.* Berlin: Max Hesse, 1921.

Ripploh, Frank, dir. *Taxi zum Klo* [*Taxi to the Toilet*]. 1980.

Roberts, J. R. *Black Lesbians: An Annotated Bibliography.* Tallahassee, FL: Naiad, 1981.

Rodgerson, Gillian. "Lesbian Erotic Explorations." Segal and McIntosh 275–79.

Roemer, Anton. "Das Sittengesetz vor dem Richterstuhl einer ärztlichen Autorität." *Streitfragen* 1 (1892): 5–15.

Roof, Judith. *A Lure of Knowledge: Lesbian Sexuality and Theory*. New York: Columbia University Press, 1991.

Rosenfeld, Hans-Friedrich. "Dietrich von der Glezze (Glesse)." *Deutsche Literatur des Mittelalters: Verfasserlexikon*. Vol. 2. General Ed. Kurt Ruh. Berlin: de Gruyter, 1980. 137-39.

Ross, Andrew. *No Respect: Intellectuals and Popular Culture*. New York: Routledge, 1989.

Rothery, Guy Cadogan. *The Amazons in Antiquity and Modern Times*. London: Griffiths, 1910.

Rubin, Gayle. "The Traffic in Women: Notes Towards a Political Economy of Sex." *Towards an Anthropology of Women*. Ed. Rayna Reiter. New York: Monthly Review, 1975. 157-210.

Rubnitz, Tom. "Rosa the Provocateur." *New York Super*, December 1987, n.p.

Rüdin, E. "Zur Rolle der Homosexuellen im Lebensprozeß der Rasse." *Archiv für Rassen- und Gesellschaftsbiologie* 1 (1904): 99-109.

Rüling, Anna. "What Interest Does the Women's Movement Have in the Homosexual Question?" Faderman and Erikson 81-91.

Russo, Mary. *The Female Grotesque*. New York: Routledge, 1994.

Russo, Vito. *The Celluloid Closet: Homosexuality in the Movies*. New York: Harper & Row, 1981. Rev. ed., 1987.

Rutledge, Leigh W. *The Gay Decades. From Stonewall to the Present: The People and Events that Shaped Gay Lives*. New York: Penguin, 1992.

Rycenga, Jennifer. "Lesbian Compositional Process: One Lover-Composer's Perspective." Brett et al. 275-96.

Sacher-Masoch, Leopold von. *Venus im Pelz*. Frankfurt/M: Insel, 1968.

Sagan, Leontine, dir. *Mädchen in Uniform*. 1931.

Said, Edward W. *Culture and Imperialism*. London: Chatto, 1993.

———. *Musical Elaborations*. New York: Columbia University Press, 1991.

Saine, Ute Margarete. "Elfriede Jelinek's 'Die Zerrissenen' und die Zusammengeflickten' as Travesties of Patriarchal Philosophy and Male Stereotypes: Descartes, Faust, Don Juan, Dracula, and Tarzan." Johns and Arens 255-69.

SAMOIS, eds. *Coming to Power. Writings and Graphics on Lesbian S/M*. 3d. Boston: Alyson Publications, 1987.

Sampath, Ursula. *Kaspar Hauser: A Modern Metaphor*. Columbia, SC: Camden House, 1991.

Sanders-Brahms, Helma, dir. *Deutschland, bleiche Mutter*. 1979.

Savoy, E. "You Can't Go Homo Again: Queer Theory and the Foreclosure of Gay Studies." *English Studies in Canada* 20.3 (1994): 129-52.

Schäfer, Anke. "Vorwort der Frauen vom LAZ zur 1. Neuauflage 1977." *Der Skorpion*. Anna E[lisabet Weirauch]. Vol. 1 of 3. 1919. Maroldweisach: Feministischer Buchverlag, 1992.

Schiller, Friedrich. *Bühnenbearbeitungen*. Ed. Herbert G. Göpfert. Munich: dtv, 1966.

Schiller, Friedrich. *Sämtliche Werke.* 5 vols. Ed. Gerhard Fricke and Herbert G. Göpfert. 5th ed. Munich: Hanser, 1965.

———. *Werke. Nationalausgabe.* (NA) Ed. Julius Petersen and Gerhard Fricke. Weimar: Böhlaus, 1942.

Schlöndorff, Volker and Margarethe von Trotta, dirs. *Die verlorene Ehre der Katharina Blum* [*The Lost Honor of Katharina Blum*]. 1975.

Schmidt, Ricarda. *Westdeutsche Frauenliteratur in den 70er Jahren.* Frankfurt/M: Fischer, 1982.

Schmitt, Carl. *Verfassungslehre.* Berlin 1957.

Schönberg, Arnold. *Style and Idea.* New York: Philosophical Library, 1950.

Schöne, Albrecht. *Johann Wolfgang Goethe. Faust: Kommentare.* I. Abteilung: *Sämtliche Werke.* Vol. 2.7 of Johann Wolfgang Goethe. *Sämtliche Werke. Briefe, Tagebücher und Gespräche.* Ed. Friedmar Apel et al. Frankfurt/M.: Deutscher Klassiker Verlag, 1994.

Schoppmann, Claudia. *"Der Skorpion": Frauenliebe in der Weimarer Republik.* Frühlings Erwachen 8. Hamburg: Libertäre Assoziation, 1985.

———. "The Position of Lesbian Women in the Nazi Period." Grau, *Hidden Holocaust* 8–15.

———. *Zeit der Maskierung: Lebensgeschichten lesbischer Frauen im "Dritten Reich."* Berlin: Orlanda Frauenverlag, 1993.

Schröder, Hannelore. "Das 'Recht' der Väter." *Feminismus: Inspektion der Herrenkultur.* Ed. Luise Pusch. Neue Folge, vol. 192. Frankfurt/M: Suhrkamp, 1983. 477–506.

Schröder, Hermann. *Die symmetrische Umkehrung in der Musik.* Leipzig: Breitkopf & Haertel, 1902.

Schuller, Marianne. "Textilien. Literaturwissenschaft in der Krise?" *Kursbuch* 97 (1989): 71–87.

Schulz, Christian. *Paragraph 175 (abgewickelt). Homosexualität und Strafrecht im Nachkriegsdeutschland – Rechtsprechung, Juristische Diskussionen und Reformen seit 1945.* Hamburg: MännerschwarmSkript, 1994.

Schulze, Gerhard. *Die Erlebnisgesellschaft. Kultursoziologie der Gegenwart.* Frankfurt/M: Campus, 1993.

Schwaibold, Matthias. "Mittelalterliche Bußbücher und sexuelle Normalität." *Ius commune* XV (1988): 107–33.

Scott, Jay. "Anita: Dances of Vice." *The Globe and Mail,* 27 February 1988, n.p.

Scott, Joan W. "The Evidence of Experience." Abelove et al. 397–415.

Sedgwick, Eve Kosofsky. "Socratic Raptures, Socratic Ruptures: Notes Toward Queer Performativity." *English Inside and Out: The Places of Literary Criticism.* Eds. Susan Gubar and Jonathan Kamholtz. New York: Routledge, 1993. 122–36.

———. *Between Men: English Literature and Male Homosocial Desire.* New York: Columbia University Press, 1985.

———. *Epistemology of the Closet.* Berkeley: University of California Press, 1990.

———. *Tendencies.* Durham: Duke University Press, 1993.

Seemüller, Joseph, ed. *Seifried Helbling.* Halle a. S. 1886, II.

Segal, Lynne and Mary McIntosh, eds. *Sex Exposed. Sexuality and the Pornography Debate.* London: Virago, 1992.

Seidel, Siegfried, ed. *Briefwechsel zwischen Friedrich Schiller und Wilhelm von Humboldt.* 2 vols. Berlin: Aufbau, 1962.

Seidman, Steven. "Deconstructing Queer Theory or the Under-Theorization of the Social and the Ethical." Nicholson and Seidman 116-41.

———. "Identity and Politics in a 'Postmodern' Gay Culture: Some Historical and Conceptual Notes." Warner, *Fear* 105-42.

Serafine, Mary-Louise. *Music as Cognition.* New York: Columbia University Press, 1987.

Shattuc, Jane. *Television, Tabloids, and Tears: Fassbinder and Popular Culture.* Minneapolis: University of Minnesota Press, 1995.

Shengold, Leonard. *Soul Murder: The Effects of Childhood Abuse and Deprivation.* New York: Fawcett Columbine, 1989.

Shubnikov, A. V., N. V. Belov, et al. *Colored Symmetry.* Trans. J. Itzkoff and J. Gollob. New York: Macmillan, 1964.

Sieg, Katrin. *Exiles, Eccentrics, Activists. Women in Contemporary German Theater.* Ann Arbor: University of Michigan Press, 1994.

Siemsen, Hans. "Drei Personen suchen einen Autor." *Die Weltbühne* 21.10 (1925): 360-61.

Sillge, Ursula. *Un-Sichtbare Frauen: Lesben und ihre Emanzipation in der DDR.* Berlin: LinksDruck, 1991.

Silverman, Kaja. "Kaspar Hauser's 'Terrible Fall' into Narrative." *New German Critique* 24/25 (1981/82): 73-93.

———. *Male Subjectivity at the Margins.* New York: Routledge, 1992.

Simon, Sunka. "De-Manning the Moon: Feminist Fantasy and Ideology from Else Lasker-Schüler to Monika Treut." Unpublished paper, 1995.

Slonimsky, Nicolas. *Lexicon of Musical Invective: Critical Assaults on Composers Since Beethoven's Time.* Seattle: University of Washington Press, 1969.

Smyth, Cherry. *Lesbians Talk Queer Notions.* London: Scarlet, 1992.

Sohncke, L. *Entwicklung einer Theorie der Kristallstruktur.* Leipzig 1879.

Sokolowski, Thomas. "Atilla Richard Lukacs." New York: 49th Parallel, 1989.

Sommerhage, Claus. *Eros und Poesis. Über das Erotische im Werk Thomas Manns.* Bonn: Bouvier, 1983.

Sontag, Susan. *Against Interpretation.* New York: Dell, 1966.

Sorlin, Pierre. *European Cinemas. European Societies 1939-1990.* London: Routledge, 1991.

Southern, Terry. "Weill and Brecht: The Original Glimmer Twins." Liner notes for CD *Lost in the Stars: The Music of Kurt Weill.* Assorted Artists. A&M Records, 1985.

Spangenberg, Eberhard. *Karriere eines Romans. Mephisto, Klaus Mann und Gustaf Gründgens. Ein dokumentarischer Bericht aus Deutschland und dem Exil 1925-1981.* Reinbek bei Hamburg: Rowohlt, 1986.

Spreitzer, Brigitte. *Die stumme Sünde. Homosexualität im Mittelalter.* Mit einem Textanhang. Göppingen: Kümmerle, 1988.

Stambolian, George. "Foreward." Ellenzweig xv–xix.

Steakley, James D. "Iconography of a Scandal: Political Cartoons and the Eulenburg Affair in Wilhelmine Germany." Duberman et al. 233–63.

Stehling, Thomas. *Medieval Latin Poems of Male Love and Friendship.* Trans. T. Stehling. New York: Garland, 1984.

Stein, Arlene. "Style Wars and the New Lesbainism." Creekmuir and Doty 476–83.

Stemmler, Theodor, ed. *Homoerotische Lyrik: Vorträge eines interdisziplinären Kolloquiums, Mannheim 1992. 6.* Kolloquium der Forschungsstelle für europäische Lyrik des Mittelalters. Tübingen: Narr, 1992.

Stenographische Berichte über die Verhandlungen des Norddeutschen Bundes. Anlagen. Berlin 1870.

Stenographische Berichte über die Verhandlungen des Reichstags. Plenum 31.03. (Abgeordneter Thaler). Berlin 1905.

Stephan, Inge and Sigrid Weigel, eds. *Feministische Literaturwissenschaft. Dokumentation der Tagung in Hamburg vom Mai 1983.* New Series, vol. 2. *Literatur im historischen Prozeß.* Berlin: Argument, 1984.

Stern, Simon. "A Bibliography of Lesbian and Gay Studies." *Yale Journal of Criticism* 3.1 (1989): 253–60.

Sternberg, Josef von, dir. *Der blaue Engel* [*The Blue Angel*]. 1930.

Steward, Samuel M. *Bad Boys and Tough Tattoos. A Social History of the Tattoo with Gangs, Sailors and Street-Corner Punks 1950–1965.* New York: Harrington Park, 1990.

Stewart, William. *Cassell's Queer Companion: A Dictionary of Lesbian and Gay Life and Culture.* London: Cassell, 1995.

Straayer, Chris. *Deviant Eyes, Deviant Bodies. Sexual Re-Orientations in Film and Video.* New York: Columbia University Press, 1996.

Straayer, Chris. "Queer Theory Sample Syllabus – Gay and Lesbian Media, Gay and Lesbian Studies." *Quarterly Review of Film and Video* 15.1 (1993): 79–87.

Strada, Famianus. *De Bello Belgico.* (1578). Rome 1640.

Strafgesetzbuch der DDR. Kommentar. Berlin: Staatsverlag, 1981.

Strafrechtskommission. *Begründungen zum Entwurf eines neuen deutschen Strafgesetzbuchs. 1. Lesung 1907.* Zentrales Staatsarchiv Potsdam. *Bestand Reichsjustizamt,* Repositur 30.01. Akte 5871, Bl. 156–57, 161, 168–70.

——. *Protokoll der Sitzung der Reichstagskommission.* 01.03.1870. Zentrales Staatsarchiv Potsdam. *Bestand Reichstag,* Repositur 01.01. Akte 826, Bl. 50, 52.

Strobel, Christina. "Vom Umgang mit Krankheit und Natur in Radclyffe Halls *The Well of Loneliness.*" *Forum Homosexualität und Literatur* 23 (1995): 83–97.

Stümke, Hans-Georg. *Homosexuelle in Deutschland: eine politische Geschichte.* Munich: Beck, 1989.

Suchomski, Joachim. *'Delectatio' und 'Utilitas': Ein Beitrag zum Verständnis mittelalterlicher komischer Literatur.* Bern: Francke, 1975.

Sweet, Denis M. "Bodies for Germany, Bodies for Socialism: The German Democratic Republic Devises a Gay (Male) Body." *Gender and Germanness: Cultural Productions of Nation*. Eds. Magda Mueller and Patricia Herminghouse. Providence, RI: Berghahn, in press.

——. "The Church, the Stasi, and Socialist Integration: Three Stages of Lesbian and Gay Emancipation in the Former German Democratic Republic." *Gay Men and the Sexual History of the Political Left*. Ed. Gert Hekma, Harry Oosterhuis, and James Steakley. New York: Haworth, 1995. 349-65.

——. "A Literature of Truth: Writing by Gay Men in East Germany." *MKF – Mitteilungen aus der kulturwissenschaftlichen Forschung* 18.36 (1995): 232-45.

Syberberg, Hans-Jürgen, dir. *Hitler. Ein Film aus Deutschland.* 1977.

——. *Karl May.* 1974.

Taeger, Angela and Rüdiger Lautmann. "Sittlichkeit und Politik. § 175 im Zweiten Deutschen Reich (1871-1919)." *Kriminologische Forschung in den 80er Jahren.* Ed. G. Kaiser, H. Kury, H. J. Albrecht. Freiburg: Eigenverlag Max-Planck-Institut für ausländisches und internationales Strafrecht, 1988. 573-90.

Taruskin, Richard. "Does Nature Call the Tune?" *New York Times,* 18 September 1994, Section II, 28.

Tervooren, Helmut. "Schönheitsbeschreibungen und Gattungsethik in der mittelhochdeutschen Lyrik." *Schöne Frauen, schöne Männer: Literarische Schönheitsbeschreibungen.* Mannheim: Forschungsstelle für europäische Lyrik des Mittelalters an der U. Mannheim, 1988. 171-98.

Theater der Zeit. Berlin: Henschel, 1946ff.

Theater heute. Hannover: Friedrich, 1960ff.

Theater-Zeitung für Deutschland. Ed. Christian August Bertram. St. 1-26. Berlin: Unger, 1789.

Theis, Wolfgang. "Verdrängung und Travestie. Das vage Bild der Homosexualität im deutschen Film (1917-1957)." *Eldorado* 102-15.

Theweleit, Klaus. *Male Fantasies.* Trans. Stephen Conway et al. 2 vols. Minneapolis: University of Minnesota Press, 1987-89.

Thietmar von Merseburg. *Chronik.* Neu übertragen und erläutert von Werner Trillmich. Darmstadt: Wissenschaftliche Buchgesellschaft, 1974.

Thomas, Gary. "'Was George Frideric Handel Gay?': On Closet Questions and Cultural Politics." Brett et al. 155-203.

Thomas, Paul. "Fassbinder: The Poetry of the Inarticulate." *Film Quarterly* (1976-77): 2-17.

Thomson, William. *Schönberg's Error.* Philadelphia: University of Philadelphia Press, 1991.

Thulin, Michael. "Sprache und Sprachkritik. Die Literatur des Prenzlauer Bergs in Berlin/DDR." Arnold 234-42.

Tobin, Robert. "Faust's Membership in Male Society: Prometheus and Ganymede as Models." Brown et al., *Interpreting* 17-28.

——. "In and Against Nature: Goethe on Homosexuality and Heterosexuality." Kuzniar 94-110, 256-57.

Todorov, Tzvetan. "The Origins of Genre." *New Literary History* 8 (1976): 159-70.

Traumann, Ernst. *Goethes Faust. Nach Entstehung und Inhalt erklärt.* Vol. 2. Munich: Beck, 1914.

Treusch-Dieter, Gerburg. "Barbie und Inzest. Das letzte Stadium der Körpermodellierung/Jeder ist der Antikörper des Anderen." *Ästhetik und Kommunikation* 87 (1994): 22-27.

Treut, Monika, dir. *Bondage.* 1983.

———. *Die Jungfrauenmaschine* [*Virgin Machine*]. 1988.

———. *Seduction. The Cruel Woman.* 1983-84.

Tyler, Carole-Ann. "Boys Will Be Girls: The Politics of Gay Drag." Fuss, *Inside/Out* 32-70.

———. "Passing: Narcissism, Identity, and Difference." *differences* 6 (1994): 212-48.

Ulrich von Liechtenstein. Mit Anmerkungen von Theodor von Karajan. Ed. Karl Lachmann. 1841. Rpt. Hildesheim: Olms, 1974.

Ulrichs, Karl Heinrich. *Memnon: Die Geschlechtsnatur des mannliebenden Urnings. Eine naturwissenschaftliche Darstellung.* Schleiz: Hübscher, 1868.

———. *The Riddle of Man-Manly Love.* Trans. M. Lombardi-Nash. Buffalo, NY: Prometheus Books, 1984.

Urania. Taschenbuch für Damen auf das Jahr 1815. Mit neun Kupfern, darstellend Scenen aus Göthe's Faust, Egmont und Tasso. Leipzig and Altenburg: Brockhaus, 1815.

van Stockum, Theodore C. and J. van Dam. *Geschichte der deutschen Literatur.* Vol. 1. Groningen, Walters, 1961.

Veeser, H. Arom, ed. *The New Historicism.* New York: Routledge, 1989.

Vermeule, Blakey. "Is There a Sedgwick School for Girls?" *Qui Parle* 5.1 (1991): 53-72.

Vester, Michael et al. *Soziale Milieus im gesellschaftlichen Strukturwandel. Zwischen Integration und Ausgrenzung.* Cologne: Bund, 1993.

Vidal, Gore. *The City and the Pillar.* London: Lehman, 1949.

Vinken, Barbara. "Der Stoff, aus dem die Körper sind." *Neue Rundschau* 4 (1993): 9-22.

Vischer, Friedrich Theodor. *Faust: Der Tragödie dritter Theil.* Stuttgart: 1862.

Vogel, Katharina. "Zum Selbstverständnis lesbischer Frauen in der Weimarer Republik: Eine Analyse der Zeitschrift *Die Freundin* 1924-1933." *Eldorado* 162-67.

Volckmann, Silvia. "'Gierig saugt sie seines Mundes Flammen.' Anmerkungen zum Funktionswandel des weiblichen Vampirs in der Literatur des 19. Jahrhunderts." *Weiblichkeit und Tod in der Literatur.* Ed. Renate Berger and Inge Stephan. Cologne: Böhlau, 1987. 155-76.

Vollmer-Heitmann, Hanna. *Wir sind von Kopf bis Fuß auf Liebe eingestellt: die zwanziger Jahre.* Hamburg: Kabel, 1993.

Vulf, G. V. *Symmetry and Its Manifestation in Nature.* Moscow 1908.

Wachenfeld, Friedrich. "Zur Frage der Strafwürdigkeit des homosexuellen Verkehrs." *Goltdammers Archiv für Strafrecht* 49 (1903): 37-66.

———. *Homosexualität und Strafgesetz.* Leipzig 1901.

Wagener, Hans, ed. *Erläuterungen und Dokumente. Johann Wolfgang Goethe. Egmont.* Stuttgart: Reclam, 1982.

Waite, Geoff. *Nietzsche's Corps/e.* Durham: Duke University Press, 1996.

Walter, Joachim. *Sicherungsbereich Literatur. Schriftsteller und Staatssicherheit in der Deutschen Demokratischen Republik.* Berlin: Links, 1996.

Warner, Michael. "From Queer to Eternity. An Army of Theorists Cannot Fail." *Village Voice. Literary Supplement* (June 1992): 18-19.

———, ed. *Fear of a Queer Planet. Queer Politics and Social Theory.* Cultural Politics, vol. 6. Minneapolis: University of Minnesota Press, 1993.

Was spielten die Theater? Werkstatistik. Cologne: Deutscher Bühnenverein. 1981ff. Superceded from 1990/91 by *Wer spielte was? Werkstatistik des Deutschen Bühnenvereins.*

Waters, John, dir. *Pink Flamingos.* 1972.

Watney, Simon. "Hollywood's Homosexual World." *Screen* 23. 3-4 (1982): 107-21.

Waugh, Thomas. "Men's Pornography." Creekmuir and Doty 307-27.

Webern, Anton von. *The Path to the New Music.* London: Universal, 1975.

"Weekend Movies." *New York Post,* 15 January 1988, n. p.

Weeks, Jeffrey. *Against Nature. Essays on History, Sexuality and Identity.* London: Rivers Oram, 1991.

———. *Coming Out: Homosexual Politics in Britain, from the Nineteenth Century to the Present.* London: Quartet, 1977.

———. *Sexuality and its Discontents.* London: Routledge, 1989.

Weigel, Sigrid. "Der schielende Blick. Thesen zur Geschichte weiblicher Schreibpraxis." *Die verborgene Frau. Sechs Beiträge zu einer feministischen Literaturwissenschaft.* Ed. Inge Stephan and Sigrid Weigel. Hamburg: Argument, 1983. 83-137.

Weine, Robert, dir. *Das Kabinett des Dr. Caligari [The Cabinet of Dr. Caligari].* 1919.

Weinrich, Harald. "Der zivilisierte Teufel." Brown et al. *Interpreting* 61-67.

Weirauch, Anna Elisabet. *Der Skorpion.* 3 Vols. Berlin: Askanischer Verlag, 1919, 1921, 1931. Rpt. Berlin: Feministischer Buchverlag, 1972; vols. 2 and 3: 1993.

Weiss, Andrea. *Vampires and Violets. Lesbians in the Cinema.* London: Cape, 1992.

Wenders, Wim, dir. *Himmel Über Berlin [Wings of Desire].* 1987.

———. *The American Friend.* 1977.

Wendland, Dorothea. "Bücher der homoerotischen Frau." *Die Freundin* 8.8 (1929): 3-4.

Westphal, Karl Friedrich Otto. "Die Sexualempfindung." *Archiv für Psychiatrie und Nervenkrankheiten* 2.1 (1869): 73-108.

Wheelock, Gretchen A. "*Schwarze Gredel* and the Engendered Minor Mode in Mozart's Operas." *Musicology and Difference.* Ed. R Solie. Berkeley, CA: University of California Press, 1993. 201-21.

White, Hayden. *The Content of the Form: Narrative Discourse and Historical Representation.* Baltimore: Johns Hopkins, 1990.

Wichner, Ernst and Herbert Wiesner, eds. *Zensur in der DDR. Geschichte, Praxis und 'Ästhetik' der Behinderung von Literatur.* Berlin: Literaturhaus, 1991.

Wilde, Oscar. *Complete Works.* London: Collins, 1966.

Wilder, Billy, dir. *The Lost Weekend.* 1945.

Wilhelm, Eugen. "Zur Frage der Strafbarkeit des gleichgeschlechtlichen Verkehrs. Eine Erwiderung." *Politisch-Anthropologische Revue* 8 (1909): 422-25.

Williams, Linda. "Pornographies on/scene or Diff'rent Strokes for Diff'rent Folks." Segal and McIntosh 233-65.

Williams, Simon. "Performing Mephisto." Brown et al., *Interpreting* 94-99.

Williamson, Judith. "A Piece of the Action: Images of 'Woman' in the Photography of Cindy Sherman." *Consuming Passions.* London: Marion Boyars, 1986.

Wilson, W. Daniel. "Amazon, Agitator, Allegory: Political and Gender Cross(-Dress)-ing in Goethe's *Egmont.*" Kuzniar 125-146, 258-64.

Winter, Jay. *Sites of Memory, Sites of Mourning: The Great War in European Cultural History.* Cambridge: Cambridge University Press, 1995.

Wisskirchen, Hans. "Republikanischer Eros. Zu Walt Whitmans und Hans Blühers Rolle in der politischen Publizistik Thomas Manns." *'Heimsuchung und süßes Gift'. Erotik und Poetik bei Thomas Mann.* Ed. Gerhard Härle. Frankfurt/M: Fischer, 1992. 17-40.

Wittig, Monique. *The Lesbian Body.* Trans. David LeVay. London: Owen, 1975.

——. "One Is Not Born a Woman." (1981) Abelove et al. 103-09.

——. "The Straight Mind." *The Straight Mind and Other Essays.* Boston: Beacon, 1992. 20-32.

Wittkower, Rudolf and Margot Wittkower. *Künstler – Außenseiter der Gesellschaft.* Stuttgart: Kohlhammer, 1965.

Wittkowski, Wolfgang, ed. *Friedrich Schiller: Kunst, Humanität und Politik in der späten Aufklärung. Ein Symposium.* Tübingen: Niemeyer, 1982.

Wood, Robin. "Don't Dream It." *The Cult film experience: Beyond all reason.* Ed. J. P. Telotte. Austin: University of Texas Press, 1991.

Worth, F. "Of Gayzes and Bodies – A Bibliographical Essay on Queer Theory, Psychoanalysis and Archaeology." *Quarterly Review of Film and Video* 15.1 (1993): 1-13.

——. "Queer Theory – Desire, Authorship and Visibility." (Includes Introduction to the Annotated Film/Videography, annotated Gay and Lesbian Film/Videography, and Selected Bibliography). *Quarterly Review of Film and Video* 15.1 (1993): 89-90, 91-119, 121-26.

Wortmann, Sönke, dir. *Der bewegte Mann* [*Maybe ... Maybe Not*]. Perf. Til Schweiger, Katja Riemann, Joachim Król, and Rufus Beck. 1994. VCL/Carolco Communications GmbH, 1995.

——. *Kleine Haie* [*Small Sharks*]. 1992.

Wright, Will. *Six Guns and Society.* Berkeley: University of California Press, 1975.

Wyatt, Justin. *High Concept: Movies and Marketing in Hollywood.* Austin: University of Texas Press, 1994.

Yaglom, I. M. *Felix Klein and Sophus Lie: Evolution of the Idea of Symmetry in the Nineteenth Century.* Boston: Birkäuser, 1988.

Yingling, Thomas. *Hart Crane and the Homosexual Text.* Chicago: University of Chicago Press, 1990.

Yunck, John A., trans. *Eneas. A Twelfth-Century French Romance.* New York: Columbia University Press, 1974.

Zarlino, Gioseffo. *The Art of Counterpoint: Part Three of Le Istitutioni Harmoniche, 1558.* Trans. G. A. Marco and C. Palisca. New York: Da Capo, 1983.

Zijderveld, A.C. "Het faible van Thomas Mann. Over de dagboeken van 1949 en 1950." *De Gids* 156.3 (1993): 169-83.

Zimmerman, Bonnie. "Daughters of Darkness. Lesbian Vampires." *Jump Cut* 24/25 (1981): 23-25.

Zinn, Alexander. *Die soziale Konstruktion des homosexuellen Nationalsozialisten. Zur Genese und Etablierung eines Stereotyps.* Frankfurt/M: Lang, 1997.

Zinnemann, Fred, dir. *High Noon.* 1952.

Zynda, Stefan. *Sexualität bei Klaus Mann.* Bonn: Bouvier, 1986.

Notes on Contributors

EVELYN ANNUß is a philologist at the Center for Interdisciplinary Women's Studies and Gender Studies (i.G.), at the TU-Berlin. Her areas of concentration are in contemporary German literature, recent trends in gender studies and queer theory. She has published on automatons in literature and on the current gender debate.

KARIN BAUER is Assistant Professor of German Studies at McGill University, Montreal. She is the author of *Nietzsche, Adorno, and the Critique of Ideology* (1998) and has published articles on Herta Müller, Botho Strauß, Petra Kelly, Christa Wolf, and Nelly Sachs.

MARTIN BLUM teaches in the Department of English and Modern Languages at Douglas College, New Westminster, BC. He has recently completed his dissertation *Body Politics: Otherness and the Representation of Bodies in Medieval Writings*. He is the author of an article on the erotic triangles in Chaucer's *Miller's Tale*.

HELMUT BRALL is Professor of German Philology and Literature at Heinrich-Heine University Düsseldorf. His publications include *Gralsuche und Adelsheil. Studien zu Wolframs "Parzival"* (1983), two books on the history of concepts (such as the devil and loneliness), and numerous articles on medieval German literature.

PIET DEFRAEYE has studied in Belgium, Ireland, and Canada and teaches modern drama and theater history at St. Thomas University in Fredericton, New Brunswick. He has published on Conor Cruise O'Brien, Howard Brenton, and Michel Marc Bouchard.

SILKE R. FALKNER is a doctoral candidate at McGill University. She wrote her M.A. thesis on Bettine von Arnim. She is interested in issues of gender, identity, and the body. She is working on her dissertation *Catharina Regina von Greiffenberg: Writing as a Woman in the Baroque*.

CARYL FLINN is Associate Professor of Cinema Studies at the University of Toronto. She is the author of *Strains of Utopia: Gender, Nostalgia and Hollywood Film Music* (1992) and several essays which have appeared in journals such as *Camera Obscura, Arachne*, and *Screen*.

NEVILLE HOAD has lectured in English at the University of the Witwatersrand, Johannesburg, South Africa, and is currently completing a Ph.D. in English and Comparative Literature at Columbia University. He is the 1997/1998 Sawyer Postdoctoral fellow in the Humanities at the University of Chicago. He has written for

Radical Teacher and *The Village Voice* and has work forthcoming from *Genders* and *Jewish Affairs.*

DAVID G. JOHN is Professor of German and Chair of the Department of Germanic and Slavic Languages at the University of Waterloo, Canada. His publications focus on eighteenth-century German theater and Goethe.

JAMES W. JONES is Professor of German at Central Michigan University. He is currently finishing a study on gay and lesbian literature published during the Weimar years, a continuation of his book *"We of the Third Sex": Literary Representations of Homosexuality in Wilhelmine Germany* (1990). He has also written extensively on AIDS discourses in Germany and in the United States.

UTE LISCHKE-MCNAB teaches as an Assistant Professor at the Department of Germanic Languages and Literatures at the University of Toronto. She has published several articles on Lili Braun. Her recent studies on "Triangulated Visions" in Helga Schübert and Jutta Brückner are forthcoming.

CHRISTOPH LOREY is Associate Professor of German at the University of New Brunswick, Fredericton. He is the author of *Lessings Familienbild* (1992), *Die Ehe im klassischen Werk Goethes* (1995), coeditor of *Analogon Rationis. Festschrift für Gerwin Marahrens* (1995), and editor of *The International Fiction Review.*

AMANDA L. MITCHELL is a graduate student at the University of Central Lancashire, England. She is currently working on a Ph.D. thesis which examines the portrayal of gynocentric relationships in German women's literature since the Reformation, centering in particular around the description of lesbian partnerships.

NANCY P. NENNO is Assistant Professor of German at the College of Charleston, South Carolina. Her dissertation *Masquerade: Woman Nature Modernity* focuses on women's performance of identity in Weimar Berlin and the figure of the actress.

HARRY OOSTERHUIS is Assistant Professor of History at the University of Maastricht. He has published extensively in the areas of the history of homosexuality in the Netherlands and Germany, male bonding in pre-Nazi Germany, the persecution of homosexuals in the Third Reich, and sexuality in fin-de-siècle Vienna.

HOLGER A. PAUSCH is Professor of German in the Division of Germanic Languages, Literatures and Linguistics at the University of Alberta. He has published extensively in the areas of German literary history and literary cultural theory, and is currently working on a book on the genealogy of the semiological relation between text and image.

JOHN L. PLEWS is a doctoral candidate at the University of Alberta, Edmonton, and recent recipient of the Izaak Walton Killam Memorial Scholarship. He is the author of articles on C. D. Grabbe's Historical Dramas and Ingeborg Drewitz's *Gestern war Heute.* He is currently writing his dissertation on physiognomy and the portrayal of intellectuals in German literature

RALPH J. POOLE, currently at Ludwig-Maximilian University, Munich, has studied American and German literature, musicology, and psychology in Heidelberg, Munich, and New York. He has published on lesbian and gay studies, transvestism, queer theory, Kathy Acker, and Harold Brodkey.

MARTIN SCHERZINGER is a composer currently enrolled in the Ph.D. program in Music Theory at Columbia University. Recipient of numerous international awards, he has published articles in *Music Analysis, Conference: A Journal of Philosophy and Theory*, and *disClosure: A Journal of Social Theory*. His compositions have received performances in South Africa, the United States, and Europe.

SUNKA SIMON currently teaches German studies, women's studies, and New German Cinema at Swarthmore College. She is in the process of completing her manuscript "Mail Orders: Contemporary Epistolary Fictions in Literature, Literary Theory, Film, Electronic Media, and the Arts." She has published on epistolary fiction, feminism and utopia, and eighteenth-century German poetry.

DENIS M. SWEET studied at Stanford and the Free University of Berlin before joining the faculty of Bates College where he teaches German. He has published articles on Nietzsche and Faust receptions in the GDR. He is currently preparing a book on East German gay literature.

ANGELA TAEGER is a research associate at the Department of History at Oldenburg University. Her main field of research is comparative social history in eighteenth- and nineteenth-century France and Prussia/Germany. She has published on family issues, sexuality, age, gender studies, and on women's and men's studies.

ROBERT TOBIN is Associate Professor of German at Whitman College in Walla Walla. He is the author of numerous articles on queer approaches to German literature. They have appeared in *Outing Goethe and His Age, Impure Reason*, and *Interpreting Goethe's "Faust" Today*, and in both the Norton Critical Edition and the Bedford Books Edition of *Death in Venice*.

CATHRIN WINKELMANN is a doctoral candidate with the Department of Germanic Studies at McGill University in Montreal. She began working in the area of queer criticism with her M.A. thesis, entitled *Distance and Desire: Homoeroticism in Thomas Mann's "Death in Venice."* She is currently writing her doctoral dissertation on the representation of desire in German lesbian literature of the twentieth century.

LES WRIGHT is Assistant Professor of Humanities and English at Mount Ida College, Boston. He is editor of *The Bear Book* (Haworth Press, 1997). His writings have appeared in *Hometowns: Gay Men Write About Where They Belong, Out in the Workplace, AIDS: The Literary Response*, and *Contemporary Gay American Novelists: A Bio-Bibliographical Critical Sourcebook.*

Index

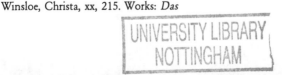
UNIVERSITY LIBRARY
NOTTINGHAM